380 SR # 1-5

389 SR # 1-4

PRENTICE HALL
EXPL⊙RING
Physical Science

Anthea Maton
Former NSTA National Coordinator
Project Scope, Sequence, Coordination
Washington, DC

Jean Hopkins
Science Instructor and Department Chairperson
John H. Wood Middle School
San Antonio, Texas

Susan Johnson
Professor of Biology
Ball State University
Muncie, Indiana

David LaHart
Senior Instructor
Florida Solar Energy Center
Cape Canaveral, Florida

Maryanna Quon Warner
Science Instructor
Del Dios Middle School
Escondido, California

Jill D. Wright
Professor of Science Education
Director of International Field Programs
University of Pittsburgh
Pittsburgh, Pennsylvania

Prentice Hall
Upper Saddle River, New Jersey
Needham, Massachusetts

EXPLORING
Physical Science

Student Text and Teacher's Edition	**Transparency Box**
Teaching Resources	**Computer Test Bank with**
Teacher's Desk Reference	**DIAL-A-TEST™ Service**
Classroom Manager	**Videos/Videodiscs**
Laboratory Manual and	**Level I Videodiscs**
Annotated Teacher's Edition	**Level III Interactive Videodiscs**
Integrated Science Activity Books	**Level III Interactive Videodiscs/CD-ROM**
Product Testing Activities	**Media Guide**

The illustration on the cover, rendered by René Milot, depicts the interactions of energy and matter in a typical city.

Credits begin on page 816.

SECOND EDITION

ISBN 0-13-418716-4

8 9 10   99

PRENTICE HALL
Simon & Schuster Education Group
A VIACOM COMPANY

STAFF CREDITS

Editorial:	Lorraine Smith-Phelan, Maureen Grassi, Joseph Berman, Christine A. Caputo, Matthew C. Hart, Rekha Sheorey, Kathleen Ventura
Design:	AnnMarie Roselli, Laura Bird, Gerry Schrenk
Production:	Suse F. Bell, Christina Burghard, Marianne Peters Riordan, Cathleen Profitko, Gregory Myers, Cleasta Wilburn
Media Resources:	Suzi Myers, Vickie Menanteaux, Martha Conway
Marketing:	Andrew Socha, Arthur C. Germano, Jane Walker Neff, Victoria Willows
Pre-Press Production:	Kathryn Dix, Paula Massenaro, Carol Barbara
Manufacturing:	Rhett Conklin, Loretta Moe
National Science Consultants	Charles Balko, Patricia Cominsky, Jeannie Dennard, Kathy French, Brenda Underwood

Contributing Writers

Linda Densman
Science Instructor
Hurst, TX

Linda Grant
Former Science Instructor
Weatherford, TX

Heather Hirschfeld
Science Writer
Durham, NC

Marcia Mungenast
Science Writer
Upper Montclair, NJ

Michael Ross
Science Writer
New York City, NY

Content Reviewers

Dan Anthony
Science Mentor
Rialto, CA

John Barrow
Science Instructor
Pomona, CA

Leslie Bettencourt
Science Instructor
Harrisville, RI

Carol Bishop
Science Instructor
Palm Desert, CA

Dan Bohan
Science Instructor
Palm Desert, CA

Steve M. Carlson
Science Instructor
Milwaukie, OR

Larry Flammer
Science Instructor
San Jose, CA

Steve Ferguson
Science Instructor
Lee's Summit, MO

Robin Lee Harris Freedman
Science Instructor
Fort Bragg, CA

Edith H. Gladden
Former Science Instructor
Philadelphia, PA

Vernita Marie Graves
Science Instructor
Tenafly, NJ

Jack Grube
Science Instructor
San Jose, CA

Emiel Hamberlin
Science Instructor
Chicago, IL

Dwight Kertzman
Science Instructor
Tulsa, OK

Judy Kirschbaum
Science/Computer Instructor
Tenafly, NJ

Kenneth L. Krause
Science Instructor
Milwaukie, OR

Ernest W. Kuehl, Jr.
Science Instructor
Bayside, NY

Mary Grace Lopez
Science Instructor
Corpus Christi, TX

Warren Maggard
Science Instructor
PeWee Valley, KY

Della M. McCaughan
Science Instructor
Biloxi, MS

Stanley J. Mulak
Former Science Instructor
Jensen Beach, FL

Richard Myers
Science Instructor
Portland, OR

Carol Nathanson
Science Mentor
Riverside, CA

Sylvia Neivert
Former Science Instructor
San Diego, CA

Jarvis VNC Pahl
Science Instructor
Rialto, CA

Arlene Sackman
Science Instructor
Tulare, CA

Christine Schumacher
Science Instructor
Pikesville, MD

Suzanne Steinke
Science Instructor
Towson, MD

Len Svinth
Science Instructor/
Chairperson
Petaluma, CA

Elaine M. Tadros
Science Instructor
Palm Desert, CA

Joyce K. Walsh
Science Instructor
Midlothian, VA

Steve Weinberg
Science Instructor
West Hartford, CT

Charlene West, PhD
Director of Curriculum
Rialto, CA

John Westwater
Science Instructor
Medford, MA

Glenna Wilkoff
Science Instructor
Chesterfield, OH

Edee Norman Wiziecki
Science Instructor
Urbana, IL

Teacher Advisory Panel

Beverly Brown
Science Instructor
Livonia, MI

James Burg
Science Instructor
Cincinnati, OH

Karen M. Cannon
Science Instructor
San Diego, CA

John Eby
Science Instructor
Richmond, CA

Elsie M. Jones
Science Instructor
Marietta, GA

Michael Pierre McKereghan
Science Instructor
Denver, CO

Donald C. Pace, Sr.
Science Instructor
Reisterstown, MD

Carlos Francisco Sainz
Science Instructor
National City, CA

William Reed
Science Instructor
Indianapolis, IN

Multicultural Consultant

Steven J. Rakow
Associate Professor
University of Houston—
  Clear Lake
Houston, TX

English as a Second Language (ESL) Consultants

Jaime Morales
Bilingual Coordinator
Huntington Park, CA

Pat Hollis Smith
Former ESL Instructor
Beaumont, TX

Reading Consultant

Larry Swinburne
Director
Swinburne Readability Laboratory

CONTENTS

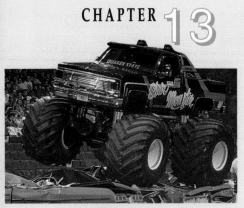
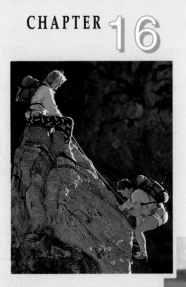

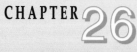
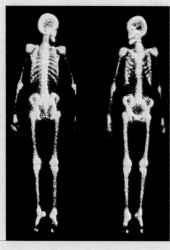

Activities for Exploring Physical Science

Doing

Calculating

Features

Problem Solving

Connections

Careers

CONCEPT MAPPING

Throughout your study of science, you will learn a variety of terms, facts, figures, and concepts. Each new topic you encounter will provide its own collection of words and ideas—which, at times, you may think seem endless. But each of the ideas within a particular topic is related in some way to the others. No concept in science is isolated. Thus it will help you to understand the topic if you see the whole picture; that is, the interconnectedness of all the individual terms and ideas. This is a much more effective and satisfying way of learning than memorizing separate facts.

Actually, this should be a rather familiar process for you. Although you may not think about it in this way, you analyze many of the elements in your daily life by looking for relationships or connections. For example, when you look at a collection of flowers, you may divide them into groups: roses, carnations, and daisies. You may then associate colors with these flowers: red, pink, and white. The general topic is flowers. The subtopic is types of flowers. And the colors are specific terms that describe flowers. A topic makes more sense and is more easily understood if you understand how it is broken down into individual ideas and how these ideas are related to one another and to the entire topic.

It is often helpful to organize information visually so that you can see how it all fits together. One technique for describing related ideas is called a **concept map**. In a concept map, an idea is represented by a word or phrase enclosed in a box. There are several ideas in any concept map. A connection between two ideas is made with a line. A word or two that describes the connection is written on or near the line. The general topic is located at the top of the map. That topic is then broken down into subtopics, or more specific ideas, by branching lines. The most specific topics are located at the bottom of the map.

To construct a concept map, first identify the important ideas or key terms in the chapter or section. Do not try to include too much information. Use your judgment as to what is really important. Write the general topic at the top of your map. Let's use an example to help illustrate this process. Suppose you decide that the key terms in a section you are reading are School, Living Things, Language Arts, Subtraction, Grammar, Mathematics, Experiments, Papers, Science, Addition, Novels. The general topic is School. Write and enclose this word in a box at the top of your map.

SCHOOL

Now choose the subtopics—Language Arts, Science, Mathematics. Figure out how they are related to the topic. Add these words to your map. Continue this procedure until you have included all the important ideas and terms. Then use lines to make the appropriate connections between ideas and terms. Don't forget to write a word or two on or near the connecting line to describe the nature of the connection.

Do not be concerned if you have to redraw your map (perhaps several times!) before you show all the important connections clearly. If, for example, you write papers for Science as well as for Language Arts, you may want to place these two subjects next to each other so that the lines do not overlap.

One more thing you should know about concept mapping: Concepts can be correctly mapped in many different ways. In fact, it is unlikely that any two people will draw identical concept maps for a complex topic. Thus there is no one correct concept map for any topic! Even

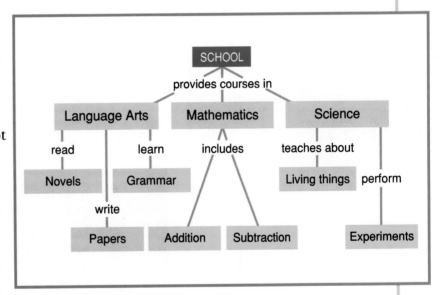

though your concept map may not match those of your classmates, it will be correct as long as it shows the most important concepts and the clear relationships among them. Your concept map will also be correct if it has meaning to you and if it helps you understand the material you are reading. A concept map should be so clear that if some of the terms are erased, the missing terms could easily be filled in by following the logic of the concept map.

U N I T O N E

Matter

Building Block of the Universe

Five hundred years ago, Christopher Columbus began a perilous journey. This journey, financed by Queen Isabella of Spain, was designed to find a new route to the riches of the Far East. In those lands, valuable spices and other treasures could be found. The rest is history: In traveling west to find the East, Columbus bumped into a New World.

People have always explored the unknown and made journeys to distant places—if only in their dreams. But no matter how far the journey or how strange the place, one observation can always be made: The universe—as near as one's feet and as far

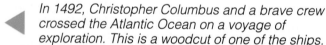

In 1492, Christopher Columbus and a brave crew crossed the Atlantic Ocean on a voyage of exploration. This is a woodcut of one of the ships.

Today's voyagers leave the comforts of city and country to begin to explore the vastness of space.

2

CHAPTERS

as the most distant star in a galaxy far, far away—is made of the same (and relatively few) kinds of materials.

In this unit you will begin your own kind of voyage. Your goal is to discover the nature of materials that form you and your universe—the matter inside and around you.

Matter surrounds everyone—whether you share space with other people in a large city or live in a house on a quiet country road.

Discovery Activity

Is Something the Matter?

1. Make a list of all the things that are found in an aquarium. Describe each item on your list. If you like, you can set up a small aquarium in your class- room. If you do, however, keep in mind that you are responsible for caring for the animals and plants that live there.

2. As you learn more about the matter that makes up the world around you, add to your list of things that are found in your aquarium.

3. Compare your "before" and "after" lists.
   - Has matter taken on any new meanings for you?

Exploring Physical Science

Soon after the launch of the *Hubble Space Telescope* on April 24, 1990, scientists discovered a problem with the primary mirror. Light striking the outer edge of the mirror was brought to a focus. about 4 centimeters behind light striking the center of the mirror. As a result, the images produced by the telescope were fuzzy and not as clear as expected. A slight miscalculation in measurement had been built into the mirror's design.

The problem with the *Hubble's* 2.4-meter primary mirror led to one of the most ambitious—and most dramatic—missions in space. In 1993, astronauts on board the space shuttle *Endeavour* embarked on an 11-day repair mission. In a series of "spacewalks," they installed a package of optical equipment that was able to correct the flaw in the mirror. Since then, the *Hubble Space Telescope* has consistently produced star-tlingly clear and sharp images of many distant objects in space.

The *Hubble Space Telescope* has been repaired. Now it can bring us pictures of the universe we have only dreamed about. But even so, it stands as a reminder to all scientists—and those who would be scientists—that careful and precise measurements can be the difference between scientific success and failure.

Journal *Activity*

You and Your World Pick a type of measurement. Perhaps length is your favorite. Or you may prefer temperature or volume. Whatever type of measurement you choose, make an entry in your journal each time you use that type of measurement on a particular day.

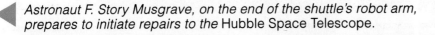

Astronaut F. Story Musgrave, on the end of the shuttle's robot arm, prepares to initiate repairs to the Hubble Space Telescope.

1–1 Science—Not Just for Scientists

You are a scientist! Does that statement surprise you? If it does, it is probably because you do not understand exactly what a scientist is. But if you have ever observed the colors formed in a drop of oil in a puddle or watched a fire burn, you were acting like a scientist. You are also a scientist when you watch waves breaking on the shore or lightning bolts darting through the night sky. Or perhaps you have walked through the grass in the morning and noticed drops of dew or have screamed with delight as you watched a roller coaster dipping up and down the track. Whenever you observe the world around you, you are acting like a scientist. Does that give you a clue to the nature of science and scientists?

Scientists observe the world around them—just as you do. For that reason, whenever you make an observation you are acting like a scientist. But scientists do more than just observe. The word *science* comes from the Latin *scire,* which means "to know." So science is more than just observation. And real scientists do more than just observe. They question what they see. They wonder what makes things the way they are. And they attempt to find answers to their questions.

No doubt you also wonder about and question what you see—at least some of the time. Hopefully, you will be better able to find answers to some of your questions as a result of reading this chapter. That is, you will be better able to approach the world as a scientist does.

Figure 1–1 *Whenever you observe and question natural occurrences, such as a lightning storm, you are acting as a scientist does.*

Figure 1-2 *The goal of science is to understand events that occur in the world around us—such as this rare desert snowstorm in Arizona.*

The Nature of Science

The universe around you and inside of you is really a collection of countless mysteries. It is the job of scientists to solve those mysteries. **The goal of science is to understand the world around us.**

How do scientists go about understanding the world? Like all good detectives, scientists use special methods to determine truths about nature. Such truths are called facts. Here is an example of a fact: The sun is a source of light and heat. But science is more than a list of facts—just as studying science is more than memorizing facts. Jules Henri Poincaré, a famous nineteenth-century French scientist who charted the motions of planets, put it this way: "Science is built up with facts, as a house is with stones. But a collection of facts is no more a science than a heap of stones is a house."

So scientists go further than simply discovering facts. Scientists try to use facts to solve larger mysteries of nature. In this sense, you might think of facts as clues to scientific mysteries. An example of a larger mystery is how the sun produces the heat and light it showers upon the Earth. Another larger mystery is how the relatively few and simple organisms of 3 billion years ago gave rise to the many complex organisms that inhabit the Earth today.

Using facts they have gathered, scientists propose explanations for the events they observe. Then they perform experiments to test their explanations. In the next section of this chapter, you will learn how scientists go about performing experiments and uncovering the mysteries of nature.

ACTIVITY
WRITING

Changing Theories

Albert Einstein once stated that he would consider his work a failure if new and better theories did not replace his own. Using the following words, write an essay describing how new evidence can change an existing theory.

data
variable
hypothesis
scientific method
control
experiment
conclusions

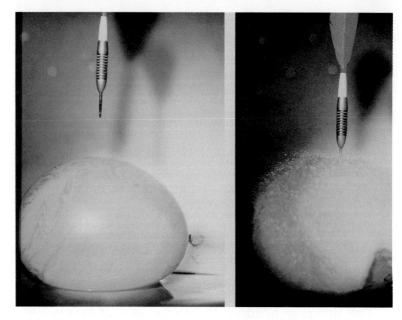

Figure 1–3 *It had long been a theory that a liquid did not retain its shape when removed from its container. However, scientists were forced to change that theory after observing the photographs shown here. The photographs show that the water in the balloon retained its balloon shape for 12 to 13 millionths of a second after the balloon had been burst by a dart.*

After studying facts, making observations, and performing experiments, scientists may develop a **theory.** A theory is the most logical explanation for events that occur in nature. Keep in mind that scientists do not use the word theory as you do. For example, you may have a theory about why your favorite soccer team is not winning. Your theory may or may not make sense. But it is not a scientific theory. A scientific theory is not just a guess or a hunch. A scientific theory is a powerful, time-tested concept that makes useful and dependable predictions about the natural world.

When a scientist proposes a theory, that theory must be tested over and over again. If it survives the

Figure 1–4 *Life science includes the study of animals such as the diamondback rattlesnake.*

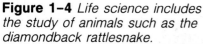

tests, the theory may be accepted by the scientific community. However, theories can be wrong and may be changed after additional tests and/or observations.

In some cases, if a hypothesis survives many tests, it becomes a **law**. A law summarizes observed experimental facts—it does not explain the facts. The explanation resides in the appropriate theory. Laws, like theories, may change as new information is provided or new experiments are performed. This points out the spirit at the heart of science: Always allow questions to be asked and new scientific explanations to be considered.

Branches of Science

One of the skills you will develop as you continue to study science is the ability to organize things in a logical, orderly way—that is, to classify things. Classification systems are an important part of science. For example, biologists classify all life on Earth into five broad kingdoms of living things. Astronomers classify stars into five main types according to their size. And chemists classify the 109 known elements according to their properties, or characteristics.

Even the study of science can be classified into groups or, in this case, what we call branches of science. There can be many branches of science, each determined by the subject matter being studied. For our purposes, however, we will consider only the three main (overarching) branches of science: life science, earth science, and physical science.

LIFE SCIENCE Life science deals with living things and their parts and actions. Smaller branches of life science include zoology (the study of animals) and botany (the study of plants).

EARTH SCIENCE Earth science is the study of the Earth and its rocks, oceans, volcanoes, earthquakes, atmosphere, and other features. Usually earth science also includes astronomy. Astronomers explore nature beyond the Earth. They study such objects as stars, planets, and moons.

PHYSICAL SCIENCE Physical science is the study of matter and energy. Some physical scientists explore what substances are made of and how they change

Figure 1–5 *What branch of science includes the study of planet Saturn?*

Figure 1–6 *Physics is the branch of physical science that studies the heat and light given off by a campfire. What branch of physical science would study the chemical changes that occur when wood burns?*

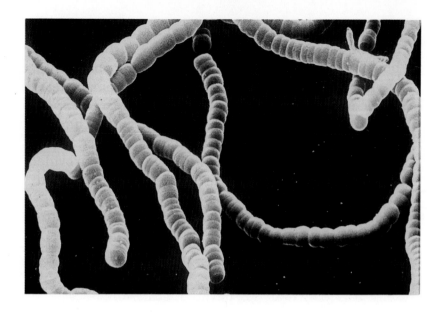

Figure 1–7 *Bacteria are among the living things examined by scientists who explore the microscopic world.*

and combine. This branch of physical science is called chemistry. Other physical scientists study forms of energy such as heat and light. This is the science of physics.

It is important for you to remember that the branches of science are a handy way to classify the subject matter scientists study. But it would be a mistake to think that any branch works independently of the others. To the contrary, the branches of science actually interweave and overlap most of the time. Science does not happen in a vacuum, and the great discoveries of science do not usually occur unless scientists from many branches work together.

ACTIVITY

DISCOVERING

Homestyle Classification

Is classification only for scientists? Not at all. Choose a room in your home and take a careful look around. Make a list of the various ways in which objects are classified. (For example, all of your socks are probably grouped together in one drawer.)

■ Does this activity suggest ways in which you might classify objects in order to organize them better?

1–1 Section Review

1. What is the goal of science?
2. Describe the three main branches of science. Give an example of a question that might be asked by scientists in each branch.

Critical Thinking—*Applying Concepts*

3. How might advances in technology affect the kinds of questions scientists ask about the world?

1–2 The Scientific Method— A Way of Problem Solving

Guide for Reading

Focus on these questions as you read.

▶ *What is the scientific method?*

▶ *How does it help scientists to discover truths about nature?*

You have read about the goal of science and the branches of science. By now you may be wondering just what separates science from other subject areas. After all, historians ask questions about the conflicts between nations, philosophers ask questions about the nature of existence, and experts on literature seek the hidden meaning in great novels. In fact, just about every area of study asks questions about the world. So what's so special about science?

What distinguishes science from other fields of study is the way in which science seeks answers to questions. In other words, what separates science is an approach called the **scientific method.** The scientific method is a systematic approach to problem solving. **The basic steps in the scientific method are**

Stating the problem
Gathering information on the problem
Forming a hypothesis
Performing experiments to test the hypothesis
Recording and analyzing data
Stating a conclusion
Repeating the work

The following example shows how the scientific method was used to solve a problem. As you will see, the steps of the scientific method often overlap.

Stating the Problem

Bundled up in warm clothing, heads bent into the wind, two friends walked along the beach. Drifts of snow rose against a fence that in the summer held back dunes of sand. Beyond the fence, a row of beach houses drew the attention of the friends.

There, from the roofs of the houses, hung glistening strips of ice. Only yesterday these beautiful icicles had been a mass of melting snow. Throughout the night, the melted snow had continued to drip, freezing into lovely shapes.

Figure 1–8 *What causes fresh water to freeze at a higher temperature than sea water? How might you find an answer to this question?*

Near the ocean's edge, the friends spied a small pool of sea water. Surprisingly, it was not frozen as were the icicles on the roofs. What could be the reason for this curious observation?

Without realizing it, the friends had taken an important step in the scientific method. They had recognized a scientific problem. A scientist might state this problem in another way: What causes fresh water to freeze at a higher temperature than sea water?

Gathering Information on the Problem

A scientist might begin to solve the problem by gathering information. The scientist would first find out how the sea water in the pool differs from the fresh water on the roof. This information might include the following facts: The pool of sea water rests on sand, while the fresh water drips along a tar roof. The sea water is exposed to the cold air for less time than the fresh water. The sea water is saltier than the fresh water.

Forming a Hypothesis

Using all of the information that has been gathered, the scientist might be prepared to suggest a possible solution to the problem. A proposed solution to a scientific problem is called a **hypothesis** (high-PAHTH-uh-sihs). A hypothesis almost always follows the gathering of information about a problem. But sometimes a hypothesis is a sudden idea that springs from a new way of looking at a problem.

Among the suggested hypotheses for our problem is this: Because fresh water does not contain salt, it freezes at a higher temperature than sea water.

Performing Experiments to Test the Hypothesis

A scientist does not stop once a hypothesis has been suggested. In science, evidence that either supports a hypothesis or does not support it must be found. This means that a hypothesis must be tested to show whether or not it is correct. Such testing is usually done by performing experiments.

Experiments are performed according to specific rules. By following these rules, scientists can be confident that the evidence they uncover will clearly support or not support a hypothesis. For the problem of the sea water and fresh water, a scientist would have to design an experiment that ruled out every factor but salt as the cause of the different freezing temperatures.

Let's see how a scientist would actually do this. First, the scientist would put equal amounts of fresh water into two identical containers. Then the scientist would add salt to only one of the containers. The salt is the **variable,** or the factor being tested. In any experiment, only one variable should be tested at a time. In this way, the scientist can be fairly certain that the results of the experiment are caused by one and only one factor—in this case the variable of salt. To eliminate the possibility of hidden or unknown variables, the scientist must run a **control** experiment. A control experiment is set up exactly like the one that contains the variable, except the control experiment does not contain the variable.

In this experiment, the scientist uses two containers of the same size with equal amounts of water. The water in both containers is at the same starting

Expanding Water?

Most substances on Earth contract, or become smaller in volume, when they freeze. Is water an exception? Using a small pan, water, and a freezing compartment, perform an experiment to discover whether or not water contracts when it freezes. Write down what you did in the form of a procedure and your results in the form of a conclusion.

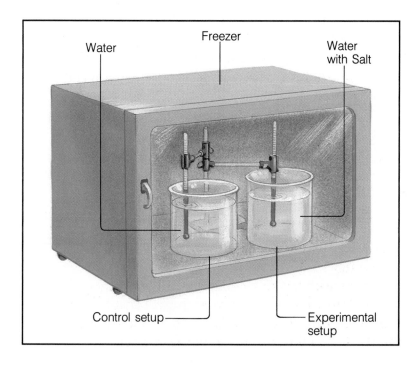

Control setup — Experimental setup

Figure 1–9 *What is the variable in this experiment? Explain your answer.*

13

temperature. The containers are placed side by side in the freezing compartment of a refrigerator and checked every five minutes. *But only one container has salt in it.* In this way, the scientist can be fairly sure that any differences that occur in the two containers are due to the single variable of salt. In such experiments, the part of the experiment with the variable is called the experimental setup. The part of the experiment with the control is called the control setup.

Recording and Analyzing Data

To determine whether salt affects the freezing temperature of water, a scientist must observe the experiment and write down important information. Recorded observations and measurements are called **data.** In this experiment, the data would include the time intervals at which the containers were observed, the temperatures of the water at each interval, and whether the water in either container was frozen or not. In most cases the data would be recorded in data tables such as those shown in Figure 1–10.

Data tables are a simple, organized way of recording information from an experiment. Sometimes, however, it is useful to visually compare the data. To do so, a scientist might construct a graph on which to plot the data. Because the data tables have two different types of measurements (time and temperature), the graph would have two axes. See Figure 1–11.

Figure 1–10 *Scientists often record their observations in data tables. According to these data tables, at what temperature did the experiment begin? (Asterisks mean the liquid started to freeze.)*

WATER (Control setup)		WATER WITH SALT (Experimental setup)	
Time (minutes)	Temperature (˚C)	Time (minutes)	Temperature (˚C)
0	25	0	25
5	20	5	20
10	15	10	15
15	10	15	10
20	5	20	5
25	0*	25	0
30	0	30	-5
35	0	35	-10*
40	0	40	-10
45	0	45	-10

The horizontal axis of the graph would stand for the time measurements in the data tables. Time measurements were made every 5 minutes. So the horizontal axis would be marked with intervals of 5 minutes. The space between equal intervals would have to be equal. For example, the space between 10 minutes and 15 minutes would be the same as the space between 20 minutes and 25 minutes.

The vertical axis of the graph would stand for the temperature measurements in the data tables. The starting temperature of the water in the experiment was 25°C. The lowest temperature reached in the experiment was -10°C. So the vertical axis would begin with 25°C and end at -10°C. Each interval of temperature would have to be equal to every other interval of temperature.

After the axes of the graph were set up, the scientist would first graph the data from the experimental setup. Each pair of data points from the data table would be marked on the graph. At 0 minutes, for example, the temperature was 25°C. So the scientist would place a dot where 0 minutes and 25°C intersect—in the upper left corner of the graph. The next pair of data points was for 5 minutes and 20°C. So the scientist would lightly draw a vertical line

Figure 1–11 *The information in data tables can be visually presented in graphs.*

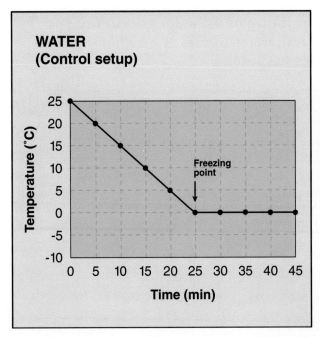

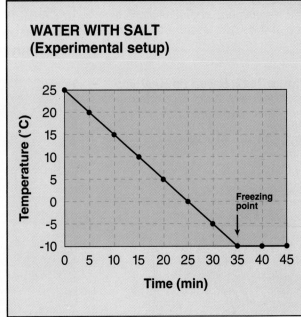

from the 5-minute interval of the horizontal axis and then a horizontal line from the 20°C interval of the vertical axis. The scientist would then put a dot at the place where the two lines intersected. This dot would represent the data points 5 minutes and 20°C. The scientist would continue to plot all of the data pairs from the data table in this manner.

When all of the data pairs were plotted, the scientist would draw a line through all the dots. This line would represent the graph of the experimental setup data. Then the scientist would follow the same procedure to graph the data pairs from the control setup. Figure 1–11 shows what the two lines would look like.

The results from a single experiment are not enough to reach a conclusion. A scientist must run an experiment over and over again before the data can be considered accurate. From the data in this experiment, the scientist would quickly find that the temperatures in both containers fall at the same rate. But the fresh water freezes at a higher temperature than the salt water.

Stating a Conclusion

If the two friends walking along the beach had followed the same steps as a scientist, they would now be ready to state a conclusion. Their conclusion would be this: When salt is dissolved in water, the freezing temperature of the water goes down. For this reason, fresh water freezes at a higher temperature than does sea water.

Figure 1–12 *Based on what you have learned, can you explain why mountain roads are often salted before a snowfall? What evidence do you have that this road was salted?*

Why does this happen, you may ask? This question sounds very much like the beginning of a new puzzle. It often happens in science that the solution of one problems leads to yet another problem. Thus the cycle of discovery goes on and on.

Repeating the Work

Although the two friends might be satisfied with their conclusion, not so with a scientist. As you read before, a scientist would want to repeat the experiment many times to be sure the data were accurate. So a scientific experiment must be able to be repeated. And before the conclusion of a scientist can be accepted by the scientific community, other scientists must repeat the experiment and check the results. So when a scientist writes a report on his or her experiment, that report must be detailed enough so that scientists throughout the world can repeat the experiment for themselves. In most cases, it is only when an experiment has been repeated by scientists worldwide is it considered to be accurate and worthy of being included in new scientific research.

Figure 1–13 *Why would it be difficult to study the effects of a single variable on these East African lions? Why is it not always possible for an experiment to have a single variable?*

The Scientific Method—Not Always So Orderly

By now it must seem as if science is a fairly predictable way of studying the world. After all, you state a problem, gather information, form a hypothesis, run an experiment, and determine a conclusion. It certainly sounds all neat and tidy. Well, sometimes it is—and sometimes it isn't!

In practice, scientists do not always follow all the steps in the scientific method. Nor do the steps always follow the same order. For example, while doing an experiment a scientist might observe something unusual or unexpected. That unexpected event might cause the scientist to discard the original hypothesis and suggest a new one. Or it might cause the scientist to suggest a new problem. Another example is that although it is a good rule that all experiments should have only one variable, it is not always practical in the real world.

Figure 1–14 *A working knowledge of prefixes and suffixes used in science vocabulary will be of great help to you. According to this chart, what is the meaning of the term converge?*

Prefix	Meaning	Prefix	Meaning	Suffix	Meaning
anti-	against	in-	inside	-ation	the act of
atmo-	vapor	inter-	between	-escent	becoming
chromo-	color	iso-	equal	-graphy	description of
con-	together	macro-	large	-logy	study of
di-	double	micro-	small	-meter	device for measuring
endo-	within	photo-	light	-scope	instrument for seeing
exo-	outside	sub-	under	-sphere	round
hetero-	different	syn-	together	-stasis	stationary condition
homo-	same	tele-	distant	-therm	heat
hydro-	water	trans-	across	-verge	turn

The Scientific Method in Your World

A common question often asked by students is "Why are we studying science? What does it have to do with my world?" The answer is—plenty! Perhaps you have little interest in the reason why fresh water freezes at a higher temperature than sea water. Maybe you live in a city or in a part of the country far removed from a beach. But regardless of where you live, people probably drive cars. And that means they may worry about the water in the car's radiator freezing in the winter and boiling over in the summer. How do we prevent these events from occurring? You probably know the answer—we add antifreeze to the radiator.

The principle behind the actions of antifreeze is exactly the same as the principle behind the fresh and salt water experiment. Adding antifreeze lowers the freezing temperature and raises the boiling temperature of water.

You should keep this example in mind whenever you study science. For very often the concepts you are learning about have very practical applications in your world. When possible, we will point out the relevance of the material you are studying. But that may not always be practical. So it's up to you to remember that science is not just for laboratory workers in white coats. Science affects all of us— each and every day of our lives.

FIND OUT BY WRITING

Prefixes and Suffixes

Study the list of common science prefixes and suffixes in Figure 1–14.

1. Select three science words that have a prefix listed on the chart.

2. Select two science words that have a suffix listed on the chart.

3. Write a paragraph using the five words you have chosen.

4. Do you know any additional science prefixes and suffixes that you think should be added to the chart? Share your findings with your class.

1–2 Section Review

1. List and describe the steps in the scientific method.
2. Explain the importance of running both an experimental setup and a control setup.

Connection—*You and Your World*

3. One morning you wake up and discover that your radio no longer works. How might you apply the steps of the scientific method to determine the cause of the problem?

Guide for Reading

Focus on this question as you read.

- *What are the basic units of measurement in the metric system?*

1–3 The Metric System

As you learned, experimenting is an important part of any scientific method. And most experiments involve measurements. Measurements made during experiments must be reliable and accurate as well as easily communicated to others. So a system of measurements based on standard units is used by scientists. With this system, scientists around the world can compare and analyze data.

The standard system used by scientists is the **metric system**. The metric system is also referred to as the International System of Units, or SI. The metric system is a decimal system. That is, it is based on the number 10 and multiples of 10.

Scientists use metric units to measure length, volume, mass, density, and temperature. Some frequently used metric units and their abbreviations are listed in Figure 1–15.

Length

The basic unit of length in the metric system is the **meter (m).** A meter is equal to about 39.4 inches. Your height would be measured in meters.

Figure 1–15 *The metric system is easy to use because it is based on units of ten. How many centimeters are there in 10 meters?*

COMMON METRIC UNITS	
Length	**Mass**
1 meter (m) = 100 centimeters (cm) 1 meter = 1000 millimeters (mm) 1 meter = 1,000,000 micrometers (μm) 1 meter = 1,000,000,000 nanometers (nm) 1 meter = 10,000,000,000 angstroms (Å) 1000 meters = 1 kilometer (km)	1 kilogram (kg) = 1000 grams (g) 1 gram = 1000 milligrams (mg) 1000 kilograms = 1 metric ton (t)
Volume	**Temperature**
1 liter (L) = 1000 milliliters (mL) or 1000 cubic centimeters (cm^3)	0°C = freezing point of water 100°C = boiling point of water
kilo- = one thousand centi- = one hundredth milli- = one thousandth	micro- = one millionth nano- = one billionth

Most students your age are between 1½ and 2 meters tall.

To measure the length of an object smaller than a meter, the metric unit called the **centimeter (cm)** is used. The prefix *centi-* means one-hundredth. So there are 100 centimeters in a meter. The height of this book is about 26 centimeters.

To measure even smaller objects, the metric unit called the **millimeter (mm)** is used. The prefix *milli-* means one-thousandth. As you might expect, there are 1000 millimeters in a meter. How many millimeters are there in a centimeter?

Sometimes scientists want to measure long distances, such as the length of the Nile River in Africa or the distance around the Earth's equator. Such lengths can be measured in meters, centimeters, or even millimeters. But when measuring long distances with small units, the numbers become very large and difficult to work with. For example, the length of the Nile River is about 6,649,000,000 millimeters. To avoid such large numbers, the metric unit called the **kilometer (km)** is used. The prefix *kilo-* means one thousand. So there are 1000 meters in a kilometer. The length of the Nile River is about 6649 kilometers. How many meters is this? How many centimeters are there in one kilometer? How many millimeters? The distance around the Earth's equator is 40,075 kilometers. Would it be easier to describe this measurement in meters?

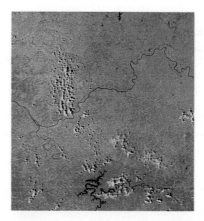

Figure 1–16 *This image showing the Missouri River was taken from a satellite in Earth orbit. In what units would you measure the length of the river?*

Volume

Volume is the amount of space an object takes up. The basic unit of volume in the metric system is the **liter (L).** A liter is slightly more than a quart. To measure volumes smaller than a liter, scientists use the **milliliter (mL).** There are 1000 milliliters in a liter. An ordinary drinking glass holds about 200 milliliters of liquid.

Liters and milliliters are used to measure the volume of liquids. The metric unit used to measure the volume of solids is called the **cubic centimeter (cm³ or cc).** A cubic centimeter is equal to a milliliter. Cubic centimeters often are used in measuring the volume of liquids as well as solids. How many cubic centimeters are there in a liter?

Figure 1–17 *A cubic centimeter (cm³, or cc) is the volume of a cube that measures 1 cm by 1 cm by 1 cm. How many milliliters are in a cubic centimeter?*

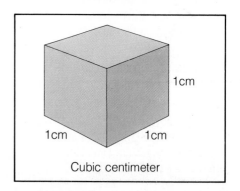

Cubic centimeter

Figure 1–18 *The hippopotamus is one of the largest land animals on the earth. Harvest field mice are the smallest mice on the earth. Which metric unit would be best for measuring the mass of a hippopotamus? Of field mice?*

Mass

The basic unit of mass in the metric system is the **kilogram (kg).** Mass is a measure of the amount of matter in an object. For example, there is more matter in a dumptruck than in a compact car. So a dumptruck has more mass than a compact car. A kilogram is about 2.2 pounds. What is your mass in kilograms?

The kilogram is used to measure the mass of large objects. To measure the mass of small objects, such as a nickel, the **gram (g)** is used. A nickel has a mass of about 5 grams. If you remember what the term *kilo-* means, then you know that a kilogram contains 1000 grams.

The mass of even smaller objects is measured in **milligrams (mg).** A milligram is one-thousandth of a gram. So there are 1000 milligrams in a gram. How many milligrams are there in a kilogram?

Density

Sometimes it is useful to know the amount of mass in a given volume of an object. This quantity is known as **density.** Density is defined as the mass per unit volume of a substance. The following formula shows the relationship between density, mass, and volume:

$$\text{density} = \frac{\text{mass}}{\text{volume}}$$

Suppose a substance has a mass of 10 grams and a volume of 10 milliliters. If you divide the mass of 10 grams by the volume of 10 milliliters, you obtain the density of the substance:

$$\frac{10 \text{ g}}{10 \text{ mL}} = \frac{1 \text{ g}}{\text{mL}}$$

As it turns out, this substance is water. The density of water is 1g/mL. Objects with a density less than that of water will float on water. Objects with a density greater than that of water will sink in water. Does wood have a density less than or greater than 1 g/mL?

Temperature

In the metric system, temperature is measured on the **Celsius** (SEHL-see-uhs) scale. On the Celsius temperature scale, water freezes at 0°C and boils at 100°C. There are exactly 100 degrees between the freezing point and boiling point of water. Each Celsius degree represents 1/100 of this temperature range. Normal body temperature in humans is 37°C. Comfortable room temperature is about 21°C.

Dimensional Analysis

Now that you know the basic units of the metric system, it is important that you understand how to go from one unit to another. The skill of converting one unit to another is called **dimensional analysis.** Dimensional analysis involves determining in what units a problem is given, in what units the answer should be, and the factor to be used to make the conversion from one unit to another.

To perform dimensional analysis, you must use a **conversion factor.** A conversion factor is a fraction that always equals 1. For example, 1 kilometer equals 1000 meters. So the fraction 1 kilometer/ 1000 meters equals 1. So does the fraction 1000 meters/1 kilometer. The top number in a fraction is called the numerator. The bottom number in a fraction is called the denominator. In a conversion fraction the numerator always equals the denominator so that the fraction always equals 1.

Activity Bank

Calculating Density, p. 712

Figure 1–19 Notice the steam rising out of Mammoth Hot Springs in Yellowstone National Park. What unit would be used to measure the temperature of the springs?

Let's see how dimensional analysis works. Suppose you are told to convert 2500 grams to kilograms. This means that grams are your given unit and you must express your answer in kilograms. The conversion factor you choose must contain a relationship between grams and kilograms that has a value of 1. You have two possible choices:

$$\frac{1000 \text{ grams}}{1 \text{ kilogram}} = 1 \quad \text{or} \quad \frac{1 \text{ kilogram}}{1000 \text{ grams}} = 1$$

To convert one metric unit to another, you must multiply the given value times the conversion factor. Remember that multiplying a number by 1 does not change the value of the number. So multiplying by a conversion factor just changes the units.

Now, which conversion factor should you use to change 2500 grams into kilograms? Since you are going to multiply by the conversion factor, you want the unit to be converted to cancel out during the multiplication. This is just what will happen if the denominator of the conversion factor has the same units as the value you wish to convert. Since you are converting grams into kilograms, the denominator of the conversion factor must be in grams and the numerator in kilograms. The first step in dimensional analysis, then, is to write out the value given, the correct conversion factor, and a multiplication symbol between them:

$$2500 \text{ grams} \times \frac{1 \text{ kilogram}}{1000 \text{ grams}}$$

The next step is to cancel out the same units:

$$2500 \text{ grams} \times \frac{1 \text{ kilogram}}{1000 \text{ grams}}$$

The last step is to multiply:

$$2500 \times \frac{1 \text{ kilogram}}{1000} = \frac{2500 \text{ kilograms}}{1000}$$

$$\frac{2500 \text{ kilogram}}{1000} = 2.5 \text{ kilograms}$$

ACTIVITY

CALCULATING

Metric Conversions

Use conversion factors to make the following metric conversions. *Do not write in this book.*

10 m = _____ km
2 km = _____ cm
250 mL = _____ L
2000 g = _____ kg
10 kg = _____ mg
1500 cc = _____ L

PROBLEM ??? Solving

Dimension Convention

You have been selected as your school's representative to the International Dimension Convention. The purpose of the convention is to select the dimensional analysis champion. In order to help you bring home the trophy, your classmates have developed the following problems for you to solve. Keep in mind that the champion will be determined on both speed and accuracy.

Making Conversions

1. Two friends are training for the track team. One friend runs 5000 meters each morning. The other friend runs about 3 kilometers. Which friend is training the hardest?

2. Data from several experiments have been sent to you for analysis. To compare the data, however, you must convert the following measurements to the same units.

> 20 kilograms
> 700 grams
> 0.004 kilograms
> 300 milligrams

3. Your cat's bowl holds 0.25 liter. You have about 300 cubic centimeters of milk. Will all the milk fit in the bowl?

4. A recipe calls for 350 grams of flour. You have used 0.4 kilogram. Did you put in too much, too little, or just the right amount?

1–3 Section Review

1. What are the basic units of length, volume, mass, and temperature in the metric system?
2. What metric unit of length would be appropriate for expressing the distance from the Earth to the sun? Why?
3. To measure the size of atoms, scientists use the unit called the Angstrom. An Angstrom is one ten-billionth of a meter. How many Angstroms are in a meter?

Critical Thinking—*Applying Concepts*
4. Without placing an object in water, how can you determine if it will float?

1–4 Tools of Measurement

Physical scientists use a wide variety of tools in order to study the world around them. Some of these tools are rather complex; others are relatively simple. In fact, you may have already used some of these tools. As you read this textbook, you will be introduced to several such tools. You will find out when and why they are used and how the development of new and more powerful tools has allowed scientists to make discoveries about the physical world. You will even have an opportunity to use some of these laboratory tools when you perform physical science experiments. **The basic laboratory tools that you will learn to use are the metric ruler, triple-beam balance, graduated cylinder, and Celsius thermometer.**

Measuring Length

A metric ruler is used to measure the length of objects. A metric ruler is divided into centimeters. Common metric rulers are 15 or 25 centimeters in length. Each centimeter is further divided into 10 millimeters. Figure 1–20 shows a metric ruler and the centimeter and millimeter divisions. Keep in mind that this ruler is not drawn to scale. You cannot use it to make calculations.

To measure an object whose length is longer than a metric ruler, you would use a meterstick. A meterstick is one meter long and contains 100 centimeters. How many millimeters are in a meterstick?

Figure 1–20 *A metric ruler is used to measure the length of small objects. What is the length of this paper clip?*

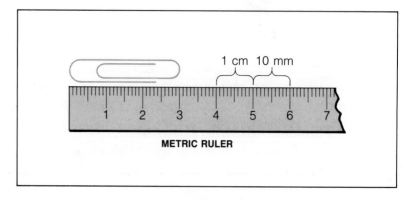

METRIC RULER

Measuring Mass

Recall that the kilogram is the basic unit of mass in the metric system. A kilogram contains 1000 grams. Most of the measurements you will make in physical science will be in grams. One of the most common tools used to measure mass in grams is the triple-beam balance shown in Figure 1–21.

As you might expect, a triple-beam balance has three beams. Each beam is marked, or calibrated, in grams. The front beam is the 10-gram beam. Markings divide the beam into 10 segments of 1 gram each. On some triple-beam balances, each 1-gram segment on the front beam is further divided into units of one-tenth gram. The middle beam, often called the 500-gram beam, is divided into 5 segments of 100 grams each. The back beam, or 100-gram beam, is divided into 10 segments of 10 grams each. What is the largest mass you can measure with a triple-beam balance?

To measure the mass of a solid, such as a small rock, follow these steps. First, place the rock on the flat pan of the balance. Then slide the rider on the middle beam notch by notch until the pointer drops below zero. Move the rider back one notch. Next, slide the rider on the back beam notch by notch until the pointer drops below zero. Move this rider back one notch. Finally, move the rider on the front

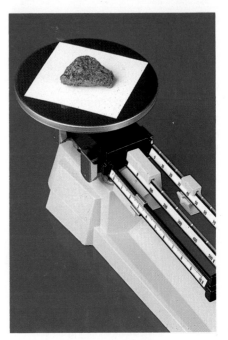

Figure 1–21 *A triple-beam balance is one of the instruments used to measure mass in grams. Can mass in kilograms be measured by using a triple-beam balance? Explain your answer.*

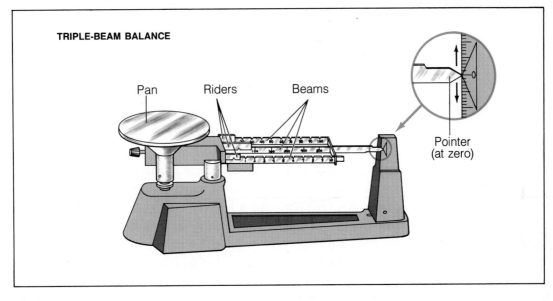

TRIPLE-BEAM BALANCE

Pan   Riders   Beams

Pointer (at zero)

ACTIVITY

DISCOVERING

A Milliliter by Any Other Name

■ Use a graduated cylinder, water, a metric ruler, and a small rectangular solid made of a material that sinks in water to prove that 1 milliliter = 1 cubic centimeter.

Figure 1–22 *A graduated cylinder is used to measure volume (top). To get an accurate measurement, where should you read the markings on the graduated cylinder? What is the volume of this rectangular block in cubic centimeters (cm³) (bottom)?*

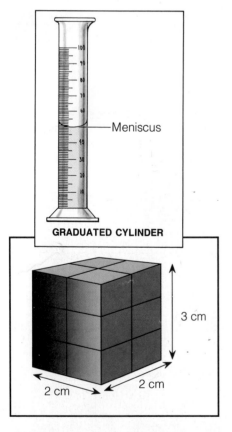

beam notch by notch until the pointer points exactly to the zero mark. The mass of the object is equal to the *sum* of the readings on the three beams.

If you want to find the mass of a powder or of crystals, you will have to place the sample on a sheet of filter paper on top of the pan. You must never place such a sample directly on the balance pan. The mass of the filter paper must first be determined. Once this is done, you can pour the sample onto the filter paper and find the mass of the filter paper and sample combined. Subtract the mass of the filter paper from the mass of filter paper and sample to determine the mass of the sample.

A similar method can be used to find the mass of a liquid. In this case, place an empty beaker or flask on the pan and find its mass. Then pour the liquid into the beaker. Find the combined mass of the beaker and liquid. Subtract the mass of the beaker from the mass of the beaker and liquid to determine the mass of the liquid.

Measuring Volume

You learned that the basic unit of volume in the metric system is the liter. Most of the measurements you will make in physical science, however, will be in milliliters or cubic centimeters. Remember there are 1000 milliliters or cubic centimeters in a liter.

To find the volume of a liquid, you will use a graduated cylinder. See Figure 1–22. A graduated cylinder is usually calibrated in milliliters. Each line on the graduated cylinder is one milliliter. To measure the volume of a liquid, pour the liquid into the graduated cylinder. You will notice that the surface of the liquid is curved. To determine the volume of the liquid, read the milliliter marking at the *bottom* of the curve. This curve is called the **meniscus** (mih-NIHS-kuhs). Keep in mind that although a graduated cylinder is marked off in milliliters, each milliliter is equal to one cubic centimeter.

To find the volume of a solid that is rectangular in shape, you will use a metric ruler. A rectangular solid is often called a regular solid. The volume of a regular solid is determined by multiplying the length of the solid times the width of the solid times the height of the solid.

The formula you can use to find the volume of a regular solid is

volume = height times length times width

or

$$v = h \times l \times w$$

Figure 1–22 shows a rectangular solid with a length of 2 centimeters, a width of 2 centimeters, and a height of 3 centimeters. If you multiply 2 cm times 2 cm times 3 cm, you obtain the volume, which is 12 cm³, or 12 cc. What is the volume of a regular solid 3 cm by 4 cm by 5 cm?

Suppose you wish to determine the volume of a solid that is not rectangular in shape, or an irregular solid. You cannot measure its height, width, or length with a metric ruler. So to determine the volume of an irregular solid, you will use a graduated cylinder again. First fill the cylinder about half full with water. Record the volume of the water. Then carefully place the solid into the liquid. Record the volume of the liquid and solid combined. Then subtract the volume of the liquid from the combined volume of the liquid and solid. The answer will be the volume of the irregular solid. Will the volume be in milliliters or in cubic centimeters?

Measuring Temperature

To measure temperature, you will use a Celsius thermometer. The two fixed points on a Celsius thermometer are the freezing point of water, 0°C, and the boiling point of water, 100°C. Some Celsius thermometers go as low as -25°C so that temperatures below the freezing point of water can be measured. Each calibration on a Celsius thermometer is equal to one degree Celsius.

Within the glass tube of a Celsius thermometer is a colored liquid. Alcohol or mercury are the two liquids most commonly used. To measure the temperature of a substance, place the thermometer in the substance. The level of the liquid in the thermometer will begin to change. When it stops changing, read the number next to the mark on the thermometer that lines up with the top of the liquid. This is the temperature of the substance.

ACTIVITY DOING

Metric Measurements

Here are some measurements you can make about yourself and your surroundings. Use the metric units of length, mass, volume, and temperature. Record your measurements in a chart.

- height
- arm length
- body temperature
- volume of water you drink in a day
- outdoor temperature
- automobile speed limit on your street
- distance to school
- total mass of ingredients in your favorite cake recipe
- mass of your favorite sports equipment

Figure 1–23 *A Celsius thermometer is used to measure temperature. What is the temperature of the ice-water mixture in the beaker?*

CONNECTIONS

Elbows to Fingertips

Have you complained to your teacher yet that you do not like the metric system? If so, perhaps you should read about some ancient systems of measurement. You might just decide that the metric system makes a lot of sense.

The Egyptians: The Egyptians are credited with having developed the most widespread system of measuring length in the ancient world. Developed around 3000 BC, the Egyptian standard of measurement was the *cubit.* The cubit was based on the length from the elbow to the fingertips. The cubit was further divided into *digits* (the length of

a finger), *palms,* and *hands.* As you can see, body parts were the basis for most measurements.

The cubit may not seem like a very accurate measurement as the length of an arm varies from person to person. To avoid any confusion, a standard cubit made of granite was developed. All cubit sticks used in Egypt were measured against the standard granite cubit. And while this may not seem all that precise, the Egyptians built the great pyramids with incredible accuracy using the cubit!

The Greeks and Romans: Around 1000 BC, the Greeks developed a new system of measuring length. The basic unit of measurement was called the *finger* (again, body parts were popular). Sixteen fingers equaled a *foot* in the Greek system. Over time the influence of the Greeks diminished and the Romans became the dominant culture in the ancient world. The Romans adjusted the Greek system and divided the Greek foot into twelve *inches.* (Although the lengths have changed, we still use feet and inches in the United States.) The Romans then decided that five feet equaled a *pace.* And finally, one thousand paces equaled what they called a *mile.*

So the next time you are asked to measure something in meters or centimeters, remember—it could be worse. You could have to measure the distance from one place to another by placing your arm down over and over again.

1-4 Section Review

1. Each side of a regular solid is 5 centimeters long. What is the volume of the solid?
2. What instrument would you use to measure length? Mass? Volume? Temperature?

Critical Thinking—*Applying Concepts*

3. If you want to find the density of an irregular object, what tools will you need? How will you go about making this measurement?

1-5 Safety in the Science Laboratory

The science laboratory is a place of adventure and discovery. Some of the most exciting events in the history of science have taken place in laboratories. The discovery of X-rays is one example. Another example is the discovery of oxygen. The relationship between electricity and magnetism was also discovered by scientists working in a laboratory. The list goes on and on.

To better understand the facts and concepts you will read about in physical science, you may work in the laboratory this year. If you follow instructions and are as careful as a scientist would be, the laboratory will turn out to be an exciting experience.

When working in the laboratory, scientists know that it is very important to follow safety procedures. All of the work you will do in the laboratory this year will include experiments that have been done over and over again. When done properly, the experiments are interesting and safe. However, if they are done improperly, accidents can occur. How can you avoid such problems?

First and foremost, always follow your teacher's directions or the directions in your textbook exactly as stated. Never try anything on your own without asking your teacher first. And when you are not sure what you should do, always ask first. As

Figure 1–24 *It is important to always point a test tube that is being heated away from yourself and your classmates (left). What two safety precautions is this student taking before picking up a hot beaker (right)?*

you read the laboratory investigations in the textbook, you will see safety alert symbols next to certain procedures that require special safety care. Look at Figure 1–25 to learn the meanings of the safety symbols and the important safety precautions you should take.

In addition to the safety procedures listed in Figure 1–25, there is a more detailed list of safety procedures in Appendix C. Before you enter the laboratory for the first time, make sure that you have read each rule carefully. Then read them over again. Make sure that you understand each rule. If you do not understand a rule, ask your teacher to explain it. You may even want to suggest further rules that apply to your particular classroom.

1–5 Section Review

1. What is the most important general rule to follow when working in the laboratory?
2. Why is it important to point a test tube away from yourself and others when it is being heated?

Connection—*Your Health and Safety*
3. Where is the nearest fire extinguisher located in your laboratory or classroom?

Glassware Safety

1. Whenever you see this symbol, you will know that you are working with glassware that can easily be broken. Take particular care to handle such glassware safely. And never use broken or chipped glassware.
2. Never heat glassware that is not thoroughly dry. Never pick up any glassware unless you are sure it is not hot. If it is hot, use heat-resistant gloves.
3. Always clean glassware thoroughly before putting it away.

Fire Safety

1. Whenever you see this symbol, you will know that you are working with fire. Never use any source of fire without wearing safety goggles.
2. Never heat anything—particularly chemicals—unless instructed to do so.
3. Never heat anything in a closed container.
4. Never reach across a flame.
5. Always use a clamp, tongs, or heat-resistant gloves to handle hot objects.
6. Always maintain a clean work area, particularly when using a flame.

Heat Safety

Whenever you see this symbol, you will know that you should put on heat-resistant gloves to avoid burning your hands.

Chemical Safety

1. Whenever you see this symbol, you will know that you are working with chemicals that could be hazardous.
2. Never smell any chemical directly from its container. Always use your hand to waft some of the odors from the top of the container toward your nose—and only when instructed to do so.
3. Never mix chemicals unless instructed to do so.
4. Never touch or taste any chemical unless instructed to do so.
5. Keep all lids closed when chemicals are not in use. Dispose of all chemicals as instructed by your teacher.

6. Immediately rinse with water any chemicals, particularly acids, that get on your skin and clothes. Then notify your teacher.

Eye and Face Safety

1. Whenever you see this symbol, you will know that you are performing an experiment in which you must take precautions to protect your eyes and face by wearing safety goggles.
2. When you are heating a test tube or bottle, always point it away from you and others. Chemicals can splash or boil out of a heated test tube.

Sharp Instrument Safety

1. Whenever you see this symbol, you will know that you are working with a sharp instrument.
2. Always use single-edged razors; double-edged razors are too dangerous.
3. Handle any sharp instrument with extreme care. Never cut any material toward you; always cut away from you.
4. Immediately notify your teacher if your skin is cut.

Electrical Safety

1. Whenever you see this symbol, you will know that you are using electricity in the laboratory.
2. Never use long extension cords to plug in any electrical device. Do not plug too many appliances into one socket or you may overload the socket and cause a fire.
3. Never touch an electrical appliance or outlet with wet hands.

Animal Safety

1. Whenever you see this symbol, you will know that you are working with live animals.
2. Do not cause pain, discomfort, or injury to an animal.
3. Follow your teacher's directions when handling animals. Wash your hands thoroughly after handling animals or their cages.

Figure 1–25 *You should become familiar with these safety symbols because you will see them in the laboratory investigations in this textbook.*

Laboratory Investigation

Uncertainty of Measurements

Problem

How accurately can matter be measured?

Materials *(per station)*

Station 1: meterstick
Station 2: metric ruler
           regular object
Station 3: graduated cylinder
           beaker with colored liquid
Station 4: triple-beam balance
           small pebble
Station 5: graduated cylinder
           beaker of water
           irregular object
Station 6: Celsius thermometer
           beaker with ice and water
           paper towel

Procedure 🔺

1. Station 1: Use the meterstick to measure the length and width of the desk or lab table. If the table is irregular, measure the shortest width and the longest length. Express your measurements in centimeters.

2. Station 2: Use the metric ruler to find the volume of the regular object. Express the volume in cubic centimeters.

3. Station 3: Use the graduated cylinder to find the volume of the colored liquid in the beaker. Then pour the liquid back into the beaker. Express your measurement in milliliters.

4. Station 4: Place the pebble on the pan of the triple-beam balance. Move the riders until the pointer is at zero. Record the mass of the pebble in grams. Remove the pebble and return all riders back to zero.

5. Station 5: Fill the graduated cylinder half full with water. Find the volume of the irregular object. Express the volume of the object in cubic centimeters. Carefully remove the object from the graduated cylinder. Pour all of the water back into the beaker.

6. Station 6: Use the Celsius thermometer to find the temperature of the ice water. Record the temperature in degrees Celsius. Remove the thermometer and carefully dry it with a paper towel.

Observations

Your teacher will construct a large class data table for each of the work stations. Record the data from each work station in the class data table.

Analysis and Conclusions

1. Do all the class measurements have the exact same value for each station?

2. Which station had measurements that were most nearly alike? Explain why these measurements were so similar.

3. Which station had measurements that were most varied? Explain why these measurements were so varied.

4. **On Your Own**   Calculate the average (mean) for the class data for each work station.

Study Guide

Summarizing Key Concepts

1–1 Science—Not Just for Scientists

▲ The goal of science is to understand the world around us.

▲ A theory is the most logical explanation for events in nature. A theory is a time-tested concept that makes useful and dependable predictions about the natural world.

▲ The three main branches of science are life, earth, and physical science.

1–2 The Scientific Method—A Way of Problem Solving

▲ The basic steps in the scientific method are stating the problem, gathering information, forming a hypothesis, experimenting, recording and analyzing data, stating a conclusion, and repeating the work.

▲ A hypothesis is a proposed solution to a scientific problem.

▲ A variable is the one factor that is being tested in an experiment.

▲ Scientists run an experimental setup and a control setup, or experiment without the variable.

1–3 The Metric System

▲ The standard system of measurement used by all scientists is the metric system.

▲ The basic unit of length in the metric system is the meter. The basic unit of mass in the metric system is the kilogram. The basic unit of volume in the metric system is the liter.

▲ Density is defined as the mass per unit volume of an object.

▲ The basic unit of temperature in the metric system is the degree Celsius.

▲ Dimensional analysis is a method of converting from one unit to another.

1–4 Tools of Measurement

▲ The metric ruler is used to measure length.

▲ The triple-beam balance is used to measure mass.

▲ A graduated cylinder is used to find the volume of a liquid or the volume of an irregular solid. The volume of a regular solid can be determined by multiplying its height by its width by its length.

▲ A Celsius thermometer is used to measure temperature.

1–5 Safety in the Science Laboratory

▲ When working in the laboratory, it is important to take all necessary safety precautions.

Reviewing Key Terms

Define each term in a complete sentence.

1–1 Science—Not Just for Scientists
theory
law

1–2 The Scientific Method— A Way of Problem Solving
scientific method   control
hypothesis   data
variable

1–3 The Metric System
metric system   kilogram
meter   gram
centimeter   milligram
millimeter   density
kilometer   Celsius
liter   dimensional analysis
milliliter   conversion factor
cubic centimeter

1–4 Tools of Measurement
meniscus

Chapter Review

Content Review

Multiple Choice

Choose the letter of the answer that best completes each statement.

1. An orderly, systematic approach to problem solving is called a(an)
   a. experiment.
   b. scientific method.
   c. conclusion.
   d. dimensional analysis.

2. A proposed solution to a scientific problem is called a
   a. conclusion.
   b. theory.
   c. data.
   d. hypothesis.

3. In any experiment, the one factor being tested is the
   a. data.
   b. control.
   c. hypothesis.
   d. variable.

4. The basic unit of length in the metric system is the
   a. kilometer.
   b. centimeter.
   c. meter.
   d. liter.

5. In volume, a cubic centimeter is equal to a
   a. liter.
   b. milliliter.
   c. gram.
   d. milligram.

6. The basic unit of mass in the metric system is the
   a. kilogram.
   b. liter.
   c. milligram.
   d. gram.

7. The amount of matter in an object is called its
   a. volume.
   b. density.
   c. mass.
   d. dimension.

8. To measure the mass of a solid, use a
   a. graduated cylinder.
   b. triple-beam balance.
   c. meterstick.
   d. Celsius thermometer.

9. A graduated cylinder is calibrated in
   a. milliliters.
   b. liters.
   c. grams.
   d. degrees.

10. In the science laboratory, always
    a. eat your lunch.
    b. reach across a flame.
    c. follow directions.
    d. taste chemicals before using.

True or False

If the statement is true, write "true." If it is false, change the underlined word or words to make the statement true.

1. An experiment should have <u>two variables</u>.
2. The <u>experimental setup</u> contains the variable.
3. Recorded observations are called <u>data</u>.
4. The prefix *kilo-* means <u>one hundred</u>.
5. A liter contains <u>100 milliliters</u>.
6. Mass is measured in <u>liters</u>.
7. Density is <u>volume</u> per unit mass.
8. A <u>conversion fraction</u> must equal one.
9. The <u>front beam</u> of a triple-beam balance is often called the 500-gram beam.
10. To find the volume of a regular solid, you <u>multiply</u> height times width times length.

Concept Mapping

Complete the following concept map for Section 1–3. Then construct a concept map for the entire chapter.

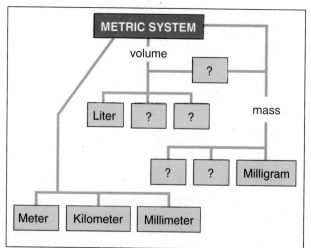

36

Concept Mastery

Discuss each of the following in a brief paragraph.

1. Describe the importance of a standard system of measurement.
2. Describe the steps of the scientific method.
3. Discuss the different metric units of length and explain when you might use each one.
4. Describe density in terms of mass and volume. Why is density such an important quantity?
5. Your friend wants you to convert kilograms to meters. Explain why that is not possible.
6. The Earth is about 5 billion years old. Yet some of the light that reaches Earth from distant stars began its journey before the Earth was formed. What does that tell you about the distance to those stars? Explain your answer.

Critical Thinking and Problem Solving

Use the skills you have developed in this chapter to answer each of the following.

1. **Applying concepts** What tool or tools would you use to make the following measurements? What units would you use to express your answers?
   a. Volume of a glass of water
   b. Length of a sheet of paper
   c. Mass of a liter of milk
   d. Length of a soccer field
   e. Volume of an irregular object
   f. Mass of a hockey puck
   g. Ocean temperature
2. **Making calculations** Use dimensional analysis to convert each of the following.
   a. A blue whale is about 33 meters in length. How many centimeters is this?
   b. The Statue of Liberty is about 45 meters tall. How tall is the statue in millimeters?
   c. Mount Everest is about 8.8 kilometers high. How high is it in meters?
   d. A Ping-Pong ball has a mass of about 2.5 grams. What is its mass in milligrams?
   e. An elephant is about 6300 kilograms in mass. What is its mass in grams?
3. **Relating concepts** Explain why every substance has a characteristic density, but no substance has a characteristic mass.

4. **Designing an experiment** A prospector is trying to sell you the deed to a gold mine. She gives you a sample from the mine and tells you it is pure gold. Design an experiment to determine if the sample is pure gold or "fools" gold. *Hint:* You will want to use the concept of density in your experiment.

5. **Using the writing process** Although the metric system is used throughout the world, it has not been officially adopted by the United States. Write a letter to the editor of your local newspaper in which you explain why the United States should or should not convert to the metric system.

General Properties of Matter

2

On July 19, 1545, a fleet of British warships sailed slowly out of Portsmouth Harbor, England, on its way to battle the French fleet. One ship, the *Mary Rose,* carried a crew of 415 sailors, 285 soldiers, and a number of very new, and very heavy, bronze cannons.

But the *Mary Rose* never met the French fleet. As the story goes, a gust of wind tipped over the *Mary Rose,* and in seconds the ship sank to the bottom of the sea. Was this the true story?

In 1965, teams of scuba divers began a search for the wreck of the *Mary Rose.* Some of the divers wore heavy weights on their belts so that they could hover above the sandy ocean bottom.

In 1967, the *Mary Rose* was found. And scientists uncovered the cause of the ship's sinking. The weight of the heavy bronze cannons had made the ship top-heavy. When the ship tipped over, water rushed into its open spaces, replacing the air. Without the air inside it, the *Mary Rose* had sunk like a stone.

But another mystery remains in this story—a mystery for you to solve. How can a diver wearing a weighted belt hover in the sea, while a ship weighted with cannons and excess water sinks to the bottom? You will uncover the solution as you read on.

Journal *Activity*

You and Your World Do you know how to swim? Think back to your first few attempts at floating in a pool or lake. What were your feelings as you moved through the water? Write your feelings in your journal. Have you ever swum in the ocean? Is it easier to remain afloat in salt water?

◀ *The secrets of the* Mary Rose—*hidden for so long under water—are revealed by a flashlight's piercing beam.*

2–1 Matter

Taking a bit of the Earth's air along, the astronaut you see in Figure 2–1 is walking over the surface of the moon. He and his fellow astronauts traveled a great distance on their journey to the moon and back, and, fortunately for us, they did not return home empty-handed. For along with tales of triumph, they brought back some of the moon itself: moon rocks for scientists to study in a laboratory and a special piece of moon rock for all to touch. This special rock, once part of the moon's surface, is now one of the great treasures on display at the Smithsonian Institution in Washington, DC. Touch this rock and your mind can journey to the moon with brave astronauts. Touch this rock and you can feel the stuff of the universe. But did you know that you can touch the stuff of the universe right here on Earth?

What Is Matter?

You see and touch hundreds of things every day. And although most of these things differ from one another, they all share one important quality: They are all forms of **matter.** Matter is what the visible universe is made of. Matter is what you are made of.

Through your senses of smell, sight, taste, and touch, you are familiar with matter. Some kinds of matter are easily recognized. Wood, water, salt, clay, glass, gold, plants, animals—even a piece of the moon—are examples of matter that are easily observed. Oxygen, carbon dioxide, ammonia, and air are kinds of matter that may not be as easily recognized. Are these different kinds of matter similar in some ways? Is salt anything like ammonia? Do water and glass have anything in common?

In order to answer these questions, you must know something about the **properties,** or characteristics, of matter. Properties describe an object. Color, odor, size, shape, texture, and hardness are properties of matter. These are specific properties of matter, however. Specific properties make it easy to tell one kind of matter from another. For example, it is

Figure 2–1 *The moon is the first body in space to feel the footprints of a human being. In this photograph you can see the ultimate "dune buggy," a specially designed vehicle that is able to scoot along the moon's soft surface. What kinds of technology make a moon visit possible?*

not hard to tell a red apple from a green one, or a smooth rock from a rough one.

Some properties of matter are more general. Instead of describing the differences among forms of matter, general properties describe how all matter is the same. **All matter has the general properties of mass, weight, volume, and density.**

Describing Properties

In a novel, the author describes the properties of the objects he or she is writing about. These details add interest to the story.

Collect at least six different kinds of objects. You might include rocks, pieces of wood or metal, and objects made by people. Identify each sample by its general properties and by its special properties. Now write a short paragraph that uses the descriptions you have developed. Be sure to include the following properties in your paragraph: color, density, hardness, mass, texture, shape, volume, and weight. Here is an example of the beginning of a paragraph:

It was a cold, wintry night as Jeff walked home from school. Small six-sided snowflakes fell to the ground. Walking past the Jefferson house, a three-story mansion with many pointed window frames, each of which had at least one broken pane of glass, Jeff was startled to see a huge shape. He had heard this house was haunted. . . .

Figure 2–2 *Rocks carved by winds, cascading water, beautiful plants, and floating magnets are all made of matter. In fact, everything on Earth—and beyond—is made of matter.*

2-1 Section Review

1. What is matter?
2. Name four general properties of matter.

Connection—*Astronomy*

3. Imagine that you have voyaged to deep space, far beyond our known universe. There you have encountered a planet inhabited by people who are much like you and who understand your language. They are very curious about Planet Earth. Describe for them the matter that makes up your home.

2-2 Mass and Weight

The most important general property of matter is that it has **mass. Mass is the amount of matter in an object.** The mass of an object is constant. It does not change unless matter is added to or removed from the object.

Mass, then, does not change when you move an object from one location to another. A car has the same mass in Los Angeles as it has in New York. You have the same mass on top of a mountain as you do at the bottom of a deep mine. In fact, you would have that exact same mass if you walked on the surface

Figure 2–3 *You know that a bowling ball has weight, for it is heavy to lift. The weight of a bowling ball depends upon gravity. The weight can change if the force of gravity acting on it changes. Does the mass of a bowling ball ever change?*

Figure 2–4 *It is not really magic—just a demonstration of inertia. As the table on which this dinner is set (left) is moved quickly, the objects are suspended in midair, but only for an instant (right).*

of the moon! Later in this chapter you will discover for yourself why this is such an important concept.

Mass and Inertia

Scientists have another definition for mass. Mass is a measure of the **inertia** (ihn-ER-shuh) of an object. Inertia is the resistance of an object to changes in its motion. Objects that have mass resist changes in their motion. Thus objects that have mass have inertia. For example, if an object is at rest, a force must be used to make it move. If you move it, you notice that it resists your push or pull. If an object is moving, a force must be used to slow it down or stop it. If you try to stop a moving object, it will resist this effort.

Suppose you were given the choice of pushing either an empty shopping cart or a cart full of groceries up a steep hill. The full cart, of course, has more mass than the empty one. And as you might know from past experience, it is much easier to push something that is empty than it is to push something that is full. Now suppose the empty cart and the full

ACTIVITY

Demonstrating Inertia

You can demonstrate that objects at rest tend to remain at rest by using a drinking glass, an index card, and a coin.

1. Place the glass on a table.

2. Lay a flat index card on top of the glass. Place the coin in the center of the card.

3. Using either a flicking motion or a pulling motion of your fingers, quickly remove the card so it flies out from under the coin. Can you remove the card fast enough so the coin lands in the glass? You might need to practice a few times.

How does this activity demonstrate inertia?

■ What happens to the coin if you remove the card slowly?

How does removing the card slowly demonstrate inertia?

Figure 2–5 *Once a bobsled is moving on the slippery sheet of ice that makes up its run, it can reach high speeds. However, to overcome its inertia and to get the bobsled moving requires the strength of four strong people.*

cart are at the top of the hill and begin to roll down. Again, you might know from experience that the full cart—the cart with more mass—will be more difficult to stop than the empty cart. In other words, it is more difficult to get the cart with more mass moving and it is more difficult to get it to stop.

The more mass an object has, the greater its inertia. So the force that must be used to overcome its inertia also has to be greater. That is why you must push or pull harder to speed up or slow down a loaded shopping cart than an empty one.

As you should remember from Chapter 1, mass is measured in units called grams (g) and kilograms (kg). One kilogram is equal to 1000 grams. The mass of small objects is usually measured in grams. The mass of large objects is usually measured in kilograms. For example, a nickel has a mass of about 5 grams. The mass of an average-sized textbook is about 1600 grams, or 1.6 kilograms. The mass of an elephant may be more than 3600 kilograms.

Weight: A Changeable Property of Matter

In addition to giving an object inertia, mass is also the reason an object has **weight.** Weight is another general property of matter. If a scientist is asked how much she weighs, she is correct in answering that it depends. This is because weight is not constant. Weight changes according to certain conditions. You probably know that your weight changes. It increases after you eat a large meal. It decreases after you spend time exercising. In these cases, your mass also changes. It increases when you eat and decreases when you exercise and burn off Calories. (Remember, mass can only change if matter is added to an object or taken away from an object.) But weight can change even when an object's mass remains the same. An object's weight, unlike its mass,

Figure 2–6 *The mass of a harvest mouse balancing itself on some strands of wheat is so small that it is measured in grams. The polar bear is a different story. Its huge mass is measured in kilograms—and many of them. Do you know the metric unit used to measure weight?*

Figure 2–7 *It is the force of Earth's gravity that determines exactly what you weigh. The same person would weigh less on a mountaintop than on the surface of the Earth. Why would a person weigh more on the surface than on a mountaintop?*

Figure 2–8 *It seems such a simple act: keeping three balls suspended in space at the same time. Remember, though, that the juggler is always acting against the force of gravity—which would surely cause the balls to fall to the ground at the first mistake.*

is also dependent on its location (where it is). In order to understand what weight is and why it is not constant, you must know something about gravity.

Weight and Gravity

You have probably noticed that a ball tossed up in the air falls to the ground. This happens regardless of how hard the ball is thrown. You also know that an apple that drops from a tree falls down to the ground, not up in the air. Both the ball and the apple fall down because of the Earth's force of attraction for all objects. This force of attraction between objects is called **gravity.**

Gravitational force is not a property of the Earth alone. All objects exert a gravitational attraction on other objects. Indeed, your two hands attract each other, and you are attracted to books, papers, and chairs. Why then are you not pulled toward these objects as you are pulled toward the Earth? In fact, you are! But the attractions between you and the objects are too weak for you to notice them. The Earth's gravity, however, is great because the Earth is so massive. In fact, the greater the mass of an object, the greater its gravitational force. How do you think the gravity of Jupiter, many times more massive than Earth, compares with that of Earth?

The pull of gravity on an object determines the object's weight. On the Earth, your weight is a direct measure of the planet's force pulling you toward the center. The pull of gravity between objects weakens as the distance between the centers of the objects becomes greater. So at a high altitude—on top of a tall mountain, for example—you actually weigh less than you do at sea level. This is because you are farther from the center of the Earth on top of a high mountain than you are at sea level. Remember this idea if you are ever on a diet. Bring a bathroom scale to the top of Mount Everest, the highest mountain on Earth, and weigh yourself there. There is no place on Earth where you will weigh less.

When an object is sent into space far from Earth, the object is said to become weightless. This is because the gravitational force of the Earth on the object decreases as the object moves away from the

ACTIVITY

CALCULATING

A Quick Weight Change

An inhabitant of Planet X weighs 243 eigers on her home planet. The gravity of Planet X is 2.7 times greater than that of Earth. How many eigers will she weigh on Earth?

Figure 2–9 *In the nineteenth century, space travel was only a dream in a writer's mind. The illustration is from a book written by the great French writer Jules Verne. Today, however, space travel is real—as this astronaut floating untethered high above the Earth's surface demonstrates. Even though this astronaut appears weightless, has his mass changed?*

Guide for Reading

Focus on this question as you read.

▶ *How can you determine the density of an object?*

center of the Earth. An object in space is a great distance from the center of the Earth—in some instances, millions of kilometers. However, although the object is said to be weightless, it really is not. The gravitational force of the Earth decreases, but it still exists.

Although an object in space is said to become weightless, it *does not* become massless. Mass, remember, does not change even though location changes. So no matter what happens to the force of gravity and the weight of an object, its mass stays the same. Only its weight can change.

The metric unit of weight is the newton (N). The newton is used because it is a unit of force, and weight is the amount of force the Earth's gravity exerts on an object. An object with a mass of 1 kilogram is pulled to the Earth with a force of 9.8 newtons. So the weight of this object is 9.8 N. An object with a mass of 50 kilograms is pulled toward the Earth with a force of 50 times 9.8, or 490 newtons. The object's weight is 490 N.

2–2 Section Review

1. What is mass? What is weight?
2. How are mass and inertia related?

Critical Thinking—*Applying Concepts*
3. The moon is smaller than the Earth. Where would you weigh less? Where would you have less matter?

2–3 Volume and Density

Let's use this textbook to help discover another general property of matter. Suppose you could wrap a piece of paper around this entire book and then remove the book inside. How would you describe what was left inside the paper? You would probably use the word space. For an important property of matter is that it takes up space. And when the book

Figure 2–10 *The volume of solids is usually measured in cubic centimeters. This cube is 1 cm on each side. What is its volume?*

$1 \times 1 \times 1$

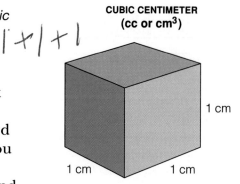

CUBIC CENTIMETER
(cc or cm³)

1 cm

1 cm   1 cm

is occupying its space, nothing else can be in that same space. You might prove this to yourself.

The amount of space an object takes up is called its **volume.** This definition should be familiar to you from Chapter 1. The metric units that are used to express volume are the liter (L), milliliter (mL), and cubic centimeter (cm³). In general, liters and milliliters are used to measure the volume of liquids, and cubic centimeters are used to measure the volume of solids. One milliliter is equal in volume to one cubic centimeter. One thousand milliliters is equal to one liter. How many milliliters are there in 2.5 liters?

Volume is an important property of matter that you use every day. Many products you may buy at a store (milk and bottled water, for example) are sold in liter containers. Cough syrups and many prescription drugs are measured in milliliters. Although you may not see cubic centimeters as frequently, you would certainly need this unit of measurement to describe the volume of a set of blocks you might want to purchase for a younger brother or sister.

You now know two important general properties of matter: Matter has mass and it occupies space. You can use these two properties to define matter in a more scientific way: **Matter is anything that has mass and volume.**

The properties of mass and volume can be used to describe another important general property of matter called density. Density is often used to describe things. A pine forest is often called a dense forest if the trees grow close together. You may have said your best friend was dense when he or she did not understand a joke you told. To a scientist, density has a specific meaning. **Density is the mass per unit volume of an object.**

Density is an important property because it allows you to compare different types of matter. Let's see how. Suppose you were asked to determine which is heavier, wood or steel. How would you go about doing it? Perhaps you would suggest comparing the masses of both on a balance. You are on the right track, but there is one problem with this solution. What size

ACTIVITY

DISCOVERING

Volume of a Solid

You can easily measure the volume of a liquid by using a graduated cylinder. Can this method be used to determine the volume of a solid?

Fill a graduated cylinder half full with water. Note the volume of the water. Now place a small solid object in the graduated cylinder. You might choose a rock, a block of wood, or a bar of soap. If the object floats, use a piece of wire to push it under the water's surface. Note the new volume of the water.

You now have two volumes for the liquid—the original volume and the new volume. Ask yourself these questions to find the volume of the solid:

What caused the change in volume?

Is the volume change different for different objects?

■ How is the change in liquid volume related to the volume of the solid object?

DENSITIES OF SOME COMMON SUBSTANCES

Substance	Density (g/cm³)
Air	0.0013
Gasoline	0.7
Wood (oak)	0.85
Water (ice)	0.92
Water (liquid)	1.0
Aluminum	2.7
Steel	7.8
Silver	10.5
Lead	11.3
Mercury	13.5
Gold	19.3

float

Figure 2–11 *This chart shows the densities of some common substances. Which substances would float on water? Which ones would sink?*

pieces of wood and steel would you use? After all, a small piece of steel might have the same mass as a large piece of wood.

You are probably beginning to realize that in order to compare the masses of two objects, you need to use an equal volume of each. When you do, you soon discover that a piece of steel has a greater mass than a piece of wood *of the same volume.* And that is the important part of that statement—of the same volume. So for our example we can say a cubic centimeter of steel is heavier than a cubic centimeter of wood. Or steel is denser than wood.

All matter has density. And the density of a specific kind of matter is a property that helps to identify it and distinguish it from other kinds of matter.

As you may recall, because density is equal to mass per unit volume, we can write a formula for calculating the density of an object:

$$\text{Density} = \frac{\text{Mass}}{\text{Volume}}$$

Figure 2–12 *Biologists use the term population density to refer to the number of individual organisms in a given area. The population density of these walruses on a crowded beach would prevent even one more walrus from squeezing in.*

Density is often expressed in grams per milliliter (g/mL) or grams per cubic centimeter (g/cm³). The density of wood is about 0.8 g/cm³. This means that a piece of wood 1 cubic centimeter in volume has a mass of about 0.8 gram. The density of steel is 7.8 g/cm³. So a piece of steel has a mass about 9.75 times that of a piece of wood of the same size.

The density of fresh water is 1 g/mL. Objects with a density less than water float. Objects with a density greater than water sink. Thus wood floats in water because its density is less than the density of water. What happens to a piece of steel when it is put in water?

If you have ever placed an ice cube in a glass of water, you know that ice floats. So frozen water (ice) must be less dense than liquid water. Actually, the density of ice is about 89 percent that of cold water. What this means is that only about 11 percent of a block of ice stays above the surface of the water. The rest is below the surface. This fact is what makes icebergs so dangerous. For it is only the "tip of the iceberg" that is visible.

Activity Bank

What "Eggs-actly" Is Going on Here?, p.714

Sample Problem	If 96.5 grams of gold has a volume of 5 cubic centimeters, what is the density of gold?
Solution	
Step 1 Write the formula.	$$\text{Density} = \frac{\text{Mass}}{\text{Volume}}$$
Step 2 Substitute given numbers and units.	$$\text{Density} = \frac{96.5 \text{ grams}}{5 \text{ cubic centimeters}}$$
Step 3 Solve for unknown variable.	$$\text{Density} = \frac{19.3 \text{ grams}}{\text{cubic centimeter}}$$

Practice Problems	1. If 96.5 g of aluminum has a volume of 35 cm³, what is the density of aluminum? How does its density compare with the density of gold?
	2. If the density of a diamond is 3.5 g/cm³, what would be the mass of a diamond whose volume is 0.5 cm³?

ACTIVITY THINKING

Archimedes and the Crown

The famous Greek mathematician and scientist Archimedes was once faced with a difficult task. He had to determine whether the new crown made by a goldsmith for King Hieron of Syracuse was pure gold or a mixture of gold and silver. And he had to accomplish this task without damaging the crown!

Pretend that you are Archimedes' assistant and describe an experiment that would help determine whether the crown is pure gold or a mixture of gold and silver. *Hint:* The concept of density is useful here.

You may have read or heard about the passenger ship *Titanic*, which sank in 1912 after it ran into an iceberg in the cold North Atlantic. The most advanced technology was used to build the *Titanic*. Special watertight doors were designed so that they could seal off a part of the ship that developed a leak. The ship was said to be unsinkable. However, its watertight doors were not able to keep the ocean waters from filling the *Titanic* when the iceberg ripped through the side of the ship. Once ocean water replaced the air in the *Titanic*, the density of the ship was no longer less than the density of water and the ship plunged to the ocean bottom on its maiden voyage!

Can you now solve the mystery posed at the beginning of this chapter? An object floats in water if its density is less than 1 g/mL. In order for the

Figure 2–13 *The "unsinkable"* Titanic *sank after striking an iceberg in the North Atlantic. As it filled with water—through the gaping hole in its hull caused by the iceberg—the density of this great ship became greater than the ocean water upon which it floated. And it sank under the waves.*

scuba diver searching for the *Mary Rose* to sink in the water, the diver's overall density has to be greater than 1 g/mL. So the diver wears a weighted belt to increase mass.

The density of water increases with depth. In other words, the density of water increases as you go deeper under the surface of the water. So the density of deep water is greater than 1 g/mL. At a certain depth, the scuba diver's density is equal to the water's density. The diver will not be able to sink below this depth.

While the *Mary Rose* moved on the surface of the ocean, her hull was partly filled with air. The air helped make the ship's overall density less than 1 g/mL, and so it floated. The large volume of air balanced the added mass of the heavy bronze cannons. However, when her hull partially filled with water, the overall density of the *Mary Rose*, her heavy cannons, and the water became greater than the density of the surrounding water at any depth. Down, down went the *Mary Rose*!

Figure 2–14 *Because of the air within it, a huge ocean liner can float on the surface of the ocean (left). By pumping water into and out of special tanks, submarines are able to sink or float at will (right). These fish can maintain their position in the water by emptying or filling an air bladder within their body (inset). How does a life preserver help a swimmer remain afloat?*

Figure 2–15 *Unlike all the other planets in our solar system, magnificent Saturn has a density less than 1 g/mL. In fact, if you could find a large enough ocean, Saturn would float in it.*

2–3 Section Review

1. What is density?
2. What determines whether an object floats or sinks in water?

Critical Thinking—*Making Comparisons*

3. Perhaps you have attended a party where balloons floated. A balloon filled with air does not rise above your head, but a balloon filled with helium gas rises in the air to the end of its string. What does this tell you about the density of helium?

PROBLEM ??? Solving

A Density Disaster

Look closely at the accompanying photograph. It shows the densities of some common substances. As you can see, some objects float in water and others sink.

Now pretend that this photograph represents a small portion of the ocean. Floating on this ocean is a steel oil tanker filled with crude oil. (Remember that because much of its volume is filled with air, a large ship such as a tanker is less dense than water and thus will float.) Suddenly the tanker runs aground on a reef. A huge hole is torn in the ship's hull. Oil gushes out of the ship into the water. This could be a major environmental disaster!

Cause and Effect

Assume that the crude oil has the same density as corn oil.

1. Why does the oil pose a great danger?

2. Is the danger greater to birds and marine mammals than it is to fish and other organisms that live on the ocean bottom?

3. How is the density of oil an advantage in the cleanup?

4. Why would an oil spill be an even greater disaster if the density of oil were the same as that of corn syrup?

Air — 0.001 g/cm³
Corn oil 0.93 g/cm³
Water — 1.00 g/cm³
Glycerine 1.26 g/cm³
Corn Syrup 1.38g/cm³

Wood 0.85 g/cm³

Plastic 1.17 g/cm³
Rubber 1.19 g/cm³
Steel 7.86 g/cm³

CONNECTIONS

Up, Up, and Away

For many thousands of years, people have dreamed of flying through the air as gracefully as birds. According to Greek *mythology,* Daedalus and his son, Icarus, escaped from the labyrinth using wings made of feathers, wax, and thread. Icarus, however, flew too close to the sun and the wax melted, plunging this early aviator to his death in the sea.

In the eighteenth century, human flight became a reality, not just mythology. The Montgolfier brothers launched the first hot-air balloon in *history*—and in so doing, captured the imagination of the French people as well. Balloonamania swept France. The principles behind their hot-air ballooning are those you learned about in this chapter.

The balloon developed by the Montgolfiers was made of silk, carefully suspended over a fire. The flames of the fire heated the air in the balloon, causing the air

to expand. As the air expanded, it occupied more space and the balloon inflated. In other words, the volume of the air increased. As the volume of the heated air increased, the density of the hot-air balloon became less than the density of the cooler air that surrounded it. The balloon—now lighter than air—rose off the ground and began its historic voyage upward.

Unlike the balloon invented by the Montgolfier brothers, modern hot-air balloons rely on tanks of flammable gas to heat the air. The height of the balloon is controlled by heating the air within the balloon. Of course, even the most avid ballooners eventually want to come back to Earth. To do so, they allow the air in the balloon to cool. When this happens, an opposite reaction occurs. The air contracts and occupies less space. Its volume decreases and it becomes denser than the surrounding air. The balloon, no longer lighter than air, descends. If the pilot wants to descend rapidly, air can also be released from special flaps at the top of the balloon. By controlling the amount of heat as well as the amount of air released, the rate of ascent or descent of the balloon can be carefully regulated.

Today, many people fly hot-air balloons, but it was the pioneering work of the Montgolfier brothers that opened up the world of flight to humans—a world once limited only to birds and beasts.

Brave Icarus tried to fly and failed.
However, the hot-air balloon took people
to heights undreamed of.

Laboratory Investigation

Inertia

Problem

How does an object's mass affect its inertia?

Materials   *(per group)*

several shoe boxes
objects of various masses to fit in the
   shoe boxes
smooth table top
household broom
meterstick or metric ruler

Procedure

1. Place an object in each shoe box and replace the lid on the shoe box. Number each box. (Your teacher may provide you with several shoe boxes that are already prepared.)

2. Position the box so that it hangs over the edge of the table by 8 cm.

3. Stand the broom directly behind the table. Put your foot on the straw part of the broom to hold it in place.

4. Slowly move the broom handle back away from the box.

5. When you release the handle, the broomstick should spring forward, striking the middle of the end of the box.

6. Measure how far the box moves across the table after it is struck by the broom.

7. Repeat this procedure with each of the boxes. Try to use the same force each time.

Observations

1. Enter the box number and the distance moved in a chart similar to the one shown here.

Box Number	Distance Traveled

2. Open the boxes and examine the contents. Record what object was in each box.

Analysis and Conclusions

1. What part of the definition of inertia applies to your observations about the movements of the boxes?

2. Why do you think some boxes moved farther than others?

3. What do you notice about the objects that moved farthest from the resting position? What do you notice about the objects that moved the shortest distance from the resting position?

4. Why was it important that you used the same force each time a box was struck?

5. **On Your Own** You can compare the masses of different objects by using a balance. Can you propose another way to determine the masses of different objects?

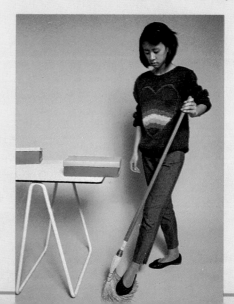

Summarizing Key Concepts

2–1 Matter

▲ All objects are made of matter.

▲ A property is a quality or characteristic that describes matter.

▲ General properties describe how all matter is the same. Specific properties describe the differences among forms of matter.

▲ All matter has the general properties of mass, weight, volume, and density.

2–2 Mass and Weight

▲ One property of matter is that it has mass. Mass is the amount of matter in an object.

▲ The property of matter that resists changes in motion is called inertia. Mass is a measure of the inertia of an object.

▲ Mass is commonly measured in grams or kilograms.

▲ The force of attraction between objects is called gravity.

▲ The gravitational attraction between objects is dependent on their masses.

▲ Gravitational attraction between objects becomes less as the distance between the objects increases.

▲ The pull of gravity on an object determines the object's weight.

▲ The weight of an object can vary with location, but its mass never changes unless matter is added to or taken from the object.

2–3 Volume and Density

▲ The amount of space an object takes up is called its volume.

▲ Volume is measured in liters, milliliters, and cubic centimeters. In general, liters and milliliters are used to measure liquid volumes and cubic centimeters are used to measure solid volumes.

▲ The density of an object is its mass per unit of volume. Density equals mass divided by volume.

▲ The density of a particular kind of matter is a specific property that helps identify it.

▲ The density of liquid water is 1 gram per milliliter (1 g/mL).

▲ Objects that float in water have a density less than 1 gram per milliliter. Objects with a density greater than 1 gram per milliliter sink in water.

Reviewing Key Terms

Define each term in a complete sentence.

2–1 Matter
matter
property

2–2 Mass and Weight
mass
inertia
weight
gravity

2–3 Volume and Density
volume

Chapter Review

Content Review

Multiple Choice

Choose the letter of the answer that best completes each statement.

1. Characteristics that describe how all matter is the same are called
   a. specific properties.
   b. universal differences.
   c. density numbers.
   d. general properties.
2. The amount of matter in an object is a measure of its
   a. volume.   c. density
   b. mass.   d. weight.
3. In describing the mass of an object, it is correct to say that
   a. mass changes with altitude.
   b. mass changes with location.
   c. mass remains unchanged.
   d. mass changes with weight.
4. The formula for finding density is
   a. volume/mass.   c. mass/volume.
   b. volume x mass. d. mass/weight.

5. As an object gets farther from Earth,
   a. its weight increases.
   b. its weight decreases.
   c. its mass decreases.
   d. its weight remains the same.
6. The amount of space an object takes up is called its
   a. volume.   c. weight
   b. density.   d. inertia.
7. An object's resistance to a change in motion is called its
   a. density.   c. mass.
   b. inertia.   d. volume.
8. The force of attraction between objects is
   a. inertia.   c. density.
   b. weight.   d. gravity.

True or False

If the statement is true, write "true." If it is false, change the underlined word or words to make the statement true.

1. All objects are made up of <u>matter</u>.
2. <u>Volume</u> is a measure of the resistance of an object to changes in its motion.
3. One liter is equal to <u>100</u> milliliters.
4. Some general properties of matter include <u>mass, weight, color, and volume</u>.
5. <u>Density</u> is the amount of space an object takes up.
6. As an object's weight increases, its mass <u>decreases</u>.
7. An object's mass per unit volume is called its <u>density</u>.
8. An object that floats in water has a density <u>greater</u> than 1 g/mL.

Concept Mapping

Complete the following concept map for Section 2–1. Then construct a concept map for the entire chapter.

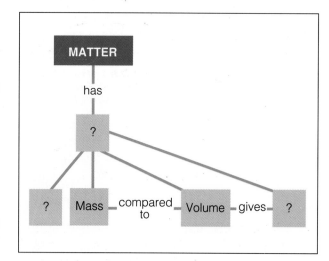

Concept Mastery

Discuss each of the following in a brief paragraph.

1. A rocket taking off from Earth needs much more fuel than the same rocket taking off from the moon. Explain why.
2. Why are astronauts floating above the Earth in a Space Shuttle really not weightless?
3. A person who cannot float in a freshwater lake can float easily in the Great Salt Lake in Utah. What does this tell you about the density of salt water?
4. Each year some college students have a contest to build and race concrete boats. What advice would you give the students to make sure their boats float?
5. Fish are able to remain at a specific depth in water without much trouble. Many fish have an organ called a swim bladder that they can fill with air and empty at will. How does a swim bladder help a fish stay at one level in the water?
6. On Earth, a ballet dancer has a great deal of trouble lifting a ballerina over his head. On the moon, however, he can lift her with ease. Explain this situation.
7. An ice cube is only frozen water. Why does an ice cube float on the surface of a glass of water and not sink to the bottom?
8. "Oil and water don't mix" is an old saying. Use what you have learned about density to explain the scientific reasons for this saying.

Critical Thinking and Problem Solving

Use the skills you have developed in this chapter to answer each of the following.

1. **Making comparisons** You are given two samples of pure copper, one with a mass of 20 grams and the other with a mass of 100 grams. Compare the two samples in terms of (a) volume, (b) weight, and (c) density.
2. **Applying concepts** Explain why selling cereal by mass rather than by volume would be more fair to consumers.
3. **Making calculations** If the density of a certain plastic used to make a bracelet is 0.78 g/cm^3, what mass would a bracelet of 4 cm^3 have? Would this bracelet float or sink in water?
4. **Designing an experiment** The common metal iron pyrite (bottom) is often called fool's gold because it can be mistaken for gold (top). Design an experiment to determine whether a particular sample is iron pyrite or real gold.
5. **Making inferences** Aluminum is used to make airplanes. Cast iron is used to make heavy machines. Based on this information, compare the densities of aluminum and cast iron.
6. **Using the writing process** Write a short poem about matter. Use at least two general properties of matter in your work.

59

Physical and Chemical Changes

At dawn's first light the weather forecast indicated the day would be sunny and bright. But throughout the day the temperature at the orange grove dropped. By afternoon it was so cold that the workers became concerned about the orange trees whose branches were heavy with fruit not yet ripe enough to be picked. Such low temperatures could wipe out the entire crop.

The workers knew that something had to be done quickly. Some workers lighted small fires in smokepots scattered throughout the groves. But they soon realized that the heat produced in this way would not save the fruit. Suddenly other workers raced into the grove hauling long water hoses! These workers began to spray the trees with water. As the temperature continued to drop, the water would freeze into ice. The ice would keep the oranges warm!

Does it seem strange to you that oranges can be protected from cold by ice? Was this some sort of magic? In a sense, yes. But it was magic that anyone who knows science can do. And as you read further, you will learn how freezing water can sometimes work better than a fire to keep things warm.

Journal *Activity*

You and Your World You know that water is a liquid. You also know that when it is frozen, water can also be a solid. Make a list of the kinds of things that you can do with liquid water. Make a second list of things you can do with solid water. Enter your lists in your journal.

To keep oranges from being destroyed by freezing temperatures, the oranges are sprayed with water that quickly freezes into ice. How does ice protect the oranges? The answer to this question lies within the pages of this chapter.

3-1 Phases of Matter

The general properties of matter that you learned about in Chapter 2—mass, weight, volume, and density—are examples of **physical properties.** Color, shape, hardness, and texture are also physical properties. Physical properties are characteristics of a substance that can be observed without changing the identity of the substance. Wood is still wood whether it is carved into a baseball bat or used to build the walls of a house.

Ice, liquid water, and water vapor may seem different to you. Certainly they differ in appearance and use. But ice, liquid water, and water vapor are all made of exactly the same substance in different states. These states are called **phases.** Phase is an important physical property of matter. Scientists use the phases of matter to classify the various kinds of matter in the world. **Matter can exist in four phases: solid, liquid, gas, and plasma.**

Solids

A pencil, a cube of sugar, a metal coin, and an ice cream cone are examples of **solids.** All solids share two important characteristics: Solids have a definite shape and a definite volume. Let's see why. The tiny particles that make up a solid are packed very close together. Because of this arrangement, the particles cannot move far out of their places, nor can they flow over or around one another. In a solid, the tightly packed particles are able only to vibrate. Little other motion occurs. Thus a solid is able to keep its definite shape.

Figure 3-1 *Living up to its name, Old Faithful geyser in Yellowstone National Park erupts on schedule. What phases of water can you observe in this photograph?*

Figure 3-2 *Sodium chloride, or table salt, and potassium chloride, which is sometimes used to season foods by people who must limit the amount of sodium they eat, are two common crystalline solids. The illustration shows how atoms are arranged in a sodium chloride crystal.*

Figure 3–3 *Crystals can vary in color and shape. Valuable ruby crystals are used to make jewelry (left). Gypsum crystals are valuable in their own right (center). Gypsum is used to make wallboard and other construction materials. Fluorite crystals (right), which can be clear or colored, are used as a source of fluorine and in glassmaking.*

If you could examine the internal structure of many solids, you would see that the particles making up the solids are arranged in a regular, repeating pattern called a **crystal.** Solids made up of crystals are called crystalline solids. A good example of a crystalline solid is common table salt. Figure 3–3 shows several other, more colorful examples of crystalline solids.

Crystals often have beautiful shapes that result from the arrangement of the particles within them. Snowflakes are crystals of water in the solid phase. If you look at them closely, you will see that all snowflakes have six sides. However, what is so amazing is that no two snowflakes in the world are ever exactly alike.

There are some solids, however, in which the particles are not arranged in a regular, repeating pattern. These solids do not keep their definite shapes permanently. Because the particles in these solids are not arranged in a rigid way, they can slowly flow around one another. Solids that lose their shape under certain conditions are called amorphous (uh-MOR-fuhs) solids. Have you ever worked with sealing wax or silicone rubber? If so, you have worked with an amorphous solid.

Actually, an amorphous solid can also be thought of as a slow-moving liquid. Candle wax, window glass, and the tar used to repair roads are amorphous solids that behave like slow-moving liquids. You were

Activity Bank

Crystal Gardening, p. 716

Figure 3–4 *The computer-generated drawing of a portion of a snowflake shows the repeating pattern of the particles of ice that make up the crystal.*

Figure 3–5 *Amorphous solids, such as sealing wax, lose their shape under certain conditions. What is one condition that could cause sealing wax to lose its shape?*

probably surprised to learn that glass is a slow-moving liquid. Although it moves too slowly to actually observe, you can see the results of its movement under certain conditions. If you look at the window-panes in a very old house, you will notice that they are thicker at the bottom than at the top. Over time, the glass has flowed slowly downward, just like a liquid. In fact, glass is sometimes described as a super-cooled liquid. Glass forms when sand and other materials in the liquid phase are cooled to a rigid condition without the formation of crystals.

Liquids

Although the particles in a **liquid** are close together, they are not held as tightly together as are the particles in a solid. So the particles in a liquid are free to move. Thus a liquid has no definite shape. It takes the shape of its container. A liquid in a square container is square. The same liquid in a round container is round.

Although liquids do not have a definite shape, they do have a definite volume. One liter of water is still one liter of water whether it is in a round container or a square one. And if that one liter of water is poured into a two-liter bottle, it will occupy only half the bottle's volume. It will not fill the bottle. One liter of water does not spread out to fill a two-liter bottle. What do you think would happen if you tried to pour that one liter of water into a half-liter bottle?

Remember that the particles in a liquid are free to move. This movement is basically a flowing around one another. Some liquids flow more easily than others, however. The resistance of a liquid to flow is called viscosity (vihs-KAHS-uh-tee). Honey has a high viscosity compared to water. This means that honey flows more slowly than water. If you have ever poured honey from a jar, you are probably familiar with this fact. The oil you put in an automobile also has a high viscosity. This is important because the oil coats the moving parts in the motor and prevents them from rubbing together and wearing out.

Observing Viscosity

Remember that some liquids flow more easily than others. Viscosity is the resistance of a liquid to flow.

1. Obtain samples of the following: catsup, corn syrup, milk, honey, maple syrup.

2. Cover a piece of cardboard with aluminum foil.

3. Place the cardboard on a plate or baking pan at about a 45- to 50-degree angle with the bottom of the plate or pan.

4. With four classmates helping you, pour a measured amount of each liquid from the top of the cardboard at the same time.

5. Determine the order in which the liquids reach the bottom of the cardboard.

Which liquid is the most viscous? The least viscous?

■ How does the viscosity of foods influence how certain foods are used?

Figure 3–6 *A gas has no definite volume and will expand to fill its container. If allowed to, it will expand without limit. That is what happened to this balloon. A hole in Donald's arm allowed the helium gas within the balloon to escape into the atmosphere. Without gas, the arm hangs limply downward.*

Gases

Another phase of matter—the **gas** phase—does not have a definite shape or a definite volume. A gas fills all of the available space in a container, regardless of the size or shape of the container.

Although the particles of a gas tend to spread far out from one another, they can be pushed close together. When you pump air into a bicycle tire or blow up a party balloon, you squeeze a large amount of gas into a small volume. Fortunately, you can do this to the particles in a gas.

Just the opposite can also happen. The particles of a small amount of gas can spread out to fill a large volume. The smell of an apple pie baking in the oven in the kitchen will reach you in another room of your house because gases given off by the pie spread out to fill the whole house. In fact, if they are allowed to, gases will expand without limit. If not for the pull of gravity, the gases that make up the atmosphere of the Earth would expand into deep space. Can you explain then why a small planet like Mercury has little or no atmosphere?

Like liquids, gases have no definite shape. The particles that make up a gas are not arranged in any set pattern. So it is easy for gas particles to move around, either spreading apart or moving close together.

Figure 3–7 *Mercury, the closest planet to the sun, is a small planet. Because of its relatively small size, it does not have a great deal of gravity. What can you predict about Mercury's atmosphere?*

Figure 3–8 *A liquid has a definite volume but not a definite shape. It takes the shape of its container. An identical volume of liquid in three differently shaped glass vessels has three different shapes. A gas has neither a definite volume nor a definite shape. How would you describe the volume of a gas?*

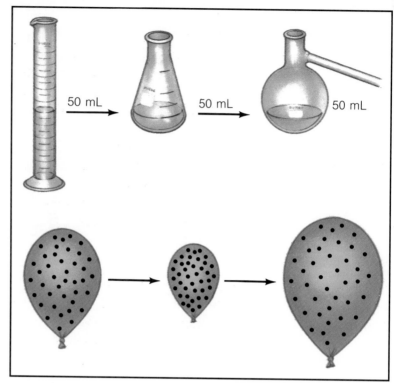

ACTIVITY

Determining Particle Space

1. Fill one 250-mL beaker with marbles, another with sand, and a third with water.

2. Describe the appearance of the beaker filled with marbles. Do the marbles occupy all the space in the beaker? Can you fit more marbles in the beaker?

3. Carefully pour some sand from its beaker into the beaker of marbles. How much sand are you able to pour? Is all the space in the beaker now occupied by marbles and sand?

4. Carefully add some water from its beaker to the beaker of marbles and sand. How much water can you add?

Is there space between the particles of a solid or a liquid?

■ How does what you observed partially explain the disappearance of rain on a lawn?

The behavior of gases can be explained in terms of the arrangement and movement of their particles. The world inside a container of gas particles is not as quiet as it may seem. Although you cannot see the particles of gas, they are in constant motion—moving about freely at speeds of nearly 100 meters per second. Whizzing around at such great speeds, the particles are constantly hitting one another. In fact, a single particle undergoes about 10 billion collisions per second! The particles are also colliding with the walls of the container. The effect of all these collisions is an outward pressure, or push, exerted by the gas. This pressure is what makes the gas expand to fill its container. What do you think would happen if the pressure in the container became too great?

BOYLE'S LAW Imagine you are holding an inflated balloon. If you press lightly on the outside of the balloon, you can feel the air inside pushing back. Now if you squeeze part of the balloon, what do you feel? You probably feel the air pressing against the wall of the balloon with even greater force.

This increase in pressure is due to a decrease in volume. By squeezing the balloon, you reduce the space the gas particles can occupy. As the particles are pushed a bit closer together, they collide with one another and with the walls of the balloon even more. So the pressure from the moving gas particles increases. The relationship between volume and pressure is explained by Boyle's law. According to Boyle's law, the volume of a fixed amount of gas varies inversely with the pressure of the gas. In other words, as one increases, the other decreases. If the volume of a gas decreases, its pressure increases. If the volume increases, its pressure decreases.

CHARLES'S LAW Imagine that you still have that inflated balloon. This time you heat it very gently. What do you think happens to the volume of gas inside the balloon? As the temperature increases, the gas particles absorb more heat energy. They speed up and move farther away from one another. So the increase in temperature causes an increase in volume. If the temperature had decreased, the volume would have decreased. This relationship between temperature and volume is described by Charles's law. According to Charles's law, the volume of a

Figure 3–9 *In a solid, such as these crystals of iron pyrite, or fool's gold (top left), the particles are packed closely together and cannot move far out of place. In a liquid, such as molten iron (top center), the particles are close together but are free to move about or flow. In a gas, such as iodine, bromine, and chlorine (top right), the particles are free to spread out and fill the available volume.*

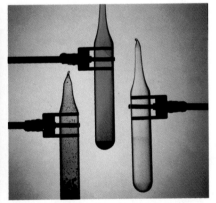

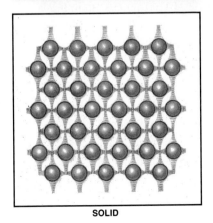

SOLID

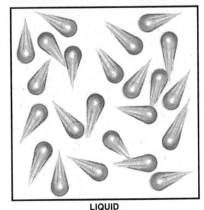

LIQUID

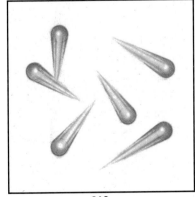

GAS

Demonstrating Charles's Law

1. Inflate a balloon. Make sure that it is not so large that it will break easily. Make a knot in the end of the balloon so that the air cannot escape.

2. Measure and record the circumference of the balloon. You can measure the circumference by placing a string around the fattest part of the balloon. Place your finger at the spot where one end of the string touches another part of the string. Now use a ruler to measure the distance between the two spots.

3. Place the balloon in an oven set at a low temperature—not more than 65°C (150°F). Leave the balloon in the oven for about 5 minutes.

4. Remove the balloon and quickly use the piece of string to measure its circumference. Record this measurement.

5. Now place the balloon in a refrigerator for 15 minutes.

6. Remove the balloon and immediately measure and record its circumference.

What happens to the size of the balloon at the higher temperature? At the lower temperature? Do the results of your investigation support Charles's law?

fixed amount of gas varies directly with the temperature of the gas. If the temperature of a gas increases, its volume increases. What do you think happens if the temperature decreases?

Boyle's law and Charles's law together are called the gas laws. The gas laws describe the behavior of gases with changes in pressure, temperature, and volume.

A third gas law, Avogadro's law, relates the amount, or number of particles, of a gas to its volume. According to Avogadro's law, equal volumes of gases at the same temperature and pressure contain equal numbers of particles, or moles. (A mole is a unit of quantity or amount.)

Plasma

The fourth phase of matter is called **plasma.** Plasma is quite rare on Earth. But the plasma phase is actually one of the most common phases in which matter is found in the universe. For example, stars such as the sun contain matter in the plasma phase.

Figure 3–10 *The illustration at top shows the effect of increasing the pressure on a fixed amount of gas. If the pressure is doubled, the volume is halved. The illustration at bottom shows the effect of increasing the temperature on the volume of a fixed amount of gas. If the temperature is doubled, the volume also doubles. What do you think happens to the volume of a fixed amount of gas when the pressure is halved? When the temperature decreases by half?*

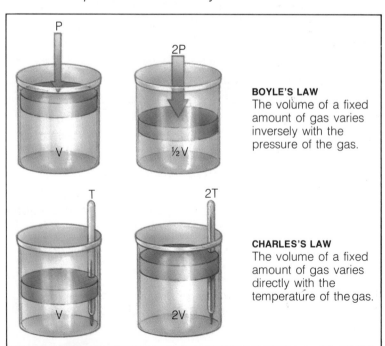

BOYLE'S LAW
The volume of a fixed amount of gas varies inversely with the pressure of the gas.

CHARLES'S LAW
The volume of a fixed amount of gas varies directly with the temperature of the gas.

Matter in the plasma phase is extremely high in energy and therefore dangerous to living things. Plasma can be made on the Earth only by using equipment that produces very high energy.

Figure 3–11 *Because the sun is a ball of matter with tremendous energy, matter exists there in the plasma phase. This photograph shows a huge solar flare erupting from the sun's surface.*

3–1 Section Review

1. What are the four phases of matter?
2. How is a crystalline solid different from an amorphous solid?

Critical Thinking—*Making Predictions*
3. Using the gas laws, predict what will happen to the volume of a gas if (a) the pressure triples, (b) the temperature is halved, (c) the pressure is decreased by a factor of five, (d) the pressure is halved and the temperature is doubled.

3–2 Phase Changes

Earth has been called the "water" planet. It is because of this abundant water that life can exist on Earth. But did you know that the water that makes up almost three fourths of the Earth's surface and about 1 percent of its atmosphere exists in three different phases? Ice, liquid water, and water vapor are all the same substance. What, then, causes the particles of a substance to be in one particular phase rather than another? The answer has to do with energy—energy that can cause the particles in a substance to move faster and farther apart.

A solid substance tends to have less energy than that same substance in the liquid phase. A gas usually has more energy than the liquid phase of the same substance. So ice has less energy than liquid

Guide for Reading

Focus on this question as you read.

▶ *What is the relationship between energy and phase changes?*

Figure 3–12 *Matter can change phase when energy is added or taken away. Is energy being added to or taken away from this ice cube?*

Melting Ice and Freezing Water

1. Place several ice cubes, a little water, and a thermometer in a glass. Wait several minutes.

2. Observe and record the temperature as the ice melts. This temperature is the melting point of ice.

3. Place a glass of water with a thermometer in it in a freezer. Observe and record the temperature every 10 minutes. Record the temperature of the water when it begins to freeze. This temperature is the freezing point of water. **Note:** *Do not let the glass of water freeze completely.*

How does the melting point of ice compare with the freezing point of water?

■ Plan an investigation to determine the effect of antifreeze on the freezing point of water.

water, and steam has more energy than ice or liquid water. The greater energy content of steam is what makes a burn caused by steam more serious than a burn caused by hot water!

Because energy content is responsible for the different phases of matter, substances can be made to change phase by adding or taking away energy. The easiest way to do this is to heat or cool the substance. This allows heat energy to flow into or out of the substance. This idea should sound familiar to you since you frequently increase or decrease heat energy to produce phase changes in water. For example, you put liquid water into the freezer to remove heat and make ice. And on a stove you add heat to make liquid water turn to steam.

The phase changes in matter are melting, freezing, vaporization, condensation, and sublimation. Changes of phase are examples of physical changes. In a physical change, a substance changes from one form to another, but it remains the same kind of substance. No new or different kinds of matter are formed, even though physical properties may change.

Solid-Liquid Phase Changes

What happens to ice cream on a hot day if you do not eat it quickly enough? It begins to melt. **Melting** is the change of a solid to a liquid. Melting occurs when a substance absorbs heat energy. The rigid crystal structure of the particles breaks down, and the particles are free to flow around one another.

The temperature at which a solid changes to a liquid is called the **melting point.** Most substances have a characteristic melting point. It is a physical

Figure 3–13 *If the children had eaten their ice cream cones quickly, the ice cream would have remained a solid until it was eaten. But because they took their time, heat energy caused the solid ice cream to become a liquid.*

LIFE SCIENCE LIBRARY/WATER. Photography by Ken Kay. Time-Life Books, Inc. Publisher ©1986 Time, Inc.

Figure 3–14 *Energy from within the Earth is great enough to melt rocks. Now in the liquid phase, the melted rocks flow from a volcano as a stream of lava.*

property that helps to identify the substance. For example, the melting point of ice is 0°C. The melting point of table salt is 801°C, whereas the melting point of a diamond is 3700°C.

The opposite phase change—that of a liquid changing to a solid—is called **freezing.** Freezing occurs when a substance loses heat energy. The temperature at which a substance changes from a liquid to a solid is called the **freezing point.** Strangely enough, the freezing point of a substance is equal to its melting point. So ice melts at 0°C and water freezes at 0°C.

Substances called alcohols have freezing points much lower than 0°C. Because of this property, these substances have an important use: They are used in automobile antifreeze. When alcohols are added to the water in an automobile's radiator, they lower the freezing point of the mixture. So even the coldest winter temperatures will not cause the water in the radiator to freeze. One such alcohol, ethylene glycol, when mixed with equal parts of water can lower the freezing point of the mixture to –37°C.

The fact that freezing involves a loss of heat energy explains the "magic" worked by the orange growers you read about at the beginning of this chapter. The liquid water sprayed onto the trees released heat energy as it froze. Some of this heat energy was released into the oranges, keeping them from freezing.

Figure 3–15 *Would you believe that freezing water can produce a violent explosion? A cast-iron ball filled with water is placed in a beaker of dry ice and alcohol. As the water freezes and expands, a huge amount of force is exerted against the walls of the cast-iron ball, causing it to eventually explode.*

Liquid-Gas Phase Changes

Have you ever left a glass of water standing on the kitchen counter overnight? If so, did you notice that the water level was lower the next morning? Some of the liquid in the glass changed phase and became a gas. The gas then escaped into the air.

The change of a substance from a liquid to a gas is called **vaporization** (vay-puhr-ih-ZAY-shuhn). During this process, particles in a liquid absorb enough heat energy to escape from the liquid phase. If vaporization takes place at the surface of the liquid, the process is called **evaporation** (ee-vap-uh-RAY-shuhn). So some of the water you left in the glass overnight evaporated.

Evaporation is often thought of as a cooling process. Does this sound strange to you? Think for a moment about perspiration on the surface of your skin. As the water in perspiration evaporates, it absorbs and carries away heat energy from your body. In this way, your body is cooled. Can you explain why it is important for you to sweat on a hot day or after you perform strenuous exercise?

Vaporization does not occur only at the surface of a liquid. If enough heat energy is supplied, particles inside the liquid can change to gas. These particles travel to the surface of the liquid and then into the air. This process is called **boiling.** The temperature at which a liquid boils is called its **boiling point.** The boiling point of water under normal conditions at sea level is 100°C. The boiling point of table salt is 1413°C, and that of a diamond is 4827°C!

The boiling point of a liquid is related to the pressure of the air above it. Since the gas particles must escape from the surface of the liquid, they

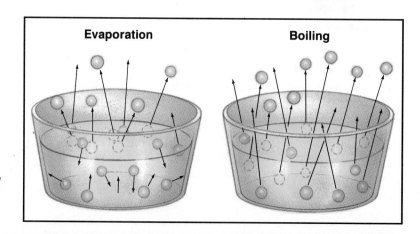

Figure 3–16 *During both evaporation (left) and boiling (right), particles of a liquid absorb heat energy and change from the liquid phase to the gas phase. Based on this illustration, what is the difference between evaporation and boiling?*

Figure 3–17 *The phase change from gas to liquid is called condensation. Water vapor in the air can condense and form rain. With the aid of cool night temperatures, water vapor in the air can also condense to form drops of dew.*

need to have enough "push" to equal the "push" of the air pressing down. So the lower the air pressure (the less the "push" of the air pressing down), the more easily the bubbles of gas can form within the liquid and then escape. Thus, lowering the air pressure lowers the boiling point.

At high altitudes, air pressure is much lower, and so the boiling point is reduced. If you could go many kilometers above the Earth's surface, the pressure of the air would be so low that you could boil water at ordinary room temperature! However, this boiling water would be cool. You would not be able to cook anything in this water. For it is the heat in boiling water that cooks food, not simply the boiling process.

Gases can change phase too. If a substance in the gas phase loses heat energy, it changes into a liquid. Scientists call this change in phase **condensation** (kahn-duhn-SAY-shuhn). You have probably noticed that cold objects, such as glasses of iced drinks, tend to become wet on the outside. Water vapor present in the surrounding air loses heat energy when it comes in contact with the cold glass. The water vapor condenses and becomes liquid drops on the glass. Can you think of another example of condensation?

ACTIVITY

WRITING

Some Fuelish Thoughts

Almost everyone in the United States depends upon the flammability of fuels to produce the energy needed to warm their homes and light their way. For the average user, these fuels are available in three phases: solids, liquids, and gases. Compile a list of several commonly used fuels and the phase in which they are used to produce energy. Then write a story that describes what would happen if all the fuels in one of the phases disappeared overnight.

PROBLEM ??? Solving

It's Only a Passing Phase

Heat plays an important role in phase changes. Heat is energy that causes particles of matter to move faster and farther apart. As particles move faster, they leave one phase and enter another. Phase changes produce changes in only the physical properties of matter. They do not produce changes in the chemical properties. A substance is still the same kind of matter regardless of its phase.

The accompanying diagram is called a phase-change diagram. It shows the heat energy-temperature relationships as an ice cube becomes steam. Study the diagram and then answer the following questions.

Interpreting Diagrams

1. At which points does the addition of heat energy cause an increase in temperature?

2. At which points is there no temperature change despite the addition of heat energy?

3. What is happening at these points?

4. What is happening to the heat energy at the points where there is no temperature drop?

5. How can you apply this information to activities and/or occurrences in your daily life?

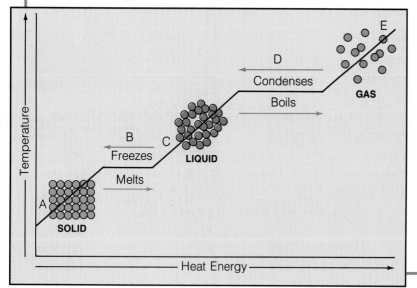

Solid-Gas Phase Changes

If you live in an area where winters are cold, you may have noticed something unusual about fallen snow. Even when the temperature stays below the melting point of the water that makes up the snow, the fallen snow slowly disappears. What happens to it? The snow undergoes **sublimation** (suhb-luh-MAY-shuhn). When a solid sublimes, its surface particles escape directly into the gas phase. They do not pass through the liquid phase.

A substance called dry ice is often used to keep other substances, such as ice cream, cold. Dry ice is solid carbon dioxide. At ordinary pressures, dry ice cannot exist in the liquid phase. So as it absorbs heat energy, it sublimes, or goes from the solid phase directly to the gas phase. By absorbing and carrying off heat energy as it sublimes, dry ice keeps materials that are near it cold and dry. Just think what would happen to an ice cream cake if it was packed with regular ice—ice that becomes liquid water before entering the gas phase—rather than with dry ice.

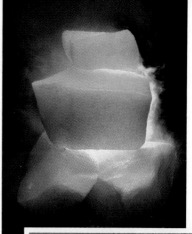

3–2 Section Review

1. How can substances be made to change phase?
2. What is a melting point? A freezing point?
3. What is the difference between evaporation and condensation?
4. Describe the changes in heat energy and particle arrangement as dry ice sublimes.

Critical Thinking—*Applying Concepts*
5. Suppose you place several ice cubes in a glass of water that is at room temperature. What happens to the ice cubes over time? What happens to the temperature of the water in the glass? What happens to the level of water in the glass? (Assume that you do not drink any of the liquid and that evaporation does not occur to any great extent.)

Figure 3–18 *Certain substances can go from the solid phase directly to the gas phase. Dry ice becomes gaseous carbon dioxide (top) and iodine crystals become gaseous iodine (bottom). What is this process called?*

3–3 Chemical Properties and Changes

At the beginning of this chapter, you learned that you could identify different substances by comparing their physical properties. It was easy to see differences in color, shape, hardness, and volume in solid objects. But now suppose you have to distinguish between two gases: oxygen and hydrogen. Both are colorless, odorless, and tasteless. Since they are

Guide for Reading

Focus on this question as you read.

▶ *What is the difference between a chemical property and a chemical change?*

Figure 3–19 *Flammability is an important chemical property that may affect your life directly—as it does this firefighter, who watches helplessly as a home is totally destroyed by flames.*

ACTIVITY
DISCOVERING

Let's Get Physical and Chemical

1. In a dry 500-mL beaker, mix 1 teaspoon of citric acid crystals with 1 tablespoon of baking soda. Observe what happens.

2. Fill another beaker halfway with water. Pour the citric acid-baking soda mixture into the water. Observe what happens.

What type of change took place in the first step of the procedure? In the second step?

Did the water have an important role in the procedure? If so, what do you think was its purpose?

■ Why are some substances marked "Store in a dry place only"?

gases, they have no definite shape or volume. And although each has a specific density, you cannot determine that density by dropping the gases into water to see what happens. In this particular case, physical properties are not very helpful in identifying the gases.

Fortunately, physical properties are not the only way to identify a substance. Both oxygen and hydrogen can turn into other substances and take on new identities. And the way in which they do this can be useful in identifying these two gases. The properties that describe how a substance changes into other new substances are called **chemical properties.**

In this case, if you collected some hydrogen in a test tube and put a glowing wooden stick in it, you would hear a loud pop. The pop occurs when hydrogen combines with oxygen in the air. What is actually happening is that the hydrogen is burning. The ability to burn is called **flammability** (flam-uh-BIHL-uh-tee). It is a chemical property. A new kind of matter forms as the hydrogen burns. Do you know what this new substance is? This substance—a combination of oxygen and hydrogen—is water.

Oxygen is not a flammable gas. It does not burn. But oxygen does support the burning of other substances. A glowing wooden splint placed in a test

Chemical properties - flammablity and ability to support burn

tube of oxygen will continue to burn until the oxygen is used up. This ability to support burning is another example of a chemical property. By using the chemical properties of flammability and supporting burning, you can distinguish between the two gases hydrogen and oxygen.

The changes that substances undergo when they turn into other substances are called **chemical changes.** Chemical changes are closely related to chemical properties, but they are not the same. **A chemical property describes a substance's ability to change into a different substance; a chemical change is the process by which the substance changes.** For example, the ability of a substance to burn is a chemical property. However, the process of burning is a chemical change. Figures 3–20 and 3–21 show several chemical changes.

Another name for a chemical change is a **chemical reaction.** Chemical reactions often involve chemically combining different substances. For example, during the burning of coal, oxygen combines chemically with carbon—the substance that makes up most of the coal. This combining reaction produces a new substance—carbon dioxide. The carbon and oxygen have changed chemically. They no longer exist in their original forms.

The ability to use and control chemical reactions is an important skill. For chemical reactions produce a range of products, from glass to pottery glazes to medicines. Your life is made easier and more enjoyable because of the products of chemical reactions.

Figure 3–20 *Nylon was one of the first synthetic fibers. Here you can see threads of nylon forming as chemicals squirted from barely visible holes undergo changes.*

77

Figure 3–21 *Many chemical changes occur in the world around you. Rust formed on the ship when iron combined with oxygen in the air. The copper in this statue reacted with sulfur in the air to form the soft green substance called verdigris. Fireworks produce beautiful colors and forms as a result of chemical changes. Chemical changes also occur in a leaf with the approach of cold winter weather.*

Synthetic fibers such as nylon and rayon, plastics, soaps, building materials, and even some of the foods you eat are the products of chemical reactions. The next time you eat a piece of cheese or a slice of bread, remember that you are eating the product of a chemical reaction.

3–3 Section Review

1. Give two examples of chemical properties.
2. What is chemical change? Give an example.

Connection—*Astronomy*

3. Suppose you visited another planet and wanted to test a sample of the planet's air. What kinds of tests would you perform to determine some physical properties of your sample? What kinds of tests would you perform to determine some chemical properties?

CONNECTIONS

The Mess We Make

Throughout history, people have lived in groups: small family groups and larger groups such as those found in towns and cities. All people, in groups large and small, produce wastes. The amount of wastes each person produces is astounding—and, unfortunately, increasing! It has been estimated that in 1900 each person living in New York City produced 538 kilograms of waste. In 1989, the amount of waste produced by each person jumped to more than 825 kilograms. In a city of 8 million people, such amounts stagger the imagination and tax the ability of a city to deal with them.

Some of the waste materials—food scraps, paper, and other natural materials—are *biodegradable.* Biodegradable materials are capable of undergoing chemical changes that cause them to break down over time. Tiny animals, plants, and microscopic organisms such as bacteria that live in the soil are responsible for these changes. The result is that biodegradable materials are broken down into simpler chemical substances. Some of these chemical substances can be used by organisms for growth and repair. Others can be used as a source of energy. Biodegradable materials also undergo physical changes.

Certain waste materials, however, such as some plastics, are not biodegradable. These materials do not break down.

They remain intact in the environment for many hundreds of years. Scientists are now working to replace many of the non-biodegradable materials we use with those that are biodegradable. This would drastically reduce the amount of nonbiodegradable wastes we produce.

The problem of *waste disposal* is sure to loom ever greater in our future. The areas where we can safely dump wastes are rapidly filling up. Other methods to deal with waste materials will have to be developed soon in order to prevent the Earth from becoming a tremendous garbage dump tomorrow. You can help even now. You can use materials that are biodegradable. For example, you can use products wrapped in biodegradable materials. You can consume less. The less waste you produce, the smaller the problem of waste disposal becomes. We must all assume responsibility for our actions—every little bit helps.

New York City, one of the world's largest cities, has the world's largest solid-waste dump site. In but a few more years, this site will be full—unable to accept another scrap of paper. It is imperative that we limit the amount of wastes we add to the environment.

Laboratory Investigation

Observing a Candle

Problem

How can physical and chemical properties be distinguished?

Materials *(per group)*

small candle
matches
metric ruler
candle holder or small empty food can
   with sand

Procedure

1. On a separate sheet of paper, prepare a data table similar to the one shown here.
2. Observe the unlighted candle. List as many physical and chemical properties as you can.
3. Place the candle in the candle holder. If you are not using a candle holder, fill the small food can with sand and place the candle in the center of the sand. Make sure that the candle is placed securely.
4. Under your teacher's supervision, carefully light the candle.
5. Observe the lighted candle. Continue to list as many physical and chemical properties as you can. Record your observations in the correct columns in your data table.

	Physical properties	Chemical properties
Unlighted candle		
Lighted candle		

Observations

1. What physical properties of the unlit candle did you observe?
2. What senses did you use when you made these observations?
3. What physical changes did you observe after you lit the candle?
4. What did you have to do to observe a chemical property of the candle?
5. What evidence of chemical change did you observe?

Analysis and Conclusions

1. What do you think is the basic difference between a physical property and a chemical property?
2. Can a physical property be observed without changing the substance?
3. What name is given to a process such as burning a candle? What is the result of such a process?
4. Which type of property—physical or chemical—is easier to determine? Why?
5. **On Your Own** Obtain a recipe for making bread. List the chemical and physical properties of the ingredients. How do the properties of the ingredients result in a loaf of bread?

Study Guide

Summarizing Key Concepts

3–1 Phases of Matter

▲ Physical properties of matter include color, shape, hardness, and density.

▲ A physical change occurs when the physical properties of a substance are altered. However, the substance remains the same kind of matter.

▲ Matter can exist in any of four phases: solid, liquid, gas, and plasma.

▲ A solid has a definite shape and volume.

▲ A crystal is the regular, repeating pattern in which the particles of some solids are arranged.

▲ Amorphous solids do not form crystals and thus do not keep a definite shape.

▲ A liquid has a definite volume but not a definite shape. A liquid takes the shape of its container.

▲ A gas has no definite shape or volume.

▲ Boyle's law states that the volume of a fixed amount of gas varies inversely with the pressure. Charles's law states that the volume of a fixed amount of gas varies directly with the temperature.

▲ Matter in the plasma state is very high in energy.

3–2 Phase Changes

▲ Phase changes are accompanied by either a loss or a gain of heat energy.

▲ Melting is the change of a solid to a liquid at a temperature called the melting point. Freezing is the change of a liquid to a solid at the freezing point.

▲ Vaporization is the change of a liquid to a gas. Vaporization at the surface of a liquid is called evaporation. Vaporization throughout a liquid is called boiling.

▲ The boiling point of a liquid is related to the air pressure above the liquid.

▲ The change of a gas to a liquid is called condensation.

▲ The change of a solid directly to a gas without going through the liquid phase is called sublimation.

3–3 Chemical Properties and Changes

▲ Chemical properties describe how a substance changes into a new substance.

▲ Flammability, the ability to burn, is a chemical property.

▲ When a substance undergoes a chemical change, or a chemical reaction, it turns into a new and different substance.

Reviewing Key Terms

Define each term in a complete sentence.

3–1 Phases of Matter
physical property
phase
solid
crystal
liquid
gas
plasma

3–2 Phase Changes
melting
melting point
freezing
freezing point
vaporization
evaporation
boiling
boiling point
condensation
sublimation

3–3 Chemical Properties and Changes
chemical property
flammability
chemical change
chemical reaction

Chapter Review

Content Review

Multiple Choice

Choose the letter of the answer that best completes each statement.

1. Color, odor, and density are
   a. chemical properties.
   b. chemical changes.
   c. physical properties.
   d. solid properties.
2. A regular pattern of particles is found in
   a. molecules.   c. compressions.
   b. crystals.   d. plasmas.
3. The phase of matter that is made up of very high-energy particles is
   a. liquid.   c. gas.
   b. plasma.   d. solid.
4. As the volume of a fixed amount of gas decreases, the pressure of the gas
   a. decreases.
   b. remains the same.
   c. first increases then decreases.
   d. increases.

5. As the temperature of a fixed amount of gas increases, the volume
   a. decreases.
   b. remains the same.
   c. increases then decreases.
   d. increases.
6. All liquids have
   a. definite shape and definite volume.
   b. no definite shape but definite volume.
   c. no definite shape and no definite volume.
   d. definite shape but no definite volume.
7. A solid changes to a liquid by
   a. evaporation.   c. melting.
   b. freezing.   d. sublimation.
8. Vaporization that takes place at the surface of a liquid is called
   a. boiling.   c. sublimation.
   b. evaporation.   d. condensation.

True or False

If the statement is true, write "true." If it is false, change the underlined word or words to make the statement true.

1. Particles that make up a <u>solid</u> are packed very close together.
2. The particles of matter are spread farthest apart in a <u>liquid</u>.
3. The relationship between the temperature of a gas and the volume it occupies is described by <u>Boyle's law</u>.
4. A liquid will freeze when it <u>absorbs</u> heat energy.
5. The process by which a liquid changes to a gas is called <u>vaporization</u>.
6. Drops of water on the outside of a cold glass are water vapor that has <u>sublimed</u> into a liquid.
7. New substances that have different properties are formed as a result of <u>physical</u> changes.

Concept Mapping

Complete the following concept map for Section 3–1. Then construct a concept map for the entire chapter.

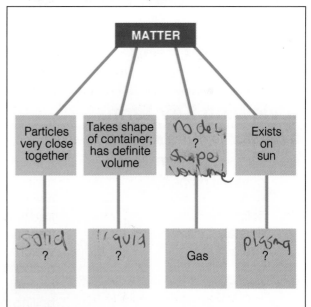

Concept Mastery

Discuss each of the following in a brief paragraph.

1. Identify the following properties as either physical or chemical. Explain your answers. (a) taste, (b) flammability, (c) color, (d) odor, (e) ability to dissolve, (f) tendency to rust

2. Identify the following changes as either physical or chemical. Explain your answers. (a) burning coal, (b) baking brownies, (c) digesting food, (d) dissolving sugar in hot water, (e) melting butter, (f) exploding fireworks, (g) rusting iron

3. Explain why both the melting point and the freezing point of water are 0°C.

4. Compare the solid, liquid, and gas phases of matter in terms of shape, volume, and arrangement and movement of molecules.

5. Explain how evaporation and boiling are similar. How are they different?

Critical Thinking and Problem Solving

Use the skills you have developed in this chapter to answer each of the following.

1. **Applying concepts** I am one of the most common substances on Earth. I am easily seen in the liquid phase and the solid phase. I am hard to observe as a gas. Identify me and explain the clues.

2. **Applying concepts** You are coming home from school one cold winter's day when you observe a neighbor filling the radiator of his car with plain tap water. What advice would you give this person? Why?

3. **Making inferences** Several campers who have set up camp on a high mountain peak decide they would like to enjoy a cup of coffee. They notice that although the water they use to make the coffee has boiled, the coffee does not seem as hot as the coffee they drink while camping out at sea level. Use your knowledge of the effects of altitude on boiling to explain their observation.

4. **Relating cause and effect** Rubbing alcohol, or isopropyl alcohol, evaporates quickly at room temperature. Explain why people with a high fever are often given rubdowns with isopropyl alcohol as a means of reducing their fevers.

5. **Applying concepts** An automobile mechanic may suggest that you test the pressure of the air in your car's tires. When should you do this—before driving or after driving?

6. **Developing a hypothesis** Solid room air fresheners "disappear" over a period of time and must be replaced. What do you think happens to the solid? How is this related to the way in which the freshener releases its pleasant odor?

7. **Using the writing process** Write a 250-word story to describe the day on which your birthday party was almost a disaster. Use the following words in your story: boiling, freezing, crystal, evaporation, liquid, melting, phase, physical change, solid, sublimation.

Mixtures, Elements, and Compounds

4

Guide for Reading

After you read the following sections, you will be able to

4–1 Classes of Matter
- Describe how matter is classified according to its makeup.

4–2 Mixtures
- List the different kinds of mixtures.
- Compare the properties of solutions with the properties of other mixtures.

4–3 Elements
- Explain why elements are considered pure substances.

4–4 Compounds
- Explain why compounds are considered pure substances.
- Describe how chemical symbols, formulas, and balanced equations are used to describe a chemical reaction.

A reddish stain on a scrap of fabric . . . some bits of dust gathered in the creases of a man's clothing . . . a seemingly unimportant clump of mud in the corner of a room . . . a few pieces of pipe tobacco found at the murder scene . . . What could all these details mean? To detective Sherlock Holmes, the creation of British author Arthur Conan Doyle, they were clues to the most mysterious crimes imaginable. By paying close attention to the evidence, Holmes was able to solve many perplexing crimes. And in so doing, he amazed not only the London police but also his own assistant, Dr. Watson.

Holmes's success had a simple, solid basis: logical thinking combined with a knowledge of chemistry. Using this knowledge, he was able to classify and analyze various substances that were clues to the mysteries. Holmes was a master at using scientific principles to solve crimes.

The whole world is a place of mystery, filled with puzzles and wonders that await the investigation of detectives like you. But before you set out on your adventure, you will need to know how chemical substances are classified. And soon you will share the delight of Holmes, who exclaimed at moments of discovery, "By Jove, Watson, I've got it!"

Journal *Activity*

You and Your World Detectives often use the scientific method to solve crimes. Pretend that you are a detective who has been asked to solve the theft of cookies from a jar in the student cafeteria. There are many suspects. Write down the method you would use to solve this "terrible" crime.

◄ *Basil Rathbone played Sherlock Holmes in a series of movies that detailed the exploits of the great fictional detective.*

![Activity Bank icon] **Activity Bank**

How to Watch the Foods You Eat, p. 718

Figure 4–1 *It is much easier to select exactly what you want to purchase if articles are grouped together. The vegetables are classified by type; the yarn, by color.*

4–1 Classes of Matter

Have you ever collected rocks, stamps, or marbles? If so, you probably know how important it is to classify, or group, the objects in a collection. To do this, you might use characteristics such as color, shape, or texture. Or maybe you would classify the objects in a collection according to their uses. In any case, you would be using a classification system based on a particular property to group the objects.

Classification systems are used all the time to organize objects. Books in a library are arranged in an organized manner. So too are the clothes in a department store and the food in a supermarket. Next time you are in a record store, notice how the records and tapes have been organized.

You can see how classifying objects—whether they be collections, books, foods, or tapes—makes it easier for you to organize them (and to locate a particular item). In order to make the study of matter easier to understand, scientists have developed different ways to classify matter. In Chapter 3, you learned that matter exists in four phases: solid, liquid, gas, and plasma. Phases are one way to classify matter.

But classifying matter by phase is not specific enough and can lead to confusion. One kind of substance can exist in more than one phase. Water is a good example. Water can be a solid in the form of ice, a liquid, or a gas in the form of water vapor. How, then, would you classify water?

Classifying matter according to phase often groups very different substances together. Table salt, gold, steel, and sand are all solids. Although they are all solids, they differ from each other in many important ways. Should they be grouped together? What about water and gasoline, which are both clear liquids? In what ways do these two liquids differ?

In order to make the study of matter easier, scientists have used a classification system based on the makeup of matter. **According to makeup, matter exists as mixtures, solutions, elements, or compounds.**

Figure 4–2 *Although they are both clear liquids, gasoline and water differ from each other in important ways. Would this truck run well if water was put into the tank instead of gasoline or diesel fuel?*

4–1 Section Review

1. According to makeup, what are the four classes of matter?
2. Why is it more useful to classify matter according to makeup rather than according to phase?

Critical Thinking—*Applying Concepts*

3. A librarian wanted to save space, so he decided to classify books according to size. By putting all the small books together and all the large books together, he was able to fit more shelves in a bookcase. Soon, the number of readers using the library decreased dramatically. Why was this method of classification not appreciated by the readers?

ACTIVITY
DOING

Classifying Common Objects

1. Obtain samples of the following materials: sugar, salt water, copper wire, taco shell, pencil eraser.
2. Observe each material. Describe its appearance in a few sentences.
3. Use simple physical tests to determine which of your samples are mixtures, solutions, elements, or compounds.
4. Present your observations in a chart.

Guide for Reading

Focus on these questions as you read.

▶ *What is a mixture?*

▶ *What are the characteristics of solutions?*

Figure 4–3 *Granite rock is made of the minerals quartz, feldspar, and mica. It is not a pure substance. Is granite a mixture? Why?*

4–2 Mixtures

Look at the photograph of a piece of granite in Figure 4–3. Granite, which is a type of rock, is made of different minerals mixed together. You can see some of these minerals—quartz, mica, and feldspar—when you look at the granite. Sand is also made of different minerals mixed together. When you pick up a handful of sand, you see dark and light grains mixed together. Granite, sand, soil, concrete, and salad dressing are examples of matter that consists of several substances mixed together.

Matter that consists of two or more substances mixed together but not chemically combined is called a mixture. A **mixture** is a combination of substances. Each substance that makes up a mixture has its own specific properties and is the same throughout. But a mixture as a whole is not the same throughout. Let's go back to granite. As you just read, granite is a mixture of minerals. The individual minerals in granite share the same properties. Every piece of a type of quartz has the same properties as every other piece of the same type of quartz. This is true of each type of mica and feldspar also.

Properties of Mixtures

The substances in a mixture are not chemically combined. The substances keep their separate identities and most of their own properties. This is an important property of mixtures. Think for a moment of a mixture of sugar and water. When sugar and water are mixed, the water is still a colorless liquid. The sugar still keeps its property of sweetness even though it is dissolved in the water. Although they may look identical, you can easily taste the difference between plain water and a sugar-water mixture.

Substances in a mixture may change in physical appearance, as when they dissolve. Some physical properties of the mixture, such as its melting point and boiling point, may also change. But the substances do not change in chemical composition. In the sugar-water mixture, the same particles of water and sugar are present after the mixing as before it. No new chemical substances have been formed.

If you eat cereal for breakfast, you are probably making a mixture. That is what you produce when you pour milk over the cereal. And if you put berries, banana slices, or raisins into your cereal, you make an even more complex mixture. But you do not use exactly the same amounts of cereal, milk, and fruit each time. This illustrates another property of mixtures.

The substances that make up a mixture can be present in any amount. The amounts are not fixed. A salt-and-pepper mixture, for example, may be one-third salt and two-thirds pepper, or one-half salt and one-half pepper. You can mix lots of sugar or only a little in a glass of iced tea. But in both cases, the mixture is still iced tea.

Because the substances in a mixture retain their original properties, they can be separated out by simple physical means. Look at Figure 4–4. A mixture of powdered iron and powdered sulfur has been made. The particles of iron are black, and the particles of sulfur are yellow. The mixture of the two has a grayish color. If you look closely at the mixture, however, you will see that particles of iron and particles of sulfur are clearly visible. You can separate the particles that make up this mixture in a rather simple way. Because iron is attracted to a magnet and sulfur is not, iron can be separated from the sulfur by holding a strong magnet near the mixture. The particles of iron can be removed from the mixture by simple

Figure 4–4 By combining powdered iron (top) with powdered sulfur (center), an iron-sulfur mixture is formed. What physical property of iron is being used to separate the mixture (bottom)?

Figure 4–5 Black sand on a Hawaiian beach, a powerful ocean wave, and a nebula far from Earth are all mixtures. What are some properties of mixtures?

What's This in My Food?

1. In a plastic sandwich bag, place half a cup of an iron-fortified breakfast cereal.

2. Squeeze the air from the bag. Seal the bag. Use your hands to crush the cereal into a fine powder.

3. Now open the bag and pour the crushed cereal into a bowl. Add just enough water to completely cover the cereal.

4. Stir the water and cereal mixture with a bar magnet for at least ten minutes.

5. Remove the magnet. Let the liquid on the magnet drain back into the bowl.

6. Use a piece of white tissue paper to remove the particles attached to the magnet. Use a hand lens to observe the particles.

What did you remove from the mixture? Is the cereal a heterogeneous or homogeneous mixture? Why?

physical means—in this case, a magnet can be used to separate the iron from the sulfur.

The methods used to separate substances in a mixture are based on the physical properties of the substances that make up the mixture. No chemical reactions are involved. What physical property of iron made it possible to separate it from sulfur in the sulfur-iron mixture? What are some other physical properties that can be used to separate the substances that make up a mixture? For example, how could you separate a mixture of sugar and water?

Types of Mixtures

You now know that granite is a mixture. Other mixtures include concrete and stainless steel. Concrete is a mixture of pieces of rock, sand, and cement. Stainless steel is a mixture of chromium and iron. (You might be interested to learn that stainless steel does "stain," or rust. However, it "stains less" than regular steel—hence, its name.) From your experience, you would probably say that stainless steel seems "better mixed" than concrete. You cannot see individual particles of chromium and iron in stainless steel, but particles of rock, sand, and cement are visible in concrete. Mixtures are classified according to how "well mixed" they are.

Figure 4–6 *This gold miner in Finland is separating heavy pieces of gold from lighter pieces of rock, sand, and soil by swirling the mixture in a shallow pan of water. The gold will settle to the bottom of the pan. Salt water is a mixture of salts and water. When the water evaporates, deposits of salt, such as these in Mono Lake, California, are left behind.*

sand — liquid salad dressing concrete — cement
sand water

HETEROGENEOUS MIXTURE A mixture that does not appear to be the same throughout is said to be heterogeneous. A **heterogeneous** (heht-er-oh-JEE-nee-uhs) **mixture** is the "least mixed" of mixtures. The particles in a heterogeneous mixture are large enough to be seen and to separate from the mixture. Concrete is an example of a heterogeneous mixture. Can you think of some other examples?

Not all heterogeneous mixtures contain only solid particles (as does concrete). Shake up some pebbles or sand in water to make a liquid-solid mixture. This mixture is easily separated just by letting it stand. The pebbles and sand will settle to the bottom of the jar. Oil and vinegar, often used as a salad dressing, make up a liquid-liquid heterogeneous mixture. When the mixture has been shaken well, drops of oil are spread throughout the vinegar. This mixture, too, will separate when allowed to stand. Now you know why you have to shake a bottle of salad dressing that has not been used for a while.

HOMOGENEOUS MIXTURE A mixture that appears to be the same throughout is said to be homogeneous (hoh-moh-JEE-nee-uhs). A **homogeneous mixture** is "well mixed." The particles that make up the mixture are very small and not easily recognizable. These particles do not settle when the mixture is allowed to stand. Stainless steel is a homogeneous mixture.

Although you may not be aware of it, many of the materials you use and eat every day are homogeneous mixtures. Milk, whipped cream, toothpaste, and suntan lotion are just a few examples. In these homogeneous mixtures, the particles are mixed together but not dissolved. As a group, these mixtures are called **colloids** (KAHL-oidz).

The particles in a colloid are relatively large in size and are kept permanently suspended. They are also continuously bombarded by other particles. This bombardment accounts for two important properties of a colloid. One property is that a colloid will not separate upon standing (as do many heterogeneous mixtures). Because the particles are constantly bombarded, they do not have a chance to settle out. Another property is that a colloid often appears cloudy. This is because the constant bombardment of particles

Figure 4–7 *Tacos are heterogeneous mixtures in which the parts are easy to recognize and to separate from the mixture.*

ACTIVITY
READING

Danger in the Air

Fog, a colloid you are probably familiar with, forms when tiny droplets of water become suspended in air. Drive along a fog-shrouded road and you will soon realize how dangerous fog can be. On a clear day, you can see forever; on a foggy day, however, your car's headlights offer scant help in piercing the gloom.

You might like to find out about the poet Carl Sandburg's impressions of this common colloid by reading his poem "Fog."

Figure 4–8 *A gelatin dessert is a colloid that contains liquid particles mixed with a solid. Whipped cream is a colloid that contains gas particles in a liquid. The smoke from a campfire is a colloid that contains solid particles mixed in a gas.*

enables a colloid to scatter light. So if a beam of light is passed through a colloid, the beam becomes visible. The white cloudy appearance of milk is due to the scattering of light by the bombarding particles in this familiar colloid. If you have ever seen a searchlight sweep through the air at night, you have observed another example of this property of colloids. Figure 4–9 is a table of several different types of colloids. Which ones are you familiar with?

Solutions

A solution (suh-LOO-shuhn) is a type of homogeneous mixture of two or more substances in a single physical state. You might say that a **solution** is the "best mixed" of all mixtures. You are probably familiar with many different solutions. Ocean water is one example. In this solution, different salts are dissolved in water. Another example of a solution is antifreeze. Lemonade and iced tea from powdered mixes are also solutions. One important solution helps keep you alive. Do you know what it is? Air is a solution of oxygen and other gases disolved in nitrogen.

All solutions have several important properties. Picture a glass of lemonade as you read about them. How do you think the lemonade was made? Lemonade mix was probably added to water and dissolved in the water. A solution always has a substance that is dissolved and a substance that does the dissolving. The substance that is dissolved is called the **solute** (SAHL-yoot). The substance that does the dissolving is called the **solvent** (SAHL-vuhnt). In the case of the lemonade, the powdered mix is the solute. The solvent is water.

Figure 4–9 *You might be surprised to learn how many commonly used materials are colloids. What type of colloid is mayonnaise? Butter?*

TYPES OF COLLOIDS	
Name	**Example**
Fog (liquid in gas)	Clouds
Smoke (solid in gas)	Smoke
Foam (gas in liquid)	Whipped cream
Emulsion (liquid in liquid)	Mayonnaise
Sol (solid in liquid)	Paint
Gel (liquid in solid)	Butter

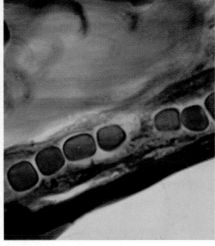

Looking at the glass of lemonade, you will notice that the particles are not large enough to be seen. Because the particles in a solution are so small, most solutions cannot easily be separated by simple physical means. Unlike many colloids, the particles in a liquid solution are too small to scatter light.

Tasting the lemonade illustrates another property of a solution. Every part of the solution tastes the same. This might lead you to believe that one property of a solution is that its particles are evenly spread out. And you would be right!

There are seven possible types of solutions, as you can see from Figure 4–12 on page 94. Many liquid solutions contain water as the solvent. Ocean water is basically a water solution that contains many salts. Body fluids are also water solutions. Because water can dissolve many substances, it is called the "universal solvent."

Figure 4–10 *Solutions are the "best mixed" of all mixtures. Seawater, the non-solid portion of blood, and lava from an erupting volcano are all solutions. What other common solutions can you name?*

Activity Bank

Acid Rain Takes Toll on Art, p. 720

Figure 4–11 *You can form three kinds of solutions using a liquid solvent. Name a common solution that is a solid dissolved in a liquid. A liquid dissolved in a liquid. A gas dissolved in a liquid.*

Solid solute

Liquid solute

Gas solute

Liquid solvent (water)

Liquid solvent (water)

Liquid solvent (water)

Figure 4–12 *Seven different types of solutions can be made from three phases of matter. Can most solutions be separated by simple physical means? Explain.*

TYPES OF SOLUTIONS

Solute	Solvent	Example
Gas Gas Gas	Gas Liquid Solid	Air (oxygen in nitrogen) Soda water (carbon dioxide in water) Charcoal gas mask (poisonous gases on carbon)
Liquid Liquid	Liquid Solid	Antifreeze (ethylene glycol in water) Dental filling (mercury in silver)
Solid Solid	Liquid Solid	Ocean water (salt in water) Gold jewelry (copper in gold)

ACTIVITY

DISCOVERING

Is It a Solution?

1. Obtain samples of the following substances: sugar, flour, powdered drink, cornstarch, instant coffee, talcum powder, soap powder, gelatin.

2. Crush each substance into pieces of equal size. Make sure you keep the substances separate.

3. Determine how much of each substance you can dissolve in samples of the same amount of water at the same temperature. Determine how quickly each substance dissolves.

4. Determine which substances dissolved fastest and to the greatest extent. Record your findings in a data table.

■ Use your knowledge of the properties of solutions to determine which substances formed true solutions.

SOLUBILITY A substance that dissolves in another substance is said to be **soluble** (SAHL-yoo-buhl). Salt and sugar are soluble in water. Mercury and oil do not dissolve, or are **insoluble,** in water.

The amount of a solute that can be completely dissolved in a given amount of solvent at a specific temperature is called its **solubility.** What is the relationship between temperature and the solubility of solid solutes? In general, as the temperature of a solvent increases, the solubility of the solute increases. What about gaseous solutes? An increase in the temperature of the solvent usually decreases the solubility of a gaseous solute. This explains why soda that warms up goes flat. The "fizz" of soda is due to bubbles of carbon dioxide dissolved in the solution. As soda warms, the dissolved CO_2 comes out of solution. It is less soluble. Without the CO_2, the soda tastes flat.

Some substances are not very soluble in water. But they dissolve easily in other solvents. For example, one of the reasons you use soap to wash dirt and grease from your skin or clothing is that soap dissolves these substances, whereas water alone does not. The soap dissolves the grease and then, along with the grease, it is washed away by the water.

ALLOYS Not all solutions are liquids. Solutions can exist in any of the three phases—solid, liquid, or gas—as the table in Figure 4–12 indicates. Metal solutions called **alloys** are examples of solids dissolved in solids. Gold jewelry is actually a solid solution of gold and copper. Brass is an alloy of copper and zinc.

Figure 4–13 *The important alloy stainless steel is a mixture of iron and chromium. Here it is being poured as a white-hot liquid from a vat. What type of mixture is stainless steel?*

Sterling silver contains small amounts of copper in solution with silver. And stainless steel, which you read about before, is an alloy of chromium and iron. You may find it interesting to learn about the make-up of other alloys, such as pewter, bronze, and solder. How do you think alloys are made?

4–2 Section Review

1. What is a mixture? What are three properties of a mixture?
2. How does a heterogeneous mixture differ from a homogeneous mixture?
3. What is a colloid?
4. What is a solution? What are the two parts of a solution? What are two properties of a solution?

Connection—*You and Your World*
5. Trout are fish that need to live in water that has a great deal of oxygen dissolved in it. What can you predict about the temperature of the water in a trout stream? Explain your answer. The correct answer may improve your luck the next time you go fishing!

ACTIVITY
DISCOVERING

Where's the Fizz?

You can determine what conditions affect the solubility of a gas in a liquid.

1. Remove the cap from a bottle of soda.

2. Immediately fit the opening of a balloon over the top of the bottle. Shake the bottle several times. Note any changes in the balloon.

3. Heat the bottle of soda very gently by placing it in a pan of hot water. Note any further changes in the balloon.

What two conditions of solubility are being tested here?

■ What general statement about the solubility of a gas in a liquid can you now make?

PROBLEM Solving

What's the Solution?

Look closely at the four photographs below. Each shows a familiar solution. For each photograph, tell what solute is dissolved in what solvent. List other solutions that are similar to the solutions shown. Use Figure 4–12 to help you. Solve this problem and you are part of the solution!

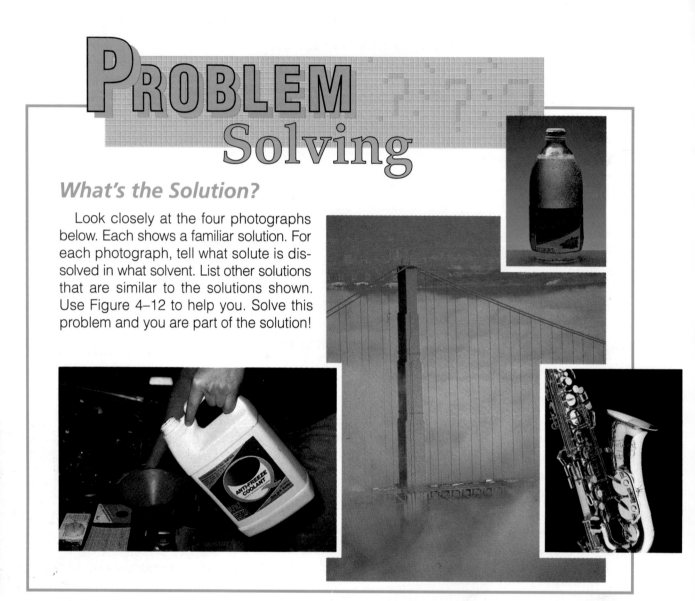

4–3 Elements

Scientists often examine, in great detail, the particles that make up a substance. Close observation shows that in some cases all the particles that make up a substance are alike; in other cases, all the particles are not alike. When all the particles are alike, the substance is called a **pure substance.** A pure substance is made of only one kind of material and has definite properties. A pure substance is the same throughout. All the particles in a pure substance are exactly the same. Iron, aluminum, water, sugar, and table salt are examples of pure substances. So is the oxygen your body uses from the air you breathe. A sample taken from any of these substances is identical to any other sample taken from that substance. For instance, a drop of pure water taken from a well in Arizona, a river in Australia, or the hard-packed snow and ice of Antarctica is the same.

Elements are the simplest pure substance. An **element** cannot be changed into a simpler substance by heating or by any chemical process. The particles that make up an element are in their simplest form. (You will learn just what these particles are in the next paragraph.) Suppose you melt a piece of iron by adding heat energy to it. You may think that you have changed the iron into a simpler substance. But the liquid iron you now have still contains only iron particles. True, the heat has changed the iron's phase—from a solid to a liquid. But it is still iron. No new or simpler substance has been formed.

ACTIVITY DOING

Name That Element

From around your home, collect several items that are made of common elements. For example, items made of iron, copper, aluminum, or carbon should be fairly easy to find. See if you can find items that are made of less common elements.

Make a display of the elements you collect. Label each element with its name and chemical symbol.

Elements and Atoms

The smallest particle of an element that has the properties of that element is called an **atom.** An atom is the basic building block of matter. All elements are made of atoms. Atoms of the same element are alike. Atoms of different elements are different.

Scientists now know that an atom is made of even smaller particles. These particles, however, do not have the properties of the elements they make up. You will learn more about the particles that make up atoms in Chapter 5.

Chemical Symbols

For many years, scientists had to spell out the full names of elements when writing about them. As you can imagine, this practice was time consuming. Then in 1813, a system of representing the elements with symbols was introduced. After all, why couldn't chemists do what mathematicians and musicians had been doing for years?

Figure 4–14 *This miner examines a rock specimen closely because if he is lucky, the rocks he mines will contain the element gold.*

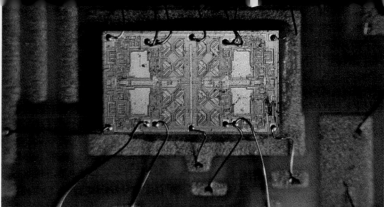

Figure 4–15 *Elements are the simplest type of pure substance. These yellow crystals are made of the element sulfur. Computer chips contain silicon. In what ways would our lives be different if there was no silicon on Earth?*

Chemical symbols are a shorthand way of representing the elements. Each symbol consists of one or two letters, usually taken from the element's name. The symbol for the element oxygen is O. The symbol for hydrogen is H; for carbon, C. The symbol for aluminum is Al; and for chlorine, Cl. Two letters are needed for a chemical symbol when the first letter of that element's name has already been used as a symbol for another element. For example, the symbol for carbon is C, for calcium it is Ca, and for copper it is Cu. You should note that when two letters are used in a symbol, the first letter is always capitalized but the second letter is never capitalized.

What do you think the symbol for gold is? The symbol for gold is Au. Does that surprise you? Gold is not spelled with an "a" or a "u." But the reason for the symbol is really not so strange. The Latin

Figure 4–16 *This table shows the chemical symbols for some of the most common elements. What is the symbol for tin? Why is Fe the symbol for iron?*

COMMON ELEMENTS

Name	Symbol	Name	Symbol	Name	Symbol
Aluminum	Al	Hydrogen	H	Oxygen	O
Bromine	Br	Iodine	I	Phosphorus	P
Calcium	Ca	Iron	Fe	Potassium	K
Carbon	C	Lead	Pb	Silicon	Si
Chlorine	Cl	Lithium	Li	Silver	Ag
Chromium	Cr	Magnesium	Mg	Sodium	Na
Copper	Cu	Mercury	Hg	Sulfur	S
Fluorine	F	Neon	Ne	Tin	Sn
Gold	Au	Nickel	Ni	Uranium	U
Helium	He	Nitrogen	N	Zinc	Zn

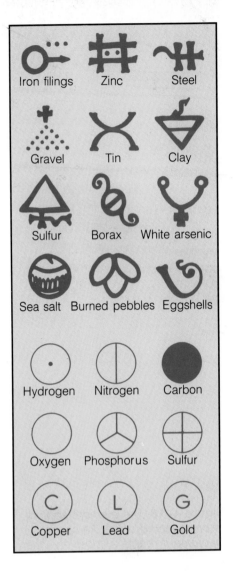

Figure 4–17 *The top four rows are symbols that were used by ancient alchemists to represent elements. The bottom three rows are part of the system developed by John Dalton. Do you think it would be easier to remember these symbols for the elements or the symbols shown in Figure 4–16?*

name for gold is *aurum*. Scientists often use the Latin name of an element as its symbol. Here are some other examples. The symbol used for silver is Ag, from the Latin word for silver, *argentum*. The Latin word for iron is *ferrum,* and the symbol for this element is Fe. The symbol for mercury is Hg, from the Latin name *hydrargyrum*. The table in Figure 4–16 lists some common elements and their symbols.

4–3 Section Review

1. What is a pure substance? Why are elements pure substances?
2. What is an atom? How do atoms of the same element compare? Of different elements?
3. Write the chemical symbols for oxygen, nitrogen, lead, sulfur, sodium, and helium.

Critical Thinking—*Relating Facts*
4. Why can elements be thought of as homogeneous matter?

4–4 Compounds

As you just learned, the simplest type of pure substance is an element. But not all pure substances are elements. Water and table salt, for example, are pure substances. Each is made of only one kind of material with definite properties. Yet water and table salt are not elements. Why? They can be broken down into simpler substances. Water can be broken down into the elements hydrogen and oxygen. Table salt can be broken down into the elements sodium and chlorine. Thus water and table salt, like many other pure substances, are made of more than one element.

Pure substances that are made of more than one element are called compounds. A **compound** is two or more elements chemically combined. Sugar is a compound that is made of the elements carbon, hydrogen, and oxygen. Carbon dioxide, ammonia, baking soda, and TNT are compounds. Can you name some other common compounds?

Unlike elements, compounds can be broken down into simpler substances. Heating is one way to separate some compounds into their elements. The compound copper sulfide, which is also known as the ore chalcocite, can be separated into the elements copper and sulfur by heating it to a high temperature.

Electric energy is often used to break down compounds that do not separate upon heating. By passing an electric current through water, the elements hydrogen and oxygen can be obtained. What elements would you obtain if you passed an electric current through melted table salt?

The properties of the elements that make up a compound are often quite different from the properties of the compound itself. Would you want to flavor your French-fried potatoes with a poisonous gas and a highly active metal? Yet, in a way, this is exactly what you are doing when you sprinkle salt on your potatoes. Chlorine is a yellow-green gas that is poisonous. Sodium is a silvery metal that explodes if placed in water. But when chemically combined, these elements produce a white compound—sodium chloride—that you cannot and probably would not want to live without. And it adds a tasty flavor to foods as well!

Figure 4–18 The element sodium is often stored under kerosene because it reacts explosively when it comes into contact with water (left). The element chlorine is a poisonous gas (center). When sodium and chlorine combine, sodium chloride forms. What is the common name for sodium chloride?

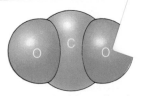

Carbon dioxide molecule

Water molecule

Figure 4–19 *As you can see from this diagram, molecules are made of two or more elements chemically bonded together. What are the chemical formulas for these two compounds?*

Compounds and Molecules

Compounds are made of **molecules** (MAHL-ih-kyoolz). A molecule is made of two or more atoms chemically bonded together. A molecule is the smallest particle of a compound that has all the properties of that compound.

Water is a compound. A molecule of water is made up of 2 atoms of hydrogen chemically bonded to 1 atom of oxygen. One molecule of water has all of the properties of a glass of water, a bucket of water, or a pool of water. If a molecule of water were broken down into atoms of its elements, would the atoms have the same properties as the molecule?

Just as all atoms of a certain element are alike, all molecules of a compound are alike. Each molecule of ammonia, for example, is like every other. Because it is made of only one kind of molecule, a compound is the same throughout. So compounds, like elements, are pure substances.

Chemical Formulas

You probably learned the alphabet before you learned to read. Well, you can think of chemical symbols as the letters of a chemical alphabet. Just as you learned to put letters together to make words, chemical symbols can be put together to make chemical "words." Combinations of chemical symbols are called **chemical formulas.** Chemical formulas are a shorthand way of representing chemical substances.

Most chemical formulas represent compounds. For example, ammonia is a compound made of the elements nitrogen (N) and hydrogen (H). The chemical formula for ammonia is NH_3. A molecule of ammonia contains 1 atom of nitrogen and 3 atoms of hydrogen. The formula for rubbing alcohol is C_3H_7OH. What elements make up this compound? How about the compound silver nitrate, $AgNO_3$?

Sometimes a formula represents a molecule of an element, not a compound. For example, the symbol

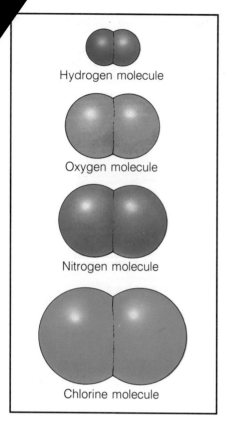

Hydrogen molecule

Oxygen molecule

Nitrogen molecule

Chlorine molecule

Figure 4–20 *Some elements are found in nature as molecules that are made of 2 atoms of that element. Hydrogen, oxygen, nitrogen, and chlorine are examples of such elements. What is the chemical formula for a molecule of each of these elements?*

for the element oxygen is O. But in nature, oxygen occurs as a molecule that contains 2 atoms of oxygen bonded together. So the formula for a molecule of oxygen is O_2. Some other gases that exist only in pairs of atoms are hydrogen, H_2, nitrogen, N_2, fluorine, F_2, and chlorine, Cl_2. Remember that the symbols for the elements just listed are the letters only. The formulas are the letters with the small number 2 at the lower right.

When writing a chemical formula, you use the symbol of each element in the compound. You also use small numbers, called **subscripts.** Subscripts are placed to the lower right of the symbols. A subscript gives the number of atoms of the element in the compound. When there is only 1 atom of an element, the subscript 1 is not written. It is understood to be 1.

Carbon dioxide is a compound of the elements carbon and oxygen. Its formula is CO_2. By looking at the formula, you can tell that every molecule is made up of 1 atom of carbon (C) and 2 atoms of oxygen (O). Sulfuric acid has the formula H_2SO_4. How many hydrogen atoms, sulfur atoms, and oxygen atoms are there in a molecule of sulfuric acid?

Can you now see the advantages of using chemical formulas? Not only does a formula save space, but it tells you a lot about the compound. It tells you the elements that make up the compound. And it tells you how many atoms of each element combine to form the compound.

Chemical Equations

If you think of chemical symbols as "letters" and chemical formulas as "words," then you can write chemical "sentences." Chemical sentences are a way to describe a chemical process, or chemical reaction. As you learned in Chapter 3, during a chemical reaction, substances are changed into new and different substances through a rearrangement of their atoms. New chemical substances with new properties

ACTIVITY

CALCULATING

Count the Atoms

List the elements that are present in each of the following compounds. Calculate how many atoms of each element are represented in the following formulas.

$NaHCO_3$

$C_2H_4O_2$

$Mg(OH)_2$

$3H_3PO_4$

are formed. By using chemical symbols and formulas, you can describe a chemical reaction.

Have you ever seen charcoal burning in a barbecue grill? If so, you were watching a chemical reaction. The carbon atoms in the charcoal were combining with the oxygen molecules in the air to form the gas carbon dioxide. The reaction could be written:

carbon atoms plus oxygen molecules
produce carbon dioxide molecules

By using symbols and formulas, this reaction can be written in a simpler way:

$$C + O_2 \longrightarrow CO_2$$

The symbol C represents an atom of carbon. The formula O_2 represents a molecule of oxygen. And the formula CO_2 represents a molecule of carbon dioxide. The arrow is read "yields," which is another way of saying "produces."

The description of a chemical reaction using symbols and formulas is called a **chemical equation.** An equation is another example of chemical shorthand. Instead of using words to describe a chemical reaction, you can use a chemical equation.

Here is another example. The chemical equation for the formation of water from the elements hydrogen and oxygen is

$$H_2 + O_2 \longrightarrow H_2O$$

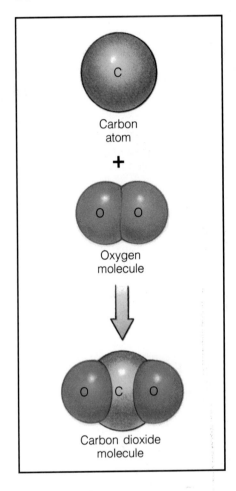

Figure 4–21 *This illustration shows the chemical reaction that occurs when carbon and oxygen combine to form carbon dioxide. What is the chemical formula for carbon dioxide?*

PROPERTIES OF ELEMENTS, COMPOUNDS, AND MIXTURES

Elements	Compounds	Mixtures
Made up of only one kind of atom	Made up of more than one kind of atom	Made up of more than one kind of molecule
Cannot be broken down by chemical means	Can be broken down by chemical means	Can be separated by physical means
Has same properties as atoms making it up	Has different properties from elements making it up	Has same properties as substances making it up
Has same properties throughout	Has same properties throughout	Has different properties throughout

Figure 4–22 *This table shows the common properties of elements, compounds, and mixtures. Which of the three substances does not have the same properties throughout?*

103

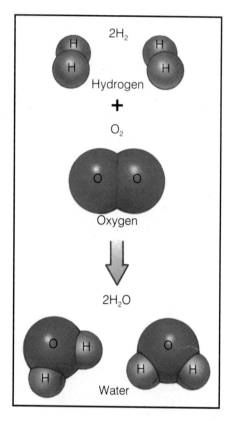

Figure 4–23 *During the formation of water, 2 hydrogen molecules combine with a molecule of oxygen to form 2 water molecules. What is the chemical equation for this reaction?*

2H$_2$

H H Hydrogen

+

O$_2$

O O Oxygen

2H$_2$O

O H H

H H O

Water

This equation (H$_2$ + O$_2$ ⟶ H$_2$O) tells you what elements are combining and what product is formed. But something is wrong with this equation. Do you know what it is?

Look at the number of oxygen atoms on each side of the equation. Are they equal? On the left side of the equation there are 2 oxygen atoms. On the right side there is only 1 oxygen atom. Could 1 oxygen atom have disappeared? Scientists know that atoms are never created or destroyed in a chemical reaction. Atoms can only be rearranged. So there must be the same number of atoms of each element on each side of the equation. The equation must be balanced. The balanced equation for the formation of water is

$$2H_2 + O_2 \longrightarrow 2H_2O$$

Now count the atoms of each element on each side of the equation. You will find that they are the same: 4 atoms of hydrogen on the left side and on the right; 2 atoms of oxygen on the left side and on the right. The equation is correctly balanced.

You have seen that an equation can be balanced by placing the appropriate number in front of a chemical formula in the equation. This number is called a **coefficient** (koh-uh-FIHSH-uhnt). The correctly balanced equation now tells you that 2 molecules of hydrogen combine with 1 molecule of oxygen to produce 2 molecules of water.

4–4 Section Review

1. What is a compound?
2. How is a compound different from an element?
3. What is a molecule? How is a molecule of an element or a compound represented?
4. Why must a chemical equation be balanced?

Connection—*You and Your World*
5. How is a recipe for baking a cake like a chemical equation? What three things must be included in a good, easy-to-follow recipe?

CONNECTIONS

Time and a Tree

You have to hurry. . . . In three minutes you will be late for class. Time has a way of ruling your days. Time tells you where to be, and when. Time also tells you what to do. Days seem short when you have a lot to do.

Time for a sugar maple is different. You probably do not give much thought to time's effects on a tree. A tree stands tall and proud for so long that time seems to have little impact on its life from one day to the next. Yet if you were able to observe a tree over a year's time, you would notice profound changes.

Take this sugar maple in the photograph. It is the middle of March and the Vermont woods where this tree grows are covered with a winter's blanket of snow. Few birds can be seen or heard, and even fewer other animals are in sight. For most forms of forest life, winter is a time of rest. But deep within the trunk of a maple tree, things are beginning to stir. Sap, a sweet juice conducted in tiny tubes in the tree trunk, is starting to move upward from the roots. Farmers are able to "tap" the tree's trunk and collect buckets of sap. Later the sap will be boiled down into delicious maple syrup. But where did this sweet sap come from?

Actually, the sugars in the sap were made by the tree the year before. In the previous spring, the maple tree leafed out. The beautiful leaves that clothed the maple then are efficient collectors of the sun's energy. The green pigment in the leaves, which is called chlorophyll, trapped the energy of sunlight and used it to make food. In a complex series of chemical reactions, water was combined with carbon dioxide to produce sugars. Scientists write a chemical equation to describe the process:

$$6CO_2 + 6H_2O \xrightarrow[\text{(chlorophyll)}]{\text{(sunlight)}} C_6H_{12}O_6 + 6O_2$$

Carbon dioxide plus water plus the energy of the sun trapped by chlorophyll yields sugar plus oxygen—a simple equation that describes the single most important chemical reaction on Earth.

You might wonder why this reaction is so important. It is important because plants are able to use the energy of the sun in ways animals never can. And in so doing, plants produce food (in the form of plant sugars) and oxygen necessary for the survival of animals on Earth.

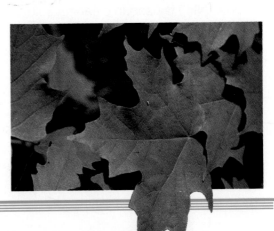

Laboratory Investigation

Making Models of Chemical Reactions

Problem

How do atoms and molecules of elements and compounds combine in chemical reactions?

Materials *(per group)*

> toothpicks
> red, yellow, green, blue, purple (red-blue), and orange (yellow-red) food coloring
> 25 large marshmallows

Procedure

A. *Making Marshmallow Atoms*

1. Prepare model atoms by applying food coloring to the marshmallows as follows:

   N (nitrogen)—red (2)

   H (hydrogen)—blue (6)

   Cu (copper)—green (4)

   O (oxygen)—yellow (7)

   K (potassium)—orange (2)

   Cl (chlorine)—purple (2)

2. Let the marshmallows dry for 2 hours.

B. *Assembling the Marshmallow Molecules*

1. Use a toothpick to join two red marshmallows to make a molecule of N_2. Use a toothpick to join two blue marshmallows to make a molecule of H_2.

2. Ammonia (NH_3) is used in cleaning solutions and in the manufacture of fertilizers. A molecule of ammonia contains 1 nitrogen atom and 3 hydrogen atoms. Use the marshmallow molecules of nitrogen and hydrogen you made in step 1 to form an ammonia molecule. You may use as many nitrogen and hydrogen molecules as you need to make ammonia molecules as long as you do not have any atoms left over. Remember, hydrogen and nitrogen must start out as molecules consisting of 2

atoms each. Now balance the equation for the chemical reaction that produces ammonia:

$$\_\_N_2 + \_\_H_2 \longrightarrow \_\_\_\_\_NH_3$$

3. Use two green marshmallows for copper and one yellow marshmallow for oxygen to make a model of a copper oxide molecule (Cu_2O). With a white marshmallow representing carbon, manipulate the marshmallow models to illustrate the reaction below, which produces metallic copper. Balance the equation.

$$\_\_Cu_2O + \_\_C \longrightarrow \_\_Cu + \_\_CO_2$$

4. Use orange for potassium, purple for chlorine, and yellow for oxygen to assemble a molecule of potassium chlorate ($KClO_3$).

Observations

1. How many molecules of N_2 and H_2 are needed to produce 2 molecules of NH_3?

2. How many molecules of copper are produced from 2 molecules of Cu_2O?

Analysis and Conclusions

1. Which substances that you made are elements? Which are compounds?

2. If you had to make 5 molecules of ammonia (NH_3), how many red marshmallows would you need? How many blue marshmallows?

Study Guide

Summarizing Key Concepts

4–1 Classes of Matter

Matter is classified according to its makeup as mixtures, solutions, elements, or compounds.

4–2 Mixtures

▲ A mixture is composed of two or more substances mixed together but not chemically combined.

▲ The substances in a mixture can be present in any amount.

▲ The substances in a mixture can be separated by simple physical means.

▲ A mixture that does not appear to be the same throughout is a heterogeneous mixture.

▲ A mixture that appears to be the same throughout is a homogeneous mixture.

▲ The particles in a colloid, a type of homogeneous mixture, are not dissolved.

▲ A solution is a type of homogeneous mixture formed when one substance, called the solute, dissolves in another substance, called the solvent.

▲ The amount of a solute that can completely dissolve in a given solvent at a specific temperature is called its solubility.

▲ Alloys are metal solutions in which solids are dissolved in solids.

4–3 Elements

▲ A pure substance is made of only one kind of material, has definite properties, and is the same throughout.

▲ Elements are the simplest type of pure substance. They cannot be broken down into simpler substances without losing their identity.

▲ Elements are made of atoms, which are the building blocks of matter.

4–4 Compounds

▲ Compounds are two or more elements chemically combined.

▲ Compounds are made of molecules. A molecule is made of two or more atoms chemically bonded together.

▲ A chemical formula, which is a combination of chemical symbols, usually represents a molecule of a compound.

▲ A chemical equation describes a chemical reaction.

Reviewing Key Terms

Define each term in a complete sentence.

4–2 Mixtures
mixture
heterogeneous mixture
homogeneous mixture
colloid
solution
solute
solvent
soluble
insoluble
solubility
alloy

4–3 Elements
pure substance
element
atom
chemical symbol

4–4 Compounds
compound
molecule
chemical formula
subscript
chemical equation
coefficient

Chapter Review

Content Review

Multiple Choice

Choose the letter of the answer that best completes each statement.

1. Matter that consists of two or more substances mixed together but not chemically combined is called a(an)
   a. element.
   c. pure substance.
   b. compound.
   d. mixture.
2. An example of a heterogeneous mixture is
   a. salt water.
   c. stainless steel.
   b. salad dressing.
   d. salt.
3. In a solution, the substance being dissolved is called the
   a. solvent.
   c. solubility.
   b. solute.
   d. insoluble.
4. The simplest type of pure substance is a (an)
   a. compound.
   c. solution
   b. alloy.
   d. element.

5. The chemical formula for a molecule of nitrogen is
   a. N.
   c. N_3.
   b. N_2.
   d. Ni.
6. Pure substances that are made of more than one element are called
   a. compounds.
   c. alloys.
   b. mixtures.
   d. solutions.
7. Which of the following is not an alloy?
   a. zinc
   c. stainless steel
   b. gold jewelry
   d. brass
8. Which of the following is not a compound?
   a. H_2 ~~molecule~~
   c. H_2SO_4
   b. H_2O
   d. CO_2

True or False

If the statement is true, write "true." If it is false, change the underlined word or words to make the statement true.

1. The basic building block of matter is the <u>compound</u>.
2. When elements combine to form compounds, their properties <u>do not</u> change.
3. One example of a <u>homogeneous</u> mixture is concrete.
4. Substances in a <u>mixture</u> keep their separate identities and most of their own properties.
5. Mixtures can be separated by simple <u>chemical</u> means.
6. Salt and sugar are <u>insoluble</u> in water.
7. The "best mixed" of mixtures is a <u>solution</u>.
8. The particles in a <u>colloid</u> are mixed together but not dissolved.

Concept Mapping

Complete the following concept map for Section 4–1. Then construct a concept map for the entire chapter.

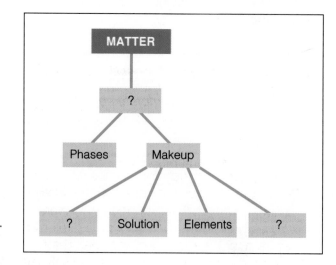

Concept Mastery

Discuss each of the following in a brief paragraph.

1. A solution is classified as a mixture instead of a compound. Why?
2. Describe a method you can use to separate the following mixtures. Your method should take into account the physical properties of the substances that make up the mixture.
   a. sugar and water
   b. powdered iron and powdered aluminum
   c. wood and gold
   d. nickels and dimes
3. What two things does a chemical formula indicate about a compound?
4. Write the symbols for the following elements and describe one use for each: (a) gold, (b) oxygen, (c) carbon, (d) hydrogen, (e) silver, (f) calcium, (g) nitrogen.
5. Chemical equations can be balanced by using coefficients but not subscripts. Explain why this is so.
6. What is a solution? What two parts make up a solution? Describe three properties of a solution.

Critical Thinking and Problem Solving

Use the skills you have developed in this chapter to answer each of the following.

1. **Making inferences** Suppose you find a chemistry book that is written in a language you cannot understand. When you look at the book, however, you realize that you can understand and duplicate the chemical reactions printed in the text. Explain how you can do this?
2. **Making calculations** Balance the following equations:
   a. $Mg + O_2 \longrightarrow MgO$
   b. $NaCl \longrightarrow Na + Cl_2$
   c. $CH_4 + O_2 \longrightarrow CO_2 + H_2O$
   d. $H_2 + O_2 \longrightarrow H_2O$
3. **Designing an experiment** Describe an experiment to show that
   a. water is a compound, not an element.
   b. salt water is a solution, not a pure substance.
4. **Relating facts** You learned that mixtures have three important properties. Use the example of a bowl of cereal with milk and strawberries to illustrate each property.
5. **Classifying data** Develop a classification system for the months of the year. State the property or properties that you will use to classify the months. Do not use the four seasons. Try to make your system as useful and as specific as possible.
6. **Making inferences** Explain whether or not you believe there exists a true "universal solvent" capable of dissolving all other substances. Include a description of the kind of container you would need to hold such a solvent.
7. **Using the writing process** Water has been accused of being an element by an assistant district attorney. You are the defense attorney whose job is to convince the jury that water is a compound. Write up a brief summation to the jury to make your case. Use only the very best scientific information in your case.

Atoms: Building Blocks of Matter

Beads of mercury gleam on a sheet of cloth. Some beads are small; others are large. But they are all still mercury, a pure substance. If you were to take the smallest bead of mercury and slice it in half once, twice, three times, even a thousand times, you would still be left with mercury—or would you?

Is there some incredibly tiny bead of mercury that if sliced one more time would no longer be mercury? It was just this kind of question that sparked the imagination and curiosity of early scientists. They hypothesized and argued as the years passed—for more than 2000 years, in fact.

Then, slowly, clues were found. Experiments were performed. New ideas were explored. And finally an answer was developed. In many ways it was quite a simple answer. To find it out, let's begin at the beginning.

Journal *Activity*

You and Your World Have you ever seen pictures of the Great Pyramids that were built in Egypt thousands of years ago? Block upon block, these great tombs were constructed with few tools and great effort. Even the tallest building is made of small parts. Draw a picture in your journal of a building you like. Next to your drawing, make another drawing of one of the pieces that make up your building.

◀ *Silvery beads of liquid mercury gleam in the photographer's lights.*

5–1 An Atomic Model of Matter

In the last few chapters, you learned several important facts about matter. All materials are made of matter. Matter is anything that has mass and volume. And the basic building blocks of matter are atoms. You have learned all of this in a rather short time. But the story of how scientists have come to know what they do about matter spans a much greater time period—thousands of years to be sure!

For more than 2400 years, philosophers and scientists have tried to determine the composition of matter using a variety of experiments and observations. Because the basic building blocks of matter (atoms) could not until recently be seen, researchers have relied on observations of how matter behaves. Such observations are called indirect evidence.

Indirect evidence about an object is evidence you get without actually seeing or touching the object. As you gather indirect evidence, you can develop a mental picture, or model. A model uses familiar ideas to explain unfamiliar facts observed in nature. A model can be changed as new information is collected. As you read further, you will learn how a model of matter was developed and changed over many years. From the early Greek concept of the atom to the modern atomic theory, scientists have built on and modified existing models of the atom. Let's see just how.

Figure 5–1 *Scientists often depend on indirect evidence to develop a model of something that cannot be observed directly. Use the two drawings in this figure to develop a model that might explain what happened during the few hours that separate the two drawings.*

Figure 5-2 *Unlike many artists working today, ancient Greek artists did not paint on canvas. This vase painting, showing a warrior carrying the body of a dead companion, was made close to the time Democritus lived.*

The Greek Model

The search for a description of matter began with the Greek philosopher Democritus (dih-MAHK-ruh-tuhs) more than 2000 years ago. He and many other philosophers had puzzled over this question: Could matter be divided into smaller and smaller pieces forever, or was there a limit to the number of times a piece of matter could be divided?

After much observation and questioning, Democritus concluded that matter could not be divided into smaller and smaller pieces forever. Eventually the smallest possible piece would be obtained. This piece would be indivisible. Democritus named this smallest piece of matter an atom. The word *atom* comes from the Greek word *atomos,* meaning "not to be cut," or "indivisible."

The Greek philosophers who shared Democritus' belief about the atom were called atomists. The atomists had no way of knowing what atoms were or how they looked. But they hypothesized that atoms were small, hard particles that were all made of the same material but were of different shapes and sizes. Also, they hypothesized that they were infinite in number, always moving, and capable of joining together.

Although Democritus and the other atomists were on the right trail, the theory of atoms was ignored and forgotten. Few people believed the idea. In fact, it took almost 2100 years before an atomic model of matter was accepted.

Dalton's Model

In the early 1800s, the English chemist John Dalton performed a number of experiments that eventually led to the acceptance of the idea of atoms. Dalton had long been interested in meteorology, the study of weather. His observations about the composition of air led him to investigate the properties of gases. He discovered that gases combine as if they were made of individual particles. These particles were the atoms of Democritus.

In 1803, Dalton combined the results of his experiments with other observations about matter and proposed an atomic theory. The basic ideas of Dalton's atomic theory are as follows:

- **All elements are composed of atoms. Atoms are indivisible and indestructible particles.**
- **Atoms of the same element are exactly alike.**
- **Atoms of different elements are different.**
- **Compounds are formed by the joining of atoms of two or more elements.**

Dalton's atomic theory of matter became one of the foundations of modern chemistry. But like many scientific theories, Dalton's theory had to be modified as scientists gained more information about the structure of matter.

Figure 5–4 *The atoms of relatively few elements make up everything in the world around you—whether it be a tranquil country landscape or a vibrant (but smoggy) city.*

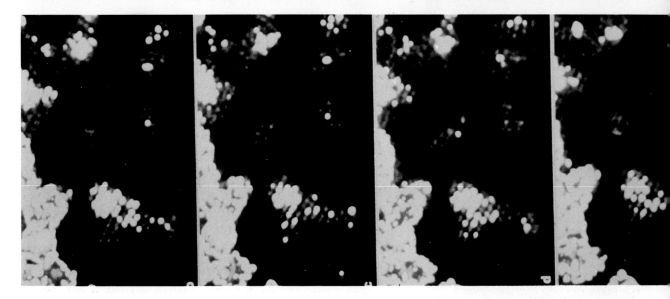

Thomson's Model

Was Dalton's theory correct? Is an atom indivisible? In 1897, the English scientist J. J. Thomson provided the first hint that an atom is made of even smaller particles. Thomson was studying the passage of an electric current through a gas. The gas gave off rays that Thomson showed were made of negatively charged particles. But the gas was known to be made of uncharged atoms. So where had the negatively charged particles come from? From within the atom, Thomson reasoned. A particle smaller than the atom had to exist. The atom was divisible! Thomson called the negatively charged particles "corpuscles." Today these particles are known as electrons.

As often happens in science, Thomson's discovery of electrons created a new problem to solve. The atom as a whole was known to be uncharged, or neutral. But if electrons in the atom were negatively charged, what balanced the negative charge? Thomson reasoned that the atom must also contain positively charged particles. But try as he might, he was unable to find this positive charge.

Thomson was so certain that these positively charged particles existed that he proposed a model of the atom that is sometimes called the "plum pudding" model. Figure 5–6 shows Thomson's model. **According to Thomson's atomic model, the atom was made of a puddinglike positively charged material throughout which negatively charged electrons were scattered, like plums in a pudding.** Thomson's

Figure 5–5 *These photographs of uranium atoms were taken by scientists working at the University of Chicago. The blue, yellow, and red spots are uranium atoms magnified more than 5 million times. In this remarkable series of photographs, you can observe the actual movement of the atoms.*

Figure 5–6 *Thomson's model of the atom pictured a "pudding" of positively charged material. Negatively charged electrons were scattered throughout like plums in a pudding. What is the overall charge on this atom? Why?*

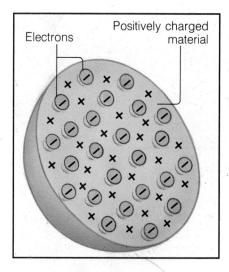

Electrons

Positively charged material

model, while far from correct, was an important step in understanding the structure of the atom.

Rutherford's Model

In 1911, the British physicist Ernest Rutherford presented a new theory about the structure of the atom. Rutherford's theory was based on an experiment that seemed to have little to do with unraveling the mysteries of atomic structure. Rutherford's experiment involved firing a stream of tiny positively charged particles at a thin sheet of gold foil. Rutherford discovered that most of the positively charged "bullets" passed right through the gold atoms in the sheet of foil without changing course at all. This could only mean that the gold atoms in the sheet were mostly empty space! Atoms were not a pudding filled with a positively charged material, as Thomson had thought.

Some of the "bullets," however, did bounce away from the gold sheet as if they had hit something solid. In fact, a few bounced almost straight back. What could this mean? Rutherford knew that positive charges repel other positive charges. So he proposed that an atom had a small, dense, positively charged center that repelled his positively charged "bullets." He called this center of the atom the **nucleus** (NOO-klee-uhs; plural: nuclei, NOO-klee-igh). The nucleus is tiny compared to the atom as a whole. To get an idea of the size of the nucleus in an atom, think of a marble in a baseball stadium!

Figure 5–7 *Artist and physicist Bill Parker created this "electric art" by passing an electric current through a glass sphere that contained certain gases. The light is produced when electrons in the gases absorb energy and release it. Who is credited with the discovery of the electron?*

Figure 5–8 *In Rutherford's experiment, most of the positively charged material passed right through the gold sheet (left). A few particles were slightly deflected, and even fewer particles bounced straight back. From these observations, Rutherford concluded that the atom was mostly empty space with a dense positively charged nucleus in the center (right).*

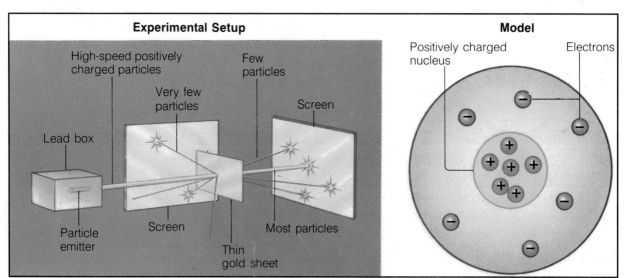

Experimental Setup

High-speed positively charged particles

Very few particles

Few particles

Screen

Lead box

Particle emitter

Screen

Thin gold sheet

Most particles

Model

Positively charged nucleus

Electrons

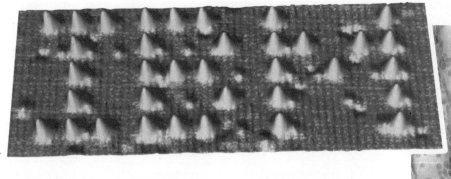

Rutherford reasoned that all of an atom's positively charged particles were contained in the nucleus. The negatively charged electrons were scattered outside the nucleus around the atom's edge. Between the nucleus and the electrons was mostly empty space! Although this model was useful in many ways, it did not adequately explain the arrangement of the electrons. It would be the job of future scientists to improve on the Rutherford atomic model.

The Bohr Model

Rutherford's model proposed that negatively charged electrons were held in an atom by the attraction between them and the positively charged nucleus. But where exactly were the electrons in the atom? In 1913, the Danish scientist Niels Bohr proposed an improvement on the Rutherford model. In his model he placed each electron in a specific energy level. **According to Bohr's atomic model, electrons move in definite orbits around the nucleus, much like planets circle the sun. These orbits, or energy levels, are located at certain distances from the nucleus.**

The Wave Model

Bohr's model worked well in explaining the structure and behavior of simple atoms such as hydrogen. But it did not explain more complex atoms.

Today's atomic model is based on the principles of wave mechanics. The basic ideas of wave mechanics are complicated and involve complex mathematical equations. Some of the conclusions of this theory, however, will help you understand the arrangement of electrons in an atom.

According to the theory of wave mechanics, electrons do not move about an atom in a definite path

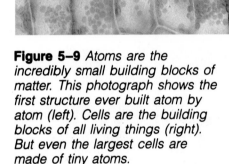

Figure 5–9 *Atoms are the incredibly small building blocks of matter. This photograph shows the first structure ever built atom by atom (left). Cells are the building blocks of all living things (right). But even the largest cells are made of tiny atoms.*

ACTIVITY
DOING

Making a Model Atom

1. Use materials such as cardboard, construction paper, colored pencils, string, and cotton to construct models of the Thomson atom and the Rutherford atom.

2. Label the models and place them on display in your classroom. Write a brief description of the experiment that each model was based on.

Figure 5-10 *This atomic model shows the nucleus with its neutrons and protons. Surrounding the nucleus are rapidly moving electrons. Can scientists know with certainty where a particular electron is located in an atom?*

like planets around the sun. In fact, it is impossible to determine the exact location of an electron. Scientists can only predict where an electron is most likely to be found. The probable location of an electron is based on how much energy the electron has.

As you can see, the modern atomic model is based on the models of Rutherford and Bohr, and on the principles of wave mechanics. **According to the modern atomic model, an atom has a small positively charged nucleus surrounded by a large region in which there are enough electrons to make the atom neutral.**

5-1 Section Review

1. How has the model of the atom changed over time?
2. Why is indirect evidence important in studying the structure of the atom?
3. What atomic particle did J. J. Thomson discover?
4. What is the center of the atom called? How was it discovered?
5. How does the wave model of electron placement differ from the model of electron position proposed by Niels Bohr?

Connection—*Science and Technology*
6. The model that explains atomic structure has changed over time. How has technology contributed to this change?

Figure 5-11 *When atomic particles collide, new and unusual particles may be produced. By studying the tracks made by these particles in a bubble chamber, scientists can learn more about the nature and interactions of atomic particles.*

CONNECTIONS

Data In . . . A Building Out

You now know that as a result of many, many years of research, scientists have developed a model that describes the structure of the atom—and they have done so without ever having seen the structure of an actual atom. Today, scientists have abundant evidence that this model of the atom is accurate.

But making a model has other, more practical uses. You can see examples of these uses almost daily as you walk down streets in your town or city. Today, models developed by *computers* serve as blueprints for the houses and buildings you see around you. Such a model can show how a building will look while it is still

only a series of ideas in an architect's mind and a few quick sketches on a sheet of paper.

Computer programs offer architects and building engineers a wide range of applications: designing a building, determining air flow and people movement, measuring wind effect on structure, to name a few. Some computer programs can even show the effects of light and shadow that will exist in a finished building. If such effects are undesirable, changes in the location and number of windows and doors, for example, can be made long before construction of the building begins.

Remember, however, that computer-assisted designs are only a tool to make the work of architects and engineers easier. The design of a wonderful building—a building that stirs the heart and lifts the spirit—still begins deep within the human mind and results from the combined talents of its creators.

Computers have become invaluable tools in many different professions. The final designs and plans for this building were developed with the help of a computer.

5-2 Structure of the Atom

When Thomson performed his experiments, he was hoping to find a single particle smaller than an atom. This task is similar to finding a particular grain of sand among the grains of sand making up all the beaches of the Earth! Certainly Thomson would be surprised to learn that today about 200 different kinds of such particles are known to exist! Because these particles are smaller than an atom, they are called **subatomic particles.**

The three main subatomic particles are the proton, the neutron, and the electron. As you read about these particles, note the location, mass, and charge of each. In this way, you will better understand the modern atomic theory. Let's begin with the nucleus, or center, of the atom.

The Nucleus

The nucleus is the "core" of the atom, the center in which 99.9 percent of the mass of the atom is located. Yet the nucleus is about a hundred thousand times smaller than the entire atom! In fact, the size of the nucleus compared to the entire atom has been likened to the size of a bee compared to a football stadium! Two of the three main subatomic particles are found in the nucleus.

PROTONS Those positively charged "bullets" that Rutherford fired at the gold sheet bounced back because of **protons** in the nucleus of the gold atoms. Protons are positively charged particles found in the nucleus. All protons are identical, regardless of the element in which they are found.

Figure 5-12 *A lithium nucleus contains 3 protons and 4 neutrons. A carbon nucleus contains 6 protons and 6 neutrons. How many electrons does a lithium nucleus contain? A carbon nucleus?*

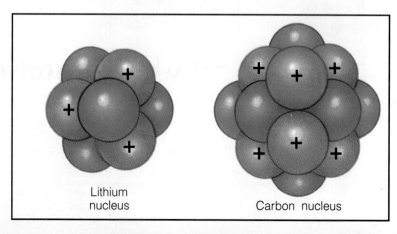

Lithium nucleus

Carbon nucleus

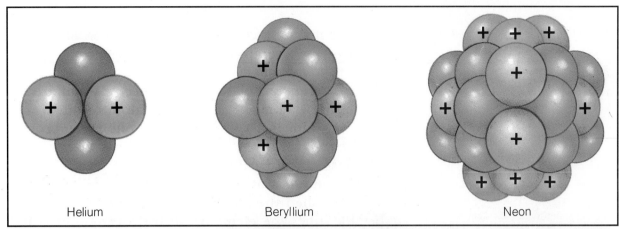

Helium   Beryllium   Neon

Figure 5–13 *The nuclei of helium, beryllium, and neon atoms all contain protons and neutrons. Yet helium, beryllium, and neon are very different elements. What accounts for these differences?*

Because the masses of subatomic particles are so small, scientists use a special unit to measure them. They call this unit an **atomic mass unit,** or amu. The mass of a proton is 1 amu. To get a better idea of how small a proton is, imagine the number 6 followed by 23 zeros. It would take that many protons to equal a mass of just 1 gram!

NEUTRONS Sharing the nucleus with the protons are the electrically neutral **neutrons.** Neutrons have no charge. Like protons, all neutrons are identical. Neutrons have slightly more mass than protons. But the mass of a neutron is still considered to be 1 amu.

Atomic Number — number of protons, electrons

You read before that atoms of different elements are different. But if all protons are identical and all neutrons are identical, what accounts for these differences? The answer lies in the particles found in the nucleus—more specifically, in the number of protons in the nucleus. Because it is the number of protons in the nucleus that determines what the element is. For example, an atom of carbon has 6 protons in its nucleus. Carbon is a dark solid. Much of the sooty remains of a burned piece of wood are made up of atoms of carbon. An atom of nitrogen has 7 protons in its nucleus—only one more proton than carbon. Nitrogen is a colorless gas that makes up most of the Earth's atmosphere.

The number of protons in the nucleus of an atom is called the **atomic number.** The atomic number identifies the element. All hydrogen atoms—and only hydrogen atoms—have 1 proton and an atomic number of 1. Helium atoms have an atomic number of 2. There are 2 protons in the nucleus of every helium atom. Oxygen has an atomic number of 8, and 8 protons are in the nucleus of each atom. How many protons does an atom of uranium—atomic number 92—have? And what are the atomic numbers of the elements carbon and nitrogen that you just read about?

Isotopes

The atomic number of an element will never change. This means that there is always the same number of protons in the nucleus of every atom of that element. But the number of neutrons is not so constant! Atoms of the same element can have different numbers of neutrons.

Atoms of the same element that have the same number of protons but different numbers of neutrons are called **isotopes** (IGH-suh-tohps). Look at Figure 5–15. You will see three different isotopes of

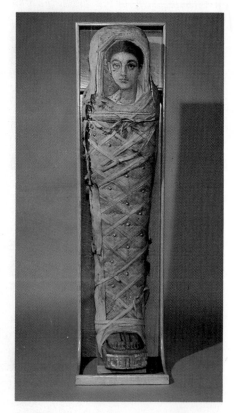

Figure 5–14 These two isotopes of carbon have the same atomic number, 6. Although this mummified boy cannot speak, he can be made to divulge his age. To do this, scientists analyze the proportions of carbon isotopes present in the mummy. What is the difference between the two carbon isotopes?

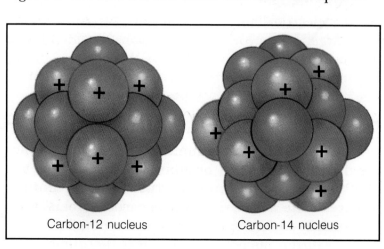

Carbon-12 nucleus   Carbon-14 nucleus

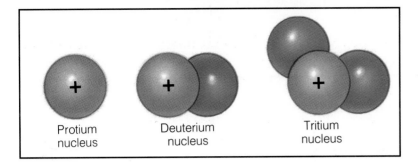

Protium nucleus

Deuterium nucleus

Tritium nucleus

Figure 5–15 *The three isotopes of hydrogen are protium, deuterium, and tritium. Which isotope contains 2 neutrons? What is the atomic number of each isotope?*

the element hydrogen. Note that the number of protons does not change. Remember that the atomic number, or number of protons, identifies a substance. No matter how many neutrons there are in the nucleus, 1 proton always means the atom is hydrogen. How many neutrons does each hydrogen isotope have?

Activity Bank

Hunting for Treasure in Trash, p. 722

Mass Number and Atomic Mass

quP + N

Figure 5–16 *This chart shows the symbol, atomic number, and mass number for some common elements. Why is the mass number always a whole number but the atomic mass is not?*

All atoms have a **mass number**. The mass number of an atom is the sum of the protons and neutrons in its nucleus. The mass number of the carbon isotope with 6 neutrons is 6 (protons) + 6 (neutrons), or 12. The mass number of the carbon isotope with 8 neutrons is 6 (protons) + 8 (neutrons), or 14. To distinguish one isotope from another, the mass number is given with the element's name.

Two common isotopes of the element uranium are uranium-235 and uranium-238. The atomic number—or number of protons—of uranium is 92. Since the mass number is equal to the number of protons plus the number of neutrons, the number of neutrons can easily be determined. The number of neutrons is determined by subtracting the atomic number (number of protons) from the mass number (number of protons + neutrons). Here are two problems for you to try. How many neutrons are there in uranium-235? In uranium-238?

Any sample of an element as it occurs in nature contains a mixture of isotopes. As a result, the **atomic mass** of the element is the average mass of all the existing isotopes of that element. For this reason, the atomic mass of an element is not usually a whole number. For example, the atomic mass of carbon is 12.011. This number indicates that there are more atoms of carbon-12 than there are of carbon-14. Can you explain why this conclusion is reasonable?

COMMON ELEMENTS		
Name	**Atomic Number**	**Mass Number**
Hydrogen H	1	1
Helium He	2	4
Carbon C	6	12
Nitrogen N	7	14
Oxygen O	8	16
Fluorine F	9	19
Sodium Na	11	23
Aluminum Al	13	27
Sulfur S	16	32
Chlorine Cl	17	35
Calcium Ca	20	40
Iron Fe	26	56
Copper Cu	29	64
Zinc Zn	30	65
Silver Ag	47	108
Gold Au	79	197
Mercury Hg	80	201
Lead Pb	82	207

PROBLEM Solving

Improving the Odds

You are trying to locate a friend on a sunny Saturday afternoon. Although you cannot say with absolute certainty where your friend is, you can estimate the chance of finding your friend in various places. Your estimates are based on past experiences.

Create a chart that lists at least seven possible locations for your friend. Next to each location, give the probability of finding your friend there. Express the probability in percent. For example, there is a 50-percent probability that your friend is at the school yard playing soccer. Remember that the total probability for the seven events should equal 100 percent.

Would a change in the weather influence your probability determination? How about a change in the day of the week? In the season of the year?

Relating Concepts

How does this activity help you better understand the concept of probability? How does it relate to an electron's location in an atom?

The Electrons

If you think protons and neutrons are small, picture this. Whirling around outside the nucleus are particles that are about 1/2000 the mass of either a proton or a neutron! These particles are **electrons.** Electrons have a negative charge and a mass of 0.0006 amu. In an uncharged atom, the number of negatively charged electrons is equal to the number of positively charged protons. The total charge of the atom is zero. Thus the atom is said to be neutral.

As you have learned, electrons do not move in fixed paths around the nucleus. In fact, the exact location of an electron cannot be known. Only the probability, or likelihood, of finding an electron at a particular place in an atom can be determined.

In fact, the entire space that the electrons occupy is what scientists think of as the atom itself. Sometimes this space is called the **electron cloud.** But do not think of an atom as a solid center surrounded by a fuzzy, blurry cloud. For the electron cloud is a space in which electrons are likely to be found. It is somewhat like the area around a beehive in which the bees move. Sometimes the electrons are near the nucleus; sometimes they are farther away from it. In a hydrogen atom, 1 electron "fills" the cloud. It fills the cloud in the sense that it can be found almost anywhere within the space.

Although the electrons whirl about the nucleus billions of times in one second, they do not do so in a random way. Each electron seems to be locked into a certain area in the electron cloud. The location of an electron in the cloud depends upon how much energy the electron has.

According to modern atomic theory, electrons are arranged in **energy levels.** An energy level represents the most likely location in the electron cloud in which an electron can be found. Electrons with the lowest energy are found in the energy level closest to the nucleus. Electrons with higher energy are found in energy levels farther from the nucleus.

The Mystery Element

You can identify the mystery element by performing the following mathematical calculations.

a. Multiply the atomic number of hydrogen by the number of electrons in mercury, atomic number 80.

b. Divide this number by the number of neutrons in helium, atomic number 2, mass number 4.

c. Add the number of protons in potassium, atomic number 19.

d. Add the mass number of the most common isotope of carbon.

e. Subtract the number of neutrons in sulfur, atomic number 16, mass number 32.

f. Divide by the number of electrons in boron, atomic number 5, mass number 11.

Which of the following elements is the mystery element: fluorine, atomic number 9; neon, atomic number 10; or sodium, atomic number 11?

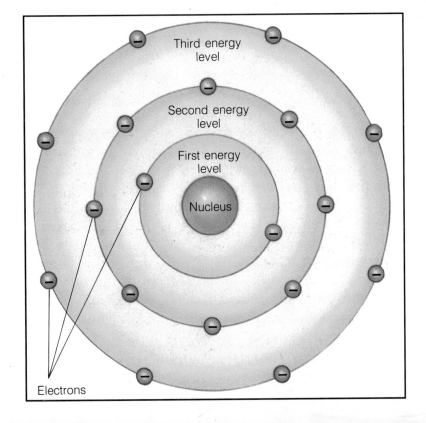

Figure 5–17 *Each energy level in an atom can hold only a certain number of electrons. How many electrons are in the first, second, and third energy levels shown here?*

SUBATOMIC PARTICLES			
Particle	Mass (amu)	Charge	Location
Proton	1.0073	+	Nucleus
Neutron	1.0087	Neutral	Nucleus
Electron	0.0006	–	Electron cloud

Figure 5–18 *The mass, charge, and location of the three basic subatomic particles are shown in this chart. Which subatomic particle has a neutral charge? Where is this subatomic particle located?*

CAREERS

Science Teacher

The weather on Saturday afternoon was ideal for gardening. But the teacher's mind was back in the classroom rather than on the tender bean sprouts that had just pushed their way through the soil's surface.

Science teachers spend much of their time developing plans to teach different topics. They try to create interesting ways to present information to their students. Activities such as lectures, demonstrations, laboratory work, and field trips are often used.

Science teachers also attend professional meetings, conferences, and workshops. If you are interested in this career, you can learn more by writing to the American Federation of Teachers, 555 New Jersey Avenue, NW, Washington, DC 20001.

Each energy level within an atom can hold only a certain number of electrons. The energy level closest to the nucleus—the lowest energy level—can hold no more than 2 electrons. The second energy level can hold 8 electrons. The third energy level can hold 18 electrons.

The properties of the different elements depend upon how many electrons are in the various energy levels of their atoms. In fact, the electron arrangement of its atoms is what gives an element its chemical properties. One of the most important chemical properties of an element is its bonding (combining) ability. Some elements easily form bonds with other elements. Some elements hardly ever form bonds. An element's bonding ability is determined by the arrangement of the electrons in its atoms—more specifically, the arrangement of the electrons in the outermost energy level, or the level farthest from the nucleus.

Can the atom be "cut"? The existence of protons, neutrons, and electrons proves it can. In fact, two of these particles can be separated into even smaller particles. Current theories explain that a different kind of particle makes up all the other known particles in the nucleus. This particle is called the **quark** (kwork). There are a number of different kinds of quarks. All nuclear particles are thought to be combinations of three quarks. One group of three quarks will produce a neutron. Another group of three quarks will produce a proton. According to current theory, quarks have properties called "flavor" and "color." There are six different flavors and three different colors.

5–2 Section Review

1. Classify the three main subatomic particles according to location, charge, and mass.
2. Why does the nucleus account for 99.9 percent of the mass of an atom?
3. Define atomic number; isotope; atomic mass; mass number.
4. Describe the arrangement of electrons in an atom. Why is electron arrangement so important?
5. Nitrogen-14 and nitrogen-15 are isotopes of the element nitrogen. Describe how atoms of these isotopes differ from each other.

Connection—*You and Your World*

6. How does a scientific model—such as the model of the structure of an atom—differ from a model airplane or boat that you might build?

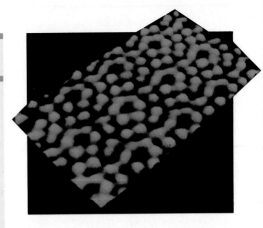

Figure 5–19 *This is the first image taken of atoms and their bonds. The bright round objects are single atoms. The fuzzy areas between atoms represent bonds.*

5–3 Forces Within the Atom

What keeps an atom together? Why don't the electrons fly out of their orbits around the nucleus? Why don't the protons move away from each other? Why don't all the atoms in the universe explode?

The answers to these questions can be found in the forces within the atom. **The four forces that account for the behavior of subatomic particles are the electromagnetic force, the strong force, the weak force, and gravity.**

The **electromagnetic force** can either attract or repel the particles on which it acts. If the particles have the same charge, such as two protons, the electromagnetic force is a force of repulsion. If the particles have opposite charges—such as an electron and a proton—the electromagnetic force is a force of attraction.

Electrons are kept in orbit around the nucleus by the electromagnetic force. The negatively charged electrons are attracted to the positively charged nucleus.

Guide for Reading

Focus on this question as you read.

▶ *What four forces are associated with atomic structure?*

127

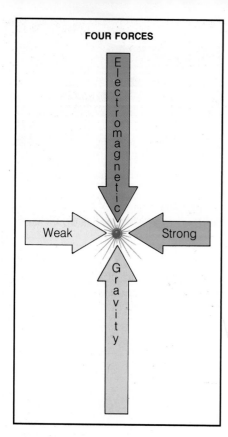

FOUR FORCES

Electromagnetic

Weak

Strong

Gravity

Figure 5–20 *The four known forces that govern all the interactions of matter and energy are the strong force, the electromagnetic force, the weak force, and gravity. Which of the four forces is the weakest?*

The electromagnetic force acts in the nucleus as a force of repulsion between positively charged protons. What keeps the protons from repelling each other and causing the atom to explode?

The **strong force** opposes the electromagnetic force of repulsion between protons. The strong force "glues" protons together to form the nucleus. Without the strong force, there would be no atoms. The strong force works only when protons are very close together, however. Although the strong force is the greatest of the four forces, it has a limited range. See Figure 5–21.

The **weak force** is the key to the power of the sun. The weak force is responsible for a process known as radioactive decay. During radioactive decay, a neutron in the nucleus changes into a proton and an electron.

The final force, **gravity,** is by far the weakest force known in nature. Yet it is probably the force most familiar to you. Gravity is the force of attraction exerted between all objects in nature. Gravity causes apples to fall from a tree and planets to remain in orbit around the sun. The effects of gravity are most easily observed in the behavior of large objects. Inside the nucleus of an atom, the effect of gravity is small compared to the effects of the other three forces. The role of gravity in the atom is not clearly understood.

As you can see, the four forces—electromagnetic, strong, weak, and gravity—are quite different. Yet physicists have tried to develop a single principle

Figure 5–21 *The strong force opposes the electromagnetic force of repulsion between two protons (top). The strong force becomes powerful enough to overcome the repulsive force and bind protons in the nucleus only when the protons are very close together (bottom).*

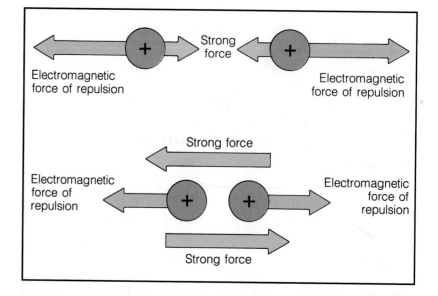

that would account for the differences between these forces. Such a principle would explain all four forces in terms of one fundamental force and all varieties of particles in terms of one basic particle. It is an awesome endeavor, indeed. But it is one that continues to challenge the knowledge and imagination of many scientists.

5–3 Section Review

1. What four forces govern the behavior of subatomic particles?
2. Which two forces are responsible for holding the atom together?
3. How does the electromagnetic force differ from the other three forces?

Critical Thinking—*Relating Concepts*
4. Gravity is the weakest of the four forces. However, it is one of the most easily observed forces in your daily life. Explain why this is so.

Figure 5–22 *In trying to unlock nature's secrets, physicists in a laboratory often study the tiny structure of the atom. Other scientists often find themselves in more precarious positions! These biologists are studying life in the treetops of a large tropical rain forest. As a result of their work, they may discover a previously unknown animal or plant, or even a new chemical that can be used to treat a once incurable disease. Often these new chemicals are analyzed atom by atom in a laboratory. Thus the knowledge uncovered in one scientific field often has applications in others.*

Laboratory Investigation

Shoe Box Atoms

Problem

How can indirect evidence be used to build a model?

Materials *(per group)*

shoe box, numbered and taped shut, containing unidentified object(s)
balance
magnet

Procedure

1. Your teacher will give you a shoe box with an object or objects inside. Do not open or damage the box.
2. Use a magnet to determine if the objects in the box have any magnetic properties.
3. Determine the mass of an empty shoe box. Then determine the mass of your shoe box. The difference between the two masses is the mass of the object(s) inside your shoe box.
4. You may be able to determine something about the object's shape by tilting the box. Does the object slide? (flat) Does it roll? (rounded) Does it collide inside? (more than one object)
5. Shake the box up and down to determine if the object bounces. How hard does it bounce? Does it flip?
6. For each test you perform, record your observations in a data table similar to the one shown here.

Observations

1. How many objects are in your shoe box?
2. Is the object soft? Magnetic? Fragile?
3. Is the object flat, or rounded?

Test Performed	Results	
	Trial 1	Trial 2
Magnet brought near		
Mass of object(s) determined		
Box tilted		
Box shaken		

Analysis and Conclusions

1. Make a sketch of what you think is in the shoe box. Draw the object(s) to show relative size.
2. What other indirect evidence did you gather to help you make the drawing?
3. How does your sketch compare with the actual objects as reported by your teacher? Make a sketch of the actual contents of the box.
4. Describe how you can develop a model of an object without directly observing the object.
5. **On Your Own** Prepare a shoe box model with two items that you select. Have a classmate see if he or she can determine what is in your shoe box.

Study Guide

Summarizing Key Concepts

5-1 An Atomic Model of Matter

▲ More than 2400 years ago, the Greek philosopher Democritus theorized the existence of the atom, the smallest particle of matter.

▲ John Dalton's atomic theory was based on experimental evidence about the behavior of matter. His theory stated that all matter is made of indivisible particles, or atoms.

▲ The discovery of the electron by J. J. Thomson proved that the atom is divisible.

▲ Thomson's model pictured the atom as being made of a positively charged, puddinglike material throughout which negatively charged electrons were scattered.

▲ Rutherford's experiments led him to propose an atomic model that states that an atom has a small, dense, positively charged nucleus surrounded by negatively charged electrons.

▲ The Bohr model of the atom pictured electrons as moving in definite orbits, or energy levels, around the nucleus.

▲ According to the theory of wave mechanics, electrons do not move about an atom in definite orbits. The exact location of an electron in an atom is impossible to determine.

5-2 Structure of the Atom

▲ Protons and neutrons are found in the nucleus.

▲ Protons have a positive charge and a mass of 1 amu.

▲ Neutrons are electrically neutral and have a mass of 1 amu.

▲ The number of protons in the nucleus of an atom is the atomic number.

▲ Atoms of the same element that have the same number of protons but different numbers of neutrons are called isotopes.

▲ The mass number of an atom is the sum of the protons and neutrons in its nucleus.

▲ The atomic mass of an element is the average mass of all the existing isotopes of that element.

▲ Electrons have a negative charge.

▲ Within the electron cloud, electrons are arranged in energy levels.

5-3 Forces Within the Atom

▲ Four forces—electromagnetic, strong, weak, and gravity—govern the behavior of subatomic particles.

Reviewing Key Terms

Define each term in a complete sentence.

5-1 An Atomic Model of Matter
nucleus

5-2 Structure of the Atom
subatomic particle
proton
atomic mass unit

neutron
atomic number
isotope
mass number
atomic mass
electron
electron cloud
energy level
quark

5-3 Forces Within the Atom
electromagnetic force
strong force
weak force
gravity

Chapter Review

Content Review

Multiple Choice

Choose the letter of the answer that best completes each statement.

1. The name Democritus gave to the smallest possible particle of matter is the
   a. molecule.
   b. atom.
   c. electron.
   d. proton.

2. The scientist J. J. Thomson discovered the
   a. proton.
   b. electron.
   c. neutron.
   d. nucleus.

3. The small, heavy center of the atom is the
   a. neutron.
   b. proton.
   c. electron.
   d. nucleus.

4. Particles smaller than the atom are called
   a. molecules.
   b. elements.
   c. ions
   d. subatomic particles.

5. The nucleus of an atom contains
   a. protons and neutrons.
   b. protons and electrons.
   c. neutrons and electrons.
   d. protons, neutrons, and electrons.

6. The number of protons in an atom with an atomic number of 18 is
   a. 10.   b. 36.   c. 18.   d. 8.

7. An isotope of oxygen, atomic number 8, could have
   a. 8 protons and 10 neutrons.
   b. 10 protons and 10 neutrons.
   c. 10 protons and 8 electrons.
   d. 6 protons and 8 neutrons.

8. All nuclear particles are thought to be made of a combination of three
   a. electrons.
   b. isotopes.
   c. molecules.
   d. quarks.

✳9. Which of the following forces within the atom is responsible for keeping electrons in orbit around the nucleus?
   a. electromagnetic   c. weak
   b. strong   d. gravity

✳10. The arrangement and location of what subatomic particles determine the chemical properties of an atom?
   a. protons
   b. neutrons
   c. quarks
   d. electrons

True or False

If the statement is true, write "true." If it is false, change the underlined word or words to make the statement true.

1. Most of the mass of the atom is located in the underlined electron cloud.
2. Electrons that have the least amount of energy are located farthest from the nucleus.
3. The idea that matter is made up of indivisible particles called atoms was proposed by Democritus.
4. In Thomson's experiment, the gas in the tube gave off rays that were made of negatively charged particles called neutrons.
5. The element chlorine has an atomic number of 17. It has 17 protons in its nucleus.

Concept Mapping

Complete the following concept map for Section 5–1. Then construct a concept map for the entire chapter.

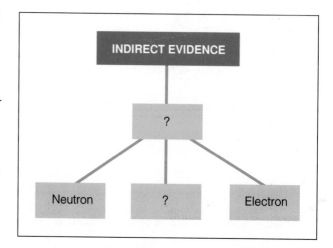

Concept Mastery

Discuss each of the following in a brief paragraph.

1. Describe the structure of the atom in terms of the three main subatomic particles. Include information about the location, charge, and atomic mass of each particle.
2. Describe the four forces and explain their role in the structure of the atom.
3. The model of the structure of the atom has changed over time. How does this illustrate the strength of the scientific method? Use specific examples in your explanation when appropriate.
4. Describe the electron configuration of each element based on atomic number: sulfur, 16; fluorine, 9; argon, 18; lithium, 3.
5. Explain how the following terms are related: atomic number, isotope, mass number, atomic mass. Be sure to define each term as you explain the relationships.
6. A certain element contains 82 percent of an isotope of mass number J and 18 percent of an isotope of mass number K. Is the atomic mass of this element closer to J or to K? Explain your answer.
7. Why must scientists use the concept of probability in describing the structure of an atom?
8. What is the significance of the atomic number of an element?

Critical Thinking and Problem Solving

Use the skills you have developed in this chapter to answer each of the following.

1. **Making inferences** Why are models useful in the study of atomic theory?
2. **Analyzing diagrams** The accompanying illustration shows the nucleus of a helium atom. Why is the nucleus positively charged? What is the mass of the nucleus? What is the atomic number of helium?

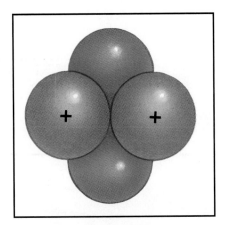

3. **Applying definitions** If the letter Z represents the atomic number of an atom and the letter A represents the mass number, explain how you could use these symbols to calculate: the number of protons, the number of electrons, and the number of neutrons.
4. **Making inferences** The element Einsteinium (named after the famous physicist Albert Einstein) has an atomic mass of 252. Einsteinium is a synthetic element, or an element that has been artificially made. How does this fact explain why the atomic mass of Einsteinium is a whole number?
5. **Using the writing process** Use the information presented in this chapter to write an update letter to Democritus. In your letter, explain how his early ideas about the atom have been modified as new pieces of indirect evidence have been uncovered. Be sure to include the names of the scientists who contributed to our current ideas about the atom and a description of their experiments.

Classification of Elements: The Periodic Table

6

Guide for Reading

After you read the following sections, you will be able to

6–1 Arranging the Elements
- Discuss the role Mendeleev played in the development of the periodic table.

6–2 Design of the Periodic Table
- Recognize how the modern periodic table is designed.
- Describe some differences between metals and nonmetals.

6–3 Chemical Families
- Describe some properties of eight families of elements.

6–4 Periodic Properties of the Elements
- Identify how the periodic law explains the physical and chemical properties of the elements.

Mary Cassatt, an American artist, lived in Paris toward the end of the nineteenth century. At that time artists were developing a "new" style of painting called Impressionism. Impressionist painters felt they no longer needed to paint with great realism. They used bright colors to give the "impression" of light and shadow in their paintings. Often, Impressionist painters moved out of their studios and into the daylight. Mary Cassatt began to paint in this new style. Today her paintings rightly share a place of honor in the history of human expression in art.

The origins of this painter's talents were firmly rooted in the human spirit. However, her paints' wondrous colors—colors that artists call pigments—have a much more ordinary origin. They are all part of the storehouse of elements in the Earth. A list of pigments reads like a chemistry textbook—zinc white, cadmium yellow, cobalt blue, iron oxide red, chromium green. All of these pigments are made from a group of elements known as the transition metals. In this chapter you will read about the transition metals and about many other groups of elements. Each group has its own properties and its own interesting—and often surprising—uses.

Journal *Activity*

You and Your World Artists often "speak" to people through drawings, paintings, and sculpture. Think back to the last time you were moved by a work of art. Maybe it was your own. Express your thoughts and feelings in your journal. Did you have any questions about what the artist was "saying"?

◀ *Mary Cassatt painted this picture entitled* Susan on a Balcony Holding a Dog.

6–1 Arranging the Elements

In some ways, your daily life contains many of the qualities of a good detective story. Unanswered questions and unexplained problems challenge your thoughts and actions all the time. And so you often act like a good detective. You discover places to go with friends and family. You learn about people who come from different cultures. You explore and gather evidence about the world around you. Like a good detective, you often try to make sense out of a series of clues and find meanings in seemingly unrelated observations.

Chemists, too, are good detectives. They gather evidence, analyze clues, follow their hunches, and make predictions. One of the most successful detective stories in the history of chemistry is the development of the periodic table of the elements. The periodic table of the elements represents a system of classifying, or logically grouping, all of the known elements. The arrangement of the elements in the periodic table was a milestone in the history of chemistry because it brought order to what had seemed to be a collection of thousands of unrelated facts. And it did something even more important: It helped chemists predict the existence of elements that had yet to be discovered!

Figure 6–1 *Each element has its own characteristic chemical and physical properties. Potassium is a soft, silvery metal that reacts explosively with water (right). Aluminum, also a silvery metal, does not easily combine with oxygen in water or in the air (left). Thus aluminum can be used for a variety of purposes, including drain pipes.*

A Hidden Pattern

The detective in this fascinating story was the Russian chemist Dmitri Mendeleev (duh-MEE-tree mehn-duh-LAY-uhf). The evidence he uncovered consisted of a huge collection of facts about the 63 elements that had been discovered by the mid-1800s. His clues were the physical and chemical properties of these elements. Based on these properties, it seemed clear to Mendeleev that some elements were similar to others. For example, sodium and potassium were both soft silver-white metals that reacted violently with water.

Mendeleev had a hunch that there had to be some order or relationship among all the elements. He was convinced that he could find a way to arrange the elements so that those with similar properties were grouped together. But what could the pattern of this arrangement be?

In his search for the pattern, Mendeleev first decided to organize his data. He did this by making a card for each of the known elements. On the card, he wrote the properties of each element. Some of the properties he included were atomic mass, density, color, and melting point. He also included the element's valence, or bonding power. Atoms form bonds with other atoms during chemical reactions (processes in which atoms join together to form molecules). When atoms form bonds, they either lose electrons, gain electrons, or share electrons. The valence, or valence number, of an element indicates the number of electrons that will be lost, gained, or shared in the bonding process.

Always looking for a pattern, Mendeleev arranged the cards in order of increasing atomic mass. If he started with lithium, the next element would be beryllium. Then would come boron, carbon, nitrogen, oxygen, and fluorine. With the cards arranged in this order, Mendeleev noticed the startling pattern of the valences: 1 2 3 4 3 2 1. Seven elements in a row, and the pattern of valences repeated itself.

As he arranged all 63 cards in order of atomic mass, Mendeleev saw the same pattern of rises and falls of valence again and again. He also saw something even more remarkable. When the elements were arranged in this way, they fell into columns,

Figure 6–2 *Mendeleev's greatest scientific contribution was the development of the periodic table. But his interests were not limited to chemistry. In 1887, he attempted to study a solar eclipse from a hot-air balloon.*

SEPTEMBER

S	M	T	W	Th	F	S
1	2	3	4	5	6	7
8	9	10	11	12	13	14
15	16	17	18	19	20	21
22	23	24	25	26	27	28
29	30					

Figure 6–3 *The days of the month are periodic because they repeat themselves according to a definite pattern. What is that pattern? Some animals also behave in a periodic manner. Geese and other birds migrate every fall and spring. What other examples of periodic behavior have you observed?*

one under the other. All the elements in a column had the same valence! All the elements in a column showed similar physical and chemical properties!

It was obvious to Mendeleev that the properties of the elements recurred at regular intervals. In Mendeleev's words, he found that "the properties of the elements were periodic functions of their atomic masses." When used this way, the word periodic means repeating according to some pattern. The days of the week are periodic because every seven days the pattern recurs. The months of the year are periodic because they also occur in a regular, repeating pattern. The notes of the musical scale are periodic, repeating a pattern with every eighth tone. In fact, you may already understand the word periodic from your familiarity with the word periodical. Sometimes magazines and newspapers are called periodicals. Their appearance on a newsstand, in a library, or at your home occurs according to a recognized repeating pattern. (You probably know when your favorite periodical is due to appear and eagerly anticipate its arrival.) Animals and plants also exhibit periodic behaviors. Birds fly south when winter's cold limits their food supply, and they return north the following spring when warmth signals an abundance of food. Can you think of other examples of periodic occurrences?

A Bold Prediction

Mendeleev designed a periodic table in which the elements were arranged in order of increasing atomic mass. Confident of the accuracy of his discovery, he left spaces in the table in order to make the known elements fit into the proper columns. Then he boldly announced that the empty spaces would be filled with elements that were not yet discovered! Indeed, he even went so far as to predict the physical and chemical properties of the unknown elements. He based his predictions on the properties of the elements above and below and to the left and right of the spaces in the table. Was he correct?

Yes, in fact, he was. Three of the unknown elements were discovered and placed in their correct positions in the periodic table during his lifetime. And the properties of the newly discovered elements

MENDELEEV'S PREDICTIONS AND ACTUAL PROPERTIES OF ELEMENT 32			
"Ekasilicon"		**Germanium**	
Date predicted	1871	Date discovered	1886
Atomic mass	72	Atomic mass	72.6
Density	5.5 g/cm³	Density	5.32 g/cm³
Bonding power	4	Bonding power	4
Color	Dark gray	Color	Grayish white

Figure 6–4 *The discovery of the element germanium in 1886 made Mendeleev the most famous chemist of the time. Notice how his predictions about the properties of element 32, or "ekasilicon," were incredibly close to the actual properties. How could Mendeleev predict the properties of an "unknown" element with such accuracy?*

were in close agreement with Mendeleev's predictions. You can see for yourself how well Mendeleev's predictions were fulfilled by looking at Figure 6–4.

The Modern Periodic Table

Despite the importance of Mendeleev's work, his periodic table was not perfect. When the elements are arranged in order of increasing atomic mass, several elements appear to be misplaced in terms of their properties. Mendeleev assumed that this was because the atomic masses of these elements had been incorrectly measured. Yet new measurements reconfirmed the original masses. What could be the problem?

It was not until 50 years after Mendeleev had developed his periodic table that the answer to the problem became clear. It was then that the British scientist Henry Moseley determined for the first time the atomic numbers of the elements. As you will recall, the atomic number of an element is the number of protons in the nucleus of each atom of that element.

The discovery of atomic numbers led to an important change in Mendeleev's periodic table. It turns out that when the elements are arranged in order of increasing atomic number (rather than increasing atomic mass), elements with similar physical and chemical properties fall into place without exception. Thus, Mendeleev's periodic table was replaced by the modern periodic table. The **periodic law** forms the basis of the modern periodic table.

Figure 6–5 *Great contributions are often made by the young. Henry Moseley was only 27 when he died in a famous battle during World War I, but his work in developing the modern periodic table lives long after him. What was Moseley's contribution?*

Figure 6–6 *Mendeleev recognized that the properties of elements are repeated in a periodic way. Thus certain elements have similar properties. Silver (top), gold (center), and copper (bottom) are all shiny elements that are good conductors of electricity. What are some other uses of these elements?*

The periodic law states that the physical and chemical properties of the elements are periodic functions of their atomic numbers.

Just in case you have the impression that all scientists are strange old people working mysteriously in musty laboratories, you might be interested to learn that Henry Moseley completed his historic work before his twenty-eighth birthday. Sadly, he died during World War I at the battle of Gallipoli. It must be left to our imaginations to wonder what other contributions to human knowledge this brilliant chemist might have made had he survived.

6–1 Section Review

1. Describe Mendeleev's periodic table. What are some properties he used to order the elements?
2. What does the word periodic mean?
3. How did Mendeleev predict the existence of undiscovered elements?
4. According to the modern periodic law, what determines the order of the elements?

Connection—*You and Your World*

5. An important series of reference books found in most libraries is entitled *Readers' Guide to Periodical Literature.* From the title, can you infer what kinds of information can be found in these books? Why do you think this series of books is important?

Guide for Reading

Focus on these questions as you read.

▶ *What information is given in each square of the periodic table?*

▶ *How do the properties of metals and nonmetals compare?*

6–2 Design of the Periodic Table

The periodic table of the elements is one of the most important tools of a scientist, especially a chemist. Why? Because the periodic table is a classification system—a way of organizing vast amounts of information in a logical, usable, and meaningful way. In some ways the periodic table is like the system used to organize books in a library. Imagine how confusing it would be if all the books in a library were placed on shelves in no particular order.

Fortunately, the books in a library are arranged by subject in a system that uses numbers and letters. You can look up a book in the card catalog, find its classification number, and locate it on the shelves. As you can see, such organization makes a book easy to locate. There is another advantage to a library's classification system. The classification number is a key to a book's subject matter. It identifies the broad topic of a book. All books with the same or similar subject matter will have essentially the same classification number. So without ever having seen a certain book, you can predict its topic from its classification number or its placement on a shelf.

The periodic table organizes the elements in a particular way. A great deal of information about an element can be gathered from its position in the periodic table. For example, you can predict with reasonably good accuracy the physical and chemical properties of the element. You can also predict what other elements a particular element will react with chemically. This means that it is not necessary to memorize a whole list of facts about many different elements. Understanding the organization and plan of the periodic table will help you obtain basic information about each of the 109 known elements. A periodic table is found on pages 142 and 143. Notice that hydrogen is the very first element in the periodic table. Hydrogen, the simplest element, is "one of a kind." For this reason, it is placed all by itself in the periodic table.

Columns in the Periodic Table

If you look at the periodic table in Figure 6–8, you will notice that it consists of vertical columns of elements. Each column is numbered. There are eighteen main columns of elements. Columns of elements are called **groups** or **families**. Elements within the same group or family have similar but not identical properties. For example, lithium (Li), sodium (Na), potassium (K), and the other members of Family 1 are all soft, white, shiny metals. They are all highly reactive elements, which means they readily combine with other elements to form compounds.

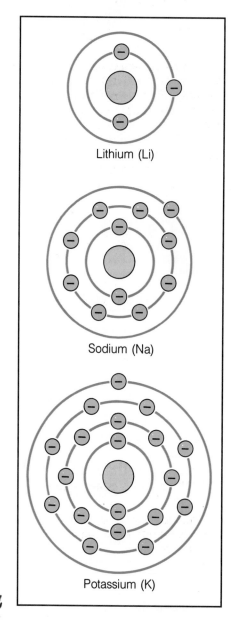

Figure 6–7 *Elements in the same family of the periodic table have similar properties. Here you see the electron arrangement of the elements lithium, sodium, and potassium. How is the electron arrangement in each element similar?*

Lithium (Li)

Sodium (Na)

Potassium (K)

PERIODIC TABLE

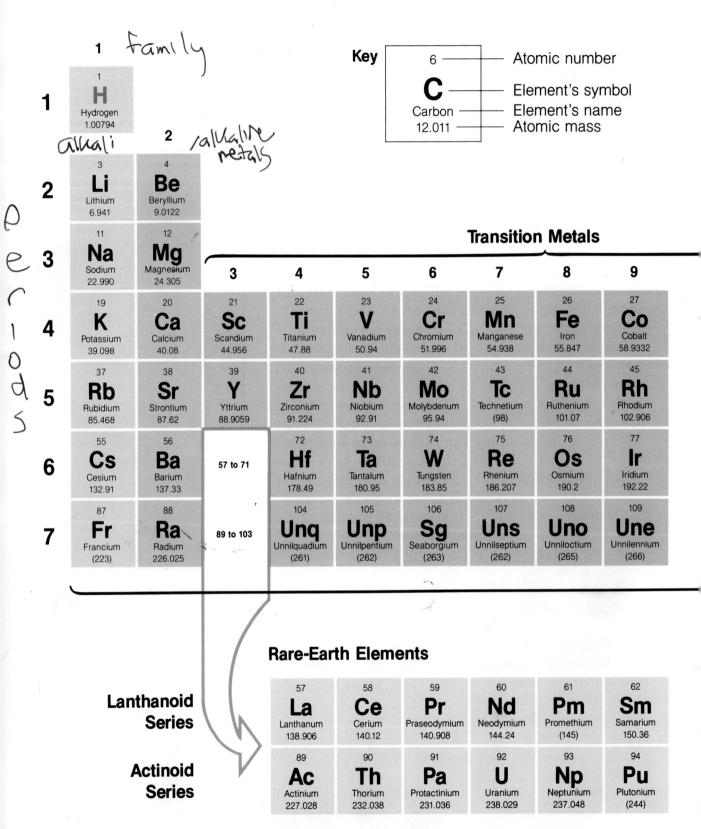

Key

6	— Atomic number
C	— Element's symbol
Carbon	— Element's name
12.011	— Atomic mass

family

alkali   *alkaline metals*

periods

Transition Metals

1								
1 **H** Hydrogen 1.00794	2	3	4	5	6	7	8	9
3 **Li** Lithium 6.941	4 **Be** Beryllium 9.0122							
11 **Na** Sodium 22.990	12 **Mg** Magnesium 24.305							
19 **K** Potassium 39.098	20 **Ca** Calcium 40.08	21 **Sc** Scandium 44.956	22 **Ti** Titanium 47.88	23 **V** Vanadium 50.94	24 **Cr** Chromium 51.996	25 **Mn** Manganese 54.938	26 **Fe** Iron 55.847	27 **Co** Cobalt 58.9332
37 **Rb** Rubidium 85.468	38 **Sr** Strontium 87.62	39 **Y** Yttrium 88.9059	40 **Zr** Zirconium 91.224	41 **Nb** Niobium 92.91	42 **Mo** Molybdenum 95.94	43 **Tc** Technetium (98)	44 **Ru** Ruthenium 101.07	45 **Rh** Rhodium 102.906
55 **Cs** Cesium 132.91	56 **Ba** Barium 137.33	57 to 71	72 **Hf** Hafnium 178.49	73 **Ta** Tantalum 180.95	74 **W** Tungsten 183.85	75 **Re** Rhenium 186.207	76 **Os** Osmium 190.2	77 **Ir** Iridium 192.22
87 **Fr** Francium (223)	88 **Ra** Radium 226.025	89 to 103	104 **Unq** Unnilquadium (261)	105 **Unp** Unnilpentium (262)	106 **Sg** Seaborgium (263)	107 **Uns** Unnilseptium (262)	108 **Uno** Unniloctium (265)	109 **Une** Unnilennium (266)

Rare-Earth Elements

Lanthanoid Series

57 **La** Lanthanum 138.906	58 **Ce** Cerium 140.12	59 **Pr** Praseodymium 140.908	60 **Nd** Neodymium 144.24	61 **Pm** Promethium (145)	62 **Sm** Samarium 150.36

Actinoid Series

89 **Ac** Actinium 227.028	90 **Th** Thorium 232.038	91 **Pa** Protactinium 231.036	92 **U** Uranium 238.029	93 **Np** Neptunium 237.048	94 **Pu** Plutonium (244)

Figure 6–8 *The modern periodic table of the elements is shown here.*

OF THE ELEMENTS

C	Solid
Br	Liquid
H	Gas

Family

Nonmetals

18

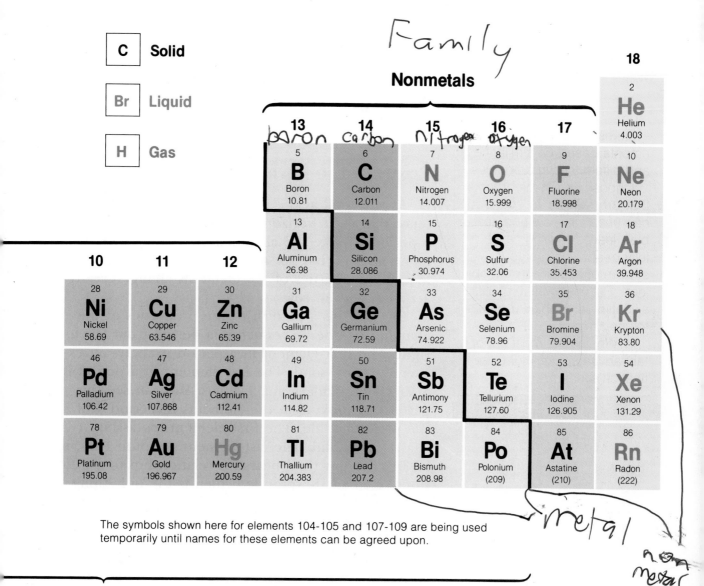

The symbols shown here for elements 104-105 and 107-109 are being used temporarily until names for these elements can be agreed upon.

metal

non metal

Metals

Mass numbers in parentheses are those of the most stable or common isotope.

63	64	65	66	67	68	69	70	71
Eu	**Gd**	**Tb**	**Dy**	**Ho**	**Er**	**Tm**	**Yb**	**Lu**
Europium	Gadolinium	Terbium	Dysprosium	Holmium	Erbium	Thulium	Ytterbium	Lutetium
151.96	157.25	158.925	162.50	164.93	167.26	168.934	173.04	174.967

95	96	97	98	99	100	101	102	103
Am	**Cm**	**Bk**	**Cf**	**Es**	**Fm**	**Md**	**No**	**Lr**
Americium	Curium	Berkelium	Californium	Einsteinium	Fermium	Mendelevium	Nobelium	Lawrencium
(243)	(247)	(247)	(251)	(254)	(257)	(258)	(259)	(260)

ACTIVITY

DISCOVERING

Classifying Objects—My Way

Mendeleev's table and the modern periodic table are systems of classifying the elements based on similarities and differences in properties.

Choose a set of objects that are familiar to you. You can use coins, stamps, marbles, leaves, playing cards, or jelly beans. Devise your own system of classifying the objects. Put your system of classification in a table for others to use.

■ What is the most important advantage of your classification system?

Fluorine (F), chlorine (Cl), bromine (Br), and iodine (I) are four of the elements in Family 17. Although fluorine and chlorine are both gases, bromine is a liquid, and iodine is a solid, they all still have many similar properties. In fact, both bromine and iodine become gases very easily. All four elements react to form the same kinds of compounds. You will learn more about each family and its properties later in this chapter.

Rows in the Periodic Table

As you look at the periodic table once again, observe that each horizontal row of elements is called a **period.** Unlike the elements in a family, the elements in a period are not alike in properties. In fact, the properties of the elements change greatly across any given row.

But there is a pattern to the properties of the elements as one moves across a period from left to right. The first element in a period is always an extremely active solid. The last element in a period is always a particularly inactive gas. You can see this pattern by looking at the elements in Period 4 of the periodic table. The first element, potassium (K), is an active solid. The last element, krypton (Kr), is an inactive gas (and bears no relationship to the fictional element Kryptonite, which is the only thing feared by Superman!). The symbols for the elements potassium and krypton should remind you of a rule for writing chemical symbols that you learned about in Chapter 4. The chemical symbol for an element consists of one or two letters. If it consists of one letter, the letter is always capitalized. If it consists of two letters, the first letter is always capitalized, but the second never is.

As you can see, there are seven periods of elements. You will also notice that one row has been separated out of Period 6 and one out of Period 7. Even though these two rows are displayed below the main part of the table, they are still part of the periodic table. They have been separated out to make the table shorter and easier to read. Elements in these two rows are rare-earth elements. You will read about these elements in just a little while.

Element Key

Look closely at the periodic table. Each element is found in a separate square. **Important information about an element is given in each square of the periodic table: its atomic number, chemical symbol, name, and atomic mass.**

The number at the top of each square is the atomic number of the element. Remember that the atomic number of an element is the number of protons in an atom of that element. The atomic number is unique to that element. In other words, no two elements have the same atomic number. Look closely at the element squares of the periodic table to see for yourself that this is true. And as you're looking, notice that the elements are arranged in order of increasing atomic number.

Just below the atomic number, near the center of the square, is the chemical symbol for the element. Below the chemical symbol, the name is spelled out. The number near the bottom of the square is the atomic mass of the element.

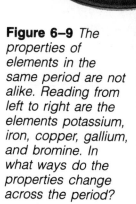

Figure 6–9 *The properties of elements in the same period are not alike. Reading from left to right are the elements potassium, iron, copper, gallium, and bromine. In what ways do the properties change across the period?*

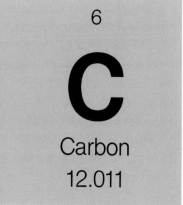

6

C

Carbon

12.011

Figure 6–10 *Four important facts about an element are supplied in each square of the periodic table: the atomic number, symbol, name, and atomic mass of that element. The element carbon is found in many things. It makes up the lead in your pencil, most of the foods you eat, and also the Hope diamond.*

A Hot Time

1. Roll a piece of aluminum foil into a small cylinder about the shape of a pencil.

2. Stand a stainless steel teaspoon, a strip of wood, a plastic spoon, and the aluminum cylinder you made in a plastic cup.

3. Add hot water to the cup. Be careful to leave the tops of the objects above the water level.

4. Wait one minute. Carefully touch the exposed ends of each object in the cup. What are your observations?

■ What conclusions does this activity help you discover?

Figure 6–11 *Unlike some metals, pure gold is actually quite soft and easily worked. This gold pin, hammered from a flat sheet of almost pure gold, can be bent out of shape with little effort. Gold used for jewelry is often combined with copper and other metals to give it strength.*

Now practice using what you have just learned. Locate the element boron in the periodic table. What is its atomic number? Its symbol? What element has the symbol Cd? What element has an atomic number of 38? What is the atomic mass of magnesium? Of bromine?

Metals

When you hear the word **metal,** what do you think of? You probably think of silver, iron, or copper. These are all familiar metals. Kitchen pots, trumpets, knives and forks, and pocket change are all familiar items made of metals. However, there are other elements that are classified as metals that you may not have thought of as metals—such as calcium, sodium, and potassium.

Of the 109 known elements, most are metals. If you look at the periodic table, you will see a dark zigzag line running like steps down the right side of the table. The 88 elements to the left of this line are metals or metallike elements.

PHYSICAL PROPERTIES OF METALS The physical properties of metals make them easy to identify. One such property is **luster,** or shininess. Hold a brand-new penny in your hand, and its gleam will convince you of this important property of metals. Most metals also allow heat and electricity to move through them easily. Therefore, metals are good conductors of heat and electricity. In general, metals have a high density. This means that they are heavy for their size. Trying to lift a metal dumbbell can easily convince you of this! Finally, metals usually have fairly high melting points. Now that you know about some of the properties of metals, explain why metal pots are used for cooking.

There are two other physical properties that are common to many metals. Most metals are **ductile,** which means they can be drawn out into thin wires. And most metals are **malleable,** which means they can be hammered into thin sheets. The ease with which metals can be drawn into wire and hammered into sheets contributes, in large part, to their use in making jewelry. The pin in Figure 6–11 is made of a thin gold sheet that was hammered by an ancient Peruvian native.

Figure 6-12 *Some of the physical properties of metals and their alloys are evident in these photographs. What properties can you identify in the cooling slabs of steel (left), steel girders (center), stainless steel artificial human hip joint (inset), and copy tubes (right)?*

Metals lose electrons

Chemical-cant see them, lose outermost electrons corrosion

CHEMICAL PROPERTIES OF METALS The chemical properties of metals are not as easily observed as are the physical properties. The chemical properties of any element depend upon the electron arrangement in the atoms of the element—more specifically, on the number of electrons in the outermost energy level. (Remember that the electrons in the outer energy level, or the valence electrons, are involved in forming bonds with other atoms.) An atom of a metal can have 1, 2, 3, or 4 electrons in its outermost energy level. The electrons in the outermost energy level of a metal are rather weakly held. So metals are elements that tend to lose their outermost electrons when they combine chemically.

Because they tend to lose electrons, most metals will react chemically with water or with elements in the atmosphere. Such a chemical reaction often results in **corrosion.** Corrosion is the gradual wearing away of a metal due to a chemical reaction in which the metal element is changed into a metallic compound. The rusting of iron is an example of corrosion. When iron rusts, it combines with oxygen in the air to form the compound iron oxide. The

Figure 6-13 *The rusting of iron and steel is actually a form of corrosion. This abandoned car shows the dramatic effects of corrosion.*

147

tarnishing of silver is another example of corrosion. Tarnishing results when silver reacts with compounds of sulfur in the air or in certain foods. Have you ever observed examples of rusting and/or tarnishing? How would you describe what you observed?

Nonmetals

Elements that are **nonmetals** are located to the right of the zigzag line in the periodic table. Fewer elements are classified as nonmetals than as metals in the periodic table. In general, the physical and chemical properties of nonmetals tend to be opposite those of metals.

PHYSICAL PROPERTIES OF NONMETALS   Nonmetals usually have no luster and are dull in appearance. Nonmetals do not conduct heat and electricity well. Nonmetals are brittle and thus break easily. They cannot be drawn out into wire or hammered into thin sheets. In other words, nonmetals are neither ductile nor malleable. Nonmetals usually have lower densities and lower melting points than metals.

Nonmetals are not as easy to recognize as a group as are metals. Nonmetals can be noticeably different from one another. For example, bromine is a brown liquid, oxygen is a colorless gas, and sulfur is a yellow solid. Yet all are nonmetals.

CHEMICAL PROPERTIES OF NONMETALS   Remember, the chemical properties of elements are determined by the number of electrons in the outermost energy level. Atoms of most nonmetals have 5, 6, 7, or 8 electrons in their outermost energy level. Atoms with 5, 6, or 7 valence electrons gain 3, 2, or 1 electron, respectively, when they combine chemically. Thus nonmetals are elements that tend to gain electrons. Perhaps you are wondering about the nonmetals whose atoms have 8 valence electrons. Atoms with 8 valence electrons have a complete outermost energy level. So elements whose atoms have 8 valence electrons tend to be nonreactive or rarely react with atoms of other elements. Knowing what you do now about metals and nonmetals, do you think they can form compounds with each other if one gives up electrons and one takes electrons?

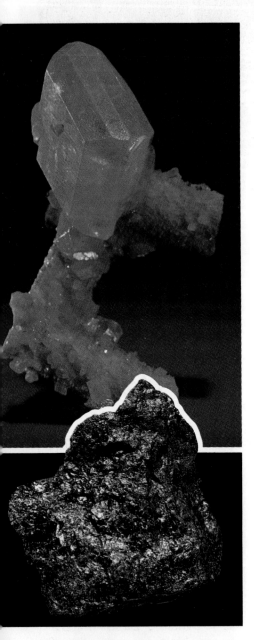

Figure 6–14 *Sulfur (top) is a nonmetal that can form beautiful crystals. Boron (bottom) is a metalloid, a word that means metallike. What are some properties of nonmetals and metalloids?*

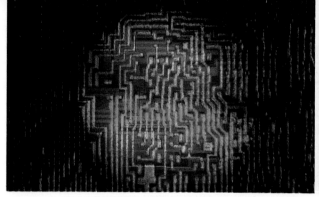

Figure 6–15 *Both silicon (left) and antimony (right) are metalloids. All metalloids are solids that can be shiny or dull. The silicon in the photograph has been made into a computer chip.*

Metalloids

The dividing line between metals and nonmetals is not quite as definite as it appears. For along both sides of the dark zigzag line are elements that have properties of both metals and nonmetals. These elements are called **metalloids** (MEHT-uh-loidz). The word metalloid means metallike. All metalloids are solids that can be shiny or dull. They conduct heat and electricity better than nonmetals but not as well as metals. Metalloids are ductile and malleable. The metalloids include boron, silicon, germanium, arsenic, antimony, tellurium, polonium, and astatine. Do any of these elements sound familiar to you? If so, in what way?

6–2 Section Review

1. What important information is given in each square of the periodic table?
2. What are the horizontal rows in the periodic table called? What are the vertical rows called?
3. What are some physical and chemical properties of metals? Of nonmetals?
4. What is a metalloid?

Critical Thinking—*Applying Concepts*
5. Electricity is, in large part, responsible for our modern lifestyle. How are some of the physical properties of metals related to the fact that a steady supply of electricity is able to reach our homes from electric generating plants?

ACTIVITY
DOING

An Elemental Hunt

1. Collect some samples of elements that are easily obtained, such as copper, iron, aluminum, nickel, and carbon.

2. Attach each element to a large square of paper or cardboard. Make each square of paper or cardboard look like a square of the periodic table.

3. On the paper square, include the atomic mass, atomic number, name, and chemical symbol of the element displayed.

Working along with your classmates, see how complete a periodic table you are able to create.

Guide for Reading

Focus on these questions as you read.

▶ What is the basis for the placement of elements in the periodic table?

▶ What are the properties of chemical families?

1	2
3 **Li** Lithium 6.941	4 **Be** Beryllium 9.0122
11 **Na** Sodium 22.990	12 **Mg** Magnesium 24.305
19 **K** Potassium 39.098	20 **Ca** Calcium 40.08
37 **Rb** Rubidium 85.468	38 **Sr** Strontium 87.62
55 **Cs** Cesium 132.91	56 **Ba** Barium 137.33
87 **Fr** Francium (223)	88 **Ra** Radium 226.025

Figure 6–16 *Family 1 metals are called the alkali metals. Family 2 metals are called the alkaline earth metals. How many electrons are in the outermost energy level of each alkali metal? Of each alkaline earth metal?*

6–3 Chemical Families

You are about to go on a "tour" of the periodic table. This trip will help you become more familiar with the basic properties of the families of elements. Remember, it is not necessary to memorize lots of facts about the elements. What we hope you will be able to do is recognize the value of the periodic table in organizing information about the elements. We also hope that you will appreciate how these elements—some of which may be unfamiliar to you—are a part of your world. After all, your world is made up of matter, and matter is ultimately made up of atoms of elements. So in some way, each and every one of the 109 elements in the periodic table is a part of your life. To help you on your tour, keep in mind the following principle: **Elements within the same family of the periodic table have similar properties because they have the same number of valence electrons.**

The Most Active Metals

The elements in Family 1, with the exception of hydrogen, are called the **alkali** (AL-kuh-ligh) **metals.** Atoms of the alkali metals have a single electron in their outermost energy level. In other words, they have 1 valence electron. Hydrogen also has 1 electron in its outer shell. In many ways, it behaves like the alkali metals.

The alkali metals are soft, silver-white, shiny metals. They are so soft, in fact, that they can be cut with a knife. The alkali metals are good conductors of heat and electricity. Because they have only 1 valence electron, these elements bond readily with other substances. In fact, they are so reactive that they are never found uncombined in nature. In other words, they are never found as free elements. In the laboratory, samples of these elements are stored in oil in order to keep them from combining with water or oxygen in the air. The reaction is violent when the alkali metals react with water. Hydrogen gas is produced, as well as extreme heat. Because of the heat produced, the hydrogen gas can begin to burn and may explode.

ALKALI METALS

Element	Properties		Uses of Compounds
Lithium (Li)	m.p. 179°C b.p. 1317°C		Medicine; metallurgy
	Soft; silvery; reacts violently with water		
Sodium (Na)	m.p. 97.8°C b.p. 883°C		Soap; table salt; lye
	Soft; silvery white; reacts violently with water		
Potassium (K)	m.p. 62.5°C b.p. 774°C		Fertilizer; medicine; photography
	Soft; silvery white; reacts violently with moisture		
Rubidium (Rb)	m.p. 39.0°C b.p. 688°C		Space vehicle engines; photocells
	Soft; lustrous; reacts violently with moisture		
Cesium (Cs)	m.p. 28.6°C b.p. 670°C		Photocells
	Silvery white; ductile; reacts with moisture		
Francium (Fr)	m.p. (27°C) b.p. (677°C)		Not widely used
	Extremely rare; radioactive isotopes		

Values in parentheses are physical properties of the most stable isotope.

Figure 6–17 *This table shows some of the properties of the alkali metals and the uses of their compounds. Which alkali metal has radioactive isotopes?*

Although the alkali metals themselves have few familiar uses, the compounds they form are some of the most important substances you use every day. Table salt and baking soda are two compounds you may be familiar with. Soap, which forms when alkali compounds react with fats, is another. Now look at the periodic table and identify the alkali metals.

Family 2 consists of the six elements known as the **alkaline** (AL-kuh-lihn) **earth metals.** Like the alkali metals, the alkaline earth metals are never found in nature as uncombined elements. Instead, they exist bonded with other elements in compounds. The alkaline earth metals have 2 valence electrons. Atoms of these elements lose their 2 electrons easily when they combine with other atoms. But since they must lose 2 electrons, they are not quite as reactive as the alkali metals.

Two of the alkaline earth metals—magnesium and calcium—are probably familiar to you. Magnesium is often combined with aluminum to make alloys that are strong yet light in weight. These alloys are used to make ladders and airplane parts. They are used where light yet strong metal parts are needed. Other compounds of magnesium are used in medicines, flares, and fireworks. Calcium is an abundant substance in the Earth's crust. Calcium compounds

ALKALINE EARTH METALS

Element	Properties		Uses of Compounds
Beryllium (Be)	m.p. 1285°C b.p. 2970°C		Radio parts; steel
	Poisonous		
Magnesium (Mg)	m.p. 650°C b.p. 1117°C		Medicine; photographic flashbulbs; auto parts; space vehicle parts; flares
	Burns with very bright flame; strong but not dense		
Calcium (Ca)	m.p. 851°C b.p. 1487°C		Plaster and plasterboard; mortar and cement; water softeners; metal bearings
	Silvery; important part of bones and teeth; tarnishes in moist air		
Strontium (Sr)	m.p. 774°C b.p. 1366°C		Fireworks; flares
	Least abundant alkaline earth metal; reactive in air		
Barium (Ba)	m.p. 850°C b.p. 1537°C		Medicine; paints; glassmaking
	Extremely reactive in air		
Radium (Ra)	m.p. (700°C) b.p. (1525°C)		Treatment of cancer; medical research
	Silvery white but turns black in air; radioactive		

Values in parentheses are physical properties of the most stable isotope.

Figure 6–18 *The properties and uses of alkaline earth metals are shown in this table. Which alkaline earth metal is important for strong teeth and bones?*

make up limestone and marble rock. Calcium is also an essential part of your teeth and bones.

The Transition Metals

Look at the periodic table between Family 2 and Family 13. What do you see? You should see several groups of elements that do not seem to fit into any other family. These elements are called the **transition metals.** Transition metals have properties similar to one another and to other metals, but they are different from the properties of any other family.

The names of the transition metals are probably well known to you. These are the metals with which you are probably most familiar: copper, tin, zinc, iron, nickel, gold, and silver, for example. You may

Figure 6–19 *An artist uses a palette of different colors to paint a picture. Many of the colors are made from the transition metals. Tungsten is a transition metal whose importance in your life is immediately apparent when you switch on an incandescent light. The tungsten wire in a light bulb glows as electricity passes through it.*

also know that the transition metals are good conductors of heat and electricity. The compounds of transition metals are usually brightly colored and are often used to color paint. (Remember Mary Cassatt and the other Impressionist painters you read about at the beginning of the chapter?) Gold and silver are used to make jewelry and eating utensils. These two metals are often used in dental fillings to replace decayed areas of a tooth. Silver is essential in the making of photographic film and paper. Mercury is an interesting transition metal because it is a liquid at temperatures above –38.8°C. How do you think this fact relates to the use of mercury in household thermometers?

Most transition elements have 1 or 2 valence electrons. When they combine with other atoms, they lose either 1 or both of their valence electrons. But transition elements can also lose an electron from the next-to-outermost energy level. In addition, transition elements can share electrons when they form bonds with other atoms. It is no wonder that transition elements form so many different compounds!

From Metals to Nonmetals

To the right of the transition elements are six families, five of which contain some metalloids. This means that certain members of these families show properties of metals as well as nonmetals. These four families are named after the first element in the family.

Family 13 is the **boron family.** Atoms of elements in this family have 3 valence electrons. Boron is a metalloid. The other elements, including aluminum, are metals.

Boron, which is hard and brittle, is never found uncombined in nature. It is usually found combined with oxygen. Compounds of boron are used to make heat-resistant glass, such as the test tubes used in your laboratory and the glass cookware used in your kitchen. Boron is also found in borax, a cleaning compound that may be familiar to you.

Aluminum is the most abundant metal and the third most abundant element in the Earth's crust. Aluminum is also found combined with oxygen in the ore bauxite. Aluminum is an extremely important

TRANSITION ELEMENTS	
Element	**Uses**
Iron (Fe)	Manufacturing; building materials; dietary supplement
Cobalt (Co)	Magnets; heat-resistant tools
Nickel (Ni)	Coins; batteries; jewelry; plating
Copper (Cu)	Electric wiring; plumbing; motors
Silver (Ag)	Jewelry; dental fillings; mirror backing; electric conductor
Gold (Au)	Jewelry; base for money systems; coins; dentistry
Zinc (Zn)	Paints; medicines; coat metals
Cadmium (Cd)	Plating; batteries; nuclear reactors
Mercury (Hg)	Liquid in thermometers, barometers, electric switches; dentistry; paints

Figure 6–20 *The transition elements have many common uses. Which transition element is liquid at room temperature?*

13	14
5 **B** Boron 10.81	6 **C** Carbon 12.011
13 **Al** Aluminum 26.98	14 **Si** Silicon 28.086
31 **Ga** Gallium 69.72	32 **Ge** Germanium 72.59
49 **In** Indium 114.82	50 **Sn** Tin 118.71
81 **Tl** Thallium 204.383	82 **Pb** Lead 207.2

Figure 6–21 *Family 13 is also known as the boron family. Elements in Family 14 are also known as the carbon family.*

Figure 6–22 *Carbon is found in oil, gas, and other petroleum products. In an oil refinery, crude oil is processed into many different products. Silicon is one of the most abundant elements in the Earth's crust.*

metal in industry. It is light, strong, and does not corrode. It is an excellent reflector of light and a good conductor of heat and electricity. Aluminum is used to make parts for cars, trains, and planes. It is also made into the pots and pans used in cooking. Because aluminum is so malleable, it can also be made into foil used to wrap food for storage.

The **carbon family** is Family 14. Atoms of the elements in this family have 4 valence electrons. Carbon is a nonmetal. But the next two elements, silicon and germanium, are metalloids. And tin and lead are metals.

Carbon atoms, with their 4 valence electrons, form an unbelievable number of different compounds—more than 5 million by some estimates! The element carbon is often called the "basis of life." Your body contains a wide variety of carbon compounds. Sugars and starches are two important examples. Fuels such as gasoline also contain carbon compounds. Carbon compounds are so numerous, in fact, that a whole branch of chemistry is devoted to their study. This branch is called organic chemistry.

Silicon is the second most abundant element in the Earth's crust. Silicon combined with oxygen to form sand is used to make glass and cement. Silicon is also used to make solar cells, which are able to convert the energy of sunlight into electricity. Solar cells are commonly found in roof panels and are also used on space satellites. One of the most important uses of silicon is probably quite familiar to you. Silicon chips are used for circuitry and memory in computers.

Figure 6–23 *Nitrogen is used to make explosives. This building is being demolished by a controlled explosion that causes the building to collapse.*

Germanium is a metalloid commonly used in transistors. Transistors are components of many electronic devices, including radios, televisions, and computer games. Tin is a metal that resists rusting and corrosion. The common "tin can" used as a container for your favorite soup is actually a steel can lined with a very thin layer of tin. The tin lining prevents the food in the can from coming into contact with the steel wall of the can.

Lead is another metal in the carbon family. In the past, lead was used to color paint. It was also an important additive in gasoline. However, because of the dangers associated with exposure to lead, it has been removed from paints and gasoline. And just so you do not become concerned about using an ordinary pencil, you should know that the "lead" in a lead pencil is not really lead but is a form of carbon known as graphite. A lead pencil is perfectly safe to use.

The **nitrogen family,** Family 15, is named after an element that makes up 78 percent of the air around you: nitrogen. The atoms of elements in this family have 5 valence electrons in their outermost energy level. These atoms tend to share electrons when they bond with other atoms.

Nitrogen is the most abundant element in the Earth's atmosphere. It is an exceptionally stable element and does not combine readily with other elements. Nitrogen is an important part of many fertilizers, which are substances used to enhance plant growth. Nitrogen is also used to produce explosives, medicines, and dyes. Ammonia, a common household cleaning agent, is a compound made of nitrogen and hydrogen.

Phosphorus is an active nonmetal that is not found free in nature. One of its main uses is in making the tips of matches. It is also used in flares. Arsenic is an important ingredient in many insecticides. Both antimony and bismuth are used in making alloys.

The elements making up Family 16 are called the **oxygen family.** Atoms of these elements have 6 valence electrons. Most elements in this family share electrons when forming compounds.

Activity Bank

What Is the Effect of Phosphates on Plant Growth?, p. 723

15	16
7 **N** Nitrogen 14.007	8 **O** Oxygen 15.999
15 **P** Phosphorus 30.974	16 **S** Sulfur 32.06
33 **As** Arsenic 74.922	34 **Se** Selenium 78.96
51 **Sb** Antimony 121.75	52 **Te** Tellurium 127.60
83 **Bi** Bismuth 208.98	84 **Po** Polonium (209)

Figure 6–24 *Which element in Family 15 shows the most metallic properties? Which member of Family 16 is a gas?*

155

HALOGENS

Element	Uses
Fluorine (F)	Etching glass; refrigerants; nonstick utensils; preventing tooth decay
Chlorine (Cl)	Bleaching agent; disinfectant; water purifier
Bromine (Br)	Medicine; dyes; photography
Iodine (I)	Medicine; disinfectant; dietary supplement in salt
Astatine (At)	Rare element

Figure 6–25 *Because of their chemical reactivity, the halogens have many uses.*

17

9
F
Fluorine
18.998
17
Cl
Chlorine
35.453
35
Br
Bromine
79.904
53
I
Iodine
126.905
85
At
Astatine
(210)

Figure 6–26 *Family 17 is known as the halogen family.*

Oxygen, the most abundant element in the Earth's crust and the second most abundant element in the atmosphere, is an extremely reactive element. It combines with almost every other element. You already know how important oxygen is to you—and to almost all other forms of life on Earth. Your body uses the oxygen you breathe to break down carbohydrates to produce energy. Plants also use oxygen to break down carbohydrates. In addition to combining with other elements, oxygen can also form molecules by bonding with itself. You might be familiar with the word ozone. Three atoms of oxygen bond to form a molecule of ozone, O_3. In the atmosphere, the ozone layer screens out harmful ultraviolet radiation from the sun, thus protecting life on Earth.

Sulfur, selenium, and tellurium are brittle solids at room temperature. They all combine with oxygen as well as with metals and with hydrogen. Sulfur is used to manufacture medicines, matches, gunpowder, and synthetic rubber. Selenium is used to color glass red and to make enamels. Tellurium is useful in making alloys. Polonium, another member of this family, is an extremely rare element.

The Halogens

The elements of Family 17 are fluorine, chlorine, bromine, iodine, and astatine. Together they are known as the **halogen family**. Halogens have 7 valence electrons, which explains why they are the most active nonmetals. Atoms of these elements need to gain only 1 electron to fill their outermost energy level. The great reactivity of the halogens explains why they are never found free in nature.

Halogens form compounds in which they share or gain 1 electron. They react with the alkali metals (Family 1) quite easily. One common compound formed when the alkali metal sodium gives up 1 electron to the halogen chlorine is called sodium chloride. You know this compound better as table salt. When halogens react with metals, they form compounds called salts. Perhaps you have heard of sodium fluoride, which is the salt used to fluoridate water and toothpaste, or of calcium chloride, which is used to melt snow and ice on streets and sidewalks. Silver bromide, another halogen salt, is used in photographic film.

Fluorine is the most active halogen. Fluorine and chlorine, which is also highly active, are never found uncombined in nature. As you can see from the periodic table, fluorine and chlorine are gases. Bromine is one of the few liquid elements, while iodine and the metalloid astatine are solids.

The Noble Gases

Your tour across the periodic table ends with Family 18, the **noble gases.** All of the elements in this family are gases that are normally unreactive. But under special conditions, certain noble gases will combine chemically with other elements. Because they do not readily form compounds with other elements, the noble gases are also called the inert gases. The noble, or inert, gases include helium (He), neon (Ne), argon (Ar), krypton (Kr), xenon (Xe), and radon (Rn). Can you figure out why they are so unreactive? Atoms of noble gases already have complete outermost energy levels. They do not need to bond with other atoms. Among the noble gases, helium has 2 valence electrons; neon, argon, krypton, xenon, and radon each has 8 valence electrons.

All of the noble gases are found in small amounts in the Earth's atmosphere. Argon, the most common of the noble gases, makes up only about 1 percent of the atmosphere. Because they are so scarce and so unreactive, the noble gases were not discovered until the end of the nineteenth century. This was roughly 30 years after Mendeleev's work.

Some common uses of the noble gases are probably quite familiar to you. No doubt you have seen a balloon filled with helium floating at the end of a string. The brightly colored signs above theaters, restaurants, and stores are filled with inert gases, often called "neon" lights. However, only the red lights are produced by neon. The other colors are produced by argon and several of the other noble gases. Some of the other uses of the noble gases may be less familiar to you. Radon is used to treat certain cancers. Argon and xenon are used in certain light bulbs and lamps.

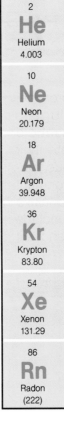

18

| 2 |
| He |
| Helium |
| 4.003 |

| 10 |
| Ne |
| Neon |
| 20.179 |

| 18 |
| Ar |
| Argon |
| 39.948 |

| 36 |
| Kr |
| Krypton |
| 83.80 |

| 54 |
| Xe |
| Xenon |
| 131.29 |

| 86 |
| Rn |
| Radon |
| (222) |

Figure 6–27 *Family 18 is known as the noble gases.*

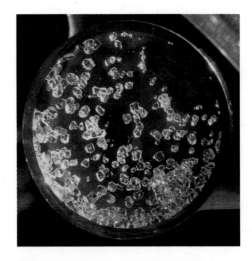

Figure 6–28 *Crystals of xenon tetrafluoride were first prepared in 1962. Before that time, it was believed that noble gases could not form compounds.*

Homely Halogens

Fluorine, chlorine, bromine, and iodine are halogens found in many household substances. Investigate their uses by locating various substances in your environment that contain halogens. Make a chart of your findings. Include examples of the substances if possible.

Rare-Earth Elements

Even though you have completed your tour across the periodic table, you probably have at least one question lurking in the back of your mind. Why are there two rows of elements standing alone at the bottom of the periodic table? The elements in these two rows are called the **rare-earth** elements. The rare-earth elements have properties that are similar to one another. They have been separated out and displayed under the main table to make the table shorter and easier to read.

The first row, called the **lanthanoid series,** is made up of soft, malleable metals that have a high luster and conductivity. The lanthanoids are used in industry to make various alloys and high-quality glass.

The elements in the second row make up the **actinoid series.** All the actinoids are radioactive. (Changes in the nucleus of radioactive atoms cause particles and energy to be given off.) Of all the actinoids, only thorium(Th) and uranium(U) occur to any extent in nature. Uranium may be familiar to you because it is used as a fuel in nuclear-powered electric generators. You won't be surprised to learn that elements 104 to 109 in period 7 are also synthetic and radioactive.

6–3 Section Review

1. What is the key to the placement of an element in the periodic table?
2. Which two families contain the most active metals?
3. To which family do the most active nonmetals belong?
4. Why are the elements in Family 18 called inert gases?

Critical Thinking—*Applying Concepts*
5. How can the arrangement of elements in the periodic table be used to predict how they will react with other elements to form compounds?

PROBLEM Solving ???

Completing the Squares

Look at the data for the five elements below. Fill in the missing data. Then construct a square for each element as it would appear in a modern periodic table. In some cases you will have to perform calculations to fill in the missing data. Do not use a completed periodic table in this activity. It is much more fun to do the calculations yourself. How would you use this information in a laboratory?

Data

■ Carbon (symbol ?); atomic mass, 12.01; number of electrons, 6; (atomic number ?)

■ More than 70 percent of the air (name ?); (symbol ?); atomic number, 7; atomic mass, 14

■ (Name ?); O; (number of protons ?); (atomic mass ?); (number of electrons ?)

■ Fluorine (atomic symbol ?); number of protons, 9; atomic mass, 18.99; (atomic number ?)

■ Inert "sign" gas (name ?); (atomic symbol ?); number of electrons, 10; atomic mass, 20.17

atomic number
symbol
name
atomic mass

6–4 Periodic Properties of the Elements

You have learned several ways in which the periodic table provides important information about the elements. Elements in the same family, or vertical column, have similar properties. Elements at the left of the table are metals. Elements at the right are nonmetals. Metalloids, which show properties of both metals and nonmetals, are located on either side of the dark zigzag line.

Additional information about the elements can be obtained from their location in a period, or

Guide for Reading

Focus on this question as you read.

▶ *What periodic trends can be identified in the elements in the periodic table?*

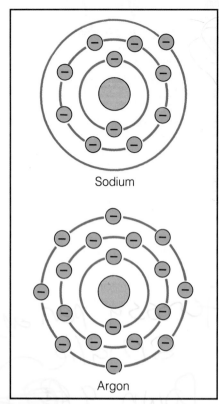

Sodium

Argon

Figure 6–29 *Sodium, an extremely reactive metal, is used in its vapor phase in street lights. Sodium vapor lights provide bright-yellow light (top center). Argon, an extremely unreactive gas, is used to make glowing works of art (top right). How does the electron arrangement of each element account for its reactivity?*

horizontal row. **Certain properties of elements vary in regular ways from left to right across a period. These properties include electron arrangement, reactivity, atomic size, and metallic properties.**

The valence number of an element is related to the electrons in the outermost energy level of an atom of that element. It is these electrons that are involved in the chemical combining of elements to form compounds.

Remember the pattern of valence numbers discovered by Mendeleev: Starting at the left of each period, the pattern of valence numbers is 1 2 3 4 3 2 1 0. An element with a valence of 1 will gain, lose, or share 1 electron in a chemical combination. An element with a valence of 4 will gain, lose, or share 4 electrons. What will happen if an element has a valence of zero? How reactive is such an element?

Elements at the left in a period tend to lose electrons easily when they combine with other elements. You know that the elements at the left of the table are metals. So an important property of metals is that they lose electrons in a chemical combination. Elements at the right in a period tend to gain electrons easily when they combine with other elements. What kinds of elements are these?

The amount of energy needed to remove an electron from an atom shows a periodic increase from left to right across a period. Since atoms of elements at the left in a period tend to lose electrons, removing an electron from such an atom requires a small amount of energy. Removing an electron from an element at the right in a period requires a great amount of energy. Why?

Another property of elements that varies periodically is atomic size. From left to right across a period, atomic size tends to decrease. The decrease can

Figure 6–30 *Fireworks! Colors and noises that astound and amaze! Such brilliant bursts are the results of explosive chemical reactions. Not all chemical reactions are explosive, however. But all chemical reactions do depend on the properties of the elements involved—properties that show a characteristic periodicity.*

be explained in terms of electron arrangement. As the atomic number increases across a period, 1 electron is added to each successive element. But this electron is still in the same energy level. The increase in the number of electrons in the energy level and the number of protons in the nucleus produces a stronger attraction between these oppositely charged particles. The electrons are pulled closer to the nucleus. The size of the atom decreases. Now explain why atomic size increases from top to bottom in a family.

Metallic properties of the elements are also periodic. From left to right across a period, elements become less metallic in nature.

[handwritten notes in right margin:] Across a period smaller. Down a family— bigger. more energy levels

6–4 Section Review

1. What properties are periodic in nature?
2. What is the pattern of valences as you move from left to right across a period?
3. How does atomic size change across a period?

Critical Thinking—*Relating Concepts*

4. A scientist claims that she has discovered a new element that should be inserted between nitrogen and oxygen in the periodic table. Why is it most likely that this scientist has made a mistake? (*Hint:* How does the number of electrons change as you move from left to right across a period?)

CONNECTIONS

The Chains That Bind

Fly from New York to Japan and after hours in the air over land and water, you become convinced of the enormous size of Planet Earth. But in many ways—some more obvious than others—humans are becoming aware of the incredibly small size of the Earth. Although this may seem like a contradiction, in some important ways it is a significant—and alarming—fact.

By now everyone is aware of the dangers of polluting the *environment*. But in the not-too-distant past, such was not the case. The economic growth of major industrial countries was based in large part on the erroneous belief that the enormous size of the Earth made it permissible to dump hazardous substances into the environment. Today we know that, in terms of pollution, the Earth is small. The effects of dumping some hazardous chemicals reach far from their point of introduction into the environment. You are probably familiar with the element mercury. Mercury is an important part of

many industrial processes. For example, it is used in the manufacture of paper and paints. Industrial processes often need a good source of water—especially for washing away the waste byproducts of the manufacturing process. So for a long time, waste mercury was dumped into rivers and streams. After all, the logic was, the water would carry the mercury far away until it eventually reached the vastness of the oceans. There it would be diluted to levels that were no longer dangerous to life.

One major flaw in this logic became evident over time, however. Mercury was found in ever-increasing amounts in the body tissues of certain fishes and other animals. How

...could the level of mercury reach dangerous proportions in certain organisms? The answer was found by biologists when they examined food chains. A food chain describes a series of events in which food, and therefore energy, is transferred from one organism to another. The first organisms in a food chain are small organisms that are able to produce their own food using simple substances. These organisms are often microscopic and make food by using the energy of the sun or the energy stored in chemicals. Some of these organisms also ingest small amounts of chemicals such as mercury, which is stored in their bodies. In turn, these small organisms are eaten by larger ones—small fishes, for example. And these small fishes store the mercury in their tissues, only in slightly larger amounts. The storage of these chemicals in ever-increasing amounts in the living tissues of organisms in a food chain is called *biological magnification.* By the time mercury has moved through a food chain to reach tuna, birds, cattle, and other larger animals, the amount of stored mercury may have reached levels high enough to threaten health and even endanger survival.

When it comes to certain things—the pollution of water by mercury, for example—the Earth is actually a small place. And the food chains that link one organism to another—the ties that bind—may hold so tightly that organisms at one link of the chain cannot survive.

Laboratory Investigation

Flame Tests

Problem

How can elements be identified by using a flame test?

Materials *(per group)*

nichrome or platinum wire
cork
Bunsen burner
hydrochloric acid (dilute)
distilled water
8 test tubes
test tube rack
8 chloride test solutions
safety goggles

Procedure 🧪 🔥 👉 🧰 👁

1. Label each of the test tubes with one of the following compounds: LiCl, $CaCl_2$, KCl, $CuCl_2$, $SrCl_2$, NaCl, $BaCl_2$, unknown.

2. Pour 5 mL of each test solution in the correctly labeled test tube. Be sure to put the correct solution in each labeled test tube.

3. Push one end of a piece of nichrome or platinum wire into a cork. Then bend the other end of the wire into a tiny loop.

4. Put on your safety goggles. Clean the wire by dipping it into the dilute hydrochloric acid and then into the distilled water. You must clean the wire after you make each test. Holding the cork, heat the wire in the blue flame of the Bunsen burner until the wire glows and no longer colors the burner flame.

5. Dip the clean wire into the first test solution. Hold the wire at the tip of the inner cone of the burner flame. Record the color given to the flame in a data table similar to the one shown here.

6. Clean the wire by repeating step 4.

7. Repeat step 5 for the other six known test solutions. Remember to clean the wire after you test each solution.

8. Obtain an unknown solution from your teacher. After you clean the wire, repeat the flame test for this compound.

Compound		Color of Flame
Lithium chloride	LiCl	
Calcium chloride	$CaCl_2$	

Observations

1. What flame colors are produced by each compound?

2. What flame color is produced by the unknown compound?

Analysis and Conclusions

1. Is the flame test a test for the metal or for the chloride in each compound? Explain your answer.

2. Why is it necessary to clean the wire before you test each solution?

3. What metal is present in the unknown solution? How do you know?

4. How can you use a flame test to identify a metal?

5. What do you think would happen if the unknown substance contained a mixture of two compounds? Could each metal be identified?

6. **On Your Own** Suppose you are working in a police crime laboratory and are trying to identify a poison that was used in a crime. How could a knowledge of flame tests help you?

Study Guide

Summarizing Key Concepts

6-1 Arranging the Elements

▲ The elements in Mendeleev's periodic table are arranged in order of increasing atomic mass.

▲ Mendeleev discovered that the properties of the elements recurred at regular intervals.

▲ Mendeleev left spaces for elements not yet discovered and predicted the properties of these missing elements based on their position in the periodic table.

▲ The modern periodic table is based on the periodic law, which states that the physical and chemical properties of the elements are periodic functions of their atomic numbers.

6-2 Design of the Periodic Table

▲ Horizontal rows of elements are called periods.

▲ Vertical columns of elements are called groups or families.

▲ Elements in the same family have similar properties.

▲ Each square in the periodic table gives the element's name, chemical symbol, atomic number, and atomic mass.

▲ According to their properties, the elements are classified as metals, nonmetals, and metalloids.

6-3 Chemical Families

▲ The number of valence electrons in an atom of an element is the key to its placement in a family in the periodic table.

6-4 Periodic Properties of the Elements

▲ Periodic properties of the elements include electron arrangement, reactivity, atomic size, and metallic properties.

Reviewing Key Terms

Define each term in a complete sentence.

6-1 Arranging the Elements
  periodic law

6-2 Design of the Periodic Table
  group
  family
  period
  metal
  luster
  ductile
  malleable
  corrosion
  nonmetal
  metalloid

6-3 Chemical Families
  alkali metal
  alkaline earth metal
  transition metal
  boron family
  carbon family
  nitrogen family
  oxygen family
  halogen family
  noble gas
  rare-earth element
  lanthanoid series
  actinoid series

Chapter Review

Content Review

Multiple Choice

Choose the letter of the answer that best completes each statement.

1. The periodic law states that the properties of elements are periodic functions of their
   a. mass.
   c. atomic number.
   b. symbol.
   d. valence.
2. Which of the following is a noble gas?
   a. sodium
   c. chlorine
   b. gold
   d. neon
3. When a metal combines with a halogen, the kind of compound formed is called a (an)
   a. organic compound.
   c. actinoid.
   b. salt.
   d. oxide.
4. If a metal can be hammered or rolled into thin sheets the metal is said to be
   a. ductile.
   c. brittle.
   b. malleable.
   d. active.
5. In the periodic table, the metallic character of the elements increases as you move in a period from
   a. right to left.
   c. left to right.
   b. top to bottom.
   d. bottom to top.
6. Which of the following is a halogen?
   a. sodium
   c. carbon
   b. silver
   d. iodine
7. Moseley was able to determine each element's
   a. atomic mass.
   c. symbol.
   b. atomic number.
   d. brittleness.
8. Each period of the table begins on the left with a
   a. highly active metal.
   b. metalloid.
   c. rare-earth element.
   d. nonmetal.
9. Which element is called the "basis of life"?
   a. neon
   c. sodium
   b. carbon
   d. oxygen
10. A brittle element that is not a good conductor of heat and electricity is
    a. inert.
    c. ductile.
    b. a metal.
    d. a nonmetal.

True or False

If the statement is true, write "true." If it is false, change the underlined word or words to make the statement true.

1. Mendeleev noticed a definite pattern in the valence numbers of the elements.
2. The property of a metal that means it can be drawn into thin wire is called luster.
3. Sodium belongs to the transition metals.
4. Nonmetals are usually poor conductors of electricity.
5. The most striking property of the noble gases is their extreme inactivity.
6. In forming compounds, nonmetals tend to lose electrons.
7. Vertical columns of elements in the periodic table are called periods.

Concept Mapping

Complete the following concept map for Section 6–1. Then construct a concept map for the entire chapter.

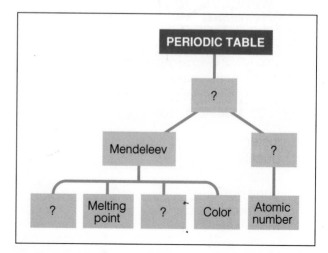

Concept Mastery

Discuss each of the following in a brief paragraph.

1. How was Mendeleev able to tell that there were elements not yet discovered?
2. Compare metals, nonmetals, and metalloids. Give an example of each.
3. Why are elements that gain or lose 1 electron the most active metals or nonmetals?
4. What happens to an atom's size as you move from left to right across a period? From top to bottom in a family?
5. What does the term periodic mean? Give two examples of daily periodic occurrences in your life.

Critical Thinking and Problem Solving

Use the skills you have developed in this chapter to answer each of the following.

1. **Applying definitions** Metals are ductile. In what three ways has this property of metals affected your daily life?
2. **Interpreting charts** Look at these three squares from the periodic table. What kinds of information can you gather from these squares? How would you use this information in a laboratory?

7	8	9
N	O	F
Nitrogen	Oxygen	Fluorine
14.007	15.999	18.998

3. **Relating concepts** Use the periodic table to help predict what will happen when the elements in each of the following pairs are brought together in a chemical reaction:
   a. barium and oxygen
   b. lithium and argon
   c. potassium and iodine
   d. sodium and bromine
4. **Applying concepts** Determine the identity of the following elements:
   a. This nonmetal has 4 valence electrons, properties similar to carbon, and an atomic mass slightly less than phosphorus.

   b. This element has 5 valence electrons, shows properties of metals and nonmetals, and has 33 protons in the nucleus of each atom.
   c. This highly active metal has 1 valence electron and 55 protons in the nucleus.
5. **Making diagrams** Draw a diagram to show the arrangement of electrons in the outermost energy level of an atom in each family in the periodic table.
6. **Classifying elements** Classify each of the following elements as very active, moderately active, fairly inactive, or inert: magnesium, mercury, fluorine, krypton, helium, gold, potassium, calcium, bromine.
7. **Using the writing process** Suppose Mendeleev was alive today and his development of the periodic table occurred yesterday. Plan and write a script for a "media event" that would bring Mendeleev's work to the attention of the public. For example, you might want to produce a television interview with Mendeleev. Or you might want to write a newspaper article.

SHIRLEY ANN JACKSON: Helping Others Through SCIENCE

▲ Shirley Ann Jackson, in her office at Bell Laboratories, is presently doing research in the field of optoelectronic materials used in communication devices.

Imagine what it would be like to catch a glimpse of the universe as it was forming—to look back in time nearly 20 billion years! Of course, no one can really see the beginning of time. But physicists such as Shirley Ann Jackson believe that learning about the universe as it was in the past will help us understand the universe as it is now and as it will be in the future.

By unraveling some of the mysteries of the universe, Dr. Jackson hopes to fulfill a basic ambition: to enrich the lives of others and to make the world a better place in which to live. This contribution, Dr. Jackson believes, can be achieved through science.

Jackson was born and raised in Washington, DC. After graduating from high school as valedictorian, she attended Massachusetts Institute of Technology, MIT. There, her role as a leader in physics began to take root. Jackson became the first

African-American woman to earn a doctorate degree from MIT. She is also the first African-American woman to earn a PhD in physics in the United States.

After graduate school, Jackson began work as a research associate in high-energy physics at the Fermi National Accelerator Laboratory in Batavia, Illinois. This branch of physics studies the characteristics of subatomic particles—such as protons and electrons—as they interact at high energies.

Using devices at Fermilab called particle accelerators, physicists accelerate subatomic particles to speeds that approach the speed of light. The particles collide and produce new subatomic particles. By analyzing these subatomic particles, physicists are able to learn more about the structure of atoms and the nature of matter.

The experiments in which Jackson participated at Fermilab helped to prove the existence of certain subatomic particles whose identity had only been theorized. This information is important in understanding the nuclear reactions that are taking place at the center of the sun and other stars.

Jackson's research is not limited to the world of subatomic particles alone. Her work also includes the study of semiconductors—materials that conduct electricity better than insulators but not as well as metal conductors. Semiconductors have made possible the development of transistor radios, televisions, and computers—inventions that have dramatically changed the ways we live.

Jackson's current work in physics at Bell Laboratories in Murray Hill, New Jersey, has brought her from the beginnings of the universe to the future of communication. This talented physicist has been doing research in the area of optoelectronic materials. This branch of electronics—which deals with solid-state devices that produce, regulate, transmit, and detect electromagnetic radiation—is changing the way telephones, computers, radios, and televisions are made and used.

Looking back on her past, Jackson feels fortunate to have been given so many opportunities at such a young age. And she is optimistic about the future. "Research is exciting," she says. Motivated by her research, Shirley Ann Jackson is happy to be performing a service to the public in the way she knows best—as a dedicated and determined scientist.

▼ **This particle-accelerator generator at Fermilab is familiar equipment to Shirley Ann Jackson.**

UNIT TWO
Chemistry of Matter

The fun of blowing bubbles is made possible by chemistry.

You have been given an assignment to perform the following steps, but you have not been told what the results of the procedure will be. What will you have made after completing the steps? Read them and see if you can figure it out. First, treat a fat called palmitin with an alkali such as sodium hydroxide in a process called saponification. The fat will break down to produce the substances sodium palmitate and glycerin. Discard the glycerin. Then add the sodium palmitate to a wetting compound to form a solution. Now dip a thin ring, preferably one with a handle, into the liquid. Finally, apply a gentle stream of air to the film on the ring.

Well, have you figured it out? Do you know what you have done? This rather complicated

The activities of the tiny particles that make up matter can be traced in patterns such as this one.

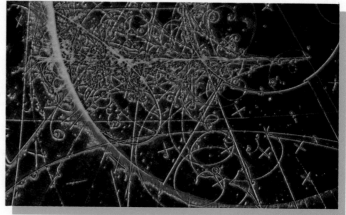

CHAPTERS

procedure has a fairly simple explanation: When you saponified the palmitin, you made soap. Then you added it to water to make a solution. And finally, you blew bubbles!

Chemical reactions such as saponification may not be familiar to you. Yet chemical reactions are occurring all around you and even in your body at this very moment. As you read this Unit, you will learn about the interactions of matter that can occur in a test tube, in nature, and even inside you!

Some of the most important chemical activities occur during the simple act of eating.

Discovery *Activity*

Chemical Mysteries

1. Dip a toothpick into a small dish of milk. Use the toothpick as a pen to write a message on a sheet of white paper.

2. Let the milk dry. Observe what happens to your message as it dries.

3. Hold the paper close to a light bulb that is lit.

   ■ How does your message change before and after you place it next to the light bulb? What can you say about the relationship between the milk and the light bulb?

4. Fill one container about half full with very cold water and another container about half full with hot water.

5. Place four or five drops of food coloring into each container at exactly the same time.

   ■ Compare the rates at which the colors spread. Explain your observations.

Atoms and Bonding

Guide for Reading

After you read the following sections, you will be able to

7–1 What Is Chemical Bonding?
- Explain chemical bonding on the basis of unfilled energy levels.

7–2 Ionic Bonds
- Describe the formation of ions and ionic bonds.

7–3 Covalent Bonds
- Describe the formation of covalent bonds.

7–4 Metallic Bonds
- Relate metallic bonding to the properties of metals.

7–5 Predicting Types of Bonds
- Explain what oxidation number is.
- Identify the relationships among an atom's position in the periodic table, its oxidation number, and the type of bonds it forms.

Salt! You are surely familiar with this abundant and important chemical substance. As a frequently used seasoning, salt enhances the flavor of many of the foods you eat. Just imagine popcorn, chow mein, or collard greens without a dash of salt!

For a long time, salt has figured prominently in human affairs. Because it was both extremely important and limited in supply, salt was highly valued. Roman soldiers were, in fact, paid in cakes of salt. It is from the Latin word *sal*, meaning salt, that our word salary is derived.

Salt has come to symbolize many characteristics of human behavior. "The salt of youth" was William Shakespeare's description of the liveliness of this time of life. A person possessing valuable qualities is often described as being "worth one's salt." And those great human beings who have improved our world are often referred to as "the salt of the earth."

Salt is the substance sodium chloride. It is made of the elements sodium and chlorine. How and why do these elements combine to form salt? And what is the process by which hundreds of thousands of other substances are formed? Throw some salt over your left shoulder for luck and read on for the answers!

Journal *Activity*

You and Your World What do you think of when you hear the word element? How about the word compound? Do you know how these substances figure in your daily life? In your journal, answer these questions and provide any other thoughts you have about this topic. When you have completed this chapter, see if you need to modify your answers.

◀ *In ancient times, no other single substance equaled the importance of salt. Crystals of salt are shown in this magnified image.*

7–1 What Is Chemical Bonding?

Look around you for a moment and describe what you see. Do you see the pages of this textbook? A window? Perhaps trees or buildings? Your friends and classmates? The air you breathe? All these objects—and many others not even mentioned—have one important property in common. They are all forms of matter. And all matter—regardless of its size, shape, color, or phase—is made of tiny particles called atoms. As you learned in Chapter 4, atoms are the basic building blocks of all the substances in the universe. As you can imagine, there are hundreds of thousands of different substances in nature. (To prove this, try to list all the different substances you can. Is there an end to your list?)

Yet, as scientists know, there are only 109 different elements. Elements are the simplest type of substance. Elements are made of only one kind of atom. How can just 109 different elements form so many different substances?

The 109 elements are each made of specific types of atoms. Atoms of elements combine with one another to produce new and different substances called compounds. You are already familiar with several compounds: water, sodium chloride (table salt), sugar, carbon dioxide, vinegar, lye, and ammonia. Compounds contain more than one kind of atom chemically joined together.

The combining of atoms of elements to form new substances is called chemical bonding. Chemical bonds are formed in very definite ways. The atoms combine according to certain rules. The rules of **chemical bonding** are determined by the structure of the atom, which you are now about to investigate.

Electrons and Energy Levels

As you learned in Chapter 5, an atom contains a positively charged center called the nucleus. Found inside the nucleus are two subatomic particles: protons and neutrons. Protons have a positive charge, and neutrons have no charge. Neutrons are

Figure 7–1 *The hundreds of thousands of different substances in nature are made up of atoms. Atoms are the basic building blocks of everything in the universe, including all forms of living things, the air, and the Lagoon Nebula in the constellation Sagittarius.*

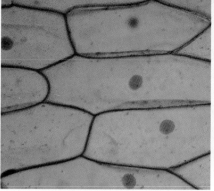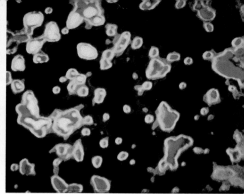

Figure 7–2 *You can think of atoms as similar to the individual stones that make up the pyramids in Giza, Egypt, or the individual cells of which all living things are made. The photograph of uranium atoms taken with an electron microscope gives you some idea of what atoms actually look like—magnified more than five million times, that is!*

neutral particles. Thus the nucleus as a whole has a positive charge.

Located outside the nucleus are negatively charged particles called electrons. The negative charge of the electrons balances the positive charge of the nucleus. The atom as a whole is neutral. It has no net charge. What do you think this means about the number of electrons (negatively charged) compared with the number of protons (positively charged)?

The negatively charged electrons of an atom are attracted by the positively charged nucleus of that atom. This electron-nucleus attraction holds the atom together. The electrons, however, are not pulled into the nucleus. They remain in a region outside the nucleus called the electron cloud.

The electron cloud is made up of a number of different energy levels. Electrons within an atom are arranged in energy levels. Each energy level can hold only a certain number of electrons. The first, or innermost, energy level can hold only 2 electrons, the second can hold 8 electrons, and the third can hold 18 electrons. The electrons in the outermost energy level of an atom are called **valence electrons.** The valence electrons play the most significant role in determining how atoms combine.

When the outermost energy level of an atom contains the maximum number of electrons, the level is full, or complete. Atoms that have complete (filled) outermost energy levels are very stable. They usually do not combine with other atoms to form compounds. They do not form chemical bonds.

ACTIVITY

DOING

A Model of Energy Levels

1. Cut a thin piece of corkboard into a circle 50 cm in diameter to represent an atom.

2. Insert a colored pushpin or tack into the center to represent the nucleus.

3. Draw three concentric circles around the nucleus to represent energy levels. The inner circle should be 20 cm in diameter; the second circle, 30 cm in diameter; and the third, 40 cm in diameter.

4. Using pushpins or tacks of another color to represent electrons, construct the following atoms: hydrogen (H), helium (He), lithium (Li), fluorine (F), neon (Ne), sodium (Na), and argon (Ar).

Are any of these elements in the same family? If so, which ones? How do you know?

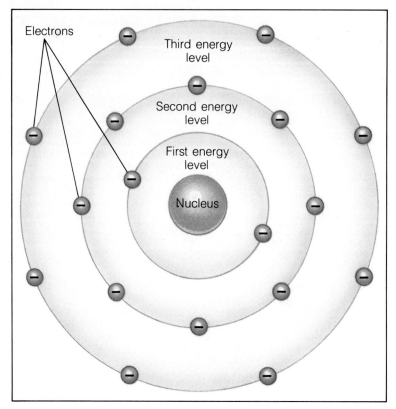

Figure 7–3 *An atom contains a positively charged nucleus surrounded by negatively charged electrons located in energy levels within the electron cloud. Each energy level can hold only a certain number of electrons. How many electrons is the first energy level holding? The second? The third?*

Turn to Chapter 6, pages 142–143, to find the periodic table. As you recall, the periodic table of the elements is one of the most important "tools" of a physical scientist. All the known elements (109) are listed in this table in a specific way. Every element belongs to a family, which is a numbered, vertical column. There are 18 families of elements. Every element also belongs to a period, which is a numbered, horizontal row. How many periods of elements do you see? Elements in the same family have similar properties, the most important of which is the number of electrons in the outermost energy level, or the number of valence electrons.

Look at Family 18 in the periodic table. It contains the elements helium, neon, argon, krypton, xenon, and radon. The atoms of these elements do not form chemical bonds under normal conditions. This is because all the atoms of elements in Family 18 have filled outermost energy levels. Remember, if the first energy level is also the outermost, it needs only 2 electrons to make it complete. Can you tell which element in Family 18 has only 2 valence electrons?

18
2 **He** Helium 4.003
10 **Ne** Neon 20.179
18 **Ar** Argon 39.948
36 **Kr** Krypton 83.80
54 **Xe** Xenon 131.29
86 **Rn** Radon (222)

Figure 7–4 *These balloons are filled with helium, a highly unreactive element. Neon gas, another unreactive element, is used in neon lights. Argon, shown here as a laser made visible through smoke, is also highly unreactive. These three elements are members of Family 18. What must be true of the outermost energy levels of atoms in this family?*

Electrons and Bonding

The electron arrangement of the outermost energy level of an atom determines whether or not the atom will form chemical bonds. As you have just read, atoms of elements in Family 18 have complete outermost energy levels. These atoms generally do not form chemical bonds.

Atoms of elements other than those in Family 18 do not have filled outermost energy levels. Their outermost energy level lacks one or more electrons to be complete. Some of these atoms tend to gain electrons in order to fill the outermost energy level. Fluorine (F), which has 7 valence electrons, gains 1 electron to fill its outermost energy level. Other atoms tend to lose their valence electrons and are left with only filled energy levels. Sodium (Na), which has 1 valence electron, loses 1 electron.

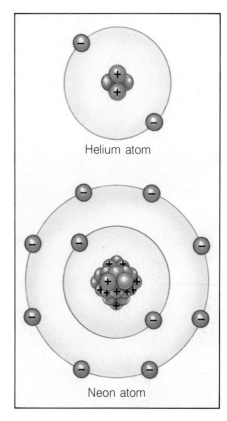

Helium atom

Neon atom

Figure 7–5 *The outermost energy level of a helium atom contains the maximum number of electrons—2. In a neon atom, the outermost energy level is the second energy level. It contains the maximum 8 electrons. What chemical property do these elements share?*

In order to achieve stability, an atom will either gain or lose electrons. In other words, an atom will bond with another atom if the bonding gives both atoms complete outermost energy levels. In the next section you will learn how bonding takes place.

7-1 Section Review

1. What is chemical bonding?
2. What is the basic structure of the atom?
3. What are valence electrons? How many valence electrons can there be in the first energy level? In the second? In the third?
4. What determines whether or not an atom will form chemical bonds?

Connection—*History*
5. On May 6, 1937, the airship (blimp) *Hindenburg* exploded in midair just seconds before completing its transatlantic voyage. On board the blimp had been 210,000 cubic meters of hydrogen gas. Since that time, airships have used helium gas rather than hydrogen gas to keep them aloft. Explain why.

Guide for Reading

Focus on this question as you read.

▶ *What is ionic bonding?*

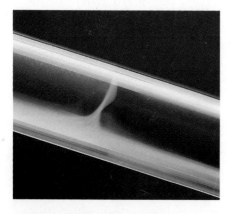

Figure 7–6 *Bonding usually results in the formation of compounds, such as ammonium chloride.*

7-2 Ionic Bonds

As you have just learned, an atom will bond with another atom in order to achieve stability, which means in order for both atoms to get complete outermost energy levels. One way a complete outermost energy level can be achieved is by the transfer of electrons from one atom to another. Bonding that involves a transfer of electrons is called **ionic bonding**. Ionic bonding, or electron-transfer bonding, gets its name from the word **ion**. An ion is a charged atom. Remember, an atom is neutral. But if there is a transfer of electrons, a neutral atom will become a charged atom.

Because ionic bonding involves the transfer of electrons, one atom gains electrons and the other atom loses electrons. Within each atom the negative and positive charges no longer balance. The atom that has gained electrons has gained a negative

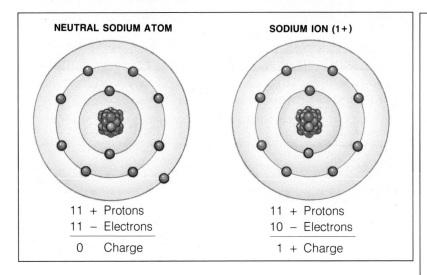

NEUTRAL SODIUM ATOM	SODIUM ION (1+)
11 + Protons	11 + Protons
11 − Electrons	10 − Electrons
0 Charge	1 + Charge

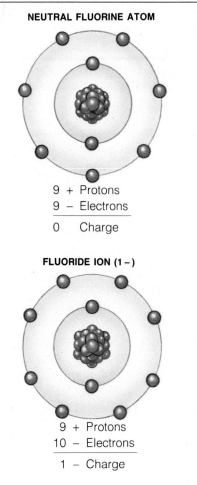

NEUTRAL FLUORINE ATOM

9 + Protons
9 − Electrons
0   Charge

FLUORIDE ION (1 −)

9 + Protons
10 − Electrons
1 − Charge

charge. It is a negative ion. For example, fluorine (F) has 7 valence electrons. To complete its outermost energy level, the fluorine atom gains 1 electron. In gaining 1 negatively charged electron, the fluorine atom becomes a negative ion. The symbol for the fluoride ion is F^{1-}. (For certain elements, the name of the ion is slightly different from the name of the atom. The difference is usually in the ending of the name—as with the fluorine atom and the fluoride ion.)

The sodium atom (Na) has 1 valence electron. When a sodium atom loses this valence electron, it is left with an outermost energy level containing 8 electrons. In losing 1 negatively charged electron, the sodium atom becomes a positive ion. The symbol for the sodium ion is Na^{1+}. Figure 7–7 shows the formation of the fluoride ion and the sodium ion.

Figure 7–7 *The formation of a negative fluoride ion involves the gain of an electron by a fluorine atom. The formation of a positive sodium ion involves the loss of an electron by a sodium atom. How many valence electrons does a fluorine atom have? A sodium atom? What is the symbol for a fluoride ion? A sodium ion?*

Figure 7–8 *The general rule that opposites attract is responsible for the formation of the ionic bond between a positive sodium ion and a negative fluoride ion. Notice the transfer of an electron during the ionic bonding. What is the formula for the resulting compound?*

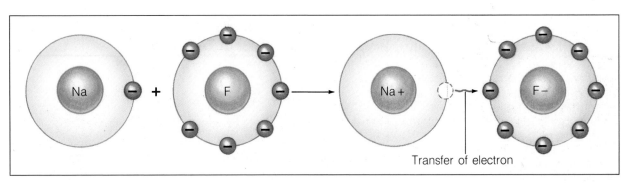

Transfer of electron

ACTIVITY

Steelwool Science

1. Place a small amount of steelwool in a jar and push it to the bottom. Pack it tightly enough so that it will remain in place when the jar is inverted.

2. Into each of two identical dishes, pour water to a height of about 2 cm. Make sure there are equal amounts of water in each dish.

3. In one dish, place the jar with the steelwool mouth down in the water. In the other dish, place an identical but empty jar in the same position.

4. Observe the jars every day for 1 week. Record your observations.

What changes did you observe in the steelwool? In the water levels?

■ Explain your observations.

■ What is the purpose of the empty jar?

In nature, it is a general rule that opposites attract. Since the two ions Na^{1+} and F^{1-} have opposite charges, they attract each other. The strong attraction holds the ions together in an ionic bond. The formation of the ionic bond results in the formation of the compound sodium fluoride, NaF. See Figure 7–8 on page 179.

Energy for Ion Formation

In order for the outermost electron to be removed from an atom, the attraction between the negatively charged electron and the positively charged nucleus must be overcome. The process of removing electrons and forming ions is called **ionization**. Energy is needed for ionization. This energy is called **ionization energy**.

The ionization energy for atoms that have few valence electrons is low. Do you know why? Only a small amount of energy is needed to remove electrons from the outermost energy level. As a result, these atoms tend to lose electrons easily and to become positive ions. What elements would you expect would have low ionization energies?

The ionization energy for atoms with many valence electrons is very high. These atoms do not lose electrons easily. As a matter of fact, these atoms usually gain electrons. It is much easier to gain 1 or 2 electrons than to lose 7 or 6 electrons! The tendency of an atom to attract electrons is called **electron affinity**. Atoms such as fluorine are said to have a high electron affinity because they attract electrons easily. What other atoms have a high electron affinity?

Figure 7–9 *During ionization, an electron is removed from an atom and an ion forms. Energy is absorbed during ionization. Energy is released when an atom gains an electron and forms an ion. What is the tendency of an atom to gain electrons called?*

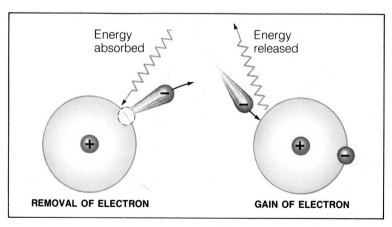

Energy absorbed   Energy released

REMOVAL OF ELECTRON   **GAIN OF ELECTRON**

Arrangement of Ions in Ionic Compounds

Ions of opposite charge strongly attract each other. Ions of like charge strongly repel each other. As a result, ions in an ionic compound are arranged in a specific way. Positive ions tend to be near negative ions and farther from other positive ions.

The placement of ions in an ionic compound results in a regular, repeating arrangement called a **crystal lattice**. A crystal lattice is made of huge numbers of ions. A crystal lattice gives the compound great stability. It also accounts for certain physical properties. For example, ionic solids tend to have high melting points. Figure 7–10 shows the crystal lattice structure of sodium chloride.

Ionic compounds are made of nearly endless arrays of ions. A chemical formula for an ionic compound shows the ratio of ions present in the crystal lattice. It does not show the actual number of ions.

Each ionic compound has a characteristic crystal lattice arrangement. This lattice arrangement gives a particular shape to the crystals of the compound. For example, sodium chloride forms cubic crystals. Figure 7–11 shows some unusual shapes that result from ionic bonding.

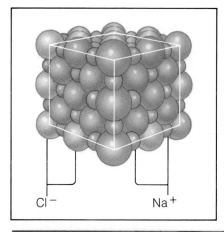

Figure 7–10 *Ionic bonding results in the formation of crystals. Crystals have a characteristic crystal lattice, or regular, repeating arrangement of ions. The lattice arrangement of sodium chloride crystals gives them their characteristic cubic shape. What is the common name for this crystal?*

Figure 7–11 *Ionic crystals often have unusual and amazingly beautiful shapes. Here you see ice crystals (left), crystals of the mineral rhodonite (center), and crystals of the mineral quartz (right). Are all these crystals ionic?*

ACTIVITY

Growing Crystals

1. Make a small sliding loop in the end of a 10-cm length of thin plastic fishing line. Attach the loop to a small crystal of sea salt (NaCl).

2. In a beaker containing 200 mL of very hot water, stir to dissolve as much sea salt as the water will hold.

3. Suspend the fishing line containing the loop and crystal in the beaker. Tie the other end of the line to a pencil. Lay the pencil across the top of the beaker to support the line. The crystal should be suspended about halfway down in the liquid.

4. Observe the growing crystals every day for 3 days.

The crystal shape of an ionic compound is of great importance to geologists in identifying minerals. There are more than 2000 different kinds of minerals, and many of them look alike! One of the properties by which minerals are classified is crystal shape. There are six basic crystal shapes, or systems, and each of the thousands of minerals belongs to one of these systems.

7–2 Section Review

1. What is ionic bonding?
2. How does an atom become a negative ion? A positive ion?
3. What is ionization energy? Electron affinity?
4. What is a crystal lattice? What is the relationship between a chemical formula for an ionic compound and its crystal lattice?

Critical Thinking—*You and Your World*

5. A general rule in nature is that opposites attract. In addition to the behavior of oppositely charged ions, what other example(s) of this rule can you think of?

Guide for Reading

Focus on these questions as you read.

▶ *What is covalent bonding?*

▶ *What is a molecule?*

7–3 Covalent Bonds

Bonding often occurs between atoms that have high ionization energies and high electron affinities. In other words, neither atom loses electrons easily, but both atoms attract electrons. In such cases, there can be no transfer of electrons between atoms. What there can be is a sharing of electrons. Bonding in which electrons are shared rather than transferred is called **covalent bonding**. Look at the word covalent. Do you see a form of a word you have just learned? Do you know what the prefix *co-* means? Why is covalent an appropriate name for such a bond?

By sharing electrons, each atom fills up its outermost energy level. So the shared electrons are in the outermost energy level of both atoms at the same time.

Figure 7–12 *Covalent bonding is bonding in which electrons are shared rather than transferred. Two substances that exhibit covalent bonding are sulfur (left) and sugar (right). Which substance is an element? A compound?*

Nature of the Covalent Bond

In covalent bonding, the positively charged nucleus of each atom simultaneously (at the same time) **attracts the negatively charged electrons that are being shared**. The electrons spend most of their time between the atoms. The attraction between the nucleus and the shared electrons holds the atoms together.

The simplest kind of covalent bond is formed between two hydrogen atoms. Each hydrogen atom has 1 valence electron. By sharing their valence electrons, both hydrogen atoms fill their outermost energy level. Remember, the outermost energy level of a hydrogen atom is complete with 2 electrons. The two atoms are now joined in a covalent bond. See Figure 7–13 on page 184.

Chemists represent the electron sharing that takes place in a covalent bond by an **electron-dot diagram**. In such a diagram, the chemical symbol for an element represents the nucleus and all the inner energy levels of the atom—that is, all the energy levels except the outermost energy level, which is the energy level with the valence electrons. Dots surrounding the symbol represent the valence electrons.

A hydrogen atom has only 1 valence electron. An electron-dot diagram of a hydrogen atom would look like this:

H·

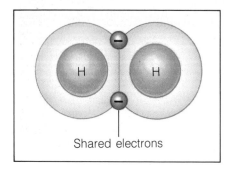

Figure 7–13 *The covalent bond between 2 atoms of hydrogen results in a molecule of hydrogen. In a covalent bond, the electrons are shared. How many valence electrons does each hydrogen atom have?*

The covalent bond between the two hydrogen atoms shown in Figure 7–13 can be represented in an electron-dot diagram like this:

$$\text{H} : \text{H}$$

The two hydrogen atoms are sharing a pair of electrons. Each hydrogen atom achieves a complete outermost energy level (an energy level containing 2 electrons).

Chlorine has 7 valence electrons. An electron-dot diagram of a chlorine atom looks like this:

$$: \overset{\displaystyle ..}{\underset{\displaystyle ..}{\text{Cl}}} \cdot$$

The chlorine atom needs one more electron to complete its outermost energy level. If it bonds with another chlorine atom, the two atoms could share a pair of electrons. Each atom would then have 8 electrons in its outermost energy level. The electron-dot diagram for this covalent bond would look like this:

$$: \overset{\displaystyle ..}{\underset{\displaystyle ..}{\text{Cl}}} : \overset{\displaystyle ..}{\underset{\displaystyle ..}{\text{Cl}}} :$$

Covalent bonding often takes place between atoms of the same element. In addition to hydrogen and chlorine, the elements oxygen, fluorine, bromine, iodine, and nitrogen bond in this way. These elements are called **diatomic elements**. When found in nature, diatomic elements always exist as two atoms covalently bonded.

The chlorine atom, with its 7 valence electrons, can also bond covalently with an unlike atom. For example, a hydrogen atom can combine with a chlorine atom to form the compound hydrogen chloride. See Figure 7–14. The electron-dot diagram for this covalent bond is

$$\text{H} : \overset{\displaystyle ..}{\underset{\displaystyle ..}{\text{Cl}}} :$$

You can see from this electron-dot diagram that by sharing electrons, each atom completes its outermost energy level.

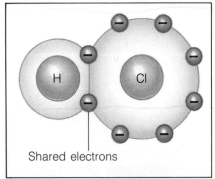

Shared electrons

Figure 7–14 *By sharing their valence electrons, hydrogen and chlorine form a molecule of the compound hydrogen chloride. When dissolved in water, hydrogen chloride forms the acid known as hydrochloric acid. Hydrochloric acid is an important part of the digestive juices found in the stomach.*

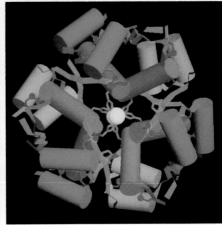

Figure 7–15 *Not all molecules are as simple as hydrogen chloride. Here you see computer-generated images of several more complex molecules: morphine (left), a common cold virus (center), and the hormone insulin (right).*

Formation of Molecules

In a covalent bond, a relatively small number of atoms are involved in the sharing of electrons. The combination of atoms that results forms a separate unit rather than the large crystal lattices characteristic of ionic compounds.

The combination of atoms formed by a covalent bond is called a **molecule** (MAHL-ih-kyool). A molecule is the smallest particle of a covalently bonded substance that has all the properties of that substance. This means that 1 molecule of water, for example, has all the characteristics of a glass of water, a bucket of water, or a pool of water. But if a molecule of water were broken down into atoms of its elements, the atoms would not have the same properties as the molecule.

Molecules are represented by chemical formulas. Like a chemical formula for an ionic crystal, the chemical formula for a covalent molecule contains the symbol of each element involved in the bond. Unlike a chemical formula for an ionic crystal, however, the chemical formula for a molecule shows the exact number of atoms of each element involved in the bond. The subscripts, or small numbers placed to the lower right of the symbols, show the number of atoms of each element. When there is only 1 atom of an element, the subscript 1 is not written. It is understood to be 1. Thus, a hydrogen chloride molecule has the formula HCl. What would be the

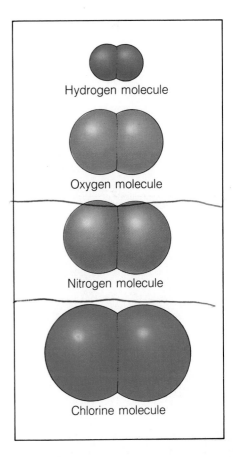

Hydrogen molecule

Oxygen molecule

Nitrogen molecule

Chlorine molecule

Figure 7–16 *Diatomic elements include hydrogen, oxygen, nitrogen, and chlorine. How many valence electrons does an atom of each element have?*

185

Figure 7–17 *Diamonds are network solids. Network solids contain bonds that are difficult to break. This accounts for the extreme hardness of diamonds. Extremely strong glues are also examples of network solids.*

formula for a molecule that has 1 carbon (C) atom and 4 chlorine (Cl) atoms?

Covalently bonded solids tend to have low melting points. Some covalent substances, however, do not have low melting points. They have rather high melting points. This is because molecules of these substances are very large. The molecules are large because the atoms involved continue to bond to one another. These substances are called **network solids**. Carbon in the form of graphite is an example of a network solid. So too is silicon dioxide, the main ingredient in sand. Certain glues also form networks of atoms whose bonds are difficult to break. This accounts for the holding properties of such glues.

Polyatomic Ions

Certain ions are made of covalently bonded atoms that tend to stay together as if they were a single atom. A group of covalently bonded atoms that acts like a single atom when combining with other atoms is called a **polyatomic ion**. Although the bonds within the polyatomic ion are covalent, the polyatomic ion usually forms ionic bonds with other atoms.

Figure 7–18 is a list of some of the more common polyatomic ions, and Figure 7–19 on page 188 shows the atomic structure of several polyatomic ions. Some of these ions may sound familiar to you. For example, the polyatomic ion hydrogen carbonate (HCO_3^{1-}) bonded to sodium produces sodium hydrogen carbonate ($NaHCO_3$), better known as baking soda. Magnesium hydroxide ($Mg(OH)_2$) is milk of magnesia. And ammonium nitrate (NH_4NO_3—two polyatomic ions bonded together) is an important fertilizer.

POLYATOMIC IONS	
Name	**Formula**
ammonium	NH_4^{1+}
acetate	$C_2H_3O_2^{1-}$
chlorate	ClO_3^{1-}
hydrogen carbonate	HCO_3^{1-}
hydroxide	OH^{1-}
nitrate	NO_3^{1-}
nitrite	NO_2^{1-}
carbonate	CO_3^{2-}
sulfate	SO_4^{2-}
sulfite	SO_3^{2-}
phosphate	PO_4^{3-}

Figure 7–18 *The name and formula of some common polyatomic ions are shown here. What is a polyatomic ion? Which polyatomic ion has a positive charge?*

Diamonds by Design

What do a razor blade, a rocket engine, and swamp gas have in common? Hardly anything, you might think. But today, researchers are working to provide an answer. Scientists involved in this endeavor are trying to find a way to coat various objects with a thin film of synthetic diamond. (Synthetic diamonds are made in the laboratory.)

Diamonds are extremely hard and resistant to wear. By placing a diamond coating on a razor blade, the blade can be made to last longer and stay sharper. Diamond coatings on rocket engines and cutting tools will increase their resistance to wear. The list of uses for diamond coatings goes on and on.

How do scientists go about making a synthetic diamond coating? They start with swamp gas, which is called methane. Methane is a chemical substance made of 1 carbon atom linked to 4 hydrogen atoms. The first step in the process is to "strip away" the hydrogen atoms from the carbon atom. When this happens, the carbon atoms from thousands of methane molecules are left behind.

Diamonds are made of carbon atoms. By carefully controlling conditions in the laboratory, scientists can make the carbon atoms link together to form synthetic diamonds. As they link together, they are deposited on the object to be coated. The synthetic diamonds are almost pure.

With continued research in this field of *chemical technology,* scientists feel certain that in any form, diamonds will continue to be extremely valuable!

Synthetic diamonds similar to these shown mixed with natural diamonds can be used to coat various objects, including silicon wafers, thereby making the objects stronger, sharper, and more durable.

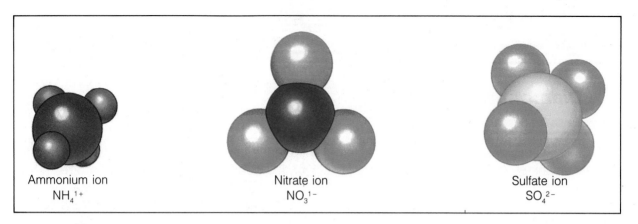

Figure 7–19 *A polyatomic ion is a group of covalently bonded atoms that act like a single atom when combining with other atoms. What kind of bond does a polyatomic ion usually form with another atom?*

Ammonium ion
NH_4^{1+}

Nitrate ion
NO_3^{1-}

Sulfate ion
SO_4^{2-}

7–3 Section Review

1. What is covalent bonding?
2. What is an electron-dot diagram? How is it used to represent a covalent bond?
3. What is a molecule? What does the chemical formula for a molecule tell you?
4. What is a polyatomic ion? Give two examples.

Critical Thinking—*Applying Concepts*
5. What elements and how many atoms of each are represented in the following formulas: Na_2CO_3, $Ca(OH)_2$, $Mg(C_2H_3O_2)_2$, $Ba_3(PO_4)_2$?

7–4 Metallic Bonds

You are probably familiar with metals such as copper, silver, gold, iron, tin, and zinc. And perhaps you even know that cadmium, nickel, chromium, and manganese are metals too. But do you know what makes an element a metal? Metals are elements that give up electrons easily.

In a metallic solid, or a solid made entirely of one metal element, only atoms of that particular metal are present. There are no other atoms to accept the electron(s) the metal easily gives up. How, then, do the atoms of a metal bond?

The atoms of metals form **metallic bonds**. In a metallic bond, the outer electrons of the atoms form

a common electron cloud. This common distribution of electrons occurs throughout a metallic crystal. In a sense, the electrons become the property of all the atoms. These electrons are often described as a "sea of electrons." **The positive nuclei of atoms of metals are surrounded by free-moving, or mobile, electrons that are all attracted by the nuclei at the same time.**

The sea of mobile electrons in a metallic crystal accounts for many properties of metals. Metals are malleable, which means they can be hammered into thin sheets without breaking. Metals are also ductile: They can be drawn into thin wire. The flexibility of metals results from the fact that the metal ions can slide by one another and the electrons are free to flow. Yet the attractions between the ions and the electrons hold the metal together even when it is being hammered or drawn into wire.

Figure 7–20 *The atoms of metals form metallic bonds. Metallic bonding accounts for many important properties of metals that make metals very useful. The metal platinum has an extremely high melting point, and so it is used in heat-resistant containers (left). The walls of this building are covered with a thin film of metal that reflects a significant amount of outdoor light (center). Metals are also excellent conductors of electricity. Some metals offer so little resistance to electric current that they can be used as superconductors (right).*

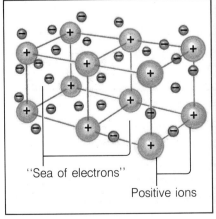

"Sea of electrons"

Positive ions

Figure 7–21 *In a metallic bond, the outer electrons of the metal atoms form a "sea of mobile electrons." Because metals are both malleable and ductile, they can be hammered and drawn into a wide variety of shapes. Here you see various forms of gold.*

Activity Bank

Hot Stuff, p. 725

The ability of the electrons to flow freely makes metals excellent conductors of both heat and electricity. Metallic bonding also accounts for the high melting point of most metals. For example, the melting point of silver is 961.9°C and of gold, 1064.4°C.

7–4 Section Review

1. What is a metallic bond?
2. What is a malleable metal? A ductile metal?
3. How does metallic bonding account for the properties of metals?

Connection—*You and Your World*
4. In terms of bonding, explain why it would be unwise to stir a hot liquid with a silver utensil.

Guide for Reading

Focus on these questions as you read.

▶ *What is oxidation number?*
▶ *What is the relationship between oxidation number and bond type?*

7–5 Predicting Types of Bonds

You have just learned about three different types of bonds formed between atoms of elements: ionic bonds, covalent bonds, and metallic bonds. By knowing some of the properties of an element, is there a way of predicting which type of bond it will form? Fortunately, the answer is yes. And the property most important for predicting bond type is the electron arrangement in the atoms of the element—more specifically, the number of valence electrons.

The placement of the elements involved in bonding in the periodic table often indicates whether the bond will be ionic, covalent, or metallic. Look again at the periodic table on pages 142–143. Elements at the left and in the center of the periodic table are metals. These elements have metallic bonds.

Compounds formed between elements that lose electrons easily and those that gain electrons easily will have ionic bonds. Elements at the left and in the center of the periodic table tend to lose valence electrons easily. These elements are metals. Elements at the right tend to gain electrons readily. These elements are nonmetals. A compound formed between a metal and a nonmetal will thus have ionic bonds.

190

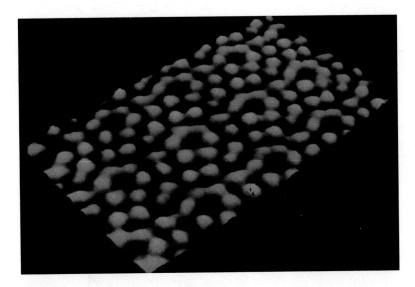

Figure 7–22 *This is the first photograph ever taken of atoms and their bonds. The bright round objects are single atoms. The fuzzy areas between atoms represent bonds.*

Compounds formed between elements that have similar tendencies to gain electrons will have covalent bonds. Bonds between nonmetals, which are at the right of the periodic table, will be covalent. What type of bonding would you expect between magnesium (Mg) and fluorine (F)? Between oxygen (O) and chlorine (Cl)? In a sample of zinc (Zn)?

Activity Bank

The Milky Way, p. 726

Combining Capacity of Atoms

The number of electrons in the outermost energy level of an atom, the valence electrons, determines how an atom will combine with other atoms. If you know the number of valence electrons in an atom, you can calculate the number of electrons that atom needs to gain, lose, or share when it forms a compound. **The number of electrons an atom gains, loses, or shares when it forms chemical bonds is called its oxidation number**. The **oxidation number** of an atom describes its combining capacity.

An atom of sodium has 1 valence electron. It loses this electron when it combines with another atom. In so doing, it forms an ion with a 1+ charge, Na^{1+}. The oxidation number of sodium is 1+. A magnesium atom has 2 valence electrons, which it will lose when it forms a chemical bond. The magnesium ion is Mg^{2+}. The oxidation number of magnesium is 2+.

An atom of chlorine has 7 valence electrons. It will gain 1 electron when it bonds with another atom. The ion formed will have a 1− charge, Cl^{1-}. The oxidation number of chlorine is 1−. Oxygen has

ACTIVITY

CALCULATING

Determining Oxidation Numbers

For each of the following compounds, determine the oxidation number of the underlined element using the clue provided.

$\underline{Ca}Br_2$ (Br 1−)
$\underline{C}H_4$ (H 1−)
$H_2\underline{S}$ (S 2−)
$Na\underline{N}O_3$ (Na 1+, O 2−)
$\underline{Mg}SO_4$ ((SO_4) 2−)

Figure 7–23 *Some elements have more than one oxidation number. Copper, seen here as pennies, can have oxidation numbers of 1+ and 2+. Mercury also exhibits these same oxidation numbers. How can you determine the oxidation number of an atom?*

ACTIVITY
READING

Dangerous Food

Sometimes an element can have adverse effects on living things and on the environment. Such unwanted effects are often the result of bonding between the element and another substance. *Minamata,* a book by W. Eugene Smith and Aileen M. Smith, describes the tragic consequences to the Japanese population from the dumping of industrial mercury into Minamata Bay. You may find this story of the poisoning of a bay fascinating and important reading.

6 valence electrons. How many electrons will it gain? What is its oxidation number?

Using Oxidation Numbers

You can use the oxidation numbers of atoms to predict how atoms will combine and what the formula for the resulting compound will be. In order to do this, you must follow one important rule: *The sum of the oxidation numbers of the atoms in a compound must be zero.*

Sodium has an oxidation number of 1+. Chlorine has an oxidation number of 1−. One atom of sodium will bond with 1 atom of chlorine to form NaCl. Magnesium has an oxidation number of 2+. When magnesium bonds with chlorine, 1 atom of magnesium must combine with 2 atoms of chlorine, since each chlorine atom has an oxidation number of 1−. In other words, 2 atoms of chlorine are needed to gain the electrons lost by 1 atom of magnesium. The compound formed, magnesium chloride, contains 2 atoms of chlorine for each atom of magnesium. Its formula is $MgCl_2$. What would be the formula for calcium bromide? For sodium oxide? Remember the rule of oxidation numbers!

PROBLEM Solving

A Little Kitchen Chemistry

While preparing lunch one day in home economics class, Monduane and Juan noticed something unusual. As they added a dash of sugar to the vegetable oil they were using to make salad dressing, the sugar dissolved completely. But when they poured in a small amount of salt, as called for in the recipe they were following, the salt did not dissolve. Curious about their observation, the two chefs decided to repeat the process. They observed the same results. What, they wondered, could account for this difference in behavior? Would other substances show differences in their ability to dissolve in vegetable oil? In water?

Anxious to find the answers to their questions, the two students sought the advice of their teacher. The answer they received was simply this: Like dissolves in like.

Developing and Testing a Hypothesis

1. Help Monduane and Juan with their problem by suggesting a hypothesis.

2. Design an experiment to test your hypothesis. Remember to include a control.

3. What other applications does your hypothesis explain?

7–5 Section Review

1. What is an oxidation number?
2. How can the oxidation number of an atom be determined?
3. How is the oxidation number related to bond type?
4. What rule of oxidation numbers must be followed in writing chemical formulas?

Critical Thinking—*Making Predictions*

5. Predict the type of bond for each combination: Ca–Br, C–Cl, Ag–Ag, K–OH, SO_4^{2-}.

Laboratory Investigation

Properties of Ionic and Covalent Compounds

Problem

Do covalent compounds have different properties from ionic compounds?

Materials *(per group)*

safety goggles	distilled water
salt	(200 mL)
4 medium-sized	2 100-mL
test tubes	beakers
glass-marking	stirring rod
pencil	3 connecting
test-tube tongs	wires
Bunsen burner	light bulb socket
timer	light bulb
sugar	dry-cell battery
vegetable oil	

Procedure

1. Place a small sample of salt in a test tube. Label the test tube. Place an equal amount of sugar in another test tube. Label that test tube.

2. Using tongs, heat the test tube of salt over the flame of the Bunsen burner. **CAUTION:** *Observe all safety precautions when using a Bunsen burner.* Determine how long it takes for the salt to melt. Immediately stop heating when melting begins. Record the time.

3. Repeat step 2 using the sugar.

4. Half fill a test tube with vegetable oil. Place a small sample of salt in the test tube. Shake the test tube gently for about 10 seconds. Observe the results.

5. Repeat step 4 using the sugar.

6. Pour 50 mL of distilled water into a 100-mL beaker. Add some salt and stir until it is dissolved. To another 100-mL beaker add some sugar and stir until dissolved.

7. Using the beaker of salt water, set up a circuit as shown. **CAUTION:** *Exercise care when using electricity.* Observe the results. Repeat the procedure using the beaker of sugar water.

Observations

1. Does the salt or the sugar take a longer time to melt?

2. Does the salt dissolve in the vegetable oil? Does the sugar?

3. Which compound is a better conductor of electricity?

Analysis and Conclusions

1. Which substance do you think has a higher melting point? Explain.

2. Explain why one compound is a better conductor of electricity than the other.

3. How do the properties of each type of compound relate to their bonding?

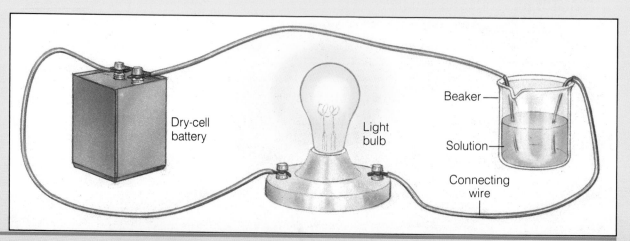

Study Guide

Summarizing Key Concepts

7–1 What Is Chemical Bonding?

▲ All matter is made of tiny particles called atoms.

▲ Chemical bonding is the combining of elements to form new substances.

▲ The atom consists of a positively charged nucleus containing protons and neutrons, and energy levels containing electrons.

▲ Bonding involves the electrons in the outer-most energy level, the valence electrons.

7–2 Ionic Bonds

▲ Ionic bonding involves a transfer of electrons and a formation of ions.

▲ Ionization energy is the amount of energy needed to remove an electron from a neutral atom. Electron affinity is the tendency of an atom to attract electrons.

▲ The placement of ions in an ionic com-pound results in a crystal lattice.

7–3 Covalent Bonds

▲ Covalent bonding involves a sharing of electrons.

▲ A molecule is the smallest unit of a covalently bonded substance.

▲ Network solids are substances whose molecules are very large because the atoms in the substance continue to bond to one another.

▲ A polyatomic ion is a group of covalently bonded atoms that acts like a single atom when it combines with other atoms.

7–4 Metallic Bonds

▲ The basis of metallic bonding is the sea of mobile electrons that surrounds the nuclei and is simultaneously attracted by them.

7–5 Predicting Types of Bonds

▲ The oxidation number, or combining capacity, of an atom refers to the number of electrons the atom gains, loses, or shares when it forms chemical bonds.

▲ The oxidation number of any atom can be determined by knowing the number of elec-trons in its outermost energy level.

Reviewing Key Terms

Define each term in a complete sentence.

7–1 What Is Chemical Bonding?
chemical bonding
valence electron

7–2 Ionic Bonds
ionic bonding
ion
ionization
ionization energy
electron affinity
crystal lattice

7–3 Covalent Bonds
covalent bonding
electron-dot diagram
diatomic element
molecule
network solid
polyatomic ion

7–4 Metallic Bonds
metallic bond

7–5 Predicting Types of Bonds
oxidation number

Chapter Review

Content Review

Multiple Choice

Choose the letter of the answer that best completes each statement.

1. Chemical bonding is the combining of elements to form new
   a. atoms.   c. substances.
   b. energy levels. d. electrons.
2. The center of an atom is called the
   a. electron.   c. octet.
   b. energy level.   d. nucleus.
3. The maximum number of electrons in the second energy level is
   a. 1.   b. 2.   c. 8.   d. 18.
4. Bonding that involves a transfer of electrons is called
   a. metallic.   c. ionic.
   b. covalent.   d. network.
5. Bonding that involves sharing of electrons within a molecule is called
   a. metallic.   c. covalent.
   b. ionic.   d. crystal.
6. The combination of atoms formed by covalent bonds is called a(an)
   a. element.   c. molecule.
   b. ion.   d. crystal.

7. Atoms that readily lose electrons have
   a. low ionization energy and low electron affinity.
   b. high ionization energy and low electron affinity.
   c. low ionization energy and high electron affinity.
   d. high ionization energy and high electron affinity.
8. An example of a polyatomic ion is
   a. SO_4^{2-} b. Ca^{2-} c. NaCl.   d. O_2.
9. A sea of electrons is the basis of bonding in
   a. metals.
   b. ionic substances.
   c. nonmetals.
   d. covalent substances.
10. Bonding between atoms on the left and right sides of the periodic table tends to be
    a. covalent.   c. metallic.
    b. ionic.   d. impossible.

True or False

If the statement is true, write "true." If it is false, change the underlined word or words to make the statement true.

1. Electrons in the outermost energy level are called <u>oxidation</u> electrons.
2. <u>Covalent</u> bonds form crystals.
3. The tendency of an atom to attract electrons is called <u>electron affinity</u>.
4. The combining capacity of an atom is described by its <u>crystal lattice</u>.
5. <u>Malleable</u> solids are substances whose molecules are very large.
6. A charged atom is called a <u>molecule</u>.
7. Bromine is a <u>diatomic</u> element.

Concept Mapping

Complete the following concept map for Section 7–1. Then construct a concept map for the entire chapter.

CHEMICAL BONDING

involves — Elements
forms — ?
determined by
Elements — made of — ?
? — consist of
? — contain — ?
Nucleus — holds — ? , ?

Concept Mastery

Discuss each of the following in a brief paragraph.

1. List the three types of chemical bonds and explain the differences among them.
2. Explain why the elements of Family 18 do not tend to form chemical bonds.
3. What are four properties of metals? How does the bonding in metals account for these properties?
4. How can you use the oxidation number of an atom to predict how it will bond?
5. Define the following structures that result from chemical bonds. Give one physical property of each.
   a. crystal lattice
   b. network solid
   c. covalently bonded solid

6. a. What is the difference between ionization energy and electron affinity?
   b. Why do atoms of high electron affinity tend to form ionic compounds with atoms of low ionization energy?
7. How can the periodic table be used to predict bond types?
8. Explain why the elements in Family 1 and in Family 17 are highly reactive.
9. How does chemical bonding account for the fact that although there are only 109 different elements, there are hundreds of thousands of different substances.
10. Describe the formation of a positive ion. Of a negative ion.

Critical Thinking and Problem Solving

Use the skills you have developed in this chapter to answer each of the following.

1. **Making predictions** Predict the type of bond formed by each pair of atoms. Explain your answers.
   a. Mg and Cl   c. I and I
   b. Na and Na   d. Li and I
2. **Making diagrams** Draw the electron configuration for a Period 2 atom from each of the following families of the periodic table: Family 1, 2, 13, 14, 15, 16, 17, 18.
3. **Identifying patterns** Use the periodic table to predict the ion that each atom will form when bonding.
   a. sulfur (S)   d. astatine (At)
   b. rubidium (Rb)   e. sodium (Na)
   c. argon (Ar)   f. aluminum (Al)
4. **Applying facts** Draw an electron-dot diagram for the following molecules and explain why they are stable: F_2, NF_3.
5. **Making predictions** Use the periodic table to predict the formulas for the compounds formed by each of the following pairs of atoms.
   a. K and S   c. Ba and S
   b. Li and F   d. Mg and N

6. **Applying concepts** Explain why a sodium ion is smaller than a sodium atom.
7. **Identifying patterns** As you can see in the accompanying photograph, a sheet of aluminum metal is being cut. The ability of a metal to be cut into sections without shattering is called sectility. How can you account for the sectility of aluminum?

8. **Using the writing process** Pretend you are an experienced electron about to give an orientation lecture for "incoming freshmen electrons." Prepare your speech, being sure to include important details about placement in the atom, ionic bonding, covalent bonding, and metallic bonding.

Chemical Reactions

Guide for Reading

After you read the following sections, you will be able to

8–1 Nature of Chemical Reactions
- Describe the characteristics of chemical reactions.

8–2 Chemical Equations
- Write balanced chemical equations.

8–3 Types of Chemical Reactions
- Classify chemical reactions.

8–4 Energy of Chemical Reactions
- Describe energy changes in exothermic and endothermic reactions.

8–5 Rates of Chemical Reactions
- Apply the collision theory to factors that affect reaction rate.

Fireworks flash brilliantly in the night sky over the dark waters of the harbor. It is Independence Day. Amidst the wonderful celebration stands a very special lady. She towers above the waters, the torch in her upraised hand reaching high into the sky. She is a symbol of freedom, justice, and the brotherhood of people of all nations. Her name is Liberty.

She has stood there for over a century. But the passage of time had not been especially kind to her. The copper of her outer structure, once bright and gleaming, had turned a dull gray-green. And the structure that supports her had begun to weaken. What had caused these changes? The answer has to do with the chemistry of atoms.

This chemistry, which damaged the Statue of Liberty, had also made possible the glorious restoration of this Lady in the Harbor. And the colorful fireworks lighting up the sky are products of the chemistry of atoms.

Chemical changes take place all the time, not just on the Fourth of July. And they take place everywhere, not just in New York Harbor. In this chapter you will learn about the nature of these chemical changes, many of which shape the world around you.

Journal *Activity*

You and Your World All around you, matter undergoes permanent changes. When bread is baked, for example, the dough changes forever. You can never turn the bread back into dough. A burned log can never be unburned. In your journal, describe several examples of substances that undergo changes and turn into new substances.

◀ *On July 4, 1986, fireworks lit up the sky in New York Harbor as the nation celebrated the one-hundredth birthday of the Statue of Liberty.*

8–1 Nature of Chemical Reactions

You have probably never given much thought to an ordinary book of matches. But stop for a minute and consider the fact that a single match in a book of matches can remain unchanged indefinitely. Yet if someone strikes that match, it bursts into a brilliant flame. And when that flame goes out, the appearance of the match will have changed forever. It can never be lighted again. The match has undergone a **chemical reaction.** What does this mean? **A chemical reaction is a process in which the physical and chemical properties of the original substances change as new substances with different physical and chemical properties are formed.** The burning of gasoline, the rusting of iron, and the baking of bread are all examples of chemical reactions.

Characteristics of Chemical Reactions

All chemical reactions share certain characteristics. One of these characteristics is that a chemical reaction always results in the formation of a new substance. The dark material on a burned match is a new substance. It is not the same substance that was originally on the match.

Another chemical reaction that you can easily observe occurs when a flashbulb lights. Because modern cameras have built-in flashes powered by a battery, you may not be familiar with traditional flashbulbs. At one time, however, all cameras used

Figure 8–1 *A burnt match has undergone a chemical reaction. So has rusted metal. Chemical reactions are also responsible for producing the vibrant colors of autumn leaves.*

flashbulbs similar to those shown in Figure 8–2 to provide the light necessary to take a photograph. Such flashbulbs can be used only once. You will now find out why.

Inside a flashbulb is a small coil of shiny gray metal. This metal is magnesium. The bulb is filled with the invisible gas oxygen. When the flashbulb is set off, the magnesium combines with the oxygen in a chemical reaction. During the reaction, energy is released in the form of light, and a fine white powder is produced. You can see this powder on the inside of the bulb. The powder is magnesium oxide, a compound with physical and chemical properties unlike those of the elements that were originally present—magnesium and oxygen. During the chemical reaction, the original substances are changed into a new substance. Now you can understand why traditional flashbulbs can be used only once.

The substances present before the change and the substances formed by the change are the two kinds of substances involved in a chemical reaction. A substance that enters into a chemical reaction is called a **reactant** (ree-AK-tuhnt). A substance that is produced by a chemical reaction is called a **product**. So a general description of a chemical reaction can be stated as reactants changing into products. In the example of the flashbulb, what are the reactants? What is the product?

In addition to changes in chemical and physical properties, chemical reactions always involve a

Flashes and Masses

1. Determine the mass of each of two unused flashbulbs. The masses should be the same.

2. Obtain a camera that uses flashbulbs. Put one flashbulb in the camera flash holder and flash the camera.

3. Allow the flashbulb to cool.

4. Again compare the masses of the used and the unused flashbulbs.

Does the mass of the used flashbulb change? What type of change has the used flashbulb undergone? How do you know?

■ What have you discovered about the mass of matter that undergoes a chemical reaction?

Figure 8–2 *Inside a flashbulb, oxygen surrounds a thin coil of magnesium. When the flashbulb is set off, a chemical reaction takes place in which magnesium combines with oxygen to form magnesium oxide. How can you tell a chemical reaction has occurred?*

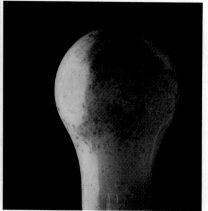

change in energy. Energy is either absorbed or released during a chemical reaction. For example, heat energy is absorbed when sugar changes into caramel. When gasoline burns, heat energy is released. Later in this chapter you will learn more about the energy changes that accompany chemical reactions.

Capacity to React

In order for a chemical reaction to occur, the reactants must have the ability to combine with other substances to form products. What accounts for the ability of different substances to undergo certain chemical reactions? In order to answer this question, you must think back to what you learned about atoms and bonding.

Atoms contain electrons, or negatively charged particles. Electrons are located in energy levels surrounding the nucleus, or center of the atom. The electrons in the outermost energy level are called the valence electrons. It is the valence electrons that are involved in chemical bonding. An atom forms chemical bonds with other atoms in order to complete its outermost energy level. As you learned in Chapter 7, having a complete outermost energy level is the most stable condition for an atom. An atom will try to fill its outermost energy level by gaining or losing electrons, or by sharing electrons. A chemical bond formed by the gain or loss of electrons is an ionic bond. A chemical bond formed by the sharing of electrons is a covalent bond.

The arrangement of electrons in an atom determines the ease with which the atom will form chemical bonds. An atom whose outermost energy level is

Figure 8–3 *The chemical reactions that occur within sea coral regulate the amount of carbon dioxide in the ocean. Why do you think this is important?*

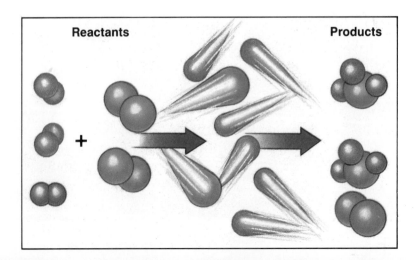

Figure 8–4 *During a chemical reaction, bonds between atoms of reactants are broken, atoms are rearranged, and new bonds in products are formed.*

Figure 8–5 *The tragic explosion of the* Hindenburg *on May 6, 1937, involved a chemical reaction. Hydrogen and oxygen combined explosively to form water. A much less dramatic chemical reaction is the corrosion of a metal such as copper, which was used to make the Statue of Liberty.*

full will not bond with other atoms. But an atom with an incomplete outermost energy level will bond readily. The ease with which an atom will form chemical bonds is known as the bonding capacity of an atom. The bonding capacity of an atom determines its ability to undergo chemical reactions. And the ability to undergo chemical reactions is an important chemical property.

During a chemical reaction, atoms can form molecules, molecules can break apart to form atoms, or molecules can react with other molecules. In any case, new substances are produced as existing bonds are broken, atoms are rearranged, and new bonds are formed.

8–1 Section Review

1. What is a chemical reaction?
2. What is a reactant? A product?
3. What is the relationship between the arrangement of electrons in an atom and the atom's chemical properties?

Critical Thinking—*Applying Concepts*

4. Cooking an egg until it is hard-boiled involves a chemical reaction. Cutting a piece of paper into a hundred little pieces does not involve a chemical reaction. Explain the difference between the two processes.

ACTIVITY
READING

The Loss of the Hindenburg

The air was thick with excitement on May 6, 1937, as the German airship *Hindenburg* headed toward its landing site in Lakehurst, New Jersey. The airship, held aloft by 210,000 cubic meters of hydrogen gas, was completing another transatlantic voyage. But before it could moor, the excitement turned to horror as the ship burst into flames. To learn about the *Hindenburg* disaster, read *Horror Overhead* by Richard A. Boning.

CAREERS

Food Chemist

Today, most methods of food processing involve chemical reactions. **Food chemists** use their knowledge of chemistry to develop these food processing methods.

Some food chemists develop new foods or new flavors. Others develop improved packaging and storage methods for foods.

If you are interested in a career as a food chemist, write to the Institute of Food Technology, Suite 300, 221 North LaSalle Street, Chicago, IL 60601.

8-2 Chemical Equations

It is important to be able to describe the details of a chemical reaction—how the reactants changed into the products. This involves indicating all the individual atoms involved in the reaction. One way of doing this is to use words. But describing a chemical reaction with words can be awkward. Many atoms may be involved, and the changes may be complicated.

For example, consider the flashbulb reaction described earlier. A word equation for this reaction would be: Magnesium combines with oxygen to form magnesium oxide and give off energy in the form of light. You could shorten this sentence by saying: Magnesium and oxygen form magnesium oxide and light energy.

Chemists have developed a more convenient way to represent a chemical reaction. Using symbols to represent elements and formulas to represent compounds, a chemical reaction can be described by a **chemical equation.** Recall that a chemical equation is an expression in which symbols and formulas are used to represent a chemical reaction.

In order to write a chemical equation, you must first write the correct chemical symbols or formulas for the reactants and products. Then you need to show that certain substances combine. This is done with the use of a + sign, which replaces the word and. Between the reactants and the products, you need to draw an arrow to show that the reactants have changed into the products. The arrow, which is read "yields," takes the place of an equal sign. It also shows the direction of the chemical change. The chemical equation for the flashbulb reaction can now be written:

$$Mg + O_2 \longrightarrow MgO + Energy$$

$$\text{Magnesium} + \text{Oxygen} \longrightarrow \text{Magnesium oxide} + \text{Energy}$$

Conservation of Mass

Chemists have long known that atoms can be neither created nor destroyed during a chemical reaction. In other words, the number of atoms of each

Figure 2-6 *Whether a chemical reaction is involved in the use of pesticides to protect crops, the breakdown of an antacid tablet in a glass of water, or the awesome explosion of fireworks, one characteristic is always the same: Mass is never lost. What law describes this observation?*

element must be the same before and after the chemical reaction (that is, the number of atoms remains the same on both sides of the arrow in a chemical equation). The changes that occur during any chemical reaction involve only the rearrangement of atoms, not their production or destruction.

Every atom has a particular mass. Because the number of atoms of each element remains the same, mass can never change in a chemical reaction. The total mass of the reactants must equal the total mass of the products. No mass is lost or gained. **The observation that mass remains constant in a chemical reaction is known as the law of conservation of mass**.

Balancing Chemical Equations

The law of conservation of mass must be taken into account when writing a chemical equation for a chemical reaction. A chemical equation must show that atoms are neither created nor destroyed. The number of atoms of each element must be the same on both sides of the equation.

Pocketful of Posies, p. 727

An equation in which the number of atoms of each element is the same on both sides of the equation is called a balanced chemical equation. Let's go back to the chemical equation for the flashbulb reaction:

$$Mg + O_2 \longrightarrow MgO + Energy$$

Is this a balanced chemical equation? Is the law of conservation of mass observed?

How many magnesium atoms do you count on the left side of the equation? You should count 1. And on the right side? You should count 1. Now try the same thing for oxygen. There are 2 oxygen atoms on the left but only 1 on the right. This cannot be correct because atoms can be neither created nor destroyed during a chemical reaction. How, then, can you make the number of atoms of each element the same on both sides of the equation?

One thing you cannot do to balance an equation is change a subscript. As you should remember from Chapter 7, a subscript is a small number placed to the lower right of a symbol. Changing the subscript would mean changing the substance. You can, however, change the number of atoms or molecules of each substance involved in the chemical reaction. You can do this by placing a number known as a coefficient (koh-uh-FIHSH-uhnt) in front of the appropriate symbols and formulas. Suppose the coefficient 3 is placed in front of a molecule of oxygen. It would be written as $3O_2$, and it would mean that there are 6 atoms of oxygen (3 molecules of 2 atoms each).

Now let's return to the flashbulb equation. To balance this equation, you must represent more than 1 atom of oxygen on the product side of the equation. If you place a coefficient of 2 in front of the formula for magnesium oxide, you will have 2 molecules of MgO. So you will have 2 atoms of oxygen. But you will also have 2 atoms of magnesium on the product side and only 1 atom of magnesium on the reactant side. So you must add a coefficient of 2 to the magnesium on the reactant side of the equation. There—the equation is balanced:

$$2\,Mg + O_2 \longrightarrow 2\,MgO + Energy$$

Figure 8–7 *These are the steps to follow in balancing a chemical equation. What law must a chemical equation obey?*

BALANCING EQUATIONS

1. Write a chemical equation with correct symbols and formulas.

$$H_2 + O_2 \rightarrow H_2O$$

2. Count the number of atoms of each element on each side of the arrow.

3. Balance atoms by using coefficients.

$$2H_2 + O_2 \rightarrow 2H_2O$$

4. Check your work by counting atoms of each element.

206

If you count atoms again, you will find 2 magnesium atoms on each side of the equation, as well as 2 oxygen atoms. The equation can be read: 2 atoms of magnesium combine with 1 molecule of oxygen to yield 2 molecules of magnesium oxide. Notice that when no coefficient is written, such as in front of the molecule of oxygen, the number is understood to be 1. Remember that to balance a chemical equation, you can change coefficients but never symbols or formulas.

Chemical equations are actually easy to write and balance. Follow the rules in Figure 8–7 and those listed here.

1. Write a word equation and then a chemical equation for the reaction. Make sure the symbols and formulas for reactants and products are correct.
2. Count the number of atoms of each element on each side of the arrow. If the numbers are the same, the equation is balanced.
3. If the number of atoms of each element is not the same on both sides of the arrow, you must balance the equation by using coefficients. Put a coefficient in front of a symbol or formula so that the number of atoms of that substance is the same on both sides of the arrow. Continue this procedure until you have balanced all the atoms.
4. Check your work by counting the atoms of each element to make sure they are the same on both sides of the equation.

ACTIVITY

CALCULATING

A Balancing Act

Rewrite each of the following equations on a sheet of paper and balance each.

$BaCl_2 + H_2SO_4 \rightarrow BaSO_4 + HCl$

$P + O_2 \rightarrow P_4O_{10}$

$KClO_3 \rightarrow KCl + O_2$

$C_3H_8 + O_2 \rightarrow CO_2 + H_2O$

$Cu + AgNO_3 \rightarrow Cu(NO_3)_2 + Ag$

8–2 Section Review

1. What is a chemical equation?
2. State the law of conservation of mass.
3. Why must a chemical equation be balanced?
4. Write a balanced chemical equation for the reaction between sodium and oxygen to form sodium oxide, Na_2O.
5. Why can't you change symbols, formulas, or subscripts in order to balance a chemical equation?

Connection—*Mathematics*

6. How are chemical equations related to equations found in mathematics?

PROBLEM ??? Solving

The Silverware Mystery

The Smith family was about to sit down to a special dinner in honor of Mr. Smith's birthday when the telephone rang. The voice on the other end of the telephone informed Mrs. Smith that the family had won a contest. The prize was a fabulous trip that began immediately.

The family excitedly packed suitcases and prepared to leave the house. They wrapped their dinner and put it into the freezer. But they decided to leave the table as it was—beautifully arranged with flowers, china dishes, and silverware. They locked the doors and went on their way!

Two weeks later, after a wonderful trip, the Smiths returned. As they entered the dining room, they noticed something odd. The once shiny silver forks, knives, and spoons were now a dull, blackish-gray color. What could have happened? Could the silverware be returned to its original condition? Being a helpful neighbor, you decide to assist the Smiths in solving the silverware mystery in the following way.

■ You tell them that it's all a matter of chemistry.

■ You give them a rubber band, which contains sulfur, to experiment with.

■ You ask them to think about what the air and the rubber band have in common.

Reaching Conclusions

1. What has happened to the Smiths' silverware?

2. How can it be returned to its original condition?

Guide for Reading

Focus on this question as you read.

▶ *What are the four types of chemical reactions?*

8–3 Types of Chemical Reactions

There are billions of different chemical reactions. In some reactions, elements combine to form compounds. In other reactions, compounds break down into elements. And in still other reactions, one element replaces another.

Chemists have identified four general types of reactions: synthesis, decomposition, single replacement, and double replacement. In each type of reaction, atoms are being rearranged and substances are being changed in a specific way.

Synthesis Reaction

In a **synthesis** (SIHN-thuh-sihs) **reaction**, two or more simple substances combine to form a new, more complex substance. So that you can easily identify synthesis reactions, it may be helpful for you to remember the form these reactions always take:

$$A + B \longrightarrow C$$

For example, the reaction between sodium and chlorine to form sodium chloride is a synthesis reaction:

$$2Na + Cl_2 \longrightarrow 2NaCl$$

Sodium + Chlorine $\longrightarrow$ Sodium chloride

Reactions involving the corrosion of metals are synthesis reactions. The rusting of iron involves the chemical combination of iron with oxygen to form iron oxide. Reactions in which a substance burns in oxygen are often synthesis reactions. Think back to the reaction that occurs in a flashbulb.

Decomposition Reaction

In a **decomposition reaction**, a complex substance breaks down into two or more simpler substances. Decomposition reactions are the reverse of synthesis reactions. Decomposition reactions take the form:

$$C \longrightarrow A + B$$

ACTIVITY

DISCOVERING

Preventing a Chemical Reaction

1. Obtain two large nails. Paint one nail and let it dry. Do not paint the other nail.

2. Pour a little water into a jar or beaker.

3. Stand both nails in the container of water. Cover the container and let it stand for several days. Compare the appearance of the nails.

Describe what happens to each nail. Give a reason for your observations. Write a word equation for any reaction that has occurred.

■ What effect does paint have on the rusting process of a nail?

Figure 8–8 *A reaction in which a substance burns in oxygen is called a combustion reaction. Why do you think smoking is not permitted in areas where oxygen is being administered?*

Figure 8–9 *Oxygen was discovered by Joseph Priestley in 1774 through a decomposition reaction in which mercury(II) oxide was broken down into its elements. Another decomposition reaction occurs during the explosion of dynamite.*

Popcorn Hop, p. 728

ACTIVITY

DOING

The Disappearing Coin

1. Place a small piece of aluminum foil in a glass filled with water.

2. Position a copper coin, such as a penny, on top of the foil.

3. Let the glass stand for one day and observe what happens.

Describe the appearance of the water at the end of the experiment. Of the aluminum foil. Of the coin.

What chemical reaction has taken place? How do you know?

One common decomposition reaction is the decomposition of water in the presence of electricity. The balanced equation for this reaction is

$$2 \text{ H}_2\text{O} \longrightarrow 2 \text{ H}_2 + \text{O}_2$$
$$\textbf{Water} \longrightarrow \textbf{Hydrogen} + \textbf{Oxygen}$$

Another decomposition occurs when marble (calcium carbonate) decomposes into calcium oxide and carbon dioxide. Write an equation for this reaction.

Single-Replacement Reaction

In a **single-replacement reaction**, an uncombined element replaces an element that is part of a compound. These reactions take the form:

$$A + BX \longrightarrow AX + B$$

Notice that the atom represented by the letter X switches its partner from B to A.

An example of a single-replacement reaction is the reaction between sodium and water. The very active metal sodium must be stored in oil, not water. When it comes in contact with water, it reacts explosively. The sodium replaces the hydrogen in the water and releases lots of energy. The balanced equation for the reaction of sodium with water is:

$$2\text{Na} + 2\text{H}_2\text{O} \longrightarrow 2\text{NaOH} + \text{H}_2$$
$$\textbf{Sodium} + \textbf{Water} \longrightarrow \textbf{Sodium hydroxide} + \textbf{Hydrogen}$$

Most single-replacement reactions, however, do not cause explosions.

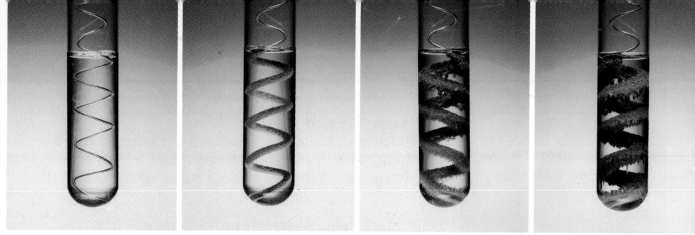

Double-Replacement Reaction

In a **double-replacement reaction**, different atoms in two different compounds replace each other. In other words, two compounds react to form two new compounds. These reactions take the form:

$$AX + BY \longrightarrow AY + BX$$

Notice that in this reaction the atoms represented by both the letters X and Y switch partners.

If you have ever had an upset stomach, you may have taken a medicine that contained the compound magnesium carbonate. This compound reacts with the hydrochloric acid in your stomach in the following way:

$$MgCO_3 + 2\ HCl \longrightarrow MgCl_2 + H_2CO_3$$

Magnesium carbonate + Hydrochloric acid $\longrightarrow$ **Magnesium chloride + Carbonic acid**

In this double-replacement reaction, the magnesium and hydrogen replace each other, or switch partners. One product is magnesium chloride, a harmless compound. The other product is carbonic acid. Do you remember what happens to carbonic acid? It decomposes into water and carbon dioxide. Your stomachache goes away because instead of too much acid, there is now water and carbon dioxide. You owe your relief to this double-replacement reaction:

$$MgCO_3 + 2HCl \longrightarrow MgCl_2 + H_2O + CO_2$$

Magnesium carbonate + Hydrochloric acid $\longrightarrow$ **Magnesium chloride + Water + Carbon dioxide**

Figure 8–10 *Because copper is a more active metal than silver, it can replace the silver in silver nitrate. In these four photos, you can see the gradual buildup of silver metal on the coil. What type of reaction is this? What other indication is there that a chemical change is taking place?*

ACTIVITY

DISCOVERING

Double-Replacement Reaction

1. Place a small amount of baking soda in a glass beaker or jar.

2. Pour some vinegar on the baking soda. Observe what happens.

Baking soda is sodium hydrogen carbonate, $NaHCO_3$. Vinegar is acetic acid, $HC_2H_3O_2$. Write the chemical equation for this reaction. What gas is produced?

■ How could you test for the presence of this gas?

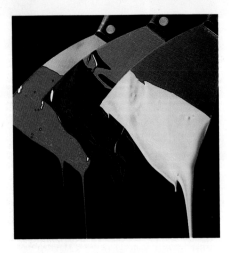

Figure 8-11 *Paints are chemical compounds produced by double-replacement reactions. What is the general form of a double-replacement reaction?*

8-3 Section Review

1. Name the four types of reactions.
2. What is the difference between a synthesis reaction and a decomposition reaction?
3. What is a single-replacement reaction? A double-replacement reaction?

Critical Thinking—*Identifying Reactions*

4. What type of reaction is represented by each of the following equations:
   a. $CaCO_3 \longrightarrow CaO + CO_2$
   b. $C + O_2 \longrightarrow CO_2$
   c. $BaBr_2 + K_2SO_4 \longrightarrow 2KBr + BaSO_4$

Guide for Reading

Focus on this question as you read.

▶ *How are chemical reactions classified according to energy changes?*

8-4 Energy of Chemical Reactions

Energy is always involved in a chemical reaction. Sometimes energy is released, or given off, as the reaction takes place. Sometimes energy is absorbed. **Based on the type of energy change involved, chemical reactions are classified as either exothermic or endothermic reactions.**

In either type of reaction, energy is neither created nor destroyed. It merely changes position or form. The energy released or absorbed usually takes the form of heat or visible light.

Exothermic Reactions

A chemical reaction in which energy is released is an **exothermic** (ek-soh-THER-mihk) **reaction.** The word exothermic comes from the root -*thermic,* which refers to heat, and the prefix *exo-,* which means out of. Heat comes out of, or is released from, a reacting substance during an exothermic reaction. A reaction that involves burning, or a combustion reaction, is an example of an exothermic reaction. The combustion of methane gas, which occurs in a gas stove, releases a large amount of heat energy.

The energy that is released in an exothermic reaction was originally stored in the molecules of the

Figure 8-12 *The explosion of a firecracker is an exothermic reaction. Why is this one reason that firecrackers are dangerous?*

reactants. Because the energy is released during the reaction, the molecules of the products do not receive this energy. So the energy of the products is less than the energy of the reactants. Energy diagrams, such as the ones shown in Figure 8–14, can be used to show the energy change in a reaction. Note that in an exothermic reaction, the reactants are higher in energy than the products are.

Endothermic Reactions

A chemical reaction in which energy is absorbed is an **endothermic reaction**. The prefix *endo-* means into. During an endothermic reaction, energy is taken into a reacting substance. The energy absorbed during an endothermic reaction is usually in the form of heat or light. The decomposition of sodium chloride, or table salt, is an endothermic reaction. It requires the absorption of electric energy.

The energy that is absorbed in an endothermic reaction is now stored in the molecules of the products. So the energy of the products is more than the energy of the reactants. See Figure 8–14 again.

Activation Energy

The total energy released or absorbed by a chemical reaction does not tell the whole story about the energy changes involved in the reaction. In order for the reactants to form products, the molecules of the reactants must combine to form a short-lived, high-energy, extremely unstable molecule. The atoms of this molecule are then rearranged to form products. This process requires energy. The molecules of

Figure 8–13 *The cooking of pancakes is an endothermic reaction. Why?*

Toasting to Good Health, p. 729

Figure 8–14 *An energy diagram for an exothermic reaction indicates that heat is released during the reaction. Heat is absorbed during an endothermic reaction, as shown by its energy diagram. How does the heat content of products and reactants compare for each type of reaction?*

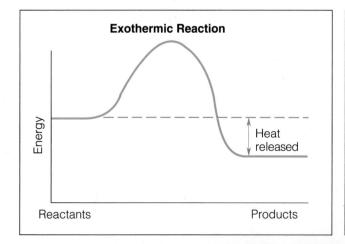

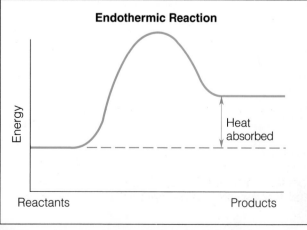

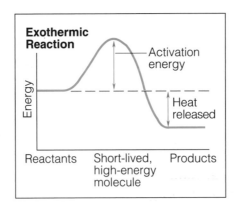

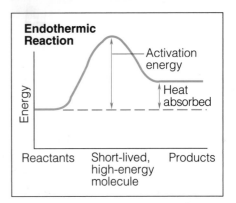

Figure 8–15 *As you can see by these energy diagrams, both an exothermic reaction and an endothermic reaction require activation energy.*

the reactants must "climb" to the top of an "energy hill" before they can form products. The energy needed to "climb" to the top of the "energy hill" is called **activation energy**. After the reactants have absorbed this activation energy, they can "slide down" the energy hill to form products.

An energy diagram indicates more than whether a reaction is exothermic or endothermic. An energy diagram shows the activation energy of the reaction. Figure 8–15 shows an energy diagram for both an exothermic reaction and an endothermic reaction.

All chemical reactions require activation energy. Even an exothermic reaction such as the burning of a match requires activation energy. In order to light a match, it must first be struck. The friction of the match against the striking pad provides the necessary activation energy.

ACTIVITY
THINKING

Kitchen Chemistry

Many interesting chemical reactions occur during various cooking processes. Observe someone preparing and cooking different kinds of food. Record your observations of the changes that take place in the properties of the food. Are the changes physical or chemical? Endothermic or exothermic? Synthesis, decomposition, or replacement?

Using books and other reference materials in the library, find out more about each of the chemical reactions you have listed.

8–4 Section Review

1. What is an exothermic reaction? An endothermic reaction?
2. On which side should the energy term be written in an equation representing an endothermic reaction? In an equation representing an exothermic reaction?
3. Compare the energy content of reactants and products in an exothermic reaction. In an endothermic reaction.

Connection—*You and Your World*
4. Using what you know about activation energy, explain why a match will not light if it is not struck hard enough.

214

8–5 Rates of Chemical Reactions

Guide for Reading

Focus on this question as you read.

▶ How is the collision theory related to the factors affecting reaction rate?

The complete burning of a thick log can take many hours. Yet if the log is ground into fine sawdust, the burning can take place at dangerously high speeds. In fact, if the dust is spread through the air, the burning can produce an explosion! In both these processes, the same reaction is taking place. The various substances in the wood are combining with oxygen. One reaction, however, proceeds at a faster speed than the other one does. What causes the differences in reaction times?

In order to explain differences in reaction time, chemists must study **kinetics**. Kinetics is the study of **reaction rates**. The rate of a reaction is a measure of how quickly reactants turn into products. Reaction rates depend on a number of factors, which you will now read about.

Collision Theory

You learned that chemical reactions occur when bonds between atoms are broken, the atoms are rearranged, and new bonds are formed. In order for this process to occur, particles must collide. As two particles approach each other, they begin to interact. During this interaction, old bonds may be broken and new bonds formed. For a reaction to occur, however, particles must collide at precisely the correct angle with the proper amount of energy. The more collisions that occur under these conditions, the faster the rate of the chemical reaction.

A theory known as the **collision theory** relates particle collisions to reaction rate. **According to the collision theory, the rate of a reaction is affected by four factors: concentration, surface area, temperature, and catalysts.**

Concentration

The concentration of a substance is a measure of the amount of that substance in a given unit of volume. A high concentration of reactants means there

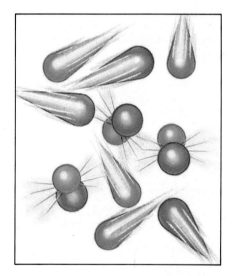

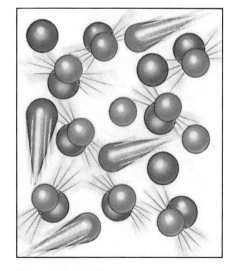

Figure 8–16 *Collisions of molecules increase when there are more molecules. The number of molecules per unit volume is called concentration. What is the relationship between the concentration of reactants and reaction rate?*

Figure 8-17 *As bellows are pumped, more oxygen is supplied to the fire and the rate of reaction increases. Why are forest fires particularly dangerous when weather conditions nearby include high winds?*

ACTIVITY

DISCOVERING

Rate of Reaction

1. Obtain two sugar cubes. Grind one of the cubes into powder.

2. Fill two clear-plastic cups with warm tap water.

3. As close to the same time as possible, put the whole sugar cube into one cup of water and the powdered sugar into the other.

4. Stir each cup briefly every 30 seconds. Observe the time required for the complete dissolving of sugar in each cup.

How do the times compare? Which reaction rate is faster?

■ What important relationship regarding reaction rate have you discovered?

are a great many particles per unit volume. So there are more particles of reactants available for collisions. More collisions occur and more products are formed in a certain amount of time. What does a low concentration of reactants mean?

Generally, most chemical reactions proceed at a faster rate if the concentration of the reactants is increased. A decrease in the concentration of the reactants decreases the rate of reaction. For example, a highly concentrated solution of sodium hydroxide (NaOH), or lye, will react more quickly to clear a clogged drain than will a less concentrated lye solution. Why would the rate of burning charcoal be increased by blowing on the fire?

Surface Area

When one of the reactants in a chemical reaction is a solid, the rate of reaction can be increased by breaking the solid into smaller pieces. This increases the surface area of the reactant. Surface area refers to how much of a material is exposed. An increase in surface area increases the collisions between reacting particles.

A given quantity of wood burns faster as sawdust than it does as logs. Sawdust has a much greater surface area exposed to air than do the logs. So oxygen particles from the air can collide with more wood particles per second. The reaction rate is increased.

Figure 8-18 *It may seem hard to believe that grains of wheat or even dust can cause the immense destruction you see here. But an explosion at a grain elevator is an ever-present danger because a chemical reaction can occur almost instantaneously. What reaction-rate factor is responsible for such an explosion?*

Many medicines are produced in the form of a fine powder or many small crystals. Medicine in this form is often more effective than the same medicine in tablet form. Do you know why? Tablets dissolve in the stomach and enter the bloodstream at a slower rate. How does the collision theory account for the fact that fine crystals of table salt dissolve more quickly in water than do large crystals of rock salt?

Temperature

An increase in temperature generally increases the rate of a reaction. Here again the collision theory provides an explanation for this fact. Particles are constantly in motion. Temperature is a measure of the energy of their motion. Particles at a high temperature have more energy of motion than do particles at a low temperature. Particles at a high temperature move faster than do particles at a low temperature. So particles at a high temperature collide more frequently. They also collide with greater energy. This increase in the rate and energy of collisions affects the reaction rate. More particles of reactants are able to gain the activation energy needed to form products. So reaction rate is increased.

At room temperature, the rates of many chemical reactions roughly double or triple with a rise in temperature of 10°C. How does this fact explain the use of refrigeration to keep foods from spoiling?

Catalysts

Some chemical reactions take place very slowly. The reactions involved with digesting a cookie are examples. In fact, if these reactions proceeded at their normal rate, it could take weeks to digest one cookie! Fortunately, certain substances speed up the rate of a chemical reaction. These substances are **catalysts**. A catalyst is a substance that increases the rate of a reaction but is not itself changed by the reaction. Although a catalyst alters the reaction, it can be recovered at the end of the reaction.

How does a catalyst change the rate of a reaction if it is not changed by the reaction? Again, the explanation is based on the collision theory. Reactions often involve a series of steps. A catalyst changes one

Figure 8–19 *These glow-in-the-dark sticks are called Cyalume light sticks. When a light stick is placed in hot water (left), it glows more brightly than when placed in cold water (right). The reaction that causes a stick to glow is faster and produces more light at higher temperatures.*

ACTIVITY
DISCOVERING

Temperature and Reaction Rate

1. Fill one glass with cold water and another with hot water.

2. Drop a seltzer tablet into each glass of water and observe the reactions that occur.

Is there any noticeable difference in the two reactions?

■ What relationship regarding reaction rate does this activity illustrate?

■ Does this activity prove that a temperature difference always has the same effect?

Figure 8–20 *A catalyst changes the rate of a chemical reaction without itself being changed by the reaction. According to this energy diagram, how does a catalyst affect the rate of a reaction?*

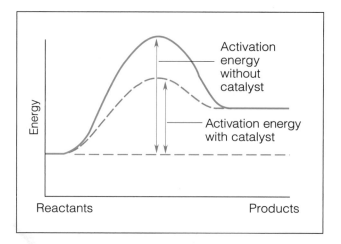

Figure 8–21 *This collection of colorful pellets actually contains catalysts used in industry. The blue catalyst in front, for example, is used in the reactions that remove sulfur and nitrogen from crude oil.*

or more of the steps. A catalyst produces a different, lower energy path for the reaction. In other words, it lowers the "energy hill," or activation energy. A decrease in the activation energy needed for the reaction allows more reactant particles to form products. Collisions need not be so energetic. Therefore, more collisions are successful at producing products.

A catalyst is usually involved in one or more of the early steps in a reaction. The catalyst is, however, re-formed during a later step. This explains why a catalyst can be recovered at the end of the reaction.

Catalysts are used in many chemical processes. Certain automobiles contain devices called catalytic converters. A catalytic converter speeds up the reaction that changes the harmful gases produced by automobile engines into harmless ones. Some of the most important catalysts are those found in your body. Catalysts in the body are called enzymes. Each enzyme increases the rate of a specific reaction involved in the body's metabolism.

8–5 Section Review

1. What is reaction rate?
2. How is reaction rate related to collision theory?
3. Name four factors that affect reaction rate.
4. How does collision theory explain the effect of a decrease in temperature on the reaction rate?

Critical Thinking—*Drawing Conclusions*
5. Do you think there is a need for catalysts that slow down a reaction? Give some examples.

CONNECTIONS

Chemical Reactions That Destroy the Environment

Stop and look around for a moment. Do you notice that you are surrounded by all sorts of devices that make life easier and more comfortable? There are cars, airplanes, air conditioners, televisions, refrigerators, radios, and industrial machinery—to mention a few. Where do all these inventions get their energy? Most of it comes from the burning of coal and petroleum.

Coal and petroleum are fuels that contain the element carbon. When they burn (a combustion reaction), carbon dioxide (CO_2) is released. The combustion of coal and petroleum releases about 20 billion tons of carbon dioxide into the atmosphere every year. And carbon dioxide in the atmosphere is of great consequence. The Earth and its inhabitants send a great deal of heat out through the atmosphere toward space. It is vital that this heat escapes the Earth's atmosphere. If it does not, the surface of the Earth will heat up, changing climates significantly. Although carbon dioxide is only a small part of the atmosphere, it has the ability to trap heat near the surface of the Earth. By absorbing heat released from the Earth, carbon dioxide acts like the glass over a greenhouse. For this reason, the warming of the Earth by carbon dioxide and other heat-trapping gases is referred to as the

greenhouse effect. Some climatologists (scientists who study climate) believe that the buildup of carbon dioxide and other gases has already begun to change the climate of our planet. They cite as evidence the fact that the six warmest years on record were all in the 1980s. The trend is continuing into the 1990s.

One long-term outcome of the warming of the Earth (global warming) is the melting of the polar icecaps. As the icecaps melt because of higher temperatures, the sea level rises, causing certain coastal areas to be flooded and destroyed. Another effect is a shift in the distribution of rainfall over the various continents. Eventually, heat and drought could become commonplace over the vast region of the United States that now provides most of the world's agricultural products.

In order to minimize and possibly reverse the greenhouse effect, new energy sources that do not release carbon dioxide into the atmosphere must be developed. Energy must also be conserved. What role do you think you can play in making sure chemical reactions do not further destroy the environment?

Laboratory Investigation

Determining Reaction Rate

Problem

How does concentration affect reaction rate?

Materials *(per group)*

safety goggles
2 graduated cylinders
120 mL Solution A
3 250-mL beakers
distilled water at room temperature
90 mL Solution B
stirring rod
sheet of white paper
stopwatch or watch with a sweep second
    hand

Procedure 🧪 🧰 👁

1. Carefully measure 60 mL of Solution A and pour it into a 250-mL beaker. Add 10 mL of distilled water and stir.
2. Carefully measure 30 mL of Solution B and pour it into a second beaker. Place the beaker of Solution B on a sheet of white paper in order to see the color change more easily.
3. Add the 70 mL of Solution A-water mixture to Solution B. Stir rapidly. Record the time it takes for the reaction to occur.
4. Rinse and dry the reaction beaker.
5. Repeat the procedure using the other amounts shown in the data table.

Observations

Solution A (mL)	Distilled Water Added to Solution A (mL)	Solution B (mL)	Reaction Time (sec)
60	10	30	
40	30	30	
20	50	30	

1. What visible indication is there that a chemical reaction is occurring?
2. What is the effect of adding more distilled water on the concentration of Solution A?
3. What happens to reaction time as more distilled water is added to Solution A?
4. Make a graph of your observations by plotting time along the X axis and volume of Solution A along the Y axis.

Analysis and Conclusions

1. How does concentration affect reaction rate?
2. Does your graph support your answer to question 1? Explain why.
3. What would a graph look like if time were plotted along the X axis and volume of distilled water added to Solution A were plotted along the Y axis?
4. In this investigation, what is the variable? The control?
5. **On Your Own** Enhance your graph by testing other concentrations.

Study Guide

Summarizing Key Concepts

8–1 Nature of Chemical Reactions

▲ When a chemical reaction occurs, there is always a change in the properties and the energy of the substances.

▲ A reactant is a substance that enters into a chemical reaction. A product is a substance that is produced by a chemical reaction.

8–2 Chemical Equations

▲ The law of conservation of mass states that matter can be neither created nor destroyed in a chemical reaction.

▲ A chemical equation that has the same number of atoms of each element on both sides of the arrow is a balanced equation.

8–3 Types of Chemical Reactions

▲ In a synthesis reaction, two or more simple substances combine to form a new, more complex substance.

▲ In a decomposition reaction, a complex substance breaks down into two or more simpler substances.

▲ In a single-replacement reaction, an uncombined element replaces an element that is part of a compound.

▲ In a double-replacement reaction, different atoms in two different compounds replace each other.

8–4 Energy of Chemical Reactions

▲ Energy is released in an exothermic reaction. Energy is absorbed in an endothermic reaction.

▲ In order for reactants to form products, activation energy is needed.

8–5 Rates of Chemical Reactions

▲ The rate of a reaction is a measure of how quickly reactants turn into products.

▲ An increase in the concentration of reactants increases the rate of a reaction.

▲ An increase in the surface area of reactants increases the rate of reaction.

▲ An increase in temperature generally increases the rate of a reaction.

Reviewing Key Terms

Define each term in a complete sentence.

8–1 Nature of Chemical Reactions
chemical reaction
reactant
product

8–2 Chemical Equations
chemical equation

8–3 Types of Chemical Reactions
synthesis reaction
decomposition reaction

single-replacement reaction
double-replacement reaction

8–4 Energy of Chemical Reactions
exothermic reaction
endothermic reaction
activation energy

8–5 Rates of Chemical Reactions
kinetics
reaction rate
collision theory
catalyst

Chapter Review

Content Review

Multiple Choice

Choose the letter of the answer that best completes each statement.

1. In a balanced chemical equation,
   a. atoms are conserved.
   b. molecules are equal.
   c. coefficients are equal.
   d. energy is not conserved.
2. Two or more substances combine to form one substance in a
   a. decomposition reaction.
   b. double-replacement reaction.
   c. single-replacement reaction.
   d. synthesis reaction.
3. In an endothermic reaction, heat is
   a. absorbed.   c. destroyed.
   b. released.   d. conserved.
4. The energy required for reactants to form products is called
   a. energy of motion.
   b. potential energy.
   c. activation energy.
   d. synthetic energy.
5. The substances to the left of the arrow in a chemical equation are called
   a. coefficients.   c. subscripts.
   b. products.   d. reactants.
6. An atom's ability to undergo chemical reactions is determined by
   a. protons.   c. innermost electrons.
   b. neutrons.   d. outermost electrons.
7. The rate of a chemical reaction can be increased by
   a. decreasing concentration.
   b. increasing surface area.
   c. removing a catalyst.
   d. all of these.
8. Adding a catalyst to a reaction increases its rate by
   a. increasing molecular motion.
   b. decreasing molecular motion.
   c. lowering activation energy.
   d. increasing concentration.

True or False

If the statement is true, write "true." If it is false, change the underlined word or words to make the statement true.

1. The substances formed as a result of a chemical reaction are called <u>reactants</u>.
2. A number written in front of a chemical symbol or formula is a(an) <u>coefficient</u>.
3. In a <u>synthesis</u> reaction, complex substances form simpler substances.
4. The formation of carbon dioxide during combustion of a fuel is an example of a <u>decomposition</u> reaction.
5. In an exothermic reaction, products have <u>more</u> energy than reactants.
6. The study of the rates of chemical reactions is <u>kinetics</u>.
7. The <u>collision theory</u> can be used to account for the factors that affect reaction rates.

Concept Mapping

Complete the following concept map for Section 8–2. Then construct a concept map for the entire chapter.

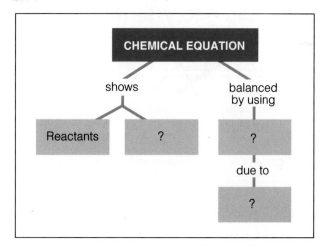

Concept Mastery

Discuss each of the following in a brief paragraph.

1. What is a chemical reaction? Why do substances react chemically?
2. Describe what a chemical equation is.
3. State the law of conservation of mass and explain its role in chemical equations.
4. What is a coefficient? What is the difference between H_2O_2 and $2H_2O$?
5. Describe each of the four types of chemical reactions. Include an equation showing the general form for each.
6. What is activation energy? How is it affected by a catalyst?
7. Explain how the energy content of the products of a reaction compares with that of the reactants when the reaction is exothermic. When it is endothermic.
8. Use the collision theory to explain the effects on reaction rate of increased concentration, catalysts, and increased surface area.
9. Give two reasons why collisions between molecules of reactants may not be effective in forming products.

Critical Thinking and Problem Solving

Use the skills you have developed in this chapter to answer each of the following.

1. **Making calculations** Balance the following equations:
   a. $PbO_2 \longrightarrow PbO + O_2$
   b. $Ca + H_2O \longrightarrow Ca(OH)_2 + H_2$
   c. $Zn + S \longrightarrow ZnS$
   d. $BaCl_2 + Na_2SO_4 \longrightarrow BaSO_4 + NaCl$
   e. $Al + Fe_2O_3 \longrightarrow Al_2O_3 + Fe$
   f. $C_{12}H_{22}O_{11} \longrightarrow C + H_2O$
2. **Classifying reactions** Identify the general type of reaction represented by each equation. Explain your answers.
   a. $Fe + 2HCl \longrightarrow FeCl_2 + H_2$
   b. $NiCl_2 \longrightarrow Ni + Cl_2$
   c. $4C + 6H_2 + O_2 \longrightarrow 2C_2H_6O$
   d. $2LiBr + Pb(NO_3)_2 \longrightarrow 2LiNO_3 + PbBr_2$
   e. $CaO + H_2O \longrightarrow Ca(OH)_2$
3. **Developing a model** Draw an energy diagram of an exothermic reaction that has a high activation energy. On your diagram, indicate how an increase in temperature would affect the rate of this reaction. Do the same for the addition of a catalyst.
4. **Applying concepts** Why can a lump of sugar be used in hot tea but granulated (small crystals) sugar is preferred in iced tea?

5. **Recognizing relationships** Potential energy is energy that is stored for later use. Explain where the potential energy is located in an exothermic reaction? Why do foods and fuel have chemical potential energy?
6. **Using the writing process** Acid rain is a serious enviromental problem that results from two successive synthesis reactions. Research the acid rain problem. Summarize your findings in a report, brochure, or pamphlet that you can show others to make them aware of the situation.

Families of Chemical Compounds

Guide for Reading

After you read the following sections, you will be able to

9–1 Acids and Bases
- Describe properties and uses of acids and bases.

9–2 Acids and Bases in Solution: Salts
- Relate pH number to acid-base strength.
- Describe the formation of salts.

9–3 Carbon and Its Compounds
- Describe organic compounds.

9–4 Hydrocarbons
- Identify three series of hydrocarbons.

9–5 Substituted Hydrocarbons
- Explain the nature of substituted hydrocarbons.

Banana, strawberry, pineapple, peach—what's your special flavor? How would you order your favorite ice cream sundae or soda? Certainly not by asking for a scoop of methyl butylacetate! Or a solution of carbonic acid, lactic acid, and ethyl butyrate! Yet that is exactly what you are eating when you enjoy a banana ice cream sundae or a pineapple ice cream soda.

Methyl butylacetate is the banana-flavored compound that makes banana ice cream different from strawberry or vanilla ice cream. And pineapple ice cream owes its characteristic flavor to the presence of ethyl butyrate.

Methyl butylacetate and ethyl butyrate belong to a much larger group of compounds known as organic compounds. Organic compounds are also found in the sugar and cream in the ice cream. But that's not all. In addition to organic compounds, your ice cream sundae or soda contains compounds known as acids, bases, and salts.

In this chapter you will learn about several groups of important compounds—compounds with a variety of surprising and sometimes delicious uses. So sit back and think about a nice big ethyl cinnemate sundae topped with isoamyl salicylate. . . .

Journal *Activity*

You and Your World What do you think of when you hear the words solution, saturated, concentration, base, salt, and neutral? In your journal, write your immediate reaction to each word. When you have finished reading this chapter, see how closely your definitions match the scientific ones.

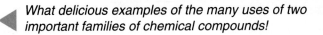

What delicious examples of the many uses of two important families of chemical compounds!

9–1 Acids and Bases

In Chapter 7 you learned that as a result of chemical bonding (the combining of atoms of elements to form new substances), hundreds of thousands of different substances exist. In Chapter 8 you were introduced to the various chemical reactions by which atoms are rearranged to form new and different substances. In this chapter you will discover how scientists have attempted to bring order to the incredible number of different types of chemical compounds that exist. In other words, you will learn about a system of classifying compounds into families based on their physical and chemical properties.

If you look in your medicine cabinet and refrigerator and on your kitchen shelves, you will find examples of groups of compounds known as **acids** and **bases.** Acids are found in aspirin, vitamin C, and eyewash. Fruits such as oranges, grapes, lemons, grapefruits, and apples contain acids. Milk and tea contain acids, as do pickles, vinegar, and carbonated drinks. Bases are found in products such as lye, milk of magnesia, deodorants, ammonia, and soaps.

Acids and bases also play an important role in the life processes that take place in your body. Acid in your stomach helps digest the foods you eat. Antacids, such as milk of magnesia, contain bases that help get rid of excess acid in the stomach.

Figure 9–1 *Acids and bases are found in many common substances, such as these appetizing breads.*

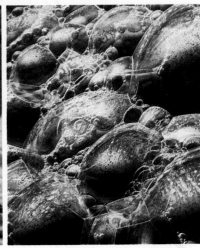

Figure 9–2 *Many of the fruits you eat contain acids. Acids are also used in the manufacture of synthetic fibers. The soap that produced these bubbles was manufactured using bases.*

Many industrial processes use acids and bases. Metals are often treated with acids to clean them. The manufacture of a wide variety of products involves the use of acids and bases. Fertilizers, synthetic fibers, and drugs are all manufactured with acids and bases.

Properties of Acids

As a class of compounds, all acids have certain physical and chemical properties when dissolved in water. One of the physical properties all acids share is sour taste. Lemons taste sour because they contain citric acid. Vinegar contains acetic acid. However, you should never use taste to identify a chemical substance. You should use other, safer properties.

Acids affect the color of indicators. Indicators are compounds that show a definite color change when mixed with an acid or a base. Litmus paper, a common indicator, changes from blue to red in an acid solution. Another indicator, phenolphthalein (fee-nohl-THAL-een), is colorless in an acid solution.

Acids react with active metals to form hydrogen gas and a metal compound. This reaction wears away, or corrodes, the metal and produces a residue. For example, sulfuric acid in a car battery often corrodes the terminals and leaves a residue.

Another property of acids can be identified by looking at the list of common acids in Figure 9–3 on page 228. What do all these acids have in common? Acids contain hydrogen. When dissolved

in water, acids ionize to produce positive hydrogen ions (H^+). A hydrogen ion is a proton. So acids are often defined as proton donors.

The hydrogen ion, or proton, produced by an acid is quickly surrounded by a water molecule. The attraction between the hydrogen ion (H^+) and the water molecule (H_2O) results in the formation of a hydronium ion, H_3O^+.

The definition of an acid as a proton donor helps to explain why all hydrogen-containing compounds are not acids. Table sugar contains 22 hydrogen atoms, but it is not an acid. When dissolved in water, table sugar does not produce H^+ ions. Table sugar is not a proton donor. So it does not turn litmus paper red or phenolphthalein colorless.

Common Acids

The three most common acids in industry and in the laboratory are sulfuric acid (H_2SO_4), nitric acid (HNO_3), and hydrochloric acid (HCl). These three acids are strong acids. That means they ionize to a high degree in water and produce hydrogen ions. The presence of hydrogen ions makes strong acids good electrolytes. An **electrolyte** is a substance whose water solution conducts an electric current.

Acetic acid ($HC_2H_3O_2$), carbonic acid (H_2CO_3), and boric acid (H_3BO_3) are weak acids. They do not ionize to a high degree in water, so they produce few hydrogen ions. Weak acids are poor electrolytes. Figure 9–3 lists the name, formula, and uses of some common acids. Remember, handle any acid—weak or strong—with care!

Properties of Bases

When dissolved in water, all bases share certain physical and chemical properties. Bases usually taste bitter and are slippery to the touch. However, bases can be poisonous and corrosive. So you should never use taste or touch to identify bases.

COMMON ACIDS	
Name and Formula	**Uses**
Strong	
Hydrochloric HCl	Pickling steel; cleaning bricks and metals; digesting food
Sulfuric H_2SO_4	Manufacturing paints, plastics, fertilizers; dehydrating agent
Nitric HNO_3	Removing tarnish; making explosives (TNT); making fertilizers
Weak	
Carbonic H_2CO_3	Carbonating beverages
Boric H_3BO_3	Washing eyes
Phosphoric H_3PO_4	Making fertilizers and detergents
Acetic $HC_2H_3O_2$	Making cellulose acetate used in fibers and films
Citric $H_3C_6H_5O_7$	Making soft drinks

Figure 9–3 *The name, formula, and uses of some common acids are given in this chart. What is the difference between a strong acid and a weak acid?*

Figure 9–4 *The name, formula, and uses of some common bases are given in this chart. What ion do all these bases contain?*

Bases turn litmus paper from red to blue and phenolphthalein to bright pink. Bases emulsify, or dissolve, fats and oils. They do this by reacting with the fat or oil to form a soap. The base ammonium hydroxide is used as a household cleaner because it "cuts" grease. The strong base sodium hydroxide, or lye, is used to clean clogged drains.

All bases contain the hydroxide ion, OH^-. When dissolved in water, bases produce this ion. Because a hydroxide ion (OH^-) can combine with a hydrogen ion (H^+) and form water, a base is often defined as a proton (H^+) acceptor.

Common Bases

Strong bases dissolve readily in water to produce large numbers of ions. So strong bases are good electrolytes. Examples of strong bases include potassium hydroxide (KOH), sodium hydroxide (NaOH), and calcium hydroxide ($Ca(OH)_2$).

Weak bases do not produce large numbers of ions when dissolved in water. So weak bases are poor electrolytes. Ammonium hydroxide (NH_4OH) and aluminum hydroxide ($Al(OH)_3$) are weak bases. See Figure 9–4.

COMMON BASES	
Name and Formula	**Uses**
Strong	
Sodium hydroxide NaOH	Making soap; drain cleaner
Potassium hydroxide KOH	Making soft soap; battery electrolyte
Calcium hydroxide $Ca(OH)_2$	Leather production; making plaster
Magnesium hydroxide $Mg(OH)_2$	Laxative; antacid
Weak	
Ammonium hydroxide NH_4OH	Household cleaner
Aluminum hydroxide $Al(OH)_3$	Antacid; deodorant

9–1   Section Review

1. What are three important properties of acids? Of bases?
2. Why are acids called proton donors?
3. Why are bases called proton acceptors?
4. If an electric conductivity setup were placed in the following solutions, would the light be bright or dim: HCl, HNO_3, H_3BO_3, $HC_2H_3O_2$, NH_4OH, KOH, NaOH, $Al(OH)_3$?

Connection—*Laboratory Safety*
5. How could you safely determine whether an unknown solution is an acid or a base?

9–2 Acids and Bases in Solution: Salts

As you have just learned, solutions can be acidic or basic. Solutions can also be neutral. To measure the acidity of a solution, the **pH** scale is used. **The pH of a solution is a measure of the hydronium ion (H_3O^+) concentration.** Remember, the hydronium ion is formed by the attraction between a hydrogen ion (H^+) from an acid and a water molecule (H_2O). So the pH of a solution indicates how acidic the solution is.

The pH scale is a series of numbers from 0 to 14. The middle of the scale—7—is the neutral point. A neutral solution has a pH of 7. It is neither an acid nor a base. Water is a neutral liquid.

A solution with a pH below 7 is an acid. Strong acids have low pH numbers. Would hydrochloric acid have a pH closer to 2 or to 6?

A solution with a pH above 7 is a base. Strong bases have high pH numbers. What would be the pH of NaOH?

Figure 9–5 *Does it surprise you to learn that many of the substances you use every day contain acids and bases? Which fruit is most acidic? What cleaner is most basic?*

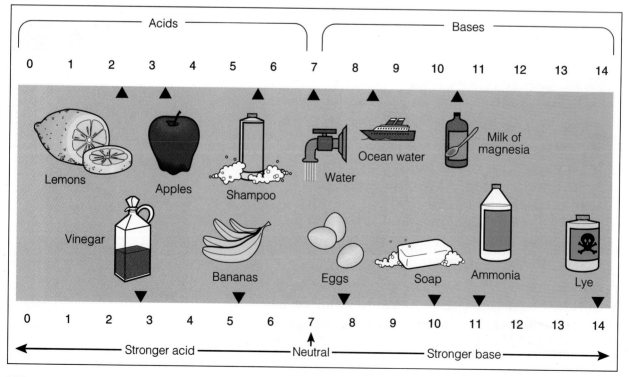

Determining Solution pH

The pH of a solution can be determined by using an indicator. You already know about two indicators: litmus paper and phenolphthalein. Other indictors include pH paper, methyl orange, and bromthymol blue. Each indicator shows a specific color change as the pH of a solution changes.

Common household materials can be used as indicators. Red-cabbage juice covers the entire pH range. Grape juice is bright pink in the presence of an acid and bright yellow in the presence of a base. Even tea can be an indicator. Have you ever noticed the color of tea change when you add lemon juice? For accurate pH measurements, a pH meter is used.

Formation of Salts

When acids react chemically with bases, they form a class of compounds called salts. A **salt** is a compound formed from the positive ion of a base and the negative ion of an acid. A salt is a neutral substance.

The reaction of an acid with a base produces a salt and water. The reaction is called **neutralization** (noo-truhl-ih-ZAY-shuhn). In neutralization, the properties of the acid and the base are lost as two neutral substances—a salt and water—are formed.

The reaction of HCl with NaOH is a neutralization reaction. The positive hydrogen ion from the acid combines with the negative hydroxide ion from the base. This produces water. The remaining positive ion of the base combines with the remaining negative ion of the acid to form a salt.

$$H^+Cl^- + Na^+OH^- \longrightarrow H_2O + NaCl$$

Many of the salts formed by a neutralization reaction are insoluble in water—that is, they do not dissolve in water. They crystallize out of solution and remain in the solid phase. An insoluble substance that crystallizes out of solution is called a precipitate (pree-SIHP-uh-tayt). The process by which a precipitate forms is called precipitation. An example of a precipitate is magnesium carbonate. Snow, rain, sleet, and hail are considered forms of precipitation because they fall out of solution. Out of what solution do they precipitate?

ACTIVITY DOING

A Homemade Indicator

1. Shred two leaves of red cabbage and boil them in some water until the liquid gets very dark. **CAUTION:** *Wear safety goggles and use extreme care .*

2. When the liquid and the shreds have cooled, squeeze all the purple juice you can from the shreds. Pour the liquid into a container.

3. Into 5 separate containers, pour about 3 to 4 mL of the following substances, one in each container: shampoo, grapefruit juice, clear soft drink, milk, ammonia cleaner.

4. Add about 2 mL of the cabbage liquid. Stir and observe any color changes.

Based on the fact that ammonia is a base, identify the other substances as either acids or bases.

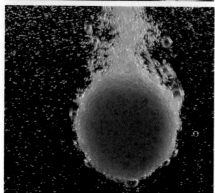

Figure 9–6 *To control dangerous acid spills, firefighters spray a blanket of base over the acid. The result is a neutral salt and water. These two substances are also produced when a person uses an antacid to relieve an upset stomach. What reaction is taking place in both of these situations?*

A neutralization reaction is a double-replacement reaction—and a very important one, too! For a dangerous acid can be combined with a dangerous base to form a harmless salt and neutral water.

9–2 Section Review

1. What is pH? Describe the pH scale.
2. What is the pH of an acid? A base? Water?
3. How can the pH of a solution be determined?
4. How does a salt form? What is a salt?
5. What is neutralization?

Critical Thinking—*Applying Concepts*
6. Use an equation to show the neutralization reaction between H_2SO_4 and NaOH.

Guide for Reading

Focus on these questions as you read.

▶ *What are organic compounds?*
▶ *What are some properties of organic compounds?*

9–3 Carbon and Its Compounds

Do you know what such familiar substances as sugar, plastic, paper, and gasoline have in common? They all contain the element carbon. Carbon is present in more than 2 million known compounds, and this number is rapidly increasing. Approximately 100,000 new carbon compounds are being isolated or synthesized every year. In fact, more than 90 percent of all known compounds contain carbon! **Carbon compounds form an important family of chemical compounds known as organic compounds.** The word organic means coming from life. Because carbon-containing compounds are present in all living things, scientists once believed that **organic compounds** could be produced only by living organisms. Living things were thought to have a mysterious "vital force" that was responsible for creating

Figure 9–7 *The element carbon is present in more than 2 million known compounds. Here you see three different forms of the pure element: diamond, graphite, and coal.*

carbon compounds. It was believed that the force could not be duplicated in the laboratory.

In 1828, the German chemist Friedrich Wöhler produced an organic compound called urea from two inorganic substances. Urea is a waste product produced by the human body. It was not long before chemists accepted the idea that organic compounds could be prepared from materials that were never part of a living organism. What is common to all organic compounds is not that they originated in living things but that they all contain the element carbon. Today, the majority of organic compounds are synthesized in laboratories.

There are some carbon compounds that are not considered organic compounds. Calcium carbonate, carbon dioxide, and carbon monoxide are considered inorganic (not organic) compounds.

The Bonding of Carbon

Carbon's ability to combine with itself and with other elements explains why there are so many carbon compounds. Carbon atoms form covalent bonds with other carbon atoms.

The simplest bond involves 2 carbon atoms. The most complex involves thousands of carbon atoms. The carbon atoms can form long straight chains, branched chains, single rings, or rings joined together.

The bonds between carbon atoms can be single covalent bonds, double covalent bonds, or triple covalent bonds. In a single bond, one pair of electrons is shared between 2 carbon atoms. In a double

ACTIVITY

DOING

Octane Rating

1. Find out what the octane rating of gasoline means.

2. Go to a local gas station and find out the octane ratings of the different grades of gasoline being sold. Compare the prices of the different grades. Ask the station attendant to describe how each grade of gasoline performs.

3. Present your findings to your class.

Figure 9-8 *Because of carbon's bonding ability, a great variety of organic compounds exists. These include synthetic rubber and plastic for firefighters' equipment, paints and dyes, and the substances of which all living things are made.*

bond, two pairs of electrons are shared between 2 carbon atoms. See Figure 9-9. How many pairs of electrons are shared in a triple bond?

Carbon atoms also bond with many other elements. These elements include oxygen, hydrogen, members of the nitrogen family, and members of Family 17. The simplest organic compounds contain just carbon and hydrogen. Because there are so many compounds of carbon and hydrogen, they form a class of organic compounds all their own. You will soon read about this class of compounds.

A great variety of organic compounds exists because the same atoms that bond together to form one compound may be arranged in several other ways in several other compounds. Each different arrangement of atoms represents a separate organic compound.

Properties of Organic Compounds

Organic compounds usually exist as gases, liquids, or low-melting-point solids. Organic liquids generally have strong odors and low boiling points. Organic liquids do not conduct an electric current. What is the name for a substance whose solution does not conduct electricity? Organic compounds generally do not dissolve in water. Oil, which is a mixture of organic compounds, floats on water because the two liquids are insoluble.

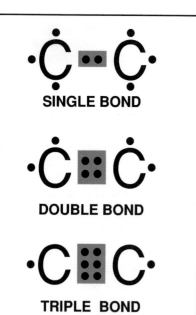

SINGLE BOND

DOUBLE BOND

TRIPLE BOND

Figure 9-9 *In a single bond, one pair of electrons is shared. In a double bond, two pairs of electrons are shared. How many pairs of electrons are shared in a triple bond?*

Structural Formulas

A molecular formula for a compound indicates what elements make up that compound and how many atoms of each element are present in a molecule. For example, the molecular formula for the organic compound ethane is C_2H_6. In every molecule of ethane, there are 2 carbon atoms and 6 hydrogen atoms.

What a molecular formula does not indicate about a molecule of a compound is how the different atoms are arranged. To do this, a **structural formula** is used. A structural formula shows the kind, number, and arrangement of atoms in a molecule. You can think of a structural formula as being a model of a molecule.

Figure 9–10 shows the structural formula for ethane and two other organic compounds: methane and propane. Note that in a structural formula, a dash (–) is used to represent the pair of shared electrons forming a covalent bond. In writing structural formulas, it is important that you remember the electron arrangement in a carbon atom.

Carbon has 4 valence electrons, or 4 electrons in its outermost energy level. Each electron will form a covalent bond with an electron of another atom to produce a stable outermost level containing 8 electrons. So when structural formulas are written, there can be no dangling bonds—no dangling dashes.

Isomers

For this activity you will need a stack of blank index cards, a felt-tipped marker, and a package of straws or pipe cleaners.

1. Take half of the index cards and label one side of each card with the letter C.

2. Take the rest of the index cards and label each card with the letter H.

3. Using the straws or pipe cleaners to represent bonds, see how many isomers you can make for the formula C_6H_{14}. Remember that each carbon atom must be bonded to four other atoms.

H	H H	H H H
H—C—H	H—C—C—H	H—C—C—C—H
H	H H	H H H
METHANE	**ETHANE**	**PROPANE**
CH_4	C_2H_6	C_3H_8

Figure 9–10 *Methane, ethane, and propane are the first three members of a series of hydrocarbons known as the alkanes. Note that each carbon atom is surrounded by four dashes, corresponding to four pairs of shared electrons.*

Isomers

Compounds with the same molecular formula but different structures are called **isomers.** Figure 9–11 on page 236 shows two isomers of butane, C_4H_{10}. Notice that one isomer is a straight chain and

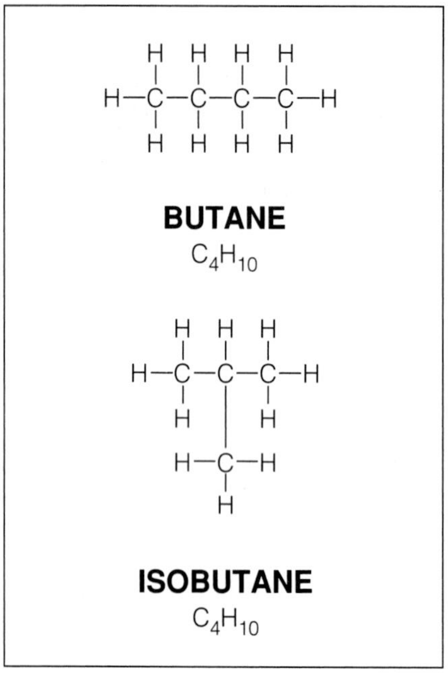

BUTANE

C_4H_{10}

ISOBUTANE

C_4H_{10}

the other isomer is a branched chain. In a branched chain, all the carbon atoms are not in a straight line. This difference in structure will account for any differences in the physical and chemical properties of these two compounds.

Figure 9–12 shows three isomers of pentane, C_5H_{12}. This time there is one straight chain and two branched chains. To see the difference between the two branched chains, count the number of carbon atoms in the straight-chain portion of each molecule. How many are there in each branched isomer? What do you think happens to the number of possible isomers as the number of carbon atoms in a molecule increases? The compound whose formula is $C_{15}H_{32}$ could have more than 400 isomers!

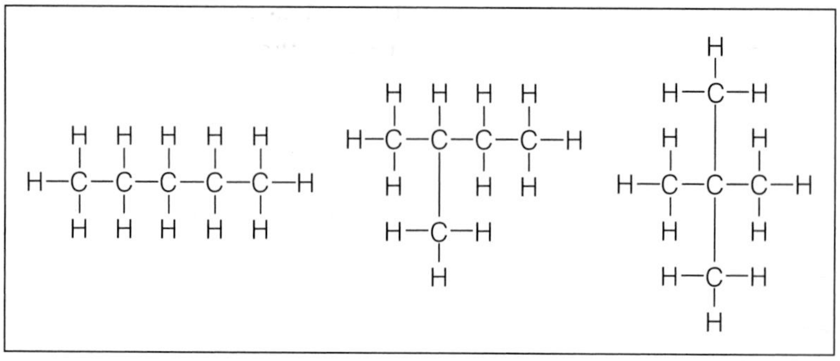

Figure 9–12 *As the number of carbon atoms increases, the number of isomers increases. What alkane is shown here? How do its three isomers differ?*

9–3 Section Review

1. What are organic compounds?
2. What four factors account for the abundance of carbon compounds?
3. What are three properties of organic compounds?

Critical Thinking—*Applying Concepts*
4. Could two compounds have the same structural formula but different molecular formulas?

9–4 Hydrocarbons

Have you ever heard of a butane lighter, seen a propane torch, or noticed a sign at a service station advertising "high octane" gasoline? Butane, propane, and octane are members of a large group of organic compounds known as **hydrocarbons.** A hydrocarbon contains only hydrogen and carbon.

Hydrocarbons can be classified as saturated or unsaturated depending on the type of bonds between carbon atoms. In **saturated hydrocarbons,** all the bonds between carbon atoms are single covalent bonds. In **unsaturated hydrocarbons,** one or more of the bonds between carbon atoms is a double covalent or triple covalent bond.

Alkanes

The **alkanes** are straight-chain or branched-chain hydrocarbons in which all the bonds between carbon atoms are single covalent bonds. Alkanes are saturated hydrocarbons. All the hydrocarbons that are alkanes belong to the alkane series. The simplest member of the alkane series is methane, CH_4. Methane consists of 1 carbon atom surrounded by 4 hydrogen atoms. Why are there 4 hydrogen atoms?

The next simplest alkane is ethane, C_2H_6. How does the formula for ethane differ from the formula for methane? After ethane, the next member of the

Guide for Reading

Focus on this question as you read.

▶ *How are hydrocarbons classified?*

Figure 9–13 *Petroleum is one of the most abundant sources of hydrocarbons. The hydrocarbons in petroleum range from 1-carbon molecules to more than 50-carbon molecules. Petroleum, which does not mix with water, is highly flammable.*

Figure 9–14 *Common alkanes include methane, of which the planet Saturn's atmosphere is composed; propane, which is burned to provide heat for hot-air balloons; and butane, which is the fuel in most lighters. What is the general formula for the alkanes?*

Alkane

$$C_nH_{2n+2}$$

ALKANE SERIES

Name	Formula
Methane	CH_4
Ethane	C_2H_6
Propane	C_3H_8
Butane	C_4H_{10}
Pentane	C_5H_{12}
Hexane	C_6H_{14}
Heptane	C_7H_{16}
Octane	C_8H_{18}
Nonane	C_9H_{20}
Decane	$C_{10}H_{22}$

alkane series is propane, C_3H_8. Can you begin to see a pattern to the formulas for each successive alkane? Ethane has 1 more carbon atom and 2 more hydrogen atoms than methane does. Propane has 1 more carbon atom and 2 more hydrogen atoms than ethane does. Each member of the alkane series is formed by adding 1 carbon atom and 2 hydrogen atoms to the previous compound.

The pattern that exists for the alkanes can be used to determine the formula for any member of the series. Because each alkane differs from the preceding member of the series by the group CH_2, a general formula for the alkanes can be written. That general formula is C_nH_{2n+2}. The letter n is the number of carbon atoms in the alkane. What would be the formula for a 15-carbon hydrocarbon? For a 30-carbon hydrocarbon?

Naming Hydrocarbons

Figure 9–15 shows the first ten members of the alkane series. Look at the names of the compounds. How is each name the same? How is each different?

Often in organic chemistry the names of the compounds in the same series will have the same ending, or suffix. Thus, the members of the alkane series all end with the suffix *-ane*, the same ending as in the series name. The first part of each name, or the prefix, indicates the number of carbon atoms

Figure 9–15 *This chart shows the names and formulas for the first ten members of the alkane series. What does the prefix hex- mean?*

present in the compound. The prefix *meth-* indicates 1 carbon atom. The prefix *eth-*, 2 carbon atoms, and the prefix *prop-*, 3. According to Figure 9–15, how many carbon atoms are indicated by the prefix *pent-*? How many carbon atoms are in octane? As you study other hydrocarbon series, you will see that these prefixes are used again and again. So it will be useful for you to become familiar with the prefixes that mean 1 to 10 carbon atoms.

Alkenes

Hydrocarbons in which at least one pair of carbon atoms is joined by a double covalent bond are called **alkenes.** Alkenes are unsaturated hydrocarbons. The first member of the alkene series is ethene, C_2H_4. The next member of the alkene series is propene, C_3H_6.

Figure 9–16 shows the first seven members of the alkene series. What do you notice about the name of each compound?

As you look at the formulas for the alkenes, you will again see a pattern in the number of carbon and hydrogen atoms added to each successive compound. The pattern is the addition of 1 carbon atom and 2 hydrogen atoms. The general formula for the alkenes is C_nH_{2n}. The letter n is the number of carbon atoms in the compound. What is the formula for an alkene with 12 carbons? With 20 carbons?

In general, alkenes are more reactive than alkanes because a double bond is more easily broken than a single bond. So alkenes can react chemically by adding other atoms directly to their molecules.

Alkynes

Hydrocarbons in which at least one pair of carbon atoms is joined by a triple covalent bond are called **alkynes.** Alkynes are unsaturated hydrocarbons. The simplest alkyne is ethyne, C_2H_2, which is commonly known as acetylene. Perhaps you have heard of acetylene torches, which are used in welding.

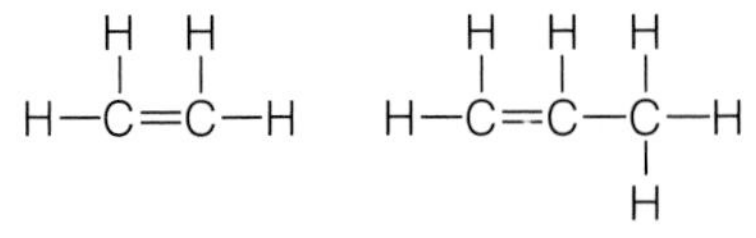

ALKENE SERIES	
Name	**Formula**
Ethene	C_2H_4
Propene	C_3H_6
Butene	C_4H_8
Pentene	C_5H_{10}
Hexene	C_6H_{12}
Heptene	C_7H_{14}
Octene	C_8H_{16}

Figure 9–16 *This chart shows the names and formulas of the first seven members of the alkene series. What would a 9-carbon alkene be called?*

·Alkenes

C_nH_{2n}

ETHENE
C_2H_4

PROPENE
C_3H_6

Figure 9–17 *The first two members of the alkene series are ethene and propene. What kind of bonds do the alkenes have?*

ALKYNE SERIES

Name	Formula
Ethyne	C_2H_2
Propyne	C_3H_4
Butyne	C_4H_6
Pentyne	C_5H_8
Hexyne	C_6H_{10}

H—C≡C—H

**ACETYLENE
(ETHYNE)**
C_2H_2

H—C≡C—C—H (with H above and below middle C)

PROPYNE
C_3H_4

Alkynes
CnH2n-2

Figure 9–18 *This chart shows the names and formulas for the first five members of the alkyne series. What is the general formula for this series? The simplest alkynes are ethyne and propyne. What is the common name for ethyne?*

The first five members of the alkyne series are listed in Figure 9–18. Here again, each successive member of the alkyne series differs by the addition of 1 carbon atom and 2 hydrogen atoms. The general formula for the alkynes is C_nH_{2n-2}.

The alkynes are even more reactive than the alkenes. Very little energy is needed to break a triple bond. Like the alkenes, alkynes can react chemically by adding other atoms directly to their molecules.

Aromatic Hydrocarbons

All the hydrocarbons you have just learned about—the alkanes, alkenes, and alkynes—are either straight-chain or branched-chain molecules. But this is not the only structure a hydrocarbon can have. Some hydrocarbons are in the shape of rings. Probably the best-known class of hydrocarbons in the shape of rings is the aromatic hydrocarbons. The name of this class comes from the fact that aromatic hydrocarbons share a common physical property. These compounds have strong and often pleasant odors (or aromas).

Figure 9–19 *The simplest aromatic hydrocarbon is benzene. Benzene is used in the manufacture of dyes. What is the basic structure of aromatic hydrocarbons?*

240

The basic structure of an aromatic hydrocarbon is a ring of 6 carbon atoms joined by alternating single and double covalent bonds. This means that within the 6-carbon ring, there are 3 carbon-to-carbon double bonds. The simplest aromatic hydrocarbon is called benzene, C_6H_6. Figure 9–20 shows the structural formula for benzene. Chemists often abbreviate this formula by drawing a hexagon with a circle in the center.

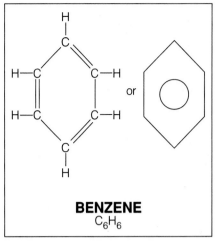

BENZENE
C_6H_6

Figure 9–20 *The structural formula for benzene shows 6 carbon atoms joined by alternating single and double covalent bonds.*

9–4 Section Review

1. What are hydrocarbons? How are hydrocarbons classified?
2. Name three series of hydrocarbons.
3. What is meant by saturated and unsaturated hydrocarbons? Classify each hydrocarbon series according to these definitions.
4. What are aromatic hydrocarbons?

Critical Thinking—*Applying Concepts*
5. Can C_6H_6 be a straight-chain hydrocarbon?

9–5 Substituted Hydrocarbons

Hydrocarbons are but one of several groups of organic compounds. Hydrocarbons contain carbon and hydrogen atoms only. But as you have learned, carbon atoms form bonds with many other elements. So many different groups of organic compounds exist. **The important groups of organic compounds include alcohols, organic acids, esters, and halogen derivatives.** These compounds are called **substituted hydrocarbons.** A substituted hydrocarbon is formed when one or more hydrogen atoms in a hydrocarbon chain or ring is replaced by a different atom or group of atoms.

Guide for Reading

Focus on this question as you read.

▶ What are some important groups of substituted hydrocarbons?

Alcohols

Alcohols are substituted hydrocarbons in which one or more hydrogen atoms have been replaced by an –OH group, or hydroxyl group. The simplest alcohol is methanol, CH_3OH. You can see from Figure 9–21 that methanol is formed when 1 hydrogen atom in methane is replaced by the –OH group. Methanol is used to make plastics and synthetic fibers. It is also used in automobile gas tank de-icers to prevent water that has condensed in the tank from freezing. Another important use of methanol is as a solvent. Methanol, however, is very poisonous— even when used externally.

As you can tell from the name methanol, alcohols are named by adding the suffix *-ol* to the name of the corresponding hydrocarbon. When an –OH group is substituted for 1 hydrogen atom in ethane, the resulting alcohol is ethanol, C_2H_5OH. Ethanol is produced naturally by the action of yeast or bacteria on the sugar stored in grains such as corn, wheat, and barley.

Ethanol is a good solvent for many organic compounds that do not dissolve in water. Ethanol is used in medicines. It is also the alcohol used in alcoholic beverages. In order to make ethanol available for industrial and medicinal uses only, it must be made unfit for beverage purposes. So poisonous compounds such as methanol are added to ethanol. The resulting mixture is called denatured alcohol.

Figure 9–21 *Methanol, an organic alcohol, is used to make plastics, such as the brightly colored insulation on telephone wires.*

H—C—OH with H above and H below the C

METHANOL

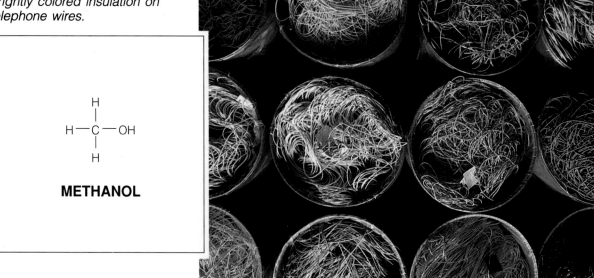

An alcohol can be in the form of a ring as well as a chain. When 1 hydrogen atom in a benzene ring is replaced by an –OH group, the resulting alcohol is called phenol. Phenol is used in the preparation of plastics and as a disinfectant.

Organic Acids

Organic acids are substituted hydrocarbons that contain the –COOH group, or carboxyl group. Figure 9–23 shows the structural formula for two common organic acids. Notice that one of the carbon-oxygen bonds in the carboxyl group is a double bond.

Organic acids are named by adding the suffix -oic to the name of the corresponding hydrocarbon. Most organic acids, however, have common names that are used more frequently. The simplest organic acid is methanoic acid, HCOOH. Methanoic acid is commonly called formic acid. Formic acid is found in nature in the stinging nettle plant and in certain ants. Formic acid produced by an ant causes the ant bite to hurt.

The acid derived from ethane is commonly called acetic acid. Acetic acid is the acid in vinegar. Citric acid, which is found in citrus fruits, is a more complicated organic acid originally derived from the hydrocarbon propane.

Figure 9–22 Denatured alcohol is ethanol to which poisonous compounds such as methanol have been added. Why is ethanol denatured?

Figure 9–23 Formic acid, also known as methanoic acid, is the simplest organic acid. It is the acid produced by ants and is responsible for the pain caused by an ant bite. Acetic acid is the acid in vinegar. What is another name for acetic acid?

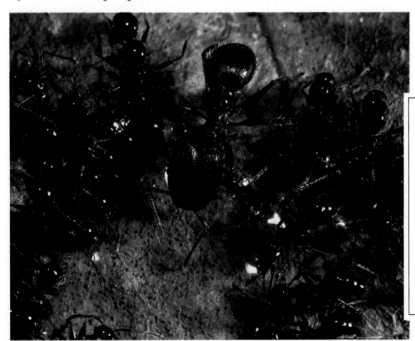

FORMIC ACID

ACETIC ACID

Figure 9–24 *Halogen derivatives have a variety of uses. Polyvinyl chloride is used to make all sorts of water-repellent gear.*

Esters

If an alcohol and an organic acid are chemically combined, the resulting compound is called an ester. Esters are noted for their pleasant aromas and flavors. The substances you read about in the chapter opener that give flavor to ice cream are esters.

Many esters occur naturally. Fruits such as strawberries, bananas, and pineapples get their sweet smell from esters. Esters can also be produced in the laboratory. Synthetic esters are used as perfume additives and as artificial flavorings.

Halogen Derivatives

Hydrocarbons can undergo substitution reactions in which one or more hydrogen atoms are replaced by an atom or atoms of fluorine, chlorine, bromine, or iodine. The family name for these elements is halogens. So substituted hydrocarbons that contain halogens are called halogen derivatives.

A variety of useful substances result from adding halogens to hydrocarbons. The compound methyl chloride, CH_3Cl, is used as a refrigerant. Tetrachloroethane, $C_2H_2Cl_4$, which consists of 4 chlorine atoms substituted in an ethane molecule, is used in dry cleaning.

When 2 hydrogen atoms in a methane molecule are replaced by chlorine atoms and the other 2 hydrogen atoms are replaced by fluorine atoms, a compound commonly known as Freon™, CCl_2F_2, is formed. The actual name of this halogen derivative is dichlorodifluoromethane. Freon™ is the coolant used in many refrigerators and air conditioners.

ACTIVITY

DISCOVERING

Saturated and Unsaturated Fats

Many of the foods you eat contain saturated and unsaturated fats. Using books and other reference materials in the library, find out what these terms mean. Find out the health risks and benefits associated with eating each.

Make a list of foods that contain saturated fats and those that contain unsaturated fats. Analyze your daily diet for a one-week period. Indicate which types of fats you eat, how much of each you eat, and how often.

■ Do you need to modify your daily diet? If so, how?

9–5 Section Review

1. What is a substituted hydrocarbon?
2. What is an alcohol? An organic acid? An ester?

Critical Thinking—*Identifying Relationships*
3. Methanol is used in car de-icers. What does this tell you about the freezing point of methanol? What role does methanol play in terms of the solution of water and methanol?

CONNECTIONS

A Chemical You

The human body is one of the most amazing chemical factories ever created. It can produce chemicals from raw materials, start complex chemical reactions, repair and reproduce some of its own parts, and even correct its own mistakes.

What is the fuel that keeps your human chemical factory going? *Nutrients* contained in the foods you eat maintain the proper functioning of all the systems of the body. The three main types of nutrients—carbohydrates, fats and oils, and proteins—are organic compounds.

Carbohydrates are organic molecules of carbon, hydrogen, and oxygen. Carbohydrates are the body's main source of energy. Carbohydrates can be either sugars or starches. The simplest carbohydrate is the sugar glucose, $C_6H_{12}O_6$. The more complex sugar sucrose, $C_{12}H_{22}O_{11}$, is common table sugar.

Starches are another kind of carbohydrate. Starches are made of long chains of sugar molecules hooked together. Starches are found in foods such as bread, cereal, potatoes, pasta, and rice.

Like carbohydrates, fats and oils contain carbon, hydrogen, and oxygen. These molecules are large, complex esters. Fats and oil store twice as much energy as do carbohydrates.

As a class of organic compounds, fats and oils are sometimes called lipids. Fats are solid at room temperature, whereas oils are liquid. Lipids include cooking oils, butter, and the fat in meat. Although fats and oils are high-energy nutrients, too much of these substances can be a health hazard. Unused fats are stored by the body. This increases body weight. In addition, scientific evidence indicates that eating too much animal fat may contribute to heart disease.

Proteins are used to build and repair body parts. Every living part of your body contains proteins. Blood, muscles, brain tissue, skin, and hair all contain proteins. Proteins contain carbon, hydrogen, oxygen, and nitrogen. Some also contain sulfur and phosphorus. Meat, fish, dairy products, and soybeans are sources of proteins.

All foods contain three basic nutrients: carbohydrates, fats and oils, and proteins. A balanced diet should provide the proper amounts of each nutrient.

A computer-generated model of a human protein molecule

Laboratory Investigation

Acids, Bases, and Salts

Problem

What are some properties of acids and bases? What happens when acids react with bases?

Materials *(per group)*

safety goggles	test-tube rack
beaker	red and blue
solutions of	litmus paper
H_2SO_4, HCl,	stirring rod
HNO_3	medicine drop-
solutions of	per
KOH, NaOH,	phenolphthalein
$Ca(OH)_2$	evaporating dish
6 medium-sized	rubber gloves
test tubes	paper towels

Procedure 🧪 ☣ 👁

A. *Acids*

1. Put on your safety goggles. Over a sink, pour about 5 mL of each acid into separate test tubes. **CAUTION:** *Handle acids with extreme care. They can burn the skin.* Place the test tubes in the rack. Test the effect of each acid on litmus paper by dipping a stirring rod into the acid and then touching the rod to the litmus paper. Test each acid with both red and blue litmus paper. *Be sure to clean the rod between uses.* Record your observations.

2. Add 1 drop of phenolphthalein to each test tube. Record your observations.

B. *Bases*

1. Over a sink, pour about 5 mL of each base into separate test tubes. **CAUTION:** *Handle bases with extreme care.* Place the test tubes in the rack. Test the contents of each tube with red and blue litmus paper. Record your observations.

2. Add 1 drop of phenolphthalein to each test tube. Record your observations.

3. Place 5 mL of sodium hydroxide solution in a small beaker and add 2 drops of phenolphthalein. Record the solution's color.

4. While slowly stirring, carefully add a few drops of hydrochloric acid until the mixture changes color. Record the color change. This point is known as the indicator endpoint. Test with red and blue litmus paper. Record your observations.

5. Carefully pour some of the mixture into a porcelain evaporating dish. Let the mixture evaporate until it is dry.

Observations

1. What color do acids turn litmus paper? Phenolphthalein?

2. What color do bases turn litmus paper? Phenolphthalein?

3. What happens to the color of the sodium hydroxide-phenolphthalein solution when hydrochloric acid is added?

4. Does the substance formed by the reaction of sodium hydroxide with hydrochloric acid affect litmus paper?

5. Describe the appearance of the substance that remains after evaporation.

Analysis and Conclusions

1. What are some properties of acids? Of bases?

2. What type of substance is formed when an acid reacts with a base? What is the name of this reaction? What is the other product? Why does this substance have no effect on litmus paper?

3. What is meant by an indicator's endpoint?

4. **On Your Own** Write a balanced equation for the reaction between sodium hydroxide and hydrochloric acid.

Study Guide

Summarizing Key Concepts

9–1 Acids and Bases

▲ Acids taste sour, turn litmus paper red and phenolphthalein colorless, and ionize in water to form hydrogen ions (H^+).

▲ Bases feel slippery, taste bitter, turn litmus paper blue and phenolphthalein pink, and produce hydroxide ions (OH^-) in solution.

9–2 Acids and Bases in Solution: Salts

▲ A neutral substance has a pH of 7. Acids have pH numbers lower than 7. Bases have pH numbers higher than 7.

▲ When an acid chemically combines with a base, the reaction is called neutralization. The products of neutralization are a salt and water.

9–3 Carbon and Its Compounds

▲ Most compounds that contain carbon are called organic compounds.

▲ Isomers have the same molecular formula but different structural formulas.

9–4 Hydrocarbons

▲ The alkanes are saturated hydrocarbons. The alkenes and the alkynes are unsaturated hydrocarbons.

▲ Aromatic hydrocarbons have a ring structure containing 6 carbon atoms.

9–5 Substituted Hydrocarbons

▲ Substituted hydrocarbons include alcohols, organic acids, esters, and halogen derivatives.

Reviewing Key Terms

9–1 Acids and Bases
acid
base
electrolyte

9–2 Acids and Bases in Solution: Salts
pH
salt
neutralization

9–3 Carbon and Its Compounds
organic compound
structural formula
isomer

9–4 Hydrocarbons
hydrocarbon
saturated hydrocarbon
unsaturated hydrocarbon
alkane
alkene
alkyne

9–5 Substituted Hydrocarbons
substituted hydrocarbon

Chapter Review

Content Review

Multiple Choice

Choose the letter of the answer that best completes each statement.

1. One of the physical properties that all acids share is
   a. no color.
   b. color.
   c. sour taste.
   d. bitter taste.

2. Weak acids do not ionize to a high degree in water, so they produce few
   a. electrolytes.
   b. hydrogen ions.
   c. hydroxide ions.
   d. carbonates.

3. You should never use taste or touch to identify bases because they can be
   a. corrosive.
   b. slippery.
   c. sour.
   d. antacids.

4. Which ion do bases contain?
   a. OH^- b. H_3O^+ c. H^+ d. NH_4^+

5. Organic compounds always contain
   a. carbon.
   b. oxygen.
   c. halogens.
   d. carboxyl groups.

6. The pH of the products formed by a neutralization reaction is
   a. 1.   b. 7.   c. 14.   d. 0.

7. The type of bonding found in organic compounds is
   a. metallic.
   b. ionic.
   c. covalent.
   d. coordinate.

8. A compound that contains only carbon and hydrogen is called a(an)
   a. isomer.
   b. hydrocarbon.
   c. carbohydrate.
   d. alcohol.

9. The simplest aromatic hydrocarbon is
   a. cyclohexane.
   b. methane.
   c. benzene.
   d. phenol.

10. The $-OH$ group is characteristic of an
    a. organic acid.
    b. aromatic compound.
    c. ester.
    d. alcohol.

True or False

If the statement is true, write "true." If it is false, change the underlined word or words to make the statement true.

1. Acids are often defined as <u>proton donors</u>.
2. Strong acids are <u>poor</u> electrolytes.
3. Weak bases produce <u>small</u> numbers of ions when dissolved in water.
4. A neutral solution has a pH of <u>10</u>.
5. In <u>neutralization</u>, an acid reacts with a base.
6. Hydrocarbons that contain only single bonds are said to be <u>unsaturated</u>.
7. The 4-carbon alkane is called <u>butane</u>.
8. An organic acid is characterized by the group <u>–COOH</u>.
9. Compounds that have the same molecular formula but different structural formulas are called <u>isotopes</u>.

Concept Mapping

Complete the following concept map for Section 9–1. Then construct a concept map for the entire chapter.

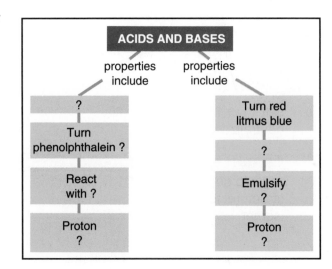

Concept Mastery

Discuss each of the following in a brief paragraph.

1. Give four different reasons why table sugar, which contains 22 hydrogen atoms, is not classified as an acid.
2. In terms of pH, explain why lemons are more acidic than bananas and why lye is more basic than ammonia.
3. Explain why water is both an acid and a base.
4. Discuss four reasons why carbon compounds are so abundant.
5. Explain the importance of structural formulas in organic chemistry.
6. In this chapter you learned that compounds called bases contain the hydroxide ion, $-OH^-$. Alcohols also contain the $-OH$ group. Why are alcohols not bases?

Critical Thinking and Problem Solving

Use the skills you have developed in this chapter to answer each of the following

1. **Classifying compounds** Identify each of the following compounds as an acid, base, or salt:
   a. $CaCO_3$ c. $CsOH$ e. $MgSO_4$
   b. HI d. H_3PO_4 f. $Ga(OH)_3$
2. **Applying concepts** Lime, $Ca(OH)_2$, is a powdery white form of calcium hydroxide. It is sometimes used to treat soils that are too acidic.
   a. How would you explain the effect of lime on acidic soil?
   b. How might you determine the correct amount of lime that should be applied to an acidic soil?
   c. How would you test the soil to see if the treatment were effective?
3. **Designing an experiment** Describe an experiment to determine if blueberry juice is a good acid-base indicator.
4. **Identifying patterns** Ten drops of phenolphthalein are added to lemon juice, tap water, and ammonia solution. Describe what happens in each case.
5. **Classifying hydrocarbons** Classify each of the following hydrocarbons as an alkane, alkene, alkyne, or aromatic compound.
   a. C_4H_{10} c. C_2H_4 e. $C_{13}H_{26}$
   b. C_3H_4 d. C_6H_6 f. $C_{42}H_{82}$
6. **Applying definitions** Draw the structural formulas for the isomers of hexane.
7. **Making diagrams** Draw structural formulas for the following compounds:
   a. hexane
   b. butene
   c. propyne
8. **Classifying substituted hydrocarbons** Classify each of the following compounds as a(an) ester, alcohol, organic acid, or halogen derivative:
   a. $C_2H_5COOC_3H_7$
   b. C_4H_9Cl
   c. C_6H_5OH
   d. C_2H_5COOH
9. **Identifying patterns** Using the general formulas for the alkanes, alkenes, and alkynes, show why the number of hydrogen atoms in each series decreases by two.
10. **Drawing a conclusion** Explain why the alkene series and the alkyne series begin with a 2-carbon hydrocarbon rather than a 1-carbon hydrocarbon, as the alkane series does. Use structural formulas to support your explanation.
11. **Using the writing process** The families of compounds discussed in this chapter play many important roles in your life. Write a short story in which you mention as many acids, bases, salts, and carbon compounds as you can. Explain the role of each compound in your everyday life.

Petrochemical Technology

Guide for Reading

After you read the following sections, you will be able to

10–1 What is Petroleum?

■ Explain what petroleum is and where it comes from.

■ Identify the major fractions of petroleum.

■ Describe the process of fractional distillation.

10–2 Petrochemical Products

■ Explain how polymers are formed from monomers.

■ Describe the process of polymerization.

■ List some important natural and synthetic polymers.

A telephone call at any time of the day or night may summon you to travel to a distant location. Once you arrive at your destination, your life will be in danger almost constantly. The situation will be explosive. One wrong move—even one unfortunate act of nature—could result in a tremendous and fatal explosion. Your role there may last only a day or perhaps several months. What is this awesome-sounding job? It is putting out oil-well fires. Does it sound like a job you might enjoy? Probably not. But one brave and unusual man who goes by the name of Red Adair loves it!

Oil wells, and the liquids and gases within them, are highly flammable. Once an oil fire begins, it will burn until all the fuel is gone. Putting out an oil-well fire requires enormous ingenuity and courage. Nonetheless, Adair has never failed to put out a fire. Some have taken six months and others only thirty seconds.

What is so important about oil that people are willing to risk their lives to find it, extract it from the Earth, and protect it? In this chapter you will learn the answer to that question. You will also find out what oil is and how it can be used.

Journal *Activity*

You and Your World Look around your home at the objects that surround you every day. Do you see a lot of plastic? You can probably find plastic in your closet, on your shelves, in your refrigerator—anywhere you look. In our journal, describe some of the objects you find that are made of plastic. Explain why plastics are useful and what materials may have been used before plastics were developed.

◄ *Only the know-how of Red Adair (inset) is enough to match an oil field burning out of control.*

Guide for Reading

*Focus on these questions as
you read.*

▶ *What is petroleum?*

▶ *How does fractional distillation separate petroleum into
its various components?*

Where Is the Oil?

Using books and other reference materials in the library,
find out where the major oil
fields in the world are located.
Make a map showing these
oil fields. Be sure to include oil
fields that have recently been
discovered, as well as areas
that are currently believed to
contain oil.

10–1 What Is Petroleum?

Have you ever seen a movie in which a group of
people gathered around a well were shouting and
cheering as a thick black liquid was rising up
through the ground and spurting high into the air?
Or have you ever read about geologists who study
the composition of the Earth in an attempt to find
oil? If so, you may have realized—correctly so—that
crude oil is a rather valuable substance. This sought-
after crude oil, one form of **petroleum,** has been
called black gold because of its tremendous importance. Fuels made from petroleum provide nearly
half the energy used in the world. And thousands of
products—from the bathing suit you wear when
swimming to the toothpaste you use when brushing
your teeth—are made from this petroleum.

**Petroleum is a substance believed to have been
formed hundreds of millions of years ago when layers of dead plants and animals were buried beneath
sediments such as mud, sand, silt, or clay at the
bottom of the oceans.** Over millions of years, heat
and great pressure changed the plant and animal
remains into petroleum. Petroleum is a nonrenewable resource. A nonrenewable resource is one that

Figure 10–1 *The sight of thick black
liquid shooting high into the air has
been a welcomed one since the first
oil well was built in Pennsylvania.*

cannot be replaced once it is used up. There is only a certain amount of petroleum in existence. Once the existing petroleum is used up, no more will be available.

Despite the huge variety of products obtained from petroleum, few people ever see the substance itself. The liquid form that gushes from deep within the Earth is a mixture of chemicals called crude oil. Petroleum can also be found as a solid in certain rocks and sand. It has been called black gold because it is usually black or dark brown. But it can be green, red, yellow, or even colorless. Petroleum may flow as easily as water, or it may ooze slowly— like thick tar. The color and thickness of petroleum depend on the substances that make it up.

Separating Petroleum Into Parts

By itself, petroleum is almost useless. But the different parts, or **fractions,** of petroleum are among the most useful chemicals in the world. **Petroleum is separated into its useful parts by a process called fractional distillation.** The process of distillation involves heating a liquid until it vaporizes (changes into a gas) and then allowing the vapor to cool until it condenses (turns back into a liquid). The different fractions of petroleum have different boiling points. So each fraction vaporizes at a different temperature than do the others. The temperature at which a substance boils is the same as the temperature at which it condenses. So if each fraction vaporizes at a different temperature, then each fraction will condense back to a liquid at a different temperature. By removing, or drawing off, each fraction as it condenses, petroleum can easily be separated into its various parts.

Fractional distillation of petroleum is done in a fractionating tower. The process of separating petroleum into its fractions is called **refining.** Refining petroleum is done at a large plant called a refinery. At a refinery, fractionating towers may rise 30 meters or more. Figure 10–3 on page 254 shows a fractionating tower. Petroleum is piped into the base of the fractionating tower and heated to about 385°C. At this temperature, which is higher than the boiling points of most of the fractions, the petroleum vaporizes.

PRODUCTS PRODUCED FROM A BARREL OF CRUDE OIL

	% Yield
Gasolines	46.7
Fuel oil	28.6
Jet fuel	9.1
Petrochemicals and Miscellaneous products	3.8
Coke	3.5
Asphalt and road oil	3.1
Liquified gases	2.9
Lubricants	1.3
Kerosene	0.9
Waxes	0.1

Figure 10–2 *Petroleum is separated into fractions in fractionating columns in an oil refinery. The numbers inside the barrel show the amount, or percentage yield, of each fraction that can be obtained from a barrel of crude oil. Which fraction represents the highest percentage yield?*

253

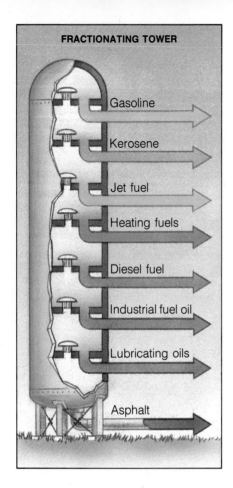

FRACTIONATING TOWER

- Gasoline
- Kerosene
- Jet fuel
- Heating fuels
- Diesel fuel
- Industrial fuel oil
- Lubricating oils
- Asphalt

Figure 10–3 *Each fraction of petroleum condenses at a different temperature and is drawn off in collecting vessels located at fixed points along the column. Where in the tower is the temperature lowest? Where is it highest?*

When the petroleum vaporizes, the fractions rise up the tower. As they rise, they cool and condense. Some fractions condense at high temperatures. These fractions condense right away near the bottom of the tower and are drawn off into collecting vessels. Other fractions continue to rise in the tower. These fractions are drawn off at higher levels in the tower. As a result of this vaporization-condensation process, the various fractions of petroleum are separated and collected.

You will notice in Figure 10–3 that asphalt is collected at the bottom of the fractionating tower. Asphalt requires a temperature even higher than 385°C to vaporize. When the other fractions vaporize, asphalt is left behind as a liquid that runs out of the bottom of the tower. Which fraction in the tower condenses at the lowest temperature?

Petroleum Products

Asphalt—the main material used for building roads—is one product that comes directly from petroleum. Wax, used in furniture polish and milk cartons, is another. Asphalt and wax fall into the category of raw materials that come from the separation of petroleum and are used in manufacturing. Many of the other raw materials in this category, however, are converted to chemicals from which a variety of products—ranging from cosmetics to fertilizers—are made. You will read about these products in the next section.

Another group of petroleum products includes lubricants. Lubricants are substances that reduce friction between moving parts of equipment. The oil applied to the gears of a bicycle is an example of a lubricant. Lubricants are used in many machines—from delicate scientific equipment to the landing gear of an aircraft. Can you think of some other uses of lubricants?

Figure 10–4 *The asphalt used to pave roadways comes directly from petroleum. Lubricants used to make machinery run more efficiently also come from petroleum.*

The greatest percentage of petroleum products includes fuels. Fuels made from petroleum burn easily and release a tremendous amount of energy, primarily in the form of heat. They are also easier to handle, store, and transport than are other fuels, such as coal and wood. Petroleum is the source of nearly all the fuels used for transportation and the many fuels used to produce heat and electricity.

10–1 Section Review

1. What is petroleum and why is it important?
2. Describe the process of fractional distillation.
3. Describe the products produced from petroleum.

Critical Thinking—*Applying Concepts*
4. How would you separate three substances—A, B, and C—whose boiling points are 50°C, 100°C, and 150°C, respectively?

ACTIVITY READING

All About Oil

Some discoveries in history are acts of genius. Others are accidents. But most are a little of both. Read Isaac Asimov's *How Did We Find Out About Oil?* to discover how oil was first discovered, extracted, and used.

Activity Bank

Oil Spill, p. 731

10–2 Petrochemical Products

Paint a picture, pour milk from a plastic container, or put on a pair of sneakers and you are using a product made from petroleum, or a **petrochemical product.**

Polymer Chemistry

The petrochemical products that are part of your life come from the chemicals produced from petroleum. (The word petrochemical refers to chemicals that come from petroleum.) Petrochemical products usually consist of molecules that take the form of long chains. Each link in the chain is a small molecular unit called a **monomer.** (The prefix *mono-* means singular, or one.) The entire molecule chain is called a **polymer.** (The prefix *poly-* means many.)

Guide for Reading

Focus on these questions as you read.

▶ What is a petrochemical product?

▶ What are some products of polymerization?

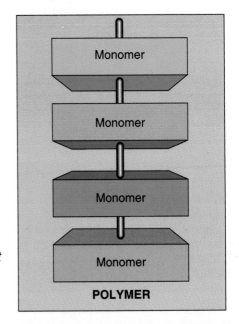

Figure 10–5 *A polymer is made up of a series of monomers. What factors distinguish one polymer from another?*

Figure 10-6 *Silk is spun from threads of silk worm cocoons. Silk is a natural polymer. Rubber obtained from rubber trees is also a natural polymer.*

The types of monomers and the length and shape of the polymer chain determine the physical properties of the polymer. Manufacturers of petrochemical products join monomers together to build polymers. A general term for this process is polymer chemistry.

Natural Polymers

Most of the polymers you will read about in this chapter are made from petrochemicals. Some polymers, however, do occur in nature. Cotton, silk, wool, and natural rubber are all **natural polymers.** Cellulose and lignin, which are important parts of wood, are natural polymers. In fact, all living things contain polymers. Yes—that includes you! Protein, an essential ingredient of living matter, is a polymer. The monomers from which proteins are made are called amino acids. Combined in groups of one hundred or more units, amino-acid monomers form many of the parts of your body—from hair to heart muscle.

Synthetic Polymers

The first polymer was manufactured in 1909. Since then, **polymerization** (poh-lihm-er-uh-ZAY-shuhn) has come a long way. Polymerization is the process of chemically bonding monomers to form polymers. Most early polymers consisted of fewer than two hundred monomers. Today's polymers may contain thousands of monomers. The many ways in which these monomers can be linked may be very complex. They include single chains, parallel chains, intertwining chains, spirals, loops, and loops of chains!

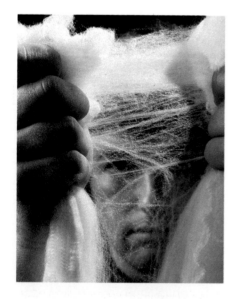

Figure 10-7 *Synthetic fibers, such as nylon, are used to make the carpets you walk on. What are some other uses of synthetic fibers?*

Polymers produced from petrochemicals are called **synthetic polymers.** Something that is synthetic does not exist naturally. Instead it is made by people. Polymer chemistry has produced synthetic materials that are strong, lightweight, heat resistant, flexible, and durable (long lasting). These properties give polymers a wide range of applications.

Although the term polymer may be new to you, you will soon discover that many polymers produced from petrochemicals are familiar to you. For example, petrochemical products such as synthetic rubber and plastic wrap are synthetic polymers. Synthetic polymers are used to make fabrics such as nylon, rayon, Orlon, and Dacron. Plastics—used in products from kitchen utensils to rocket engines—are petrochemical products made of polymers.

In medicine, polymers are used as substitutes for human tissues, such as bones and arteries. These polymers must last a lifetime and must withstand the wear and tear of constant use. Polymer adhesives, rather than thread, may be used to hold clothes together. Polymers are replacing glass, metal, and paper as containers for food. The cup of hot chocolate you may have held today did not burn your hand because it was made of a white insulating polymer. Polymer materials are also used to make rugs, furniture, wall coverings, and curtains. Look around and see how many polymers you can spot. And remember: You have petroleum to thank for all these useful materials.

Polymer materials also can be mixed and matched to produce substances with unusual properties.

Figure 10–8 *Applications of synthetic polymers include rubber tires, leaf and trash bags, and waterproof rain gear.*

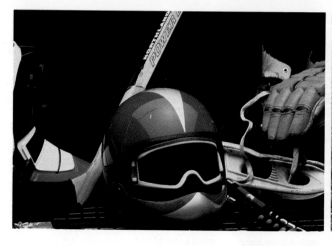

Figure 10–9 *Different forms of plastics are made by melting and processing small bits of plastic grain. The plastic grain can be made into a variety of products, each with characteristics suited for a specific use.*

Different plastics and synthetic fibers are combined to make puncture-proof tires and bulletproof vests. Layers of polymer materials can be combined to make waterproof rain gear.

Polymer chemistry is also important in the transportation industry. Every year the number of polymer parts in cars, planes, and trains increases. A plastic car engine has been built and tested. This engine is lighter, more fuel efficient, and more durable than a metal engine. As you can see, polymers made from petroleum are extremely important today. And they will be even more important in the future.

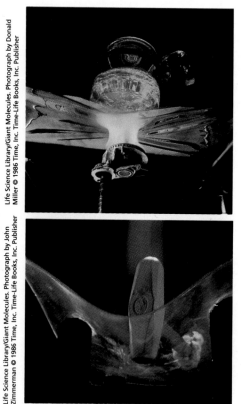
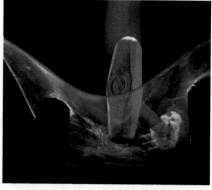

Figure 10–10 *Polymer technology has produced some amazing materials. This sheet of plastic bends no matter how hard it is struck by a hammer (bottom). This extra-thin sheet of plastic is not damaged by temperatures greater than 1000°C (top).*

10–2 Section Review

1. What is a petrochemical product? Give several examples.
2. What is the relationship between a monomer and a polymer?
3. List three examples of natural polymers.
4. What is polymerization?
5. What are some characteristics of synthetic polymers?

Connection—*You and Your World*
6. What might be some of the economic side effects of increased use of polymers in automobiles?

CONNECTIONS

Life-Saving Chemistry

The human body is an amazing collection of systems that interact with one another to sustain life. The systems are made up of tissues and cells that each have a certain function. For example, thin, soft, flexible layers of tissue control the flow of chemicals into and out of the cells. These layers are called *biological membranes.* Some biological membranes allow harmful chemicals to pass out of a cell while keeping needed chemicals inside the cell. The kidneys contain membranes that do this kind of job. Biological membranes are natural polymers.

Like other parts of the human body, biological membranes sometimes do not work correctly or become damaged. The failure of a biological membrane to perform its necessary function can be fatal. That is why healthy kidneys are so important. In the human body, two kidneys constantly filter waste materials from the blood. If the kidneys fail to do this vital job, wastes will remain in the blood, causing damage to other parts of the body.

In 1944, a synthetic membrane that worked like a natural biological membrane was developed. This synthetic membrane made possible the invention of the artificial kidney. The artificial kidney is essentially a large filtering machine. A tube from the machine is inserted into an artery in the patient's arm. Blood flows from the patient into the machine, where the blood is filtered by a synthetic membrane. The purified blood is then pumped back into the patient's system.

Synthetic membranes have a variety of other applications. Some are used as skin substitutes for people who have been badly burned. Others are used in artificial body parts. Polymer chemistry has had a significant impact on human health.

No, the bird is not drowning. It is surrounded by a synthetic membrane that allows oxygen to pass from the water to the bird.

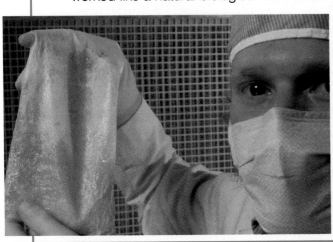

Laboratory Investigation

Comparing Natural and Synthetic Polymers

Problem

How do natural and synthetic polymers compare in strength, absorbency, and resistance to chemical damage?

Materials *(per group)*

3 samples of natural polymer cloth: wool, cotton, linen

3 samples of synthetic polymer cloth: polyester, nylon, acetate

12 Styrofoam cups

mild acid (lime or lemon juice or vinegar)

marking pen	liquid bleach
metric ruler	medicine dropper
scissors	oil
rubber gloves	paper towel

Procedure 🧪 🎲 👁 🔩

1. Record the color of each cloth.
2. Label 6 Styrofoam cups with the names of the 6 cloth samples. Also write the word Bleach on each cup.
3. Cut a 2-square-cm piece from each cloth. Put each piece in its cup.
4. Wearing rubber gloves, carefully pour a small amount of bleach into each cup.
5. Label the 6 remaining cups with the names of the 6 cloth samples and the word Acid. Then pour a small amount of the mild acid into each and repeat step 3.

6. Set the cups aside for 24 hours. Meanwhile, proceed with steps 7 through 9.
7. Using the remaining samples of cloth, attempt to tear each.
8. Place a drop of water on each material. Note whether the water forms beads or is absorbed. If the water is absorbed, record the rate of absorption.
9. Repeat step 8 using a drop of oil.
10. After 24 hours, wearing rubber gloves, carefully pour the liquids in the cups into the sink or a container provided by your teacher. Dry the samples with a paper towel.
11. Record any color changes.

Observations

1. Which material held its color best in bleach? In acid?
2. Which materials were least resistant to chemical damage by bleach or mild acid?
3. Which material has the strongest fiber or is hardest to tear?
4. Which materials are water repellent?

Analysis and Conclusions

1. Compare the natural and synthetic polymers' strength, absorbency, and resistance to chemical change.
2. Which material would you use to manufacture a laboratory coat? A farmer's overalls? A raincoat? An auto mechanic's shirt?
3. **On Your Own** Confirm your results with additional samples of natural and synthetic polymers. What additional tests can you add for comparison?

Summarizing Key Concepts

10–1 What Is Petroleum?

▲ Petroleum is a substance believed to have been formed when plant and animal remains were subjected to tremendous pressure for millions of years.

▲ Petroleum is a mixture of chemicals that can be divided into separate parts, or fractions.

▲ Petroleum is separated into its components through a process call fractional distillation.

▲ During fractional distillation, petroleum is heated and pumped into a fractionating tower. As the fractions rise up the tower, they cool and condense. Because they condense at different temperatures, they can be drawn off at different heights.

▲ Different groups of products are produced from petroleum: raw materials used in manufacturing, raw materials converted to chemicals, lubricants, and fuels.

10–2 Petrochemical Products

▲ Substances derived from petroleum are called petrochemical products.

▲ Most petrochemical products are polymers.

▲ A polymer is a series of molecular units called monomers.

▲ The process of chemically combining monomers to make a polymer is called polymerization.

▲ Natural polymers include cotton, silk, wool, natural rubber, cellulose, protein, and lignin.

▲ Synthetic polymers include synthetic rubber, plastics, and fabrics such as nylon, Orlon, rayon, and Dacron.

▲ Polymers are usually strong, lightweight, heat resistant, flexible, and durable.

▲ Polymers can be mixed and matched to form substances that are waterproof, puncture proof, or electrically conductive.

Reviewing Key Terms

Define each term in a complete sentence.

10–1 What Is Petroleum?
petroleum
fraction
refining

10–2 Petrochemical Products
petrochemical product
monomer
polymer
natural polymer
polymerization
synthetic polymer

Chapter Review

Content Review

Multiple Choice

Choose the letter of the answer that best completes each statement.

1. Crude oil is
   a. a single element.   c. asphalt.
   b. gasoline.   d. a mixture.
2. The physical property used to separate petroleum into its parts is
   a. melting point.   c. density.
   b. boiling point.   d. solubility.
3. The highest temperature in the fractionating tower is
   a. below the boiling point of most petroleum fractions.
   b. above the boiling point of most petroleum fractions.
   c. equal to the boiling point of most petroleum fractions.
   d. below the melting point of most petroleum fractions.
4. A substance unlikely to vaporize in a fractionating tower is
   a. kerosene.   c. asphalt.
   b. gasoline.   d. heating fuel.

5. The process of distillation involves
   a. vaporization and condensation.
   b. freezing and melting.
   c. vaporization and melting.
   d. freezing and condensation.
6. A polymer is made of a series of
   a. atoms.   c. fuels.
   b. monomers.   d. synthetic molecules.
7. An example of a natural polymer is
   a. wool.   c. crude oil.
   b. plastic.   d. copper.
8. An example of a synthetic polymer is
   a. natural rubber.   c. rayon.
   b. protein.   d. cotton.
9. The process of chemically bonding monomers to form polymers is called
   a. distillation.   c. polymerization.
   b. fractionation.   d. refining.
10. An example of a polymer product is
    a. lead tubing.   c. water.
    b. crude oil.   d. plastic.

True or False

If the statement is true, write "true." If it is false, change the underlined word or words to make the statement true.

1. Petroleum taken directly from the Earth is called <u>asphalt</u>.
2. Petroleum can be separated into its different parts, or <u>fractions</u>.
3. The process of separating petroleum into its components is called <u>condensing</u>.
4. <u>Polymerization</u> involves the chemical bonding of monomers into polymers.
5. Plastics are examples of <u>natural</u> polymers.
6. When a vapor <u>evaporates</u>, it changes back to a liquid.
7. A <u>monomer</u> is a long chain of <u>polymers</u>.
8. Silk is an example of a <u>natural</u> polymer.

Concept Mapping

Complete the following concept map for Section 10–1. Then construct a concept map for the entire chapter.

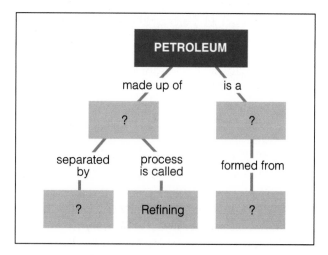

Concept Mastery

Discuss each of the following in a brief paragraph.

1. How did petroleum most likely form?
2. Explain how petroleum is separated into parts during fractional distillation.
3. What happens in the fractionating tower to fractions with extremely high boiling points? With extremely low boiling points?
4. Why is petroleum an important source of fuel?
5. What are natural polymers? Give some examples.
6. What is polymerization? Why is this process useful?
7. What are synthetic polymers? Give some examples.
8. What characteristics of synthetic polymers make them so useful?

Critical Thinking and Problem Solving

Use the skills you have developed in this chapter to answer each of the following.

1. **Drawing conclusions** Petroleum is believed to have been formed at the bottom of oceans. However, oil is often found under dry land—even in deserts. How can you explain this?

2. **Relating facts** Describe some of the uses of synthetic polymers in your life. Then describe what changes you would have to make in your lifestyle if these polymers were not available.
3. **Identifying patterns** The achievements and inventions of the United States space program—originally directed outside planet Earth—have found dramatic uses in our everyday lives. Why do you think space-technology spinoffs have been so widely and successfully used?

4. **Applying concepts** Describe several ways in which polymer chemistry can be used in medicine other than those mentioned in the chapter.
5. **Analyzing information** The United States has been said to have undergone a chemical revolution during the last fifty years. Having read this chapter, explain what the term chemical revolution means to you.
6. **Applying technology** Imagine that you are an engineer whose task is to design a fuel-efficient car that meets all the current standards for safety and durabilty. What kinds of materials would you consider using? What properties must the materials used in the engine have? How about the materials used in safety belts and seat cushions?
7. **Using the writing process** Many people use and enjoy the products derived from petroleum. However, some of the chemical processes used to make these products—as well as the burning of petroleum fuels—add to the pollution of the air, land, and water. Should the manufacturing of certain products be stopped in order to protect the environment? Write a composition expressing your opinion and explaining the reason for it.

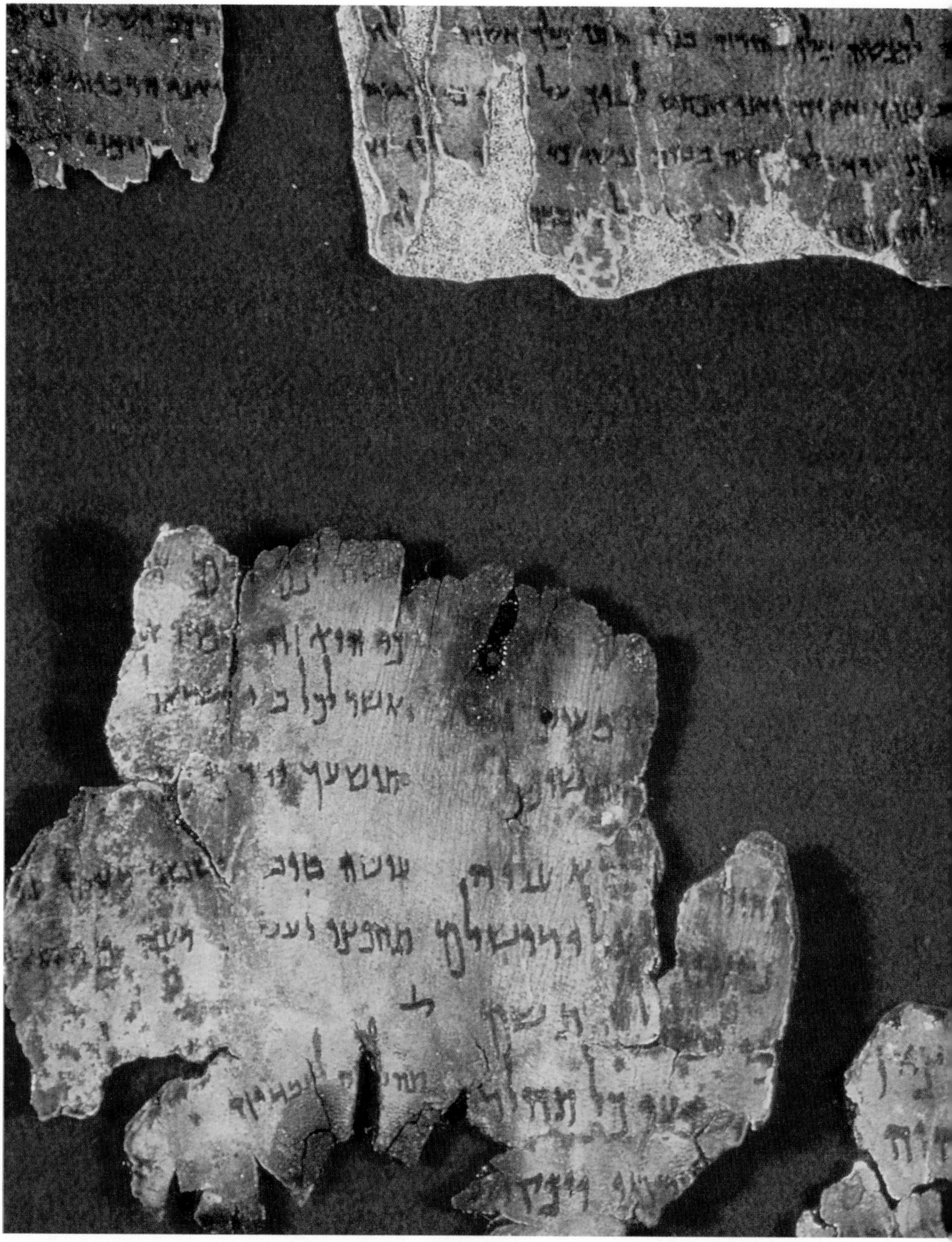

Radioactive Elements

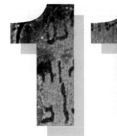

Carbon is one of the most familiar and versatile of all the elements. From plastics to paper, more than 90 percent of all known compounds contain carbon. In addition to forming a huge variety of compounds, carbon has another useful property: One naturally occurring form of carbon—called carbon-14—is radioactive. Why is radioactivity a useful property of carbon-14? By measuring the radioactivity of carbon-14, scientists are able to ascertain the age of any substance that contains carbon. The age of the Dead Sea Scrolls, for example, was determined by means of carbon-14 dating.

Carbon-14 is only one of several radioactive elements. Others include cobalt-60, which is used in the treatment of cancer, and uranium-235, which is used as fuel in nuclear reactors that supply electricity for thousands of communities. As you can see, radioactive elements have many important and beneficial uses. Unfortunately, radioacive elements, such as uranium and plutonium, are also the key components of so-called "atomic" bombs.

In order to understand the risks and benefits involved in their use, you need to learn about radioactive elements and the mysteries hidden deep within them—the subjects of the pages that follow.

Journal *Activity*

You and Your World You have probably heard the terms atomic bomb (A-bomb) and hydrogen bomb (H-bomb). Perhaps you even know about the nuclear radiation associated with them. In your journal, describe the thoughts and/or questions that come to mind when you hear these terms.

◀ *Here you see a fragment from the Book of Deuteronomy from the Dead Sea Scrolls, the age of which was determined using carbon-14 dating.*

11–1 Radioactivity

Some discoveries are made by performing experiments to find out whether hypotheses are true. Other discoveries are stumbled upon purely by accident. The majority of scientific discoveries, however, are a combination of the two—both genius and luck. One such discovery was made by the French scientist Henri Becquerel (beh-KREHL) in 1896. Becquerel was experimenting with a uranium compound to determine whether it gave off X-rays. His experiments did indeed provide evidence of X-rays. But they also showed something else—something rather exciting. Quite by accident, Becquerel discovered that the uranium compound gave off other types of rays that had never before been detected. Little did Becquerel know then that these mysterious rays would open up a whole new world of modern science.

An Illuminating Discovery

At the time of Becquerel's work, scientists knew that certain substances glowed when exposed to sunlight. Such substances are said to be fluorescent. Becquerel wondered whether in addition to glowing, fluorescent substances gave off X-rays.

To test his hypothesis, Becquerel wrapped some photographic film in lightproof paper (paper that does not allow light through it). He placed a piece

Figure 11–1 *The image on the photographic film (right) convinced Becquerel that an invisible "something" had been given off by uranium. The photograph on the left shows rectangular blocks containing the element cesium. The photograph was taken through a heavy glass window 1 meter thick with no source of illumination other than the cesium.*

of fluorescent uranium salt on top of the film and the paper and set both in the sun. Becquerel reasoned that if X-rays were produced by the uranium salt when it fluoresced, the X-rays would pass through the lightproof paper and produce an image on the film. The lightproof paper would prevent light from reaching the film and creating an image, however.

When Becquerel developed the film, he was delighted to see an image. The image was evidence that fluorescent substances give off X-rays when exposed to sunlight. In order to confirm his results, he prepared another sample of uranium salt and film to repeat his experiment the following day. But much to his disappointment, the next two days were cloudy. Impatient to get on with his work, Becquerel decided to develop the film anyway. What he saw on the film amazed him. Once again there was an image of the sample, even though the uranium salt had not been made to fluoresce. In fact, the image on the film was just as strong and clear as the image that had been formed when the sample was exposed to sunlight.

Becquerel realized that an invisible "something" given off by the salt had gone through the lightproof paper and produced an image. In time, this invisible "something" was named **nuclear radiation.** Becquerel tested many more uranium compounds and concluded that the source of nuclear radiation was the element uranium. An element that gives off nuclear radiation is said to be **radioactive.**

Marie Curie, a Polish scientist working in France and a former student of Becquerel's, became interested in Becquerel's pioneering work. She and her husband, French scientist Pierre Curie, began searching for other radioactive elements. In 1898, the Curies discovered a new radioactive element in a uranium ore known as pitchblende. They named the element polonium in honor of Marie Curie's native Poland. Later that year they discovered another radioactive element. They named this element radium, which means "shining element." Both polonium and radium are more radioactive than uranium. Since the Curies' discovery of polonium and radium, many other radioactive elements have been identified and even artificially produced.

Figure 11–2 *Marie Curie and her husband, Pierre, were responsible for the discovery of the radioactive elements radium and polonium. Since that time, many other radioactive elements have been identified.*

The Nature of Nuclear Radiation

Nuclear radiation cannot be seen. So radioactive elements were difficult to identify at first. But it was quickly realized that radioactive elements have certain characteristic properties. The first of these is the property observed by Becquerel. Nuclear radiation given off by radioactive elements alters photographic film. Another property of many radioactive elements is that they produce fluorescence in certain compounds. A third characteristic is that electric charge can be detected in the air surrounding radioactive elements. Finally, nuclear radiation damages cells in most organisms.

Today, scientists use the term **radioactivity** to describe the phenomenon discovered by Becquerel. **Radioactivity is the release of nuclear radiation in the form of particles and rays from a radioactive element.** The radiation given off by radioactive elements consists of three different particles or rays. The three types of radiation have been named alpha (AL-fuh) particles, beta (BAYT-uh) particles, and gamma (GAM-uh) rays after the first three letters of the Greek alphabet.

Figure 11–3 *The three types of radiation can be separated according to charge and penetrating power. When passed through a magnetic field, alpha particles are deflected toward the negative magnetic pole, beta particles are deflected toward the positive pole, and gamma rays are not deflected. Which type of radiation is the most penetrating?*

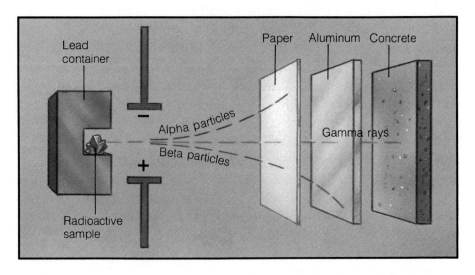

Figure 11–4 *This chart shows the three types of nuclear radiation. What is an alpha particle? A beta particle? Describe gamma rays.*

TYPES OF NUCLEAR RADIATION		
Type	Atomic Mass	Atomic Number
Alpha (α)	4	2
Beta (β)	0	–1
Gamma (γ)	0	none

ALPHA PARTICLES   An **alpha particle** is actually the nucleus of a helium atom—2 protons and 2 neutrons. An alpha particle has a positive charge because it contains 2 positive protons and no other charges. Alpha particles are the weakest type of nuclear radiation. Although they can burn flesh, alpha particles can be stopped by a sheet of paper.

BETA PARTICLES   A **beta particle** is an electron. However, a beta particle should not be confused with an electron that surrounds the nucleus of an atom. A beta particle is an electron that is formed inside the nucleus when a neutron breaks apart. Beta particles have a penetrating ability 10 times greater than alpha particles. Beta particles can pass through as much as 3 millimeters of aluminum.

GAMMA RAYS   A **gamma ray** is an electromagnetic wave of extremely high frequency and short wavelength. Gamma rays are the same kind of waves as the visible light that enables you to see. That is, both are forms of electromagnetic waves. Gamma rays, however, carry a lot more energy. They are the most penetrating radiation given off by radioactive elements. Gamma rays can pass through several centimeters of lead!

11–1 Section Review

1. Describe radioactivity. How did Becquerel discover radioactivity?
2. How did the Curies use Becquerel's discovery?
3. What is a radioactive element?
4. Describe an alpha particle, a beta particle, and a gamma ray. How are they alike? How are they different?

Critical Thinking—*Forming a Hypothesis*
5. There are several theories that attempt to explain how a beta particle is produced. Develop a hypothesis to explain what a neutron—since it is neutral—may actually be composed of while still containing an electron.

11–2 Nuclear Reactions

Although Becquerel and the Curies observed radioactivity, they could not explain its origin. The reason for this is understandable: The source of radioactivity is the nucleus of an atom. But Becquerel discovered radioactivity well before the nucleus was discovered. Several years after Becquerel's and the Curies' work, it was determined that radioactivity results when the nuclei of atoms of certain elements change, emitting particles and/or rays. What still remained unknown, however, was what makes a nucleus break apart and why only some elements are radioactive.

Nuclear Stability

The answers to these puzzling questions would be found in the atom—specifically, in the nucleus. The nucleus of an atom contains protons and neutrons. Protons are positively charged particles. Neutrons are neutral particles; they have no charge. It is a scientific fact that particles with the same charge (positive or negative) repel each other. Thus protons repel each other. How, then, does the nucleus hold together? A force known as the **nuclear strong force** overcomes the force of repulsion between protons and holds protons and neutrons together in the nucleus. The energy required to break up the nucleus is called **binding energy.**

The binding energy is essential to the stability of a nucleus. In some atoms, the binding energy is great enough to hold the nucleus together permanently. The nuclei of such atoms are said to be stable. In other atoms, the binding energy is not as great. The nuclei of these atoms are said to be unstable. An unstable nucleus will come apart. Atoms with unstable nuclei are radioactive.

Some elements that are not radioactive have radioactive forms, or isotopes (IGH-suh-tohps). What is

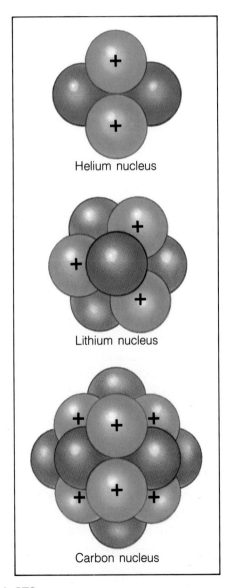

Helium nucleus

Lithium nucleus

Carbon nucleus

Figure 11–5 *The nucleus of an atom contains positively charged protons and neutral neutrons that are held together by the nuclear strong force. A helium nucleus has 2 protons and 2 neutrons. How many protons and neutrons does a lithium nucleus contain? A carbon nucleus?*

NONRADIOACTIVE AND RADIOACTIVE ISOTOPES OF SOME COMMON ELEMENTS

Element	Nonradioactive Isotope	Radioactive Isotope
Hydrogen	1 proton 0 neutrons	1 proton 2 neutrons
Helium	2 protons 2 neutrons	2 protons 4 neutrons
Lithium	3 protons 4 neutrons	3 protons 5 neutrons
Carbon	6 protons 6 neutrons	6 protons 8 neutrons
Nitrogen	7 protons 7 neutrons	7 protons 9 neutrons
Oxygen	8 protons 8 neutrons	8 protons 6 neutrons
Potassium	19 protons 20 neutrons	19 protons 21 neutrons

Figure 11–6 *An isotope is an atom of an element that has the same number of protons but a different number of neutrons. Often, if the number of neutrons greatly differs from the number of protons, the isotope does not have enough binding energy to hold the nucleus together and is therefore radioactive.*

an isotope? The number of protons in the atoms of a particular element cannot vary. An atom is identified by the number of protons it contains. (The number of protons is called the atomic number.) Carbon atoms would not be carbon atoms if they had 5 protons or 7 protons—only 6 protons will do. Yet there are some carbon atoms that have 6 neutrons, and others that have 8 neutrons. The difference in the number of neutrons affects the characteristics of the atom but not its identity. Now you may recall from Chapter 5 that atoms that have the same number of protons (atomic number) but different numbers of neutrons are called isotopes.

Many elements have at least one radioactive isotope. For example, carbon has two common isotopes—carbon-12 and carbon-14. Carbon-12, which you are familiar with as coal, graphite, and diamond, is not radioactive. Carbon-14, used in dating fossils, is radioactive. Figure 11–6 shows the radioactive and nonradioactive isotopes of some common elements.

ACTIVITY

WRITING

What Is a Quark?

Scientists have proposed that all nuclear subatomic particles are composed of basic particles called quarks. Using books and other reference materials in the library, look up the word quark. Find out what quarks are and how they were discovered. Describe some different types of quarks and what they do. Find out about the recent discoveries that have been made involving quarks. Report your findings to the class.

ACTIVITY

WRITING

The Nuclear Age

Often when you learn about discoveries or developments in science, you do not consider the lives and personalities of the scientists involved or the conditions of the time period during which they worked. These factors are important in appreciating the significance of the discovery. The production of the atomic bomb at the end of World War II is a good example of a discovery that grew out of the expectations and concerns of the people involved.

After completing thorough research, write a paper describing the events that led to an enormous research project known as the Manhattan Project. Be sure to include information about these people: Enrico Fermi, Otto Hahn, Lise Meitner, Otto Frisch, Albert Einstein, and President Franklin D. Roosevelt. Also discuss the impact of these developments on history.

Becoming Stable

Imagine a large rock hanging over the edge of a cliff. How might you describe the rock's precarious position? You would probably say it is unstable, meaning that it cannot remain that way for long. Most likely, the rock will fall to the ground below, where it will be in a stable condition. Once it has fallen, the rock will certainly never move itself back to the cliff. Perhaps now you can think of an answer as to why an unstable nucleus breaks apart.

A nucleus that is unstable can become stable by undergoing a nuclear reaction, or change. There are four types of nuclear reactions that can occur. In each type, the identity of the original element is changed as a result of the reaction. You will now learn about each type of nuclear reaction.

Radioactive Decay

The process in which atomic nuclei emit particles or rays to become lighter and more stable is called **radioactive decay.** Radioactive decay is the spontaneous breakdown of an unstable atomic nucleus. There are three types of radioactive decay, each determined by the type of radiation released from the unstable nucleus.

ALPHA DECAY Alpha decay occurs when a nucleus releases an alpha particle. The release of an alpha particle (2 protons and 2 neutrons) decreases the mass number of the nucleus by 4. The mass number is the sum of the number of protons and neutrons in the nucleus. Each proton and each neutron has a mass of 1. The release of an alpha particle decreases the number of protons, or the atomic number, by 2. Thus the original atom is no longer the same. A new atom with an atomic number that is 2 less than the original is formed.

An example of an element that undergoes alpha decay is an isotope of uranium called uranium-238. The number 238 to the right of the hyphen is the mass number for this particular nucleus. An isotope of an element is often represented by using the element's symbol, mass number, and atomic number. The mass number is written to the upper left of the symbol. At the lower left, the atomic number (or number of protons) is written. Uranium has 92 protons. So this is the way uranium-238 would be represented:

$$^{238}_{92}\text{U}$$

The number of neutrons in the nucleus can be determined by subtracting the number of protons from the mass number. In this example, the number of neutrons is the mass number 238 minus the number of protons, 92, or 146 (238 − 92 = 146).

When uranium-238 undergoes alpha decay, or loses an alpha particle, it changes into an atom of thorium (Th), which has 90 protons and 144 neutrons. What is the mass number of thorium?

BETA DECAY   Beta decay occurs when a beta particle is released from a nucleus. As you have learned, a beta particle is an electron formed inside the nucleus when a neutron breaks apart. The other particle that forms when a neutron breaks apart is a proton. So beta decay produces a new atom with the same mass number as the original atom but with an atomic number one higher than the original atom. The atomic number is one higher because there is now an additional proton.

An example of an element that undergoes beta decay is carbon-14. An atom of carbon-14 has 6 protons and 8 neutrons. During beta decay it changes into an atom of nitrogen-14. An atom of nitrogen-14 has 7 protons and 7 neutrons.

When a nucleus releases either an alpha particle or a beta particle, the atomic number, and thus the identity, of the atom changes. **The process in which one element is changed into another as a result of changes in the nucleus is known as transmutation.** The word **transmutation** comes from the word *mutation*, which means change, and the prefix *trans-*, which means through.

GAMMA DECAY   Alpha and beta decay are almost always accompanied by gamma decay, which involves the release of a gamma ray. When a gamma ray is emitted by a nucleus, the nucleus does not change into a different nucleus. But because a gamma ray is an extremely high-energy wave, the nucleus makes a transition to a lower energy state.

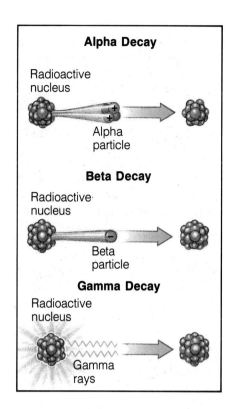

Figure 11–7 *Radioactive elements emit mass and energy during three different types of decay processes. During alpha decay, a helium nucleus and energy are released. A beta particle, or electron, and energy are released during beta decay. During gamma decay, high-energy electromagnetic waves are emitted. Which type of decay does not result in a different element?*

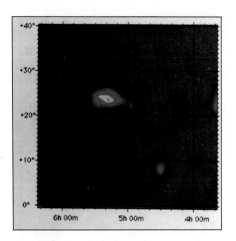

Figure 11–8 *Gamma rays are not as rare as you may think. For example, energy in the form of gamma rays is constantly being emitted from objects in space. This image of a solar flare was recorded by detecting gamma rays from the sun.*

Radioactive Half-Life

A sample of any radioactive element consists of a vast number of radioactive nuclei. These nuclei do not all decay at one time. Rather, they decay one by one over a period of time in a continuous process. The period of time in which a radioactive element decays is called the **half-life.** The half-life is the amount of time it takes for half the atoms in a given sample of an element to decay.

The half-life of carbon-14 is 5730 years. In 5730 years, half the atoms in a given sample of carbon-14 will have decayed to another element: nitrogen-14. In yet another 5730 years, half the remaining carbon-14 will have decayed. At that time, one fourth—or one half of one half—of the original sample will be left. One fourth of the original sample will be carbon-14, and three fourths will be nitrogen-14.

Suppose you had 20 grams of pure barium-139. Its half-life is 86 minutes. So after 86 minutes, half the atoms in the sample would have decayed into another element: lanthanum-139. You would have 10 grams of barium-139 and 10 grams of lanthanum-139. After another 86 minutes, half the atoms in the 10 grams of barium-139 would have decayed into lanthanum-139. You would then have 5 grams of barium-139 and 15 grams of lanthanum-139. What would you have after the next half-life?

Figure 11–9 *The half-life of a radioactive element is the amount of time it takes for half the atoms in a given sample of the element to decay. After the first half-life, half the atoms in the sample are the radioactive element. The other half are the decay element, or the element into which the radioactive element changes. What remains after the second half-life? After the third?*

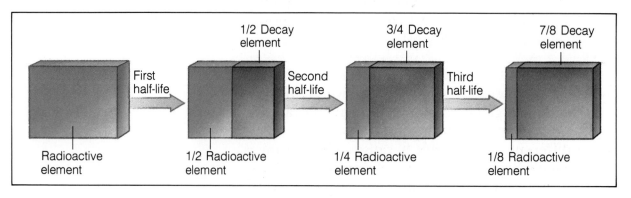

The half-lives of certain radioactive isotopes are useful in determining the ages of rocks and fossils. Scientists can use the half-life of carbon-14 to determine the approximate age of organisms and objects less than 50,000 years old. The technique is called carbon-14 dating. Other radioactive elements, such as uranium-238, can be used to date objects many millions of years old.

Half-lives vary greatly from element to element. Some half-lives are only seconds; others are billions of years. For example, the half-life of rhodium-106 is 30 seconds. The half-life of uranium-238 is 4.5 billion years!

Decay Series

As radioactive elements decay, they change into other elements. These elements may in turn decay, forming still other elements. The spontaneous breakdown continues until a stable, nonradioactive nucleus is formed. The series of steps by which a radioactive nucleus decays into a nonradioactive nucleus is called a **decay series.** Figure 11–11 on page 276 shows the decay series for uranium. What stable nucleus results from this decay series?

Because of the occurrence of decay series, certain radioactive elements are found in nature that otherwise would not be. In the 5-billion-year history of the solar system, many isotopes with short half-lives have decayed quickly. Thus they should not exist in

HALF-LIVES OF SOME RADIOACTIVE ELEMENTS	
Element	**Half-Life**
Bismuth-212	60.5 minutes
Carbon-14	5730 years
Chlorine-36	400,000 years
Cobalt-60	5.26 years
Iodine-131	8.07 days
Phosphorus-32	14.3 days
Polonium-215	0.0018 second
Polonium-216	0.16 second
Radium-226	1600 years
Sodium-24	15 hours
Uranium-235	710 million years
Uranium-238	4.5 billion years

Figure 11–10 *The half-lives of radioactive elements vary greatly. Using the known half-lives of certain radioactive elements, such as carbon-14 and uranium-238, scientists can determine the age of ancient objects. Radioactive dating has been essential to the discovery of information about the Earth's history and about the evolution of organisms such as this ancient turtle.*

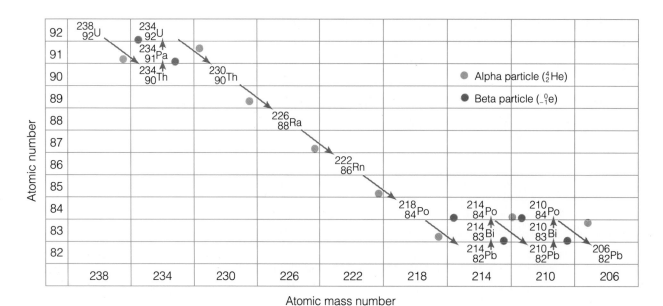

Figure 11–11 *The decay series for uranium-238 is shown in this graph. Radioactive uranium forms nonradioactive lead as a result of the decay series. What happens to the atomic mass number during a decay series? The atomic number?*

ctivity Bank

The Domino Effect, p. 733

nature today. This is hardly the case, however. For example, radium, whose half-life is 1600 years, should have disappeared long ago. Yet it still exists on Earth today. This is because radium is part of the decay series for an isotope with a much longer half-life: uranium-238. Recall that uranium-238 has a half-life of 4.5 billion years.

Artificial Transmutation

Once scientists understood how natural transmutation occurred, they worked to produce **artificial transmutation.** The key was to find a way to change the number of protons in the nucleus of an atom. Ernest Rutherford, the same scientist who discovered the nucleus of the atom, produced the first artificial transmutation. By using alpha particles emitted during the radioactive decay of radium to bombard (hit forcefully) nitrogen nuclei, he produced an isotope of oxygen.

Getting the particles to hit the target nuclei with enough force to alter them is extremely difficult. In order to more effectively produce collisions of high-energy particles, scientists have developed devices for accelerating (speeding up) charged particles. One such device is the Tevatron shown in Figure 11–12 on page 277. Other devices are the cyclotron, synchrotron, betatron, and linear accelerator. These devices use magnets and electric fields to speed up particles and produce collisions.

Before the discovery of the neutron in 1932, mainly alpha particles and protons were used as the "bullets" to bombard nuclei. But because both these particles are positively charged, they are repelled by the positive charge of the target nucleus. A large amount of extra energy is required simply to overcome this repulsion.

Enrico Fermi (FER-mee), an Italian scientist, and his co-workers realized that because neutrons are neutral, they are not repelled by the nucleus. These researchers discovered that neutrons can penetrate the nucleus of an atom more easily than a charged particle can. Neutrons can go through the nucleus without changing it; they can cause the nucleus to disintegrate; or they can become trapped by the nucleus, causing it to become unstable and break apart.

After a great deal of experimentation, the elements neptunium and plutonium were created. They were the first **transuranium elements.** Transuranium elements (also known as synthetic elements) are those with more than 92 protons in their nuclei. In other words, transuranium elements have atomic numbers greater than 92. A whole series of transuranium elements have been formed by bombarding atomic nuclei with neutrons, alpha particles, or other nuclear "bullets."

Figure 11–12 *Artificial transmutation of elements is done in a particle accelerator, such as the one at Fermilab in Illinois. This aerial view shows the outline of the underground tunnel. Particles traveling through long tubes will reach a final speed greater than 99.999 percent of the speed of light!*

Figure 11–13 *Some elements present at the origin of the universe no longer exist. Others, whose half-lives are so short that they should no longer exist, do exist because they are part of the decay series of other radioactive elements. Scientists study decay series in an effort to learn more about the universe and its structures, such as the Tarantula Nebula.*

Radioactive isotopes of natural elements can be made by using a similar technique. Marie Curie's daughter, Irene, and Irene's husband, Frederic Joliot, discovered that stable atoms can be made radioactive when they are bombarded with neutrons. For example, by shooting neutrons at the nucleus of an iodine atom, scientists have been able to make I-131, a radioactive isotope of iodine.

11–2 Section Review

1. How is the binding energy related to the stability of a nucleus? How can an unstable nucleus become stable?
2. What happens during radioactive decay? What are three types of radioactive decay?
3. What is half-life? What is a decay series?
4. What is transmutation? Artificial transmutation?

Critical Thinking—*Making Calculations*
5. The half-life of radium-222 is 38 seconds. How many grams of radium-222 remain in a 12-gram sample after 76 seconds? After 114 seconds? How many half-lives have occurred when 0.75 gram remains?

CONNECTIONS

An Invisible Threat

When you think of the greatest threats to the environment and to your health and safety, scenes of polluted waterways and dirty landfills probably come to mind. So you might be surprised to learn that one of the most widespread and serious environmental threats cannot even be seen. This dangerous menace is radon.

Radon-222 is a radioactive element (atomic number 86) that is produced as part of the decay series for uranium-238. Because of uranium's long half-life, radon is continuously being generated. Since the mid-1980s, radon has become a priority concern for the United States Environmental Protection Agency (EPA). In addition to producing the effects normally associated with nuclear radiation, highly concentrated radon in the air can cause lung cancer if inhaled in large quantities. Radon represents one of the few naturally existing pollutants.

The EPA has set limits for radon levels in the home. However, many homes have radon levels nearly 1000 times greater than the limit. One reason for this is that many buildings are constructed on land rich in uranium ore. Radon is released from soil and rocks containing this ore. In the outdoors, radon is diluted to safe levels. But when it leaks into buildings through cracks in basement floors and walls, radon is trapped—and dangerous.

The concentration of radon in a building depends on the type of construction

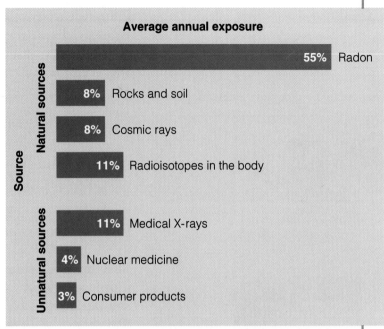

Average annual exposure

Source

Natural sources
- 55% Radon
- 8% Rocks and soil
- 8% Cosmic rays
- 11% Radioisotopes in the body

Unnatural sources
- 11% Medical X-rays
- 4% Nuclear medicine
- 3% Consumer products

and the materials used. New energy-efficient buildings, which are designed to keep heated or cooled air in, also trap radon. One way to protect against radon, especially in areas with a high natural concentration, is to seal cracks in foundation walls and floors. Another way is to improve air ventilation by circulating outside air into a building, thereby diluting existing radon concentrations.

Over the long term, everyone is exposed to potentially damaging radiation from both natural sources and human activity. But radon exposure currently accounts for more than half the average annual exposure to radiation. Home radon-testing kits have become a common household item in many parts of the country. One of the most important protections against the health hazards of radon is the awareness that something that cannot be seen, touched, or smelled can be life-threatening.

11–3 Harnessing the Nucleus

Radioactive decay and the bombardment of a nucleus with particles are two ways in which energy is released from the nucleus of an atom. The amount of energy released, however, is small compared with the tremendous amount of energy known to bind the nucleus together. Long ago, scientists realized that if somehow they could release more of the energy holding the nucleus together, huge amounts of energy could be gathered from tiny amounts of mass.

Nuclear Fission

During the 1930s, several other scientists built upon the discovery of Fermi and his co-workers. In 1938, the German scientists Otto Hahn and Fritz Strassman discovered that when the nucleus of an atom of uranium-235 is struck by a neutron, two smaller nuclei of roughly equal mass were produced. Two other scientists, Lise Meitner and Otto Frisch, provided an explanation for this event: The uranium nucleus had actually split into two. What made the discovery and the explanation so startling was that until then the known nuclear reactions had involved only knocking out a tiny fragment from the nucleus—not splitting it into two!

This reaction—the first of its kind ever to be produced—is an example of **nuclear fission** (FIHSH-uhn). It was so named because of its resemblance to cell division, or biological fission. **Nuclear fission is the splitting of an atomic nucleus into two smaller nuclei of approximately equal mass.**

In one typical fission reaction, a uranium-235 nucleus is bombarded by a neutron, or nuclear "bullet." The products of the reaction are a barium-141 nucleus and a krypton-92 nucleus. Three neutrons are also released: the original "bullet" neutron and 2 neutrons from the uranium nucleus.

The amount of energy released when a single uranium-235 nucleus splits is not very great. But the neutrons released in the first fission reaction become nuclear "bullets" that are capable of splitting other

Figure 11–14 *In the midst of the social and political strife of the late 1930s, scientists such as Lise Meitner and Otto Hahn succeeded in recognizing and explaining the events of nuclear fission. What is nuclear fission?*

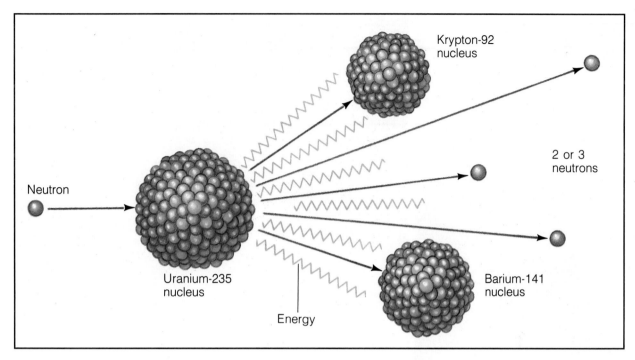

Krypton-92
nucleus

2 or 3
neutrons

Neutron

Uranium-235
nucleus

Barium-141
nucleus

Energy

Figure 11–15 *In this diagram, a uranium-235 nucleus is bombarded with a neutron. The nucleus breaks up, producing a nucleus of krypton-92 and a nucleus of barium-141. Large amounts of energy as well as 2 or 3 additional neutrons are released. Each neutron is capable of splitting another uranium-235 nucleus. What is this repeating process called?*

uranium-235 nuclei. Each uranium nucleus that is split releases 2 or 3 neutrons. These neutrons may then split even more uranium nuclei. The continuous series of fission reactions is called a nuclear chain reaction. In a **nuclear chain reaction,** billions of fission reactions may take place each second!

When many atomic nuclei are split in a chain reaction, huge quantities of energy are released. This energy is produced as a result of the conversion of a small amount of mass into a huge amount of energy. The total mass of the barium, krypton, and 2 neutrons is slightly less than the total mass of the original uranium plus the initial neutron. The missing mass has been converted into energy. An uncontrolled chain reaction produces a nuclear explosion. The atomic bomb is an example of an uncontrolled chain reaction.

All currently operating nuclear power plants use controlled fission reactions to produce energy. The energy is primarily in the form of heat. The heat is carried away and used to produce electricity.

ACTIVITY
READING

An Event That Would Change History Forever

With the excitement of science and the versatility of technology come serious responsibilities and social concerns. The development and use of the atomic bomb was one such ramification of the discovery of nuclear fission. Read *Hiroshima* by John Hersey to gain some insight into the effects such an event has had on people, politics, and history.

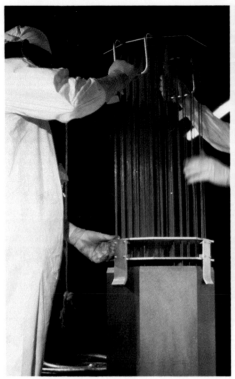

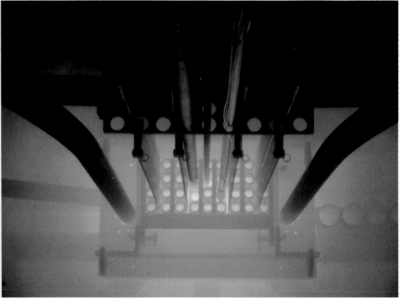

Figure 11–16 *Inside a nuclear reactor, radioactive fuel rods give off energy that produces a blue glow in the water. Before being placed in the reactor, a bundle of uranium-containing rods must be carefully checked.*

Nuclear Fusion

Another type of nuclear reaction that certain radioactive elements can undergo is called **nuclear fusion** (FYOO-zhuhn). Like fission, this kind of nuclear reaction produces a great amount of energy. But unlike fission, which involves the splitting of a high-mass nucleus, this reaction involves the joining of two low-mass nuclei. The word fusion means joining together. **Nuclear fusion is the joining of two atomic nuclei of smaller masses to form a single nucleus of larger mass.**

Nuclear fusion is a thermonuclear reaction. The prefix *thermo-* means heat. For nuclear fusion to take place, temperatures well over a million degrees Celsius must be reached. At such temperatures, the phase of matter known as plasma is formed. Plasma consists of positively charged ions, which are the nuclei of original atoms, and free electrons.

The temperature conditions required for nuclear fusion exist on the sun and on other stars. In fact, it is nuclear fusion that produces the sun's energy. In the sun's core, temperatures of about 20 million degrees Celsius keep fusion going continuously. In a series of steps, hydrogen nuclei are fused into a helium-4 nucleus. See Figure 11–18.

Nuclear fusion produces a tremendous amount of energy. The energy comes from matter that is converted into energy during the reaction. In fact,

the products formed by fusion have a mass that is about 1 percent less than the mass of the reactants. Although 1 percent loss of mass may seem a small amount, its conversion produces an enormous quantity of energy.

Nuclear fusion has several advantages over nuclear fission. The energy released in fusion reactions is greater for a given mass than that in fission reactions. Fusion reactions also produce less radioactive waste. And the possible fuels used for fusion reactions are more plentiful. Unfortunately, considerable difficulties exist with producing useful

Figure 11–17 *The light and heat that make life on Earth possible are the result of nuclear fusion within the sun. The destruction caused by a hydrogen bomb is also the result of nuclear fusion. The only source capable of delivering the energy required to trigger a fusion reaction in the hydrogen bomb is an atomic explosion.*

Figure 11–18 *In the process of nuclear fusion, hydrogen nuclei fuse to produce helium and tremendous amounts of energy. What other products are formed during the fusion reaction?*

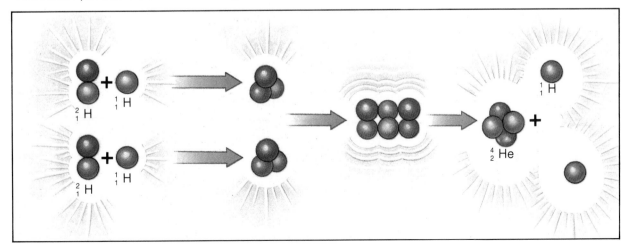

Figure 11–19 *Different elements will give off energy and become more stable by undergoing either fusion or fission. For most elements lighter than iron-56, nuclear fusion will give off energy. For most elements heavier than iron-56, nuclear fission will give off energy. Elements gain stability by moving closer on the graph to iron-56.*

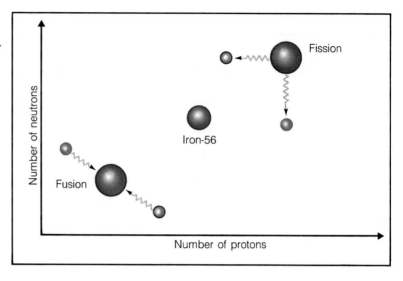

fusion reactions on Earth. Fusion reactions are more difficult to begin, to control, and to maintain than nuclear fission reactions are. After all, no known vessel can contain reactions occurring at such tremendous temperatures. And such high temperatures are extremely difficult to achieve. In fact, a hydrogen bomb, which uses fusion, is started by an atomic bomb, which uses fission. It is the only way of achieving the necessary temperatures.

Scientists are continuing their search for ways to control this powerful reaction and to tap a tremendous energy resource. As an example, experiments using high-powered laser beams and electrons as ways of starting fusion reactions are being conducted.

11–3 Section Review

1. What is nuclear fission? Nuclear fusion?
2. How is the sun's energy produced?
3. Where does the energy produced in both fission and fusion reactions come from?
4. Compare the energy produced by fission and fusion reactions with the energy produced by radioactive decay.

Connection—*You and Your World*

5. Why is the production of less radioactive waste considered an advantage of nuclear fusion?

11–4 Detecting and Using Radioactivity

Guide for Reading

Focus on these questions as you read.

▶ *What instruments are used to detect and measure radioactivity?*

▶ *What are some uses of radioactive substances?*

Radioactivity cannot be seen or felt. Becquerel discovered radioactivity because it left marks on photographic film. Although film is still used today to detect radioactivity, scientists have more specialized instruments for this purpose. **The instruments scientists use to detect and measure radioactivity include the electroscope, the Geiger counter, the cloud chamber, and the bubble chamber.**

Instruments for Detecting and Measuring Radioactivity

ELECTROSCOPE An **electroscope** is a simple device that consists of a metal rod with two thin metal leaves at one end. If an electroscope is given a negative charge, the metal leaves separate. In this condition, the electroscope can be used to detect radioactivity.

Radioactive substances remove electrons from molecules of air. As a result, the molecules of air become positively charged ions. When a radioactive substance is brought near a negatively charged electroscope, the air molecules that have become positively charged attract the negative charge on the leaves of the electroscope. The leaves discharge, or lose their charge, and collapse.

GEIGER COUNTER In 1928, Hans Geiger designed an instrument that detects and measures radioactivity. Named the **Geiger counter** in honor of its inventor, this instrument produces an electric current in the presence of a radioactive substance.

A Geiger counter consists of a tube filled with a gas such as argon or helium at a reduced pressure. When radiation enters the tube through a thin window at one end, it removes electrons from the atoms of the gas. The gas atoms become positively charged ions. The electrons move through the positively charged ions to a wire in the tube, setting up an electric current. The current, which is amplified and fed into a recording or counting device, produces a flashing light and a clicking sound. The number of

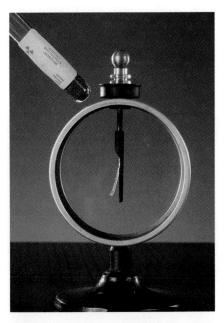

Figure 11–20 *Because radioactive substances will cause an electroscope to discharge, an electroscope can be used to detect radiation. What do radioactive substances do to molecules of air?*

285

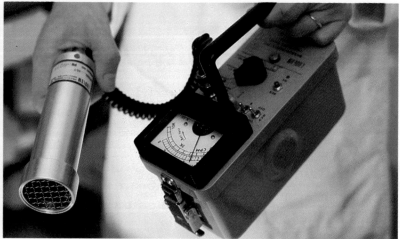

Figure 11–21 *A Geiger counter detects and measures radioactivity. A spiderwort plant is nature's radiation detector. The stamens of the spiderwort flower are usually blue. In the presence of radiation the stamens turn pink.*

flashes and clicks per unit time indicates the strength of the radiation. A counter attached to the wire is able to measure the amount of radioactivity by measuring the amount of current.

CLOUD CHAMBER A **cloud chamber** contains a gas cooled to a temperature below its usual condensation point (point at which it becomes a liquid). When a radioactive substance is put inside the chamber, droplets of the gas condense around the radioactive particles. The process is similar to what happens in "cloud seeding," when rain droplets condense around particles that have been injected into the clouds. The droplets formed around the particles of radiation in a cloud chamber leave a trail that shows up along the chamber lining. An alpha particle leaves a short, fat trail, whereas a beta particle's trail is long and thin. The trails left by alpha particles are shown in Figure 11–22.

BUBBLE CHAMBER The **bubble chamber** is similar in some ways to the cloud chamber, although its construction is more complex. A bubble chamber contains a superheated liquid. A superheated liquid is hot enough to boil—but does not. Instead, it remains in the liquid phase. The superheated liquid most often contained in a bubble chamber is hydrogen.

When radioactive particles pass through the chamber, they cause the hydrogen to boil. The boiling liquid leaves a trail of bubbles, which is used to track the radioactive particle.

Figure 11–22 *This cloud chamber photograph shows an upward stream of alpha particles.*

Putting Radioactivity to Work

Radioactive substances have many practical uses. Dating organic objects, which you learned about earlier, is one such use. In industry, radioactive isotopes, or **radioisotopes,** have additional uses. Radioisotopes can be used to find leaks or weak spots in metal pipes, such as oil pipe lines. Radioisotopes also help study the rate of wear on surfaces that rub together. One surface is made radioactive. Then the amount of radiation on the other surface indicates the wear.

Because radioisotopes can be detected so readily, they can be used to follow an element through an organism, or through an industrial process, or through the steps of a chemical reaction. Such a radioactive element is called a **tracer,** or radiotracer. Tracers are possible because all isotopes of the same element have essentially the same chemical properties. When a small quantity of radioisotope is mixed with the naturally occurring stable isotopes of the same element, all the isotopes go through the same reactions together.

An example of a tracer is phosphorus-32. The nonradioactive element phosphorus is used in small amounts by both plants and animals. If phosphorus-32 is given to an organism, the organism will use the radioactive phosphorus just as it does the nonradioactive phosphorus. However, the path of the radioactive element can be traced. In this way, scientists can learn a great deal about how plants and animals use phosphorus.

Another area in which radioisotopes make an important contribution is in the field of medicine. The branch of medicine in which radioactivity is used is known as nuclear medicine. Tracers are extremely valuable in diagnosing diseases. For example, radioactive iodine—iodine-131—can be used to study the function of the thyroid gland, which absorbs iodine. Sodium-24 can be used to detect diseases of the circulatory system. Iron-59 can be used to study blood circulation.

Another procedure, known as radioimmunoassay, developed by Dr. Rosalyn Yalow—who won the Nobel prize for her work—involves using tracers to detect the presence of minute quantities of substances in

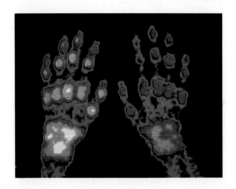

Figure 11–23 *Radioisotopes can be used as tracer elements to produce images such as this one of a person's hands. The different-colored areas help doctors diagnose conditions in order to prescribe treatment. This person has arthritis.*

Radioactivity in Medicine

Obtain permission to visit the radiation laboratory at a local hospital. Observe the instruments used and the safety precautions taken for both patients and technicians when using the devices. Interview a technician, if possible. Make a report on your visit.

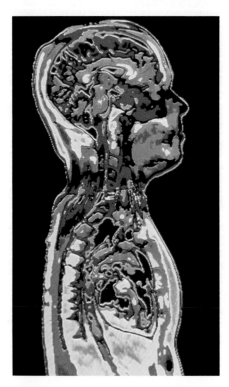

Figure 11–24 *Observing changes in the nuclei of atoms has many important applications. Through nuclear magnetic resonance imaging, doctors can form detailed images of various parts of the human body. What is an advantage of this procedure over exploratory surgery?*

the body. These tests can be used to detect pregnancy as well as the early signs of a disease. Another powerful research tool—nuclear magnetic resonance imaging (MRI)—has become invaluable in a variety of fields, from physics to chemistry and biochemistry. MRI involves recording changes in the energy of atomic nuclei in response to external energy changes, without altering the cells of the body in any way.

Radiation is also used to destroy unhealthy cells, such as those that cause cancer. Radiation in large doses destroys living tissues, especially cells undergoing division. Because cancer cells undergo division more frequently than normal cells do, radiation kills more cancer cells than it does normal cells. As early as 1904, physicians attempted to treat masses of unhealthy cells, known as tumors, with high-energy radiation. This treatment is called radiation therapy.

Radioisotopes can also be used to kill bacteria that cause food to spoil. Radiation was used to preserve the food that the astronauts ate while on the moon and in orbit.

Dangers of Radiation

Although radioactivity has tremendous positive potential, radioactive materials must be handled with great care. Radioactive materials are extremely dangerous. Radiation can ionize—or knock electrons out of—atoms or molecules of any material it passes through. For this reason, the term ionizing radiation is sometimes used. So, oddly enough, the same radiation that is used to treat disease can also cause it.

Ionization can cause considerable damage to materials, particularly to biological tissue. When ionization is produced in cells, ions may take part in chemical reactions that would not otherwise have occurred. This may interfere with the normal operation of the cell. Damage to DNA is particularly serious. An alteration in the DNA (substance responsible for carrying traits from one generation to another) of a cell can interfere with the production of proteins and other essential cellular materials. The result may be the death of the cell. If many cells die, the organism may not be able to survive.

Large doses of radiation can cause reddening of the skin, a drop in the white blood cell count, and numerous other unpleasant symptoms, including nausea, fatigue, and loss of hair. Such effects are sometimes referred to as radiation sickness. Large doses of radiation can also be fatal. Marie Curie's death in 1934 was caused by exposure to too much radiation.

Even metals and other structural materials can be weakened by intense radiation. This is a considerable problem in nuclear-reactor power plants and for space vehicles that must pass through areas of intense cosmic radiation.

We are constantly exposed to low-level radiation from natural sources such as cosmic rays from space, radioactivity in rocks and soil, and radioactive isotopes that are present in food and in our bodies.

Today, people who work with radioactive materials take extreme precautions. They wear radiation-sensitive badges that serve as a warning of unsafe levels of radiation. Specially designed clothing is worn to block radiation. Scientists continue to search for greater understanding and control of radiation so that its benefits can be enjoyed without the threat of danger.

Figure 11–25 *The hands and numbers of a luminous watch contain minute amounts of radium. The radioactive decay of radium causes the watch to glow in the dark. People who painted the dials on clocks in the early 1900s suffered from radiation poisoning because they often licked the tips of their brushes to make fine lines.*

Figure 11–26 *Workers handling radioactive materials must use extreme caution and wear specially designed clothes for protection.*

11–4 Section Review

1. Name four instruments used to detect and measure radioactivity.
2. Compare a bubble chamber and a cloud chamber.
3. What is a radioisotope? What are its uses?
4. What is a tracer? Describe several uses of tracers.

Connection—*Life Science*

5. A mutation is a change that occurs in the genetic material of a cell (the code that determines what traits will be carried on from generation to generation). Why does nuclear radiation cause mutations?

Laboratory Investigation

The Half-Life of Sugar Cubes

Problem

How can the half-life of a large sample of sugar cubes be determined?

Materials *(per group)*

250 sugar cubes	large bowl
food coloring	medicine dropper

Procedure 🧪

1. Place a small drop of food coloring on one side of each sugar cube.

2. Put all the sugar cubes in a bowl. Then gently spill them out on the table. Move any cubes that are on top of other cubes.

3. Remove all the sugar cubes that have the colored side facing up. If you have room on the table, arrange in a vertical column the sugar cubes that you removed. Put the rest of the cubes back in the bowl.

4. Repeat step 3 several more times until five or fewer sugar cubes remain.

5. On a chart similar to the one shown, record the number of tosses (times you spilled the sugar cubes), the number of sugar cubes removed each time, and the number of sugar cubes remaining. For example, suppose after the first toss you removed 40 sugar cubes. The number of tosses would be 1, the number of cubes removed would be 40, and the number of cubes remaining would be 210 (250 – 40).

Observations

1. Make a full-page graph of tosses versus cubes remaining. Place the number of tosses on the X (horizontal) axis and the number of cubes remaining on the Y (vertical) axis. Start at zero tosses with all 250 cubes remaining.

2. Determine the half-life of the decaying sugar cubes in the following way. Find the point on the graph that corresponds to one half of the original sugar cubes (125). Move vertically down from this point until you reach the horizontal axis. Your answer will be the number of tosses.

Tosses	Sugar Cubes Removed	Sugar Cubes Remaining
0	0	250
1	40	210
2		
3		

Analysis and Conclusions

1. What is the shape of your graph?

2. How many tosses are required to remove one half of the sugar cubes?

3. How many tosses are required to remove one fourth of the sugar cubes?

4. Assuming tosses are equal to years, what is the half-life of the sugar cubes?

5. Using your answer to question 4, how many sugar cubes should remain after 8 years? After 12 years? Do these numbers agree with your observations?

6. What factor(s) could account for the differences in your observed results and those calculated?

7. **On Your Own** Repeat the experiment with a larger number of sugar cubes. Predict whether the determined half-life will be different. Is it?

Study Guide

Summarizing Key Concepts

11–1 Radioactivity

▲ An element that gives off nuclear radiation is said to be radioactive.

▲ Nuclear radiation occurs in three forms: alpha particles, beta particles, and gamma rays.

11–2 Nuclear Reactions

▲ If the binding energy—the energy required to break up the nucleus—is not strong, an atom is said to be unstable. Atoms with unstable nuclei are radioactive.

▲ Atoms that have the same atomic number but different numbers of neutrons are called isotopes.

▲ An unstable nucleus eventually becomes stable by undergoing a nuclear reaction.

▲ Radioactive decay is a nuclear reaction that involves the spontaneous breakdown of an unstable nucleus. During radioactive decay, alpha particles, beta particles, and/or gamma rays are emitted.

▲ The length of time needed for half of a given sample of a radioactive element to decay is called the half-life.

▲ The series of steps by which a radioactive nucleus decays is known as a decay series.

▲ Artificial transmutation involves the nuclear reactions in which atomic nuclei are bombarded with high-speed particles.

11–3 Harnessing the Nucleus

▲ Nuclear fission is the splitting of an atomic nucleus to form two smaller nuclei of roughly equal mass.

▲ Nuclear fusion is the joining together of two atomic nuclei to form a single nucleus of larger mass.

11–4 Detecting and Using Radioactivity

▲ Four devices that can detect radioactivity are the electroscope, Geiger counter, cloud chamber, and bubble chamber. The Geiger counter can also measure radioactivity.

▲ Radioactive substances must be handled carefully because large amounts of radiation can be harmful to living things.

Reviewing Key Terms

Define each term in a complete sentence.

11–1 Radioactivity
nuclear radiation
radioactive
radioactivity
alpha particle
beta particle
gamma ray

11–2 Nuclear Reactions
nuclear strong force

binding energy
radioactive decay
transmutation
half-life
decay series
artificial transmutation
transuranium element

11–3 Harnessing the Nucleus
nuclear fission

nuclear chain reaction
nuclear fusion

11–4 Detecting and Using Radioactivity
electroscope
Geiger counter
cloud chamber
bubble chamber
radioisotope
tracer

Chapter Review

Content Review

Multiple Choice

Choose the letter of the answer that best completes each statement.

1. The particle given off by a radioactive element that is actually a helium nucleus is a(an)
   a. beta particle.
   c. isotope.
   b. gamma ray.
   d. alpha particle.

2. Atoms with the same atomic number but different numbers of neutrons are
   a. isotopes.
   c. alpha particles.
   b. radioactive.
   d. beta particles.

3. In relation to the original atom, the atom that results from alpha decay has an atomic number that is
   a. 2 less.
   c. the same.
   b. 1 less.
   d. 2 more.

4. The process in which one element changes into another as a result of nuclear changes is
   a. fluorescence.
   c. transuranium.
   b. transmutation.
   d. synthesis.

5. An atomic nucleus splits into two smaller nuclei in
   a. fusion.
   c. fission.
   b. alpha decay.
   d. transmutation.

6. A device in which radioactive materials leave a trail of liquid droplets is a(an)
   a. bubble chamber.
   c. decay chamber.
   b. cloud chamber.
   d. electroscope.

7. A Geiger counter detects radioactivity when the radioactive substance
   a. leaves a trail of bubbles.
   b. condenses around particles of a gas.
   c. causes liquid gas to boil.
   d. produces an electric current.

8. An artificially produced radioactive isotope of an element is called a
   a. alpha isotope.
   c. radioisotope.
   b. transmutation.
   d. gamma isotope.

True or False

If the statement is true, write "true." If it is false, change the underlined word or words to make the statement true.

1. One of the radioactive elements discovered by the Curies was <u>uranium</u>.
2. The energy that holds the nucleus together is the <u>binding energy</u>.
3. <u>Gamma rays</u> are electromagnetic waves of very high frequency and energy.
4. The spontaneous breakdown of an unstable nucleus is <u>artificial transmutation</u>.
5. Two atomic nuclei join together during nuclear <u>fission</u>.
6. Gas molecules are ionized by a radioactive substance in a <u>bubble chamber</u>.
7. <u>Iodine-131</u> can be used to study the function of the thyroid gland.
8. <u>Radioisotopes</u> are used to kill bacteria.

Concept Mapping

Complete the following concept map for Section 11–1. Then construct a concept map for the entire chapter.

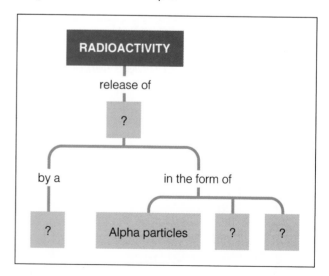

Concept Mastery

Discuss each of the following in a brief paragraph.

1. Describe how Becquerel's work illustrates the scientific method.
2. Describe the penetrating power of each of the three types of radiation.
3. How was the existence of the nuclear strong force deduced? What is the energy associated with the strong force, and how is it related to the stability of an element?
4. What do isotopes of a given element have in common? How are they different?
5. Describe the four types of nuclear reactions.
6. Describe how a Geiger counter works. How is it different from a bubble chamber, cloud chamber, and an electroscope?
7. Explain why the amount of helium in the sun is increasing.
8. Why must the fission process release neutrons if it is to be useful?
9. What are some of the uses of radioactivity?

Critical Thinking and Problem Solving

Use the skills you have developed in this chapter to answer each of the following.

1. **Making graphs** Sodium-24 has a half-life of 15 hours. Make a graph to show what happens to a 100-gram sample of sodium-24 over a 5-day period.
2. **Interpreting a graph** The dots on the accompanying graph represent stable nuclei. The straight line represents equal numbers of protons and neutrons. Describe the relationship between the number of protons and the number of neutrons as the atomic number increases.

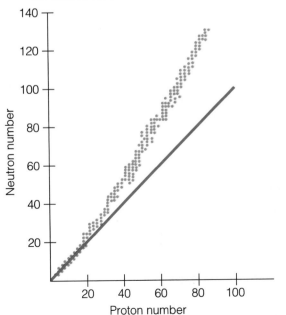

3. **Making comparisons** Describe the three types of radiation and relate them to the three types of radioactive decay.
4. **Analyzing data** A skeleton of an ancient fish is found to contain one eighth the amount of carbon-14 that it contained when it was alive. How old is the skeleton?
5. **Making calculations** The half-life of cobalt-60 is 5.26 years. How many grams of a 20-gram sample of cobalt-60 remain after 10.52 years? After 15.78 years?
6. **Drawing conclusions** Why do you think it is more dangerous for a woman of child-bearing age to be exposed to nuclear radiation than it is for a younger or an older woman to be exposed?
7. **Using the writing process** Food spoils because organisms such as bacteria and mold grow on it and decompose it. Gamma rays can destroy such organisms. So foods treated with gamma rays, or irradiated foods, last longer. Many people, however, are afraid that irradiated foods may be dangerous. Others do not want to live near gamma-ray treatment centers. Write a letter to your state representative describing your thoughts about irradiated foods.

GAZETTE

CARBON BALLS:
New Adventures in Chemistry

You can't kick it through goalposts, dribble it down a basketball court, or hit it with a bat or a tennis racket. But scientists are extremely excited about a ball that has much more to do with atoms than with athletics!

The special sphere is called the "bucky ball." It is a molecular form of pure carbon shaped like the geodesic domes designed by the famous architect R. Buckminster Fuller. Thus its nickname—bucky ball—and its complete name: Buckminsterfullerene.

The humorous scientists who named the fullerene—as well as discovered it—include teams of chemists led by Richard Smalley of Rice University in Texas and Harry Kroto of the University of Sussex in England. In 1985, while researching the clustering properties of carbon atoms, the chemists noticed what they considered to be a curious trend: All the carbon molecules they produced contained an even number of atoms. Their measurements also indicated that a large proportion of the molecules consisted of 60 atoms. After further investigation—with equipment that ranged from sophisticated lasers to simple scraps of paper—the scientists theorized the existence of a special crystal form of carbon. Under the right circumstances, they claimed, 60 carbon atoms could bond together to form a hollow perfect sphere: the bucky ball. The sphere has 32 facets, or sides, of which 12 are pentagons (5-sided) and 20 are hexagons (6-sided). Its structure makes it an incredibly stable molecule.

Smalley and Kroto were offering the world a startling discovery: a third molecular form of pure carbon. The only other known forms of carbon are graphite and diamond. In light of its implications, Smalley and Kroto's proposal was first met with skepticism from

Dr. Richard Smalley is shown here at work in his laboratory blasting bits of carbon with a laser. His research, along with that of Dr. Kroto, resulted in the discovery of the bucky ball—seen here as a computer-generated image.

(a)

C_{60}

(b)

C_{70}

▲ ▶ A three-dimensional model of Buckminsterfullerene shows its pattern. Scientists hope that they can produce molecules that keep the same shape yet contain more carbon atoms. On the right is the first microscopic image of buckminsterfullerenes.

fellow scientists. Some said that Smalley and Kroto had failed to provide enough concrete evidence to prove their discovery. Some critics even said that the theory was too good, too simple, and too elegant to be true. But Smalley and Kroto refused to abandon their ideas. They were convinced that the Buckminsterfullerene molecule did indeed exist.

While Smalley and Kroto continued their research, other scientists around the globe began to investigate the possible existence of the bucky ball. In the fall of 1990, a good five years after Smalley and Kroto first published their findings, two major discoveries confirmed their theory. Researchers at the University of Arizona, the Max Planck Institute in Germany, and the International Business Machines Almaden Research Center in San Jose, California, produced and published the first photographs of the carbon balls. In addition, two physicists found a way to mass-produce the ball-shaped molecules. The laboratories in Arizona and Germany pioneered a method of producing the molecules by passing an electric arc between graphite electrodes. Carbon from the electrodes, which are kept in a vacuum with a small amount of helium, vaporizes and then condenses as soot. About 5 percent of this soot results in fullerene molecules.

Now scientists—even the skeptics—are excited about the fullerene's future. Because of its exceptional stability, the ball-shaped molecule has many potential applications. As a researcher at the University of Arizona explained, the fullerene may introduce a "brand new kind of chemistry." Scientists imagine that fullerenes may be able to make a new type of lubricant because the molecules roll like invisible ball bearings. The bucky balls may also be used to produce new organic compounds and in the development of better batteries. Other areas of research include the use of bucky balls on new telecommunications systems as building blocks for a new generation of high-speed computers based on light waves rather than on electricity. There is also hope of encapsulating drugs for cancer treatments in bucky balls to preserve the drugs until they reach the intended therapy site. But the busiest and most exciting area of research is in the application of fullerenes as superconductors.

So despite the fact that the bucky ball doesn't have much use on the playing fields, it undoubtedly has tremendous potential in the laboratory, as well as in the marketplace.

UNIT THREE
Motion, Forces, and Energy

▲ Although this volcanic eruption may look like a fireworks display, it is actually an extremely violent release of energy.

Poised high upon the edge of a jagged rock, the cheetah seems almost motionless. Yet every muscle is tensed and ready to spring into action. A gentle breeze blows the familiar scent of an antelope toward the cheetah's quivering nostrils. Its head turns. The prey is in sight. The cheetah silently readies itself for attack, while the unsuspecting antelope calmly grazes on the plain just below.

With one swift leap, the cheetah pounces forcefully on the ground and sets into motion. The antelope takes off fast and furiously to spare itself an untimely death at the paws of the cheetah. The powerful cheetah can run as fast as 110 kilometers per hour. The antelope seems doomed. Speeding across the grassy plain with the cheetah at its tail, the antelope suddenly darts into the bush. The cheetah lags behind. The antelope escapes—this time. A meal of antelope would have given the cheetah its fill of energy.

An anxious cheetah cub awaits an opportunity to pounce on and capture a handsome meal. ▶

CHAPTERS

But for tonight, the cheetah will go hungry.

The interaction of forces that made this motion-packed scene possible is not limited to the jungle. Almost everything you do every day of your life involves the same basic characteristics of motion, forces, and energy that spared this antelope's life. In this Unit you will learn all about motion and forces and the relationship between them. You will also learn how forces are altered by machines to make them more helpful to you. Finally, you will learn about energy and its role in motion, forces, and machines.

 This pipeline wave may give the surfer the ride of his life or a crushing blow. Where do you think the wave gets its energy?

Discovery *Activity*

Tabletop Raceway

1. On a smooth surface such as a floor or long tabletop, make a ramp by placing one end of a sturdy piece of cardboard on one textbook. Make another ramp using three or four textbooks.

2. Release a small toy car from the top of the low ramp. Do not push it. Observe how far and how fast the car travels.

3. Repeat step 2 using the high ramp.

4. Tape a stack of washers to the car. Repeat steps 2 and 3. Observe the movement of the car.

   What effect does the height of the ramp have on the movement of the car?

   How would the movement of the car have changed if you had pushed it down the ramp?

   How do the washers affect the movement of the car?

   ■ Is it more difficult to stop a heavily loaded truck or a compact car?

What Is Motion?

12

The eyes of the crowd are fixed on the sleek, dazzling skier as he sweeps down the ski-jump track at 100 kilometers per hour. Reaching the bottom of the track, he leaps into the air. The icy wind lashes at his face. Even with goggles on, he is blinded by the glare of the snow on the mountainside below— far below.

Then, in an attempt to defy gravity, he leans forward. His body and skis take the form of an airplane wing as he rides the wind farther. Finally, his skis make contact with the snow-covered landing area. The snow flies up in his face in two streams. The sound of the cheering crowd mingles with the sound of the wind. His ride is over.

The scene is the Winter Olympics. And the ski jumper has just flown 117 meters through the air to set a new record for distance. He owes his gold medal not only to courage and years of training but also to an understanding of motion.

In this sense, ski jumping is not merely a sport; it is also a science. Learning about the science of motion may not earn you an Olympic medal, but it can be a leap into adventure and discovery.

Journal *Activity*

You and Your World Recall an experience in which you were moving at a fairly rapid speed. Perhaps you were running, bicycling, or riding in a car, train, or airplane. Describe the situation in detail in your journal. Explain how you felt speeding up from rest and then slowing down again to stop. Tell how the speed affected your movement. How would your movement have been different if your speed was slower?

◀ *Although this ski jumper seems to be floating in midair, his body is really in motion. You would quickly observe this fact if you were watching the ski jump from the ground below.*

12–1 Frames of Reference

The conductor blows the whistle, and your train pulls away from the station. As the train picks up speed, the people on the platform watch you whiz by them. But to the person sitting next to you on the train, you are not moving at all. How can this be? Are you or are you not moving? Actually, you are doing both! The answer to the question depends on the background with which the observer is comparing you.

The people on the platform are comparing you with the Earth. Because the Earth is not moving out from under their feet, you appear to be moving. The person sitting next to you is comparing you with the train. Because you are moving with the train (the train is not moving out from under you), you do not appear to be moving when compared with the train. If, however, the person on the train had compared you with a nearby tree or the ground, you would have appeared to move.

Whenever you describe something that is moving, you are comparing it with something that is assumed to be stationary, or not moving. The background or object that is used for comparison is called a **frame of reference.** All movement, then, is described relative to a particular frame of reference. For the people on the platform, the frame of reference is the Earth. For the person sitting next to you, the frame

Figure 12–1 *From your frame of reference, the sun seems to be dropping below the horizon in southern Spain. But is the sun really falling or are you moving?*

Figure 12–2 *The Russian space station* Mir *and the American space shuttle* Atlantis, *in orbit high above the Earth's surface, move at speeds greater than 28,000 kilometers per hour relative to an observer on the ground. But because they are moving at the same speed, they are not moving relative to one another. This enabled them to rendezvous and dock in June, 1995.*

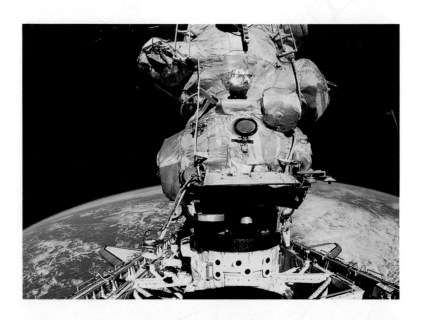

of reference is the train. Perhaps the term frame of reference sounds new to you. But it is an idea you use often in your daily life as you describe different movements. The frame of reference you use depends on the type of movement and the position from which you are observing.

The fact that movement is related to a frame of reference is often used in movies to achieve certain effects. Sometimes an actor stays in one place and just the background moves. On the screen it looks as if the actor is moving. This is because your frame of reference is the background. You have assumed that the background is the stationary object—which it is most of the time.

No frame of reference is more correct than any other. If you are riding on a train, you may describe movement as if the train were your frame of reference. However, the train is moving relative to the Earth. So, if you use the trees and the ground as your background, the Earth could become your frame of reference. But the Earth is moving around the sun. Thus the sun could be your frame of reference. Even the sun is moving as part of the galaxy. So you see, everything in the universe is moving. There is no frame of reference that is truly not moving relative to all other frames of reference. What is not moving in one frame of reference is moving in another. But all movement is described according to some frame of reference. The most common frame of reference is the Earth, but no single frame of reference is "correct" in any situation.

Figure 12–3 *No need to turn this photograph right-side-up. Fred Astaire is dancing on the ceiling, or so it seems. How is this effect achieved in the movies?*

ACTIVITY

DOING

Stargazing

The Big Dipper is a dipper-shaped group of stars familiar to most people. If you have ever tried to locate the Big Dipper in the nighttime sky, you know that it is not always in the same place. In January, you may look out your window in one direction to find it. In June, however, you will have to look in another direction.

Obtain star charts for 12 months in a row. Observe how the stars are in different locations in the course of the year. Is the motion a result of the movement of the Earth or of the stars? What does your description of motion depend on?

12–1 Section Review

1. What is a frame of reference?
2. What is the most common frame of reference?
3. How is it possible that an actress can be shown dancing on the ceiling in a movie?

Critical Thinking—*Applying Concepts*

4. Suppose you are standing on a sidewalk and your friend rides past you on her skateboard. Which one of you is moving relative to the Earth? Are you moving relative to your friend?

12–2 Measuring Motion

A cool autumn breeze sends a leaf on a spiraling journey to the ground. An army of ants marches past your feet on their way to your fallen ice cream. A meteor leaves a brilliant streak of light in its path as it hurtles through the atmosphere. In each one of these examples, something is changing position, or moving from one place to another. And although it might take the ants a while to reach their destination whereas the meteor is gone in a few blinks of the eye, all of these movements take place over some particular amount of time. **A change in position in a certain amount of time is motion.** When you say that something has moved, you are describing **motion.** But always remember that when you describe movement, or motion, you are comparing it with some frame of reference.

Speed

Suppose that at one instant runners are poised at the starting blocks ready for a race. Seconds later, the winner breaks the tape at the finish line. The runners got from the starting blocks to the finish line because they moved, or changed their position.

Figure 12–4 *Just as the runners move from one place to another during their race, so do the small ants as they carry bits of a leaf back to their home. Which photo shows movement at a greater speed?*

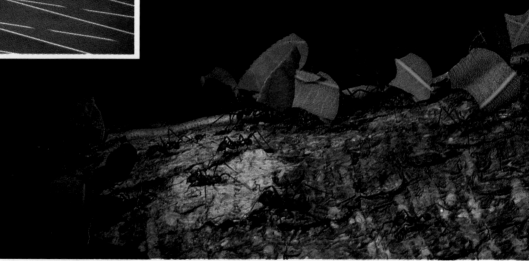

| 1 km/hr | 80 km/hr | 110 km/hr | 3600 km/hr |
| Baby crawling | Cyclist | Cheetah | Concorde SST |

And they did so in a certain amount of time. So you can be sure that the runners were in motion. But to better describe the motion of the runners, you need to know the distance they traveled and how long it took them to travel that distance (that is, to reach the finish line). Distance is the length between two places. In the metric system, distance is measured in units called meters (m) and kilometers (km). One kilometer is equal to 1000 meters. How many meters are there in 10 kilometers?

If you know the distance the runners traveled and the time it took them to travel that distance, then you can determine how fast each runner moved. In other words, you can calculate the **speed** of each runner. You probably use the words fast and slow often to describe motion. But what you may not realize is that by using these words, you are actually describing speed. **Speed is the rate at which an object moves.** The faster a runner's rate of motion, the faster the runner's speed.

You can find the speed of an object by dividing the distance it traveled by the time it took to travel that distance:

$$\text{Speed} = \frac{\text{Distance}}{\text{Time}}$$

Using this formula, you can see that if two runners ran the same distance, the runner who took the longer time must have run at a slower speed. The runner who took the shorter time must have run at a faster speed. And as you know, only the runner who ran faster won the race. If, on the other hand, two runners took the same amount of time but one runner ran a longer distance, that runner must have run at a faster speed.

Figure 12–5 *You can compare the speeds of some common objects on this scale. Where do you think your walking speed would fit?*

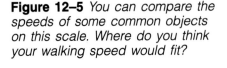

Trotting Into Your Heart

When you think of speed, the image of a beautiful sleek horse may come to mind. That same image must have come to Walter Farley's mind because he wrote an entire collection of books about a black stallion. Read *The Black Stallion* by Walter Farley and enjoy the adventures of a very special horse. And if you get hooked on his stories, which you may easily do, go ahead and indulge in the rest of the series.

Distance is usually measured in meters or kilometers. Time is usually measured in seconds or hours. So the unit of speed is often meters per second (m/sec) or kilometers per hour (km/hr) This idea should be pretty familiar to you. After all, if someone asked you for the speed of a car, would you say 80 kilometers? No! You would

Figure 12–6 *Microscopic red blood cells crowd together as they move through the body at a particular speed. This huge glacier moves through part of Alaska at a different speed—obviously slower!*

say 80 kilometers per hour. This means that traveling at this speed the car will go a distance of 80 kilometers in a time of one hour.

Speed is not used to describe only runners, cars, or trains. Anything that is changing its position has speed. This includes ocean currents, wind, glaciers, the moon, and even the Earth. For example, from the sun's frame of reference, the Earth is orbiting the sun at an average speed of about 30 kilometers per second, or 30 km/sec.

CONSTANT SPEED So far, we have been discussing the motion of objects whose speed is the same throughout their movement. Their speed does not change. Speed that does not change is called constant speed. When you calculate the speed of an object traveling at constant speed, you are figuring out its speed at every point in its path. Let's see how this works. Look at Figure 12–7. This is a

hey mike
whats goin on!
nuttin much here
well we're in
science and we're
leaving geg
tryl
always
-kt

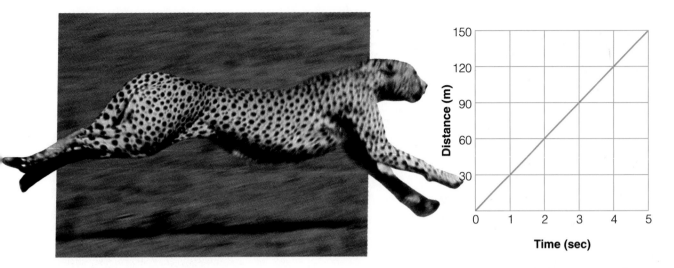

Figure 12–7 *One of the Earth's swiftest land animals, the cheetah can attain great speeds for short periods of time. The graph shows the distance the cheetah travels as a function of time. How do you know the cheetah ran at a constant speed?*

distance–time graph showing several seconds of a cheetah's motion. Distance is plotted on the vertical, or Y, axis. Time is plotted on the horizontal, or X, axis. According to the graph, how many meters did the cheetah travel after 1 second? You are right if you said 30 meters. The cheetah's speed was 30 m/1 sec, or 30 m/sec. After 3 seconds, the cheetah traveled 90 meters. So its speed was 90 m/3 sec, or 30 m/sec. The cheetah's speed did not change. When you divide the total distance by the total time, 150 m/5 sec, you get 30 m/sec. Thus, for constant speed, total distance divided by total time gives the speed for every point in the cheetah's path because

Sample Problem	At what speed did a plane fly if it traveled 1760 meters in 8 seconds?
Solution	
Step 1 Write the formula.	**Speed = Distance/Time**
Step 2 Substitute given numbers and units.	**Speed = 1760 meters/8 seconds**
Step 3 Solve for the unknown.	**Speed = 220 meters/second (m/sec)**
Practice Problems	**1.** A car travels 240 kilometers in 3 hours. What is the speed of the car during that time?
	2. The speed of a cruise ship is 50 km/hr. How far will the ship travel in 14 hours?

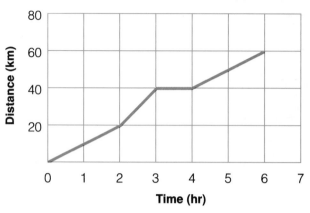

Figure 12–8 *Riding merrily along on a lovely spring day, the cyclist travels quite a distance. The graph shows how her speed changed during the course of the trip. During which hours was her speed the greatest?*

Activity Bank

Flying High, p. 735

the speed of the cheetah is the same at every point. Notice that the distance–time graph for constant speed is a straight line.

AVERAGE SPEED   The speed of a moving object is not always constant. In fact, this is usually the case. Suppose a cyclist takes a long ride. She begins slowly for the first two hours and picks up speed for the third hour. After three hours, she takes a break before finishing the final two hours of her ride. Clearly, her speed changes many times throughout her journey. Dividing the total distance by the total time does not tell you her speed for every point of her journey. Instead it gives you her average speed. What is the average speed of the cyclist in Figure 12–8? Actually, the formula you just learned for calculating speed—distance/time—always gives you the average speed. For things that move at constant speed (such

Figure 12–9 *If you have ever walked into the wind, you know you expend more energy than you do if you walk with the wind at your back. Why?*

as the cheetah in the previous example), the speed at any point is the same as the average speed.

Velocity

In addition to speed, another characteristic is needed to describe motion. It is the direction in which an object moved. Did it go east? West? North? South? To describe both the speed and the direction of motion, **velocity** is used. **Velocity is speed in a given direction.** Suppose a runner moves eastward at 10 m/sec. Her *speed* is 10 m/sec. Her *velocity,* however, is 10 m/sec east. If the runner was moving westward, her speed would be the same, but her velocity would change.

You may not think that there is much difference between speed and velocity. But the direction given by velocity is very important. Airplane pilots and air-traffic controllers use velocity measurements to fly and land airplanes. It would be dangerous to know only that one airplane is taking off at a speed of 100 km/hr and that another airplane is landing at 150 km/hr. Instead, air-traffic controllers must know the airplanes' directions so that the airplanes will not head directly into each other. Weather forecasters must know the velocity of air masses to predict the weather correctly. And anyone traveling from one city to another knows that it is not only the speed that counts, but also the direction!

COMBINING VELOCITIES Suppose you are rowing a boat downstream at 16 km/hr. Would it surprise you to learn that you are actually going faster than 16 km/hr? How is this possible? The river is also moving, say at 10 km/hr. Since you are rowing

ACTIVITY DISCOVERING

Marble Motion

1. On a level floor or a table top about 1.5 m long, place a 30-cm metric ruler at an incline of about 1.5 cm. Use a book at one end of the ruler to raise it.

2. Roll a marble down the incline.

3. Record the distance the marble rolls from the bottom of the incline across the floor or table top in two seconds. Repeat this procedure two more times.

4. Record the distance the marble travels in three seconds, again making three trials.

What is the marble's average speed in two seconds? Three seconds?

Which average speed is greater?

■ What must be true about the marble's speed during the third second?

Figure 12–10 *These adventurous white-water rafters are spared a little work by the river. Why does the river make them move much faster than they are rowing?*

Figure 12-11 *A rocket launched in the same direction as the Earth rotates gets an added boost. Without this boost, Space Shuttles would have to attain much greater speeds in order to leave the Earth's atmosphere and enter space. How much of a boost does a rocket get?*

1800 km/hr

39,200 km/hr

41,000 km/hr

downstream, you are going in the same direction as the river. The two velocities combine. So you are moving at 26 km/hr. Velocities that have the same direction are added together. You must use subtraction when combining velocities in opposite directions. For example, if you were rowing 16 km/hr upstream, you would be going 16 km/hr – 10 km/hr, or 6 km/hr.

This idea of combining velocities is very important, especially for launching rockets and flying planes. Space engineers launch rockets in the same direction as the Earth rotates. The speed of the Earth's rotation is about 1800 km/hr. Thus the rocket gets an added boost of 1800 km/hr to its speed.

ACTIVITY

READING

Just Floating Away

Sometimes you may wish that a gust of wind or a swoosh of water could carry you off on a wonderful adventure. Tom Sawyer got such an adventure courtesy of the motion of the Mississippi River. Read Mark Twain's *The Adventures of Tom Sawyer* and join him in his escapades.

12-2 Section Review

1. Define motion. Give an example.
2. How is the speed of an object calculated?
3. What is constant speed? How does it compare with average speed?
4. What quantity gives both the speed and the direction of an object?

Connection—*You and Your World*

5. It is 2:00 PM. The local weather bureau is tracking a violent storm that is traveling eastward at 25 km/hr. It is 75 kilometers west of Suntown, USA. If everyone works until 5:00 PM, will the residents of Suntown be able to get home safely before the storm hits?

PROBLEM Solving

In Search of Buried Treasure

The *Sea Queen,* a majestic research ship, drops anchor in the area where a great treasure is believed to have been lost on the ocean floor. Here, however, the ocean floor is far too deep for divers to explore. So instead, the scientists on board send out a series of sound waves at different locations around the ship. Sound waves travel at 1.5 km/sec in ocean water. When a sound wave reaches the ocean bottom, it bounces back to the ship, where it is recorded. Each sound wave travels the same distance on the way up from the ocean floor as it does on the way down.

After a long day, the researchers have gathered many pages of data describing the sound waves. Now it is time to call in an expert to interpret the information. And guess what—you are the expert! It will be your job to figure out the depth of the ocean at each point in the area surrounding the ship.

Organizing Resources and Information

1. What other measurement do you need to do this?

On board is a map of the ocean floor in that area. The map was made on the basis of measurements taken before the treasure was lost.

2. How can you use the map to find the treasure?

3. Do you think you will be able to find the lost treasure?

12–3 Changes in Velocity

Have you ever ridden on a roller coaster? You are pulled up to the top of the first hill at constant speed. But as you roll down the other side, your speed rapidly increases. At the bottom of the hill you make a sharp right turn, changing your direction once again. Then your speed rapidly decreases as you climb the second hill. On a roller-coaster ride, you experience rapid changes in velocity. Remember, velocity measures both speed and direction. **The rate of change in velocity is known as acceleration.** If something is accelerating, it is

Guide for Reading

Focus on these questions as you read.

▶ *What is the relationship between velocity and acceleration?*

▶ *How is acceleration calculated?*

Figure 12–12 *Up, down, and around go the roller-coaster cars. If a car begins its final descent at 4 km/hr and zooms down the hill in 5 seconds, what other information do you need to calculate its acceleration?*

speeding up, slowing down, or changing direction. The **acceleration** of an object is equal to its change in velocity divided by the time during which this change occurs. The change in velocity is the difference between the final velocity and the original velocity:

$$\text{Acceleration} = \frac{\text{Final Velocity} - \text{Original Velocity}}{\text{Time}}$$

Acceleration, like speed, tells you how fast something is happening—in this case, how fast velocity is changing. And like velocity, acceleration has direction. A car on an entrance ramp to a highway begins at rest and gradually increases its speed in the

---

Sample Problem

A roller coaster's velocity at the top of a hill is 10 meters/second. Two seconds later it reaches the bottom of the hill with a velocity of 26 meters/second. What is the acceleration of the roller coaster?

Solution

Step 1 Write the formula. $\text{Acceleration} = \dfrac{\text{Final Velocity} - \text{Original Velocity}}{\text{Time}}$

Step 2 Substitute given numbers and units. $\text{Acceleration} = \dfrac{26 \text{ meters/second} - 10 \text{ meters/second}}{2 \text{ seconds}}$

Step 3 Solve for the unknown. $\text{Acceleration} = \dfrac{16 \text{ meters/second}}{2 \text{ seconds}}$

$\text{Acceleration} = 8 \text{ meters/second/second (m/sec/sec)}$

Practice Problems

1. A roller coaster is moving at 25 m/sec at the bottom of a hill. Three seconds later it reaches the top of the next hill, moving at 10 m/sec. What is the deceleration of the roller coaster?

2. A car is traveling at 60 km/hr. It accelerates to 85 km/hr in 5 seconds. What is the acceleration of the car?

direction of the highway. The car is accelerating in the direction of the highway.

You can determine the unit of acceleration by looking at the formula. The change in velocity is measured in kilometers per hour or meters per second. Time is measured in hours or seconds. So acceleration is measured in kilometers per hour per hour (km/hr/hr) or meters per second per second (m/sec/sec). This means that if an object is accelerating at 5 m/sec/sec, each second its velocity increases by 5 m/sec. The speed of the object is 5 m/sec greater each second.

If there is a decrease in velocity, the value of acceleration is negative. Negative acceleration is called deceleration. When a roller coaster climbs a hill, it decelerates because it is slowing down. Can you think of another example of deceleration?

The data table in Figure 12–13 is a record of a professional drag-strip race. The driver had traveled a distance of 5 meters after the first second. The

ACTIVITY
WRITING

Race Around the World

Most people enjoy a race of some type or another. Whether you take part in it, photograph it, or just watch and enjoy it, a race is exciting. The following list includes a number of famous races. Find out what is racing or being raced in each case. Then choose one race and write an essay in which you describe the race, its significance, and its history.

America's Cup
Boston Marathon
Tour de France
Kentucky Derby
Indianapolis 500

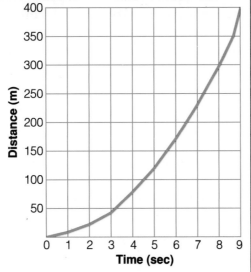

Time (sec)	Distance (m)
0	0
1	5
2	20
3	45
4	80
5	125
6	180
7	245
8	320
9	405

Figure 12–13 *The data from a professional drag race are shown on the left. A distance–time graph of the racer's motion is shown on the right.*

Figure 12–14 *Although these photos may make you dizzy, they each illustrate important properties of circular motion. Why are both the gymnast and a passenger on the Ferris wheel experiencing acceleration?*

distance covered in the next second was 15 meters (20 m – 5 m). By the end of four seconds, the driver had traveled 80 meters. Figure 12–13 on page 311 also shows a distance–time graph of the racing car's motion. The graph is a curve rather than a straight line. A distance–time graph for acceleration is always a curve. How far did the driver travel in the first five seconds of the race? In the last five seconds?

Circular Motion

Acceleration and deceleration are easy to recognize when the motion is in a straight line. After all, motion in a straight line does not involve a change in direction. It involves only a change in speed. And it is rather easy to recognize an object speeding up or slowing down. When the path of motion is curved, however, the results can be surprising. To understand why, you must remember that acceleration is a change in velocity. And velocity expresses direction as well as speed. In circular motion, the velocity is continuously changing because direction is continuously changing. An object in circular motion is accelerating even though its speed may be constant.

You experience circular motion in many common activities. When you ride a Ferris wheel, pedal a bike on a curved track, or travel in a car turning a corner, you are constantly changing direction. So you are accelerating. In fact, because the Earth is continuously rotating, you are constantly accelerating—even when you are fast asleep!

12-3 Section Review

1. What is acceleration?
2. What is another name for negative acceleration?
3. Why does an object traveling in a circular path at constant speed accelerate?
4. A car at a stoplight has a velocity of 0 km/hr. Three seconds after the light turns green, the car has a velocity of 30 km/hr. What is the acceleration of the car?

Critical Thinking—*Making Calculations*
5. Despite his mother's warnings, Timothy was playing ball in the house when his ball bounced out the window. A freely falling body accelerates at about 10 m/sec/sec. What is the velocity of Timothy's ball after 2 seconds? *Hint:* What is its original downward velocity?

Figure 12–15 *Powering the spinning wheel with her foot, this woman takes advantage of circular motion. Can you think of other devices that use circular motion?*

12-4 Momentum

Guide for Reading

Focus on these questions as you read.

▶ *How is momentum related to velocity and mass?*
▶ *What does it mean that momentum is conserved?*

The 100-kg fullback runs up the middle of the football field. Suddenly he collides with a 75-kg defensive back running toward him. The more massive fullback is thrown back two meters! How can a 75-kg defensive back stop a 100-kg fullback?

The answer is that the defensive back has more **momentum.** All moving objects have momentum. And the more momentum an object has, the harder it is to stop. **Momentum depends on the mass of the object and the velocity with which it is traveling.** If either of these measurements is large, the object will have a large momentum.

Momentum is equal to the mass of an object multiplied by its velocity:

$$\text{Momentum} = \text{Mass} \times \text{Velocity}$$

Although he has less mass, the defensive back has more momentum because he is moving faster than the fullback. His greater velocity makes up for his smaller mass. If both players had the same velocity,

313

Figure 12–16 *It has been said that football is a game of momentum. What must be true of the smaller player's velocity if his momentum is enough to stop the larger player?*

who would have more momentum? You can determine the unit of momentum by looking at the formula. Mass is often measured in kilograms and velocity in meters per second. So the unit of momentum is usually kilogram-meters per second (kg-m/sec). And momentum is in the same direction as the velocity of the object.

A train has a large momentum because of its mass. That is probably obvious to you. But what do you think about the momentum of a bullet fired from a rifle? Do you think it is small? Do not be fooled by the small mass of a bullet. Bullets are fired at extremely high velocities. A bullet has a large momentum because of its velocity. What is the momentum of a bullet before it is fired from a rifle?

Why do you think it is harder to stop a car moving at 100 km/hr than it is to stop the same car moving at 25 km/hr? You are right if you said the car moving at 100 km/hr has more momentum. A car having greater momentum requires a longer distance in which to stop. The stopping distance of a car is directly related to its momentum. People who design roadways must take this into account when determining safe stopping distances and speed limits.

Conservation of Momentum

If you have ever played billiards, you may know about an important property of momentum. If you send a moving ball into a stationary ball, you can cause the stationary ball to move and the moving ball to become stationary. This is because the momentum of the moving object is transferred to the stationary object when the two objects collide. None of the momentum is lost. **The total momentum of any group of objects remains the same unless outside forces act on the objects.** This is what we mean when we say that momentum is conserved. One object may lose momentum, but the momentum lost by this object is gained by another. Momentum is always conserved.

Now suppose that you send two moving billiard balls into each other. After they hit, both balls are still moving. This means that neither ball transferred all of its momentum to the other. But as you just learned, momentum is conserved. So the total momentum of the billiard balls before they hit and after they hit must be the same. Although their

Figure 12–17 *Although the King of Diamonds may not appreciate the importance of momentum, the bullet is able to cut right through the card because of this physical phenomenon. Similarly, the momentum of the bowling ball enables it to knock the pins down. Why must the engines of supertankers be shut off several kilometers before they need to stop?*

Figure 12–18 *Like a long jumper who uses her momentum to carry her a great distance, an agile frog also takes advantage of momentum. Why do long jumpers run before jumping?*

individual momentums may change, because of either a change in speed or mass, the total momentum does not change. For example, if one ball speeds up after they hit, the other must slow down.

There are many common examples of conservation of momentum. The momentum of a baseball bat is transferred to the ball when the bat and the ball meet. The more momentum the bat has, the more momentum is transferred to the ball. The act of throwing an object off a boat causes the boat to move in the opposite direction. The more massive the object and the faster it is thrown, the faster the boat will move away. Why do you think a pitcher winds up before throwing the baseball? In each of these situations, the total momentum is conserved.

12–4 Section Review

1. What is momentum?
2. How is momentum conserved?
3. What is the momentum of an 0.30 kg bluejay flying at 17 m/sec?
4. Which object has more momentum: a car traveling at 10 km/hr or a baseball pitched at 150 km/hr? Explain your answer.

Critical Thinking—*Making Inferences*
5. When a person jumps from a tree to the ground, what happens to the momentum of the person upon landing on the ground?

CONNECTIONS

In a Flash

Think about some of the photographs you or your family have taken. Most likely, they are of events or people who are not moving—a snowcapped mountain, a famous statue, some friends posing. But have you ever tried to photograph things that are in motion—perhaps friends who moved just as you pushed the button on your camera? If so, you know that the photograph comes out blurry. So you might wonder how cameras can photograph moving objects—particularly those that move too quickly even for the human eye to see.

Cameras depend on light. When light bounces off an object it will form a picture on a material that is sensitive to light. That material is film. This picture can then be chemically processed into a photograph. A device on a camera called a shutter controls the length of time that the film is exposed to light. If the subject moves at any time while the film is exposed to light, the movement will be recorded as a blur.

By decreasing the length of time the shutter is open to only fractions of a second, photographers are able to take sharp pictures of moving subjects. Remember that motion involves a change in position during a certain amount of time. When the speed with which the shutter opens and closes is increased, the time segment studied becomes so small that the change in position is too small to be

recorded as a blur. The camera actually catches a tiny segment of motion.

At a setting of 1/1000 of a second, the shutter is open for such a short time that the motion of a race car appears to be "stopped." To freeze the beating of an insect's wings needs an even shorter exposure. Even at 1/1000 of a second, the wings are a blur. To record this type of motion, high-speed cameras capable of exposures 10 or 20 times shorter have been developed.

Photography has become a universal means of communication and a valuable tool in many fields. Photographs made at high speeds are very important in science and technology. This is because they record a phase of a fast event or photograph a rapid sequence of events that can be slowed down for study. The ability to photograph moving subjects has opened up a whole new world of study and has shed light on important aspects of the physical world. Some wonderful contributions to science have been made by creative and ambitious shutterbugs.

Laboratory Investigation

Measuring Constant Speed

Problem

What is the shape of a distance–time graph of constant speed?

Materials *(per student)*

pencil
graph paper
metric ruler

Procedure

1. The illustration on this page represents a series of flash shots taken of a dry-ice puck sliding across the floor. The time between each flash is 0.1 second. Study the illustration carefully.

2. Copy the sample data table on a piece of graph paper.

3. Position the 0-cm mark of the metric ruler on the front edge of the first puck. This position will represent distance 0.0 cm at time 0.0 second. Record these data in your data table.

4. Without moving the ruler, determine the distance of each puck from the first one.

5. Record each distance to the nearest 0.1 cm in your data table.

Observations

Time (sec)	Distance (cm)
0.0	0.0
0.1	
0.2	
0.3	
0.4	
0.5	
0.6	

Make a distance–time graph using the data in your table. Plot the distance on the vertical, or Y, axis and the time on the horizontal, or X, axis.

Analysis and Conclusions

1. What is the shape of the graph?
2. Is the speed constant? Explain your answer.
3. Calculate the average speed.
4. How will the graph change as time goes on?
5. **On Your Own** Suppose you are ice skating around a rink at a constant speed. Then you get tired so you stop moving your feet and glide along the ice. How would your distance–time graph look?

| 0.0 sec | 0.1 sec | 0.2 sec | 0.3 sec | 0.4 sec | 0.5 sec | 0.6 sec |

Study Guide

Summarizing Key Concepts

12–1 Frames of Reference

▲ All movement is compared with a background that is assumed to be stationary. This background is called a frame of reference.

▲ An object that is stationary in one frame of reference may be moving in another frame of reference. Any frame of reference can be chosen to describe a given movement, but the most common frame of reference is the Earth.

12–2 Measuring Motion

▲ Motion involves a change in position during a certain amount of time. The characteristics of position and time are used to measure motion.

▲ The rate at which an object moves is speed. Any object that is changing its position has speed. Speed can be determined by dividing the distance traveled by the time taken to travel that distance.

▲ Speed that does not change is called constant speed. For an object moving at constant speed, the speed at any point is the same as the average speed. For an object whose speed varies, you calculate the average speed.

▲ Speed in a given direction is velocity.

▲ Velocities that have the same direction combine by addition. Velocities that have opposite directions combine by subtraction.

12–3 Changes in Velocity

▲ Acceleration is the rate of change in velocity. It is equal to the change in velocity divided by the time it takes to make the change.

▲ An object that is accelerating is speeding up, slowing down, or changing direction.

▲ Negative acceleration is also known as deceleration.

▲ Circular motion always involves acceleration because the object's direction is constantly changing.

12–4 Momentum

▲ Momentum is equal to the mass of an object multiplied by its velocity. An object with a large momentum is very difficult to stop.

▲ The total momentum of any group of objects remains the same unless outside forces act on the objects.

Reviewing Key Terms

Define each term in a complete sentence.

12–1 Frames of Reference
frame of reference

12–2 Measuring Motion
motion
speed
velocity

12–3 Changes in Velocity
acceleration

12–4 Momentum
momentum

Chapter Review

Content Review

Multiple Choice

Choose the letter of the answer that best completes each statement.

1. All movement is compared with a
   a. car.   c. tree.
   b. frame of reference.   d. train.
2. The most commonly used frame of reference is the
   a. sun.   c. moon.
   b. Earth.   d. ocean.
3. A change in position relative to a frame of reference is
   a. motion.   c. acceleration.
   b. momentum.   d. direction.
4. The rate at which an object changes position is called
   a. distance.   c. speed.
   b. acceleration.   d. momentum.
5. Velocity is speed and
   a. motion.   c. distance.
   b. mass.   d. direction.
6. If a motorboat travels 25 km/hr down a river that has a velocity of 4 km/hr, what is the boat's actual velocity?
   a. 21 km/hr   c. 100 km/hr
   b. 29 km/hr   d. 6.2 km/hr
7. The rate of change of velocity is called
   a. speed.   c. momentum.
   b. motion.   d. acceleration.
8. A distance-time graph is a straight line for
   a. constant speed.   c. momentum.
   b. acceleration.   d. speed.
9. An object traveling in circular motion is constantly changing
   a. speed.   c. distance.
   b. mass.   d. direction.
10. Momentum is mass times
    a. acceleration.   c. motion.
    b. velocity.   d. distance.

True or False

If the statement is true, write "true." If it is false, change the underlined word or words to make the statement true.

1. Motion must be measured relative to a <u>frame of reference</u>.
2. A change in position of an object is called <u>momentum</u>.
3. The measurement of how fast or slow something is traveling is <u>speed</u>.
4. An object whose speed does not change is traveling at <u>constant</u> speed.
5. The quantity that gives speed and direction is <u>momentum</u>.
6. Velocities in opposite directions combine by <u>subtraction</u>.
7. Acceleration is a change in speed or <u>direction</u>.
8. The measurement of how hard it is to stop an object (mass times velocity) is <u>acceleration</u>.

Concept Mapping

Complete the following concept map for Section 12–2. Then construct a concept map for the entire chapter.

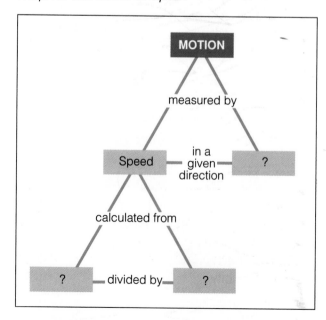

Concept Mastery

Discuss each of the following in a brief paragraph.

1. A car is traveling along the road at a moderate speed. One person describes the velocity of the car as 30 km/hr forward. Another person describes the car as moving 20 km/hr in reverse. Explain how both observers can be correct.

2. You are flying in an airplane whose speed is programmed to be 400 km/hr. However, the airplane is really traveling at 460 km/hr. Explain how this can be true.

3. Explain why you are being accelerated on a Ferris wheel moving at constant speed.

Critical Thinking and Problem Solving

Use the skills you have developed in this chapter to answer each of the following.

1. **Making calculations** Complete the following problems:
   a. What is the average speed of a jet plane that flies 7200 km in 9 hours?
   b. The speed of a cruise ship is 50 km/hr. How far will the ship travel in 14 hours?
   c. A car accelerates from 0 km/hr to 60 km/hr in 5.0 seconds. What is the car's acceleration? Watch your units!

2. **Applying definitions** Samantha ran 90 meters in 35 seconds to catch up with her dog. When she got to him, she played with him for 70 seconds before they walked back in 75 seconds. Did Samantha travel at constant speed? What was Samantha's average speed?

3. **Applying concepts**

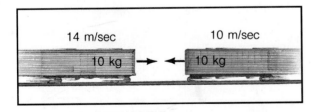

14 m/sec   10 m/sec
10 kg → ← 10 kg

   a. What is the momentum of the train car moving at 14 m/sec? Of the car moving at 10 m/sec? What is the total momentum of the system?
   b. If the two cars collide and stick together, what will be the direction of their resulting motion?

4. **Relating cause and effect** Use the following information to explain the launch of a rocket: Hot gases that escape from a rocket have a very small mass but a high velocity. As fuel is used up, the mass of the rocket decreases.

5. **Applying concepts** An old legend tells the story of a stingy man who never let go of his bag of coins. One winter's day, he slipped in the snow and suddenly found himself in the middle of a frozen pond. The ice on the pond was so smooth and slippery that he could not grab on to the ice to stand up. In fact, he could not get enough traction to move on it at all. What could he do to save himself?

6. **Using the writing process** The distance–time graph describes your walk to the local store and back home. Write a brief story describing your walk that would correspond to the graph.

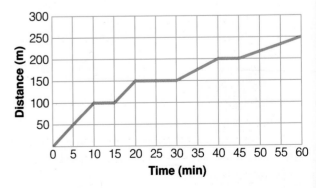

The Nature of Forces

13

Guide for Reading

After you read the following sections, you will be able to

13–1 What Is Force?
- Describe the nature of force.
- Compare balanced and unbalanced forces.

13–2 Friction: A Force Opposing Motion
- Identify different types of friction.

13–3 Newton's Laws of Motion
- Discuss Newton's three laws of motion.
- Explain why Newton's laws of motion are important for describing common examples of motion.

13–4 Gravity
- Describe the relationship between gravitational force, mass, and distance.
- Compare weight and mass.

The year was 1665. Throughout Cambridge, schools and businesses had closed. The deadly bubonic plague raged through the city, causing twenty-two-year-old Isaac Newton to return to his mother's farmhouse in Woolsthorpe.

You are probably familiar with the famous story in which Newton began to wonder why an apple falls down to the Earth. Isaac Newton went on to conclude that the force that pulls an apple to the ground is the same force that helps keep the moon in orbit around the Earth. He was also able to show that this force keeps the planets in their orbits around the sun. While Newton was making this profound dicovery, he was also uncovering the secrets of light and color, and inventing a branch of mathematics called calculus. Incredibly, Newton accomplished all this in just 18 months!

Isaac Newton is considered the founder of modern physics and "one of the greatest names in the history of human thought." In this chapter, you will gain an appreciation for Newton and his contribution to science as you read about his beautifully simple explanation of forces and motion.

Journal *Activity*

You and Your World   Have you ever tried to pull something that just wouldn't budge? Maybe it was a stubborn dog avoiding a bath or a heavy piece of furniture. In your journal, describe a situation in which you pulled, or tried to pull, something. Include any details that made the job more or less difficult for you. What might have made your task easier?

◀ *Isaac Newton discovered the force that keeps the moons orbiting around Saturn and also holds you on the Earth.*

13–1 What Is Force?

Do you play baseball or tennis? Have you raked a pile of leaves or shoveled snow? Have you ever hammered a nail into a piece of wood or moved a large piece of furniture? How about something as simple as riding a bicycle, lifting this textbook, or opening a door? If so, you know that there is some type of motion involved in all of these activities. But what causes a tennis ball to suddenly zoom across the court or a bicycle to skid to a halt? The answer is **force.** In each of these activities, a force is involved. You are exerting a force on an object. And although you may not know it, the object is exerting a force on you! What is force? How is it related to motion?

A force is a push or pull. The wind pushes against the flag on a flagpole. A magnet pulls iron toward it. A jet engine pushes an airplane forward. The moon pulls on the oceans, causing the daily tides. A nuclear explosion pushes nearby objects outward with tremendous force. A negatively charged particle and a positively charged particle are attracted to each other. In each of these examples, a force is involved. **A force gives energy to an object, sometimes causing it to start moving, stop moving, or change direction.** For example, if you want to open a door, you exert a force on it to cause it to move. Increasing your force will make it move faster. If you want to stop the door from opening, you also exert a force. This time the force stops the motion of the door. And if you want to change the direction in which the door is moving, you must exert a force on it.

Figure 13–1 *Quite a force is required to send a soccer ball hurtling down a field. What is the source of the force?*

Figure 13–2 *Powerful ocean waters smash into coastal rocks all day. If you have ever been hit by ocean waves, you know just how forceful they can be.*

Figure 13-3 *The force exerted by a powerful pooch overcomes the opposing force of a reluctant child. Pulling a stubborn cow, however, may not be as enjoyable an adventure.*

Combining Forces

Have you noticed by now that most measurements involving motion—velocity, acceleration, and momentum, for example—include direction? Forces also act in a particular direction. Suppose you were trying to pull a wagon filled with rocks. To get the wagon to move, you would have to exert a force on the wagon and rocks. If your force was not large enough, you might ask a friend to help you. Your friend might pull with you or push from the back of the wagon. In either case, the two forces (yours and your friend's) would be exerted *in the same direction*. When two forces are acting in the same direction, they add together. The total force on the wagon would be the sum of the individual forces. When the total force on an object is in one direction, the force is called unbalanced. An unbalanced force changes the motion of an object.

If your friend pulled *in the opposite direction*, the forces would combine in a different way. When two forces act in opposite directions, they combine by subtraction. If one force was greater than the other force, the wagon would move in the direction of the greater force. And the total force on the wagon would be the difference between the individual forces. In this case, your friend would certainly not be helpful! What do you think would happen if your force and your friend's force were equal? When you subtracted one force from the other, you would be

Figure 13-4 *Moving this pumpkin is a hard job to do alone! So these two children are combining forces in the same direction. Are the children exerting a balanced or an unbalanced force?*

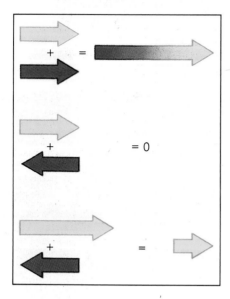

Figure 13–5 *Two forces can combine so that they add together (top), cancel each other (center), or subtract from each other (bottom).*

left with zero. This means that there would be no force acting on the object. The wagon would not move! Forces that are in opposite directions and equal in size are called balanced forces. When forces are balanced, there is no change in motion.

You should remember that in describing forces, a number value, a unit of measurement, and a direction must be given. It is helpful to think of forces as arrows. The length of the arrow shows the strength of the force. The head of the arrow points in the direction of the force. Using such arrows, you can tell what the resulting size and direction of combined forces will be.

13–1 Section Review

1. What is force?
2. How are forces related to motion?
3. What are unbalanced forces? Balanced forces?

Connection—*Life Science*
4. How is your heart able to produce a force? Why is this force vital to life?

Guide for Reading

Focus on these questions as you read.

▶ What are the effects of friction on motion?
▶ What are three types of friction?

13–2 Friction: A Force Opposing Motion

Have you ever tried to slide a piece of furniture, such as a desk, across a floor? If you have, you know that as you push, the rubbing of the desk against the floor makes it difficult to push the desk. This is because whenever two surfaces are touching, such as a desk and a floor, a force called **friction** exists. Friction is a force that acts in a direction opposite to the motion of the moving object. **Friction will cause a moving object to slow down and finally stop.**

Friction arises from the fact that objects and surfaces are not perfectly smooth. On a microscopic scale, the surfaces are rough. Jagged edges on one object rub against and get caught on jagged edges on the other object. Thus the amount of friction

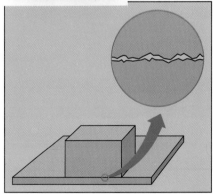

Figure 13–6 Wheels enable roller skaters to overcome sliding friction. Yet rolling friction will cause them to slow down. How does rolling friction affect the little girls' toy?

between two surfaces depends on how hard the surfaces are forced together and on the materials of which the surfaces are made. A heavy desk will force the surfaces together more than a light desk will. The heavier the desk you try to move, the more difficult it will be to push it across the floor. Likewise, if the floor is covered with a rough material such as carpeting, the desk will be harder to push.

The force you exert to move an object is in one direction. The force of friction is in the opposite direction. Because the two forces combine by subtraction, you must exert a force that is larger than the force of friction in order to move the object.

When solid objects slide over each other, the type of friction that results is called sliding friction. From your experience you know that sliding friction can oppose motion rather effectively. Can sliding friction be reduced? Suppose you place the object you wish to move on wheels. You can push it across the room with greater ease. You have to apply only a small amount of force because there is only a small amount of friction between the wheels and the floor. The friction produced by objects such as wheels or ball bearings is called rolling friction. Rolling friction tends to be less than sliding friction. So wheels are often placed under objects that are being moved. Just imagine how much force would have to be used if automobiles had to overcome sliding friction instead of rolling friction!

Figure 13–7 No matter how fast a bobsled moves, it is still slowed by friction. When highly magnified, surfaces appear quite uneven and rough, making it difficult for them to slide over each other.

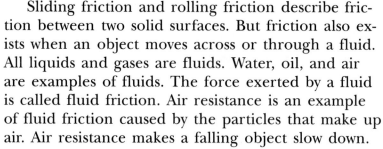

Sliding friction and rolling friction describe friction between two solid surfaces. But friction also exists when an object moves across or through a fluid. All liquids and gases are fluids. Water, oil, and air are examples of fluids. The force exerted by a fluid is called fluid friction. Air resistance is an example of fluid friction caused by the particles that make up air. Air resistance makes a falling object slow down.

Fluid friction is usually less than sliding friction. Substances called lubricants, which are "slippery" substances such as grease, change sliding friction to fluid friction, thus reducing friction. Lubricants such as oil, wax, and grease are often used in devices that have moving parts, such as engines. Why?

Friction is not always a troublesome force. Friction can often be very helpful. In fact, without friction, you would not be able to walk. The friction between the soles of your shoes and the ground keeps you from slipping and sliding around. Automobiles are able to stop because the action of the brakes increases friction between the tires and the road. Cars often skid on icy streets because the friction between the tires and the road is reduced.

Figure 13–8 *Friction is quite often helpful. For example, gymnasts use chalk on their hands to increase friction. Cyclists rely on friction to hold their bicycles on the ground during turns. And without friction, cars and other vehicles would not be able to start or stop.*

13–2 Section Review

1. What is friction? How does it affect motion?
2. Describe three types of friction.

Critical Thinking—*Making Inferences*
3. Sand is often thrown on icy walkways to prevent people from falling. Explain how the sand is helpful.

13-3 Newton's Laws of Motion

During the years 1665 and 1666, Isaac Newton developed three laws that describe all of the states of motion—rest, constant motion, and accelerated motion. In addition, these three laws explain how forces cause all of the states of motion. The importance of Newton's laws has been recognized for hundreds of years. But the significance of his contribution was perhaps best expressed by the *Apollo* crew as they were hurtling toward the moon. They radioed a message to mission control saying: "We would like to thank the person who made this trip possible . . . Sir Isaac Newton!"

Newton's First Law of Motion

Have you ever coasted on your bike along a level street? If so, you know that you continue to move for a while even though you have stopped pedaling. But do you keep on moving forever? Your experience tells you the answer to this question is no. You finally come to a stop because you are no longer exerting a force by pedaling.

The early Greek philosophers made similar observations about objects in motion. It seemed to them that in order to set an object in motion, a force had to be exerted on the object. And if that force was removed, the object would come to rest. They logically concluded that the natural state of an object was that of rest. From your everyday experiences, you would probably agree. A ball rolled along the ground comes to rest. A book pushed along a table stops sliding. A sled gliding on the snow soon stops.

But the Greeks (and perhaps you) were wrong! What brings an object to rest is friction. If there was no friction, an object would continue to travel forever. The force exerted on an object to keep it moving is simply to overcome friction. Perhaps this idea is difficult for you to imagine. After all, friction is always present in your everyday experiences. Isaac Newton, however, recognized that if friction was not present, an object in motion would continue to

Figure 13-9 *Although they would probably enjoy it, these kids will not keep moving forever. The friction between the sled and the snow will slow their movement and eventually bring them to a stop.*

Figure 13–10 *More than just going for a stroll on the cold Alaskan terrain, these sled dogs are displaying important physical properties. Sled dogs join together to exert a force great enough to overcome the inertia of the sled. What would happen if the team stopped or started suddenly?*

move forever. And an object at rest would stay at rest unless it was acted upon by an unbalanced force. You would probably agree that a football lying on a field will not suddenly fly off by itself. It will move only when thrown or kicked.

Newton called this tendency of objects to remain in motion or stay at rest **inertia** (ihn-ER-shuh). Inertia is the property of matter that tends to resist any change in motion. The word inertia comes from the Latin word *iners*, which means "idle" or "lazy." Why do you think Newton used this word? The more massive an object is, the more difficult it is to change its motion. This means that the more massive an object is, the more inertia it has. Thus the inertia of an object is related to its mass.

The concept of inertia forms the basis for Newton's first law of motion. **The first law of motion states that an object at rest will remain at rest and an object in motion will remain in motion at constant velocity unless acted upon by an unbalanced force.** Remember, constant velocity means the same speed and the same direction. In order for an object to change its velocity, or accelerate, a force must act on it. Thus, Newton's first law tells us that acceleration and force are related. There is acceleration only in the presence of forces. Any time you observe acceleration, you know that there is a force at work.

You feel the effects of inertia every day. When you are riding in a car and it stops suddenly, you keep moving forward. If you did not have a safety

Figure 13–11 *The pitch is hit and the batter strains as he begins his sprint to first base. A runner must exert more energy to start running from a stopped position than to continue running once he has begun. Why?*

belt on to stop you, your inertia could send you through the windshield. Perhaps you never thought about it this way, but safety belts protect passengers from the effects of inertia.

When you are standing on a bus you experience inertia in two ways. When the bus starts to move forward, what happens to you? You are thrown off balance and fall backward. Your body has inertia. It is at rest and tends to stay at rest, even though the bus is moving. When the moving bus stops, you fall forward. Even though the bus stops, you do not. You are an object in motion.

Because of inertia, a car traveling along a road will tend to move in a straight line. What happens, then, if the road curves? The driver turns the steering wheel and the car moves along the curve. But the people in the car continue to move in a straight line. As a result, they bump into the walls of the car. The force exerted on the people by the walls of the car keeps the people in the curved path.

Newton's Second Law of Motion

Forre = Mass + acceleration

Newton's first law of motion tells you that acceleration and force are related: Acceleration cannot occur without a force. Newton's second law of motion explains how force and acceleration are related. Have you ever pushed a shopping cart along the aisles in a grocery store? If you push on the cart, it begins to move. The harder you push, the faster the cart accelerates. Thus, the greater the force, the more the acceleration. If the cart is filled with groceries, you have to push harder than you do when it is empty. This is because the cart filled with

Demonstrating Inertia

Obtain a playing card or index card, several coins of different sizes, and an empty glass. Place the card on top of the glass.

Use the coins to design an experiment whose results can be explained using Newton's first law of motion. You should show that an object with more mass has more inertia.

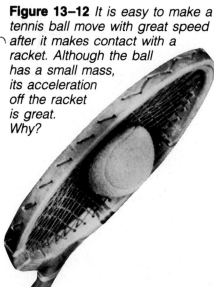

Figure 13–12 *It is easy to make a tennis ball move with great speed after it makes contact with a racket. Although the ball has a small mass, its acceleration off the racket is great. Why?*

Figure 13–13 *Crush. Crinkle. Crash. Looks easy, but it's not. Huge trucks must exert a greater amount of force to accelerate than a small vehicle must. How does Newton's second law of motion explain this?*

ACTIVITY

CALCULATING

Move That Barge

Tugboat A exerts a force of 4000 N on a barge. Tugboat B exerts a force of 8000 N on the barge in the same direction. What is the combined force on the barge? Using arrows, draw the individual and combined forces acting on the barge. Then draw the forces involved if the tugboats were pulling in opposite directions.

groceries has more mass, or inertia. A greater force is required to accelerate an object with greater inertia. Thus force and acceleration must be related to an object's mass.

Newton's second law of motion shows how force, mass, and acceleration are related.

Force = Mass x Acceleration

When mass is in kilograms and acceleration is in meters/second/second, force is in **newtons** (N). One newton equals the force required to accelerate one kilogram of mass at one meter/second/second.

1 N = 1 kg x 1 m/sec/sec

Newton's second law of motion explains one reason why a small car has better gas mileage than a large car. Suppose the acceleration of both cars is 2 m/sec/sec. The mass of the small car is 750 kg. The mass of the large car is 1000 kg. According to the second law of motion, the force required to accelerate the small car is 750 kg x 2 m/sec/sec, or 1500 N. The force required to accelerate the large car is 1000 kg x 2 m/sec/sec, or 2000 N. More gasoline will have to be burned in the engine of the large car to produce the additional force.

Sample Problem	How much force is needed to accelerate a 1400-kilogram car 2 meters/second/second?
Solution	
Step 1 Write the formula.	**Force = Mass x Acceleration**
Step 2 Fill in given numbers and units.	**Force = 1400 kilograms x 2 meters/second/second**
Step 3 Solve for the unknown.	**Force = 2800 kilogram-meters/second/second (kg-m/sec/sec) or 2800 N**
Practice Problems	**1.** How much force is needed to accelerate a 66-kg skier 1 m/sec/sec?
	2. What is the force on a 1000-kg elevator that is falling freely at 9.8 m/sec/sec?

Figure 13–14 *Which of Newton's three laws of motion explains why the jumper lands in the water, not on the dock?*

Newton's Third Law of Motion

Suppose you are an astronaut making a spacewalk outside the Space Shuttle. In your excitement about your walk, you use up all of the gas in your reaction jet. How do you get back to the Shuttle?

In order to save yourself, you need to know Newton's third law of motion. **The third law of motion states that for every action, there is an equal and opposite reaction.** Another way to state the third law is to say that every force must have an equal and opposite force. All forces come in pairs.

Now, back to your problem of being stranded in space. You have no walls or floor to push against. So you throw your jet pack in the opposite direction of the Shuttle. In throwing the jet pack, you push on it and it pushes on you. The jet pack moves away from the Shuttle. You move toward safety!

You probably associate forces with active objects such as humans, animals, and machines. So it may be difficult for you to imagine that an object such as a wall or floor exerts a force. But indeed it does. This is because every material is somewhat elastic. You know that a stretched rubber band can be pulled back in such a way that it can propel a wad of paper across the room. Although other materials do not stretch as easily as rubber, they do stretch somewhat (even if you cannot see it) when a force is applied to them. And just as a stretched rubber band exerts a force to return to its original condition, so do these materials.

Take a minute now to prove this fact for yourself. Push down on the edge of your desk with your hand. The desk may not move, but your hand will have a mark on it. This mark is evidence that a

ACTIVITY

DISCOVERING

Newton's Third Law of Motion

1. Obtain a rigid cardboard strip, about 15 cm x 75 cm, a skateboard, and a motorized or windup toy car.

2. Position the skateboard upside down on the floor Place the cardboard strip and the car on top. The cardboard is the road for the car.

3. Start the car and observe what happens.

Does the car or the road move?

■ Why don't you see the road moving away from you when you are in a real car?

■ Would you be able to drive forward if you were not attached to the Earth?

Figure 13–15 *Flying gracefully through the air, birds depend on Newton's third law of motion. Could a bird fly if there was no air?*

Activity Bank

Smooth Sailing, p. 737

Figure 13–16 *How does the third law of motion explain the movement of a water sprinkler?*

Movement of water

Movement of sprinkler arm

force is being exerted on your hand. The desk is exerting the force. The harder you push on the desk, the harder the desk pushes back on your hand.

One of the most basic examples of Newton's third law of motion is walking. As you walk, your feet push against the floor. At the same time, the floor pushes with an equal but opposite force against your feet. You move forward. If the floor is highly polished, you cannot push against it with much force. So the force it exerts against your feet is also less. You move more slowly, or perhaps not at all. If you were suspended a few meters above the Earth, could you walk forward? The flight of a bird can also be explained using Newton's third law of motion. The bird exerts a force on the air. The air pushing back on the bird's wings propels the bird forward.

The reaction engine of a rocket is another application of the third law of motion. Various fuels are burned in the engine, producing hot gases. The hot gases push against the inside tube of the rocket and escape out the bottom of the tube. As the gases move downward, the rocket moves in the opposite direction, or upward.

Have you noticed that many of these examples could have been used in Chapter 12 to describe how momentum is conserved? Well, it is no coincidence. In fact, Newton arrived at his third law of motion by studying the momentum of bodies before and after collisions. The two laws are actually different ways of describing the same interactions.

Newton's three laws of motion can explain all aspects of an object's motion. His first law explains that forces are necessary to change the motion of an object. His second law describes how force and acceleration are related to mass, or inertia. His third law explains that forces act in pairs.

13–3 Section Review

1. What is inertia? How is it involved in Newton's first law of motion? *Inertia must be overcome by force*
2. What three quantities are related in Newton's second law of motion? What is the relationship among them?
3. What does Newton's third law of motion say about action–reaction forces?

Connection—*You and Your World*
4. A person wearing a cast on one leg becomes more tired than usual by the end of each day. Explain this on the basis of Newton's first and second laws of motion.

ACTIVITY WRITING

A View of the World

It is certainly not big news to you that the sun is in the center of the solar system. But for a long time, people believed that the arrangement of the planets and the sun was completely different. In fact, when scientists first suggested that the Earth moved around the sun (rather than vice versa) they were laughed at, criticized, and condemned.

Using books in the library and other research materials, find out about the lives and work of the people involved in providing an accurate understanding of the solar system. A list of such people would include Galileo, Copernicus, Kepler, and Newton. Write a paper describing the contributions of each to the growing body of scientific knowledge.

13–4 Gravity

Legend has it that in the late 1500s, the famous Italian scientist Galileo dropped two cannonballs at exactly the same time from the top of the Leaning Tower of Pisa in Italy. One cannonball had ten times the mass of the other cannonball. According to the scientific theories of that day, the more massive ball should have landed first. But Galileo wanted to prove that this was not correct. He believed that the cannonballs would land at the same time. What would have been your hypothesis? According to the legend, Galileo proved to be right: Both cannonballs did land at exactly the same time! Galileo's experiment displays the basic laws of nature that govern the motion of falling objects.

Guide for Reading

Focus on these questions as you read.

▶ How is gravity related to motion?
▶ How is weight different from mass?

335

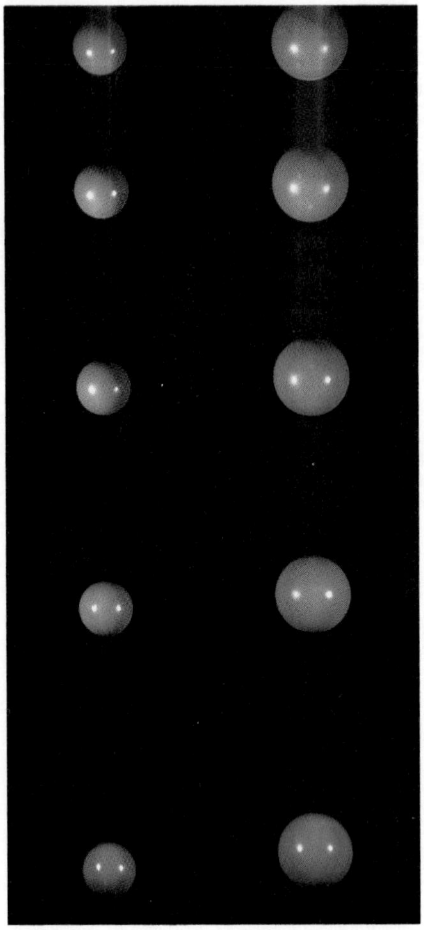

Falling Objects

What was so important about Galileo's discovery that a heavy object and a lighter object would land at the same time? To Isaac Newton, it meant that both objects were speeding up at the same rate, regardless of their masses. In other words, all falling objects accelerate at the same rate. A marble, a rock, and a huge boulder dropped from the top of a building at the same moment will all hit the ground at exactly the same time! According to Newton's laws of motion, if an object is accelerating, a force must be present. This force is called gravity. **The acceleration of a falling object is due to the force of gravity between the object and the Earth.**

Near the surface of the Earth, the acceleration due to the force of **gravity** (which is abbreviated as g) is 9.8 meters per second per second, or 9.8 m/sec/sec. This means that for every second an object is falling, its velocity is increasing by 9.8 m/sec. Here is an example. Suppose an object is dropped from the top of a mountain. Its starting velocity is 0 m/sec. At the end of the first second of fall, the object has a velocity of 9.8 m/sec. After two seconds, its velocity is 19.6 m/sec (9.8 m/sec + 9.8 m/sec).

Figure 13–17 *Two objects will fall to the Earth at exactly the same rate, regardless of their masses.*

Activity Bank

At the Center of the Gravity Matter, p. 738

Figure 13–18 *Without the force of gravity, these sky-diving acrobats would simply float in the sky. Thanks to gravity, however, they receive a thrilling adventure as they fall to Earth.*

After three seconds, 29.4 m/sec (9.8 m/sec + 9.8 m/sec + 9.8 m/sec). If it takes five seconds for the object to reach the ground, how fast will it be traveling? Perhaps you can now understand why even a dime can cause damage if it is dropped from a great height!

Activity Bank

Light Rock, p.739

PROBLEM ??? Solving

All in a Day's Work

On a colorful autumn day you head out on your newspaper route. As you are about to leave, your mother reminds you to take out the garbage. So you pick up the bag, place it on top of the newspapers that fill your wagon, and drop it off at the curb. On your way along the sidewalk, you come across the neighbor's cat, which you lift up and briefly pet before it jumps down and runs off. You continue on your way, pulling your wagon filled with newspapers behind you. At the next house, you strategically throw the paper from the sidewalk to the front step. Perfect shot! As you head for your next stop, you see a few acorns hanging from a tree. You pull them off the tree and throw them on the sidewalk ahead of you. Shortly after that, you see two of your friends trying to push a heavy bag of leaves. They are not having much success, so you join in and the three of you move the bag to the side of the house. You say goodbye to your friends and continue on your way until your red wagon is totally empty and it's time to go home—just in time for dinner.

Making a Diagram

During this short walk, a number of forces were exerted. Draw a series of diagrams showing each activity you performed. Use stick figures and arrows to show the forces involved. Do not forget about friction and gravity! When you finish, think of some other activities that might have taken place during your walk: catching a ball, moving a branch, lifting a rock. Add these to your drawings.

ACTIVITY

DISCOVERING

Science and Skydiving

1. Design a parachute using a large bandana and a piece of string or thread. Attach a clothespin to it.

2. Drop the parachute and a second clothespin from the same height at the same time. **CAUTION:** *Do not climb on any object without adult approval and supervision.* Which do you expect to hit the ground first? Why? Are you correct?

3. Describe the motion of the objects as they fell.

■ Redesign your parachute to decrease its velocity.

■ Can you now explain why insects can fall from tremendous heights yet walk away unharmed? (*Hint:* Compare their masses to their surface areas.)

Figure 13–19 *Although gravity pulls both a leaf and a rock toward the Earth, the two objects do not accelerate at the same rate on the Earth. Astronauts, however, have found that the two objects land at the same time on the moon. Why?*

Air Resistance

Do a leaf, a piece of paper, and a feather fall at 9.8 m/sec/sec? Because you have probably seen these objects fluttering through the air to the ground, you know the answer is no. Their acceleration is much less than 9.8 m/sec/sec. Why? As a leaf falls, air resistance opposes its downward motion. So it moves more slowly. Air resistance also opposes the downward motion of a falling rock. But the shape of the leaf causes greater air resistance, and so its downward motion is more significantly slowed. If both the leaf and the rock were dropped in a vacuum, they would accelerate at 9.8 m/sec/sec.

Any falling object meets air resistance. You can think of the object as being pushed up by this opposing force of the air. As the object falls, the air resistance gradually becomes equal to the pull of gravity. The forces are then balanced. According to the first law of motion, when forces are balanced there is no acceleration. The object continues to fall, but it falls at a constant velocity. There is no further acceleration. When a falling body no longer accelerates (but continues to fall at a constant velocity), it has reached its terminal (final) velocity. Sky divers cannot accelerate any further once they reach a

338

terminal velocity of about 190 km/hr. At this point, the sky divers continue their descent, although there is no longer any sensation of falling!

Newton's Law of Universal Gravitation

Although his work had provided answers to so many questions about falling objects and gravity, Newton did not stop there. He went even further. He wondered if the force that was making the apple fall to the Earth was the same force that kept the moon in its path around the Earth. After all, since the direction of the moon was constantly changing in its circular path, it too was accelerating. Therefore a force must be involved.

Newton calculated the acceleration of the apple and compared it with the acceleration of the moon. Using laws already presented by Johannes Kepler (1571–1630), a brilliant astronomer, Newton was able to derive a formula to calculate the force acting on both the apple and the moon. He concluded that the force acting on the moon was the same force that was acting on the apple—gravity.

In Newton's day, most scientists believed that forces on the Earth were different from forces elsewhere in the universe. Newton's discovery represented

ACTIVITY DOING

Science and the Leaky Faucet

1. Adjust a faucet so that it slowly drips. Use a deep sink, if possible.

2. Measure the distance from the tip of a hanging drop to the bottom of the sink.

3. Use a stopwatch to measure the time it takes for the drop to fall to the bottom of the sink.

4. Calculate the average velocity of the drop. Repeat steps 3 and 4 three more times.

5. Use your average value of velocity to calculate the acceleration of the water drop. This is the acceleration due to gravity.

How close does your value come to the accepted value of 9.8 m/sec/sec? If your value does not match the accepted value, what reasons can you give for the difference?

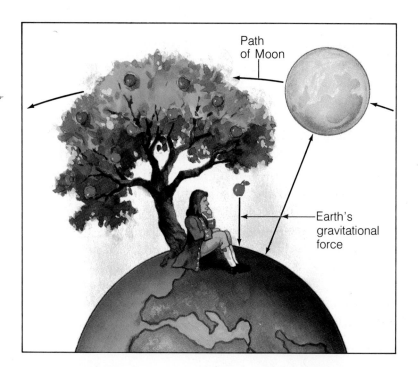

Path of Moon

Earth's gravitational force

Activity Bank

Putting Gravity to Work, p. 740

Figure 13–20 *Newton's universal law of gravitation explains why an apple falls to the ground as well as why the moon stays in its orbit around the Earth.*

Figure 13–21 *Although the Earth's gravitational attraction decreases as distance increases, a force is still exerted at a distance as great as that of the moon. In fact, the Earth's gravitational attraction is responsible for holding the moon in its path. How is gravity related to the organization of the solar system?*

ACTIVITY

DOING

Faster Than a Speeding Snowball?

A snowball is dropped over a cliff. If its starting velocity is 0 m/sec, how fast will it be traveling after 5 seconds? After 7 seconds? Right before it hits the ground at the end of its 11-second fall?

Now place a penny, a quarter, and a half dollar along the edge of a table. Place a ruler behind the coins, parallel with the table edge. Keeping the ruler parallel, push all three coins over the edge of the table at the same time. Record your observations.

Do all the coins, regardless of mass, hit the floor at the same time? Explain.

With this in mind, do you think the coins would fall faster than the snowball? Explain.

If a quarter was dropped with the snowball, how fast would the quarter be traveling after 7 seconds?

the first universal law of forces. A universal law applies to all objects in the universe. Newton's **law of universal gravitation** states that all objects in the universe attract each other by the force of gravity. The size of the force depends on two factors: the masses of the objects and the distance between them.

The force of gravity increases as the masses of the objects increase. Although gravitational forces always exist between objects, they only become observable when the masses of the objects are as large as those of the planets, moon, and stars. For example, there is a force of gravity between you and this textbook. Yet the textbook is not pulled over to you. Why? The force of gravity depends on the masses of the objects. The gravitational force between a book and you is extremely small because your mass and the book's mass are small compared with the mass of the Earth.

Gravitational force decreases rapidly as the distance between objects increases. The gravitational force between an apple and the Earth is about 2 N on the surface of the Earth. At 380,000 km—the distance to the moon—the gravitational force between the apple and the Earth is only 0.001 N.

Gravity is of great importance in the interactions of large objects. It is gravity that binds us to the Earth and holds the Earth and other planets in the solar system. The force of gravity plays an important role in the evolution of stars and in the behavior of galaxies. In a sense, it is gravity that holds the universe together.

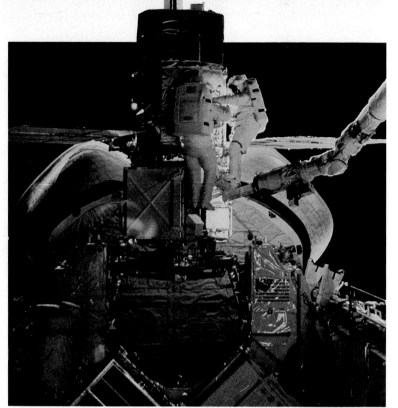

Figure 13–22 *Making repairs or performing experiments is quite a different experience in an almost weightless environment. For example, grabbing a huge piece of machinery in only one hand would be a great advantage. However, the fact that forgetting to tie oneself onto the work station would result in floating up and away would not be as favorable.*

ACTIVITY READING

Voyage to the Moon

Before it was possible to travel to the moon, Jules Verne envisioned such a trip. In Verne's *From the Earth to the Moon*, he described how people would get to the moon and how they would have to adjust to the conditions outside the Earth's atmosphere. Read the book and discover situations Verne's space travelers encounter.

Weight and Mass

You are all familiar with the term weight. Each time you step on a scale, you are looking to see what you weigh. **Weight is a measure of the force of gravity on an object.** In this case, the object is you! Since weight is a force, its unit is the newton (N). This textbook weighs about 15 N. A medium-sized car probably weighs between 7000 and 9500 N.

Your weight varies according to the force of gravity pulling on you. And the force of gravity varies according to distance from the center of the Earth. Suppose you weigh yourself in the morning at sea level. Later that day you ride to the top of a tall mountain, weigh yourself again, and find that you weigh less. What has happened? Is there less of you on top of the mountain than there was at sea level? After all, you weigh less. The answer, of course, is no. In a given day, you have the same amount of

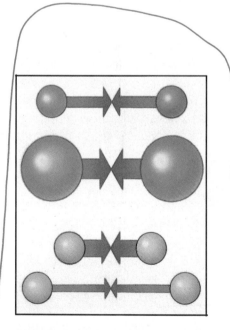

Figure 13–23 *The force of attraction between two objects increases as mass increases (top). It decreases as distance increases (bottom). The wider the arrow, the greater the force.*

mass regardless of your location. Your mass does not change, unless of course you diet and exercise. Your mass is the same anywhere on the Earth (on top of a mountain or at sea level), on the moon, and even on Jupiter. It is your weight that changes. Because you are farther from the center of the Earth when you are on top of a mountain than when you are at sea level, the pull of gravity on you decreases. Thus you weigh less on top of the mountain than you do at sea level.

Although mass and weight are not the same thing, they are related. This may be obvious to you because you know that more massive objects weigh more than less massive objects. Newton's second law of motion, force = mass × acceleration, can be rewritten in terms of weight to show the relationship.

Weight = Mass × Acceleration due to gravity
$$w = m \times g$$

Remember that the unit of weight is the newton and the unit of mass is the kilogram.

On the surface of the Earth, the acceleration due to gravity is 9.8 m/sec/sec. A 10-kg mass would weigh 10 kg × 9.8 m/sec/sec, or 98 N. If your mass is 50 kg, your weight would be 490 N. What would be the weight of a 100-kg mass?

13–4 Section Review

1. How is gravity related to falling objects?
2. How would all objects accelerate if they fell in a vacuum? Why?
3. What does the law of universal gravitation state?
4. Compare weight and mass.

Critical Thinking—*Making Calculations*
5. An astronaut who weighs 600 N on Earth is standing on an asteroid. The gravitational force of the asteroid is one hundredth of that of the Earth. What is the astronaut's weight on the asteroid?

CONNECTIONS

Which Way Is Up?

You know that the sky is up and the ground is down because you can see it. But would you know the same if you closed your eyes? Yes, you would! Astronauts in space can spin comfortably in all directions, but you cannot. Even with your eyes closed, you can tell which way is up and which way is down. You can even determine if you are moving and in what direction. You have your *ears* to thank for all this!

In one area of the inner ear, special structures called otoliths determine whether the body is speeding up, slowing down, or changing direction. They do this by comparing the body's movement with something that is always in the same direction—the downward force of gravity. When the otoliths move, they pull on hair cells that relay a nerve impulse to the brain describing the position or motion of the head. For example, when your head is in the upright position, gravity pulls the otoliths down. The otoliths in turn push the sensory hairs down, rather than to one side or the other. When your head is tilted, the pull of gravity shifts the otoliths to the side. This causes the sensory hairs to send a different signal to the brain.

Additional balance comes from another section of the inner ear. Here three tiny canals called semicircular canals lie at right angles to each other. A fluid flows through each canal in response to motion in a particular direction. If, for example, you move your head from right to left when you say "no," the fluid in the semicircular canal that detects horizontal motion will be forced to move. When the fluid moves, it disturbs hair cells that send messages about the movement to the brain. Because each semicircular canal detects motion in one dimension, the arrangement of the canals enables a person to detect movement in all directions.

So the next time you find yourself upside down, give some thought to what your ears have to do with it!

The otoliths (left) and the semicircular canals (right) enable a gymnast to maintain balance as she completes a back flip.

343

Laboratory Investigation

Will an Elephant Fall Faster Than a Mouse?

Problem

Does mass affect the rate of fall?

Materials (per group)

wood block, 10 cm x 15 cm x 2.5 cm
Styrofoam pad, 10 cm x 15 cm x 2.5 cm
sheet of notebook paper
triple-beam balance

Procedure

1. Use the triple-beam balance to determine the masses of the block, Styrofoam pad, and paper. Record each mass to the nearest 0.1 gram.
2. Hold the block and foam pad horizontally at arm's length. The largest surface area of each object should be parallel to the ground.
3. Release both the block and the foam pad at the same time. Observe if they land at the same time or if one hits the ground before the other.
4. Repeat step 3 several times. Record your results.
5. Repeat steps 2 to 4 for the foam pad and the paper.
6. Crumple the paper into a tight ball.

7. Compare the falling rates of the crumpled paper and the foam pad. Record your observations.
8. Compare the falling rates of the crumpled paper and the wood block. Record your observations.

Observations

Object	Mass	Falling Rate (comparative)
Wood block		
Styrofoam pad		
Paper (uncrumpled)		
Paper (crumpled)		

1. Which reaches the ground first, the wood block or the foam pad?
2. Are your results the same in each trial?
3. Which reaches the ground first, the foam pad or the uncrumpled paper?
4. Which reaches the ground first, the foam pad or the crumpled paper?

Analysis and Conclusions

1. Galileo stated that two bodies with different masses fall at the same rate. Do your observations verify his hypothesis? Explain your answer.
2. Did crumpling the paper have any effect on its falling rate? Explain your answer.
3. Now answer this question: Would an elephant fall faster than a mouse? Explain your answer.
4. **On Your Own** Design and perform an experiment that compares different objects made out of the same material.

Study Guide

Summarizing Key Concepts

13–1 What Is Force?

▲ A force is a push or pull. A force may give energy to an object, setting the object in motion, stopping it, or changing its direction.

▲ Forces in the same direction combine by addition. Forces in opposite directions combine by subtraction.

▲ Unbalanced forces cause a change in motion. When forces are balanced, there is no change in motion. Balanced forces are opposite in direction and equal in size.

13–2 Friction: A Force Opposing Motion

▲ Friction is a force that opposes motion.

▲ The three kinds of friction are sliding, rolling, and fluid friction.

13–3 Newton's Laws of Motion

▲ Inertia is the tendency of matter to resist a change in motion.

▲ Newton's first law of motion states that an object at rest will remain at rest and an object in motion will remain in motion at constant velocity unless acted upon by an unbalanced force.

▲ Newton's second law of motion describes how force, acceleration, and mass are related. Force equals mass times acceleration.

▲ Newton's third law of motion states that forces always occur in pairs. Every action has an equal and opposite reaction.

13–4 Gravity

▲ The acceleration due to gravity at the surface of the Earth is 9.8 m/sec/sec.

▲ Gravity is a force of attraction that exists between all objects in the universe.

▲ The size of the force of gravity depends on the masses of the two objects and the distance between them.

▲ Weight and mass are different quantities. Weight is a measure of the pull of gravity on a given mass. Mass is a measure of the amount of matter in an object. Mass is constant; weight can change.

Reviewing Key Terms

Define each term in a complete sentence.

13–1 What Is Force?
force

13–2 Friction: A Force Opposing Motion
friction

13–3 Newton's Laws of Motion
inertia
newton

13–4 Gravity
gravity
law of universal gravitation

Chapter Review

Content Review

Multiple Choice

Choose the letter of the answer that best completes each statement.

1. Force is
   a. a push.   c. the ability to change motion.
   b. a pull.   d. all of these answers

2. Forces that are opposite and equal are called
   a. balanced.   c. unbalanced.
   b. friction.   d. gravitational.

3. The force that opposes the motion of an object is called
   a. acceleration.   c. density.
   b. friction.   d. gravity.

4. The type of friction that exists for a shark swimming in the ocean is
   a. sliding.   c. rolling.
   b. hydraulic.   d. fluid.

5. The property of matter that resists a change in motion is
   a. inertia.   c. gravity.
   b. friction.   d. weight.

6. According to Newton's second law of motion, force equals mass times
   a. inertia.   c. direction.
   b. weight.   d. acceleration.

7. The force of attraction that exists between all objects in the universe is
   a. friction.   c. momentum.
   b. inertia.   d. gravity.

8. A change in the force of gravity pulling on you will change your
   a. mass.   c. inertia.
   b. air resistance.   d. weight.

True or False

If the statement is true, write "true." If it is false, change the underlined word or words to make the statement true.

1. A <u>force</u> can set an object in motion, stop its motion, or change the speed and direction of its motion.
2. The combined force of <u>unbalanced</u> forces is always zero.
3. Friction is a force that always acts in a direction <u>opposite</u> to the motion of the moving object.
4. "Slippery" substances such as oil, wax, and grease that reduce friction are called <u>lubricants</u>.
5. Objects in constant motion will remain in constant motion unless acted upon by <u>balanced</u> forces.
6. Force equals mass times <u>velocity</u>.
7. In a vacuum, a heavier object will fall to the Earth <u>faster than</u> a lighter object will.
8. <u>Mass</u> is the measure of the force of gravity.

Concept Mapping

Complete the following concept map for Section 13–3. Then construct a concept map for the entire chapter.

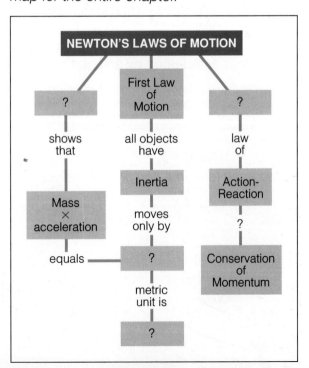

346

Concept Mastery

Discuss each of the following in a brief paragraph.

1. Why is there a force involved when the sails of a windmill turn?
2. Distinguish between balanced and unbalanced forces.
3. Why do athletes' shoes often have cleats on them?
4. Explain how Newton's three laws explain all aspects of an object's motion.
5. Explain why a single force cannot exist.
6. When a golf ball is dropped to the pavement, it bounces up. Is a force needed to make it bounce up? If so, what exerts the force?
7. Why does a raindrop fall to the ground at exactly the same rate as a boulder?
8. Explain why a flat sheet of paper dropped from a height of 2 meters will not accelerate at the same rate as a sheet of paper crumpled into a ball.
9. What is the relationship between weight and mass?

Critical Thinking and Problem Solving

Use the skills you have developed in this chapter to answer each of the following.

1. **Applying concepts** How is inertia responsible for removing most of the water from wet clothes in a washing machine?
2. **Making connections** Although Newton's first law of motion has two parts, they actually say the same thing. Explain how this can be true using what you learned about frames of reference.
3. **Applying concepts** Suppose a 12-N force is required to push a crate across a floor when friction is not present. In reality, friction exerts a force of 3 N. If you exert a force of 7 N, what size force must your friend exert so that you can move the crate together? Draw a diagram showing the forces involved.

4. **Making generalizations** What happens to the force of gravity if mass increases? If distance increases? Write a statement that explains how gravity, mass, and distance are related according to Newton's law of universal gravitation.
5. **Making calculations** A heavy object is dropped from the top of a cliff. What is its velocity at the end of 2 seconds? At the end of 5 seconds? Just before it hits the ground after 12 seconds?
6. **Identifying relationships** Suppose the acceleration due to gravity on a planet called Zorb is 20 m/sec/sec. What is the weight of a 100-kg Zorbian?
7. **Using the writing process** Pretend you live on a planet whose size is the same but whose mass is four times greater than the mass of the Earth. Using the words listed below, write a 200-word story about a typical day in your life. Include information about how your planet's mass affects you and the life forms around you.

    acceleration   law of universal gravitation
    gravity   momentum
    inertia   weight

Forces in Fluids

Guide for Reading

After you read the following sections, you will be able to

14–1 Fluid Pressure
- Describe how the particles of a fluid exert pressure.

14–2 Hydraulic Devices
- Explain how a hydraulic device operates.

14–3 Pressure and Gravity
- Relate fluid pressure to altitude and depth.

14–4 Buoyancy
- Describe the relationship between the buoyant force and Archimedes' principle.

14–5 Fluids in Motion
- Explain why an object floats or sinks.
- Recognize how Bernoulli's principle is related to flight.

It is December 17, 1903. Wilbur and Orville Wright stand on a deserted beach near Kitty Hawk, North Carolina. Orville climbs into a strange-looking seat made of wood and canvas. A 12-horsepower gasoline engine is connected to two large propellers by a chain and sprocket. The Wright brothers are about to try something no one has ever succeeded in doing before. They are going to fly this machine!

They have prepared well for their attempt at flight. For the past 7 years they have studied the dynamics of air flight. They have experimented with more than 200 different wing surfaces in their homemade wind tunnel. They have observed and analyzed the flight of buzzards, carefully noting how the birds turn in the sky without losing balance.

Now they are finally ready. In a flight that lasts just 12 seconds, the plane manages to travel about 36 meters. It is a small distance, but a significant step in science: Human flight has become a reality!

The first flying machine was designed in the sixteenth century by Leonardo da Vinci. Why did it take so long to fly the first plane? How can a jumbo jet fly over 800 kilometers per hour? As you read this chapter, you will learn the answers.

Journal *Activity*

You and Your World Can you remember a time when you got caught in a storm? Did the wind pushing against you almost stop you in your tracks? In your journal, describe the storm and how it felt to get caught in it. Include details such as the puddle you stepped in or the snow that blew into your coat or gloves.

◀ *As Wilbur Wright stood watching on the deserted beach at Kitty Hawk, North Carolina, his brother Orville took one of the most important trips in history—a 12-second, 36-meter leap toward the attainment of human flight.*

14–1 Fluid Pressure

When you think of forces and Newton's laws of motion, do you think only of solid objects—pushing a box, pulling a wagon, lifting a crate? Although you may not realize it, forces exist naturally in fluids as well. Fluids are substances that do not have a rigid shape. Liquids and gases are fluids. When you breathe, when you swim, when you drink from a straw, you are experiencing forces created by fluids. As a matter of fact, there is a force approximately equal to the weight of an automobile pushing down on you right now! Do you know why?

What Is Pressure?

All matter is made up of tiny particles. **The forces that exist in fluids are caused by the mass and motion of the particles making up the fluid.** In a solid, the particles are packed very tightly together. There is very little movement of the particles in a solid. In liquids and gases, however, the particles are not packed together so tightly. Thus they are able to move about more freely. The particles that make up fluids are moving constantly in all directions. As each particle moves, it pushes against other particles and against the walls of its container with a force that depends on the mass and acceleration of the particle. The "push," or force, particles exert over a certain area is called **pressure**. Fluid pressure is exerted equally in all directions.

Perhaps you are familiar with the word pressure as it is used to describe water, air, and even blood. Scientists define pressure as force per unit area. Pressure can be calculated by dividing the force exerted by a fluid by the total area over which the force acts:

$$\text{Pressure} = \frac{\text{Force}}{\text{Area}}$$

Figure 14–1 *Although they may not realize it, these wind surfers and cliff divers could not enjoy their activities without the forces exerted by fluids. What fluids are involved in the actions shown in these photos?*

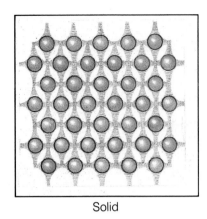

Solid

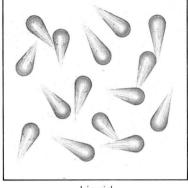

Liquid

Gas

Figure 14–2 *The arrangement and movement of the particles that make up a substance determine the characteristics of the substance. Notice that as you move from solids to gases, the particles become more spread out and motion increases. How does this explain why gases exert the greatest pressure?*

When force is measured in newtons (N) and area is measured in square centimeters (cm^2), pressure is measured in newtons per square centimeter (N/cm^2).

Air in the atmosphere exerts a pressure of 10.13 N/cm^2 at sea level. If your back has an area of approximately 1000 cm^2, then you have a force of 10,130 N pushing on your back. This is the force approximately equal to the weight of an automobile you read about earlier. What keeps this force from crushing you? The fluids inside your body also exert pressure. The air pressure outside your body is balanced by the fluid pressure inside your body. So you do not feel the outside force.

You are probably familiar with some important consequences of pressure. Many devices must be inflated to a particular pressure before they can operate properly. For example, a car whose tires are not properly inflated may not ride correctly or get its expected gas mileage. What will happen if a basketball is not filled to the proper pressure? Meteorologists also pay careful attention to pressure. Atmospheric pressure is an important indicator of weather conditions. High and low pressure areas are each associated with specific weather characteristics.

Differences in Pressure

You probably did not give much thought to what you were doing the last time you drank through a straw. But what you actually do when you suck on a straw is remove most of the air from inside the straw. This causes the pressure inside the straw to

Activity Bank

Watering Your Garden Green, p. 742

Figure 14–3 *This can was crushed because of a change in air pressure. Was the air pressure greater inside the can or outside it?*

351

Figure 14–4 *It would be very difficult for this girl to enjoy her ice cream soda if it were not for unequal air pressure. The air pressure pushing down on the liquid outside the straw is greater than the air pressure inside the straw. This difference in pressure forces the liquid up.*

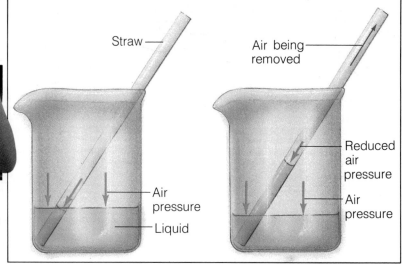

ACTIVITY

DOING

Air Pressure

1. Obtain an empty plastic 1-liter bottle that has an airtight top.

2. Fill the bottle one-quarter full with hot water.

3. Tightly secure the top to the bottle so that no air can enter or escape.

4. Place the bottle in a refrigerator for about five minutes. At the end of this time, record the shape of the bottle.

When the hot air in the bottle cools, the particles slow down and do not push into each other as often. Thus, the air pressure inside the bottle decreases.

What causes the bottle to collapse?

decrease. Standard air pressure, which is now greater than the air pressure inside the straw, pushes down on the surface of your drink. This push forces the drink up through the straw and into your mouth! See Figure 14–4. The principle that enables you to drink from a straw is an important property of fluids. **Fluids will move from areas of higher pressure to areas of lower pressure.**

The operation of a vacuum cleaner is another example of the principle of unequal air pressure. It may surprise you to learn that a vacuum cleaner does not suck up only dirt. A fan inside the cleaner causes the air pressure within the machine to become less than the pressure of the air outside the machine. The outside air pressure pushes the air and dirt into the vacuum cleaner. A filter then removes the dirt and releases the air. In addition to vacuum cleaners, all devices that involve suction take advantage of differences in pressure. This includes plungers, suction cups, and even medicine droppers.

One extremely important consequence of the principle of unequal pressure is your ability to breathe. When you breathe, you use a large muscle at the base of your rib cage to change the volume and pressure of the chest cavity. This muscle is called the diaphragm. When you inhale, the diaphragm flattens, giving your lungs room to expand. In turn, the air particles inside your lungs have more room to move about, which means that the pressure decreases. When the pressure inside your lungs is less than the air pressure outside your body, air is forced through your mouth or nose into your lungs. When you exhale, the diaphragm moves upward, reducing the size of your lungs. This causes the pressure inside your lungs to increase to a pressure greater than that outside your body. Air is now forced out.

14–1 Section Review

1. Why does fluid pressure exist?
2. How is pressure calculated?
3. Explain how a woman weighing 500 N and wearing high-heeled shoes can exert a pressure on the floor equal to about three times the pressure exerted by a 45,000-N elephant.

Connection—*Life Science*
4. What can happen to a person's blood vessels if his or her blood pressure gets too high?

Figure 14–5 *Pop. Fizz. These are familiar sounds associated with opening certain containers. Many liquids are put into cans or bottles under high pressure. When the container is opened, that pressure is released.*

14–2 Hydraulic Devices

If there are no outside forces acting on a fluid, the pressure exerted by the fluid will be the same throughout. And the pressure will be exerted in every direction—up, down, sideways. Suppose you have a balloon filled with air and you poke your finger into it without popping it. Your finger adds pressure to the air at that point inside the balloon. The particles of the air are already packed tightly together and cannot escape. So what happens to this additional pressure applied to the air? The pressure at any point in a fluid is transmitted, or sent out, equally in all directions throughout the fluid. This means that the pressure is increased in every direction.

You have probably experienced this event without even knowing it. If you have a bottle completely filled with water and you try to push a stopper into it, what happens? You probably get wet as the water squirts out the top. The pressure applied to the water by

Guide for Reading

Focus on this question as you read.

▶ *How do the properties of fluid pressure make hydraulic devices operate?*

353

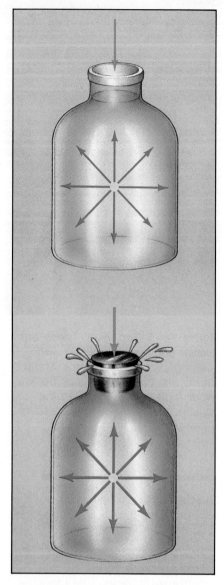

the stopper acts equally in all directions—including up! **The transmission of pressure equally in all directions in a liquid is the principle behind hydraulic devices.** The brakes on your family car and a hydraulic lift used to raise heavy objects are examples of **hydraulic devices.** Hydraulic devices produce enormous forces with the application of only a very small force. In other words, hydraulic devices multiply forces. Let's see just how this works in the case of hydraulic brakes.

You may have wondered how it is possible that a rapidly moving car with a mass of more than 1000 kilograms can be stopped with a relatively light push on the brake pedal—a push certainly much lighter than you would need to exert if you were trying to stop the car from the outside. Imagine two movable pistons connected to a container of liquid as shown in Figure 14–7. The smaller piston can be pushed downward. This piston is like the piston connected to the brake pedal. When a force is exerted on the piston, the pressure created by the force pushes against the liquid. The pressure is transmitted equally throughout the liquid.

Now for the surprising part. The force experienced by the larger piston is greater than the force used to move the smaller piston. How does

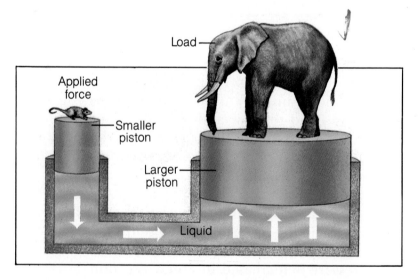

Load
Applied force
Smaller piston
Larger piston
Liquid

Figure 14–7 *In a hydraulic lift, the applied force moves the smaller piston down and adds pressure to the liquid. That pressure is transmitted equally in all directions, so the same pressure is exerted on the larger piston. But because the area of the larger piston is greater than the area of the smaller piston, more force is produced. The larger piston and its load move up.*

Figure 14–8 *Besides being practical, hydraulic devices sometimes sustain life, as for this sea anemone, or provide endless fun, as for these children at the amusement park. No matter what the application, hydraulic devices are used to multiply force.*

this happen? The pressure on every square centimeter of the larger piston is equal to the pressure on every square centimeter of the smaller piston. The force exerted on a piston is the pressure of the liquid times the area of the piston. Since the number of square centimeters (or area) is greater on the larger piston, the force is greater. In the case of hydraulic brakes, the larger piston would be connected to the brake pads that slow the tires down. This is how a push on the brake pedal can bring a car to a halt.

You may already be familiar with some hydraulic devices. Barbers' chairs, automobile lifts, rescue ladders, and robotic equipment all use such devices. In addition, a number of living organisms make use of hydraulic pressure. A sea anemone can achieve a variety of shapes by the action of muscles on its seawater-filled body cavity. Earthworms move forward by repeated contractions of circular muscles along the body that act on their fluid-filled body cavities. The legs of some spiders are not extended only by muscles. Instead, the legs are extended by fluid driven into them under pressure.

14–2 Section Review

1. Explain the principle used in the operation of hydraulic devices.
2. Name four hydraulic devices with which you are familiar.

Critical Thinking—*Applying Concepts*

3. Without changing the size of the applied force or the small piston, how can you increase the amount of force that comes out of a hydraulic lift or ladder?

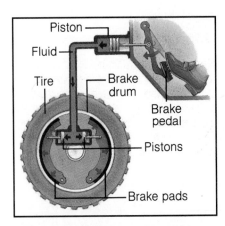

Figure 14–9 *Fluid in the brake system of a car multiplies the force exerted by the driver into a force great enough to stop the moving car. What force is used by the brake pads to stop the tire from turning?*

14–3 Pressure and Gravity

You learned that the pressure exerted by a fluid is the same throughout the fluid if there are no forces acting on the fluid. But there is one force that is always present. That force is gravity. Gravity pulls downward on all of the particles in a fluid.

The force of gravity produces some familiar results. For example, if you have ever swum to the bottom of a pool, then you remember how your ears began to ache as you went deeper. This happened because the pressure of the water increased rapidly with depth. **Due to the force of gravity, the pressure of any fluid varies with its depth.** The greater the depth, the greater the pressure. Let's see why.

The pool of water in Figure 14–10 has been broken up into five different levels. Because gravity pulls down on the particles in the top level, the entire level has a certain weight. The force of the weight of the first level pushes down on the second level. The second level, then, has the pull of gravity on its own particles plus the force of the weight of the first level. Therefore, the pressure at the second level is greater than the pressure at the first level. What about at the third level? The third level has the pull of gravity on its own particles plus the weight of the first two levels pushing down on it. So the pressure at the third level is greater than at either level above it. The bottom level (or greatest depth) of any fluid will have the greatest pressure because it has the greatest force pushing down on it from all the levels above it.

The increase in pressure that accompanies an increase in depth has some important effects.

Figure 14–10 *As any diver knows, the pressure in a fluid increases with depth. Where is the pressure greatest in a swimming pool?*

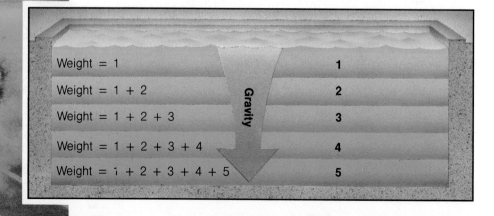

Weight = 1		1
Weight = 1 + 2		2
Weight = 1 + 2 + 3	Gravity	3
Weight = 1 + 2 + 3 + 4		4
Weight = 1 + 2 + 3 + 4 + 5		5

Figure 14–11 *Because pressure increases downward, the stream from the bottom hole in this container of water is strongest. Try it and see! The horizontal supporting ribs of a silo are closer together at the bottom than at the top. Why?*

Submarines that have descended too deep in the ocean have on occasion been crushed by the tremendous pressure. Divers cannot go too deep without experiencing serious problems caused by the increased pressure. Under high-pressure conditions, more nitrogen gas than usual dissolves in a diver's blood. When the diver resurfaces, the pressure on the body greatly decreases and the nitrogen gas leaves the blood. If the nitrogen leaves too quickly, it forms tiny bubbles that are often quite painful and can be dangerous. This condition is sometimes referred to as the bends. In order to prevent the bends, a diver must rise slowly to allow the dissolved nitrogen to be released gradually from the blood.

Water is not the only fluid in which pressure varies with depth. Our planet is surrounded by a fluid atmosphere. The pressure of our atmosphere also varies. In this case, the pressure varies with altitude, or height above the ground. The higher the altitude, the lower the pressure. In addition, at higher altitudes, there are fewer particles of air in a given area. Fewer particles pushing against one another results in lower pressure. At higher altitudes, the pressure inside your body becomes greater than the air pressure outside your body. You may feel the difference in pressure as a pain in your eardrums. When this happens, some air rushes out of your ears and you hear a "pop." As a result of the release of some of the air from inside your eardrum, the pressure inside your eardrum is again equal to the pressure outside your body.

ACTIVITY

DISCOVERING

A Plumber's Magic

1. Wet the bottom rim of a plumber's plunger.

2. Push the plunger tight against the seat of a stool, the chalkboard, or some other smooth surface.

What happens when you try to lift the plunger?

■ Using what you know about air pressure, explain how a plunger works.

14–3 Section Review

1. What force causes fluid pressure to vary with depth? Why?
2. Why must divers rise slowly?
3. Why are dams thicker at the bottom than at the top?

Connection—*Life Science*

4. Explain why it is more difficult to breathe at higher altitudes than at sea level.

Guide for Reading

Focus on these questions as you read.

▶ *What is buoyancy?*
▶ *How does Archimedes' principle explain why an object floats or sinks?*

14–4 Buoyancy

Here is an experience that you have probably had. You have been able to lift a friend or heavy object while you were in or under water that you could not lift while you were out of the water. Objects submerged in a fluid appear to weigh less than they do out of the fluid. Why? Force (pressure) increases with depth. Thus the force at the bottom of an object in a fluid is greater than the force at the top of the object. The overall force is in the upward direction and acts against the downward weight of the object. The upward force is called the **buoyant** (BOI-uhnt) **force.** This phenomenon is known as **buoyancy.**

Think for a moment about what happens to the level of water in a bathtub when you sit down in it. The level rises. It does so because you move aside some of the water and take its place. Any object placed in water displaces, or moves aside, a certain amount of water. The amount of water that is displaced has a definite weight. Because the buoyant force was able to support this weight, this weight must be related to the size of the buoyant force.

More than 2000 years ago, the Greek scientist Archimedes discovered the nature of this relationship. **The buoyant force on an object is equal to the weight of the fluid displaced by the object.** This relationship between buoyancy and the weight of the displaced fluid is called **Archimedes' principle.**

The size of the buoyant force determines what will happen to an object placed in a fluid—that is,

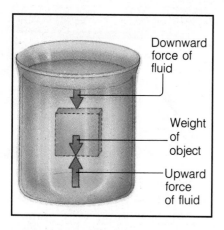

Figure 14–12 *Fluids exert an upward force that acts against the downward force exerted by the weight of the object. What is this upward force called?*

Downward force of fluid

Weight of object

Upward force of fluid

whether it will sink or float. The buoyant force can be greater than, less than, or equal to the weight of an object placed in the fluid. What do you think happens when the weight of an object placed in a fluid is less than or equal to the weight of the fluid it displaces—and therefore the buoyant force? You are correct if you said the object floats. **An object floats when it displaces a volume of fluid whose weight is greater than or equal to its own weight.**

Have you ever heard the expression "tip of the iceberg" applied to a situation in which only a few facts are known (the rest are hidden). This expression is based in science—in particular, in Archimedes' principle. An iceberg is a massive chunk of ice that has broken away from a glacier and is floating in the ocean. Because it is floating, you know that its weight must be less than or equal to the weight of the salt water it displaces. A volume of ice weighs slightly less than the same volume of salt water. Therefore, the buoyant force of the ocean pushes the iceberg upward. But because the weight of the iceberg and the weight of the displaced water are so close, the iceberg is pushed upward only a small amount. Close to 90 percent of the iceberg remains submerged. Icebergs can be extremely dangerous because a passing ship may see only the small portion that is above water—the tip—and thus be damaged by the much larger portion floating beneath the surface.

Exactly why do some substances float and others sink? The answer has to do with a physical property of both the object and the fluid called **density.** As you learned in Chapter 2, density is the ratio of the mass of a substance to its volume. In other words, density is mass divided by volume (D = M/V). Here is an example. A block of wood placed in water will float. But the same size block of aluminum placed in water sinks. Why? For the displaced water to have a greater weight than the object (the condition for floating), the fluid must have a greater density than the object. Water, then, must be more dense than this block of wood, but less dense than aluminum.

The conditions for floating can now be stated in terms of density: **An object will float in a fluid if the density of that object is less than the density of the fluid.** The density of water is 1 gram per cubic

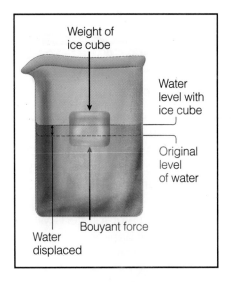

Figure 14–13 *An object placed in a fluid displaces an amount of fluid causing the level to rise. The buoyant force is equal to the weight of the displaced fluid. How can you measure the amount of water displaced by this ice cube?*

Activity Bank

Density Dazzlers, p. 744

Figure 14–14 *Do not worry about the tip of an iceberg. It is what lies beneath the surface that is the problem! Because the density of ice is slightly less than the density of water, only a portion of an iceberg is above the surface, even though the whole iceberg is floating.*

ACTIVITY

An Archimedean Trick

1. Obtain a cubic object such as a die.

2. Measure the volume of the cube. Volume equals length times width times height.

3. Obtain a graduated cylinder or small beaker into which you can place the cube. Fill half of the container with water. Record the volume of the water either by reading the level on the graduated cylinder or making a mark on the beaker with a glass-marking pencil.

4. Place the cube into the water. Make sure the cube is entirely under water. Record the volume shown on the container again.

5. Subtract the first volume measurement from the second volume measurement. Compare this difference with the volume of the cube you calculated.

Why is the second volume measurement greater than the first? Is there more water?

■ What does this experiment tell you about the fluid an object displaces?

■ Suppose the container of water was filled to the top. What would have happened when you placed the cube into the container?

centimeter (1 g/cm³). The wood block floats because the density of wood is about 0.8 g/cm³. The density of aluminum is 2.7 g/cm³—more than twice the density of water. So the aluminum block sinks. Aluminum can never displace a weight of water equal to its own weight. The density of lead is 11.3 g/cm³. It, too, sinks in water. What happens to lead and aluminum when they are placed in mercury, which has a density of 13.6 g/cm³?

You may wonder how objects such as steel ships are able to float in water, since the density of steel is 7.8 g/cm³. A ship is built of a shell of steel that is hollow inside. So the volume of the ship is made up mostly of air. The ship and air together have a density that is less than that of water. They can displace a weight of water equal to or greater than their weight. Can you explain why a ship will sink if its hull fills with water?

Air is also a fluid. So air exerts a buoyant force. You are buoyed up by the air. But because its buoyant force is so small, you cannot actually feel it. The density of air is only 0.00121 g/cm³. A balloon filled with helium gas will float in air because the density of helium is 0.000167 g/cm³. The density of carbon dioxide is almost twice the density of air. Will a balloon filled with carbon dioxide float in air?

Certain organisms and objects need to float at a certain depth, rather than at the surface. If the weight of a submerged object is exactly equal to the weight of the displaced fluid, the object will not move up or down. Instead, it will float at a constant depth. Most fishes have a gas-filled bladder whose

Figure 14–15 *This bather in the Dead Sea in Israel relaxes with the newspaper as she enjoys the results of density differences. Because the Dead Sea is very salty, it is very dense. Is the woman's density greater or less than that of the water?*

Figure 14-16 *At first glance you may see no relationship between hot-air balloons that rise high in the sky and a submarine that sinks deep into the ocean. But both must adjust their masses to rise, sink, or float at a certain level depending on the buoyant force. Why?*

volume changes to adjust to the buoyant force at various depths. Submerged submarines take on and discharge sea water as needed for the same reason. And the pilot of a hot-air balloon adjusts its weight to match the buoyant force of the air.

The concept of buoyancy is useful in many fields. Geology is a good example. According to the modern theory of plate tectonics and continental drift, the continents can be thought of as floating in a sea of slightly soft rock that acts like a fluid. The height of any continent in a particular area depends in part on the difference between its density and the density of the rock in which it is floating.

14-4 Section Review

1. Why does the buoyant force exist?
2. State Archimedes' principle in terms of buoyancy. In terms of density.
3. The density of ocean water is 1.02 g/cm³. Will a boat float higher in ocean water than in fresh water? Explain your answer.

Critical Thinking—*Designing an Experiment*

4. Suppose a friend finds a strange-looking object with no particular shape. Explain how you can determine the density of the object in order to identify the substance.

14–5 Fluids in Motion

Now it is time for you to do a little discovering. Try this experiment. Get a long, thin strip of paper. Put the paper in a book by inserting about 5 centimeters of it between two pages. Hold the book upright in front of your mouth so that the paper hangs over the far side of the book as shown in Figure 14–17. Now blow gently across the top of the paper. What happens? If you do this experiment correctly, the piece of paper is pushed upward, or lifted.

What you have demonstrated is the principle formulated by the eighteenth-century Swiss scientist Daniel Bernoulli. **Bernoulli's principle** explains why all forms of flight are possible. **Bernoulli's principle explains that the pressure in a moving stream of fluid is less than the pressure in the surrounding fluid.** The faster a fluid moves, the less pressure it exerts.

When you blow across the top of the paper, you produce a moving stream of air. The pressure in this moving stream is less than the pressure in the surrounding air. So the air pressure under the paper is now greater than the air pressure above it. The paper is pushed up into the moving air. What has this to do with how airplanes fly?

Look at Figure 14–18, which shows the shape of an airplane wing. You will notice that the wing is round in the front, thickest in the middle, and narrow at the back. The bulge in the upper surface makes this surface longer than the lower surface. So when the wing moves forward, the air above the wing must travel a longer distance than the air

Figure 14–17 *You can demonstrate Bernoulli's principle by doing this simple experiment.*

ACTIVITY

DISCOVERING

Rolling Uphill

1. Place a hard-boiled egg or a potato in a small saucepan filled with water.

2. Hold the saucepan under running water so that the water runs between the egg (or potato) and the rim.

3. Tilt the saucepan toward you slightly. Where do you think the egg (or potato) will go? Are you correct?

■ Explain your observations.

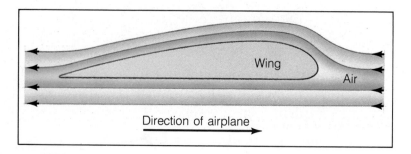

Figure 14–18 *An airplane wing is designed so that air passing over the wing travels faster than air passing beneath it. According to Bernoulli's principle, less pressure is exerted by a fluid that is flowing faster than another fluid. How does this explain how airplanes can fly?*

below the wing. Recalling what you know about speed, what must be true if the air above the wing travels a longer distance in the same amount of time? The air above the wing must be moving faster. According to Bernoulli's principle, then, the air above the wing exerts less pressure on the wing than the air below the wing. This creates an upward un-balanced force that keeps the airplane in the air.

Activity Bank

Baffling With Bernoulli, p. 746

PROBLEM ??? Solving

Attack of the Shower Curtain

Smash! You forcefully shut off your alarm clock and drag yourself out of bed. With your eyes only half open, you stumble into the shower. Blindly, you reach over and turn on the water. Aaaah! Suddenly, your eyes pop open as the shower curtain attacks you. You push it away but it comes right back. In-stinctively, you shut off the water. To your relief, the shower curtain calms back down. You are a little confused. Could you have imagined all this? You turn the water back on and again the shower curtain moves toward you, climbing on your legs and encircling you. What is going on?

This is no horror story. In fact, it is a common experience you may have had.

Drawing Conclusions

Can you explain why some shower curtains are pulled into the shower with you? What are some ways you can stop the shower curtain from attacking?

Figure 14-19 *Animals that live underground must take advantage of Bernoulli's principle to keep air flowing through their burrows. These prairie dogs, for example, design their mounds so that air pressure above the hole is lower than air pressure inside the burrow. This causes the air inside to be pushed out. What other animals might use similar tactics?*

Figure 14-20 *Up, up, and away goes the beautiful kite as you run vigorously on a windy day. Where is the pressure greater, above or below the kite?*

You can use a simple kite to illustrate the basic ideas of flight. As you run with the kite, the air pushes upward on the kite and the kite rises. And once the kite's weight is balanced by the upward force, the kite remains up. You might want to demonstrate these ideas yourself. Go ahead—fly a kite!

Bernoulli's principle can be used to explain much more than just the flight of an airplane or a kite. You can also use Bernoulli's principle to explain why smoke goes up a chimney. In addition to the fact that hot air rises, smoke goes up a chimney because wind blows across the top of the chimney. This makes the pressure lower at the top of the chimney than at the bottom in the house. This difference in pressure causes the smoke to be pushed up.

14-5 Section Review

1. Explain Bernoulli's principle.
2. How is the shape of an object related to the effects of Bernoulli's principle?
3. Why do airplanes normally take off into the wind?

Critical Thinking—*Relating Cause and Effect*
4. Roofs of houses are sometimes pushed off from the inside by very strong winds. Explain this using Bernoulli's principle.

CONNECTIONS

What a Curve!

It's the bottom of the ninth inning. There are two outs and two strikes on the batter as the pitcher winds up. The batter waits as the ball heads straight for his bat. The batter begins to swing. But wait! In the middle of his swing the ball swerves out of the bat's way. The game is over!

The key to a game-winning *curve ball* is spin. Why do spinning balls curve in flight?

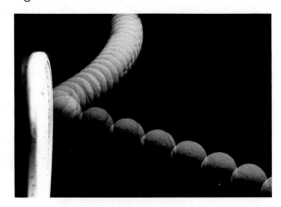

As a spinning ball passes through the air, it drags air around itself in the direction of the spin. For example, consider a tennis ball that is spinning so that the top is being carried in the direction of motion of the ball and the bottom is being carried in the opposite direction. As the ball spins, some of the air will be dragged around in a circular pattern. This will happen as long as the surface of the ball is rough (which is why the fuzz is important). As the ball moves, the air through which it travels appears to move in the opposite direction. Thus the air dragged around the top of the ball is moving in the opposite direction from the air passing the ball.

You know that velocities in opposite directions combine by subtraction. Because of this, the air above the ball slows down. Below the ball, however, the air passing the ball and the air being dragged around the ball are in the same direction. This causes the air below the ball to speed up, as the velocities add together. The air on top of the ball is moving at a slower speed than the air below the ball.

According to Bernoulli's principle, the slower speed means a higher pressure. Thus the air on top of the ball exerts a greater pressure on the ball than the air beneath the ball. This forces the ball downward. A good tennis player can hit the ball with just enough topspin so that it appears to be going out of the court but drops sharply before the baseline.

If a pitcher wishes to make a ball curve, sidespin must be applied to the ball. The direction of the curve will depend on the direction of the sidespin. A spin to the right will curve the ball to the right. A spin to the left will curve the ball to the left. On a baseball, it is the seams that create the airflow around the ball.

So go out and practice Bernoulli's principle for yourself . . . Plaaaay ball!

CURA

365

Laboratory Investigation

A Cartesian Diver

Problem

What is the relationship between the density of an object and its buoyancy in a fluid?

Materials (per group)

copper wire
medicine dropper
large, clear-plastic bottle with an airtight lid
glass
water

Procedure 🧪

1. Wrap several turns of wire around the middle of the medicine dropper.

2. Fill the glass with water and place the dropper in the glass. The dropper should barely float, with only the very top of it above the surface of the water.

3. If the dropper floats too high, add more turns of wire. If the dropper sinks, remove some turns of wire.

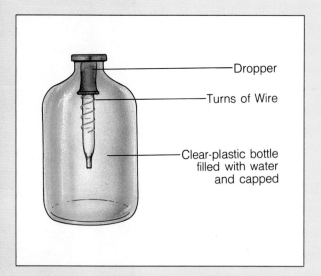

Dropper

Turns of Wire

Clear-plastic bottle filled with water and capped

4. Completely fill the large plastic bottle with water.

5. Place the dropper in the bottle of water. The water should overflow.

6. Screw the cap tightly on the bottle. No water or air should leak out when the bottle is squeezed.

7. Squeeze the sides of the bottle. Record your observations. If the dropper does not move, take it out and add more turns of wire.

8. Release the sides of the bottle. Record your observations.

Observations

1. What happens to the dropper when the sides of the bottle are squeezed?

2. What happens to the dropper when the sides of the bottle are released?

Analysis and Conclusions

1. What happens to the pressure of the water when you squeeze the sides of the bottle?

2. When you squeeze the bottle, some of the water is pushed up into the dropper. Why?

3. Why does the dropper sink when you squeeze the sides of the bottle?

4. Why does the dropper rise when you release the sides of the bottle?

5. How is the density of an object related to its buoyancy in a fluid?

6. **On Your Own** Leave the experimental setup in a place where you can observe it at various times of the day. What does it show about air pressure over a period of several days?

Study Guide

Summarizing Key Concepts

14–1 Fluid Pressure

▲ Pressure is a force that acts over a certain area.

▲ The pressure a fluid exerts is due to the fact that the fluid is made up of particles that have mass and motion.

▲ All liquids and gases are fluids. All fluids exert pressure equally in all directions.

▲ Fluids can be pushed from areas of higher pressure to areas of lower pressure.

14–2 Hydraulic Devices

▲ Pressure applied to a fluid is transmitted equally in all directions throughout the fluid.

▲ In hydraulic devices, a small force acting on a small area is multiplied into a larger force acting on a larger area.

14–3 Pressure and Gravity

▲ As a result of gravity, the pressure a liquid exerts increases as the depth increases.

▲ Air pressure decreases as altitude increases.

14–4 Buoyancy

▲ Buoyancy is the phenomenon caused by the upward force of fluid pressure.

▲ The buoyant force on an object is equal to the weight of the fluid displaced by the object. This relationship is called Archimedes' principle.

▲ An object floats in a fluid when the buoyant force on the object is greater than or equal to the weight of the object.

▲ Density is the ratio of the mass of an object to its volume ($D = M/V$).

▲ An object will float in a fluid if its density is less than the density of the fluid.

14–5 Fluids in Motion

▲ Bernoulli's principle states that the pressure in a moving stream of fluid is less than the pressure in the surrounding fluid.

▲ The faster a fluid moves, the less pressure it exerts.

Reviewing Key Terms

Define each term in a complete sentence.

14–1 Fluid Pressure
pressure

14–2 Hydraulic Devices
hydraulic device

14–4 Buoyancy
buoyant force
buoyancy
Archimedes' principle
density

14–5 Fluids in Motion
Bernoulli's principle

Chapter Review

Content Review

Multiple Choice

Choose the letter of the answer that best completes each statement.

1. Force that acts over a certain area is called
   a. density.   c. pressure.
   b. hydraulic.   d. gravity.
2. Pressure in a fluid is exerted
   a. upward only.   c. downward only.
   b. sideways only.   d. in all directions.
3. The weight and motion of fluid particles create
   a. volume.   c. pressure.
   b. mass.   d. density.
4. The pressure of a fluid varies with depth because of
   a. volume.   c. Bernoulli's principle.
   b. gravity.   d. Archimedes' principle.
5. The force of a fluid that pushes an object up is called
   a. hydraulics.   c. buoyancy.
   b. gravity.   d. weight.

6. The relationship between buoyant force and weight of displaced fluid was stated by
   a. Archimedes.   c. Orville Wright.
   b. Newton.   d. Bernoulli.
7. The buoyant force on an object is equal to the weight of the
   a. object.   c. container
   b. displaced fluid. d. entire fluid.
8. Compared with the slow-moving water along the edge of a river, the rapidly-moving stream in the middle exerts
   a. less pressure.   c. more pressure.
   b. no pressure.   d. the same pressure.
9. When compared with the air that travels under an airplane wing, the air that travels over the wing
   a. is more dense.   c. moves more slowly.
   b. is less dense.   d. moves faster.

True / False

If the statement is true, write "true." If it is false, change the underlined word or words to make the statement true.

1. Pressure is force per unit <u>mass</u>.
2. Fluids will move from areas of <u>high</u> pressure to areas of <u>low</u> pressure.
3. Pressure varies with depth due to the force of <u>gravity</u>.
4. The force of a fluid that pushes an object up is called <u>buoyant</u> force.
5. The buoyant force on an object equals the <u>volume</u> of the displaced fluid.
6. An object will float in a fluid whose density is <u>less</u> than the density of the object.
7. Pressure in a moving stream of fluid is <u>greater than</u> the pressure in the surrounding fluid.
8. The flight of an airplane can be explained using <u>Bernoulli's</u> principle.

Concept Mapping

Complete the following concept map for Section 14–1. Then construct a concept map for the entire chapter.

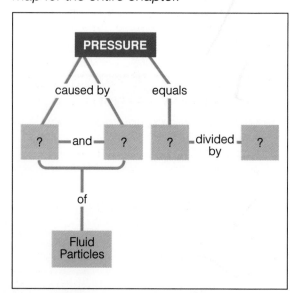

Concept Mastery

Discuss each of the following in a brief paragraph.

1. What is fluid pressure?
2. Explain why an astronaut must wear a pressurized suit in space.
3. Heating a fluid causes its pressure to increase. Why should you poke holes in the skin of a potato before it is baked?
4. Using the principle of fluid pressure, explain how a medicine dropper works.
5. Describe how a hydraulic device works.
6. Why does fluid pressure increase as depth increases?
7. What is the effect of increased water depth on a scuba diver?
8. Explain why you weigh more in air than you do in water.
9. Why does the canvas top of a convertible car bulge out when the car is traveling at high speed?
10. Hummingbirds expend 20 times as much energy to hover in front of a flower as they do in normal flight. Explain.

Critical Thinking and Problem Solving

Use the skills you have developed in this chapter to answer each of the following.

1. **Applying concepts** Air exerts a downward force of 100,000 N on a tabletop, producing a pressure of 1000 N/cm^2.
   a. What would be the force if the tabletop were twice as large?
   b. What would be the pressure if the tabletop were twice as large?
2. **Designing an experiment** The density of gold is 19.3 g/cm^3. The density of pyrite, or fool's gold, is 5.02 g/cm^3. Using mercury, density 13.6 g/cm^3, describe an experiment by which you could tell the difference between samples of the two substances.
3. **Applying concepts** Explain why salad dressing made of oil and vinegar must be shaken before use.
4. **Applying concepts** Describe how you could make a sheet of aluminum foil float in water. How could you change its shape to make it sink?
5. **Applying concepts** A barge filled with sand approaches a bridge over the river and cannot quite pass under it. Should sand be added to or removed from the barge?
6. **Applying concepts** A student holds two sheets of paper a few centimeters apart and lets them hang down parallel to each other. Then the student blows between the two papers. What happens to the papers? Why?
7. **Relating facts** A Ping-Pong ball can be suspended in the air by blowing a stream of air just above it. Explain how this works.

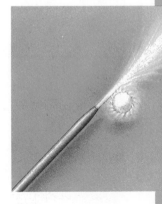

8. **Identifying relationships** Airplanes are riveted together at the seams. The rivets are installed so they are even with the outside surface. Why is it important that the outside surface be so smooth?
9. **Using the writing process** It's your first assignment as a cub reporter. You are to interview the Wright brothers after their pioneering flight. Make a list of five questions you would ask.

Work, Power, and Simple Machines

Guide for Reading

After you read the following sections, you will be able to

15–1 What It Means to Do Work
- Relate force, work, and distance.
- Calculate work.

15–2 Power
- Calculate power.

15–3 Machines
- Describe the role of machines in doing work.

15–4 Simple and Compound Machines
- Name the six simple machines.
- Show how simple machines are related to compound machines.

The Great Pyramid of Khufu in Egypt is one of the Seven Wonders of the World. It stands over 137 meters high. Its base covers an area large enough to hold ten football fields. More than 2 million stone blocks, each weighing about 20,000 newtons (about the weight of two large cars), make up its structure.

The Great Pyramid is a tribute to human effort and ingenuity. For it is exactly these two qualities that enabled the Egyptians to chisel the stone blocks from limestone quarries, to transport them to the pyramid site, and to raise them to the top of the magnificent structure.

The Egyptians had only simple machines with which to work. Their only source of power was human effort. Several hundred thousand people toiled for twenty years to build the Great Pyramid. Today, with modern machinery, it could be built with only a few hundred workers and in one fifth the time!

In this chapter you will learn about work, power, and simple machines. And you will gain an understanding of how machines make work easier—certainly easier than it was for the Egyptians who built the Great Pyramid.

Journal *Activity*

You and Your World Doorknobs, wheels, shovels, ramps, screwdrivers, and buttons are but a few examples of the many tools and machines you use each day. In your journal, explore how different your day would be if you lived during the time in which the pyramids were built—a time in which most of these devices did not exist. What devices would you miss most?

◀ *The Great Pyramid of Khufu stands at Giza, Egypt.*

Figure 15–1 *A scientist knows that work is done only when a force moves an object through a distance. The karate student is doing work; the lifeguards are not. Why?*

15–1 What It Means to Do Work

People use the word work in many different ways. You say that you work when you study for a test. A lifeguard may use the word work to describe watching people swim in a pool or lake. A television newscaster thinks of work as reporting the news. All these people believe they are doing work. But a scientist would not agree!

The term **work** has a special meaning in science. Work is done only when a force moves an object. When you push, lift, or throw an object, you are doing work. Your force is acting on the object, causing it to move a certain distance. **A force acting through a distance is work.** You do work whenever you move something from one place to another.

Work is not done every time a force is applied, however. A force can be exerted on an object without work being done on the object. How can this be so? Suppose you push as hard as you can against a wall for several minutes. Obviously, the wall does not move. And although you may be extremely tired, you have not done any work. According to the definition of work, a force must be exerted over a distance. Although you have applied a force to the wall, the wall did not move. Thus no work has been done.

Figure 15–2 *In the scientific sense, why is no work being done by the person's arms in carrying the bag of groceries? Why is work being done in lifting the bag?*

Figure 15–3 *Everyone knows it's hard work being a mother—in more ways than one. Just observe this mother chimpanzee as she carries her baby, who has decided to take a free ride.*

Another important requirement for work to be done is that the distance the object moves must be in the same direction as the force applied to the object. Let's see just what this means. Imagine that you are given a heavy bag of groceries to carry. Your muscles exert an upward force on the bag in order to hold it up. Now suppose you walk toward the door. Have your arms done any work on the bag of groceries? The answer is no. The direction of movement of the bag is not the same as the direction of the applied force. The applied force is upward, whereas the direction of movement is forward. What would you have to do with the bag in order to do work on it?

The amount of work done in moving an object is equal to the force applied to the object times the distance through which the force is exerted (the distance the object moves):

$$\text{Work} = \text{Force} \times \text{Distance}$$

Force is measured in newtons. Distance is measured in meters. So the unit of work is the newton-meter (N-m). In the metric system, the newton-meter is called the **joule** (J). A force of 1 newton exerted on an object that moves a distance of 1 meter does 1 newton-meter, or 1 joule, of work.

If you lifted an object weighing 200 N through a distance of 0.5 m, how much work would you do? The force needed to lift the object up must be equal to the force pulling down on the object. This is the object's weight. So the force is 200 N. The amount of work is equal to 200 N x 0.5 m, or 100 J.

ACTIVITY

CALCULATING

It Takes Work to Catch a Flight

There was an announcement made over the loudspeaker. The flight to Los Angeles was about to depart. A 600-newton woman who was waiting for the flight lifted her 100-newton suitcase a distance of 0.5 meter above the airport floor and ran 25 meters.

Calculate how much work was done by the woman's arms in moving the suitcase. Draw a diagram showing the forces and distances involved in this situation.

Explain how the work done would change if she had dragged her suitcase along horizontally instead of lifting it. Draw a diagram showing this situation.

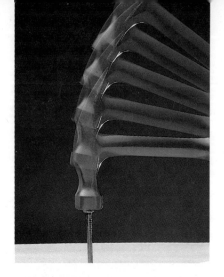

Figure 15–4 *A hammer pounding a nail exerts a force on the nail causing it to move a certain distance into the wood. Is work done on the hammer?*

15–1 Section Review

1. What is work?
2. How are force, work, and distance related?
3. What are the units of work?
4. A 900-N mountain climber scales a 100-m cliff. How much work is done by the mountain climber?

Critical Thinking—*Analyzing Information*

5. A small turtle slowly crawls along carrying a fallen bird feather on its back. After quite some time, the turtle passes an elephant standing still with five large lions on its back. Who is doing more work, the turtle or the elephant? Explain.

Guide for Reading

Focus on this question as you read.

▶ *How is power related to work and time?*

15–2 Power

The word **power** is like the word "work." It has different meanings to different people. But in science, power has a very specific meaning. Like speed, velocity, and acceleration, power tells you how fast something is happening—in this case, how fast work is being done. **Power is the rate at which work is done, or the amount of work per unit of time.**

Power, then, is calculated by dividing the work done by the time it takes to do it:

$$\text{Power} = \frac{\text{Work}}{\text{Time}}$$

Since work equals force times distance, the equation for power can also be written:

$$\text{Power} = \frac{\text{Force} \times \text{Distance}}{\text{Time}}$$

The unit of power is simply the unit of work divided by a unit of time, or the joule per second. This unit is also called a **watt** (W). One watt is equal to 1 joule per second (1 J/sec).

You are probably familiar with the watt as it is used to express electric power. Electrical appliances and light bulbs are rated in watts. A 50-watt light

Figure 15–5 *Both the man and the snowplow are doing work, but there is little doubt that the machine is doing more work in the same amount of time. So the machine has more power. How is power calculated?*

bulb does work at the rate of 50 joules per second. In the same second, a 110-watt light bulb does 110 joules of work. The 110-watt light bulb has more power than the 50-watt light bulb. Large quantities of power are measured in kilowatts (kW). One kilowatt equals 1000 watts. The electric company measures the electric power you use in your home in kilowatts.

Perhaps you can now see why a bulldozer has more power than a person with a shovel. The bulldozer does more work in the same amount of time. As the process of doing work is made faster, power is increased. Can you explain why it takes more power to run up a flight of stairs than it takes to walk up?

15–2 Section Review

1. What is power? What is the relationship among power, work, and time?
2. What is a watt?
3. A small motor does 4000 J of work in 20 sec. What is the power of the motor in watts?

Critical Thinking—*Relating Concepts*

4. Suppose you ride in a sleigh being pulled by horses at 16 kilometers per hour. Another sleigh being pulled at 10 kilometers per hour travels the same distance you do. Which horses are more powerful? How is speed related to power?

ACTIVITY

DOING

Work and Power

1. Determine your weight in newtons. (Multiply your weight in pounds by 4.5).

2. Determine how many seconds it takes you to walk up a flight of stairs.

3. Determine how many seconds it takes you to run up the same flight of stairs. Be careful as you run.

4. Measure the vertical height of the stairs to the nearest 0.01 meter.

5. Using the formula work = weight x height, calculate the work done in walking and running up the stairs.

6. Calculate the power needed for walking and for running up the stairs.

Is there a difference in the work done in walking and running? In the power?

CONNECTIONS

The Power of Nature

■ Nebraska: Buildings are blown apart. Houses and cars are thrown about like toys. A beautiful town is leveled in a matter of minutes.

■ New York: A defenseless city is crippled by a two-foot blanket of snow.

■ Florida: Tall, stately palm trees are bent over as far as they can go. Fierce winds break windows and knock off roofs while sheets of rain batter coastal cities.

■ Ohio: A rural area is evacuated as flood waters approach.

What force is powerful enough to cause so much destruction? What force is capable of doing the work required to move people, buildings, and water? As you may have already guessed, the source of this awesome power is nature!

Powerful *weather* conditions are a result of the interactions of several factors in the Earth's atmosphere. In particular, changes in weather are caused by move-ments of air masses. An air mass is a large volume of air that has the same temperature and contains the same amount of moisture throughout. When two different air masses meet, an area called a front is created. The weather at a front is usually unsettled and stormy. And when two fronts collide—watch out! The results are rainstorms, thunderstorms, hail storms, or snowstorms, depending on the characteristics of the various air masses.

Weather affects people daily and it influences them and the world around them. The type of homes people build, the clothes they wear, the crops they grow, and the jobs they work at are all determined by the weather. It is important to appreciate the fact that despite all of our technological advances, the greatest source of power is still found in nature. And when this power is destructive, or even inconvenient, we are ultimately defenseless.

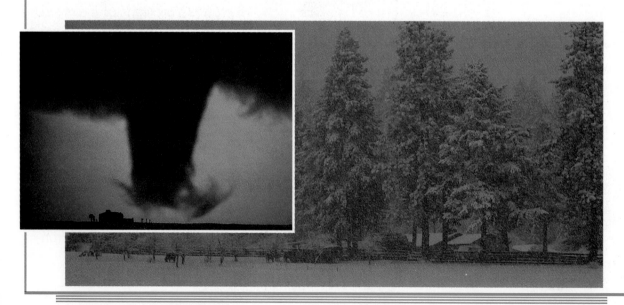

15–3 Machines

Think about performing some common activities without the devices you normally use. Consider eating soup without a spoon, opening the door without a doorknob, removing snow without a shovel, cutting the lawn without a lawn mower. For centuries, people have looked for ways to make life more enjoyable by using devices that make work easier.

An instrument that makes work easier is called a **machine.** Machines are not limited to the complicated devices you may be thinking of—car engines, airplanes, computers, factory equipment. In fact, some machines do not even have moving parts. A machine is any device that helps you to do something.

How Do Machines Make Work Easier?

There are always two types of work involved in using a machine: the work that goes into the machine and the work that comes out of the machine. The work that goes into the machine is called the **work input.** The work input comes from the force that is applied to the machine, or the effort force. When you use a machine, you supply the

Guide for Reading

Focus on this question as you read.

▶ *How do machines affect work?*

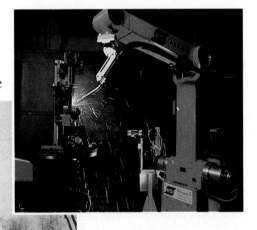

Figure 15–6
Machines have come a long way— from simple water wheels to automated robots. Regardless of their complexity, all machines have the same purpose: to make work easier.

ACTIVITY

READING

effort force. Because you exert this force over some distance, you put work into the machine.

Of course the machine does work too. The machine exerts a force, called an output force, over some distance. The work done by the machine is called the **work output.** The work output is used to overcome the force you and the machine are working against. This force, which opposes the effort force, is called the resistance force. The resistance force is often the weight of the object being moved. For example, when you use a shovel to move a rock, your effort is opposed by the rock's weight. The rock's weight is the resistance force.

Machines do not increase the work you put into them. This is a very important idea that you should keep in mind as you continue to read about machines. The work that comes out of a machine can never be greater than the work that goes into the machine. Like momentum, work is conserved. Why, then, do we say that machines make work easier?

What machines do is change the factors that determine work. **Machines make work easier because they change either the size or the direction of the force put into the machine.** Any change in the size of a force is accompanied by a change in the distance through which the force is exerted. If a machine multiplies the force you put into it, the output force (the force you get out of a machine) will be exerted over a shorter distance. If a machine exerts an output force over a longer distance than the

Figure 15–7 *A machine can make a task easier in one of three ways. It can multiply the size of the force, but decrease the distance over which the force moves. It can multiply the distance over which the force moves, but decrease the size of the force. Or it can leave both force and distance unchanged, but change the direction in which the force moves.*

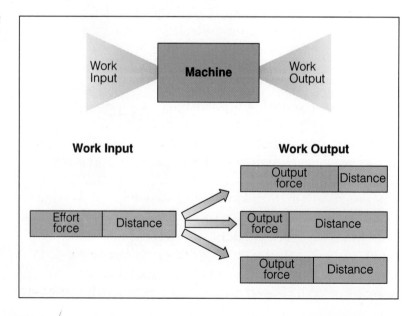

effort force, the output force will be less than the effort force. Because work is conserved (it does not change), what you increase in force you pay for in distance, and what you increase in distance is at the expense of force. In other words, most machines make work easier by multiplying either force or distance—but never both. No machine can multiply both force and distance!

Determining How Helpful a Machine Is

As you just learned, the work that comes out of a machine (work output) can never be greater than the work that goes into the machine (work input). In reality, the work output is always less than the work input. Do you know why? The operation of any machine always involves some friction. Some of the work the machine does is used to overcome the force of friction. Scientists have a way of comparing the work output of a machine to its work input—and thereby knowing how much work is lost to friction. The comparison of work output to work input is called the **efficiency** of a machine. The closer work output is to work input, the more efficient the machine. What does this mean in terms of friction?

Efficiency is expressed as a percentage. Efficiency can never be greater than 100 percent, because the work output can never be greater than the work input. In fact, there is no machine that has an efficiency of 100 percent. Machines with the smallest

Figure 15–9 *Many attempts have been made to create a machine with 100 percent or more efficiency—a perpetual motion machine. So far, this has proved impossible. What force reduces the efficiency of a machine?*

Figure 15–10 *Many household appliances come with guides that inform potential customers of the efficiency of the appliance. A more efficient appliance will be easier to run and will save the owner money on the electric bill.*

amount of friction are the most efficient. For this reason, it is important to keep a machine well lubricated and in good condition.

In addition to knowing how efficient a machine is, we can also determine how helpful a machine is. What we mean by helpful is how many times the machine multiplies the effort force to overcome the resistance force. The number of times a machine multiplies the effort force is called the **mechanical advantage** of the machine. The mechanical advantage tells you how much force is gained by using the machine. The more times a machine multiplies the effort force, the easier it is to do the job.

15–3 Section Review

1. What is a machine?
2. What advantage is there to using a machine if it does not multiply the work put into it?
3. What is effort force? Resistance force?
4. What is efficiency? Mechanical advantage?

Critical Thinking—*Drawing Conclusions*
5. Describe the relationship between friction and the efficiency of a machine.

Guide for Reading

Focus on these questions as you read.

▶ How are the six simple machines the basis for all machines?
▶ What is a compound machine?

15–4 Simple and Compound Machines

The devices you think of when you hear the word "machine" are actually combinations of two or more simple machines. **There are six types of simple machines: the inclined plane, the wedge, the screw, the lever, the pulley, and the wheel and axle.**

Inclined Plane

Suppose you had to raise a car to a height of 10 centimeters. How would you do it? Certainly not by lifting the car straight up. But you could do it if you pushed the car up a ramp. A ramp would make the job easier to do. Although a ramp does not alter the amount of work that is needed, it does alter the way in which the work is done. A ramp decreases the amount of force you need to exert, but it increases the distance over which you must exert your force. Remember, what you gain in force, you pay for in distance.

A ramp is an example of an **inclined plane**. An inclined plane is simply a flat slanted surface. An inclined plane is a simple machine with no moving parts. The less slanted the inclined plane, the longer the distance over which the effort force is exerted and the more the effort force is multiplied. Thus the mechanical advantage of an inclined plane increases as the slant of the plane decreases. The principle of the inclined plane was of great importance in ancient times. Ramps enabled the Egyptians to build their pyramids and temples. Since then, the inclined plane has been put to use in many devices from door locks to farming plows to zippers.

WEDGE In many devices that make use of the inclined plane, the inclined plane appears in the form of a **wedge.** A wedge is an inclined plane that moves. In a wedge, instead of an object moving along the inclined plane, the inclined plane itself moves to raise the object. As the wedge moves a greater distance, it raises the object with greater force. A wedge is usually a piece of wood or metal that is thinner at one end. Most wedges are made up of two inclined planes. A knife and an ax are two examples.

The longer and thinner a wedge is, the less the effort force required to overcome the resistance force. (This is true of the inclined plane as well.) When you sharpen a wedge, you are increasing its mechanical advantage by decreasing the effort force that must be applied in using it. A sharpened ax requires less effort force because the edge is thinner.

A lock is another device that depends on the principle of the wedge. Think for a moment about the shape of a key. The edges go up and down in a certain pattern. The edges of a key are a series of wedges. The wedges lift up a number of pins of different lengths inside the lock. When all of the pins are lifted to the proper height, which is accomplished by the shape of the key, the lock opens.

Figure 15–11 An inclined plane is a slanted surface used to raise an object. An inclined plane decreases the size of the effort force needed to move an object. What happens to the distance through which the effort force is applied?

Figure 15–12 As a wedge is moved through an object to be cut, a small effort force is able to overcome a large resistance force. How can the mechanical advantage of a wedge be increased?

381

Figure 15–13 *A plow is a device that uses a combination of wedges to cut, lift, and turn over the soil. You have probably never given much thought to the zipper that fastens your clothes. But zippers consist of wedges. One wedge is used to open the zipper. Two different wedges are used to push the two sides together.*

The zipper is another important application of the wedge. Zippers join or separate two rows of interlocking teeth. Have you ever tried to interlock the two sides of a zipper with your hands? It is almost impossible to create enough force with your fingers to join the two rows of teeth. However, the part of the zipper that you pull up or down contains three small wedges. These wedges turn the weak effort force with which you pull into a strong force that either joins or separates the two sides. Without these wedges, you would not be able to use the zipper.

SCREW Just as the wedge is an inclined plane that moves, the **screw** is an inclined plane wrapped around a central bar, or cylinder, to form a spiral. A screw rotates, and with each turn moves a certain distance up or down. A screw multiplies an effort force by acting through a long distance. The closer

Figure 15–14 *Screws come in a variety of shapes and sizes. A bolt and a spark plug are but two examples. How is a screw related to an inclined plane?*

together the threads, or ridges, of a screw, the longer the distance over which the effort force is exerted and the more the force is multiplied. Thus the mechanical advantage of a screw increases when the threads are closer together.

The wood screw and the corkscrew are two obvious examples of the screw. Another example is a nut and bolt. In a nut and bolt, the nut has to turn several times to move forward a short distance. However, the nut moves along the bolt with a much greater force than the effort force used to turn it. Faucets and jar lids also take advantage of the principle of a screw. It is important for a jar lid to close tightly, but it requires a great deal of force to achieve a tight seal. Inside a jar lid are the threads of a screw. They fit into those on the top of the jar. You exert a small effort force when you turn the lid. However, your effort force is multiplied because you exert it over a long distance as you turn the lid many times. The large output force seals the jar.

Lever

Have you ever ridden on a seesaw or pried open a can with a screwdriver? If so, you are already familiar with the simple machine called a **lever.** A lever is a rigid bar that is free to pivot, or move about, a fixed point. The fixed point is called the **fulcrum.** When a force is applied on a part of the bar by pushing or pulling it, the lever swings about the fulcrum and overcomes a resistance force. Here is an example. Let's suppose you are using a crowbar to remove a nail from a piece of wood. When you push down on one end of the crowbar, the nail moves in the other direction—in this case, up. The crowbar changes the direction of the force. But the force exerted on the nail by the crowbar moves a shorter distance than the effort force you exert on the crowbar. In other words, you push down through a longer distance than the nail moves up. Because work is conserved, this must mean that the crowbar multiplies the effort force you apply.

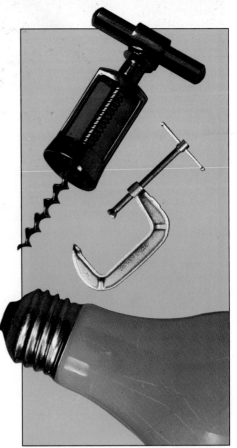

Figure 15–15 *These screws increase the amount of force applied in turning them, but decrease the distance over which the force is applied.*

Figure 15–16 *An essential attraction of any playground, a seesaw, is a lever. Why is a seesaw a simple machine?*

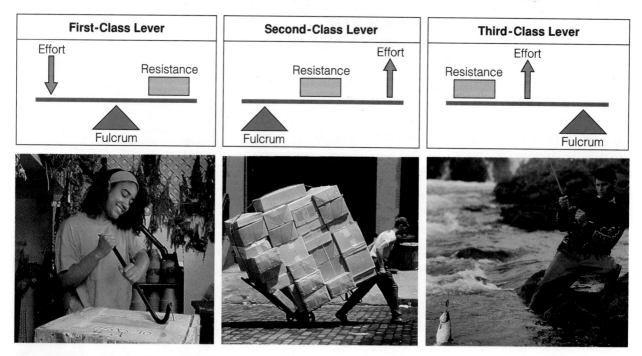

First-Class Lever	Second-Class Lever	Third-Class Lever
Effort ↓ Resistance / Fulcrum	Resistance / Effort ↑ / Fulcrum	Resistance / Effort ↑ / Fulcrum

Figure 15–17 *The relative positions of the effort force, resistance force, and fulcrum determine the three classes of levers. Which lever multiplies effort force as well as changes its direction? Which lever multiplies the distance of the effort force?*

Figure 15–18 *One person may be able to lift a large rock with a sturdy lever. The same rock, however, would require a much greater effort force if the length of the lever was shortened. Should the effort force be applied closer to or farther away from the fulcrum to make a chore easier?*

In the case of the crowbar, the fulcrum is between the effort force (your push) and the resistance force (the nail). The fulcrum of a lever is not always between the effort force and the resistance force, however. Sometimes it is at the end of the lever. In fact, levers are divided into three groups, or classes, depending on the location of the fulcrum and the forces. Levers such as a crowbar, seesaw, and pliers are in the first class.

A wheelbarrow is a second-class lever. In a wheelbarrow, the fulcrum is at the end. The wheel acts as the fulcrum. The resistance force is the weight of the load in the wheelbarrow (often rock or soil). And the effort force, which is at the other end of the lever, is the force that you apply to the handles to lift the wheelbarrow. In this case, the effort force is exerted over the distance you lift the handles. The load moves a much shorter distance than you actually lift the handles. Keeping in mind that work is always conserved, you can see that because distance is decreased by the wheelbarrow, force must be increased. So you must exert a smaller force with

Figure 15–19 *"Row. Row. Row" shouts the captain as the crew team sweats through an early morning practice. Although they may hardly be aware of it, their work is made much easier by the action of levers. Where are the levers in this photo?*

the wheelbarrow than you would need to if you lifted the soil directly, but you must exert your force for a longer distance. Like most first-class levers, levers in this second class multiply force but decrease distance. In this second class of levers, however, the direction in which you lift is the same as the direction in which the load moves. A second-class lever does not change the direction of the force applied to it. Doors, nutcrackers, and bottle openers are additional examples of second-class levers. Can you explain why by identifying the location of the fulcrum and forces?

A surf-casting rod is a third-class lever. The fixed point, or fulcrum, is at the end of the rod where you are holding it. The effort force is applied by your other hand as you pull back on the rod. At the top of the rod is the resistance force. In this case, you need to move your effort force only a short distance to make the end of the rod move a greater distance. A lever in the third class reduces the effort force but multiplies the distance through which the output force moves. Shovels, hoes, hammers, tweezers, and baseball bats are third-class levers.

Have you ever tried to pry open a can of paint with a short stick? If so, you know that it is rather difficult to do. But what if you use a longer stick or even a screwdriver? The task becomes much easier. What this example illustrates is that where you push or pull on a lever is just as important as the amount of force you apply to it. Less effort force can move the same load if that force is applied farther

ACTIVITY
DOING

Levers

1. Tape five large washers together to form a resistance force.

2. Obtain a rigid 30-centimeter (cm) ruler to use as a lever and a pen to use as a fulcrum.

3. Place the washers on the 1-cm mark. Place the pen under the ruler at the 10-cm mark.

4. Push down on the ruler at the 30-cm mark. Your push is the effort force.

5. Move the pen to the 15-cm mark and again push down at the 30-cm mark.

6. Compare your effort force in steps 4 and 5.

7. Move the pen to the 20-cm mark and again push down on the 30-cm mark.

What is the effect on the effort force of decreasing the distance between it and the fulcrum? What class lever is this?

away from the fulcrum. As long as the resistance force (the load) is closer to the fulcrum than the effort force, the lever will multiply the effort force. This is true for first- and second-class levers. For third-class levers, however, the resistance force is always farther away from the fulcrum than the effort force. So these levers cannot multiply force. But this should not surprise you because you learned that a fishing pole does not multiply force, only distance.

Some familiar instruments are examples of combinations of levers. A pair of scissors, for example, is a combination of two first-class levers. The fulcrum is the center of the scissors, where the two blades are connected. The object to be cut exerts the resistance force. The effort force is exerted by the person using the scissors.

A grand piano is another example of levers working together. Each key on the piano is linked to a complex system of levers. The levers transmit movement from the player's fingers to the felt-tipped hammer, which strikes the tight piano wire and sounds a note. These levers multiply movement so that the hammer moves a greater distance than the player's fingertips. Similarly, a manual typewriter converts a small movement of the fingertip into a long movement of the key to the paper.

Pulley

Have you ever raised or lowered a window shade? If so, you were using another type of simple machine, the **pulley.** A pulley is a rope, belt, or chain wrapped around a grooved wheel. A pulley can function in two ways. It can change the direction of a force or the amount of force.

Suppose you had to lift a very heavy object by yourself. How would you do it? It would be quite difficult, if not impossible, to lift the object directly off the ground. It would be easier to attach the object to a rope that moves through a pulley attached to the ceiling, and then pull down on the rope. After all, pulling down on a rope is a lot easier than lifting the object directly up. By using a pulley, you can change the direction in which you have to apply the force. A pulley that is attached to a structure is called a fixed pulley. A fixed pulley does not multiply

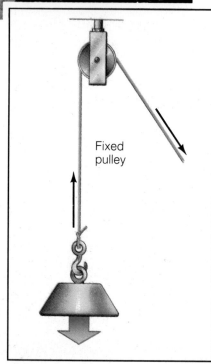

Figure 15–20 *A fixed pulley makes lifting an object easier by changing the direction of the effort force. These unlucky lobsters have been hoisted up with the use of a fixed pulley.*

Fixed pulley

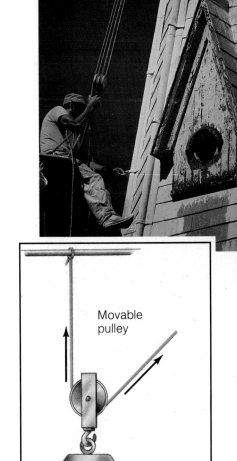

an effort force. It only changes the direction of the effort force. The fact that the effort force is not changed tells you something about the distance the object moves. Because work output can never be greater than work input, if the pulley does not change the amount of force, it does not change the distance the force moves. So the distance you pull is the same as the distance the object moves.

Pulleys can be made to multiply the force with which you pull on them. This is done by attaching a pulley to the object you are moving. This type of pulley is called a movable pulley. Look at the pulley in Figure 15–21. For each meter the load moves, the force must pull two meters. This is because as the load moves, both the left and the right ropes move. Two ropes each moving one meter equals two meters. So although a movable pulley multiplies the effort force, you must exert that effort force for a greater distance than the distance the output force moves the object. Movable pulleys, however, cannot change the direction of an effort force.

A greater mechanical advantage can be obtained by combining fixed and movable pulleys into a pulley system. As more pulleys are used, more sections of rope are attached to the system. Each additional section of rope helps to support the object. Thus less force is required. This increases the mechanical advantage. A block and tackle is a pulley system.

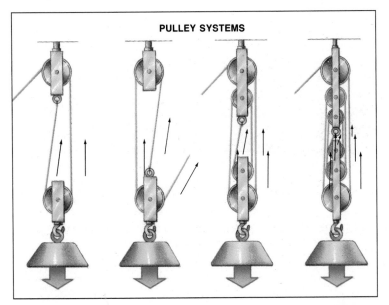

PULLEY SYSTEMS

Figure 15–22 *By combining fixed and movable pulleys into a pulley system, the mechanical advantage is increased. The block and tackle on this boat is an example of a pulley system.*

1. Make a data table with six columns. Head each column with one of the six simple machines.

2. Walk around your house, garage, yard, and school. Identify all of the simple machines you see. Record your observations on the data table.

3. Extend your observations by noticing simple machines in other locations, such as a department store, supermarket, bank, and playground.

Which is the most common simple machine? The least common?

Wheel and Axle

Do you think you would be able to insert a screw into a piece of wood using your fingers? Why not try it and see. You will find it is almost impossible to do—which is precisely why you use a screwdriver! A screwdriver enables you to turn the screw with relative ease. A screwdriver is an example of a tool that uses the principle of a **wheel and axle.**

A wheel and axle is a simple machine made up of two circular objects of different sizes. The wheel is the larger object. It turns about a smaller object called the axle. Because the wheel is larger than the axle, it always moves through a greater distance than the axle. A force applied to the wheel is multiplied when it is transferred to the axle, which travels a shorter distance than the wheel. Remember, work must remain the same. The mechanical advantage depends on the radius of the wheel and of the axle. If the radius of the wheel is four times greater than the radius of the axle, every time you turn the wheel once, your force will be multiplied by four.

Bicycles, Ferris wheels, gears, wrenches, doorknobs, and steering wheels are all examples of wheels and axles. Water wheels also use the principle of a wheel and axle. The force of the water on the

Figure 15–23 *A youngster enjoys a ride with the help of several wheels and axles. Can you identify them? Applying a small effort force to the wheel causes it to move through a greater distance than the axle. Thus the force is multiplied at the axle. The same principle is responsible for the operation of a wheelchair and of gears.*

paddles at the rim produces a strong driving force at the central shaft. Windmills use sails to develop power from the wind. The force of wind along the sails produces a strong driving force at the central shaft. A less pleasant but direct descendant of the windmill is the dentist's drill, which uses a stream of air to turn the drill.

Compound Machines

A car is not one of the six simple machines you have just learned about. Rather, a car is a combination of simple machines: wheels and axles; a gearshift lever; a set of transmission gears; a brake lever; and a steering wheel, to name just a few.

Cars, bicycles, watches, and typewriters are all examples of compound machines. Most of the machines you use every day are compound machines. **A compound machine is a combination of two or more simple machines.**

You are surrounded by a great variety of compound machines. How many compound machines do you have in your home? A partial list might include a washing machine, VCR, blender, sewing machine, and vacuum cleaner. Compound machines make doing work easier and more enjoyable. But remember that machines, simple or compound, cannot multiply work. You can get no more work out of a machine than you put into it!

Figure 15–24 *The wheel and gears of a bicycle consist of a combination of simple machines. How many can you identify?*

15–4 Section Review

1. Describe the six simple machines.
2. How is slant related to the mechanical advantage of an inclined plane, wedge, and screw?
3. How can you increase the mechanical advantage of a wheel and axle? A lever?

Connection—*You and Your World*
4. An elevator is continously lifted up and lowered down. Which of the six simple machines would be most important to the operation of an elevator? Explain your reasoning.

ACTIVITY

DOING

Compound Machines

Design a machine that uses all six simple machines. Your machine should do something useful, like wash a pet snail or scratch your back. Draw a diagram or build a model of your machine. Label each simple machine. Accompany your model with a short written explanation of what your machine does.

Laboratory Investigation

Up, Up, and Away!

Problem

How do pulleys help you to do work?

Materials *(per group)*

ring stand and ring
spring balance calibrated in newtons
weight
string
single pulley

Procedure

1. Tie one end of a small piece of string around the weight. Tie the other end to the spring balance. Weigh the weight. Record the weight in newtons. Untie the string and weight.
2. Attach the ring about one half to three fourths of the way up the ring stand.
3. To construct a single fixed pulley, hang the pulley directly onto the ring as shown.
4. Tie the weight to one end of a string.
5. Pass the other end of the string over the pulley and tie it to the spring balance.
6. Pull down slowly and steadily on the spring balance and record the force needed to raise the weight.

7. To make a single movable pulley, tie one end of a string to the ring.
8. Pass the other end of the string under the pulley and tie it to the spring balance as shown.
9. Attach the weight directly onto the pulley.
10. Raise the weight by pulling the spring balance upward. Record the force shown on the spring balance.

Observations

1. How much force was needed to lift the weight using the fixed pulley?
2. How much force was needed to lift the weight using the movable pulley?

Analysis and Conclusions

1. How does a fixed pulley help you do work?
2. How does a movable pulley help you do work?
3. What could you do to lift an object with greater ease than either the fixed pulley or the movable pulley alone?
4. **On Your Own** Using what you learned about pulleys, figure out how many movable pulleys you would need to lift a 3600-N boat using a force of 450 N.

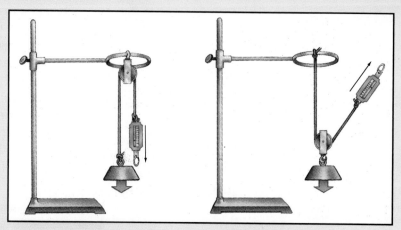

Study Guide

Summarizing Key Concepts

15–1 What It Means to Do Work

▲ Work is the product of force applied to an object times the distance through which the force is applied.

▲ The metric unit of work is the joule.

15–2 Power

▲ Power is the rate at which work is done.

▲ The metric unit of power is the watt.

15–3 Machines

▲ A machine changes either the size or direction of an applied force.

▲ Effort force is force applied to a machine. Work put into a machine is work input.

▲ Work that comes out of a machine is work output. Work output overcomes the resistance force.

▲ The comparison of work output to work input is called efficiency.

▲ The mechanical advantage of a machine is the number of times the machine multiplies the effort force.

15–4 Simple and Compound Machines

▲ There are six simple machines: the inclined plane, the wedge, the screw, the lever, the pulley, and the wheel and axle.

▲ The inclined plane is a slanted surface.

▲ The wedge is a moving inclined plane.

▲ The screw is an inclined plane wrapped around a cylinder.

▲ The lever is a rigid bar that is free to move about the fulcrum when an effort force is applied. There are three classes of levers depending upon the locations of the fulcrum, the effort force, and the resistance force.

▲ A pulley is a chain, belt, or rope wrapped around a grooved wheel. A fixed pulley changes the direction of an effort force. A movable pulley multiplies the effort force.

▲ A wheel and axle is a simple machine made up of two circular objects with different diameters.

▲ A compound machine is a combination of two or more simple machines.

Reviewing Key Terms

Define each term in a complete sentence.

15–1 What It Means to Do Work
work
joule

15–2 Power
power
watt

15–3 Machines
machine
work input
work output

efficiency
mechanical advantage

15–4 Simple and Compound Machines
inclined plane
wedge
screw
lever
fulcrum
pulley
wheel and axle

Chapter Review

Content Review

Multiple Choice

Choose the letter of the answer that best completes each statement.

1. Even if a large force is exerted on an object, no work is performed if
   a. the object moves.
   b. the object does not move.
   c. the power is too large.
   d. the power is too small.
2. The rate at which work is done is called
   a. energy.   c. power.
   b. efficiency.   d. mechanical advantage.
3. Two forces always involved in using a machine are
   a. effort and fulcrum.
   b. friction and fulcrum.
   c. resistance and wattage.
   d. effort and resistance.
4. The comparison between work output and work input is
   a. power.   c. mechanical advantage.
   b. efficiency.   d. friction.
5. Decreasing the slant of an inclined plane increases its
   a. mechanical advantage.
   b. effort force.
   c. power.
   d. work output.
6. The effort force is multiplied in a
   a. corkscrew.   c. baseball bat.
   b. fixed pulley.   d. fishing pole.
7. An example of a second-class lever is a
   a. seesaw.   c. door.
   b. shovel.   d. crowbar.
8. Neither force nor distance is multiplied by a (an)
   a. inclined plane.   c. movable pulley.
   b. wheel and axle. d. fixed pulley.
9. A gear in a watch is an example of a
   a. pulley.   c. lever.
   b. wheel and axle. d. screw.
10. An example of a compound machine is a
    a. school bus.   c. crowbar.
    b. pliers.   d. ramp.

True or False

If the statement is true, write "true." If it is false, change the underlined word or words to make the statement true.

1. Work equals force times <u>time</u>.
2. The unit of work in the <u>metric</u> system is the newton-meter or <u>joule</u>.
3. Power is work divided by <u>force</u>.
4. In the metric system, the unit of power is the <u>newton</u>.
5. Work done by a machine is called <u>work output</u>.
6. <u>Friction</u> reduces the efficiency of a machine.
7. A <u>pulley</u> is an inclined plane that moves.
8. An ax is an example of a <u>wheel and axle</u>.

Concept Mapping

Complete the following concept map for Section 15–1. Then construct a concept map for the entire chapter.

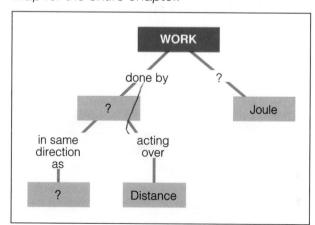

Concept Mastery

Discuss each of the following in a brief paragraph.

1. The mythical god Atlas is known for the fact that he holds up a stationary Earth. Does Atlas perform any work? Explain your answer.
2. Explain how machines make work easier. Use several examples in your answer.
3. Why is a dull razor less helpful than a sharp razor?
4. What is the difference between a screw whose threads are close together and a screw whose threads are far apart?
5. You have been given the task of moving a huge box of baseballs to a shelf that is 1 meter above the floor. There are three ramps available for you to use. They all have a height of 1 meter. However, the first one is 1 meter long, the second is 2 meters long, and the third is 3 meters long. Which ramp will make your task easiest? Why?
6. How can you increase the efficiency of a pulley?
7. Why is a bicycle a compound machine?

Critical Thinking and Problem Solving

Use the skills you have developed in this chapter to answer each of the following.

1. **Applying information** You are walking along the road when you stop to help someone who is changing a tire. Using a jack like the one shown on the right, you lift the rear end of the car with one hand. What type of simple machine is a car jack? How does it work? Does a car jack multiply force or distance? How does the length of the arm affect the use of the jack?

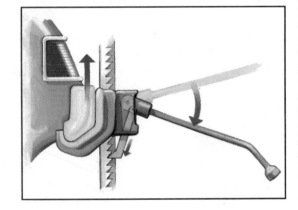

2. **Applying definitions** For each of the following situations, determine whether work is being done. Explain each answer.
   a. You are babysitting for a friend by watching the child while it naps.
   b. You are doing homework by reading this chapter.
   c. You are doing homework by writing answers to these questions.
3. **Developing a model** Suppose you have a large crate you wish to lift off the floor. To accomplish this you have been given a pulley and some rope. The crate has a hook on it, as does the ceiling. Describe two ways in which you could use this equipment to raise the crate. Accompany each description with a diagram showing how you would set it up.
4. **Using the writing process** You are a brilliant and creative inventor famous for your unusual machines. You have recently completed your most outstanding project—an odd-looking, but very important machine. Write an explanation that will be given to the scientific world describing your machine, how you built it, what it is composed of, and what it does.

393

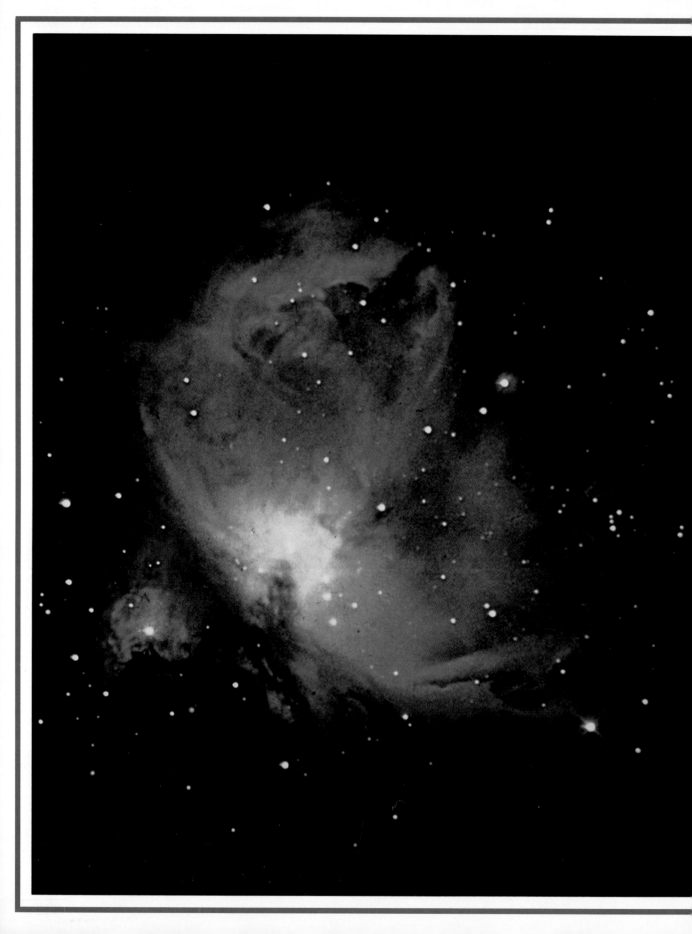

Energy: Forms and *Changes*

Guide for Reading

After you read the following sections, you will be able to

16–1 Nature of Energy
- Identify five forms of energy.

16–2 Kinetic and Potential Energy
- Compare kinetic energy and potential energy.
- Relate kinetic energy to mass and velocity.

16–3 Energy Conversions
- Describe different types of energy conversions.

16–4 Conservation of Energy
- Explain what Einstein said about the relationship between matter and energy.

16–5 Physics and Energy
- Relate the law of conservation of energy to motion and machines.

Within the large, cold clouds of gas and dust, small particles begin to clump together. Their own gravitational force and the pressure from nearby stars cause these small clumps to form a single large mass. Like a monstrous vacuum cleaner, gravitational force attracts more and more particles of dust and gas. The gravitational force becomes so enormous that the bits of matter falling faster and faster to the center begin to heat up. The internal temperature reaches 15 million degrees. Subatomic particles called protons collide with one another at tremendous speeds. The normal electromagnetic force of repulsion between protons is overcome by the force of particle collisions. The protons fuse together to form helium. During this process, part of the matter is transformed into energy. A star is born!

What is energy? How can energy from our sun be changed into useful energy on the Earth? Is the total energy in the universe constant? As you read further, you will find answers to these questions.

Journal *Activity*

You and Your World Think about the last time you were awakened by a violent thunderstorm. Were you frightened or excited? Did you pay more attention to the lightning or to the thunder? What did you think might happen? In your journal, explore the ideas and feelings you had on this occasion. Include any questions you have about thunderstorms.

◀ *The formation of the Orion Nebula is evidence of the interaction of matter and energy.*

16–1 Nature of Energy

On July 4, 1054, the sudden appearance of a new star was recorded by the Chinese. The star shone so brightly that it could be seen even during the day. After 23 days, the distant star began to disappear. What the Chinese had observed was an exploding star, or supernova. The energy released by a supernova is capable of destroying a nearby solar system in just a few hours. A supernova is one of the greatest concentrations of energy in the universe.

A supernova is a very dramatic example of energy release. But not all forms of energy are quite that dramatic. In fact, you live in an ocean of **energy**. Energy is all around you. You can hear energy as sound, you can see it as light, and you can feel it as wind. You use energy when you hit a tennis ball, compress a spring, lift a grocery bag. Living organisms need energy for growth and movement. Energy is involved when a bird flies, a bomb explodes, rain falls from the sky, and electricity flows in a wire.

Figure 16–1 *Energy is all around you, continually shaping and reshaping the Earth and maintaining all the life that exists upon it.*

What is energy that it can be involved in so many different activities? **Energy can be defined as the ability to do work.**

If an object or organism does work (exerts a force over a distance to move an object), the object or organism uses energy. You use energy when you swim in a race. Electric charges in a current use energy as they move along a wire. A car uses energy to carry passengers from one place to another. Because of the direct connection between work and energy, energy is measured in the same unit as work. Energy is measured in joules (J).

In addition to using energy to do work, objects can gain energy because work is being done on them. If work is done on an object, energy is given to the object. When you kick a football, you give some of your energy to the football to make it move. When you throw a bowling ball, you give it energy. When that bowling ball hits the pins, it loses some of its energy to the pins, causing them to fall down.

Figure 16–2 *Although he may not realize it, this young boy has energy simply because he is in motion. The same is true of the cascading waterfall.*

Forms of Energy

Energy appears in many forms. **The five main forms of energy are mechanical, heat, chemical, electromagnetic, and nuclear.** It may surprise you to learn that your body is an "energy factory" that stores and converts various forms of energy. After reading about each form of energy, see if you can describe how your energy factory works.

MECHANICAL ENERGY Matter that is in motion has energy. The energy associated with motion is called **mechanical energy.** Water in a waterfall has a great amount of mechanical energy. So does wind. An automobile traveling at 95 km/hr has mechanical energy. A jet plane cruising at 700 km/hr has even more! When you walk, ride a bike, or hit a ball, you use mechanical energy. Sound is a type of mechanical energy. Even the blood flowing through your blood vessels has mechanical energy.

HEAT ENERGY All matter is made up of tiny particles called atoms that are constantly moving. The internal motion of the atoms is called **heat energy**. The faster the particles move, the more heat energy is produced. Rub your hands together for several

ACTIVITY

DOING

Energy in the News

1. Make five columns on a sheet of paper.

2. Write one of the following headings at the top of each column: Mechanical Energy, Heat Energy, Chemical Energy, Electromagnetic Energy, and Nuclear Energy.

3. Read through a newspaper and place a check mark in the appropriate column every time a particular form of energy is mentioned.

What form of energy is most often mentioned? Would this form of energy always be the most discussed?

Figure 16-3 *Lots of delicious foods to eat have an added benefit. They are a source of energy. What type of energy is stored in food?*

seconds. Did you feel heat? Using the friction between your hands, you converted mechanical energy (energy of motion) into heat energy! Heat energy usually results from friction. Heat energy causes changes in the temperature and phase (solid, liquid, gas) of any form of matter. For example, it is heat energy that causes your ice cream cone to melt and drip down your hand.

CHEMICAL ENERGY Energy exists in the bonds that hold atoms together. This energy is called **chemical energy**. Often, when bonds are broken, this chemical energy is released. The fuel in a rocket engine has stored chemical energy. When the fuel is burned, chemical energy is released and converted into heat energy. When you start a fire in a charcoal grill, you are releasing chemical energy. When you digest food, bonds are broken to release energy for your body to store and use. When you play field hockey or lacrosse, you are using the chemical energy stored in your muscles that you obtained from food.

ELECTROMAGNETIC ENERGY Moving electric charges have the ability to do work because they have **electromagnetic energy.** Power lines carry electromagnetic energy into your home in the form of electricity. Electric motors are driven by electromagnetic energy. Light is another form of electromagnetic energy. Each color of light—red, orange, yellow, green, blue, violet—represents a different amount of electromagnetic energy. Electromagnetic energy is also carried by X-rays, radio waves, and laser light.

NUCLEAR ENERGY The nucleus, or center, of an atom is the source of **nuclear energy.** When the nucleus splits, nuclear energy is released in the form of heat energy and light energy. Nuclear energy is also released when lightweight nuclei collide at high speeds and fuse (join). The sun's energy is produced from a nuclear fusion reaction in which hydrogen nuclei fuse to form helium nuclei. Nuclear energy is the most concentrated form of energy.

Figure 16-4 *Light, whether seen as a beautiful rainbow or used as laser beams, is an important part of everyday life. No matter how it is used, light is a form of energy. What form of energy is light?*

16-1 Section Review

1. What is energy?
2. Can energy be transferred from one object to another? Explain.
3. What are the different forms of energy?
4. Why is energy measured in the same unit as work?

Connection—*You and Your World*

5. It is energy you must pay for on your electric bill. Electric companies usually express the total amount of energy used in kilowatt-hours (kW-h)—the flow of 1 kilowatt of electricity for 1 hour. How many joules of energy do you get when you pay for 1 kW-h? (1 J = 1 watt x 1 second; 1 kW = 1000 watts; 1 hour = 3600 seconds)

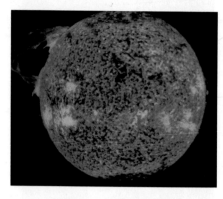

Figure 16–5 *A solar flare erupts from the sun at temperatures greater than 50,000°C. What form of energy is responsible for the characteristics of the sun?*

16-2 Kinetic and Potential Energy

Stretch a rubber band between your thumb and index finger. Keep the rubber band stretched without any motion. How long can you hold it this way? After a short while, as your fingers begin to tire, you become aware of the energy in the rubber band. Yet the rubber band is not moving! This is because the energy of the stretched rubber band is stored in it. Remember that energy is the ability to do work. Release your thumb and the rubber band moves. As the rubber band moves back to its normal shape, it does work.

The energy that you felt when you stretched the rubber band was different from the energy displayed when the rubber band snapped back to its original shape. They are two different states of energy. The five different forms of energy you just learned about can be classified into either one of these states of energy. The two states are called **kinetic energy** and **potential energy.**

Guide for Reading

Focus on this question as you read.

▶ *What is the difference between kinetic energy and potential energy?*

399

Figure 16–6 *One powerful bang and the energy in a moving hammer enables this youngster to win a prize. The same type of energy—energy of motion—can demolish a building. What is this type of energy called?*

Figure 16–7 *Although this horse and colt may be running at the same velocity, they each have a different amount of kinetic energy because they have different masses.*

Kinetic Energy

An object that is moving can do work on another object by colliding with that object and moving it through a distance. A flying rubber band does work when it flattens a house of cards. A swinging hammer does work on a nail as it drives the nail into a piece of wood. A wrecking ball does work as it knocks down a wall. Because an object in motion has the ability to do work, it has energy. **The energy of motion is called kinetic energy.** The word kinetic comes from the Greek word *kinetikos* which means "motion." Why do the particles in matter have kinetic energy?

Suppose you are accidentally hit with a tennis ball that has been tossed lightly toward you. It probably does not hurt you. Now suppose you are hit with the same tennis ball traveling at a much greater speed. You can certainly feel the difference! The faster an object moves, the more kinetic energy it has. So kinetic energy is directly related to the velocity of an object. You have more kinetic energy when you run than when you walk. In baseball, a fast ball has more kinetic energy than a slow curve. When does a skier have more kinetic energy, when skiing downhill or cross-country?

Do all objects with the same velocity have the same kinetic energy? Think about the tennis ball again. Suppose this time it rolls across the tennis court and hits you in the foot. Compare this with getting hit in the foot by a bowling ball traveling at the same speed as the tennis ball. The bowling ball is much more noticeable because the bowling ball has more kinetic energy than the tennis ball. A battleship moving at 40 km/hr has much more kinetic energy than a mosquito moving at the same velocity. So kinetic energy must depend on something other than just velocity. The battleship has more kinetic energy because it has greater mass. Kinetic energy depends on both mass and velocity. The mathematical relationship between kinetic energy (K.E.), mass, and velocity is:

$$\text{K.E.} = \frac{\text{mass} \times \text{velocity}^2}{2}$$

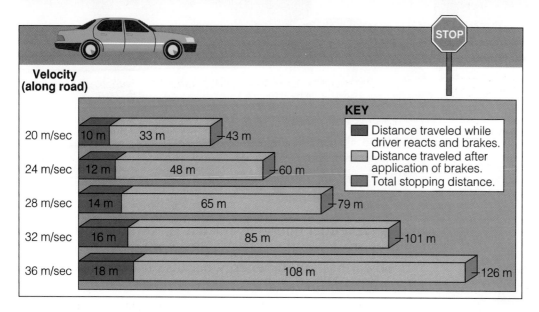

Velocity
(along road)

Velocity	Distance traveled while driver reacts and brakes	Distance traveled after application of brakes	Total stopping distance
20 m/sec	10 m	33 m	43 m
24 m/sec	12 m	48 m	60 m
28 m/sec	14 m	65 m	79 m
32 m/sec	16 m	85 m	101 m
36 m/sec	18 m	108 m	126 m

KEY
■ Distance traveled while driver reacts and brakes.
□ Distance traveled after application of brakes.
■ Total stopping distance.

Figure 16–8 *A car requires a longer distance in which to stop when traveling at faster velocities. Notice how quickly the distance increases for a small increase in velocity.*

According to this equation, an increase in either mass or velocity will mean an increase in kinetic energy. Which of these two factors, mass or velocity, will have a greater effect on kinetic energy? Why?

Now suppose you want to push a heavy box across the floor. You must exert a force on the box to move it. Thus you do work on the box. Before you moved the box, it did not have kinetic energy because it did not have velocity. As you give it kinetic energy, the box picks up velocity. The more work you do, the faster the box will move. When you increase the velocity of an object, you increase its kinetic energy. The change in the kinetic energy of the box is equal to the work you have done on it.

Potential Energy

You just read that some objects are able to do work as a result of their motion. Other objects can do work because of their position or shape. **Potential energy is energy of position.** A stretched rubber band has the potential, or ability, to fly across the room. A wound-up watch spring also has potential energy. It has the potential to move the hands of the watch around when it unwinds. An archer's taut (tightly stretched) bow has the potential to send an arrow gliding toward a target. A brick being held high above the ground has the potential to drive a stake into the ground when it falls onto it.

ACTIVITY

CALCULATING

Computing Kinetic Energy

Complete the following table.

Which has the greater effect on the kinetic energy of a body, mass or velocity?

Object	Mass (kg)	Velocity (m/sec)	Kinetic Energy (J)
A	1	1	
B	2	1	
C	1	2	
D	2	2	

Figure 16–9 *A jack-in-the-box uses potential energy to burst out of its container. How does the archer use potential energy?*

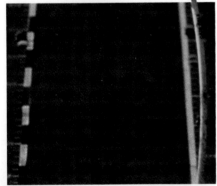

Figure 16–10 *Tightly wound springs store potential energy that can be used to turn the hands of time. What kind of potential energy does a pole vaulter have at the top of a vault?*

Potential energy is related to work in a different way than kinetic energy is. Remember that a moving object has kinetic energy because it can do work as it moves. But an object with potential energy is not moving or doing work. Instead, it is storing the energy that was given to it when work was done on it. It has the ability, or potential, to give that energy back by doing work. The spring acquired potential energy because work was done on it by the person winding the watch. Work was done by the person who pulled back on the bow's arrow. The brick acquired potential energy because work was done in lifting it.

Potential energy is not always mechanical, or associated with movement. For example, the chemical energy stored in food is an example of potential energy. The energy is released when the food is broken down in digestion and respiration. Similarly, fuels such as coal and oil store chemical potential energy. The energy is released when the fuel is burned. The nucleus of an atom consists of a number of particles held together by a strong force. The potential energy stored in the nucleus of an atom can be released if the nucleus is split in a nuclear reactor.

GRAVITATIONAL POTENTIAL ENERGY Imagine that you are standing on the edge of a 1-meter diving board. Do you think you have any energy? You probably think you do not because you are not moving. It is true that you do not have kinetic energy. But you do have potential energy. Your potential energy is due to your position above the water.

If you stand on a 3-meter diving board, you have three times the potential energy you have on the 1-meter board. Potential energy that is dependent on height is called **gravitational potential energy.** A waterfall, suspension bridge, and falling snowflake all have gravitational potential energy.

Weight also determines the amount of gravitational potential energy an object has. The old saying "The bigger they are, the harder they fall" is an observation of the effect of weight on gravitational potential energy. From your experiences, you may already know that gravitational potential energy is dependent on weight. You have a lot more gravitational potential energy with a heavy pack on your back than you do with a light pack.

The relationship between gravitational potential energy (G.P.E.), weight, and height can be expressed by the following formula:

G.P.E. = Weight x Height

You can see from this formula that the greater the weight, the greater the gravitational potential energy. The higher the position above a surface, the greater the gravitational potential energy.

Figure 16–11 *This huge boulder in Arches National Park in Utah has a great deal of gravitational potential energy. So does a falling drop of water in a leaky faucet. The drop of water could not fall without the help of energy. Rock climbers, on the other hand, must do a tremendous amount of work to increase their gravitational potential energy.*

16–2 Section Review

1. What is kinetic energy? Potential energy?
2. Use the formula for kinetic energy to describe the relationship between the kinetic energy of an object, its mass, and its velocity.
3. What is gravitational potential energy? How is it calculated?

Critical Thinking—*Relating Concepts*
4. If you use the sun as your frame of reference, you always have kinetic energy. Why?

Figure 16–12 *As a basketball player throws the ball in the air, various energy conversions take place. What are these conversions?*

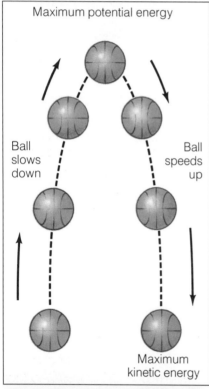

16–3 Energy Conversions

When you think of useful energy, you may think of the energy involved in moving a car or the energy you get from the food you eat. But in both these examples, the useful energy was obtained by first converting energy from one form to another. The mechanical energy of the car came from burning the chemical energy of fuel. Your energy also comes from chemical energy—the chemical energy stored in the food you eat. Energy can be transferred from one object to another and energy can be changed from one form to another. Changes in the forms of energy are called **energy conversions.**

Kinetic–Potential Energy Conversions

One of the most common energy conversions involves the changing of potential energy to kinetic energy or kinetic energy to potential energy. A stone held high in the air has potential energy. As it falls, it loses potential energy because its height decreases. At the same time its kinetic energy increases because its velocity increases. Thus potential energy is converted into kinetic energy. Similarly, the potential energy stored in a bent bow can be converted into the kinetic energy of the arrow.

Conversions between kinetic energy and potential energy are taking place around you every day. Think of tossing a ball up into the air. When you throw the ball up, you give it kinetic energy. As the ball rises, it slows down. As its velocity decreases, its kinetic energy is reduced. But at the same time its height above the Earth is increasing. Thus its potential energy is increasing. At the top of its path, the ball has slowed down to zero velocity so it has zero kinetic energy. All of its kinetic energy from the beginning of its flight has been converted to potential energy.

Then the ball begins to fall. As it gets closer to the Earth's surface, its potential energy decreases. But it is speeding up at the same time. Thus its kinetic energy is increasing. When you catch it, it has its maximum velocity and kinetic energy. The potential energy of the ball has changed into kinetic energy.

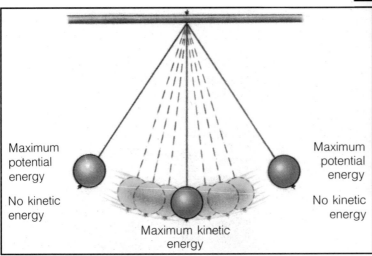

Figure 16–13 *A continuous conversion between kinetic energy and potential energy takes place in a pendulum. Potential energy is greatest at the two highest points in the swing and zero at the bottom. Where is kinetic energy greatest?*

Other Conversions

Although conversions between kinetic energy and potential energy are common, they are not the only changes in energy that take place. **All forms of energy can be converted to other forms.** For example, the sun's energy is not used merely as heat energy or light energy. It is converted to other forms of energy as well. Solar products convert the energy of sunlight directly into electricity. Green plants use the energy of the sun to trigger a process in which sugars and starches are made. These substances store the energy as chemical energy. In this process, electromagnetic energy is converted to chemical energy.

In an electric motor, electromagnetic energy is converted to mechanical energy. In a battery, chemical energy is converted to electromagnetic energy. The mechanical energy of a waterfall is converted to electromagnetic energy in a generator. Solar cells convert the sun's energy directly into electrical energy. In a heat engine (such as an automobile engine), fuel is burned to convert chemical energy into heat energy. The heat energy is then changed to mechanical energy. In a microphone-loudspeaker system, the microphone converts mechanical energy in the form of sound into electromagnetic energy in the form of electricity. The electromagnetic energy goes to the loudspeaker that then converts the electric signal back into sound.

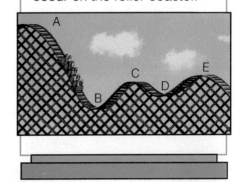

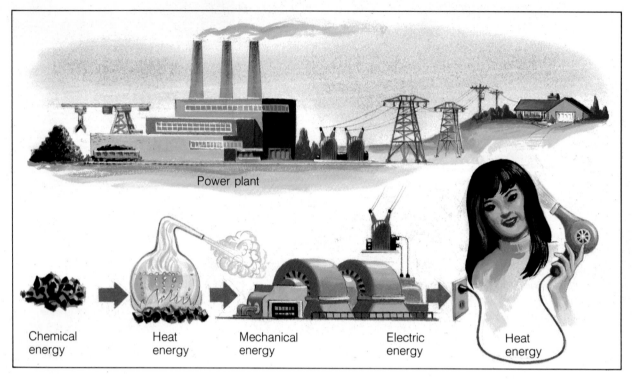

Power plant

Chemical energy → Heat energy → Mechanical energy → Electric energy → Heat energy

Figure 16–14 *A series of energy conversions is needed to produce the heat energy of the hair dryer. Trace the conversions.*

ACTIVITY

DOING

Mixing It Up

1. Fill two mixing bowls with cold water. Record the temperature of the water in each bowl.

2. Run an electric or hand mixer in one bowl for a few minutes.

3. Take the temperature of the water in each bowl again. You must read the thermometer with great precision.

How did you expect the temperatures to compare after you used the mixer?

How do the final temperatures actually compare? Why?

Often a whole series of energy conversions is needed to do a particular job. The operation of a hair dryer is a good example of this. See Figure 16–14. The electromagnetic energy used by the dryer is generated from some fuel source, such as gas. The chemical energy of the fuel is released by burning it. The fuel provides heat energy, which in turn is changed to mechanical energy. This mechanical energy is used to make a generator do the work of providing the dryer with electromagnetic energy in the form of electricity. When you turn the dryer on, the electricity is changed back to heat energy.

Figure 16–15 *This cute little animal is enjoying an afternoon snack totally unaware that the complex process of energy conversion is taking place. Describe the energy conversions.*

16–3 Section Review

1. Describe the conversions between potential energy and kinetic energy as a tennis ball drops, hits the ground, and bounces back up.
2. What energy conversions take place in a pendulum? Why does the pendulum eventually stop?
3. Describe the energy conversions that you think take place when a flashlight is turned on.

Critical Thinking—*Analyzing Information*

4. Identify the various energy conversions involved in the following events: An object is raised and then allowed to fall. As it hits the ground it stops, produces a sound, and becomes warmer.

Crazy Eights, p. 748

16–4 Conservation of Energy

When you turn on a lamp, not all of the electricity flowing through the filament of the light bulb is converted into light. This may lead you to think that energy is lost. But it is not. It is converted into heat. Although heat is not useful in a lamp, it is still a form of energy. Energy is never lost. Scientists have found that even when energy is converted from one form to another, no energy is gained or lost in the process. **The law of conservation of energy states that energy can be neither created nor destroyed by ordinary means.** Energy can only be converted from one form to another. So energy conversions occur without a loss or gain in energy.

The **law of conservation of energy** is one of the foundations of scientific thought. If energy seems to disappear, then scientists look for it. Important discoveries have been made because scientists believed so strongly in the conservation of energy.

One such discovery was made by Albert Einstein in 1905. Part of his famous theory of relativity deals with the concept that mass and energy are directly related. According to Einstein, even the tiniest mass can form a tremendous amount of energy. With this mass-energy relationship, Einstein was saying that mass and energy can be converted into each other.

Guide for Reading

Focus on this question as you read.

▶ *What is the law of conservation of energy?*

Figure 16–16 *You have probably felt the heat given off by a light bulb. The heat released is energy that did not become light.*

407

With this relationship, Einstein clarified the law of conservation of energy. He showed that if matter is destroyed, energy is created and if energy is destroyed, matter is created. The total amount of mass and energy is conserved.

PROBLEM ??? Solving

How Energy Conscious Are You?

Years ago, most people believed that the Earth's energy resources were endless. People used energy at an astonishing rate with no concern that the resources might someday run out. Today, ideas are changing. People have begun to face the reality that we can no longer afford to waste these precious resources. Until practical alternatives are found, we must make every effort to conserve those resources we have. Answer the following questions to find out how energy conscious you are.

1. If you leave a room for at least an hour, do you leave the electrical appliances in the room on—lights, television, radio?

2. When you want something from the refrigerator, do you stare into the open refrigerator while you slowly decide what you want?

3. Suppose you are running in and out of a room every few minutes. Do you turn the light on and off every time you walk into or out of the room?

4. Do you open and close the oven to peek at the brownies cooking?

5. Do you wait for a ride in a car or bus rather than riding your bike or walking to nearby locations?

6. Do you take the elevator instead of the stairs?

7. Do you throw away bottles and cans rather than saving them for recycling?

If you answered "no" to all or most of these questions, you are in good shape. If not, you may be hazardous to the environment! And what's more, your monthly electric bill reflects the energy you use. If you save energy, you save money.

Relating Cause and Effect

Think about the questions to which you answered "no." How do your actions conserve energy? Think about the questions to which you answered "yes." Why are your actions not energy efficient? Make a list of ways in which you could start saving energy every day. Think of as many additional examples as you can.

During nuclear reactions—such as those that take place in the sun—energy and mass do not seem to be conserved. But Einstein showed that a loss in mass results in a gain in energy. Mass is continuously changed to energy in our sun through a process called nuclear fusion. During this process, a small loss in mass produces a huge amount of energy.

16–4 Section Review

1. What is the law of conservation of energy? How does it relate to energy conversions?

Critical Thinking—*Making Inferences*

2. Using the law of conservation of energy, explain why you become tired from pushing your bicycle along the road.

16–5 Physics and Energy

The topic of energy is essential to learning about any subject in physical science. You may wonder, then, why you have not studied energy earlier. Would it surprise you to know that you have actually been learning about energy for the past several chapters? For example, you learned that you travel at a faster *speed* when you run than when you walk. Now it should be clear that you can travel at a faster speed if you use more energy. You must exert more energy to pedal your bicycle quickly than to ride along slowly.

You learned that a moving object, such as a billiard ball, has *momentum* (mass × velocity.) The quantities mass and velocity are also used to measure the kinetic energy of an object. Thus an object that has momentum also has kinetic energy. Momentum must be conserved because energy is conserved. A moving billiard ball that collides with a stationary one gives some or all of its energy to the other ball, causing it to move.

You learned that a *force* is required to change the motion of an object. A force acting on an object to change its motion is doing work. If a force does

Guide for Reading

Focus on this question as you read.

▶ *How is the law of conservation of energy related to other physical principles?*

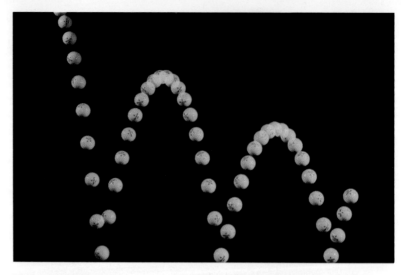

Figure 16–18 *If you follow the bouncing ball, you will see that it gets lower and lower. The forces of friction and gravity are responsible for this behavior. Is the energy of the ball lost?*

work on an object, it changes the energy of the object. When a ball is bounced off the head of a soccer player, the player exerts a force on the ball. In so doing, the player gives energy to the ball, causing a change in its motion.

You learned that *power* is the rate at which work is done. Thus power must be the rate at which energy is consumed. When you run instead of walk up the stairs, you use the same amount of energy (do the same amount of work), but you use the energy at a faster rate. Your monthly electric bill measures the electromagnetic energy you use. The electric company multiplies the power you used by the length of time it was used.

Another quantity you learned about is *work*. Now you know that work is directly related to energy. When you read about machines, you also learned that the work that comes out of a machine can never be greater than the work that goes into a machine. Work done on a machine means that energy goes into the machine. Because energy is conserved, the same amount of energy must come out of the machine. Thus, since energy is conserved, work must also be conserved. The only energy that does not come directly out of a machine is that taken by friction. But this energy is not lost, it is simply converted to another form—heat.

Have you begun to see that almost nothing happens without the involvement of energy? It is interesting to note that the concept of energy was not yet developed in Newton's time. However, once energy was described, Newton's detailed descriptions of motion could be easily explained in terms of energy. In addition, the laws of motion did not violate the law of conservation of energy. In fact, no physical phenomena have yet violated the law of conservation of energy.

Figure 16–19 *This art by M. C. Escher shows an unusual waterfall that violates the law of conservation of energy. When the water falls, part of its potential energy is converted into the kinetic energy of the water wheel. But how does the water get back up to the top?*

16–5 Section Review

1. How is energy related to motion?
2. How is energy related to force?
3. How is energy related to power?

Critical Thinking—*Making Calculations*

4. Two cars have the same momentum. One car weighs 5000 N and the other weighs 10,000 N. Which car has a greater kinetic energy? Explain your answer.

411

CONNECTIONS

Our Energetic World

Start looking around. Imagine that you are standing on the edge of the Grand Canyon in Arizona. In the distance you see a wonderful snowcapped mountain.

Mountains result from great forces that push up through the Earth's surface. Think about the tremendous amount of work, and therefore energy, that was required to create the mountain. The huge amount of energy located within the Earth's interior not only creates mountains, it also causes volcanic eruptions, earthquakes, and movement of the continents. There, you have seen the effect of energy already without too much trouble.

Look some more—this time downward. Think about the amount of work required to chisel out such a masterpiece as the Grand Canyon. Clearly, a great deal of energy was involved. The Grand Canyon was dug out by the Colorado River over millions of years. Water and other natural forces continually reshape the face of the *Earth*. Glaciers, ocean waves, winds, and rough storms are examples of the natural forces that not only create some of the most beautiful sights in the world,

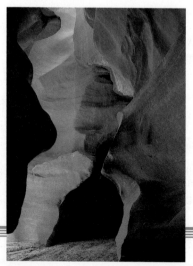

but also can be some of the most destructive forces on Earth.

Perhaps all this thinking is making you hungry. Why not sit down and eat lunch. Guess what! Energy is there again. It's in the food you eat. Food, like any fuel, has chemical potential energy stored in it. When you eat it, your digestive and respiratory systems break down the food and release energy into your system. You use this energy to keep all your body systems working and to power your daily activities. You would not be able to walk around, run, play, or even think without the energy you obtain from the food you eat.

Now you might wonder where the food you eat gets its energy. The sun is the ultimate source of energy for all *living things*. Green plants and certain bacteria trap the energy of sunlight. They use about half of this energy for their own activities and store the rest in compounds that they manufacture called carbohydrates. Animals that either eat the plants or eat other animals that eat plants obtain this stored energy.

Wow! You can't seem to get away from energy. Take a deep breath and relax. Oh, there it is again. The oxygen in the air you breathe is released in the

process by which plants convert the energy of the sun into the chemical energy of food. So without the energy that is required to drive these conversion processes, there would not be any oxygen for you to breathe.

Maybe you should walk around a bit and organize your thoughts. Surprise! Energy is involved once again. When you walk, you convert chemical energy in your body to mechanical energy and heat. In fact, you use mechanical energy for your movements, chemical energy in your body processes, and electrical energy to control many of your body systems. And when you move something by throwing it, pushing it, or picking it up, you give some of your energy to the object, causing it to move.

Boy it's sure getting hot out there thinking about energy. Speaking of heat leads us to the sun. The sun is the main source of energy for living things. Without the sun, there would be no life on Earth. The sun releases energy in a process called nuclear fusion. Within the core of the sun, ex-

tremely strong gravitational forces pull the atoms of hydrogen gas together so tightly that they fuse into helium atoms. During this process, some mass is changed to energy, mostly in the form of heat and light. A portion of this energy reaches the Earth.

The sun is only one of the trillions and trillions of stars in the universe. Nonetheless, the sun is the center of our solar system. It showers the Earth and the eight other planets with a constant supply of energy. And as you have been learning, thanks to the sun, the Earth is alive with energy.

Have you begun to see things a little differently? Energy in one form or another is everywhere and is necessary for every activity and process you can imagine. From the cry of a baby to the falling of rain to the rumble of an earthquake, energy is involved. You use energy constantly—even when you are asleep. In fact, because the Earth moves around the sun, you and everything on the Earth always have kinetic energy. So the next time you need a little energy, just look around!

Laboratory Investigation

Relating Mass, Velocity, and Kinetic Energy

Problem

How does a change in mass affect the velocity of an object if its kinetic energy is constant?

Materials *(per group)*

> rubber band
> 3 thumbtacks
> 12 washers glued together in groups of 2, 4, and 6
> wooden board, 15 cm x 100 cm
> meterstick

Procedure 👁 ⬛

1. Place three thumbtacks at one end of the wooden board, as shown in the figure.

2. Stretch the rubber band over the three thumbtacks to form a triangle.

3. In front of the rubber band, place two washers that have been stuck together.

4. Pull the washers and the rubber band back about 2 cm, as in the figure. Release the rubber band. The washers should slide about 70 to 80 cm along the board.

5. Practice step 4 until you can make the double washer travel 70 to 80 cm each time.

6. Mark the point to which you pulled the rubber band back to obtain a distance of 70 to 80 cm. This will be your launching point for the entire experiment.

7. Launch the double washer three times. In a data table, record the distance in centimeters for each trial. Remember to use the same launching point each time.

8. Repeat step 7 for a stack of 4 washers.

9. Repeat step 7 for a stack of 6 washers.

Observations

Calculate the average distance traveled by 2 washers, 4 washers, and 6 washers.

Analysis and Conclusions

1. What is the relationship between the mass, or number of washers, and the average distance traveled?

2. What kind of energy was in the washers when you held them at the launching point? How do you know?

3. After the washers were launched, what kind of energy did they have?

4. You launched all the washers from the same position. Was the energy the same for each launch?

5. Assume that the farther the washers slid, the greater their initial velocity. Did the heavier group of washers move faster or slower than the lighter group?

6. If the kinetic energy is the same for each set of washers, what happens to the velocity as the mass increases?

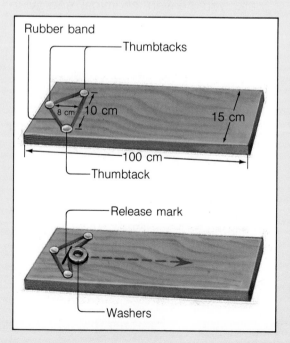

Study Guide

Summarizing Key Concepts

16-1 Nature of Energy

▲ Energy is the ability to do work.

▲ Energy appears in many forms: mechanical, heat, chemical, electromagnetic, and nuclear.

16-2 Kinetic and Potential Energy

▲ Energy that an object has due to its motion is called kinetic energy.

▲ Kinetic energy equals one half the product of the mass times the square of the velocity.

▲ Energy that an object has due to its shape or position is called potential energy.

▲ Potential energy that an object has due to its height above the Earth's surface and its weight is called gravitational potential energy.

16-3 Energy Conversions

▲ Energy can change from one form to another. Changes in the form of energy are called energy conversions.

▲ The most common energy conversions occur between kinetic energy and potential energy. But all forms of energy can be converted to another form.

16-4 Conservation of Energy

▲ The law of conservation of energy states that energy can neither be created nor destroyed by ordinary means.

16-5 Physics and Energy

▲ Energy is involved in every physical activity or process.

▲ An increase in speed or velocity is accompanied by an increase in kinetic energy.

▲ An object that has kinetic energy also has momentum.

▲ A force doing work on an object to change its motion is giving energy to the object.

▲ Power is the rate at which energy is used.

▲ The conservation of work can be understood because energy is conserved.

Reviewing Key Terms

Define each term in a complete sentence.

16-1 Nature of Energy
energy
mechanical energy
heat energy
chemical energy
electromagnetic energy
nuclear energy

16-2 Kinetic and Potential Energy
kinetic energy
potential energy
gravitational potential energy

16-3 Energy Conversions
energy conversion

16-4 Conservation of Energy
Law of Conservation of Energy

Chapter Review

Content Review

Multiple Choice

Choose the letter of the answer that best completes each statement.

1. Energy is the ability to do
   a. motion.
   c. acceleration.
   b. work.
   d. power.
2. The unit in which energy is measured is the
   a. newton.
   c. electron.
   b. watt.
   d. joule.
3. X-rays, lasers, and radio waves are forms of
   a. mechanical energy.
   b. heat energy.
   c. electromagnetic energy.
   d. nuclear energy.
4. Gravitational potential energy is dependent on
   a. speed and height.
   b. weight and height.
   c. time and weight.
   d. acceleration and kinetic energy.
5. Gasoline and rocket fuel store
   a. electromagnetic energy.
   b. chemical energy.
   c. mechanical energy.
   d. gravitational potential energy.
6. A stretched rubber band has
   a. potential energy.
   b. kinetic energy.
   c. nuclear energy.
   d. electromagnetic energy.
7. Energy of motion is
   a. potential energy.
   b. nuclear energy.
   c. kinetic energy.
   d. electromagnetic energy.
8. According to Einstein, matter is another form of
   a. mass.
   c. time.
   b. light.
   d. energy.

True or False

If the statement is true, write "true." If it is false, change the underlined word or words to make the statement true.

1. Energy is the ability to do <u>work</u>.
2. The food you eat stores <u>chemical</u> energy.
3. Light is <u>nuclear</u> energy.
4. Sound is a form of <u>mechanical</u> energy.
5. Energy stored in an object due to its position is called <u>kinetic</u> energy.
6. <u>Potential</u> energy is energy of motion.
7. Kinetic energy equals the mass of an object times the square of its velocity divided by <u>two</u>.
8. Gravitational potential energy is dependent on both the weight and <u>height</u> of an object.

Concept Mapping

Complete the following concept map for Section 16–1. Then construct a concept map for the entire chapter.

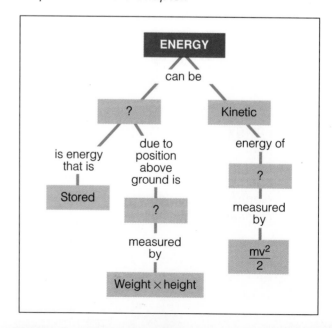

416

Concept Mastery

Discuss each of the following in a brief paragraph.

1. Describe five different examples of mechanical energy.
2. From the standpoint of kinetic energy, why is a loaded truck more dangerous than a small car in a collision even though they are traveling at the same speed?
3. How does bouncing on a trampoline illustrate both kinetic and potential energies?
4. Water is boiled. The resulting steam is blown against huge turbine blades. The turning blades spin in a magnetic field, producing electricity. Describe in order the energy conversions.
5. How does the law of conservation of energy relate to the following situations: a bat hitting a baseball, a person throwing a frisbee, a person breaking a twig over his or her knee.
6. The concept of energy links the various scientific disciplines—physical science, life science, and earth science. Explain why.

Critical Thinking and Problem Solving

Use the skills you have developed in this chapter to answer each of the following.

1. **Applying concepts** Sound is produced by vibrations in a medium such as air. The particles of air are first pushed together and then pulled apart. Why is sound considered a form of mechanical energy?
2. **Relating concepts** A bear in a zoo lies sleeping on a ledge. A visitor comments: "Look at that lazy bear. It has no energy at all." Do you agree? Explain your answer.
3. **Making calculations and graphs** The gravitational potential energy of a boulder at 100 m is 1000 J. What is the G.P.E. at 50 m? At 20 m? At 1 m? At 0 m? Make a graph of height versus energy. What is the shape of your graph?
4. **Applying concepts** Two cyclists are riding their bikes up a steep hill. Jill rides her bike straight up the hill. Jack rides the bike up the hill in a zigzag formation. Jack and Jill have identical masses. At the top of the hill, does Jack have less gravitational potential energy than Jill? Explain your answer.
5. **Identifying relationships** The diagram shows a golfer in various stages of her swing. Compare the kinetic and potential energies of the golf club at each labeled point in the complete golf swing.
6. **Using the writing process** Imagine that the Earth's resources of coal and oil were suddenly used up. Describe how your typical day would change from morning until night. Give details about what you and your family would do about such things as cooking, transportation, entertainment, heat, and light. Discuss the importance of finding alternative energy resources.

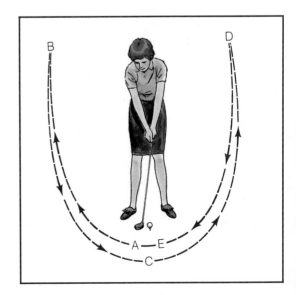

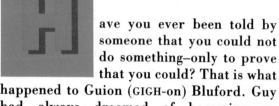

Guion Bluford:
CHALLENGER
in Space

Have you ever been told by someone that you could not do something–only to prove that you could? That is what happened to Guion (GIGH-on) Bluford. Guy had always dreamed of becoming an aerospace engineer. As a boy, he built model airplanes and read his father's engineering books. He analyzed the game of table tennis to find out how many different ways he could hit a Ping-Pong ball in order to alter its flight. Yet when Guy reached his last year in high school, his guidance counselors told him that he was "not college material" and that he should go to a technical school instead. Little did they know that this young man would someday earn a Ph.D. in aerospace engineering and join the NASA space program–and become the first African American to fly in space.

Guy admits, "I really wasn't too concerned about what the counselors said. I just ignored it. I had such a strong interest in aerospace engineering by then that nothing a counselor said was going to stop me."

With his parents' encouragement, Guy applied to Pennsylvania State University and was accepted into the aerospace engineer-

ing program. The courses were tough, but he did well. After receiving a bachelor's degree from Penn State, Guy joined the Air Force and went to Vietnam as a pilot. When he returned to the United States after the war, he was accepted into the Air Force Institute of Technology. There he earned a master's degree and a Ph.D. in aerospace engineering.

Guy decided that NASA would be the best place for him to learn about the latest aerospace technology. In 1978, he applied for a position in the astronaut program. Out of 8878 applicants, only 35 were chosen–and Guy was one of them. He was sent to work at the Johnson Space Flight Center in Houston, Texas.

At the Johnson Space Flight Center, Guy took different courses for the first year. Then he spent the next few years flying in "shuttle simulators"–machines that imitate the look and feel of a space shuttle. The work was so interesting and enjoyable that Guy could not have been happier. In his own words, "The job is so fantastic, I don't need a hobby. My hobby is going to work!"

One day while he was at the Johnson Space Flight Center, Guy received a message that

NASA's "top brass" wanted to see him. Guy's first reaction was to think that he had done something wrong! Much to his amazement, he learned that he had been chosen to fly in the third mission of the *Space Shuttle Challenger*. Guy was so thrilled that he was walking on air–and soon he really would be!

The *Challenger* took off from Cape Canaveral, Florida at 2:00 AM on August 30, 1983. Two of the five astronauts on board were designated as pilots and three were designated as mission specialists. Pilots fly the shuttle, while mission specialists are in charge of scientific experiments. Guy's job was that of mission specialist. In particular, his special task was to send out a satellite for the nation of India.

Guy's training in shuttle simulators had prepared him for the experience of space travel–almost. Once in orbit, Guy found that life in zero gravity took some getting used to.

"There is no feeling of right side up or upside down," he recalls, "When you're floating around in space, you feel the same when you're upside down as you do when you're right side up. You don't feel any different when you're standing on the ceiling than you do when you're standing on the floor. [You can] walk across the ceiling or

along the walls as easily as y[ou]
the floor!"

Ordinary tasks such as eating a[nd]ing become real challenges in a weig[htless] environment. Food has to be something [that] sticks to a plate, like macaroni and cheese. You cannot eat anything like peas because they will just float away. Knives and forks have to be held to eating trays with little magnets–otherwise they, too, will float away.

Sleeping also presents problems. A weightless astronaut who falls asleep will soon find himself floating all over the spaceship and bumping into things. Some astronauts aboard the *Challenger* slept strapped in their seats, but Guy preferred to tie one end of a string to his waist and the other end to something stable on the walls of the cockpit. Then he would float into the middle of the room and fall asleep. Guy recalls, "Occasionally I'd float up against the lockers and be jarred awake. It felt funny waking up and not knowing if I was upside down or not."

Challenger stayed in orbit for six days, from August 30 to September 5. During that time, the crew received a special telephone message from then President Reagan. Mr. Reagan praised all of the astronauts, but had a special message for Guy Bluford: "You, I think, are paving the way for others, and you are making it plain that we are in an era of brotherhood here in our land."

How does Guion Bluford feel about being the first African American in space? Guy has always stressed that he wants to be known for doing a good job–not for the color of his skin. Yet he is glad to be a role model for others who are African American. He hopes that young people will look at him and say, "If this guy can do it, maybe I can do it too." And he is quick to add that his story has a message for all young people. "They can do it. They can do whatever they want. If you really want to do something and are willing to put in the hard work it takes, then some-day–bingo, you've done it!"

UNIT FOUR
Heat Energy

This colorful photograph of a girl and her dog is a special kind of image called a thermogram. Notice that the dog's nose appears dark blue in the thermogram. Does this mean that the dog's nose is hot or cold?

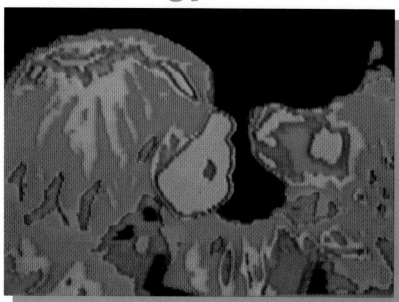

▲ Fire is useful when it is properly controlled. However, it is also quite dangerous. An out-of-control forest fire can be extremely destructive.

The colorful picture above is not a cartoon or a computer graphic. It is a thermogram of a young girl and her pet dog. A thermogram (from *thermo-* meaning heat and *-gram* meaning something recorded) is an image formed by the invisible heat given off by an object. In this thermogram, the hottest areas are bright and the coolest areas are dark. Doctors can use thermograms to determine whether parts of the body are functioning properly.

Thermograms illustrate only one way in which heat is important in our lives. Heat is also important because of its many uses. Thousands of years ago, early humans discovered fire and began using it to heat their cave dwellings and to cook their food. Today, central heating and cooling systems make our homes, schools, and office buildings comfortable places in which to live and work. Heat engines—from steam engines to modern gasoline engines—help make our work easier. But heat can also damage the environment if we are not careful.

What exactly is heat? You will find the answer to that question in this Unit. You will also learn about the many applications of heat in your daily life.

As this painting of cowboys gathered around an open fire in the Old West illustrates, the ability to use fire for heating and cooking was one of the most important discoveries in human history.

Burning coals glow reddish yellow. In the heart of the fire, the hottest coals glow white hot.

Discovery *Activity*

In Hot Water

1. Fill three bowls with water. Put cold water in one bowl, warm water in the second bowl, and hot (but not too hot to touch) water in the third bowl.

2. Now place one hand in the cold water and one hand in the hot water.

3. After about a minute, place both hands in the warm water. Does the temperature of the warm water feel the same to both hands?

   ■ Is using your hands a good way to measure heat? Could a scientist measure heat in this way?

   ■ What does this experiment tell you about the relationship between heat and temperature?

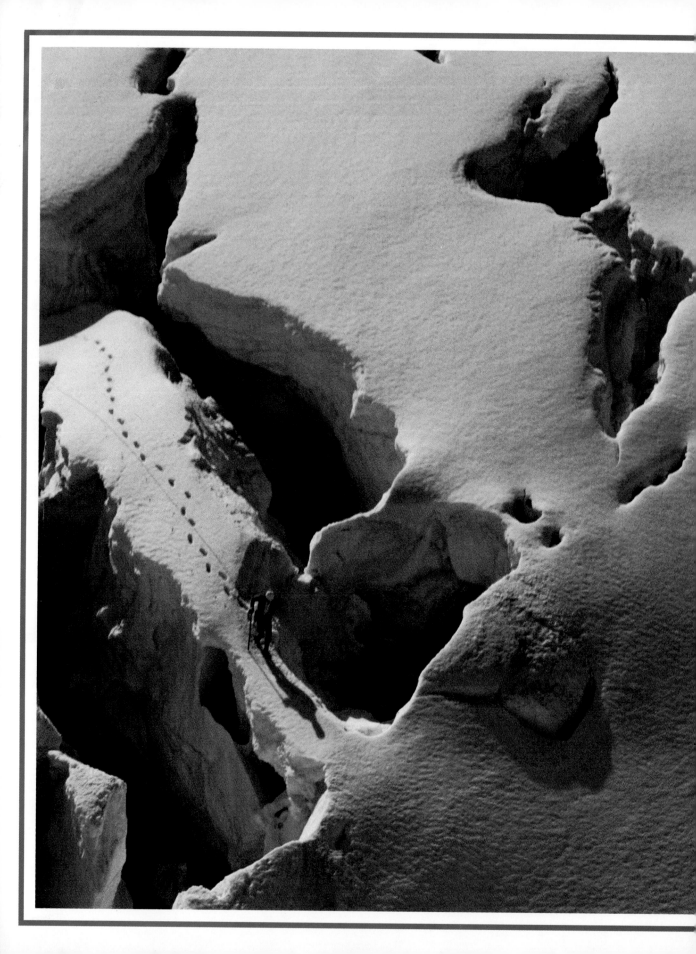

What Is Heat?

Guide for Reading

After you read the following sections, you will be able to

17–1 Heat: A Form of Energy
- ■ Describe how scientists discovered that heat is a form of energy.

17–2 Temperature and Heat
- ■ Define temperature in terms of the kinetic energy of molecules.

17–3 Measuring Heat
- ■ Describe how heat can be measured indirectly.

17–4 Heat and Phase Changes
- ■ Explain how a transfer of heat energy causes a phase change.

17–5 Thermal Expansion
- ■ Explain why thermal expansion occurs.
- ■ Describe some practical applications of thermal expansion.

Alone and lost in a snowy, barren wilderness, a man wanders in search of warmth and shelter. He is rapidly losing his body heat to the much colder surroundings. Although he is dressed in layers of thick clothing, he cannot hold enough heat to keep his body functioning. He is slowly freezing to death. If he could find some wood to burn, the fire would produce enough heat to warm him. But he is surrounded by snow and ice!

This exciting adventure story, called "To Build a Fire," was written by the American author Jack London. But it is more than just a thrilling tale of a man's struggle to survive in the wilderness. It is also a story about heat and the attempt to understand and control it. In this sense, it is a story about scientific knowledge.

An understanding of heat and the many roles it plays in the lives of real people is important to you, too. Who knows? Someday this knowledge may even save your life. As you read this chapter you will find out what heat is, how it is measured, and how it affects the world around you. As for the man in the snow, you will have to read the story to find out what happened to him!

Journal *Activity*

You and Your World Try to remember a situation when you were really cold or really hot. How did you feel? What did you do to make yourself warmer or cooler? Describe your feelings and actions in your journal. After reading this chapter, is there anything you would do differently?

◀ *Lost in a snowy wilderness*

Guide for Reading

Focus on these questions as you
read.
▶ What is heat?
▶ What are the three methods
  of heat transfer?

17–1 Heat: A Form of Energy

An open fire casts a warm glow on your face and the faces of your fellow campers as you toast marshmallows over the flames. Sitting near an open fire, you know that the fire gives off **heat.** You might be tempted to think that heat is some kind of substance flowing from the fire, through the air, and into your marshmallow. Actually, that is just what eighteenth-century scientists believed. They thought that heat was an invisible, weightless fluid capable of flowing from hotter objects to colder ones. They called this substance caloric.

In 1798, the American scientist Benjamin Thompson (who moved to England after the American Revolution and became known as Count Rumford) challenged the caloric theory. Rumford had noticed that when holes were drilled in cannon barrels, the barrels and the drills became hot. Heat was being produced. Rumford decided to find out how. He designed an experiment to test his observation. A cannon barrel to be drilled was first placed in a box filled with water. After several hours of drilling, the water began to boil. The water boiled as long as the drilling continued. Rumford concluded that it was

ACTIVITY WRITING

Rumford and Joule

The investigations of Count Rumford and James Prescott Joule illustrate the importance of careful observation and experimentation. Using books and other reference materials in the library, find out more about these two scientists, their experiments, and their contributions to the understanding of heat. Write a report of your findings.

Figure 17–1 At one time people believed that the heat from a fire was a substance called caloric. Heat is now known to be a form of energy related to the motion of molecules.

the action of drilling, not a flow of caloric, that was producing heat. Since drilling represents work being done and energy is the ability to do work, energy and heat must be related. Rumford concluded that heat must be a form of energy.

Molecules in Motion

Forty years after Count Rumford's experiment, the British scientist James Prescott Joule investigated the relationship between heat and motion. He performed a series of experiments which supported the idea that objects in motion can produce heat. The amount of heat produced depends on the amount of motion. You have probably already noticed this effect in your everyday life. Rub your hands together rapidly. What happens? Your hands feel warmer. Similarly, sliding too quickly down a rope can produce a "rope burn." These examples demonstrate that motion produces heat. Can you think of any other examples?

Other scientists working at the same time as Joule knew that energy is needed to set an object in motion. They also knew that matter is made up of tiny particles called **molecules** (MAHL-ih-kyoolz), which are always in motion. Combining these facts with the results of the experiments of Rumford and Joule, scientists correctly concluded that heat is a form of energy and that it is somehow related to the motion of molecules. **In fact, heat is a form of energy caused by the internal motion of molecules of matter.**

Activity Bank

May the Force (of Friction) Be With You, p.750

Figure 17–2 *Heated molecules (right) move faster and are farther apart than cooler molecules (left).*

Heat Transfer

Try holding an ice cube in your hand for a short time. What happens? After several seconds, you notice that your hand begins to feel cold and the ice cube begins to melt. You might think that the coldness of the ice cube is moving from the ice cube to your hand. But there is no such thing as "coldness." Cold is simply the absence of heat. So it must be heat that is moving. The ice cube in your hand is melting because heat is moving from your hand to the ice cube. If you have ever accidentally touched a hot pan, you have discovered for yourself (most likely in a painful way) that heat energy moves from a warmer object to a cooler object. The heat moves from the hot pan, through the handle, to your hand!

The movement of heat from a warmer object to a cooler one is called **heat transfer.** There are three methods of heat transfer. **Heat energy is transferred by conduction, convection, and radiation.** Let's see how each of these processes takes place.

CONDUCTION   In the process of **conduction** (kuhn-DUHK-shuhn), heat is transferred through a substance, or from one substance to another, by the

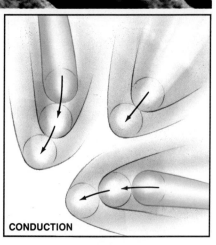

CONDUCTION

Figure 17–4 *Heat transfer by conduction involves the direct contact of molecules. As fast-moving molecules collide with slow-moving molecules, heat energy is transferred from the faster molecules to the slower molecules. Conduction by direct contact is one reason this lizard steps gingerly on a hot rock.*

Figure 17–5 *Why do several layers of clothing keep these children better insulated from the cold than a single layer of clothing?*

direct contact of molecules. All molecules are constantly in motion. Fast-moving molecules have more heat energy than slow-moving molecules.

When fast-moving molecules collide with slow-moving molecules, heat energy is transferred from the faster molecules to the slower molecules, causing the slower molecules to move faster. Now these molecules have enough energy to collide with other slow-moving molecules. This process is repeated over and over. In this way, heat energy is transferred from molecule to molecule throughout a substance. Because all matter is made of molecules, conduction can take place in solids, liquids, and gases. But conduction takes place best in solids, because the molecules of a solid are in direct contact with one another.

Some substances conduct heat better and more rapidly than other substances. These substances are good **conductors** of heat. Metals, such as iron and aluminum, are good heat conductors. Silver is one of the best conductors of heat. Copper is another good conductor of heat. Why do you think the bottoms of pots and pans are often made of copper?

Substances that do not conduct heat easily are called **insulators.** Glass, wood, plastic, and rubber are examples of good insulators. Why should the handles of pots and pans be made of wood or plastic instead of iron or aluminum?

ACTIVITY

DISCOVERING

Heat and Electricity

Good conductors of heat are usually also good conductors of electricity.

1. Set up a battery, a light bulb, wires, and alligator clips according to your teacher's directions.

2. Test different materials to find out if they are good conductors of electricity. For example, you might test a rubber band, a metal paper clip, a plastic spoon, and a wooden pencil. To test each object, place it between the clips on the free ends of the wires. If the material conducts electricity, the bulb will light.

■ Which of the materials you tested conduct electricity?

■ Which materials would probably conduct heat easily? Which would not?

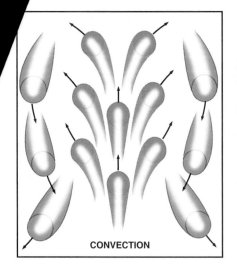

CONVECTION

Figure 17–6 *Heat transfer by convection involves the motion of molecules in currents in liquids and gases. Heated molecules speed up and spread out, causing the warmer part of the liquid or gas to become less dense than the cooler part. The heated portion rises, creating currents that carry heat. How do hot-air balloons make use of convection to float high above Earth's surface?*

ACTIVITY

DISCOVERING

Using Convection Currents

Suppose you want to let air into a stuffy room. Should you open the window from the top or the bottom if the outside temperature is warmer than the room temperature? What if the outside temperature is cooler than the room temperature? Draw a diagram to explain your answers.

■ With an adult's permission, determine if your explanations are correct.

Air is also a good insulator. That is why the best way to stay warm in extremely cold weather is to wear several layers of clothing. Layers of clothing will trap air close to your body and prevent the loss of body heat.

CONVECTION Heat transfer by **convection** (kuhn-VEHK-shuhn) takes place in liquids and gases. Heat energy is transferred through liquids and gases by means of up-and-down movements called convection currents. When a liquid or gas is heated, the molecules begin to move faster. (They have more energy as a result of being heated.) As the molecules move faster, they move farther apart. This means that the heated liquid or gas is now less dense than the surrounding liquid or gas. The less-dense liquid or gas rises, carrying heat with it.

Warm air near the surface of the Earth is heated by the Earth and becomes less dense than the cooler air above it. The warm air tends to rise. Hang gliders and soaring birds rely on updrafts of warm air to help keep them aloft. Because cooler air is denser than warmer air, it tends to sink, just as a dense rock sinks in water. As warm air rises and cool air sinks, convection currents are formed. These currents transfer heat throughout the Earth's atmosphere and contribute to the Earth's weather. Convection currents are also formed in the Earth's oceans as warm water rises to the surface and cold water sinks to the bottom.

RADIATION Heat energy is transferred through empty space by **radiation** (ray-dee-AY-shuhn). Heat from the sun reaches the Earth by means of radiation. The heat energy is in the form of invisible light called infrared radiation. Other familiar forms of heat transfer by radiation include the heat you can feel around an open fire or a candle flame, the heat near a hot stove, and the heat given off by an electric heater. Now can you explain why you can toast marshmallows over a fire even if the flames do not touch the marshmallows?

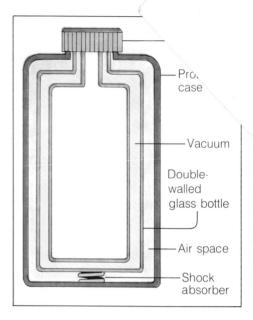

Figure 17–7 A thermos bottle keeps liquids hot or cold by preventing heat transfer by conduction, convection, or radiation. The glass bottle reduces conduction. The air space between the bottles, which is a partial vacuum, prevents heat transfer by convection because there are so few air molecules to carry the heat. A silvered coating on the surface of the bottle prevents heat transfer by radiation. Why is the cap usually made of plastic?

Figure 17–8 Radiation is the transfer of heat energy in the form of invisible infrared rays. How is radiation from the sun related to the heating of the Earth?

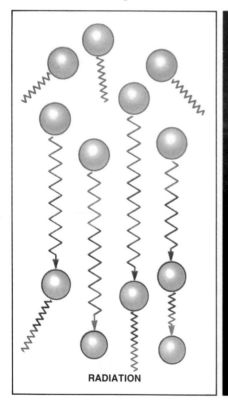

RADIATION

ACTIVITY
DISCOVERING

Heat Loss

Make a list of places in your home or school where heat may be escaping to the outside. Determine whether the heat loss is due to conduction, convection, or radiation.

■ How can the heat loss from the building be reduced?

PROBLEM ??? Solving

Too Hot to Fly

One day in July, passenger jets at the airport in Phoenix, Arizona, were grounded. The problem? The air temperature—a sizzling 50°C—was just too hot for the planes to get off the ground! The planes had to wait several hours until the temperature dropped a few degrees before they could take off.

Applying Concepts

Why do you think the planes were unable to take off in the hot air? (*Hint:* When a plane is moving fast enough to take off, air moving past the plane's wings normally provides enough "lift" for the plane to get off the ground. But what happens to air when it is heated?)

17–1 Section Review

1. What is heat? How did the experiments of Rumford and Joule help contribute to an understanding of the nature of heat?
2. What are the three methods of heat transfer? How does each method work?
3. What are molecules? What factors caused scientists to make a connection between heat and the motion of molecules?

Connection—*You and Your World*

4. Identify the method of heat transfer illustrated by each of the following: an egg cooking in a frying pan; a warm air mass bringing a change in weather; the wire of an electric appliance becoming hot; heat from a fireplace warming a room.

17-2 Temperature and Heat

If a weather forecaster predicts temperatures between 30°C and 35°C, you know you can expect a hot day. Many people—perhaps even you—think that temperature and heat are the same thing. But they are not. Temperature and heat are related, but they are not the same. In order to understand the difference between temperature and heat, you will need to look more closely at how energy and the motion of molecules are related.

Kinetic Energy

Count Rumford observed that heat was produced when a hole was drilled in a cannon barrel. James Prescott Joule observed that objects in motion produce heat. In both cases, work is being done. What do you think of when you hear the word work? You may think of doing chores, such as washing dishes or raking leaves. Or perhaps going to work in an office comes to mind. But when scientists speak of work, they are referring to a force (a push or a pull) acting on an object and causing it to move. A moving hammer can do work by hitting a nail and driving it into a piece of wood. Moving objects can do work because they have energy. Energy of motion is called **kinetic** (kih-NEHT-ihk) **energy.** The faster an object moves, the more kinetic energy it has. So a fast-moving hammer can do more work than a slow-moving one. You can test this by hammering a nail

Guide for Reading

Focus on this question as you read.

▶ *What is the difference between temperature and heat?*

Figure 17–9 *Heat within the Earth increases the kinetic energy of water molecules so that they escape from the Earth as an eruption of hot water and steam. How does Old Faithful geyser in Yellowstone National Park, Wyoming, illustrate the relationship between heat and temperature?*

Figure 17–10 *Kinetic energy is defined as the energy of motion. How does the kinetic energy of the gazelles change when they are running from a predator that wants to eat them?*

ACTIVITY

DISCOVERING

Exploring Molecular Motion

1. Fill a beaker about two thirds full with water at or near room temperature.

2. Fill a second beaker about two thirds full with cold water. (You can use ice cubes to cool the water, but be sure to remove the ice before adding the cold water to the beaker.)

3. Using a medicine dropper, place one drop of dark food coloring on the surface of the water in each beaker. Do not stir. What changes do you see in each beaker? How quickly do the changes occur in each beaker?

■ How are your observations related to the effect of heat on the motion of molecules?

into a piece of wood. The faster you swing the hammer, the farther the nail is driven into the wood.

Like all moving objects, molecules have kinetic energy because of their motion. **Temperature is a measure of the average kinetic energy of molecules.** Adding heat to a substance increases the average kinetic energy of the molecules and causes a rise in temperature. Thus **temperature** is a measure of how hot or how cold something is. The higher the temperature of a substance, the faster the molecules in that substance are moving, on the average. Likewise, a lower temperature indicates that the molecules are moving more slowly. In which pot of water would most of the water molecules be moving faster—a pot at 90°C or one at 70°C?

Unlike temperature, heat depends on the mass of the substance present. For instance, 10 grams of water at 90°C have more heat energy than 5 grams of water at the same temperature. This means that if you were to spill hot water on your hand by accident, 10 grams of water at 90°C would produce a more severe burn than 5 grams of water at 90°C!

Measuring Temperature

You would not want to put your hand into a pot of boiling water to find out how hot the water is! And you might not always agree with someone else on how hot or how cold something is. So you need a safe and accurate way of measuring temperature. A **thermometer** is an instrument for measuring temperature. Most common thermometers consist of a thin tube filled with a liquid, usually alcohol or mercury. Remember that as a liquid is heated, its molecules move faster and farther apart. So as the liquid in a thermometer gets warmer, it expands and rises in the tube. The opposite happens as the liquid gets cooler. The molecules move slower and closer together. The liquid contracts and drops in the tube.

Along the tube of a thermometer is a set of numbers, called a scale, that allows you to read the temperature. The **Celsius scale** is used to measure

Figure 17–11 *At a temperature of –195.8°C, nitrogen gas becomes a liquid. A banana dipped in liquid nitrogen becomes so frozen it can be used to hammer a nail into a block of wood.*

Figure 17–12 *A comparison of the Celsius and Kelvin temperature scales is shown here. Notice that absolute zero is –273°C. Uranus, located farther from the sun than Earth, has temperatures near absolute zero.*

temperature in the metric system. The unit of temperature on the Celsius scale is the degree Celsius (°C). Water freezes at 0°C and boils at 100°C.

Another metric temperature scale often used by scientists is the **Kelvin scale.** On this scale, temperature is measured in units called kelvins (K). You can convert Celsius degrees to kelvins simply by adding 273 to the Celsius temperature. For example, if a thermometer reads 10°C, the same temperature on the Kelvin scale would be 273 + 10 = 283 K. A temperature of –5°C equals 268 K [273 + (–5)]. At what temperature does water freeze on the Kelvin scale? At what Kelvin temperature does water boil?

The main reason the Kelvin scale is useful to scientists is that the lowest reading on this scale, 0 K, is the lowest temperature that can be reached. This temperature is often called **absolute zero.** Scientists have now been able to reach a temperature only one billionth of a degree Celsius above absolute zero.

You may not have guessed that there is a lowest possible temperature. Recall that temperature is a measure of the energy of motion of molecules. What do you think happens at absolute zero?

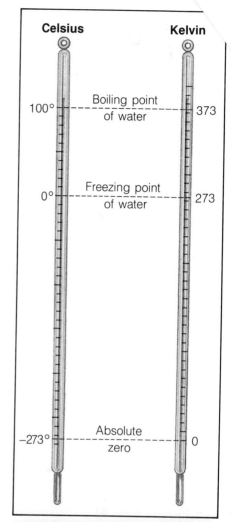

Celsius   Kelvin

100° — Boiling point of water — 373

0° — Freezing point of water — 273

–273° — Absolute zero — 0

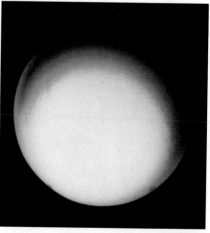

17–2 Section Review

1. What is temperature? What is the difference between temperature and heat?
2. How does a thermometer measure temperature?
3. What is the most common metric scale used to measure temperature? What temperature scale is most often used by scientists?
4. How would you convert a temperature in kelvins to degrees Celsius?

Critical Thinking—*Relating Concepts*
5. Do you think a temperature of absolute zero can ever be reached? Why or why not?

Activity Bank

One Hundred Degrees of Separation, p.751

Suspended Animation

A concept once found only in science fiction has moved into the operating rooms of modern hospitals. In science fiction movies, astronauts embarking on a long space voyage are put into a state of "suspended animation" from which they can be revived when they reach their destination. Actually, this physical state is called hypothermic arrest (from the prefix *hypo-,* meaning lower than normal, and *-therm,* meaning heat). In hypothermic arrest, the heart stops beating and blood circulation comes to a halt. Hypothermic arrest is deadly under normal circumstances.

Today, hypothermic arrest is used in *medicine.* Doctors can cool the body of a patient to a state of near death in order to perform brain surgery without a flow of blood! A person can survive hypothermic arrest because the brain can survive longer without oxygen at low temperatures.

In 1990, surgeons at Columbia Presbyterian Medical Center in New York City used the procedure to correct an aneurysm (AN-yoo-rihz-uhm) in the brain of a 24-year-old man. In an aneurysm, the wall of a blood vessel puffs out like a little balloon. The ballooning blood vessel presses on the brain, causing paralysis and eventual death.

In the case of the patient at Columbia, the aneurysm was buried deep in the brain. A team of surgeons lowered the patient's temperature until his heart stopped. Then they drained his blood and repaired the aneurysm. Once the surgery was completed, blood was again allowed to flow through the patient's body, his temperature rose, and his heart began to beat. A week later, he left the hospital! A normally deadly process had saved his life.

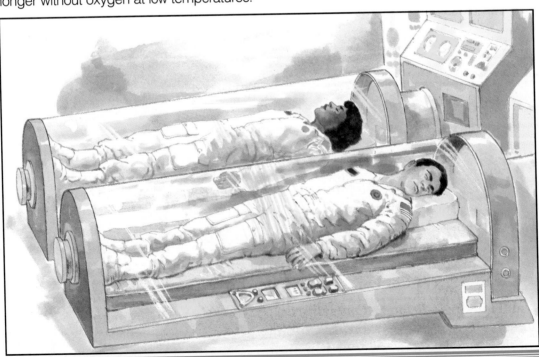

17–3 Measuring Heat

You know that when you cook soup or boil water, heat energy must be added to the liquid in order to raise its temperature. Heat energy is needed to set molecules in motion. Temperature is a measure of this molecular motion.

Heat cannot be measured directly. But changes in temperature—which can be measured directly—provide a way to measure heat indirectly. **An increase in temperature indicates that heat is being added. A decrease in temperature indicates that heat is being removed.**

Heat is measured in units called **calories.** One calorie (cal) is defined as the amount of heat needed to raise the temperature of 1 gram of water 1 degree Celsius. For example, to raise the temperature of 1 gram of water from 4°C to 5°C or from 20°C to 21°C, 1 calorie of heat is needed. Another unit that can be used to measure heat is the joule (J), named after James Prescott Joule. One calorie is equal to 4.19 joules (1 cal = 4.19 J).

Notice that the amount of heat needed for a given temperature change depends on the mass of the water being heated. For example, 10 calories of heat

Figure 17–13 *Although heat cannot be measured directly, a change in temperature provides an indirect measurement of heat. Higher temperatures indicate more heat whereas lower temperatures indicate an absence of heat.*

TABLE OF SPECIFIC HEATS	
Substance	Specific Heat (cal/g·°C)
Air	0.25
Aluminum	0.22
Copper	0.09
Glass	0.20
Ice (−20°C to 0°C)	0.50
Iron	0.11
Mercury	0.03
Ocean water	0.93
Water	1.00
Wood	0.42

Figure 17–14 *According to this table of specific heats, which heats up more quickly: aluminum or mercury?*

will raise the temperature of 1 gram of water 10°C. If you had 10 grams of water instead of 1 gram, the same 10 calories would raise the temperature of the water only 1°C. How many calories would be needed to raise the temperature of 10 grams of water 10°C?

Specific Heat Capacity

Mass is not the only factor that determines temperature change. The same amount of heat will produce a different temperature change in different substances even if their masses are the same. That is because some substances absorb heat energy more readily than other substances.

The ability of a substance to absorb heat energy is called its **specific heat.** The specific heat of a substance is the number of calories needed to raise the temperature of 1 gram of that substance 1 degree Celsius. The specific heat of water is 1 calorie per gram per degree Celsius (1.00 cal/g·°C). This is high compared with the specific heats of most other substances.

The high specific heat of water explains why the climate near an ocean or a large lake is usually mild. Water tends to heat up slowly, but it also loses heat slowly. This slow heating and cooling tends to keep the climate near a large body of water relatively uniform.

Figure 17–14 lists the specific heat values of some other common substances. Specific heat is an important property because it can be used to help decide which substance should be used for a specific purpose. For example, you can see by looking at Figure 17–14 that the specific heat of aluminum is almost twice that of iron. That means that aluminum pots and pans hold about twice as much heat as pots and pans of the same mass made of iron.

Calculating Heat Energy

Specific heat can be used to calculate the amount of heat gained or lost by a substance. The heat gained or lost by a substance is equal to the product of its mass times the change in temperature (ΔT) times its specific heat. (The symbol Δ is the Greek letter delta; ΔT means change in temperature.)

Figure 17–15 *The calorimeter shown here can be used to measure the heat given off during a chemical reaction. What principle of heat transfer is the basis of operation of the calorimeter?*

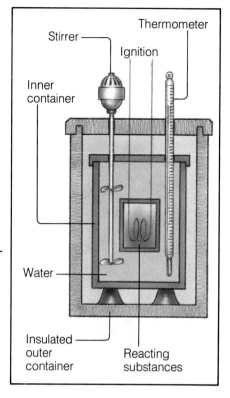

Heat gained or lost = Mass × ΔT × Specific heat

Within a closed container, the heat lost by one substance must equal the heat gained by another substance. A device that makes use of this principle is called a **calorimeter** (kal-uh-RIHM-uht-er). A calorimeter can be used to measure the heat given off in chemical reactions.

Figure 17–15 shows how a calorimeter is constructed. An insulated outer container surrounds an inner container filled with water. Inside the inner container is a chamber in which a chemical reaction takes place. Because the heat given off by the chemical reaction equals the heat gained by the water, the heat of the chemical reaction can be calculated. The temperature change, mass, and specific heat of the water must be known in order to make the calculation. For example, suppose the surrounding water has a mass of 300 grams. If the temperature of the

Sample Problem	How much heat is needed to raise the temperature of 4 grams of aluminum 5°C?

Solution

Step 1	Write the formula.	
Step 2	Substitute given numbers and units.	**Heat gained = Mass × ΔT × Specific heat**
		Heat gained = 4 g × 5°C × 0.22 cal/g·°C
Step 3	Solve for unknown variable.	**Heat gained = 4.4 cal**

Practice Problems

1. Calculate the heat lost by 10 g of copper if it is cooled from 35°C to 21°C.

2. Suppose that 10 grams of a certain substance gained 16.5 cal of heat when the temperature increased from 70°C to 85°C. What would be the specific heat of the substance?

water increases 5°C, the heat given off by the chemical reaction is equal to 300 g x 5°C x 1 cal/g·°C = 1500 calories. How much heat would be given off by a chemical reaction that raised the temperature of 150 grams of water 10°C?

Potential Energy

When does heat energy not cause a change in the temperature of a substance? The answer to this question is quite simple: when the heat energy is stored. Stored energy—in the form of heat or any other kind of energy—is called **potential** (poh-TEHN-shuhl) **energy.** Potential heat energy is present in chemical substances such as gasoline and other fuels. The stored heat energy is released when the fuels are burned, for example, in a car engine.

Foods also contain potential heat energy. The energy stored in foods can be measured in calories because when foods are "burned," they release heat energy. ("Burning" food in your body involves the process of respiration, in which food that is broken

Activity Bank

These "Fuelish" Things, p.752

Figure 17–16 *The stored, or potential, energy in rocket fuel provides the boost needed to launch a Space Shuttle. Stored energy in food provides a similar boost to you.*

down into sugar is combined with oxygen to release energy.) When sugars are burned in your body, heat energy needed to keep your body functioning is produced. The amount of heat a food gives off is indicated by the number of calories it contains. There is one big difference, however. "Food calories" are really kilocalories (kcal). And 1 kilocalorie is equal to 1000 calories. Food calories are usually written with a capital C to differentiate them from calories with a small c. So the next time you are on a diet, you can tell your friends that you are watching your kilocalories!

17–3 Section Review

1. How can heat be measured? What unit is used to measure heat?
2. What is specific heat? Why is it important?
3. What is a calorimeter? How does it work?

Critical Thinking—*Making Calculations*

4. Which would require more heat energy—raising the temperature of 100 grams of water from 40°C to 100°C or raising the temperature of 1000 grams of water from 80°C to 90°C? Show your calculations.

Counting Calories

All foods contain Calories. But not all substances in food contain the same number of Calories per gram. Carbohydrates and proteins contain 4 Calories per gram. Fats contain 9 Calories per gram.

1. Obtain a nutrition information label from a food product, such as yogurt or peanut butter.

2. Read the label to find the number of grams of carbohydrate, protein, and fat contained in one serving.

3. Calculate the number of Calories of carbohydrate, protein, and fat for one serving.

4. Add your three values to find the total number of Calories. How does your value compare with the total number of Calories listed on the label for one serving?

17–4 Heat and Phase Changes

Have you ever watched an ice cube melt in a glass of water? If so, have you been curious about why this happens? Heat always moves from a warm substance to a cooler substance. Because the water is warmer than the ice, heat moves from the water to the ice. As the ice absorbs heat, it melts, or changes into a liquid. Eventually all the solid ice will change into liquid water.

Matter can exist in three phases: solid, liquid, and gas. The physical change of matter from the solid phase (ice) to the liquid phase (water) is called a

Guide for Reading

Focus on this question as you read.

▶ *What causes a phase change?*

Figure 17–17 *Matter can exist in three phases. Which phases of matter can be observed in this photograph?*

Figure 17–18 *With the addition of heat, these water droplets will change phase and become gaseous water in the atmosphere. What term is used for the amount of heat needed to change a liquid to a gas?*

phase change. Matter can undergo several different phase changes. Phase changes occur when a solid becomes a liquid, which is called melting, and when a liquid becomes a solid, which is called freezing. The change of a liquid to a gas, or evaporation, and the change of a gas to a liquid, or condensation, are also phase changes.

What causes a phase change? **A change in phase requires a change in heat energy.** When ice melts and changes into water, energy in the form of heat is being absorbed by the ice. The energy is needed to overcome the forces of attraction that hold the water molecules together in the solid phase (ice). Where do you think the heat energy needed to melt the ice in a glass of water is coming from?

Heat of Fusion and Heat of Vaporization

The amount of heat needed to change 1 gram of a substance from the solid phase to the liquid phase is called **heat of fusion.** The heat of fusion of ice is 80 calories per gram (cal/g). This means that in order to melt 1 gram of ice, 80 calories of heat are needed. What do you think happens when 1 gram of liquid water changes into ice? You are right if you said that 80 calories of heat are lost by 1 gram of liquid water as it changes into ice. How much heat is needed to change 10 grams of ice into water?

The amount of heat needed to change 1 gram of a substance from the liquid phase to the gas phase is called **heat of vaporization.** The heat of vaporization of water is 540 calories per gram. This means that 540 calories of heat must be added to 1 gram of water in order to change it into steam. How much heat is needed to change 10 grams of water into steam? How much heat is given off if 10 grams of steam are condensed into water?

Melting, Freezing, and Boiling Points

In order for a substance to undergo a phase change, the substance must be at a certain temperature. The temperature at which a substance changes from the liquid phase to the solid phase is called its **freezing point.** The freezing point of water is 0°C. The temperature at which a substance changes from the solid phase to the liquid phase is its **melting point.** A substance's freezing point and melting point are the same. Can you explain why? The

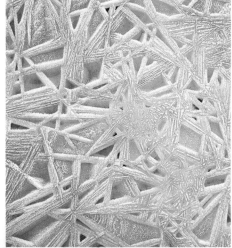

Figure 17–19 *The temperature at which a liquid changes to a solid is called its freezing point. At what temperature does liquid water change to ice crystals?*

Figure 17–20 *A heating curve, or phase-change diagram, illustrates the fact that during a phase change the addition of heat produces no change in temperature. According to the graph, how many calories per gram are required for ice to melt? For water to vaporize?*

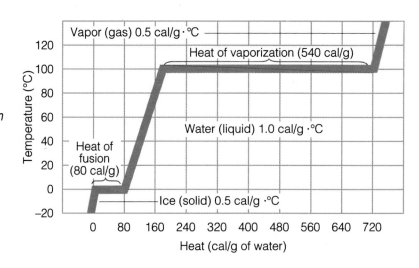

temperature at which a substance changes from the liquid phase to the gas phase is called its **boiling point.** The boiling point of water is 100°C.

During a phase change, something unusual happens. Although there is a change in heat energy (heat is either added or removed), there is no change in temperature. The forces of attraction between molecules are overcome, but the average kinetic energy of the molecules remains the same. Once the melting point or boiling point of a substance has been reached, adding or removing heat results in more of the substance changing phase, not in a change in temperature. Only after a phase change is complete will a change in heat energy result in a change in temperature.

The graph in Figure 17–20 shows the relationship among heat energy, temperature, and phase for water. This type of graph is called a phase-change diagram or a heating curve. According to the diagram, what happens as ice is heated from –20°C to 0°C? The temperature rises as heat is added. For every degree Celsius that the temperature rises, an amount of heat equal to 0.5 cal/g is required. At 0°C the ice undergoes a phase change—the solid ice melts and becomes liquid water. There is no change in temperature during the phase change. How much heat, in calories per gram, is required for this phase change? What is this amount of heat called?

As heat is added to the liquid water after the phase change, the temperature rises again until it reaches 100°C. At this point, even though heat is still being added, the temperature remains at 100°C while the liquid water changes to a gas (steam). This fact has an important application in your daily life. Remember, the heat of vaporization of water is 540 cal/g. So although boiling water and steam have the same temperature, the steam contains 540 cal/g more heat than the water. This means that you can get a more serious burn from steam at 100°C than from boiling water at 100°C.

Once the phase change is complete, the temperature rises again as heat is added to the steam. How many calories of heat are needed to change 1 gram of ice at 0°C to 1 gram of steam at 100°C?

17–4 Section Review

1. What is necessary for a phase change to occur?
2. What is heat of fusion? What is heat of vaporization?
3. What happens to the temperature of a substance during a phase change? What happens to heat energy?

Critical Thinking—*Making Comparisons*
4. Compare the amount of heat released when 54 grams of water freeze to ice with the amount of heat released when 8 grams of steam condense to water.

ACTIVITY

DISCOVERING

Changing the Boiling Point

1. Obtain three clean beakers.

2. Pour 100 mL of water into each beaker.

3. Add 10 g of salt to the first beaker and 20 g of salt to the second beaker. Do not add anything to the third beaker. Stir to dissolve the salt in each beaker.

4. Heat the water in each beaker until it begins to boil. Record the temperature at which the water in each beaker begins to boil.

What is the boiling point of the water in the first beaker? The second beaker? The third beaker?

■ What effect does adding salt to water have on the boiling point of the water?

■ What is the relationship between the amount of salt added and the boiling point?

17–5 Thermal Expansion

Have you ever wondered why sidewalks have spaces between the squares of concrete? The reason is that concrete expands in hot weather. Without the spaces, the surface of the sidewalk would buckle as it expanded. Spaces are left in bridge roadways and between railroad tracks for the same reason.

Have you ever seen a hot-air balloon? As the air inside the balloon is heated, its volume increases and the balloon expands. When the volume of air increases, its density decreases. This is why a hot-air balloon rises.

Guide for Reading

Focus on this question as you read.

▶ *What is meant by thermal expansion?*

And you might have noticed that the tires on your bicycle tend to look "higher" in warm weather than they do in cold weather. All of these examples illustrate the process of **thermal expansion.** Thermal expansion is the expansion, or increase in size, of a substance caused by heat. **Most substances—solids, liquids, and gases—expand when their temperature is increased.**

Expansion in Solids

Why do solids expand when they are heated? Knowing something about how molecules are arranged in a solid will help you to answer this question. The molecules of a solid are arranged in fixed positions about which they vibrate, or move in place. As heat energy is added to the solid, the kinetic energy of the molecules increases and their vibrations speed up. The molecules move farther away from their fixed positions and farther away from each other. The increased distance between the molecules accounts for the expansion of the solid.

Expansion in Liquids

The kinetic energy of the molecules in a liquid also increases when the liquid is heated. As the molecules begin to move faster, they move farther apart. So most liquids expand when they are heated.

Figure 17–21 *Thermal expansion is the expansion of a substance due to heat. Solids expand when heated, so expansion links are provided in bridge surfaces. When the temperature is low, the gap between the metal links is large. What happens when the temperature rises?*

Figure 17–22 *Unlike all other substances on Earth, water expands when it freezes. This fact explains why ice floats, an important consideration when ice fishing. How does this fact contribute to potholes on concrete roadways?*

There is one exception to this rule, however. Between the temperatures of 4°C and 0°C, water expands as it cools. Because of this expansion, the volume of water increases as it cools from 4°C to 0°C. As the volume increases, the density decreases. As you learned in Chapter 2, density is an important property of matter. The density of a substance is equal to the mass of the substance divided by its volume (Density = Mass/Volume). This equation shows why the density of water changes when its volume changes.

Recall that 0°C is the freezing point of water. So solid ice is less dense than liquid water. You can see this for yourself when you look at ice cubes floating in a glass of water or chunks of ice floating on the surface of a pond. What do you think would be the effect on living things if ice were more dense than liquid water?

ACTIVITY
DOING

A Model Pothole

1. Fill a balloon with water and tie the end securely.

2. In a bowl, mix together equal amounts of flour and salt. Add enough water to the mixture to make a paste.

3. Spread a thick layer of paste over the surface of the balloon. Let the paste dry.

4. Leave the balloon in the freezer compartment of a refrigerator overnight.

What happened to the balloon? What caused this to happen?

You may have noticed "potholes" in roads, especially in the early spring. Potholes are caused when water under the road surface freezes and expands during the winter. The colder the winter, the more potholes in the spring! The expansion of water as it freezes should also remind you not to fill an ice tray to the top with water before putting it in the freezer. Why?

Expansion in Gases

Gas molecules are already farther apart and moving faster than molecules in a solid or a liquid. As the temperature of a gas increases, the molecules move faster and faster. They begin to collide with one another and with the sides of their container. Because the molecules in a gas have considerable freedom of motion, thermal expansion in a gas can be quite dramatic. An explosion may result when a tightly closed container of a gas becomes too hot. Why should you never heat food or anything else in a closed container?

Applications of Thermal Expansion

You are already familiar with one application of thermal expansion—the expansion of a liquid in a thermometer tube as it is heated. The principle of thermal expansion can also be useful in constructing heat-regulating devices. These devices make use of the fact that different solids expand at different rates.

A device that is used to control temperature is called a **thermostat** (THER-muh-stat). Thermostats are used to control the air temperature in homes, schools, and other indoor areas. They are also useful in adjusting the temperature of electric appliances. The switch in a thermostat is a **bimetallic strip,** which consists of two different metals joined together. The two metals have different rates of thermal expansion. When the bimetallic strip is heated, one of the metals expands faster than the other, causing the strip to bend. The metal that expands faster is on the outside of the bimetallic strip. As the temperature changes, the bending and unbending of the bimetallic strip opens and closes an electric circuit

A CTIVITY

DISCOVERING

Thermal Expansion

1. Obtain a metal ball and ring. Pass the ball through the ring.

2. Heat the ball in a candle flame. **CAUTION:** *Be careful when using an open flame.* Pass the heated ball through the ring again.

3. Keep heating the ball and trying to pass it through the ring. Then heat the ring and see if the ball will pass through. Record your observations.

■ Based on your observations, what can you conclude about how solids behave when they are heated?

that controls the heat-regulating device. Thermostats are used on air conditioners, electric blankets, refrigerators, and home heating systems. What are some other uses of thermostats?

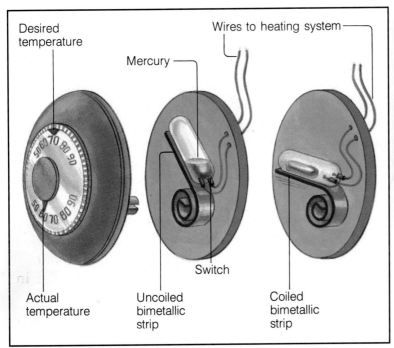

Figure 17–23 *Because the two heated metals in a bimetallic strip expand at different rates, the strip bends. A bimetallic strip is an important part of a thermostat. When the temperature gets too low, the bimetallic strip uncoils. This action causes a drop of mercury to close a switch and start the heating system. What happens when the room temperature then reaches the desired level?*

17–5 Section Review

1. What is meant by thermal expansion?
2. What happens to the molecules of a substance when the substance is heated?
3. How does a bimetallic strip in a thermostat make use of the principle of thermal expansion? What are some uses of thermostats?

Critical Thinking—*Applying Concepts*
4. Use the concept of density to explain why icebergs float in water.

Laboratory Investigation

Finding the Temperature of a Mixture

Problem

When hot and cold water are mixed together, what will be the temperature of the mixture?

Materials   *(per group)*

3 Styrofoam cups
2 100-mL graduated cylinders
thermometer
ice cubes
2 250-mL beakers
stirring rod
hot plate

Procedure 🧪 🧤 🌡

1. Place several ice cubes in a beaker and fill the beaker about two thirds full with water. Cool the water until the temperature is 10°C or lower.

2. Fill a second beaker about two thirds full with water and heat the beaker until the temperature is at least 75°C. **Note:** *Do not boil the water.*

3. Line up three Styrofoam cups. Pour 40 mL of cold water into the first cup. **Note:** *Be sure that there is no ice in the water.* Pour 40 mL of hot water into the second cup.

4. Measure and record the temperature of the water in each cup.

5. Pour the samples of hot and cold water into the third cup and stir to mix. Measure and record the temperature of the mixture.

6. Discard the water and save the cups for the next steps.

7. Repeat steps 3 through 6 using 80 mL of hot water and 40 mL of cold water.

8. Repeat steps 3 through 6 using 40 mL of hot water and 80 mL of cold water.

9. For each trial, record your observations in a data table.

Observations

For each trial, was the temperature of the mixture closer to the temperature of the hotter sample or of the colder sample? How much closer?

Analysis and Conclusions

1. Explain your observations in each trial.

2. When hot and cold water are mixed, what is one factor that determines the temperature of the mixture?

3. What types of heat transfer are involved when you mix hot and cold water?

4. What are some sources of error in this experiment?

5. **On Your Own** What would you predict the approximate temperature of the mixture to be if you mixed 20 mL of water at 10°C with 100 mL of water at 80°C? Carry out the experiment to test your prediction.

	Cold Water		Hot Water		Mixture	
Trial	*Volume*	*Temperature*	*Volume*	*Temperature*	*Volume*	*Temperature*
1						
2						

Study Guide

Summarizing Key Concepts

17–1 Heat: A Form of Energy

▲ Heat is a form of energy related to the motion of molecules.

▲ The three types of heat transfer are conduction, convection, and radiation.

▲ Substances that conduct heat effectively are called conductors. Substances that do not conduct heat easily are called insulators.

17–2 Temperature and Heat

▲ Kinetic energy is energy of motion.

▲ Temperature is the measure of the average kinetic energy of molecules. The unit used to measure temperature is the degree Celsius.

17–3 Measuring Heat

▲ Heat can be measured indirectly by measuring changes in temperature.

▲ A calorie is the amount of heat needed to raise the temperature of 1 gram of liquid water 1 degree Celsius.

▲ The ability of a substance to absorb heat energy is called its specific heat.

▲ Heat gained or lost by a substance is equal to its mass times the change in temperature times its specific heat.

17–4 Heat and Phase Changes

▲ A phase change involves a gain or loss of heat energy but no change in temperature.

▲ The amount of heat needed to change a substance from the solid phase to the liquid phase is called heat of fusion.

▲ The amount of heat needed to change a substance from the liquid phase to the gas phase is called heat of vaporization.

17–5 Thermal Expansion

▲ Thermal expansion, or the expansion of a substance due to heat, can be explained in terms of the kinetic energy of molecules.

Reviewing Key Terms

Define each term in a complete sentence.

17–1 Heat: A Form of Energy

heat
molecule
heat transfer
conduction
conductor
insulator
convection
radiation

17–2 Temperature and Heat

kinetic energy
temperature
thermometer
Celsius scale
Kelvin scale
absolute zero

17–3 Measuring Heat

calorie
specific heat
calorimeter
potential energy

17–4 Heat and Phase Changes

phase change
heat of fusion
heat of vaporization
freezing point
melting point
boiling point

17–5 Thermal Expansion

thermal expansion
thermostat
bimetallic strip

449

Chapter Review

Content Review

Multiple Choice

Choose the letter of the answer that best completes each statement.

1. The tube of a thermometer is usually filled with a(an)
   a. solid.
   b. liquid.
   c. gas.
   d. insulator.
2. When a substance is heated, its molecules
   a. move faster and farther apart.
   b. move slower and closer together.
   c. stay in the same place.
   d. become larger.
3. Heat is measured in units called
   a. degrees Celsius.
   b. kelvins.
   c. calories.
   d. specific heat units.
4. The freezing point of a substance is the same as its
   a. boiling point.
   b. evaporation point.
   c. melting point.
   d. condensation point.

5. All of the following materials are good conductors of heat except
   a. copper.
   b. silver.
   c. wood.
   d. aluminum.
6. The energy that is stored in fuels and foods is called
   a. kinetic energy.
   b. food energy.
   c. caloric energy.
   d. potential energy.
7. The phase change that takes place when a gas becomes a liquid is called
   a. evaporation.
   b. condensation.
   c. boiling.
   d. freezing.
8. A temperature of $20°C$ is equal to
   a. 293 K.
   b. 253 K.
   c. −253 K.
   d. −293 K.

True or False

If the statement is true, write "true." If it is false, change the underlined word or words to make the statement true.

1. Heat is transferred through liquids and gases by <u>radiation</u>.
2. Fast-moving molecules have <u>less</u> heat energy than slow-moving molecules.
3. An instrument used to measure temperature is a <u>calorimeter</u>.
4. Heat can be measured in calories or <u>kelvins</u>.
5. During a phase change, the temperature <u>does not</u> change.
6. Solid ice is <u>more</u> dense than liquid water.
7. Absolute zero is equal to the lowest reading on the <u>Kelvin</u> temperature scale.

Concept Mapping

Complete the following concept map for Section 17–1. Then construct a concept map for the entire chapter.

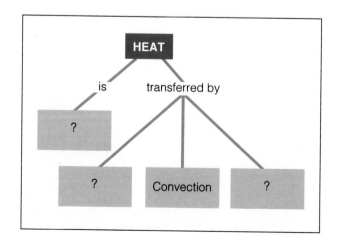

Concept Mastery

Discuss each of the following in a brief paragraph.

1. How did Count Rumford's experiment challenge the caloric theory of heat?
2. Explain why a temperature of –273°C is called absolute zero.
3. What is the relationship among work, heat, and energy?
4. Compare temperature and heat.
5. How does a thermometer make use of the property of thermal expansion?
6. Describe how a thermostat controls the temperature in a house.
7. Why does an ice cube float in water instead of sinking to the bottom of the glass?

Critical Thinking and Problem Solving

Use the skills you have developed in this chapter to answer each of the following.

1. **Applying concepts** Why is the air pressure in a car's tires different before and after the car has been driven for several hours?
2. **Interpreting graphs** Using the heating curve in Figure 17–20, explain what would happen to a 5-gram ice cube at 0°C if it were to gain 1000 calories of heat.
3. **Interpreting diagrams**
   a. In which container(s) is the heat content greatest?
   b. In which containers is the motion of molecules the same?
   c. Compare the motion of molecules in containers A and C.
   d. Compare the average kinetic energy of containers A and B.
   e. Which container needs the greatest number of calories to raise the temperature by 1 Celsius degree?

4. **Making comparisons** Compare the three methods of heat transfer in terms of how heat moves and the types of substances in which the transfer takes place.
5. **Applying concepts** Refer to the drawing of a thermos bottle in Figure 17–7 on page 429. Explain the importance of the cap, vacuum, double-walled glass bottle, and air space in preventing heat transfer.
6. **Analyzing data** A chemical reaction takes place in a calorimeter. The following data are obtained:

mass of water	500 g
initial temperature of water	30°C
final temperature of water	45°C

   How much heat, in calories and kilocalories, is released in this reaction?
7. **Using the writing process** Haiku is a form of poetry that began in Japan. A haiku has three lines. The first and third lines have five syllables each. The second line has seven syllables. Haiku may be used to describe scenes in nature and to express feelings. Write a haiku describing how you might feel on a frosty winter day or a sweltering summer day.

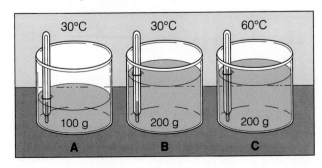

Uses of Heat

Guide for Reading

After you read the following sections, you will be able to

18–1 Heating Systems
- Distinguish among various types of heating systems.

18–2 Insulation
- Explain how insulation prevents heat loss.

18–3 Cooling Systems
- Describe the operation of a cooling system.

18–4 Heat Engines
- Explain how heat engines convert heat energy into mechanical energy.

18–5 Thermal Pollution
- Define thermal pollution and discuss its effects on the environment.

The year is 2064. Across the Midwest, an area at one time called the breadbasket of the nation, desert sands cover the once-fertile fields. In Arizona, the former desert is covered with the green, leafy canopy of a rain forest. Much of the coastline of eastern New York, including the skyscrapers of Manhattan, is under water.

Does this sound like a science fiction story? Although you may think these scenes are unbelievable, they are within the realm of possibility. Scientists report that the temperature of the Earth is gradually rising due to the greenhouse effect. Like the glass in a greenhouse, carbon dioxide and other gases in the Earth's atmosphere trap infrared radiation (heat) from the sun. The result is a kind of "heat blanket" wrapped around the Earth.

If the greenhouse effect continues to raise the Earth's temperature, heat may dramatically affect your life in the future. But did you know that heat plays an important role in your daily life right now? In this chapter you will learn how heat is obtained, used, and controlled. The more we understand about heat today, the better our chances may be of avoiding the greenhouse effect in the future.

Journal *Activity*

You and Your World In your journal, describe what you think your life might be like 20 or 30 years from now if the greenhouse effect continues to cause an increase in the Earth's temperature.

◀ *An artist's conception of what Manhattan may look like in the future if the greenhouse effect continues to raise Earth's average temperature*

Guide for Reading

Focus on this question as you read.

▶ *How do central heating systems work?*

Figure 18–1 *Heating systems have certainly changed over the years as people have progressed from fires in caves to warm hearths in a country home to a modern building heated entirely by the heat given off by computers.*

18–1 Heating Systems

Controlling the temperature of an indoor environment is one way to use an understanding of heat for a practical application. If you have ever been in a building that was either too hot or too cold, you know the importance of a good heating system. Most office buildings, homes, and apartment houses in the United States have **central heating systems** that provide comfortable environments for daily activities. **A central heating system generates heat for an entire building or group of buildings from one central location.** After the heat is generated, it is delivered where it is needed.

Based on how the heat is delivered, central heating systems are divided into two main groups: direct systems and indirect systems. A direct system circulates warm air throughout the area to be heated. An indirect system circulates hot water or steam through

pipes that lead to convectors or radiators. The convectors or radiators then give off heat in the area to be heated. Look around your home or classroom as you read this section. Can you tell what kind of heating system is in use? How do you know?

Although there are different types of central heating systems, they all require a source of heat, such as electricity or the burning of a fuel. All central heating systems also have automatic controls. These controls regulate the temperature of the area being heated, turn off the system if any part of it becomes dangerously overheated, and prevent the system from starting if conditions are unsafe.

Hot-Water Heating

A **hot-water system** consists of a network of pipes and convectors connected to a hot-water heater. Fuel burned in the hot-water heater raises the temperature of the water to about 82°C. (Remember, the boiling point of water is 100°C.) Then the water is pumped through pipes to a convector in each room. The hot water heats the convector. The heat given off by the convector is circulated throughout the room by convection currents. After the water has lost some of its heat, it returns to the hot-water heater through another pipe.

Figure 18–2 *A hot-water heating system (left) and a steam-heating system (right) are two common central heating systems that are quite similar. What is the major difference between the two systems?*

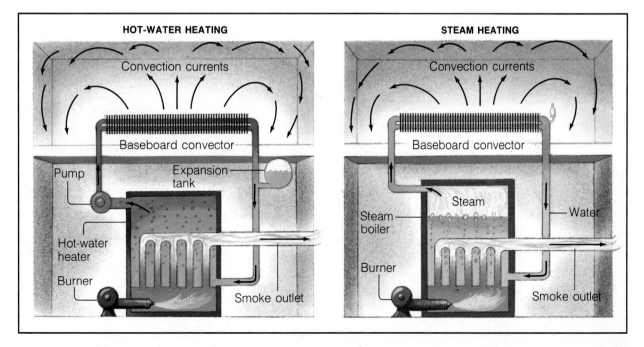

Steam Heating

A **steam-heating system** is similar to a hot-water system except that the water is changed into steam in a boiler. The steam is then forced through pipes to the convectors, where it gives off heat to the room. In giving off heat, the steam condenses, or changes from the gas phase to the liquid phase. The condensed steam, or water, then flows back to the boiler, where it is heated and changed into steam again.

Radiant Hot-Water Heating

In a **radiant hot-water system,** water is heated in a hot-water heater and then transferred to a continuous coil of pipe in the floor of each room. As heat radiates from the pipe, a nearly uniform temperature is maintained from floor to ceiling. This means that the temperature difference between the floor and the ceiling is only a few degrees. Why do you think radiant hot-water heating provides a more even temperature than steam heating or hot-water heating?

Figure 18–3 *In these central heating systems, heat is transferred by radiation. The source of heat in a radiant hot-water system (left) is hot water. In a radiant electric system (right), the source of heat is electricity.*

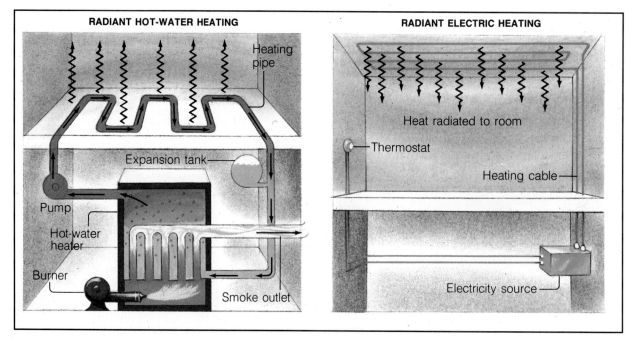

RADIANT HOT-WATER HEATING

Heating pipe

Expansion tank

Pump

Hot-water heater

Burner

Smoke outlet

RADIANT ELECTRIC HEATING

Heat radiated to room

Thermostat

Heating cable

Electricity source

Radiant Electric Heating

The source of heat for a **radiant electric system** is electricity. As electricity passes through wires or cables, the wires or cables resist the flow of electricity. As a result of this resistance, heat is produced. Think of the coils of wire in a toaster. As electricity passes through the wire, the heat produced toasts your bread or muffin.

The wires or cables in a radiant electric system can be installed in the ceiling, floor, baseboards, or walls of a room. The heat produced is radiated to all parts of the room. A thermostat, which is often installed in each room or local area, controls the amount of heat produced by the wires or cables.

Warm-Air Heating

A **warm-air system** consists of a furnace, a blower, pipelike connections called ducts, and vents that open into each room to be heated. The furnace heats the air, which is then forced by the blower through the ducts to the vents. Convection currents keep the warm air moving as it transfers its heat to the surrounding air. Cool air returns to the furnace by a separate duct. As the air circulates, filters remove dust particles.

Figure 18–4 *In a warm-air system (left), hot air from a furnace is forced to vents through pipelike connections called ducts. How is heat transferred in this system? A heat-pump system (right) takes heat from the outside and brings it inside—even in cold weather! What two phase changes are involved in this heating system?*

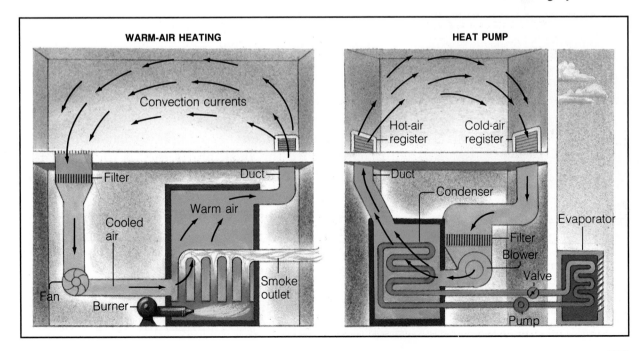

WARM-AIR HEATING — Convection currents — Filter — Duct — Warm air — Cooled air — Smoke outlet — Fan — Burner

HEAT PUMP — Hot-air register — Cold-air register — Duct — Condenser — Filter — Blower — Valve — Evaporator — Pump

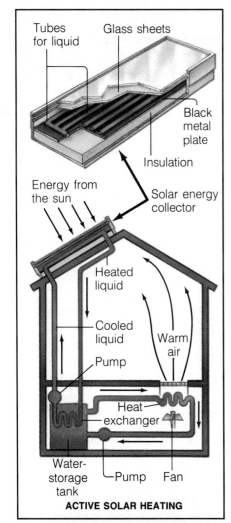

Tubes for liquid
Glass sheets
Black metal plate
Insulation
Energy from the sun
Solar energy collector
Heated liquid
Cooled liquid
Warm air
Pump
Heat exchanger
Water-storage tank
Pump
Fan

ACTIVE SOLAR HEATING

Figure 18–5 *Water in the solar panel of an active solar system is heated by the sun and piped to a storage tank. Here it heats water in the water tank. This heated water then circulates through pipes to heat the house. Why is the metal plate in the solar panel painted black?*

Heat Pumps

A **heat-pump system** is based on the principle that the Earth or outside air contains heat energy that can be used to heat an indoor area—even in cold weather! What a heat pump actually does is take heat from outside a building and bring it inside.

Through a coil outside the building that is to be heated, a heat pump circulates a liquid that evaporates (changes from the liquid phase to the gas phase) at a low temperature. As the liquid passes through the coil, it picks up heat from the air or the ground. Eventually the liquid gains enough heat to change to a gas. The gas travels into a compressor, where an increase in pressure results in an increase in temperature. The hot gas then passes to a coil inside the building, where it heats the air. The warm air is forced through ducts and circulated through each room just as in a warm-air system.

Once the hot gas has given off its heat, it condenses into a hot liquid. The hot liquid is then cooled as it passes through a pressure-reducing valve. Finally, the cooled liquid is pumped into the outdoor coil to begin the process all over again. What might be some disadvantages in this type of heating system?

Solar Heating

A **solar-heating system** uses the energy of the sun to produce heat. There are two basic types of solar-heating systems: active solar heating and passive solar heating.

An **active solar-heating system** includes a device for collecting solar energy (called a solar collector), a place to store the heat, and a means for circulating the heat throughout a building. The diagram in Figure 18–5 shows a typical active solar-heating system. Refer to the diagram as you read the description that follows.

The solar collector, also called a flat-plate collector, consists of a metal plate painted black on the side that faces the sun. (Black absorbs sunlight better than any other color.) As the sunlight is absorbed, the plate heats up. On the surface of

Activity Bank

Let the Sun Shine In, p.754

Figure 18–6 *In the Mojave Desert, California, hundreds of mirrors in an array called Solar One reflect solar radiation onto a tower filled with water. How might the heated water in the tower be used?*

the plate is an array of metal tubing. Water, or some other liquid, circulates through the tubing. The tubing is covered by glass or clear plastic to keep it from losing heat. Why do you think glass or clear plastic is used for this purpose?

As sunlight strikes the collector, heat is absorbed. The heat absorbed by the collector is transferred to the water. The heated water flows through a tube into a storage tank. Here the heat from the water in the tube is transferred to the water in the tank by a heat exchanger in the tank. The hot water circulates through pipes to heat the building or to heat air blown into the building. In the meantime, a pump returns the cool water to the collector to be reheated by the sun. On cloudy days, when the solar collector cannot absorb enough solar energy to produce hot water and the storage system has cooled, a backup heating system is used.

In a **passive solar-heating system,** a building is heated directly by the rays of the sun. To get the most heat from a passive solar system, the building must be designed with the placement, size, and orientation of the windows in mind.

ACTIVITY

DISCOVERING

Black and White

Try this activity to demonstrate the effect of color on heat. You will need a piece of black construction paper, a piece of white construction paper, a candle, and an electric light bulb.

1. Light the candle. **CAUTION:** *Be careful when using an open flame.* Let one drop of wax from the candle fall on each piece of construction paper. Blow out the candle.

2. Hold both pieces of construction paper exactly the same distance from an electric light bulb. On which piece of paper does the wax melt first?

■ If you want to keep cool on a hot summer day, should you wear dark-colored clothes or light-colored clothes? Why?

Heat From the Sun

1. Place a piece of paper on a flat surface in direct sunlight.

2. Hold a small magnifying glass (such as a hand lens) above the paper.

3. Position the magnifying glass so that the sun's rays are focused to a point on the paper. What happens to the paper? Why?

Because of the variations in the amount of solar energy received at a particular location, passive solar systems are usually not the only source of heat for a building. A backup heating system usually must be used with a passive solar system. The backup system provides heat when sunlight is not available or when the heat collected during the day is not enough to keep the building warm on a cold night. What conditions do you think affect the amount of solar energy a location receives?

Figure 18–7 *To keep itself warm on cold days, this iguana basks in the sun. Is the iguana using a form of active or passive solar heating?*

18–1 Section Review

1. What is a central heating system?
2. How does a steam-heating system differ from a hot-water system?
3. Describe how a radiant electric system produces heat. Why is this system different from other central heating systems?
4. What is the basic difference between an active solar-heating system and a passive solar-heating system?

Critical Thinking—*Sequencing Events*
5. Describe in order the heat transfers and phase changes involved in a heat-pump system.

18–2 Insulation

What happens after a central heating system brings heat into a building? Once heat is brought into a room or building, it will quickly begin to escape if the area does not have proper **insulation.** Recall from Chapter 17 that insulating materials reduce heat transfer because they are poor conductors of heat. **Insulation prevents heat loss by reducing the transfer of heat that occurs by conduction and convection.**

A common insulating material is **fiberglass.** Fiberglass consists of long, thin strands of glass packed together. In between the strands of glass are air spaces. Glass is a poor conductor of heat. So is the air that is trapped between the glass fibers. A down-filled vest or jacket uses the same principle to keep you warm in winter. Air trapped in the spaces between the down prevents the loss of body heat. (Down is the inner layer of soft, fluffy feathers on birds such as ducks and geese. How do you think down feathers help keep birds warm?)

Insulating materials are packed beneath roofs and in the outside walls of buildings. Insulation can also be used around doors and windows. This type

Activity Bank

Turn Down the Heat, p.755

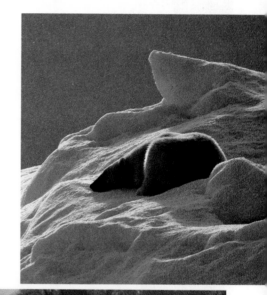

Figure 18–8 *How does insulation protect the polar bear, the bison, and the geese from the cold?*

Figure 18–9 *Invisible heat energy, or infrared energy, can be "seen" by using a device called a thermograph. This thermogram, or heat picture, reveals heat loss from a house. Generally, the lighter and brighter the color, the greater the heat loss. How can a thermogram be useful to homeowners?*

ACTIVITY

WRITING

What Is the Value of Insulation?

The effectiveness of an insulating material is measured according to its R-value. Using books and other reference materials from the library, find out what the R-value of insulating materials is based on. Look up the R-values of common insulating materials such as brick, concrete, ceramic tile, stucco, fiberglass, wood, and plastic foam. Rank the materials according to their effectiveness.

of insulation is called weatherstripping. Weatherstripping prevents heat loss by closing off spaces through which heat can be transferred by convection. Double-pane window glass is another effective insulator. The air trapped between the panes of glass does not conduct heat well. In addition, the air space is so small that heat transfer by convection cannot take place.

A well-insulated building is as comfortable in hot weather as it is in cold weather. In cold weather, insulation keeps heat inside the building. In hot weather, the insulation keeps heat out. The building is kept relatively cool as heat from the outside is prevented from entering the building by either conduction or convection. Good insulation also helps lower fuel costs. Why do you think this is so?

18–2 Section Review

1. What is insulation? What is the purpose of insulation?
2. How does fiberglass prevent heat loss?
3. Why is good insulation important in both hot weather and cold weather?
4. Explain how insulation prevents heat loss by both conduction and convection.

Connection—*You and Your World*

5. The cardboard used to make pizza boxes is naturally brown in color. Why would the companies that manufacture the boxes spend extra money to make them white? What else could they do to the boxes to make them better insulators?

Figure 18–10 *Believe it or not, blocks of ice can be used to insulate a home, as this Eskimo of the Arctic Circle well knows. How is an igloo insulated?*

18–3 Cooling Systems

Have you ever had this experience? On a hot summer day, you jump into a swimming pool to cool off. After climbing out of the swimming pool, you feel a chill—even though the sun is just as hot as it was before you got wet. What causes this cooling effect? The cooling effect is due to evaporation. The water molecules on your skin absorb heat from your body as the water evaporates, or changes from the liquid phase to the gas phase. This absorption of heat lowers your body temperature. Thus evaporation is a cooling process.

You can test the cooling effect of evaporation for yourself. Put a drop of water on the back of your hand. Now blow gently on your hand. Which feels cooler: the wet skin or the dry skin? How does perspiration help cool you when you are overheated?

The process of evaporation is used by cooling systems to remove heat energy from a room, building, or other enclosed space. Refrigerators, air conditioners, and dehumidifiers all contain **cooling systems.**

A cooling system consists of four basic parts: a storage tank, a freezer unit, a compressor, and condenser coils. A cooling system also contains a refrigerant. The refrigerant is the liquid that is evaporated. Refrigerants evaporate at a low temperature. Many cooling systems use Freon (FREE-ahn) as the refrigerant. Another common refrigerant is ammonia.

The diagram in Figure 18–11 shows how a typical refrigerator system works. Liquid Freon in the storage tank is pumped to the freezer unit. As the liquid refrigerant evaporates, it absorbs heat from the freezer compartment. So the inside of the refrigerator becomes cool. The Freon gas then flows to a compressor, where the pressure of the gas (and its temperature) is increased. The hot gaseous Freon then passes through the condenser coils, where it loses its heat and changes back into a liquid. The liquid Freon then returns to the storage tank and the process begins again.

The heat removed from the freezer compartment of a refrigerator is radiated from the condenser coils to the outside air. The condenser coils are often

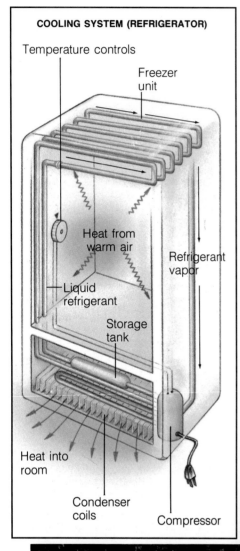

COOLING SYSTEM (REFRIGERATOR)

Temperature controls

Freezer unit

Heat from warm air

Liquid refrigerant

Refrigerant vapor

Storage tank

Heat into room

Condenser coils

Compressor

Figure 18–11 *Without refrigeration systems, ice hockey could not be an indoor sport. In this diagram, you can see how the basic parts of a refrigerator work as a cooling system. What phase change takes place in the freezer unit? In the condenser coils?*

PROBLEM Solving

Freon and the Ozone Layer

High in the Earth's atmosphere is a layer of gas called the ozone layer. Ozone is a form of oxygen. The ozone layer blocks harmful ultraviolet radiation from the sun from reaching the Earth. (Ultraviolet radiation can cause certain types of skin cancer.) The Freon used in refrigerators eventually escapes into the atmosphere and reaches the ozone layer, where it changes some of the ozone into oxygen. Not too long ago, scientists discovered a "hole" in the ozone layer over Antarctica.

This satellite map shows severe holes (blue areas) in the ozone layer over Antarctica.

Relating Cause and Effect

1. What might happen to the ozone layer if more and more Freon is produced and released into the atmosphere?

2. What effect might this have on human health?

3. What do you think might be done in the future to help protect the ozone layer?

located on the back of a refrigerator. Fans are sometimes used to blow away the air that is heated by the coils. You should be careful not to touch the coils, which can become quite hot. Although you may think it sounds strange, you can burn yourself on a refrigerator!

18–3 Section Review

1. How does a cooling system use the process of evaporation?
2. What are the basic parts of a cooling system?
3. What is a refrigerant? What happens to the refrigerant in a cooling system?

Connection—*You and Your World*

4. Is it a good idea to try to cool a room by opening the door of the refrigerator? Why or why not?

ACTIVITY DOING

Evaporation and Cooling

1. Place a drop of water on the back of your hand. How does your hand feel as the water evaporates?

2. Repeat step 1 using a drop of rubbing alcohol. Is there any difference in the rate of evaporation?

3. Wrap a small piece of wet cotton around the bulb of a thermometer. Fan it gently with a piece of cardboard. What happens to the temperature?

Guide for Reading

Focus on this question as you read.

▶ *How do heat engines use heat energy to do work?*

18–4 Heat Engines

You learned in Chapter 17 that the experiments of Rumford and Joule showed that work produces heat. **Heat engines** make use of the reverse process. **Heat engines are machines that convert heat energy into mechanical energy in order to do work.** (Any form of energy, such as heat, can be converted into any other form of energy.) Mechanical energy is the energy associated with motion. What is another name for energy of motion?

All heat engines involve **combustion.** Combustion is the burning of a fuel. During combustion, a fuel is heated to a temperature at which it combines with oxygen in the air and gives off heat. Heat engines are classified into two main types according to where combustion takes place.

External-Combustion Engines

In an **external-combustion engine,** fuel is burned outside the engine. The steam engine is an example of an external-combustion engine. In a steam engine, steam is heated in a boiler outside the engine and then passed through a valve into the engine. In early steam engines, the steam pushed

Figure 18–12 *An external-combustion engine, as shown in the diagram, converts heat energy into mechanical energy. The wheels of a steam train are powered by an external-combustion engine.*

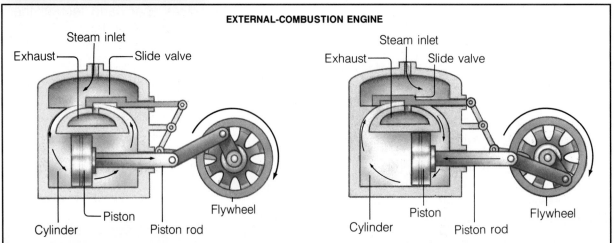

EXTERNAL-COMBUSTION ENGINE

against a metal plate called a piston, which moved back and forth in a tube called a cylinder. The movement of the piston transferred mechanical energy to a connecting rod, which then did some kind of work, such as turning the wheels of a train or the propellers of a steamship.

Modern steam engines do not use a piston and a cylinder. Instead, steam under great pressure is passed through holes onto paddle wheels called turbines. The turbines, which rotate like high-speed windmills, produce mechanical energy. A steam turbine is more efficient than a piston and a cylinder because it wastes less energy.

Internal-Combustion Engine

When the burning of a fuel takes place inside an engine, the engine is called an **internal-combustion engine.** A familiar type of internal-combustion engine is the gasoline engine, which powers most cars.

Most gasoline engines are four-stroke engines. The diagram in Figure 18–13 on page 468 shows the four strokes that make up each cycle in a gasoline engine. In the first stroke, the piston inside the cylinder moves down and the intake valve opens. Gasoline that was changed from a liquid to a gas and mixed with air in the carburetor (KAHR-buh-rayt-er) enters the cylinder through the intake valve. This process is the intake stroke.

The intake valve closes and the piston moves to the top of the cylinder. As it does, the gaseous mixture is compressed, or squeezed together, so that the volume of the mixture is greatly reduced. This process is the compression stroke.

At this point in the four-stroke cycle, with both valves closed, a spark plug produces an electric spark that ignites the compressed fuel mixture. The explosion of hot gases increases the volume of the mixture and forces the piston back down in the cylinder. This is the power stroke. At this point energy is transferred from the piston to the wheels of the car by a series of shafts and gears.

In the final stroke, the exhaust valve opens. The piston moves to the top of the cylinder and expels gases through the exhaust valve. This process is called the exhaust stroke.

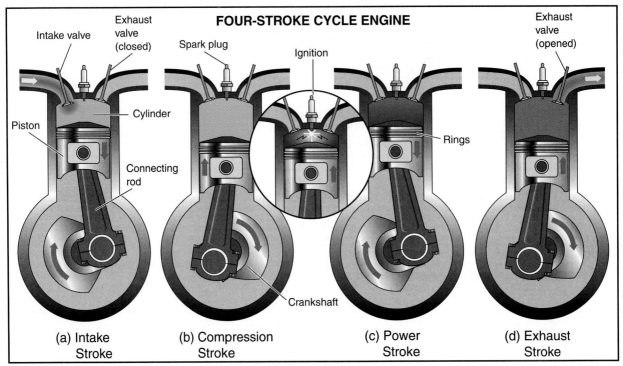

FOUR-STROKE CYCLE ENGINE

Intake valve

Exhaust valve (closed)

Spark plug

Ignition

Exhaust valve (opened)

Piston

Cylinder

Connecting rod

Rings

Crankshaft

(a) Intake Stroke

(b) Compression Stroke

(c) Power Stroke

(d) Exhaust Stroke

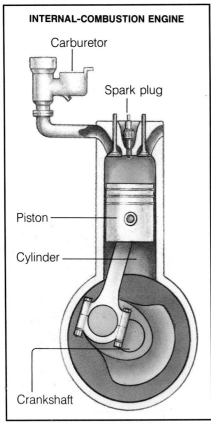

INTERNAL-COMBUSTION ENGINE

Carburetor

Spark plug

Piston

Cylinder

Crankshaft

Figure 18–13 *A gasoline engine is a four-stroke internal-combustion engine. Here you see the processes involved in each stroke. During which stroke is energy transferred from the piston to the wheels of the car?*

As the piston moves back down, more gaseous fuel and air mixture from the carburetor enters the cylinder to begin the four-stroke cycle again. A fixed amount of gasoline is used in each cycle, and waste products are given off as exhaust at the end of each cycle. It is important to use clean-burning fuel in car engines to reduce the amount of impurities given off in the exhaust.

A diesel engine, like a gasoline engine, is an internal-combustion engine. But in a diesel engine, only air is taken in during the intake stroke. At the end of the compression stroke, a measured amount of fuel is injected into the compressed air in the cylinder. The compression of the air raises its temperature high enough so that the fuel ignites at once. For this reason a diesel engine does not need spark plugs. Why do you think a diesel engine might more correctly be called a compression-ignition engine?

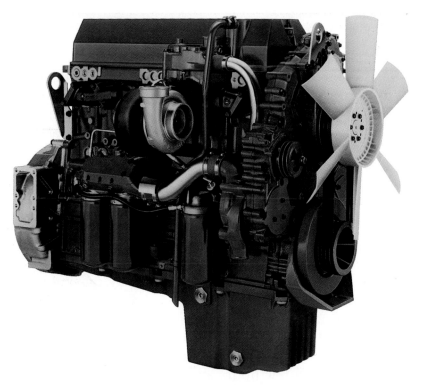

Figure 18–14 *Diesel engines are more efficient than gasoline engines. However, diesel engines have some drawbacks. They may be difficult to start in cold weather and tend to be noisier than gasoline engines.*

18–4 Section Review

1. How does a heat engine work?
2. What are the two main types of heat engines? How are they different?
3. Describe what happens in the four-stroke cycle of a gasoline engine. How is this different from what happens in a diesel engine?

Critical Thinking—*Applying Concepts*

4. Several car manufacturers are working on cars that use two-stroke engines instead of four-stroke engines. These two-stroke engines eliminate the intake stroke and the exhaust stroke, and they make use of modern fuel-injection techniques during the compression stroke. Why do you think a two-stroke engine might be more efficient than a four-stroke engine?

ACTIVITY
READING

Earth's Future?

How could such human activities as thermal pollution, the greenhouse effect, and the thinning of the ozone layer possibly affect the Earth's future? For a look at what the Earth might be like in the year 2038, read the science-fiction novel *Earth* by David Brin.

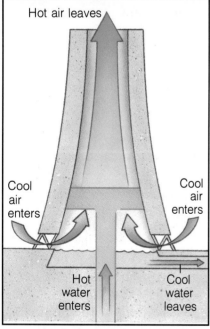

Hot air leaves

Cool air enters

Cool air enters

Hot water enters

Cool water leaves

Figure 18–15 *These cooling towers at a nuclear-power plant are used to reduce thermal pollution. Hot water from the power plant is cooled as it flows through pipes suspended in the tower. Why is thermal pollution harmful?*

18–5 Thermal Pollution

Modern technology could not exist without the use of heat energy. Yet like many aspects of technology, heat energy can be harmful to the environment. The environment includes the air, land, and water.

Much of the heat generated by industrial processes and power plants cannot be used. It is waste heat. This waste heat is often released directly into the atmosphere. Or it may be released as hot water—just dumped into nearby rivers and lakes. **Thermal pollution** results. Pollution is anything that damages the environment. **Thermal pollution occurs when waste heat damages the environment by causing an unnatural rise in temperature.**

Thermal pollution endangers the survival of plants and animals. Fishes are especially vulnerable to increases in water temperature. Some species can survive only a few hours at temperatures above 25°C.

What can be done to reduce thermal pollution from factories and power plants? One solution is the use of a cooling tower. In a cooling tower, hot water from a factory or power plant is cooled as it flows through pipes. By the time the water is released into a nearby river or lake, it has cooled enough so that it is no longer a threat to fishes and other wildlife.

18–5 Section Review

1. What is thermal pollution? What types of wildlife are threatened by thermal pollution?
2. What is the source of the heat that causes thermal pollution?
3. According to Figure 18–15 what happens to the excess heat after the water is cooled in the cooling tower?

Connection—*Life Science*

4. Manatees are aquatic mammals that live in warm rivers and streams in Florida. These animals are attracted to the hot water released by power plants. How might the manatees be affected if the power plants were shut down?

CONNECTIONS

Using Cold to Fight Cancer

What does heat—or rather the lack of it—have to do with cancer? Doctors are presently testing a new way to use *cryosurgery* to combat some forms of cancer. The prefix *cryo-* means cold or freezing. Cryosurgery is the use of extreme cold to destroy diseased tissue. This is not a new technique. Dermatologists have used cryosurgery for years to destroy skin tumors. What is new is the way in which cryosurgery can now be used to destroy cancerous tumors inside the body.

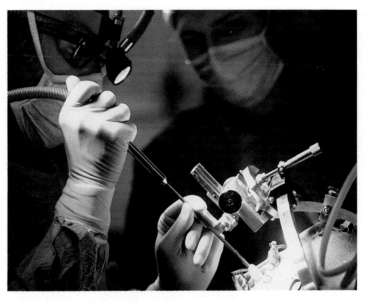

When cancer cells spread through the body, one of the internal organs in which they may settle is the liver. Today, more than 65,000 people in the United States develop liver cancer every year. Conventional surgery for liver cancer is complicated and dangerous (and sometimes impossible). Few liver cancer patients survive more than a few years after surgery.

Cryosurgery involves using a thin probe to freeze tumors. Once the probe has been inserted into the liver, liquid nitrogen at a temperature of about −200°C flows through the probe and freezes the tumor, destroying the cancer cells. Surgeons can watch this process, which takes about 15 minutes, on an ultrasound monitor.

The long-term survival rate for liver cancer patients following cryosurgery has been found to be much higher than for conventional surgery. Doctors are now attempting to refine this technique and to expand its use to destroy tumors in other parts of the body, including the brain.

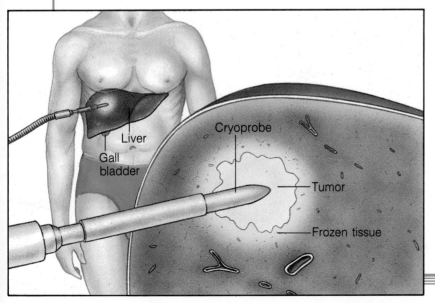

Liver

Gall bladder

Cryoprobe

Tumor

Frozen tissue

Laboratory Investigation

Building a Solar Collector

Problem

How can solar energy be collected?

Materials *(per group)*

shoe box, painted black on the inside
newspaper, painted black
rubber or plastic tubing, 1 mm diameter x
  1 m long
funnel   container, 1 L capacity
ring stand and ring   graduated cylinder
thermometer   plastic wrap
250-mL beaker   pencil

Procedure 🧪

1. Fill the inside of the shoe box with crumpled newspaper. Using a pencil, punch a hole in each end of the shoe box, as shown in the diagram.

2. Insert the tubing through the holes and position it inside the box as shown. Be sure to leave at least 10 cm of tubing sticking out each end of the box.

3. Cover the box tightly with plastic wrap.

4. Place the box in direct sunlight, tilting one end so that it is about 5 cm higher than the other end.

5. Attach the funnel to the tubing at the higher end of the box. Use the ring stand and ring to hold the funnel in place.

6. Position a beaker at the other end of the box to serve as the collecting beaker.

7. Fill the container with 1 L of water at room temperature. Measure and record the temperature of the water.

8. Pour 200 mL of water from the container into the graduated cylinder.

9. Now pour the 200 mL of water from the graduated cylinder into the funnel.

10. Repeat steps 8 and 9 for a total of five trials. After every trial, record the number of the trial and the temperature of the water in the collecting beaker. **Note:** *Empty the collecting beaker after every trial.*

11. Record your data on a graph. Plot the trial number along the X axis and the water temperature along the Y axis.

Observations

What happened to the water temperature as the number of trials increased? Does your graph support this observation?

Analysis and Conclusions

1. How can you explain the different temperatures that you recorded?

2. **On Your Own** How could you make your solar collector more effective?

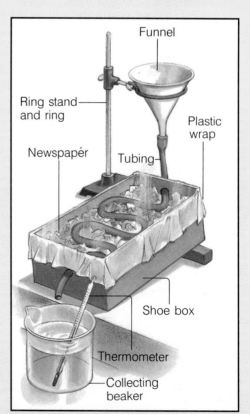

Funnel

Ring stand and ring

Plastic wrap

Newspaper

Tubing

Shoe box

Thermometer

Collecting beaker

Study Guide

Summarizing Key Concepts

18–1 Heating Systems

▲ Based on the way heat is delivered, central heating systems are classified as direct or indirect systems.

▲ Major types of central heating systems include hot water, steam, radiant hot water, radiant electric, warm air, heat pump, and solar.

18–2 Insulation

▲ Insulation prevents heat loss by reducing the transfer of heat from a building by conduction and convection.

▲ Insulating a building is as important in hot weather as it is in cold weather.

18–3 Cooling Systems

▲ Cooling systems use the process of evaporation to remove heat from the surroundings.

▲ A cooling system consists of a storage tank, freezer unit, compressor, condenser coils, and refrigerant.

▲ A refrigerant is a liquid that evaporates at a low temperature.

18–4 Heat Engines

▲ Heat engines convert heat energy into mechanical energy to do work.

▲ All heat engines involve combustion, or the burning of a fuel.

▲ In an external-combustion engine, fuel is burned outside the engine.

▲ In an internal-combustion engine, such as a gasoline engine, fuel is burned inside the engine.

▲ The four strokes in a gasoline engine are the intake stroke, the compression stroke, the power stroke, and the exhaust stroke.

18–5 Thermal Pollution

▲ Thermal pollution occurs when waste heat damages the environment by causing an unnatural rise in temperature.

Reviewing Key Terms

Define each term in a complete sentence.

18–1 Heating Systems
central heating system
hot-water system
steam-heating system
radiant hot-water system
radiant electric system
warm-air system
heat-pump system
solar-heating system
active solar-heating system
passive solar-heating system

18–2 Insulation
insulation
fiberglass

18–3 Cooling Systems
cooling system

18–4 Heat Engines
heat engine
combustion
external-combustion engine
internal-combustion engine

18–5 Thermal Pollution
thermal pollution

Chapter Review

Content Review

Multiple Choice

Choose the letter of the answer that best completes each statement.

1. The heating system that uses the energy of the sun to produce heat is a
   a. radiant hot-water system.
   b. radiant electric system.
   c. solar-heating system.
   d. warm-air system.
2. Heat engines convert heat energy into
   a. chemical energy.
   b. mechanical energy.
   c. light energy.
   d. nuclear energy.
3. Which of the following is an insulating material?
   a. fiberglass   c. copper
   b. Freon   d. ammonia
4. Thermal pollution damages the environment by increasing
   a. dust particles in the air.
   b. engine exhaust.
   c. infrared radiation.
   d. temperature.

5. A cooling system contains all of the following parts except a(an)
   a. compressor.   c. freezer unit.
   b. storage tank.   d. exhaust valve.
6. All central heating systems require a(an)
   a. refrigerant.   c. insulator.
   b. heat source.   d. compressor.
7. One way to reduce thermal pollution is by using a
   a. turbine.   c. cooling system.
   b. cooling tower.   d. heating system.
8. In a cooling system, condenser coils are used to
   a. change the refrigerant from a liquid to a gas.
   b. increase the pressure of the refrigerant.
   c. change the refrigerant from a gas back into a liquid.
   d. increase the temperature of the refrigerant.

True or False

If the statement is true, write "true." If it is false, change the underlined word or words to make the statement true.

1. A solar collector is part of a <u>passive</u> solar-heating system.
2. Double-pane window glass prevents heat loss by reducing heat transfer by convection and <u>radiation</u>.
3. Thermal pollution probably <u>would not</u> be a problem for fishes living in a lake near a power plant.
4. In a diesel engine, fuel is injected into the cylinder during the <u>intake</u> stroke.
5. The type of heating system that produces a nearly uniform temperature in a room is a <u>steam-heating system</u>.

Concept Mapping

Complete the following concept map for Section 18–1. Then construct a concept map for the entire chapter.

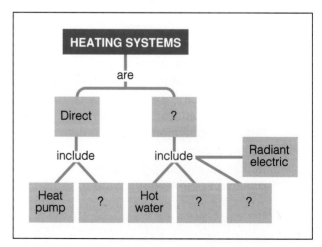

Concept Mastery

Discuss each of the following in a brief paragraph.

1. Assume that a factory or power plant is located near each of the following: an ocean, a river, and a lake. Which body of water would probably be most affected by thermal pollution? Which would be least affected? Explain your answers.
2. Choose one type of heat engine and describe how it changes heat energy into mechanical energy to do work.
3. Choose one type of central heating system and describe how it works.
4. Explain the difference between a passive solar-heating system and an active solar-heating system.
5. Why is fiberglass a good insulating material?
6. Explain how a cooling system works.

Critical Thinking and Problem Solving

Use the skills you have developed in this chapter to answer each of the following.

1. **Making diagrams** Draw a diagram showing how a heat-pump system gathers heat from the outside air and uses this heat to warm air inside a building. Be sure to label your diagram.
2. **Classifying** Classify each of the following central heating systems as direct or indirect: warm air, hot water, steam, heat pump, radiant hot water, solar.
3. **Interpreting photographs** Does the building in the photograph make use of an active solar-heating system or a passive solar-heating system? How can you tell?

4. **Making inferences** Why do you think an alcohol rub might at one time have been used to help a person with a high fever?
5. **Applying concepts** Explain how each of the following insulating materials works: plastic foam used in a picnic cooler; goose down used in a ski jacket; aluminum foil used to wrap hot food for a takeout order.
6. **Making comparisons** Describe how a gasoline engine and a diesel engine are alike and how they are different.
7. **Using the writing process** Pretend that you are James Watt, the eighteenth-century Scottish engineer who is credited with developing an efficient steam engine. Write a letter to a friend describing your invention and explaining how it works. Include a sketch of your steam engine and some suggestions for practical applications.

GAZETTE

JENEFIR ISBISTER:
SHE DOES DIRTY WORK FOR CLEANER COAL

Jenefir Isbister knelt in the blackened soil outside a Pennsylvania coal mine. With a garden trowel, she scooped some dry black soil into a plastic box. The next day, she dug up some soil from outside a coal-processing plant near the laboratory in which she works. She even scooped up a little mud from the bank of a creek in her own backyard.

Why was Dr. Isbister collecting all this soil? "My boss asked me to find a microor-ganism to remove sulfur from coal," she explains. And such a microorganism might make its home in coal-rich soil. Dr. Isbister is an expert on microorganisms, or living things that are too small to be seen without special equipment. Microorganisms include a variety of bacteria.

Many microorganisms—often called microbes—feed upon nature's garbage, such as fallen leaves and the remains of dead animals and plants. The microbe that Dr. Isbister was searching for was one that eats the sulfur in coal—a sulfur-eating coal bug.

But why would Isbister be looking for such a thing? As she puts it, "A coal bug could help solve the problem of acid rain." In many parts of the world, acid rain is a serious problem whose effects include the death of trees, fishes, and other living things.

Acid rain is often caused by burning coal that contains high levels of sulfur. The coal smoke produced contains sulfur dioxide. Sulfur dioxide chemically combines with water in the air to form sulfuric acid, a very strong acid. The acid falls to the Earth as acid rain, acid snow, and even acid fog.

One way to reduce acid rain, then, is to remove as much sulfur as possible from the coal. Washing the coal before burning it is the simplest method of scrubbing out the sulfur. But coal washing is expensive and removes only some of the sulfur. Prying more sulfur out of coal requires a chemical reaction—the kind of chemical reaction microbes produce when they dine.

"A sulfur-eating microbe would let us use high-sulfur coal," Dr. Isbister explains. And high-sulfur coal is relatively inexpensive and plentiful.

So Dr. Isbister began collecting soil in the hope of finding a microbe that eats sulfur. "Soil is the best place to look for microorganisms that will grow under many conditions," she explains. "We didn't want bugs we had to baby!"

In the first step of experimentation, Dr. Isbister and Dr. Richard Doyle, a coworker at the Atlantic Research Corporation in Alexandria, Virginia, crushed each soil sample and placed a small amount of each in separate flasks of salt solution. "The solution keeps the microbes alive while we separate them from the soil," Isbister explains.

A special machine was then used to wash the bugs out of the soil in each flask. Liquid from the top of each flask was then added to another flask filled with nutrient broth. "It's a kind of soup that feeds the microorganisms," explains Isbister.

Next, the researchers added sulfur to each microbe broth. "We did lots of tests. After a long time, we found one solution that contained less sulfur than we had put in," says Isbister. The microbes in this broth had done the best job of eating sulfur. Surprisingly, the sulfur-eating microbes were the ones from her own backyard! Unfortunately, it had taken the microbes 7 days to lower the sulfur level by only 7 percent. "Seven percent is very little; seven days is horrible," says Isbister. "But it was a start. We had a little celebration."

Now the team added powerful chemicals to the broth, hoping to change the microbes' basic metabolism, or cell processes. The goal was to make the microbes even hungrier for sulfur.

"I tested 250 chemical combinations," Isbister recalls. Finally, she found one combination that caused the microbes to eat 80 percent of the sulfur in just 18 hours. "Then we really celebrated, and Dr. Doyle and I applied for a patent on Coal Bug One." Coal Bug One is the nickname the researchers have given their sulfur-eating microbe. Two and one-half years of research had finally resulted in success.

Will Coal Bug One solve the problem of high-sulfur coal? "Coal Bug One eats just one of the many kinds of sulfur found in coal," Isbister replies. "So we'll need to find more bugs. But Coal Bug One is the first step."

▼ Coal Bug One, shown here in an electromicrograph (left), may solve the problem of burning high-sulfur coal (right).

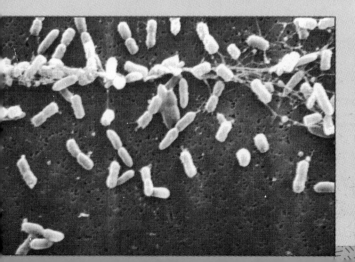

Electricity and Magnetism

As if made of flesh and blood, these computer-controlled dinosaurs appear to be munching on assorted fruits.

Huge dinosaurs roar wildly as they tower over your head. Some cause the ground to tremble merely by walking past you. Have you been transported back in time? No. You are at Epcot Center in Walt Disney World where animated creatures are designed and controlled by computers.

Although this computer application is specifically designed to amuse and entertain you, other computer applications have more scientific and informational uses. Researchers can enter available data into computers in order to build complete, moving models of subjects that can only be imagined—not observed. For example, computers have enabled scientists to design a wide range of new products, simulate various aspects of prehistoric life, and hypothesize about the features of distant planets and galaxies. The beauty of such applications is that designers—whether they are interested in the past, present, or future—can build, experiment with, and improve upon models with the speed, accuracy, and safety of a computer and its display devices.

The design of many new products is aided by computers. In this way designers can observe a new product, such as this shoe, and test various features of the product before it is manufactured.

CHAPTERS

Much of the technology that makes computer applications possible is more familiar than you might think. In this Unit you will discover that the phenomona of electricity and magnetism reach far beyond household appliances and industrial devices. They reach into the heart of present and future technology.

It would be quite costly for automobile manufacturers to constantly build test models of new cars. Instead, computers enable designers to create models on a screen. This computer model is being tested for aerodynamic efficiency. ▶

Discovery *Activity*

Flying Through Air With the Greatest of Ease

1. Inflate a balloon and tie the end.

2. Bring the balloon within centimeters of a plate filled with a mixture of salt and pepper. Observe for 3 to 5 minutes.

3. Take the balloon away from the plate. Rub the balloon with a piece of wool. Repeat step 2.

   ■ How is the behavior of the salt and pepper different before and after you rub the balloon with wool?

4. Arrange small piles of each of the following materials: paper clips, rubber bands, pieces of paper, assorted metal and plastic buttons. Make sure that each of the piles is separated from the others.

5. Hold a magnet above the first pile without touching it. Observe what happens. Repeat this procedure over each of the remaining piles.

   ■ What happens to each of the materials when you place the magnet above it? What can you conclude about how different materials are affected by a magnet?

Electric Charges and Currents

Guide for Reading

After you read the following sections, you will be able to

19–1 Electric Charge
- Relate electric charge to atomic structure.
- Describe the forces that exist between charged particles.

19–2 Static Electricity
- Describe the effects of static electricity.

19–3 The Flow of Electricity
- Describe the nature of current electricity.

19–4 Electric Circuits
- Identify the parts of an electric circuit.
- Compare a series and a parallel circuit.

19–5 Electric Power
- Explain how electric power is calculated and purchased.

Have you ever experienced a severe thunderstorm accompanied by cracks of thunder and flashes of lightning? One of the most spectacular sights in nature is a forked bolt of lightning lancing downward from a black storm cloud and illuminating everything in its path with its ghostly light. Of all the forces of nature, lightning is one of the most powerful. Every year thousands of forest fires are started by lightning strikes. And many people are injured or even killed when they are struck by lightning. As you will learn in this chapter, lightning is a form of electricity.

For hundreds of years, many people were frightened by electricity and believed it to have mysterious powers. Today a great deal is known about electricity and the powerful role it plays in your world. Electricity is involved in all interactions of everyday matter—from the motion of a car to the movement of a muscle to the growth of a tree. Electricity makes life easier and more comfortable. In this chapter you will discover what electicity is, how it is produced and used, and why it is so important.

Journal *Activity*

You and Your World Did you switch on a light, shut off an alarm clock, listen to the radio, or turn on a hair dryer today? In your journal, describe the importance of electricity in your daily life. Include any questions you may have about electricity.

A summer lightning storm breaks over the Saguaro National Monument outside Tucson, Arizona.

19–1 Electric Charge

Have you ever rubbed a balloon on your clothing to make it stick to you or to a wall? Or have you ever pulled your favorite shirt out of the clothes dryer only to find socks sticking to it? How can objects be made to stick to one another without glue or tape? Believe it or not, the answer has to do with electricity. And the origin of electricity is in the particles that make up matter.

Atoms and Electricity

All matter is made of atoms. Recall from Chapter 5 that an atom is the smallest particle of an element that has all the properties of that element. An element contains only one kind of atom. For example, the element lead is made of only lead atoms. The element gold is made of only gold atoms.

Atoms themselves are made of even smaller particles. Three of the most important particles are protons, neutrons, and electrons. Protons and neutrons are found in the nucleus, or center, of an atom. Electrons are found in an area outside the nucleus often described as an electron cloud. **Both protons and electrons have a basic property called charge.** Unlike many other physical properties of matter, **charge** is not something you can see, weigh, or define. However, you can observe the effects of charge—more specifically, how charge affects the behavior of particles.

The magnitude, or size, of the charge on the proton is the same as the magnitude of the charge on the electron. The kind of charge, however, is not the same for both particles. Protons have a positive charge, which is indicated by a plus symbol (+). Electrons have a negative charge, which is indicated by a minus symbol (−). Neutrons are neutral, which means that they have no electric charge. The terms positive and negative, which have no real physical

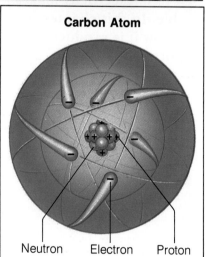

Carbon Atom

Neutron   Electron   Proton

Figure 19–1 *The diagram of the carbon atom shows the arrangement of subatomic particles known as protons, neutrons, and electrons. Carbon is found in all living organisms, including this hungry hippo.*

significance, were originally decided upon by Benjamin Franklin when he first discovered charge. They have been used ever since.

Charge and Force

The difference between the two charges has to do with how they behave and the forces they exert. Recall that force is a pull or push on an object. You are already familiar with various types of forces. Your foot exerts a force (a push) on a ball when you kick it. An ocean wave exerts a force (a push) on you when it knocks you over. The Earth exerts a force (a pull) on the moon to keep it in its orbit. Charged particles exert similar pushes and pulls.

When charged particles come near one another, they give rise to two different forces. A force that pulls objects together is a force of attraction. **A force of attraction exists between oppositely charged particles.** So negatively charged electrons are attracted to positively charged protons. This force of attraction holds the electrons in the electron cloud surrounding the nucleus.

A force that pushes objects apart is a force of repulsion. **A force of repulsion exists between particles of the same charge.** Negatively charged electrons repel one another, just as positively charged protons do. Electric charges behave according to this simple rule: *Like charges repel each other; unlike charges attract each other.*

ACTIVITY

DOING

Electric Forces

1. Take a hard rubber (not plastic) comb and rub it with a woolen cloth.

2. Bring the comb near a small piece of cork that is hanging from a support by a thread.

3. Allow the comb to touch the cork, and then take the comb away. Bring the comb toward the cork again.

4. Repeat steps 1 to 3 using a glass rod rubbed with silk. Then bring the rubber comb rubbed with wool near the cork.

Record and explain your observations.

Figure 19–2 *When charged particles come near each other, a force is produced. The force can be either a force of attraction or a force of repulsion. What is the rule of electric charges?*

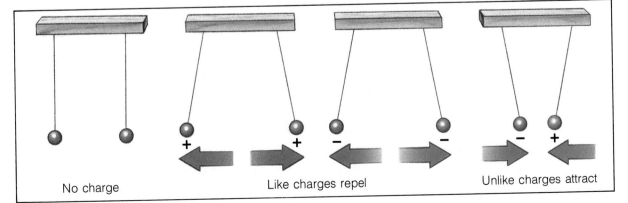

No charge   Like charges repel   Unlike charges attract

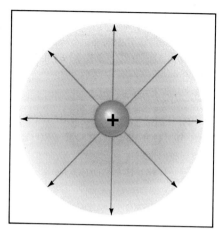

Figure 19–3 *Lines of force show the nature of the electric field surrounding a charged particle. When two charged particles come near each other, the electric fields of both particles are altered as shown. Arrows point in the direction that a positive charge would be pushed by the charge shown.*

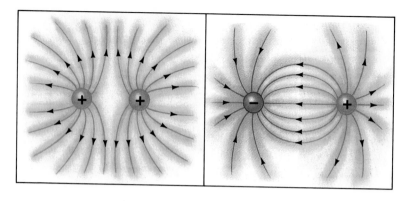

Electric Field

To explain why one charged particle exerts a force on another charged particle, scientists use the concept of an **electric field.** An electric field extends outward through space from every charged particle. When a charged particle moves into the electric field of another charged particle, it is either pushed or pulled depending on the charges of the two particles.

The electric field is the strongest near the charged particle. As the distance from the charged particle increases, the strength of the electric field decreases. As shown in Figure 19–3, the electric field can be visualized by drawing lines extending outward from a charged particle.

19–1 Section Review

1. Describe the charged particles in an atom.
2. What is a force? Give some examples.
3. What is the rule of electric charges?
4. Describe an electric field.

Critical Thinking—*Drawing Diagrams*
5. A positively charged particle is placed 1 centimeter from positively charged particle X. Describe the forces experienced by each particle. Compare these forces with the forces that would exist if a negatively charged particle were placed 10 centimeters from particle X. Draw the electric field surrounding each particle.

19–2 Static Electricity

From your experience, you know that when you sit on a chair, pick up a pen, or put on your jacket, you are neither attracted nor repelled by these objects. Although the protons and electrons in the atoms of these objects have electric charges, the objects themselves are neutral. Why?

An atom has an equal number of protons and electrons. So the total positive charge is equal to the total negative charge. The charges cancel out. So even though an atom contains charged particles, it is electrically neutral. It has no overall charge.

How then do objects such as balloons and clothing develop an electric charge if these objects are made of neutral atoms? The answer lies in the fact that electrons, unlike protons, are free to move. In certain materials, some of the electrons are only loosely held in their atoms. Thus these electrons can easily be separated from their atoms. If an atom loses an electron, it becomes positively charged because it is left with more positive charges (protons) than negative charges (electrons). If an atom gains an electron, it becomes negatively charged. Why? An atom that gains or loses electrons is called an ion.

Figure 19–4 *Is it magic that makes these pieces of paper rise up to the comb? No, just static electricity. Have you ever experienced static electricity?*

Guide for Reading

Focus on these questions as you read.

▶ How do neutral objects acquire charge?
▶ What is static electricity?

ACTIVITY

DISCOVERING

Balloon Electricity

1. Blow up three or four medium-sized balloons.

2. Rub each balloon vigorously on a piece of cloth. Wool works especially well.

3. "Stick" each balloon on the wall. Record the day, time, and weather conditions.

4. Every few hours, check the position of the balloons.

5. Repeat your experiment on a day when the weather conditions are different—for example, on a dry day versus on a humid or rainy day.

How long did the balloons stay attached to the wall? Why did they eventually fall off the wall?

■ Does weather have any effect? Explain.

ACTIVITY

DOING

Spark, Crackle, Move

1. Comb your hair several times in the same direction. Then bring the comb near your hair, but do not touch it.

2. Repeat step 1 but now bring the comb near a weak stream of water from a faucet.

3. In a darkened room, walk across a wool carpet and then touch a doorknob with a metal pen or rod.

Provide an explanation for each observation.

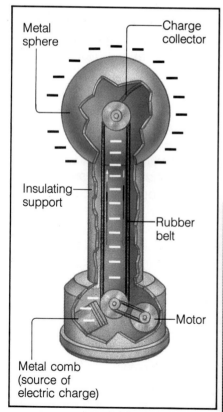

Metal sphere

Charge collector

Insulating support

Rubber belt

Motor

Metal comb (source of electric charge)

Just as an atom can become a negatively or positively charged ion, so can an entire object acquire a charge. **A neutral object acquires an electric charge when it either gains or loses electrons.** Remember, only electrons move. Also remember that charge is neither being created nor destroyed. Charge is only being transferred from one object to another. This is known as the Law of Conservation of Charge.

Methods of Charging

When you rub a balloon against a piece of cloth, the cloth loses some electrons and the balloon gains these electrons. The balloon is no longer a neutral object. It is a negatively charged object because it has more electrons than protons. As the negatively charged balloon approaches a wall, it repels the electrons in the wall. The electrons in the area of the wall nearest the balloon move away, leaving that area of the wall positively charged. See Figure 19–6. Using the rule of charges, can you explain why the balloon now sticks to the wall?

Rubbing two objects together is one method by which an object can become charged. This method is known as the **friction** method. In the previous example, the balloon acquired a charge by the friction method. That is, it was rubbed against cloth.

Figure 19–5 *A Van de Graaff generator produces static electricity by friction. Electrons ride up a rubber belt to the top of the generator, where they are picked off and transferred to the metal sphere. The charge that has built up on the generator at the Ontario Science Center is large enough to make this girl's hair stand on end.*

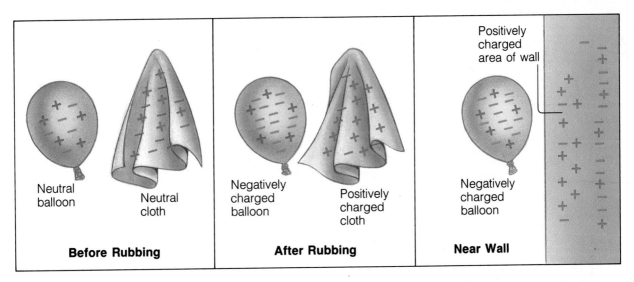

| Before Rubbing | After Rubbing | Near Wall |

Before Rubbing: Neutral balloon, Neutral cloth

After Rubbing: Negatively charged balloon, Positively charged cloth

Near Wall: Positively charged area of wall, Negatively charged balloon

Another method of charging is **conduction.** In conduction, which involves the direct contact of objects, electrons flow through one object to another object. Certain materials permit electric charges to flow freely. Such materials are called **conductors.** Most metals are good conductors of electricity. This is because some electrons in the atoms are free to move throughout the metal. Silver, copper, aluminum, and mercury are among the best conductors. The Earth is also a good conductor.

Materials that do not allow electric charges to flow freely are called **insulators.** Insulators do not conduct electric charges well because the electrons in the atoms of insulators are tightly bound and cannot move throughout the material. Good insulators include rubber, glass, wood, plastic, and air. The rubber tubing around an electric wire and the plastic handle on an electric power tool are examples of insulators.

Figure 19–6 *Rubbing separates charges, giving the cloth a positive charge and the balloon a negative charge. When the negatively charged balloon is brought near the wall, it repels electrons in the wall. The nearby portion of the wall becomes positively charged. What happens next?*

Activity Bank

Give It a Spin, p.757

Figure 19–7 *A metal rod can be charged negatively (left) or positively (right) by conduction.*

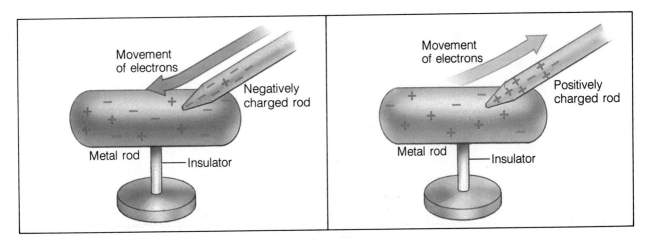

Left: Movement of electrons, Negatively charged rod, Metal rod, Insulator

Right: Movement of electrons, Positively charged rod, Metal rod, Insulator

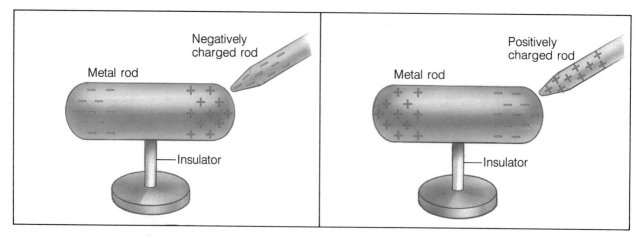

Figure 19–8 *A charged rod brought near a conductor induces an electric charge in the conductor. How is this different from conduction?*

ctivity Bank

Snake Charming, p.758

Figure 19–9 *The discharge of static electricity from one metal object to another can be seen as a spark.*

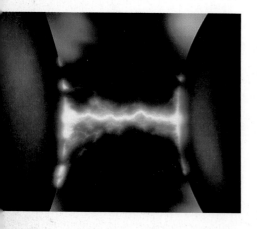

The third method of charging is by **induction.** Induction involves a rearrangement of electric charges. For induction to occur, a neutral object need only come close to a charged object. No contact is necessary. For example, a negatively charged rubber rod can pick up tiny pieces of paper by induction. The electric charges in the paper are rearranged by the approach of the negatively charged rubber rod. The electrons in the area of the paper nearest to the negatively charged rod are repelled, leaving the positive charges near the rod. Because the positive charges are closer to the negative rod, the paper is attracted. Does this description sound familiar? What method of charging made the wall positive in the area nearest the balloon?

The transfer of electrons from one object to another without further movement is called **static electricity.** The word static means not moving, or stationary. **Static electricity is the buildup of electric charges on an object.** The electric charges build up because electrons have moved from one object to another. However, once built up, the charges do not flow. They remain at rest.

Electric Discharge—Lightning

Electrons that move from one object to another and cause the buildup of charges at rest, or static electricity, eventually leave the object. Sometimes they move onto another object. Usually, these extra electrons escape onto water molecules in the air. (This is why static electricity is much more noticeable on dry days. On dry days the air contains fewer water molecules. Objects are more easily charged because charges cannot escape into the air.) When the charged object loses its static electricity, it becomes neutral once again. The balloon eventually falls off the wall because it loses its charge and there is no longer a force of attraction between it and the wall.

The loss of static electricity as electric charges move off an object is called **electric discharge.** Sometimes electric discharge is slow and quiet. Sometimes it is very rapid and accompanied by a shock, a spark of light, or a crackle of noise.

One of the most dramatic examples of the discharge of static electricity is lightning. During a storm, particles contained in clouds are moved about by the wind. Charges may become separated, and there are buildups of positive and negative charges

Figure 19–10 Lightning is a spectacular discharge of static electricity between two areas of different charge. Lightning can occur between a portion of a cloud and the ground, between different clouds, or between different parts of the same cloud. Benjamin Franklin's famous experiments provided evidence that lightning is a form of static electricity.

in different parts of the cloud. If a negatively charged edge of a cloud passes near the surface of the Earth, objects on the Earth become electrically charged by induction. Negative charges move away from the cloud, and positive charges are left closest to the cloud. Soon electrons jump from the cloud to the Earth. The result of this transfer of electrons is a giant spark called lightning.

Lightning can also occur as electrons jump from cloud to cloud. As electrons jump through the air, they produce intense light and heat. The light is the bolt of lightning you see. The heat causes the air to expand suddenly. The rapid expansion of the air is the thunder you hear.

One of the first people to understand lightning as a form of electricity was Benjamin Franklin. In the mid-1700s, Franklin performed experiments that provided evidence that lightning is a form of static electricity, that electricity moves quickly through certain materials, and that a pointed surface attracts electricity more than a flat surface. Franklin suggested that pointed metal rods be placed above the roofs of buildings as protection from lightning. These rods were the first lightning rods.

Lightning rods work according to a principle called grounding. The term grounding comes from the fact that the Earth (the ground) is extremely large and is a good conductor of electric charge.

Figure 19-11 *Lightning rods, such as this one on the Canadian National Tower, provide a safe path for lightning directly into the ground. Scientists studying lightning build up large amounts of electric charge in order to create their own lightning.*

The Earth can easily accept or give up electric charges. Objects in electric contact with the Earth are said to be grounded. A discharge of static electricity usually takes the easiest path from one object to another. So lightning rods are attached to the tops of buildings, and a wire connects the lightning rod to the ground. When lightning strikes the rod, which is taller than the building, it travels through the rod and the wire harmlessly into the Earth. Why is it dangerous to carry an umbrella during a lightning storm?

Unfortunately, other tall objects, such as trees, can also act as grounders. That is why it is not a good idea to stand near or under a tree during a lightning storm. Why do you think it is dangerous to be on a golf course during a lightning storm?

The Electroscope

An electric charge can be detected by an instrument called an **electroscope.** A typical electroscope consists of a metal rod with a knob at the top and a pair of thin metal leaves at the bottom. The rod is inserted into a one-hole rubber stopper that fits into a flask. The flask contains the lower part of the rod and the metal leaves. See Figure 19–12.

In an uncharged electroscope, the leaves hang straight down. When a negatively charged object

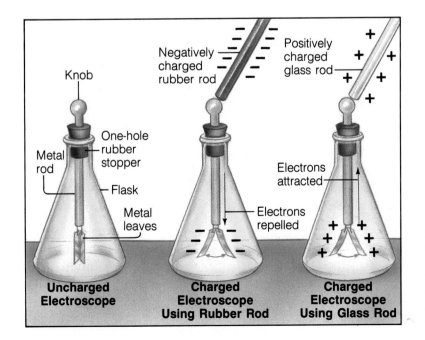

Figure 19–12 *An electroscope is used to detect electric charges. Why do the leaves in the electroscope move apart when either a negatively charged rubber rod or a positively charged glass rod makes contact?*

491

touches the metal knob, electric charges travel down the rod and into the leaves. The leaves spread apart, indicating the presence of an electric charge. Since the charge on both leaves is the same, the leaves repel each other and spread apart.

If a positively charged object touches the knob of the electroscope, free electrons in the leaves and metal rod are attracted by the positive object. The loss of electrons causes the leaves to become positively charged. Again, they repel each other and spread apart.

19–2 Section Review

1. What are three ways an object can acquire an electric charge?
2. What is static electricity?
3. What is electric discharge? Give an example.
4. If the body of a kangaroo contains millions of charged particles, why aren't different kangaroos electrically attracted to or repelled by one another?

Critical Thinking—*Making Inferences*
5. What would happen if a lightning rod were made of an insulating material rather than of a conducting material?

Guide for Reading

Focus on these questions as you read.

▶ *How can a flow of charges be produced?*

▶ *What is the relationship among electric current, voltage, and resistance?*

19–3 The Flow of Electricity

The electricity that you use when you plug an electrical appliance into a wall outlet is certainly not static electricity. If it were, the appliance would not run for long. Useful electricity requires moving electric charges.

Making Electric Charges Move

What makes an electric charge move? You know that you must do work to move, or lift, an object such as a book because the Earth's gravitational field is pulling down the book. When you let go, the book falls to the ground. In a similar fashion, you must do work to move a charged particle against an electric field. And just as you do less work in lifting a light book than a heavy book, the amount of work required to move a charge depends upon the strength of the charge. The amount of work required to move a charge between two points, or the work per unit charge, is called the **electric potential difference** between those two points. The unit of potential difference is called the **volt (V).** The term **voltage** is often used for potential difference. Although the two terms do not have the same exact meaning, the differences are not important at this point.

Potential difference can be positive or negative depending upon the direction in which a charge is moving. Consider rolling a ball up and down a hill. You must do work to roll the ball up the hill, but the ball will roll down the hill on its own once set into motion. Moving a positive charge through a positive potential difference can be likened to rolling a ball uphill. And moving a positive charge through a negative potential difference can be likened to rolling a ball downhill.

So what can make electric charges move and keep moving? The answer is a device that uses some form of energy to do the work required to move electric charges. Such devices include batteries, electric generators, thermocouples, and photo cells. On the following page you will find a brief description of three of these devices. Electric generators will be discussed in Chapter 21.

Figure 19–13 *Imagine plugging a car into the nearest outlet rather than going to the gas station! Researchers have been attempting to design efficient cars that use a rechargeable battery as a source of power.*

Figure 19–14 *Electrochemical cells, which include dry cells and wet cells, convert chemical energy into electric energy. What is a series of dry cells called? What is an example of a wet cell?*

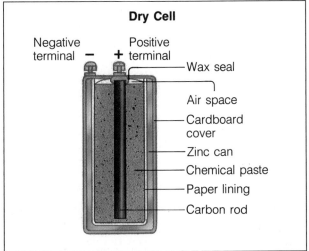

Dry Cell

Negative terminal —
Positive + terminal
Wax seal
Air space
Cardboard cover
Zinc can
Chemical paste
Paper lining
Carbon rod

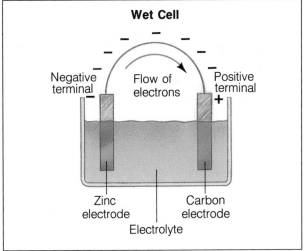

Wet Cell

Negative terminal
Flow of electrons
Positive terminal +
Zinc electrode
Carbon electrode
Electrolyte

BATTERIES   A **battery** is a device that produces electricity by converting chemical energy into electrical energy. A battery is made of several smaller units called electric cells, or electrochemical cells. Each cell consists of two different materials called electrodes as well as an electrolyte. The electrolyte is a mixture of chemicals that produces a chemical reaction. The chemical reaction releases electric charges.

Electric cells can be either dry cells or wet cells, depending on the type of electrolyte used. In a wet cell, such as a car battery, the electrolyte is a liquid. In a dry cell, such as the battery in a flashlight, the electrolyte is a pastelike mixture.

Figure 19-14 on page 493 will help you to understand how a simple electrochemical cell works. In this cell, one of the electrodes is made of carbon and the other is made of zinc. The part of the electrode that sticks up is called the terminal. The electrolyte is sulfuric acid. The acid attacks the zinc and dissolves it. In this process, electrons are left behind on the zinc electrode. Thus the zinc electrode becomes negatively charged. At the same time, a series of chemical reactions causes eletrons to be pulled off the carbon electrode. The carbon electrode becomes positively charged. Because there are opposite charges on the electrodes, charge will flow between the terminals if a wire connects them.

THERMOCOUPLES   A **thermocouple** is a device that produces electrical energy from heat energy. A thermocouple releases electric charges as a result of temperature differences. In this device the ends of two different metal wires, such as copper and iron, are joined together to form a loop. If one iron-copper junction is heated while the other is cooled, electric charges will flow. The greater the temperature difference between the junctions, the faster the charges will flow. Figure 19-15 shows a thermocouple.

Thermocouples are used in thermometers in cars to show engine temperature. One end of the thermocouple is placed in the engine, while the other end is kept outside the engine. As the engine gets warm, the temperature difference produces a flow of charge. The warmer the engine, the greater the temperature difference—and the greater the flow of charge. The moving charges in turn operate a gauge that shows engine temperature. Thermocouples are also used in ovens and in gas furnaces.

Figure 19–15 *The temperature difference between the hot junction and the cold junction in a thermocouple generates electricity. What is the energy conversion involved in the operation of a thermocouple?*

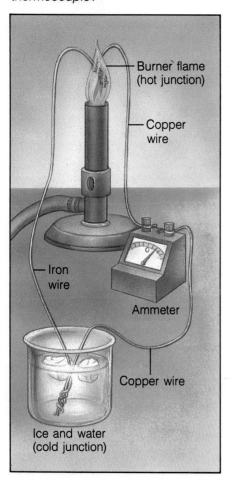

Burner flame (hot junction)

Copper wire

Iron wire

Ammeter

Copper wire

Ice and water (cold junction)

Figure 19–16 *On November 9, 1965, a major blackout plunged the illuminated skyline of New York City into darkness and left more than 30 million people in the Northeast without electricity.*

PHOTOCELLS The most direct conversion of energy occurs in a device known as a **photocell.** A photocell takes advantage of the fact that when light with a certain amount of energy shines on a metal surface, electrons are emitted from the surface. These electrons can be routed through a wire to create a constant flow of electric charge.

Electric Current

When a wire is connected to the terminals of a source, a complete path called a **circuit** is formed. Charge can flow through a circuit. A flow of charge is called an electric **current.** More precisely, electric current is the amount of charge that passes a given point per unit of time. The higher the electric current in a wire, the more electric charges that are passing through.

The symbol for current is the letter I. And the unit in which current is expressed is the amphere (A). The amphere, or amp for short, is the amount of charge that flows past a point per second. Scientists use instruments such as ammeters and galvanometers to measure current.

You may wonder how charge can flow through a wire. Recall that conductors are made from elements whose atoms have some loosely held electrons. When a wire is connected to the terminals of a source, the potential difference causes the loose electrons to be

Life on the Prairie

Not very long ago, people just like you grew up without the electrical devices that make your life easy, comfortable, and entertaining. In *Little House on the Prairie* and its related books, Laura Ingalls Wilder tells delightful stories about growing up in the days before electricity. These stories are especially wonderful because they are not tainted by fictional drama. The author simply describes life as it actually was.

Figure 19–17 *When the switch in the diagram is closed, the students each pass a ball to the right. Thus a ball reaches the switch almost instantly. Similarly, when you flip on a switch to a light, for example, current flows to the light almost immediately.*

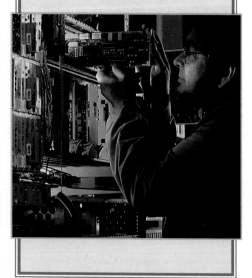

pulled away from their atoms and to flow through the material.

You may also wonder how lights and other electrical appliances can go on as soon as you turn the switch even though the power plant may be quite a distance away. The answer is that you do not have to wait for the electrons at the power plant to reach your switch. All the electrons in the circuit flow as soon as the switch is turned. To help understand this concept, imagine that each student in Figure 19–17 has a red ball. When the switch is turned on, each student passes the ball to the person on the right. So almost as soon as the switch is turned on, a red ball reaches the switch. When the switch is turned off, each person still holds a ball—even though it may not be the original ball. This is basically how electrons shift through a conductor. The electrons shift positions, but no electrons leave the circuit.

So now you know what constitutes an electric current and you know that a potential difference is required to produce an electric current. But did you know that electric currents are not limited to the electric circuits that are used to run your appliances? In fact, you depend on the potential difference that exists across the surface of your heart. If the heart stops beating, doctors sometimes apply a potential difference across the heart to make it start beating again. Many aquatic animals use electricity as well. The electric eel, for example, kills its prey by creating a potential difference of several hundred volts along its length. The result is an electric current around the eel.

Whatever the application, there is a clear relationship between electric current and potential difference. A scientist named Georg Simon Ohm (1787–1854) was the first person to establish this relationship experimentally. He found that the current in a metal wire is proportional to the potential difference applied to the ends of the wire. Thus for example, if a wire is connected to an 8-V battery, the current flow will be twice what it would be if the wire were connected to a 4-V battery.

To better understand this relationship, consider the flow of water in a pipe. If one end of the pipe is somewhat higher than the other, the rate at which the water flows is greater than when the pipe is nearly level. Since the rate at which the water flows can be likened to electric current and the difference in height between the two ends of the pipe can be likened to potential difference, you can conclude that a greater potential difference causes a greater current flow.

Figure 19–18 *The greater the difference in height between the ends of the pipe, the greater the flow of water. How can this relationship be likened to the relationship between voltage and current?*

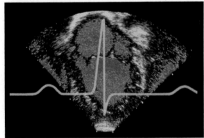

Figure 19–19 *This electric ray is capable of producing an electric current. Electric currents are also found in the human body. An electrocardiogram (EKG) records changes in the potential differences that exist across the heart.*

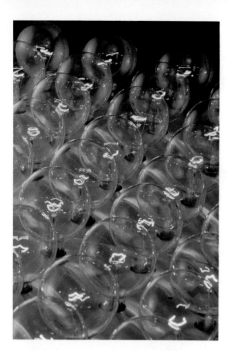

Figure 19–20 *Light bulbs light because of the phenomenon of resistance. The metal filament in the center of the bulb offers enough resistance to the electric current flowing through it so that heat and light are given off.*

A Shocking Combination, p.761

Resistance

The amount of current that flows through a wire does not depend only on the voltage. It also depends on how the wire resists the flow of electric charge. Opposition to the flow of electric charge is known as **resistance.** The symbol for resistance is the letter R.

Imagine a stream of water flowing down a mountain. Rocks in the stream resist the flow of the water. Or think about running through a crowd of people. The people slow you down by resisting your movement. Electric charges are slowed down by interactions with atoms in a wire. So the resistance of a wire depends on the material of which it is made. If the atoms making up the material are arranged in such a way that it is difficult for electric charge to flow, the resistance of the material will be high. As you might expect, resistance will be less for a wider wire, but more for a longer wire. Higher resistance means greater opposition to the flow of charge. The higher the resistance of a wire, the less current for a given voltage.

The unit of resistance is the ohm (Ω). Different wires have different resistances. Copper wire has less resistance than iron wire does. Copper is a good conductor; iron is a poor conductor. Nonconductors offer such great resistance that almost no current can flow. All electric devices offer some resistance to the flow of current. And although it may not seem so at first, this resistance is often quite useful—indeed, necessary.

You know that light bulbs give off light and heat. Have you ever wondered where the light and heat come from? They are not pouring into the bulb through the wires that lead from the wall. Rather, some of the electric energy passing through the filament of the bulb is converted into light and heat energy. The filament is a very thin piece of metal that resists the flow of electricity within it. The same principle is responsible for toasting your pita bread when you place it in the toaster.

How much resistance a material has depends somewhat on its temperature. The resistance of a metal increases with temperature. At higher temperatures, atoms move around more randomly and thus get in the way of flowing electric charges. At very

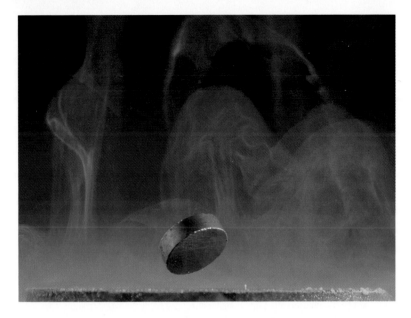

Figure 19–21 *This is no magic trick. At low temperatures, certain materials that have almost no resistance are said to be superconducting. Superconducting materials, such as the one at the bottom of the photograph, repel magnets. For this reason the magnet floats in midair.*

low temperatures, however, the resistance of certain metals becomes essentially zero. Materials in this state are said to be **superconductors.** In superconductors, almost no energy is wasted. However a great deal of energy must be used to keep the material cold enough to be superconducting.

Scientists are currently working to develop new materials that are superconducting at higher temperatures. When this is accomplished, superconductors will become extremely important in industry. Superconductors will be used in large generating plants and in motors where negligible resistance will allow for very large currents. There are also plans for superconducting transmission cables that will reduce energy loss tremendously. Electric generating plants are usually located near major population centers rather than near the fuel source because too much energy is lost in carrying a current. Superconducting transmission lines will make it practical for generating plants to be situated next to fuel sources rather than near population centers. Superconductors are also being tested in high-speed transportation systems.

Ohm's Law

The complete expression called **Ohm's Law** identifies the relationship among current, voltage, and resistance. **Ohm's law states that the current in a wire (I) is euqal to the voltage (V) divided by the resistance (R).**

ACTIVITY

CALCULATING

Ohm's Law

Complete the following chart.

I (amps)	V (volts)	R (ohms)
	12	75
15	240	
5.5		20
	6	25
5	110	

As an equation, Ohm's Law is

$$\text{Current} = \frac{\text{Voltage}}{\text{Resistance}}$$

$$I = \frac{V}{R} \qquad \text{Amperes} = \frac{\text{Volts}}{\text{Ohms}}$$

If the resistance in a wire is 100 ohms and the voltage is 50 volts, the current is 50/100, or 0.5 ampere. You can rearrange the equation in order to calculate resistance or voltage. What is the resistance if the voltage is 10 volts and the current 2 amperes?

Current Direction

Electrons moving through a wire can move continuously in the same direction, or they can change direction back and forth over and over again.

When electrons always flow in the same direction, the current is called **direct current,** or DC. Electricity from dry cells and batteries is direct current.

When electrons move back and forth, reversing their direction regularly, the current is called **alternating current,** or AC. The electricity in your home is alternating current. In fact, the current in your home changes direction 120 times every second. Although direct current serves many purposes, alternating current is better for transporting the huge amounts of electricity required to meet people's needs.

19–3 Section Review

1. How does an electrochemical cell produce an electric current?
2. What is a thermocouple? A photocell?
3. What is electric current? Explain how current flows through a wire.
4. What is resistance? Voltage? How is electric current related to resistance and voltage?
5. What is direct current? Alternating current?

Critical Thinking—*Drawing Conclusions*
6. If the design of a dry cell keeps electrons flowing steadily, why does a dry cell go ''dead''?

19–4 Electric Circuits

Perhaps you wonder why electricity does not flow from the outlets in your home at all times? You can find the answer to this question if you try the following experiment. Connect one wire from a terminal on a dry cell to a small flashlight bulb. Does anything happen? Now connect another wire from the bulb to the other terminal on the dry cell. What happens? With just one wire connected, the bulb will not light. But with two wires providing a path for the flow of electrons, the bulb lights up.

In order to flow, electrons need a closed path through which to travel. **An electric circuit provides a complete, closed path for an electric current.**

Parts of a Circuit

An electric circuit consists of a source of energy; a load, or resistance; wires; and a switch. Recall that the source of energy can be a battery, a thermocouple, a photocell, or an electric generator at a power plant.

The load is the device that uses the electric energy. The load can be a light bulb, an appliance, a machine, or a motor. In all cases the load offers some resistance to the flow of electrons. As a result, electric energy is converted into heat, light, or mechanical energy.

Guide for Reading

Focus on these questions as you read.

▶ *What is an electric circuit?*
▶ *What is the difference between series and parallel circuits?*

Figure 19–22 *No electricity can flow through an open circuit (left). When the switch is flipped, the circuit is closed and electrons have a complete path through which to flow (right). What indicates that a current is flowing through the circuit?*

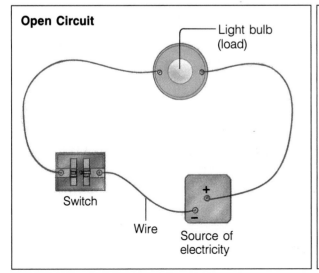

Open Circuit

Light bulb (load)

Switch

Wire

Source of electricity

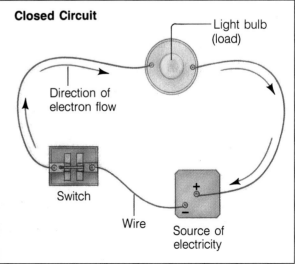

Closed Circuit

Light bulb (load)

Direction of electron flow

Switch

Wire

Source of electricity

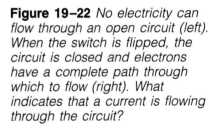

Figure 19–23 *When severe weather conditions—such as the tornado that caused this destruction—damage power lines, the flow of electricity is interrupted. Why?*

The switch in an electric circuit opens and closes the circuit. You will remember that electrons cannot flow through a broken path. Electrons must have a closed path through which to travel. When the switch of an electric device is off, the circuit is open and electrons cannot flow. When the switch is on, the circuit is closed and electrons are able to flow. Remember this important rule: *Electricity cannot flow through an open circuit. Electricity can flow only through a closed circuit.*

Series and Parallel Circuits

There are two types of electric circuits. The type depends on how the parts of the circuit (source, load, wires, and switch) are arranged. If all the parts of an electric circuit are connected one after another, the circuit is a **series circuit.** In a series circuit there is only one path for the electrons to take. Figure 19–24 illustrates a series circuit. The disadvantage of a series circuit is that if there is a break in any part of the circuit, the entire circuit is opened and no current can flow. Inexpensive holiday tree lights are often connected in series. What will happen if one light goes out in a circuit such as this?

In a **parallel circuit,** the different parts of an electric circuit are on separate branches. There are several paths for the electrons to take in a parallel circuit. Figure 19–24 shows a parallel circuit. If there is a break in one branch of a parallel circuit, electrons can still move through the other branches. The

Figure 19–24 *A series circuit provides only one path for the flow of electrons. A parallel circuit provides several paths. How are the circuits in your home wired? Why?*

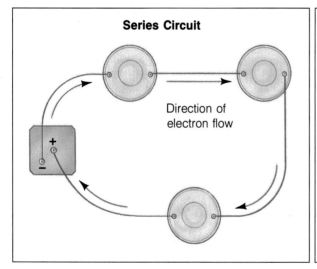

Series Circuit

Direction of electron flow

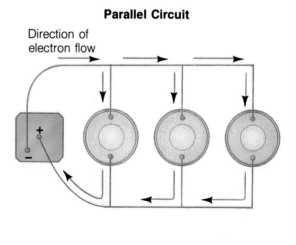

Parallel Circuit

Direction of electron flow

current continues to flow. Why do tree lights connected in parallel have an advantage over tree lights connected in series? Why do you think the electric circuits in your home are parallel circuits?

Household Circuits

Have you ever wondered what was behind the outlet in the wall of your home? After all, it is rather amazing that by inserting a plug into the wall outlet, you can make your television, refrigerator, vacuum cleaner, hair dryer, or any other electrical appliance operate.

Connected to the outlet is a cable consisting of three wires enclosed in a protective casing. Two of the wires run parallel to each other and have a potential difference of 120 volts between them. The third wire is connected to ground. (Recall that a wire that is grounded provides the shortest direct path for current to travel into the Earth.) For any appliance in your home to operate, it must have one of its terminals connected to the high potential wire and the other terminal connected to the low potential wire. The two prongs of a plug of an appliance are connected to the terminals inside the appliance. When the switch of the appliance is closed, current flows into one prong of the plug, through the appliance, and back into the wall through the other prong of the plug.

Many appliances have a third prong on the plug. This prong is attached to the third wire in the cable, which is connected directly to ground and carries no current. This wire is a safety feature to protect against short circuits. A short circuit is an accidental connection that allows current to take a shorter path around a circuit. A shorter path has less resistance and therefore results in a higher current. If the high-potential wire accidentally touches the metal frame of the appliance, the entire appliance will become part of the circuit and anyone touching the appliance will suffer a shock. The safety wire provides a shorter circuit for the current. Rather than flowing through the appliance, the current will flow directly to ground—thereby protecting anyone who might touch the appliance. Appliances that have a plastic casing do not need this safety feature. Can you explain why?

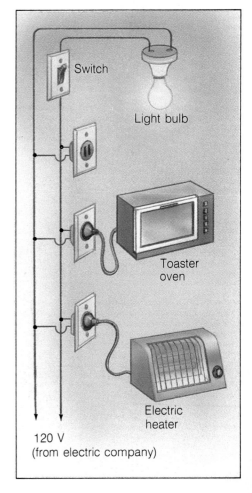

Figure 19–25 *The outlets in a home are connected in such a way that several may rely on the same switch. A home must have several circuits so that different switches control only certain outlets. What happens when the switch in the diagram is flipped off? What if all the appliances in the home are attached to this circuit?*

Switch

Light bulb

Toaster oven

Electric heater

120 V
(from electric company)

Circuit Safety Features

Your home has a great amount of electricity running through it. If too many appliances are running at once on the same circuit or if the wires have become old and frayed, heat can build up in the wiring. If the wires in the walls get too hot, there is the danger of fire. Two devices protect against this potential danger.

FUSES To protect against too much current flowing at once, your home may have **fuses** in a fuse box. Inside each fuse is a thin strip of metal through which current flows. If the current becomes too high, the strip of metal melts and breaks the flow of electricity. So a fuse is an emergency switch.

CIRCUIT BREAKERS One disadvantage of fuses is that once they burn out, they must be replaced. For this reason, **circuit breakers** are often used instead of fuses. Like fuses, circuit breakers protect a circuit from becoming overloaded. Modern circuit breakers have a switch that flips open when the current flow becomes too high. These circuit breakers can easily be reset and used again once the problem has been found and corrected. Circuit breakers are easier to use than fuses.

19–4 Section Review

1. What is an electric circuit?
2. Compare a series circuit and a parallel circuit.
3. Can a circuit be a combination of series connections and parallel connections? Explain your answer.
4. What would happen if your home were not wired in parallel?

Connection—*You and Your World*
5. Does your home have fuses or circuit breakers? Explain the purpose of each device.

PROBLEM ? ? ?
Solving

Faulty Wiring

You and your family arrive at the site of your summer vacation—an old but quaint cabin situated at the edge of a beautiful lake. As you pile out of the car, you are greeted by the superintendent responsible for taking care of all the cabins in the area. The neighbors call her Ms. Fix-It.

Ms. Fix-It tells you that everything in the cabin is in working order. However, when she was working on the wiring, she must have made a mistake or two. The kitchen light must remain on in order to keep the refrigerator going. In order to turn on the television, the fan must be on. And the garbage disposal will work only when the oven is on.

Drawing Diagrams

How must the cabin be wired? How should the cabin be rewired? Draw a diagram showing the mistakes and the corrections.

19–5 Electric Power

You probably use the word power in a number of different senses—to mean strength, or force, or energy. To a scientist, **power** is the rate at which work is done or energy is used. **Electric power is a measure of the rate at which electricity does work or provides energy.**

POWER USED BY COMMON APPLIANCES	
Appliance	Power Used (watts)
Refrigerator/ freezer	600
Dishwasher	2300
Toaster	700
Range/oven	2600
Hair dryer	1000
Color television	300
Microwave oven	1450
Radio	100
Clock	3
Clothes dryer	4000

Figure 19–27 *The table shows the power used by some common appliances. Do any of the values surprise you?*

If you can, pick up a cool light bulb and examine it. Do you notice any words written on it? For example, do you see "60 watts" or "100 watts" on the bulb? Watts (W) are the units in which electric power is measured. To better understand the meaning of watts, let's look at the concept of electric power more closely.

As you have just read, electric power measures the rate at which electricity does work or provides energy. Electric power can be calculated by using the following equation:

$$\textbf{Power = Voltage} \times \textbf{Current}$$
$$\text{or}$$
$$\textbf{P = V} \times \textbf{I}$$

Or, put another way:

$$\textbf{Watts = Volts} \times \textbf{Amperes}$$

Now think back to the light bulb you looked at. The electricity in your home is 120 volts. The light bulb itself operates at 0.5 ampere. According to the equation for power, multiplying these two numbers gives the bulb's wattage, which in this case is 60 watts. The wattage tells you the power of the bulb, or the rate at which energy is being delivered. As you might expect, the higher the wattage, the brighter the bulb—and the more expensive to run.

To measure large quantities of power, such as the total used in your home, the kilowatt (kW) is used. The prefix *kilo-* means 1000. So one kilowatt is 1000 watts. What is the power in watts of a 0.2-kilowatt light bulb?

Electric Energy

Have you ever noticed the electric meter in your home? This device measures how much energy your household uses. The electric company provides electric power at a certain cost. Their bill for this power is based on the total amount of energy a household uses, which is read from the electric meter.

The total amount of electric energy used depends on the total power used by all the electric appliances

Figure 19–28 *Electricity for your home is purchased on the basis of the amount of energy used and the length of time for which it is used. Power companies install an electric meter in your home to record this usage in kilowatt-hours.*

and the total time they are used. The formula for electric energy is

$$\textbf{Energy} = \textbf{Power} \times \textbf{Time}$$
$$\text{or}$$
$$\textbf{E} = \textbf{P} \times \textbf{t}$$

Electric energy is measured in kilowatt-hours (kWh).

$$\textbf{Energy} = \textbf{Power} \times \textbf{Time}$$
$$\textbf{Kilowatt-hours} = \textbf{Kilowatts} \times \textbf{Hours}$$

One kilowatt-hour is equal to 1000 watts of power used for one hour of time. You can imagine how much power this is by picturing ten 100-watt bulbs in a row, all burning for one hour. One kilowatt-hour would also be equal to a 500-watt appliance running for two hours.

To pay for electricity, the energy used is multiplied by the cost per kilowatt-hour. Suppose the cost of electricity is $0.08 per kilowatt-hour. How much would it cost to burn a 100-watt bulb for five hours? To use a 1000-watt air conditioner for three hours?

Electric Safety

Electricity is one of the most useful energy resources. But electricity can be dangerous if it is not used carefully. Here are some important rules to remember when using electricity.

1. Never handle appliances when your hands are wet or you are standing in water. If you are wet, you could unwillingly become part of an electric circuit.

2. Never run wires under carpets. Breaks or frays in the wires may go unnoticed. These breaks cause short circuits. A short circuit represents a shorter and easier path for electron flow and thus can cause shocks or a fire.

ACTIVITY
THINKING

Power and Heat

Examine the appliances in your home for their power rating. Make a chart of this information.

What is the relationship between an appliance's power rating and the amount of heat it produces?

3. Never overload a circuit by connecting too many appliances to it. Each electric circuit is designed to carry a certain amount of current safely. An overloaded circuit can cause a fuse to blow.

4. Always repair worn or frayed wires to avoid short circuits.

5. Never stick your fingers in an electric socket or stick a utensil in an appliance that is plugged in. The electricity could be conducted directly into your hand or through the utensil into your hand. Exposure to electricity with both hands can produce a circuit that goes through one arm, across the heart, and out the other arm.

6. Never come close to wires on power poles or to wires that have fallen from power poles or buildings. Such wires often carry very high voltages, resulting in strong currents.

ACTIVITY

CALCULATING

How Much Electricity Do You Use?

1. For a period of several days, keep a record of every electrical appliance you use. Also record the amount of time each appliance is run.

2. Write down the power rating for each appliance you list. The power rating in watts should be marked on the appliance. You can also use information in Figure 19–27.

3. Calculate the amount of electricity in kilowatt-hours that you use each day.

4. Find out how much electricity costs per kilowatt-hour in your area. Calculate the cost of the electricity you use each day.

19–5 Section Review

1. What is electric power? What is the formula for calculating electric power? In what unit is electric power measured?

2. What is electric energy? What is the formula for calculating electric energy? In what unit is electric energy measured?

3. What happens if you touch an exposed electric wire? Why is this situation worse if you are wet or standing in water?

Critical Thinking—*Making Calculations*

4. If left running unused, which appliance would waste more electricity, an iron left on for half an hour or a television left on for one hour?

CONNECTIONS

Electrifying Personalities

Your hair color, eye color, height, and other personal traits are not the haphazard results of chance. Instead, they are determined and controlled by a message found in every one of your body cells. The message is referred to as the *genetic code*. The genetic information passed on from generation to generation in all living things is contained in structures called chromosomes, which are made of genes.

The genetic information contained in a gene is in a molecule of DNA (deoxyribonucleic acid). A DNA molecule consists of a long chain of many small molecules known as nucleotide bases. There are only four types of bases in a DNA molecule: adenine (A), cytosine (C), guanine (G), and thymine (T). The order in which the bases are arranged determines everything about your body.

A chromosome actually consists of two long DNA molecules wrapped around each other in the shape of a double helix. The two strands are held together in a precise shape by electric forces — the attraction of positive charges to negative charges.

In addition to holding the two strands of DNA together, electric forces are responsible for maintaining the genetic code and reproducing it each time a new cell is made. Your body is constantly producing new cells. It is essential that the same genetic message be given to each cell. When DNA is reproduced in the cell, the two strands unwind, leaving the charged parts of the bases exposed. Of the four bases, only certain ones will pair together. A is always paired with T, and G is always paired with C.

Suppose, for example, that after DNA unwinds, a molecule of C is exposed. Of the four bases available for pairing with C, only one will be electrically attracted to C. The charges on the other three bases are not arranged in a way that makes it possible for them to get close enough to those on C.

Electric forces not only hold the two chains together, they also operate to select the bases in proper order during reproduction of the genetic code. Thus the genetic information is passed on accurately to the next generation. So, although it may surprise you, it is a fact: Electricity is partly responsible for your features, from your twinkling eyes to your overall size.

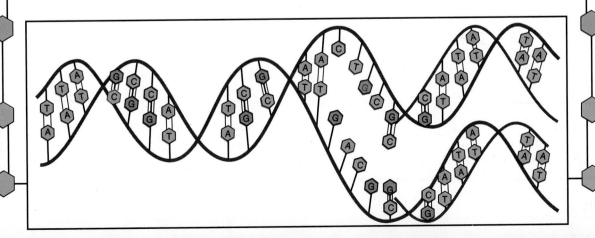

Laboratory Investigation

Electricity From a Lemon

Problem

Can electricity be produced from a lemon, a penny, and a dime?

Materials *(per group)*

bell wire	scissors
cardboard box	sandpaper
compass	dime
lemon	2 pennies

Procedure ▪️ 🔌

1. Wrap 20 turns of bell wire around the cardboard box containing the compass, as shown in the accompanying figure.
2. Roll the lemon back and forth on a table or other flat surface while applying slight pressure. The pressure will break the cellular structure of the lemon.
3. Use the pointed end of the scissors to make two slits 1 cm apart in the lemon.
4. Sandpaper both sides of the dime and two pennies.
5. Insert the pennies in the two slits in the lemon as shown in the figure.

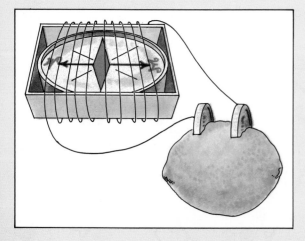

6. Touch the two ends of the bell wire to the coins. Observe any deflection of the compass needle.
7. Replace one of the pennies with the dime. Repeat step 6. Observe any deflection of the compass needle. If there is deflection, observe its direction.
8. Reverse the connecting wires on the coins. Observe any deflection of the compass needle and the direction of deflection.

Observations

1. Is the compass needle deflected when the two ends of the bell wire touch the two pennies?
2. Is the compass needle deflected when the two ends of the bell wire touch the penny and the dime?
3. Is the direction of deflection changed when the connecting wires on the coins are reversed?

Analysis and Conclusions

1. A compass needle will be deflected in the presence of an electric current. Is an electric current produced when two pennies are used? When a dime and a penny are used?
2. What is the purpose of breaking the cellular structure of the lemon? Of sandpapering the coins?
3. What materials are necessary to produce an electric current?
4. An electric current flowing through a wire produces magnetism. Using this fact, explain why a compass is used in this investigation to detect a weak current.
5. A dime is made of copper and nickel. What would happen if the dime were made of pure copper?

Summarizing Key Concepts

19–1 Electric Charge

▲ All matter is made of atoms. Atoms contain positively charged protons, negatively charged electrons, and neutral neutrons.

▲ Opposite charges exert a force of attraction on each other. Similar charges exert a force of repulsion.

19–2 Static Electricity

▲ A neutral object can acquire charge by friction, conduction, or induction.

▲ The buildup of electric charge is called static electricity.

19–3 The Flow of Electricity

▲ Electric charges can be made to flow by a source such as a battery, thermocouple, photocell, or electric generator.

▲ The flow of electrons through a wire is called electric current (I). Electric current is measured in units called amperes (A).

▲ A measure of the potential difference across a source is voltage (V), which is measured in units called volts (V).

▲ Opposition to the flow of charge is called resistance (R). Resistance is measured in units called ohms (Ω).

▲ Ohm's law states that the current in a wire is equal to voltage divided by resistance.

▲ In direct current (DC), electrons flow in one direction. In alternating current (AC), electrons reverse their direction regularly.

19–4 Electric Circuits

▲ An electric circuit provides a complete closed path for an electric current. Electricity can flow only through a closed circuit.

▲ There is only one path for the current in a series circuit. There are several paths in a parallel circuit.

19–5 Electric Power

▲ Electric power measures the rate at which electricity does work or provides energy. The unit of electric power is the watt (W).

Reviewing Key Terms

Define each term in a complete sentence.

19–1 Electric Charge
charge
electric field

19–2 Static Electricity
friction
conduction
conductor
insulator
induction
static electricity
electric discharge
electroscope

19–3 The Flow of Electricity
battery
potential difference
thermocouple
photocell
circuit
current
voltage
resistance
superconductor
Ohm's law
direct current
alternating current

19–4 Electric Circuits
series circuit
parallel circuit
fuse
circuit breaker

19–5 Electric Power
power

Chapter Review

Content Review

Multiple Choice

Choose the letter of the answer that best completes each statement.

1. An atomic particle that carries a negative electric charge is called a(n)
   a. neutron.
   b. positron.
   c. electron.
   d. proton.
2. Between which particles would an electric force of attraction occur?
   a. proton-proton
   b. electron-electron
   c. neutron-neutron
   d. electron-proton
3. Electricity cannot flow through which of the following?
   a. series circuit
   b. open circuit
   c. parallel circuit
   d. closed circuit
4. Electric power is measured in
   a. ohms.
   b. watts.
   c. electron-hours.
   d. volts.
5. The three methods of giving an electric charge to an object are conduction, induction, and
   a. friction.
   b. resistance.
   c. direct current.
   d. alternating current.
6. Electricity resulting from a buildup of electric charges is
   a. alternating current.
   b. magnetism.
   c. electromagnetism.
   d. static electricity.
7. When electrons move back and forth, reversing their direction regularly, the current is called
   a. direct current.
   b. series current.
   c. electric charge.
   d. alternating current.

True or False

If the statement is true, write "true." If it is false, change the underlined word or words to make the statement true.

1. The number of electrons in a neutral atom equals the number of <u>protons</u>.
2. A neutral object develops a negative charge when it <u>loses</u> electrons.
3. An instrument that detects charge is a(n) <u>electroscope</u>.
4. Materials that do not allow electrons to flow freely are called <u>insulators</u>.
5. Rubber is a relatively <u>poor</u> conductor of electricity.
6. A <u>photocell</u> generates electricity as a result of temperature differences.
7. Once a <u>circuit breaker</u> burns out, it must be replaced.
8. An electric circuit provides a complete <u>open</u> path for an electric current.
9. Electric <u>power</u> is the rate at which work is done.

Concept Mapping

Complete the following concept map for Section 19–1. Then construct a concept map for the entire chapter.

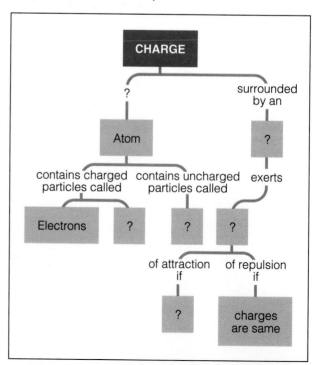

512

Concept Mastery

Discuss each of the following in a brief paragraph.

1. Describe the structure of an atom. How are atoms related to electric charge?
2. How does the force exerted by a proton on a proton compare with the force exerted by a proton on an electron at the same distance?
3. Describe the three ways in which an object can become charged.
4. Describe how a simple electrochemical cell operates? How are electrochemical cells related to batteries?
5. Compare an insulator and a conductor. How might each be used?
6. Describe two ways in which the resistance of a wire can be increased.
7. What is a circuit? A short circuit?
8. Explain why a tiny 1.5-V cell can operate a calculator for a year, while a much larger 1.5-V cell burns out in a few hours in a toy robot.
9. Discuss three safety rules to follow while using electricity.

Critical Thinking and Problem Solving

Use the skills you have developed in this chapter to answer each of the following.

1. **Making calculations** A light bulb operates at 60 volts and 2 amps.
   a. What is the power of the light bulb?
   b. How much energy does the light bulb need in order to operate for 8 hours?
   c. What is the cost of operating the bulb for 8 hours at a rate of $0.07 per kilowatt-hour?

2. **Identifying relationships** Identify each of the following statements as being a characteristic of (a) a series circuit, (b) a parallel circuit, (c) both a series and a parallel circuit:
   a. $I = V/R$
   b. The total resistance in the circuit is the sum of the individual resistances.
   c. The total current in the circuit is the sum of the current in each resistance.
   d. The current in each part of the circuit is the same.
   e. A break in any part of the circuit causes the current to stop.

3. **Applying concepts** Explain why the third prong from a grounded plug should not be removed to make the plug fit a two-prong outlet.

4. **Making inferences** Electric current can be said to take the path of least resistance. With this in mind, explain why a bird can perch with both feet on a power line and not be injured?

5. **Using the writing process** Imagine that from your window you can see the farm that belongs to your neighbors, whom you have never met. You rarely notice the neighbors, except when it rains. During rainstorms, they protect themselves with huge umbrellas as they walk out to check the crops. Write them a friendly but direct letter explaining why it is dangerous for them to use umbrellas during thunderstorms.

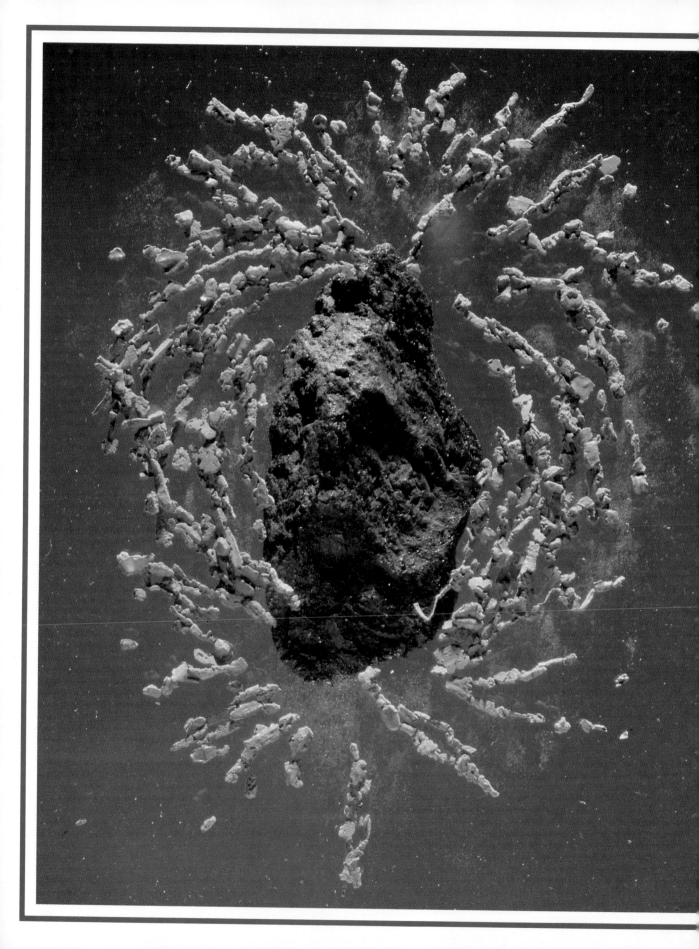

Magnetism

Guide for Reading

After you read the following sections, you will be able to

20–1 The Nature of Magnets

■ Describe magnetism and the behavior of magnetic poles.

■ Relate magnetic fields and magnetic field lines of force.

■ Explain magnetism in terms of magnetic domains.

20–2 The Earth As a Magnet

■ Describe the Earth's magnetic properties.

■ Explain how a compass works.

■ Identify other sources of magnetism in the solar system.

20–3 Magnetism in Action

■ Explain what happens to a charged particle in a magnetic field.

More than 2000 years ago, the Greeks living in a part of Turkey known as Magnesia discovered an unusual rock. The rock attracted materials that contained iron. Because the rock was found in Magnesia, the Greeks named it magnetite. As the Greeks experimented with their new discovery, they observed another interesting thing about this peculiar rock. If they allowed it to swing freely from a string, the same part of the rock would always face in the same direction. That direction was toward a certain northern star, called the leading star, or lodestar. Because of this property, magnetite also became known as lodestone.

The Greeks did not know it then, but they were observing a property of matter called magnetism. In this chapter you will discover what magnetism is, the properties that make a substance magnetic, and the significance of magnetism in your life.

Journal *Activity*

You and Your World You probably use several magnets in the course of a day. In your journal, describe some of the magnets you encounter and how they are used. Also suggest other uses for magnets.

◀ *Magnetite, or lodestone, is a natural magnet that exhibits such properties as attracting iron filings.*

Guide for Reading

Focus on these questions as you read.

▶ What are the characteristics of a magnetic field?

▶ How is magnetism related to the atomic structure of a material?

ACTIVITY

DISCOVERING

Magnetic Forces

1. Take two bar magnets of the same size and hold one in each hand.

2. Experiment with the magnets by bringing different combinations of poles together. What do you feel in your hands?

■ Explain your observations in terms of magnetic forces.

20–1 The Nature of Magnets

Have you ever been fascinated by the seemingly mysterious force you feel when you try to push two magnets together or pull them apart? This strange phenomenon is known as **magnetism.** You may not realize it, but magnets play an extremely important role in your world. Do you use a magnet to hold notes on your refrigerator or locker door? Do you play video- and audiotapes? Perhaps you have used the magnet on an electric can opener. Did you know that a magnet keeps the door of your freezer sealed tight? See, you do take advantage of the properties of magnets.

Magnetic Poles

All magnets exhibit certain characteristics. Any magnet, no matter what its shape, has two ends where its magnetic effects are strongest. These regions are referred to as the **poles** of the magnet. One pole is labeled the north pole and the other the south pole. Magnets come in different shapes and sizes. The simplest kind of magnet is a straight bar of iron. Another common magnet is in the shape of a horseshoe. In either case, the poles are at each end. Figure 20–1 shows a variety of common magnets.

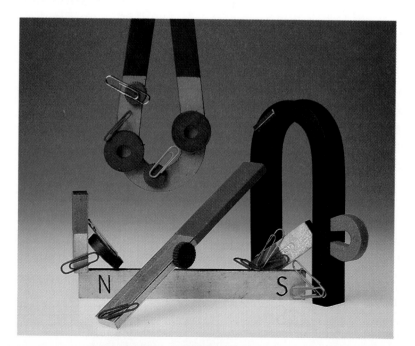

Figure 20–1 *Modern magnets come in a variety of sizes and shapes, including bar magnets, horseshoe magnets, and disc magnets.*

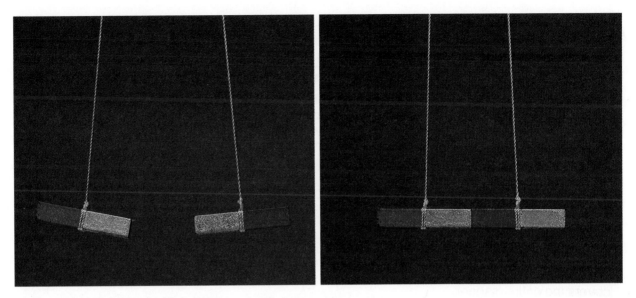

Figure 20–2 *Two bar magnets suspended by strings are free to move. What force is occurring between the magnets in each photograph? Why?*

When two magnets are brought near each other, they exert a force on each other. Magnetic forces, like electric forces, involve attractions and repulsions. If the two north poles are brought close together, they will repel each other. Two south poles do the same thing. However, if the north pole of one magnet is brought near the south pole of another magnet, the poles will attract each other. The rule for magnetic poles is: Like poles repel each other and unlike poles attract each other. How does this rule compare with the rule that describes the behavior of electric charges?

Magnetic poles always appear in pairs—a north pole and a south pole. For many years, physicists have tried to isolate a single magnetic pole. You might think that the most logical approach to separating poles would be to cut a magnet in half. Logical, yes; correct, no. If a magnet is cut in half, two smaller magnets each with a north pole and a south pole are produced. This procedure can be repeated again and again, but a complete magnet is always produced. Theories predict that it should be possible to find a single magnetic pole (monopole), but experimental evidence does not agree. A number of scientists are actively pursuing such a discovery because magnetic monopoles are believed to have played an important role in the early history of the universe.

Figure 20–3 *No matter how many times a magnet is cut in half, each piece retains its magnetic properties. How are magnetic poles different from electric charges?*

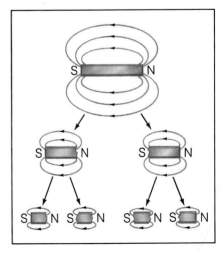

Mapping Lines of Magnetic Force

For this activity you need iron filings, a horseshoe magnet, a thin piece of cardboard, a pencil, and a sheet of paper.

1. Place the horseshoe magnet on a flat surface. Place the cardboard on top of it. Be sure the cardboard covers the entire magnet.

2. Sprinkle iron filings over the cardboard. Make a drawing of the pattern you see.

■ Explain why this particular pattern is formed.

■ What does the pattern tell you about the location of the poles of a horseshoe magnet?

You may think that science has all the answers and that everything has been discovered that can be discovered. But the quest for monopoles illustrates that scientific knowledge is continually developing and changing. It is often the case that a scientific discovery creates a whole new collection of questions to be answered—perhaps by inquisitive minds like yours.

Magnetic Fields

Although magnetic forces are strongest at the poles of a magnet, they are not limited to the poles alone. Magnetic forces are felt around the rest of the magnet as well. The region in which the magnetic forces can act is called a **magnetic field.**

It may help you to think of a magnetic field as an area mapped out by magnetic lines of force. Magnetic lines of force define the magnetic field of an object. Like electric field lines, magnetic field lines can be drawn to show the path of the field. But unlike electric fields, which start and end at charges, magnetic fields neither start nor end. They go around in complete loops from the north pole to the south pole of a magnet. **A magnetic field, represented by lines of force extending from one pole of a magnet to the other, is an area over which the magnetic force is exerted.**

Magnetic lines of force can be easily demonstrated by sprinkling iron filings on a piece of cardboard placed on top of a magnet. See Figure 20–4. Where are the lines of force always the most numerous and closest together?

Figure 20–4 *You can see the magnetic lines of force mapped out by the iron filings placed on a glass sheet above a magnet. The diagram illustrates these lines of force. Where are the lines strongest?*

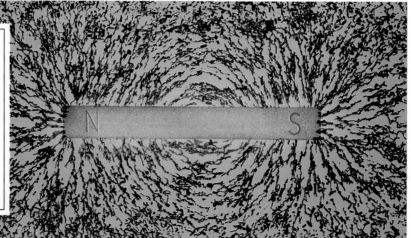

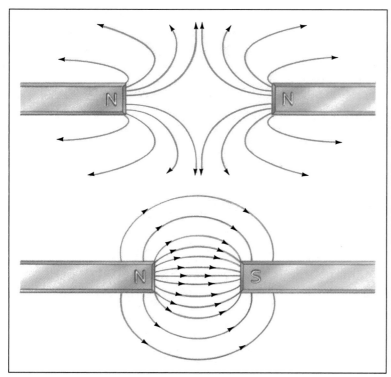

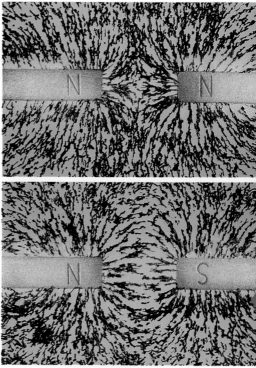

Figure 20–5 *What do the lines of force around these magnets tell you about the interaction of like and unlike magnetic poles?*

Figure 20–5 shows the lines of force that exist between like and unlike poles of two bar magnets. The pattern of iron filings shows that like poles repel each other and unlike poles attract each other.

Magnetic Materials

If you bring a magnet near a piece of wood, glass, aluminum, or plastic, what happens? You are right if you say nothing. There is no action between the magnet and any of these materials. In addition, none of these materials can be magnetized. Yet materials such as iron, steel, nickel, and cobalt react readily to a magnet. And all these materials can be magnetized. Why are some materials magnetic while others are not?

The most highly magnetic materials are called ferromagnetic materials. The name comes from the Latin name for iron, *ferrum*. Ferromagnetic materials are strongly attracted to magnets and can be made into magnets as well. For example, if you bring a strong magnet near an iron nail, the magnet will attract the nail. If you then stroke the nail several times in the same direction with the magnet, the nail itself becomes a magnet. The nail will remain magnetized even after the original magnet is removed.

Paper Clip Construction

1. How many paper clips can you make stick to the surface of a bar magnet?

Explain your results.

2. How many paper clips can you attach in a single row to a bar magnet?

Explain your results.

What would happen if you placed a plastic-coated paper clip in the second position?

Magnetic Domains

1. Cut several index cards into small strips to represent magnetic domains. Label each strip with a north pole and a south pole.

2. On a sheet of posterboard, arrange the strips to represent an unmagnetized substance.

3. On another sheet of posterboard, arrange the strips to represent a magnetized substance.

Provide a written explanation for your model.

Some materials, such as soft iron, are easy to magnetize. But they also lose their magnetism quickly. Magnets made of these materials are called temporary magnets. Other magnets are made of materials that are more difficult to magnetize, but they tend to stay magnetized. Magnets made of these materials are called permanent magnets. Cobalt, nickel, and iron are materials from which strong permanent magnets can be made. Many permanent magnets are made of a mixture of aluminum nickel, cobalt, copper, and iron called Alnico.

An Explanation of Magnetism

The magnetic properties of a material depend on its atomic structure. Scientists know that the atom itself has magnetic properties. These magnetic properties are due to the motion of the atom's electrons. Groups of atoms join in such a way that their magnetic fields are all arranged in the same direction, or aligned. This means that all the north poles face in one direction and all the south poles face in the other direction. A region in which the magnetic fields of individual atoms are lined up together is called a **magnetic domain.**

You can think of a magnetic domain as a miniature magnet with a north pole and a south pole. All materials are made up of many domains. In unmagnetized material, the domains are arranged randomly (all pointing in different directions). Because the domains exert magnetic forces in different directions, they cancel out. There is no overall magnetic force in the material. In a magnet, however, most of the domains are aligned. See Figure 20–6.

A magnet can be made from an unmagnetized material such as an iron nail by causing the domains to become aligned. When a ferromagnetic material is placed in a strong magnetic field, the poles of the magnet exert a force on the poles of the individual domains. This causes the domains to shift. Either

Figure 20–6 *The sections represent the various domains of a material. The arrows point toward the north pole of each domain. What is the arrangement of the domains in an unmagnetized material? In a magnetized material?*

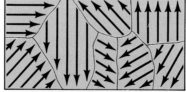

Unmagnetized material

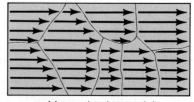

Magnetized material

most of the domains rotate (turn) to be in the direction of the field, or the domains already aligned with the field become larger while those in other directions become smaller. In both situations, an overall magnetic force is produced. Thus the material becomes a magnet.

This also explains why a magnet can pick up an unmagnetized object, such as a paper clip. The magnet's field causes a slight alignment of the domains in the paper clip so that the clip becomes a temporary magnet. Its north pole faces the south pole of the permanent magnet. Thus it is attracted to the magnet. When the magnet is removed, the domains return to their random arrangement and the paper clip is no longer magnetized.

Even a permanent magnet can become unmagnetized. For example, if you drop a magnet or strike it too hard, you will jar the domains into randomness. This will cause the magnet to lose some or all of its magnetism. Heating a magnet will also destroy its magnetism. This is because the additional energy (in the form of heat) causes the particles of the material to move faster and more randomly. In fact, every material has a certain temperature above which it cannot be made into a magnet at all.

Now that you have learned more about the nature of magnets, you can better describe the phenomenon of magnetism. **Magnetism is the force of attraction or repulsion of a magnetic material due to the arrangement of its atoms—particularly its electrons.**

Figure 20–7 *This iron nail attracts metal paper clips. How can an iron nail be turned into a magnet?*

20–1 Section Review

1. How is a magnetic field related to magnetic poles and lines of force?
2. State the rule that describes the behavior of magnetic poles.
3. What is magnetism?
4. What is a magnetic domain? How are magnetic domains related to magnetism?

Critical Thinking—*Applying Concepts*
5. From what you know about the origin of magnetism, explain why cutting a magnet in half produces two magnets.

ACTIVITY

Where It All Began

The phenomenon of magnetism has been known for many centuries, well before it was actually understood. Various references to this "magical" property can be found in ancient Chinese and Greek mythology. Using reference materials from your library, find out about the discovery and history of lodestones. Write a report describing how lodestone was discovered, what people first thought of it, and how it has come to be understood and used.

PROBLEM ? ? ? Solving

Mix-Up in the Lab

You are working in a research laboratory conducting experiments regarding the characteristics of magnets. You have several samples of magnetic materials and several samples of materials that are not magnetic. Unfortunately, you also have a problem. One of your inexperienced laboratory assistants has removed the label identifying one particular sample as magnetic or not magnetic. To make matters worse, you must complete this part of your research before your boss returns.

Drawing Conclusions

All you have is this photograph showing the pattern of the magnetic domains of the sample. Is the sample a magnet?

Explain how you reached your conclusion. Devise an experiment for your lab assistant to perform to prove your conclusion so that the sample can be correctly labeled.

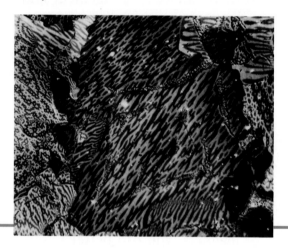

Guide for Reading

Focus on these questions as you read.

▶ *What are the magnetic properties of the Earth?*

▶ *How does a compass work?*

Activity Bank

Just Ducky, p.763

20–2 The Earth As a Magnet

You have read earlier that as the ancient Greeks experimented with magnetite, they discovered that the same part of the rock always pointed in the same direction. Why does one pole of a bar magnet suspended from a string always point north and the other pole always point south? After all, the poles of a magnet were originally labeled simply to describe the directions they faced with respect to the Earth.

The first person to suggest an answer to this question was an English physician named William Gilbert. In 1600, Gilbert proposed the idea that the Earth itself is a magnet. He predicted that the Earth would be found to have magnetic poles.

Gilbert's theory turned out to be correct. Magnetic poles of the Earth were eventually discovered.

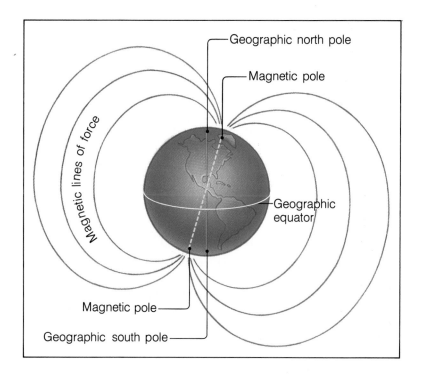

- Geographic north pole
- Magnetic pole
- Magnetic lines of force
- Geographic equator
- Magnetic pole
- Geographic south pole

Figure 20-8 *You can see in this illustration that the magnetic poles are not located exactly at the geographic poles. Does a compass needle, then, point directly north?*

Today, scientists know that the Earth behaves as if it has a huge bar magnet buried deep within it. **The Earth exerts magnetic forces and is surrounded by a magnetic field that is strongest near the north and the south magnetic poles.** The actual origin of the Earth's magnetic field is not completely understood. It is believed to be related to the motion of the Earth's outer core, which is mostly iron and nickel.

Scientists have been able to learn a great deal about the Earth's magnetic field and how it changes over time by studying patterns in magnetic rocks formed long ago. Some minerals have magnetic properties and are affected by the Earth's magnetism. In molten (hot liquid) rocks, the magnetic mineral particles line up in the direction of the Earth's magnetic poles. When the molten rocks harden, a permanent record of the Earth's magnetism remains in the rocks. Scientists have discovered that the history of the Earth's magnetism is recorded in magnetic stripes in the rocks. Although the stripes cannot be seen, they can be detected by special instruments. The pattern of the stripes reveals that the magnetic poles of the Earth have reversed themselves completely many times throughout Earth's history—every half-million years or so.

Activity Bank

Magnetic Personality, p.764

Figure 20-9 *When volcanic lava hardens into rock, the direction of the Earth's magnetic field at that time is permanently recorded.*

Figure 20–10 *Without the use of compasses, early discoverers would have been unable to chart their courses across the seas and make maps. This photograph shows the earliest surviving Portuguese compass.*

Compasses

If you have ever used a compass, you know that a compass needle always points north. The needle of a compass is magnetized. It has a north pole and a south pole. The Earth's magnetic field exerts a force on the needle just as it exerts a force on a bar magnet hanging from a string.

The north pole of a compass needle points to the North Pole of the Earth. But to exactly which north pole? As you have learned, like poles repel and unlike poles attract. So the magnetic pole of the Earth to which the north pole of a compass points must actually be a magnetic south pole. In other words, the north pole of a compass needle points toward the geographic North Pole, which is actually the magnetic south pole. The same is true of the geographic South Pole, which is actually the magnetic north pole.

The Earth's magnetic poles do not coincide directly with its geographic poles. Scientists have discovered that the magnetic south pole is located in northeastern Canada, about 1500 kilometers from the geographic North Pole. The magnetic north pole is located near the Antarctic Circle. The angular difference between a magnetic pole and a geographic pole is known as magnetic deviation, or declination. The extent of magnetic deviation is not the same for all places on the Earth. Near the equator, magnetic deviation is slight. As you get closer to the poles, the error increases. This must be taken into account when using a compass.

Other Sources of Magnetism in the Solar System

Magnetic fields have been detected repeatedly throughout the galaxy. In addition to Earth, several other planets produce magnetic fields. The magnetic field of Jupiter is more than 10 times greater than that of Earth. Saturn also has a very strong magnetic field. Like Earth, the source of the field is believed to be related to the planet's core.

The sun is another source of a magnetic field. The solar magnetic field extends far above the sun's surface. Streamers of the sun's corona (or outermost

Figure 20–11 *A total solar eclipse provides a glimpse of the sun's corona. The flares of the solar corona are shaped by the sun's magnetic field.*

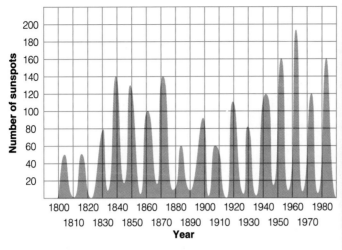

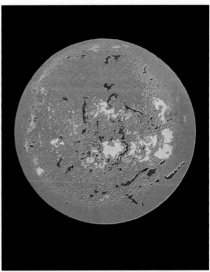

Figure 20–12 *The dark regions on the surface of the sun, or sunspots, are produced by the sun's magnetic field. The pattern of sunspots changes regularly in an 11-year cycle. Notice from the graph how the number of sunspots rises and falls.*

layer) trace the shape of the field. Within specific regions of the sun are very strong magnetic fields. Where magnetic lines of force break through the sun's surface, the temperature of the surface gases is lowered somewhat. These cooler areas appear as dark spots on the surface of the sun. These dark areas are known as sunspots. Sunspots always occur in pairs, each one of the pair representing the opposite poles of a magnet. The annual number of sunspots varies in an eleven-year cycle. The cycle is believed to be related to variations in the sun's magnetic field. Every eleven years the sun's magnetic field reverses, and the north and the south poles switch.

20–2 Section Review

1. In what ways is the Earth like a magnet?
2. How does a compass work?
3. What does it mean to say that the Earth's geographic North Pole is really near the magnetic south pole?
4. What is meant by magnetic declination?
5. How are sunspots related to the sun's magnetic field?

Connection—*Astronomy*

6. If the magnetic field of Earth is related to its inner core, how can astronomers learn about the inner cores of distant planets?

ACTIVITY
DOING

Cork-and-Needle Compass

1. Fill a nonmetal bowl about two-thirds full with water.

2. Magnetize a needle by stroking it with one end of a magnet.

3. Float a cork in the water; then place the needle on the cork. You may need to tape the needle in place.

4. Hold a compass next to the bowl. Compare its needle with the needle on the cork.

Explain how the cork-and-needle compass works. What is one disadvantage of a cork-and-needle compass?

525

20–3 Magnetism in Action

You learned in Chapter 19 that when a charged particle enters an electric field, an electric force is exerted on it (it is either pulled or pushed away). But what happens when a charged particle enters a magnetic field? The magnetic force exerted on the particle, if any, depends on a number of factors, especially the direction in which the particle is moving. **If a charged particle moves in the same direction as a magnetic field, no force is exerted on it. If a charged particle moves at an angle to a magnetic field, the magnetic force acting on it will cause it to move in a spiral around the magnetic field lines.** See Figure 20–14.

SOLAR WIND   The Earth and the other planets are immersed in a wind of charged particles sent out by the sun. These particles sweep through the solar system at speeds of 300 to 1000 kilometers per second. If this tremendous amount of radiation (emitted charged particles) reached the Earth, life as we know it could not survive.

Figure 20–13 *Because of its interaction with the solar wind, the Earth's magnetic field differs from that of a bar magnet. The solar wind causes the magnetosphere to stretch out into a tail shape on the side of the Earth that is experiencing nighttime.*

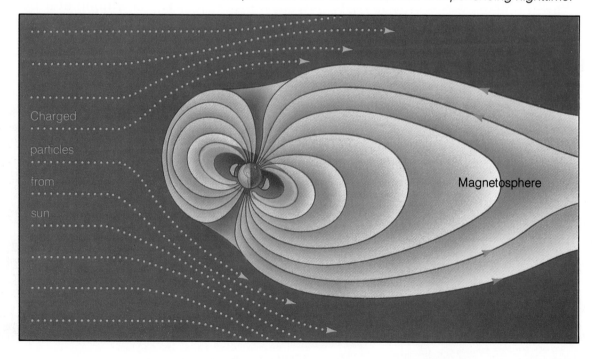

Charged

particles

from

sun

Magnetosphere

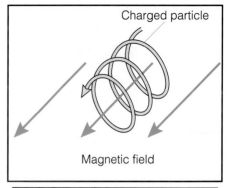

Charged particle

Magnetic field

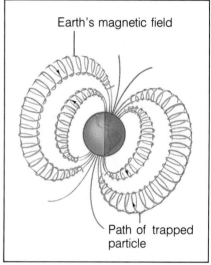

Earth's magnetic field

Path of trapped particle

Figure 20–14 *Charged particles from the sun become trapped in spiral paths around the Earth's magnetic field lines. What are the two regions in which the particles are confined called?*

Fortunately, however, these charged particles are deflected by the Earth's magnetic field. The magnetic field acts like an obstacle in the path of the solar wind. The region in which the magnetic field of the Earth is found is called the **magnetosphere.** Without the solar wind, the magnetosphere would look like the lines of force surrounding a bar magnet. However, on the side of the Earth facing away from the sun the magnetosphere is blown into a long tail by the solar wind. The solar wind constantly reshapes the magnetosphere as the Earth rotates on its axis.

Sometimes charged particles from the sun do penetrate the field. The particles are forced to continually spiral around the magnetic field lines, traveling back and forth between magnetic poles. Generally, these charged particles are found in two large regions known as the Van Allen radiation belts, named for their discoverer, James Van Allen.

When a large number of these particles get close to the Earth's surface, they interact with atoms in the atmosphere, causing the air to glow. Such a glowing region is called an **aurora.** Auroras are continually seen near the Earth's magnetic poles, since these are the places where the particles are closest to the Earth. The aurora seen in the northern hemisphere is known as the aurora borealis, or northern lights. In the southern hemisphere, the aurora is known as the aurora australis, or southern lights.

Many scientists believe that short-term changes in the Earth's weather are influenced by solar particles and their interaction with the Earth's magnetic field. In addition, during the reversal of the Earth's magnetic field, the field is somewhat weakened. This allows more high-energy particles to reach the Earth's surface. Some scientists hypothesize that these periods during which the magnetic field reversed might have caused the extinction of certain species of plants and animals.

Figure 20–15 *A band of colors called an aurora dances across the sky near the Earth's magnetic poles. This one is in northern Alaska. Why do auroras form?*

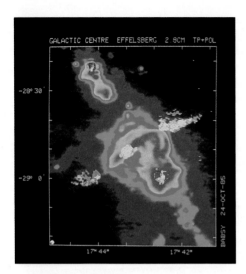

GALACTIC CENTRE EFFELSBERG 2.8CM TP+POL

BRABSY 24-OCT-85

Figure 20–16 *This map of the constellation Sagittarius was made from information collected by a radio telescope.*

ACTIVITY

READING

A Lonely Voyage

The dangerous quest to reach the North Pole was at one time only a vision in the minds of adventurous explorers. But during the 1800s several different explorers set out on difficult and sometimes fatal missions to the North Pole. Two different explorers reached the pole, but the matter of who arrived first still remains controversial. The answers lie in whether the explorers made appropriate corrections for magnetic declination. Read *To Stand at the Pole: The Dr. Cook-Admiral Peary North Pole Controversy* by William Hunt to discover the details of the story.

ASTRONOMY Radiation from particles spiraling around in magnetic fields also plays an important role in learning about the universe. Particles trapped by magnetic fields emit energy in the form of radio waves. Radioastronomers study the universe by recording and analyzing radio waves rather than light waves. In this way, scientists have been able to learn a great deal about many regions of the galaxy. For example, energy received from the Crab Nebula indicates that it is a remnant of a supernova (exploding star).

NUCLEAR ENERGY Utilizing the behavior of charged particles in magnetic fields may be a solution to the energy problem. A tremendous amount of energy can be released when two small atomic nuclei are joined, or fused, together into one larger nucleus. Accomplishing this, however, has been impossible until now because it is extremely difficult to overcome the repulsive electric forces present when two nuclei approach each other. At high temperatures, atoms break up into a gaseous mass of charged particles known as plasma. In this state, nuclear reactions are easier to achieve. But the required temperatures are so high that the charged particles cannot be contained by any existing vessels. By using magnetic fields, however, scientists have briefly created "magnetic bottles" to contain the particles at the required temperatures. Research is continuing in an effort to produce a self-sustaining fusion reaction.

20–3 Section Review

1. Describe what happens to a charged particle in a magnetic field.
2. How does the magnetosphere protect the Earth from the sun's damaging radiation?
3. What are Van Allen radiation belts? How are they related to auroras?
4. How might magnetic fields enable scientists to utilize energy from atomic nuclei?

Connection—*Earth Science*
5. Why would a planet close to the sun have to possess a strong magnetic field in order to sustain life?

CONNECTIONS

Magnetic Clues to Giant-Sized Mystery

Have you ever looked at a world map and noticed that the Earth's landmasses look like pieces of a giant jigsaw puzzle? According to many scientists, all the Earth's land was once connected. How then, did the continents form?

In the early 1900s, a scientist named Alfred Wegener proposed that the giant landmass that once existed split apart and its various parts "drifted" to their present positions. His theory, however, met with great opposition because in order for it to be true, it would involve the movement of sections of the solid ocean floor. Conclusive evidence to support his *theory of continental drift* could come only from a detailed study of the ocean floor.

In the 1950s, new mapping techniques enabled scientists to discover a large system of underwater mountains, called midocean ridges. These mountains have a deep crack, called a rift valley, running through their center. A great deal of volcanic activity occurs at the midocean ridges. When lava wells up through the rift valley and hardens into rock, new ocean floor is formed. This process is called *sea-floor spreading*. This evidence showed that the ocean floor could indeed move.

Further evidence came from information about the Earth's magnetic field. When the molten rocks from the midocean ridges harden, a permanent record of the Earth's magnetism remains in the rocks. Scientists found that the pattern of magnetic stripes on one side of the ridge matches the pattern on the other side. The obvious conclusion was that as magma hardens into rocks at the midocean ridge, half the rocks move in one direction and the other half move in the other direction. If it were not for knowledge about magnetism and the Earth's magnetic field, such a conclusion could not have been reached. Yet thanks to magnetic stripes, which provide clear evidence of ocean-floor spreading, the body of scientific knowledge has grown once again.

Laboratory Investigation

Plotting Magnetic Fields

Problem

How can the lines of force surrounding a bar magnet be drawn?

Materials *(per group)*

bar magnet	horseshoe magnet
sheet of white paper	compass
pencil	

Procedure

1. Place a bar magnet in the center of a sheet of paper. Trace around the magnet with a pencil. Remove the magnet and mark the ends of your drawing to show the north and the south poles. Put the magnet back on the sheet of paper in its outlined position.

2. Draw a mark at a spot about 2 cm beyond the north pole of the magnet. Place a compass on this mark.

3. Note the direction that the compass needle points. On the paper, mark the position of the north pole of the compass needle by drawing a small arrow. The arrow should extend from the mark you made in step 2 and point in the direction of the north pole of the compass needle. This arrow indicates the direction of the magnetic field at the point marked. See the accompanying diagram.

4. Repeat steps 2 and 3 at 20 to 30 points around the magnet. You should have 20 to 30 tiny arrows on the paper when you have finished.

5. Remove the magnet from the paper. Observe the pattern of the magnetic field you have plotted with your arrows.

6. Using a clean sheet of paper, repeat steps 1 through 5 using a horseshoe magnet.

Observations

1. Describe the pattern of arrows you have drawn to represent the magnetic field of the bar magnet. How does it differ from that of the horseshoe magnet?

2. From which pole does the magnetic field emerge on the bar magnet? On the horseshoe magnet?

Analysis and Conclusions

1. What evidence is there that the magnetic field is strongest near the poles of a magnet?

2. What can you conclude about the path of magnetic field lines between the poles of any magnet?

3. **On Your Own** The pattern of magnetic field lines for a bar magnet will change if another bar magnet is placed near it. Design and complete an investigation similar to this one in which you demonstrate this idea for both like poles and unlike poles.

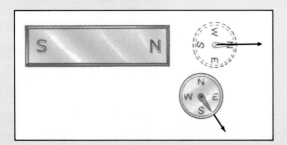

Study Guide

Summarizing Key Concepts

20–1 The Nature of Magnets

▲ Every magnet has two poles—a north pole and a south pole. Like magnetic poles repel each other; unlike poles attract each other.

▲ The region in which magnetic forces can act is called a magnetic field. Magnetic fields are traced by magnetic lines of force.

▲ Magnetic domains are regions in which the magnetic fields of all the atoms line up in the same direction. The magnetic domains of a magnet are aligned. The magnetic domains of unmagnetized material are arranged randomly.

▲ Magnetism is the force of attraction or repulsion exerted by a magnet through its magnetic field.

20–2 The Earth As a Magnet

▲ The Earth is surrounded by a magnetic field that is strongest around the magnetic north and the south poles.

▲ A compass needle does not point exactly to the Earth's geographic poles. It points to the magnetic poles. The difference in the location of the Earth's magnetic and geographic poles is called magnetic declination.

▲ Sunspots on the surface of the sun are related to the sun's magnetic field.

20–3 Magnetism in Action

▲ The deflection of charged particles in a magnetic field is responsible for several phenomena: the protection of the Earth from solar wind; radio astronomy; and future applications of nuclear reactions to produce energy.

▲ The region in which the magnetic field of Earth is exerted is known as the magnetosphere.

▲ Some charged particles from the sun become trapped by Earth's magnetic field. They are located in two regions known as the Van Allen radiation belts. If charged particles reach Earth's surface, usually at the poles, they create auroras.

Reviewing Key Terms

Define each term in a complete sentence.

20–1 The Nature of Magnets
magnetism
pole
magnetic field
magnetic domain

20–3 Magnetism in Action
magnetosphere
aurora

Chapter Review

Content Review

Multiple Choice

Choose the letter of the answer that best completes each statement.

1. The region in which magnetic forces act is called a
   a. line of force.
   b. pole.
   c. magnetic field.
   d. field of attraction.

2. A region in a magnet in which the magnetic fields of atoms are aligned is a
   a. ferrum.
   b. domain.
   c. compass.
   d. magnetosphere.

3. The idea of the Earth as a magnet was first proposed by
   a. Dalton.
   b. Faraday.
   c. Oersted.
   d. Gilbert.

4. The results of the sun's magnetic field can be seen as
   a. sunspots.
   b. solar winds.
   c. magnetic stripes.
   d. ridges.

5. Which of the following is not a magnetic material?
   a. lodestone
   b. glass
   c. cobalt
   d. nickel

6. The region of the Earth's magnetic field is called the
   a. atmosphere.
   b. stratosphere.
   c. aurora.
   d. magnetosphere.

7. Charged particles from the sun that get close to the Earth's surface produce
   a. supernovas.
   b. volcanoes.
   c. plasma.
   d. auroras.

True or False

If the statement is true, write "true." If it is false, change the underlined word or words to make the statement true.

1. The north pole of a magnet suspended horizontally from a string will point <u>north</u>.
2. <u>Like</u> poles of a magnet <u>attract</u> each other.
3. The region in which magnetic forces act is called a <u>magnetic field</u>.
4. Steel <u>cannot</u> be magnetized.
5. In a magnetized substance, <u>magnetic domains</u> point in the same direction.
6. Magnetic domains exist because of the magnetic fields produced by the motion of <u>electrons</u>.
7. A compass needle points to the Earth's <u>geographic pole</u>.
8. The Earth's magnetic field protects against the harmful radiation in <u>solar winds</u>.

Concept Mapping

Complete the following concept map for Section 20–1. Then construct a concept map for the entire chapter.

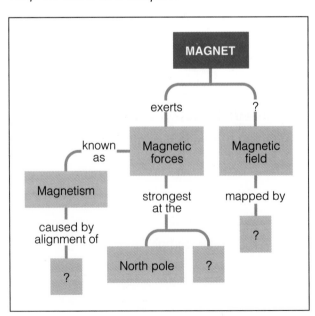

Concept Mastery

Discuss each of the following in a brief paragraph.

1. What are magnetic poles? How do magnetic poles behave when placed next to each other?
2. What happens when a magnet is cut in half? Why?
3. How is a magnetic field represented by magnetic field lines of force?
4. How are magnetic domains related to the atomic structure of a material?
5. How can evidence of changes in the Earth's magnetic field be found in rocks?
6. Why are some materials magnetic while others are not? How can a material be magnetized? How can a magnet lose its magnetism?
7. Like what type of magnet does the Earth act? How?
8. Describe several sources of magnetism in the solar system.
9. Explain how an aurora is produced.
10. What is the significance of the fact that charged particles can become trapped by magnetic fields?

Critical Thinking and Problem Solving

Use the skills you have developed in this chapter to answer each of the following.

1. **Making comparisons** How do the lines of force that arise when north and south poles of a magnet are placed close together compare with the lines of force that arise when two like poles are placed close together? Use a diagram in your explanation.
2. **Applying concepts** Why might an inexperienced explorer using a compass get lost near the geographic poles?
3. **Making comparisons** One proton is traveling at a speed of 100 m/sec parallel to a magnetic field. Another proton is traveling at a speed of 10 m/sec perpendicular to the same magnetic field. Which one experiences the greater magnetic force? Explain.
4. **Identifying patterns** Describe the difference between a permanent magnet and a temporary magnet.
5. **Relating cause and effect** Stroking a material with a strong magnet causes the material to become magnetic. Explain what happens during this process.
6. **Making inferences** Why might a material be placed between two other materials so that magnetic lines of force are not allowed to pass through?
7. **Using the writing process** Write a poem or short story describing the importance of magnets in your daily life. Include at least five detailed examples.

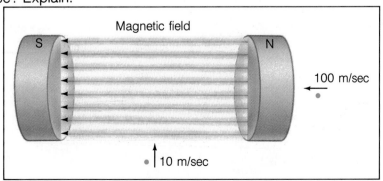

Electromagnetism

Guide for Reading

After you read the following sections, you will be able to

21–1 Magnetism From Electricity
- Describe how a magnetic field is created by an electric current.
- Discuss the force exerted on an electric current by a magnetic field.
- Apply the principles of electromagnetism to devices such as the electric motor.

21–2 Electricity From Magnetism
- Explain how electricity can be produced from magnetism.
- Apply the principle of induction to generators and transformers.

Traveling by train can be convenient. But by today's standards, a long train ride can also be time-consuming. The speed of modern trains is limited by the problems associated with the movement of wheels on a track. Engineers all over the world, however, are now involved in the development of trains that "float" above the track. The trains are called maglev trains, which stands for magnetic levitation. Because a maglev train has no wheels, it appears to levitate. While a conventional train has a maximum speed of about 300 kilometers per hour, a maglev train is capable of attaining speeds of nearly 500 kilometers per hour.

Although this may seem to be some sort of magic, it is actually the application of basic principles of electricity and magnetism. Maglev trains are supported and propelled by the interaction of magnets located on the train body and on the track.

In this chapter, you will learn about the intricate and useful relationship between electricity and magnetism. And you will gain an understanding of how magnets can power a train floating above the ground.

Journal *Activity*

You and Your World Have you ever wondered where the electricity you use in your home comes from? In your journal, describe the wires you see connected across poles to all the buildings in your area. If you cannot see them, explain where they must be. Describe some of the factors you think would be involved in providing electricity to an entire city.

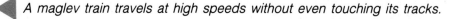

A maglev train travels at high speeds without even touching its tracks.

21–1 Magnetism From Electricity

When you think of a source of magnetism, you may envision a bar magnet or a horseshoe magnet. After reading Chapter 20, you may even suggest the Earth or the sun. But would it surprise you to learn that a wire carrying current is also a source of magnetism?

You can prove this to yourself by performing a simple experiment. Bring a compass near a wire carrying an electric current. The best place to hold the compass is just above or below the wire, with its needle parallel to it. Observe what happens to the compass needle when electricity is flowing through the wire and when it is not. What do you observe?

This experiment is similar to one performed more than 150 years ago by the Danish physicist Hans Christian Oersted. His experiment led to an important scientific discovery about the relationship between electricity and magnetism, otherwise known as **electromagnetism.**

Figure 21–1 *A current flowing through a wire creates a magnetic field. This can be seen by the deflection of the compasses around the wire. Notice that the magnetic field is in a circle around the wire and that the direction of the magnetic field lines changes when the wires connected to the battery are reversed. What then determines the direction of the magnetic lines of force?*

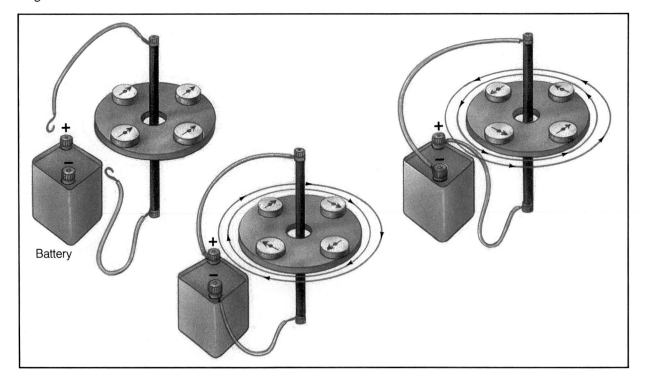

Battery

Oersted's Discovery

For many years, Oersted had believed that a connection between electricity and magnetism had to exist, but he could not find it experimentally. In 1820, however, he finally obtained his evidence. Oersted observed that when a compass is placed near an electric wire, the compass needle deflects, or moves, as soon as current flows through the wire. When the direction of the current is reversed, the needle moves in the opposite direction. When no electricity flows through the wire, the compass needle remains stationary. Since a compass needle is deflected only by a magnetic field, Oersted concluded that an electric current produces a magnetic field. **An electric current flowing through a wire gives rise to a magnetic field whose direction depends on the direction of the current.** The magnetic field lines produced by a current in a straight wire are in the shape of circles with the wire at their center. See Figure 21–1.

Electromagnets

Oersted then realized that if a wire carrying current is twisted into loops, or coiled, the magnetic fields produced by each loop add together. The result is a strong magnetic field in the center and at the two ends, which act like the poles of a magnet. A long coil of wire with many loops is called a **solenoid.** Thus a solenoid acts as a magnet when a current passes through it. The north and the south poles change with the direction of the current.

The magnetic field of a solenoid can be strengthened by increasing the number of coils or the amount of current flowing through the wire. The greatest increase in the strength of the magnetic field, however, is produced by placing a piece of iron in the center of the solenoid. The magnetic field of the solenoid magnetizes—or aligns the magnetic domains of—the iron. The resulting magnetic field is the magnetic field of the wire plus the magnetic field of the iron. This can be hundreds or thousands of times greater than the strength of the field produced by the wire alone. A solenoid with a magnetic material such as iron inside it is called an **electromagnet.**

Making an Electromagnet

Obtain a low-voltage dry cell, nail, and length of thin insulated wire.

1. Remove the insulation from the ends of the wire.

2. Wind the wire tightly around the nail so that you have at least 25 turns.

3. Connect each uninsulated end of the wire to a post on the dry cell.

4. Collect some lightweight metal objects. Touch the nail to each one. What happens?

Explain why the device you constructed behaves as it does.

Activity Bank

Slugging It Out, p. 765

Figure 21–2 *A coil of wire carrying current is a solenoid. As a wire is wound into a solenoid, the magnetic field created by the current becomes strongest at the ends and constant in the center, like that of a bar magnet.*

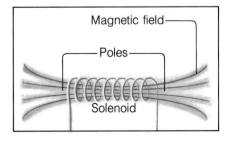

Magnetic field

Poles

Solenoid

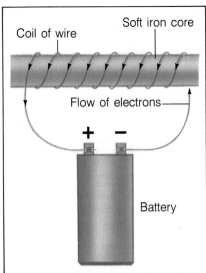

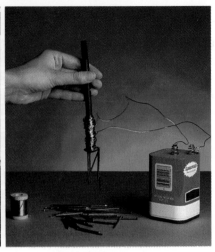

Figure 21–3 *An electromagnet is produced when a piece of soft iron is placed in the center of a solenoid. Large electromagnets can be used to pick up heavy pieces of metal. What factors determine the strength of an electromagnet?*

The type of iron used in electromagnets acquires and loses its magnetism when the electric current is turned on and off. This makes electromagnets strong, temporary magnets. Can you think of other ways in which this property of an electromagnet might be useful?

Magnetic Forces on Electric Currents

You have just learned that an electric current exerts a force on a magnet such as a compass. But forces always occur in pairs. Does a magnetic field exert a force on an electric current?

To answer this question, consider the following experiment. A wire is placed in the magnetic field between the poles of a horseshoe magnet. When a current is sent through the wire, the wire jumps up as shown in Figure 21–4. When the direction of the

Figure 21–4 *A magnetic field will exert a force on a wire carrying current. On what does the direction of the force depend?*

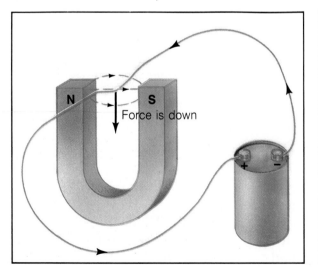

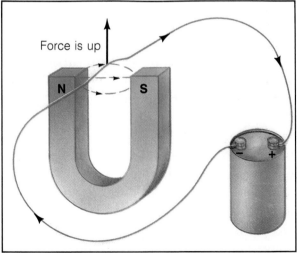

current is reversed, the wire is pulled down. So the answer is yes. **A magnetic field exerts a force on a wire carrying current.** Actually, this fact should not surprise you. After all, as you learned in Chapter 20, a magnetic field can exert a force on a charged particle. An electric current is simply a collection of moving charges.

Applications of Electromagnetism

A number of practical devices take advantage of the relationship that exists between electric currents and magnetic fields.

ELECTRIC MOTOR An **electric motor** is a device that changes electrical energy into mechanical energy that is used to do work. (Mechanical energy is energy related to motion.) An electric motor contains a loop, or coil, of wire mounted on a cylinder called an armature. The armature is attached to a shaft that is free to spin between the poles of a permanent magnet. In some motors, the permanent magnet is replaced by an electromagnet.

When a current flows through the coil of wire, the magnetic field of the permanent magnet exerts a force on the current. Because the current flows up one side of the coil and down the other, the magnetic field pushes one side of the coil up and one side down. This makes the coil rotate until it lines up with the magnetic field of the magnet. A motor, however, must turn continuously. This is achieved by changing the direction of the current just as the armature is about to stop turning. When the current changes direction, the side of the coil that had been pushed up is pushed down and the side that had been pushed down is pushed up. So the armature continues to turn. This process occurs over and over.

A current that switches direction every time the armature turns halfway is essential to the operation of an electric motor. The easiest way to supply a changing current is to use AC, or alternating current, to run the electric motor.

An electric motor can be made to run on DC, or direct current, by attaching a device known as a commutator to the armature. In a simple motor, the commutator is a ring that is split in half and

ACTIVITY

DISCOVERING

Changing Direction

Obtain a dry cell, a compass, and a length of thin insulated wire.

1. Remove the insulation from both ends of the wire.

2. Place the compass flat on the table. Observe the direction of the needle.

3. Connect each uninsulated end of the wire to a post on the dry cell. Put the center of the wire across the compass. Observe the needle.

4. Disconnect the wires and reconnect them to the opposite terminals without moving the wire over the compass. What happens? Repeat this procedure.

■ How is the magnetic field produced by an electric current related to the direction of the current?

Figure 21–5 *A motor can be found within most practical devices.*

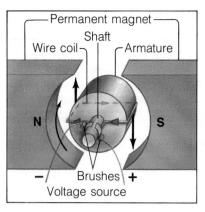
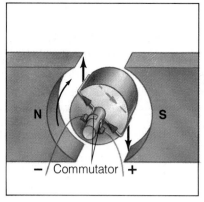
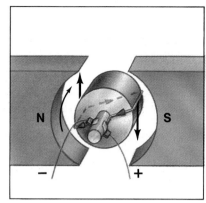

Figure 21–6 *When current travels into the motor through the brush on the left, it first enters through the side of the coil attached to the commutator marked in green in the illustration. The magnetic field of the permanent magnet then pushes the left side of the coil up and the right side down. When the armature turns far enough, the green part moves to the opposite brush and the commutator marked in yellow moves to the brush on the left. At this point, current travels into the side of the coil attached to the yellow commutator, causing its direction to change within the coil, and the coil to rotate further.*

Figure 21–7 *As current flows through the wire in a galvanometer, the magnet forces the wire to turn and deflect the needle attached to it. The greater the current, the greater the deflection.*

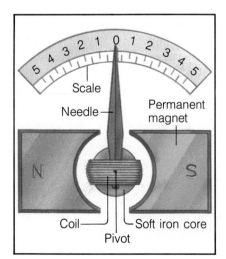

connected to the ends of the coil. See Figure 21–6. Electric current is supplied to the commutator through two contacts called brushes that do not move, but simply touch the commutator as it spins. At first, current travels from the source through one of the brushes to the commutator and into one side of the coil. But by the time the coil rotates half way, each commutator moves to the opposite brush. Thus current enters through the same brush but into the other side of the coil. This reverses the direction of the current in the coil.

Most motors actually contain several coils, each located in a different place on the armature. This allows the current to be fed into whichever coil is in the right position to get the greatest force from the magnetic field.

GALVANOMETER Another instrument that depends on electromagnetism is a **galvanometer.** A galvanometer is an instrument used to detect small currents. It is the basic component of many meters, including the ammeter and voltmeter you read about in Chapter 19. A galvanometer consists of a coil of wire connected to an electric circuit and a needle. The wire is suspended in the magnetic field of a permanent magnet. When current flows through the wire, the magnetic field exerts a force, causing the wire to move the needle of the galvanometer. The size of the current will determine the amount of force on the wire, and the amount the needle will move. Because the needle will move in the opposite direction when the current is reversed, a galvanometer can be used to measure the direction of current as well as the amount.

OTHER COMMON USES A simple type of electromagnet consists of a solenoid in which an iron rod is only partially inserted. Many doorbells operate with this type of device. See Figure 21–8. When the doorbell is pushed, the circuit is closed and current flows through the solenoid. The current causes the solenoid to exert a magnetic force. The magnetic force pulls the iron into the solenoid until it strikes a bell.

The same basic principle is used in the starter of an automobile. When the ignition key is turned, a circuit is closed, causing an iron rod to be pulled into a solenoid located in the car's starter. The movement of the iron rod connects the starter to other parts of the engine and moves a gear that enables the engine to turn on. Another example of the application of this principle can be found in a washing machine. The valves that control the flow of water into the machine are opened and closed by the action of an iron rod moving into a solenoid.

Some other uses of electromagnets include telephones, telegraphs, and switches in devices such as tape recorders. Electromagnets also are important in heavy machinery that is used to move materials, such as moving scrap metal from one place to another.

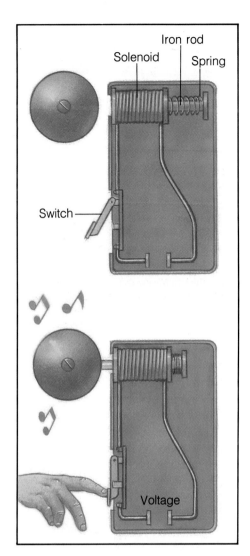

Figure 21–8 *Whenever you ring a doorbell, you are using a solenoid. When the button is pushed, current flows through the wire causing the solenoid to act as a magnet. Once magnetic, the solenoid attracts the bar of iron until the iron strikes the bell, which then rings.*

21–1 Section Review

1. How is magnetism related to electricity?
2. What is an electromagnet? What are some uses of electromagnets?
3. How is an electromagnet different from a permanent magnet?
4. How does an electromagnet change electric energy to mechanical energy in an electric motor?

Critical Thinking—*Making Comparisons*
5. How is the effect of an electric current on a compass needle different from the effect of the Earth's magnetic field on a compass needle?

21–2 Electricity From Magnetism

If magnetism can be produced from electricity, can electricity be produced from magnetism? Scientists who learned of Oersted's discovery asked this very question. In 1831, the English scientist Michael Faraday and the American scientist Joseph Henry independently provided the answer. It is interesting to note that historically Henry was the first to make the discovery. But because Faraday published his results first and investigated the subject in more detail, his work is better known.

Electromagnetic Induction

In his attempt to produce an electric current from a magnetic field, Faraday used an apparatus similar to the one shown in Figure 21–9. The coil of wire on the left is connected to a battery. When current flows through the wire, a magnetic field is produced. The strength of the magnetic field is increased by the iron, as in an electromagnet. Faraday hoped that the steady current would produce a magnetic field strong enough to create a current in the wire on the right. But no matter how strong the current he used, Faraday could not achieve his

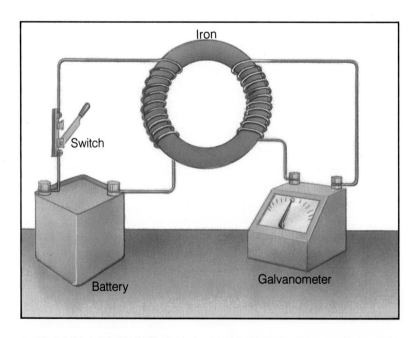

Figure 21–9 *Using this setup, Faraday found that whenever the current in the wire on the left changed, a current was induced in the wire on the right. The changing current produced a changing magnetic field, which in turn gave rise to a current.*

desired results. The magnetic field did not produce a current in the second wire. However, something rather strange caught Faraday's attention. The needle of the galvanometer deflected whenever the current was turned on or off. Thus a current was produced in the wire on the right, but only when the current (and thus the magnetic field) was changing.

Faraday concluded that although a steady magnetic field produced no electric current, a changing magnetic field did. Such a current is called an **induced current.** The process by which a current is produced by a changing magnetic field is called **electromagnetic induction.**

Faraday did many other experiments into the nature of electromagnetic induction. In one, he tried moving a magnet near a closed loop of wire. What he found out was that when the magnet is held still, there is no current in the wire. But when the magnet is moved, a current is induced in the wire. The direction of the current depends on the direction of movement of the magnet. In another experiment he tried holding the magnet still while moving the wire circuit. In this case, a current is again induced.

The one common element in all Faraday's experiments is a changing magnetic field. It does not matter whether the magnetic field changes because the magnet moves, the circuit moves, or the current

Compass Interference

Use a compass to explore the magnetic properties of a room. Take the compass to different parts of the room to see which way the needle points. Can you find places where the compass does not point north? Why does it point in different directions?

■ What precautions must a ship's navigator take when using a compass?

Figure 21–10 *A current is induced in a wire that is exposed to a changing magnetic field. Here the magnet is moved past a stationary wire. On what does the direction of the current depend?*

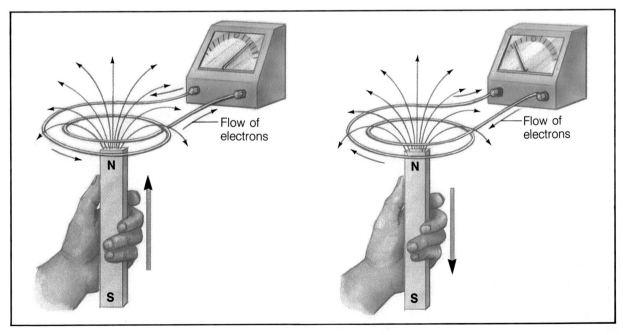

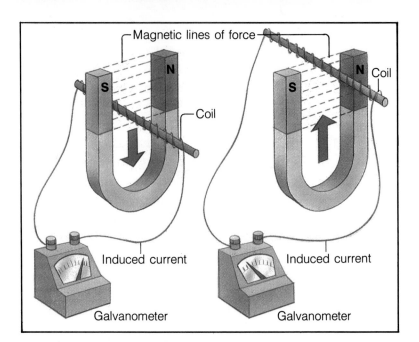

Figure 21–11 *A current is also induced in a wire when the wire is moved through a stationary magnetic field.*

giving rise to the magnetic field changes. It matters only that a changing magnetic field is experienced. **An electric current will be induced in a circuit exposed to a changing magnetic field.**

It may help you to think about electromagnetic induction in terms of magnetic lines of force. In each case magnetic lines of force are being cut by a wire. When a conducting wire cuts across magnetic lines of force, a current is produced.

GENERATORS An important application of electromagnetic induction is a **generator.** A generator is a device that converts mechanical energy into electrical energy. How does this energy conversion compare with that in an electric motor? Generators in power plants are responsible for producing about 99 percent of the electricity used in the United States.

A simple generator consists of a loop of wire mounted on a rod, or axle, that can rotate. The loop of wire, which is attached to a power source, is placed between the poles of a magnet. When the loop of wire is rotated by the power source, it moves through the field of the magnet. Thus it experiences a changing magnetic field (magnetic lines of force are being cut). The result is an induced current in the wire.

As the loop of wire continues to rotate, the wire moves parallel to the magnetic lines of force. At this point the field is not changing and no lines of force

ACTIVITY

WRITING

The History of Electromagnetism

Several scientists were responsible for establishing the relationship between electricity and magnetism. Using books and reference materials in the library, write a report about the scientists listed below. Include information about their lives as well as their contributions to a better understanding of electromagnetism.

Hans Christian Oersted
André Ampère
Michael Faraday
Joseph Henry
Nikola Tesla

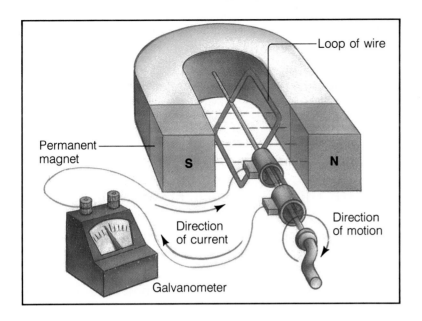

Figure 21–12 *Inside a basic generator, a loop of wire is rotated through a stationary magnetic field. Because the wire continuously changes its direction of movement through the field, the induced current keeps reversing direction. What type of current is produced?*

are cut, so no current is produced. Further rotation moves the loop to a position where magnetic lines of force are cut again. But this time the lines of force are cut from the opposite direction. This means that the induced current is in the opposite direction. Because the direction of the electric current changes with each complete rotation of the wire, the current produced is AC, or alternating current.

The large generators in power plants have many loops of wire rotating inside large electromagnets. The speed of the generators is controlled very carefully. The current is also controlled so that it reverses direction 120 times each second. Because two reversals make one complete cycle of alternating

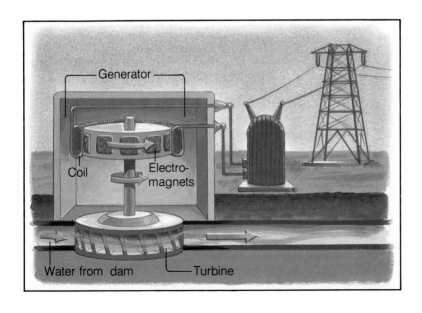

Figure 21–13 *In the operation of a modern generator, a source of mechanical energy—such as water—spins a turbine. The turbine moves large electromagnets encased in coils of insulated wire. As the electromagnets move, the coiled wire cuts through a magnetic field, inducing an electric current in the wire.*

current, the electricity generated has a frequency of 60 hertz. (Frequency is the number of cycles per second, measured in hertz.) Alternating current in the United States has a frequency of 60 hertz. In many other countries, the frequency of alternating current is 50 hertz.

Generators can also be made to produce direct current. In fact, the system proposed and developed by Thomas Edison distributed direct-current electricity. However, the method of alternating current, developed by Edison's rival Nikola Tesla, eventually took its place. When only direct current is used, it has to be produced at high voltages, which are extremely dangerous to use in the home and office. Alternating current, however, can be adjusted to safe voltage levels.

You may wonder about what type of power source is responsible for turning the loop of wire in a generator. In certain generators it can be as simple as a hand crank. But in large generators turbines provide the mechanical energy to turn the axles. Turbines are wheels that are turned by the force of moving wind, water, or steam. Most of the power used in the United States today is generated at steam

Figure 21–14 *The force of moving water can be used to spin turbines in generators located in a power plant such as this one at Hoover Dam. What energy conversion takes place in a generator?*

plants. There the heat from the burning of fossil fuels (coal, oil, natural gas) or from nuclear fission boils water to produce high-pressure steam that turns the turbines. In many modern generators, the loop remains stationary, but the magnetic field rotates. The magnetic field is produced by a set of electromagnets that rotate.

If you own a bicycle that has a small generator attached to the wheel to operate the lights, you are the source of power for the generator. To turn the lights on, a knob on the generator is moved so that it touches the wheel. As you pedal the bike, you provide the mechanical energy to turn the wheel. The wheel then turns the knob. The knob is attached to a shaft inside the generator. The shaft rotates a coil of wire through a magnetic field. What happens to the lights when you stop pedaling?

A small electric generator, often called an alternator, is used to recharge the battery in a car while the engine is running. Even smaller electric generators are used extensively in the conversion of information into electric signals. When you play a conventional record, for example, the grooves in the record cause the needle to wiggle. The needle is connected to a tiny magnet mounted inside a coil. As the magnet wiggles, a current is induced that corresponds to the sounds in the record grooves. This signal drives loudspeakers, which themselves use magnetic forces to convert electric signals to sound.

When you play a videotape or an audiotape, you are again taking advantage of induced currents. When information is taped onto a videotape or audiotape, it is in the form of an electric signal. The electric signal is fed to an electromagnet. The strength of the field of the electromagnet depends on the strength of the electric signal. The tape is somewhat magnetic. When it passes by the electromagnet, the magnetic field pulls on the magnetic domains of the tape. According to the electric signal, the domains are arranged in a particular way. When the recorded tape is played, a tiny current is induced due to the changing magnetic field passing the head of the tape player. The magnetic field through the tape head changes with the changing magnetic field of the tape, inducing a current that corresponds to

Figure 21–15 *A light powered by a generator on a bicycle uses the mechanical energy of the spinning tire to rotate the wire. Can the light be on when the bicycle is not in use?*

the information—audio, video, or computer data—recorded on the tape. Magnetic disks used for information storage in computers work on the same principle. For this reason, placing a tape next to a strong magnet or a device consisting of an electromagnet can destroy the information on the tape.

Devices that use electromagnetic induction have a wide variety of applications. In the field of geophysics, a device called a geophone, or seismometer, is used to detect movements of the Earth—especially those associated with earthquakes. A geophone consists of a magnet and a coil of wire. Either the magnet or the wire is fixed to the Earth and thus moves when the Earth moves. The other part of the geophone is suspended by a spring so that it does not move. When the Earth moves, a changing magnetic field is experienced and an electric current is induced. This electric current is converted into an electric signal that can be detected and measured. Why is a geophone a valuable scientific instrument?

TRANSFORMERS A **transformer** is a device that increases or decreases the voltage of alternating current. A transformer operates on the principle that a current in one coil induces a current in another coil.

A transformer consists of two coils of insulated wire wrapped around the same iron core. One coil is called the primary coil and the other coil is called the secondary coil. When an alternating current passes through the primary coil, a magnetic field is created. The magnetic field varies as a result of the alternating current. Electromagnetic induction causes a current to flow in the secondary coil.

If the number of loops in the primary and the secondary coils is equal, the induced voltage of the secondary coil will be the same as that of the primary coil. However, if there are more loops in the secondary coil than in the primary coil, the voltage of the secondary coil will be greater. Since this type of transformer increases the voltage, it is called a step-up transformer.

In a step-down transformer, there are fewer loops in the secondary coil than there are in the primary coil. So the voltage of the secondary coil is less than that of the primary coil.

Transformers play an important role in the transmission of electricity. Power plants are often situated

ACTIVITY

DISCOVERING

An Electrifying Experience

1. Remove the insulation from both ends of a length of thin insulated wire.

2. Coil the wire into at least 7 loops.

3. Connect each uninsulated end of the wire to a terminal of a galvanometer.

4. Move the end of a bar magnet halfway into the loops of the wire. Observe the galvanometer needle.

5. Move the magnet faster and slower. Observe the needle.

6. Increase and decrease the number of loops of the wire. Observe the needle.

7. Move the magnet farther into the loops and not as far. Observe the needle.

8. Use a strong bar magnet and a weak one. Observe the needle.

■ What process have you demonstrated?

■ Explain all your observations.

■ What variables affect the process the most? The least?

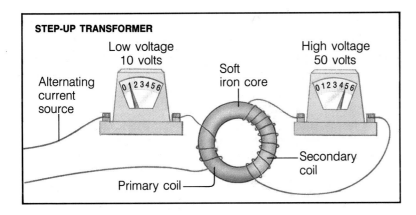

STEP-UP TRANSFORMER

Low voltage
10 volts

Alternating
current
source

Soft
iron core

High voltage
50 volts

0 1 2 3 4 5 6

0 1 2 3 4 5 6

Secondary
coil

Primary coil

Figure 21–16 *A transformer either increases or decreases the voltage of alternating current. A step-up transformer increases voltage. A step-down transformer decreases voltage. Which coil has the greater number of loops in each type of transformer?*

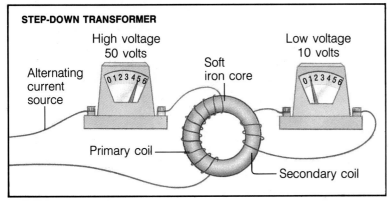

STEP-DOWN TRANSFORMER

High voltage
50 volts

Alternating
current
source

Soft
iron core

Low voltage
10 volts

0 1 2 3 4 5 6

0 1 2 3 4 5 6

Primary coil

Secondary coil

long distances from metropolitan areas. As electricity is transmitted over long distances, there is a loss of energy. At higher voltages and lower currents, electricity can be transmitted with less energy wasted. But if power is generated at lower voltages and also used at lower voltages, how can high-voltage transmission be achieved? By stepping up the voltage before transmission (step-up transformer) and stepping it back down before distribution (step-down transformer), power can be conserved.

Step-up transformers are used by power companies to transmit high-voltage electricity. Step-down transformers are then used to lower the voltage to 120 volts before it can be used in homes and offices. Step-up transformers are also used in fluorescent lights and X-ray machines. In television sets, step-up transformers increase ordinary household voltage from 120 volts to 20,000 volts or more.

Figure 21–17 *Electric current is most efficiently transmitted at high voltages. However, it is produced and used at low voltages. For this reason, electric companies use transformers such as these to adjust the voltage of electric current. Why is alternating current more practical than direct current?*

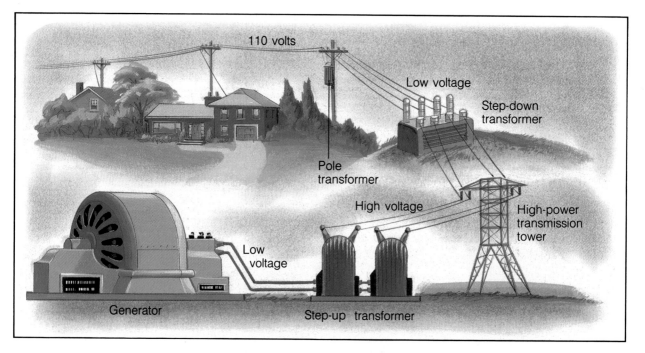

110 volts

Low voltage

Step-down transformer

Pole transformer

High voltage

High-power transmission tower

Low voltage

Generator

Step-up transformer

Figure 21–18 *Low-voltage current produced at a power plant is stepped-up before being sent over long wires. Near its destination, high-voltage current is stepped-down before it is distributed to homes and other buildings. Current may be further transformed in appliances that require specific voltages.*

Step-down transformers reduce the voltage of electricity from a power plant so it can be used in the home. Step-down transformers are also used in doorbells, model electric trains, small radios, tape players, and calculators.

21–2 Section Review

1. What is electromagnetic induction?
2. How can an electric current be produced from a magnetic field?
3. What is the purpose of a generator?
4. What is the difference between a step-up and a step-down transformer?

Connection—*You and Your World*
5. What are some common objects that use either electromagnetism or electromagnetic induction?

Smaller Than Small

When you have difficulty seeing a very small object, do you use a magnifying glass to help you? A magnifying glass enlarges the image of the object you are looking at. If you want to see an even smaller object, you may need a *microscope.* A microscope is an instrument that makes small objects appear larger. The Dutch biologist Anton van Leeuwenhoek is given credit for developing the first microscope. His invention used glass lenses to focus light.

The light microscope, which has descended from Van Leeuwenhoek's original device, still uses lenses in such a way that an object is magnified. Light microscopes are very useful. But due to the properties of light, there is a limit to the magnification light microscopes can achieve. How then can objects requiring greater magnification be seen? In the 1930s, scientists realized that a beam of electrons could be used in much the same way as light was. But microscopes that use electron beams cannot use glass lenses. Instead, they use lenses consisting of magnetic fields that exert forces on the electrons to bring them into focus. The magnetic fields are produced by electromagnets.

Electron microscopes have one major drawback. The specimens to be viewed under an electron microscope must be placed in a vacuum. This means that the specimens can no longer be alive. Despite this disadvantage, electron microscopes are extremely useful for studying small organisms, parts of organisms, or the basic structure of matter. Electron microscopes have opened up a new world!

High-precision microscopes have enabled researchers to peer into the world of the tiny. On this scale you may hardly recognize an ant's head, the cells responsible for pneumonia, or a stylus traveling through the grooves of a record.

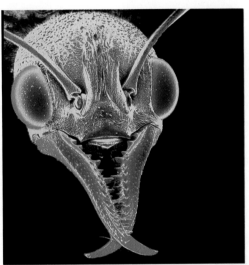

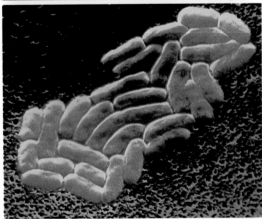

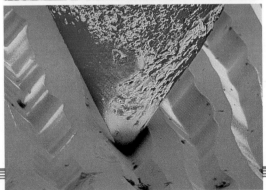

Laboratory Investigation

Electromagnetism

Problem

What factors affect the strength of an electro-magnet? What materials are attracted to an electromagnet?

Materials *(per group)*

dry cell	nickel
6 paper clips	dime
5 iron nails, 10 cm long	
2 meters of bell wire	
small piece of aluminum foil	
penny or copper sheet	
other objects to be tested	

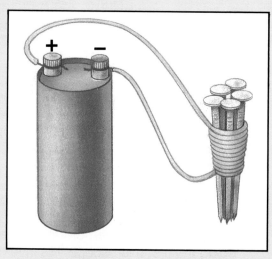

Procedure

1. Hold the five nails together and neatly wrap the wire around them. Do not allow the coils to overlap. Leave about 50 cm of wire at one end and about 100 cm at the other end.
2. Attach the shorter end of the wire to one terminal of the dry cell.
3. Momentarily touch the 100-cm end of the wire to the other terminal of the dry cell. **CAUTION:** *Do not operate the electro-magnet for more than a few seconds each time.*
4. When the electromagnet is on, test each material for magnetic attraction. Record your results.
5. During the time the electromagnet is on, determine the number of paper clips it can hold.
6. Wrap the 100-cm end of wire over the first winding to make a second layer. You should use about 50 cm of wire. There should be approximately 50 cm of wire remaining.
7. Connect the wire once again to the dry cell. Determine the number of paper clips the electromagnet can now hold. Record your results.
8. Carefully remove three nails from the windings. Connect the wire and deter-mine the number of paper clips the elec-tromagnet can hold. Record your results.
9. Determine whether the electromagnet at-tracts the penny, nickel, dime, and other test objects.

Observations

What materials are attracted to the electromagnet?

Analysis and Conclusions

1. What do the materials attracted to the magnet have in common?
2. When you increase the number of turns of wire, what effect does this have on the strength of the electromagnet?
3. How does removing the nails affect the strength of the electromagnet?
4. **On Your Own** How can you increase or decrease the strength of an electro-magnet without making any changes to the wire or to the nails? Devise an experi-ment to test your hypothesis.

Study Guide

Summarizing Key Concepts

21-1 Magnetism From Electricity

▲ A magnetic field is created around a wire that is conducting electric current.

▲ The relationship between electricity and magnetism is called electromagnetism.

▲ A coiled wire, known as a solenoid, acts as a magnet when current flows through it. A solenoid with a core of iron acts as a strong magnet called an electromagnet.

▲ A magnetic field exerts a force on a wire conducting current.

▲ An electric motor converts electric energy into mechanical energy that is used to do work.

▲ A galvanometer is a device consisting of an electromagnet attached to a needle that can be used to measure the strength and direction of small currents.

21-2 Electricity From Magnetism

▲ During electromagnetic induction, an electric current is induced in a wire exposed to a changing magnetic field.

▲ One of the most important uses of electromagnetic induction is in the operation of a generator, which converts mechanical energy into electric energy.

▲ A transformer is a device that increases or decreases the voltage of alternating current. A step-up transformer increases voltage. A step-down transformer decreases voltage.

Reviewing Key Terms

Define each term in a complete sentence.

21-1 Magnetism From Electricity

electromagnetism
solenoid
electromagnet
electric motor
galvanometer

21-2 Electricity From Magnetism

induced current
electromagnetic induction
generator
transformer

Chapter Review

Content Review

Multiple Choice

Choose the letter of the answer that best completes each statement.

1. The strength of the magnetic field of an electromagnet can be increased by
   a. increasing the number of coils in the wire only.
   b. increasing the amount of current in the wire only.
   c. increasing the amount of iron in the center only.
   d. all of these.
2. A generator can be considered the opposite of a(an)
   a. galvanometer.   c. electric motor.
   b. transformer.   d. electromagnet.
3. A device that changes the voltage of alternating current is a(an)
   a. transformer.   c. generator.
   b. electric motor. d. galvanometer.

4. The scientist who discovered that an electric current creates a magnetic field is
   a. Faraday.   c. Henry.
   b. Oersted.   d. Maxwell.
5. A device with an electromagnet that continually rotates because of a changing electric current is a(an)
   a. doorbell.   c. galvanometer.
   b. solenoid.   d. electric motor.
6. The creation of an electric current by a changing magnetic field is known as
   a. electromagnetic induction.
   b. generation.
   c. transformation.
   d. stepping-up.

True or False

If the statement is true, write "true." If it is false, change the underlined word or words to make the statement true.

1. The relationship between electricity and magnetism is called <u>electromagnetism</u>.
2. A solenoid with a piece of iron in the center is called an <u>electromagnet</u>.
3. A <u>commutator</u> and <u>brushes</u> are found in an electric motor running on direct current.
4. A <u>generator</u> is used to detect small currents.
5. In a generator, <u>mechanical</u> energy is converted to <u>electric</u> energy.
6. Large generators at power plants often get their mechanical energy from <u>steam</u>.
7. An induced current is produced by a changing <u>electric</u> field.
8. A <u>transformer</u> changes the voltage of an electric current.

Concept Mapping

Complete the following concept map for Section 21–1. Then construct a concept map for the entire chapter.

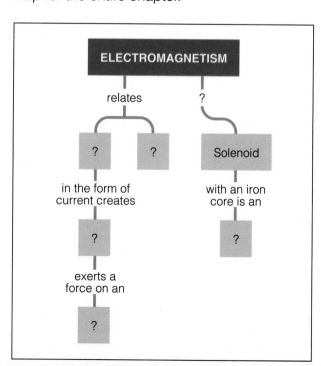

554

Concept Mastery

Discuss each of the following in a brief paragraph.

1. Does a magnetic field exert a force on a wire carrying electric current? Explain.
2. Describe how an electric motor operates. How does its operation differ depending on the type of current used to run the motor?
3. Explain how a galvanometer works.
4. Describe how a generator operates.
5. Describe the discoveries of Oersted and Faraday. How are these discoveries related?
6. What is a solenoid? An electromagnet?
7. What is a step-up transformer? A step-down transformer? Why are transformers important for the transmission of electricity?

Critical Thinking and Problem Solving

Use the skills you have developed in this chapter to answer each of the following.

1. **Making comparisons** Explain the difference between an electric motor and an electric generator in terms of energy conversion.
2. **Making diagrams** Use a diagram to show how the rotation of a wire loop in a generator first induces a current in one direction and then a current in the other direction.
3. **Applying concepts** The process of electromagnetic induction might seem to disobey the law of conservation of energy, which says that energy cannot be created. Explain why this is actually not so.
4. **Applying definitions** Indicate whether each of the following characteristics describes (a) a step-up transformer, (b) a step-down transformer, (c) both a step-up and a step-down transformer.
   a. Voltage in the secondary coil is greater.
   b. Involves electromagnetic induction.
   c. Voltage in the primary coil is greater.
   d. Used in doorbells and model trains.
   e. Consists of two insulated coils wrapped around opposite sides of an iron core.
   f. More loops in the secondary coil.
5. **Making inferences** Explain why a transformer will not operate on direct current.

6. **Making comparisons** Thomas Edison originally designed a power plant that produced direct current. Alternating current, however, has become standard for common use. Compare and contrast the two types of currents in terms of production and use.
7. **Using the writing process** Several devices that work on the principle of electromagnetism and electromagnetic induction have been mentioned in this chapter. Choose three of these devices and imagine what your life would be like without them. Write a short story or a poem that describes your imaginings.

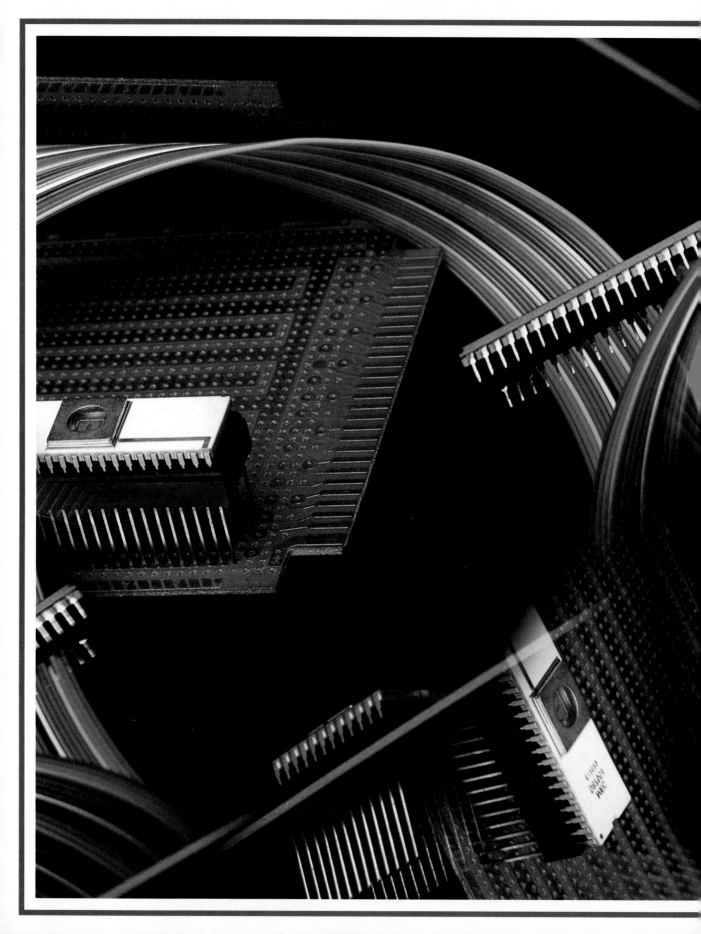

Electronics and Computers

Guide for Reading

After you read the following sections, you will be able to

22–1 Electronic Devices
- Define electronics.
- Describe the structure and applications of vacuum tubes.
- Relate semiconductors to the operation of transistors and integrated circuits.

22–2 Transmitting Sound
- Explain how a radio and a telephone work.

22–3 Transmitting Pictures
- Describe the operation of a cathode-ray tube and its use in a television set.

22–4 Computers
- Discuss the development and the components of a modern computer.

It was 1952—and not many people were familiar with computers. In fact, there were some who had never heard the word. But on Election Day of that year, millions of Americans came face to face with the computer age.

The presidential contest that year pitted Republican Dwight D. Eisenhower against Democrat Adlai E. Stevenson. Early in the evening, even before the voting polls had closed, newscaster Walter Cronkite announced to viewers than an "electronic brain" was going to predict the outcome of the election. The "electronic brain" was the huge UNIVAC I computer.

What UNIVAC predicted, based on just 3 million votes, was a landslide victory for Eisenhower. An amazed nation sat by their television sets into the early hours of the morning, convinced that the "electronic brain" could not have predicted as it did.

UNIVAC was not wrong, however. When all the votes were counted, the computer's prediction turned out to be remarkably close to the actual results. In this chapter you will learn about some of the devices that have brought the computer age and the electronic industry to where it is now.

Journal *Activity*

You and Your World Do you watch television often? If so, what kinds of shows do you watch? If not, why not? Television is an electronic device in widespread use in modern society. In your journal, compare the positive contributions television has made with its negative aspects. Explain how you would improve the use of television.

◀ *A photographer's view of some of the electronic components that make computer technology possible.*

22–1 Electronic Devices

Were you awakened this morning by the buzz of an alarm clock? Did you rely on a radio or a cassette player to get the day started with music? Did your breakfast include food that was warmed in a microwave oven? Can you get through the day without using the telephone or watching television?

You probably cannot answer these questions without realizing that electric devices have a profound effect on your life. The branch of technology that has developed electric devices is called **electronics.** Electronics is a branch of physics closely related to the science of electricity. **Electronics is the study of the release, behavior, and control of electrons as it relates to use in helpful devices.**

Although electronic technology is relatively new—it can be traced back only 100 years or so—electronics has rapidly changed people's lives. For example, telephones, radio, television, and compact disc players have revolutionized communication and

Figure 22–1 *Familiar electronic devices such as these have shaped the way people live and work. Have you used any of these devices?*

entertainment. Computers and robots have increased speed in business and industry. Electronic devices help physicians diagnose diseases and save lives. Most modern forms of travel depend on electronic devices.

Perhaps you wonder how electronics differs from the study of electricity. After all, both deal with electrons and electric currents. The study of electricity concentrates on the use of electric currents to power a wide range of devices, such as lamps, heaters, welding arcs, and other electrical appliances. In such devices, the kinetic energy of moving electrons is converted into heat and light energy. Electronics treats electric currents as a means of carrying information. Currents that carry information are called electric signals. Carefully controlled, electrons can be made to carry messages, magnify weak signals, draw pictures, and even do arithmetic.

Vacuum Tubes

To appreciate the electronics industry as it exists today, it is important to recognize its historical origins. For this reason, it is necessary to briefly review the development and application of some early devices. These devices were able to carefully control electrons even though such devices are not found in modern electronic instruments.

In 1883, Thomas Edison found that the heated wire filament in his incandescent light bulb gave off a material that blackened the inside of the bulb. This discovery, known as the Edison effect, led to much experimentation. It turned out that when a current flows through a filament, the resulting heat gave some electrons in the filament enough energy to overcome the attractive forces holding them in the metal.

In 1904, John Fleming of England took advantage of the Edison effect in a **vacuum tube**. A vacuum tube is essentially a sealed glass tube from which almost all of the air has been removed. Fleming used an electric current to heat a metal filament that had been placed inside the vacuum tube. The heat drove the electrons from the filament out into the surrounding space. When a metal plate connected to the filament by an outside electric circuit was also placed in the vacuum tube, the electrons moved

ACTIVITY
DISCOVERING

Electronics in Your Home

Over the course of a day, observe and make a list of all the electronic appliances you use in your home.

■ Which of these appliances contain transistors? Cathode-ray tubes? Vacuum tubes? Integrated circuits?

■ Do some appliances contain multiple types of devices? If so, which ones?

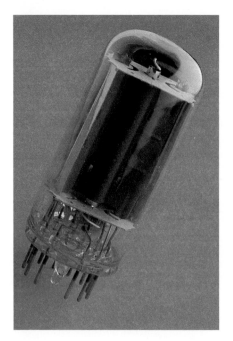

Figure 22–2 *Vacuum tubes, such as the one shown, are no longer used in modern electronic devices. At one time, however, numerous vacuum tubes were required for the operation of a simple television or radio. Have you ever seen a vacuum tube?*

from the filament to the plate. Because the electrons moved in only one direction, this vacuum tube acted as a one-way valve, or gate, for a flow of electrons. Such a vacuum tube is called a **diode**.

In 1906, the American inventor Lee DeForest transformed the diode into a device now called a **triode**. He did this by inserting a grid of fine wire mesh between the filament and the plate. When variable voltages were placed on the filament and grid, they caused variations in the flow of electrons to the plate. Moreover, the variations in current were much stronger than those caused by the voltage of the incoming signal alone. Thus a triode acts as an **amplifier** because it strengthens the signal.

Vacuum tubes had a wide variety of applications in early electronics. They became the basis of radio, television, and computers. In fact, from the 1920s until the 1950s, vacuum tubes dominated the world of electronics.

Solid-State Devices

In the 1950s, a new group of electronic devices took over the electronics industry. They resulted from research into the atoms that make up matter and the behavior of the particles that make up atoms. This research has been a great tool for understanding the structure of solids, and even liquids. The field of research is known as solid-state physics and the devices that result from it are known as **solid-state devices**.

Solid-state devices have several advantages over vacuum tubes. They are much smaller and lighter than vacuum tubes and give off much less heat. They also use far less electric power, are more dependable, and last longer. And in most cases, they are less expensive.

In solid-state devices, an electric signal flows through certain solid materials instead of through a vacuum. The use of solid-state devices was made possible by the discovery of **semiconductors**. Semiconductors are solid materials that are able to conduct electric currents better than insulators do but not as well as true conductors do. More accurately, a semiconductor is a material that conducts electricity, but only under certain conditions. In contrast, conductors always conduct well and insulators always conduct poorly.

To understand how a semiconductor works, let's take a look at some properties of one of the most commonly used semiconductors—silicon. An atom of silicon has four outer electrons that act to hold the atoms firmly in a crystal structure. Silicon acquires useful properties for use in electronics only when a tiny amount of an impurity is introduced into the structure. By impurity we mean atoms of another element. This process of adding an impurity is called **doping.**

Two types of semiconductors can be made, depending on the type of impurity used. If the impurity is a material whose atoms have five outer electrons, such as arsenic, only four arsenic's electrons fit into the crystal structure as shown in Figure 22–3. The fifth electron does not fit and can move relatively freely throughout the structure producing a current, much like the electrons in a conductor. Because of this small number of extra electrons, a doped semiconductor becomes slightly conducting. An arsenic-doped silicon crystal is called an n-type semiconductor because negative electrons carry the electric current.

Figure 22–3 *A silicon crystal is shown on the left. Notice the four electrons for each silicon atom. On the right, an atom of arsenic has been added. The extra electron does not fit into the crystal structure and is free to move about.*

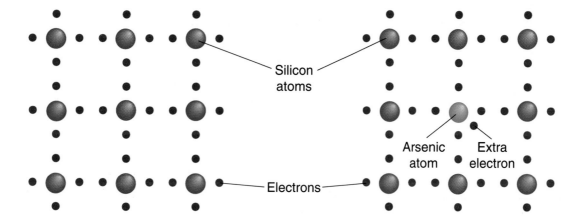

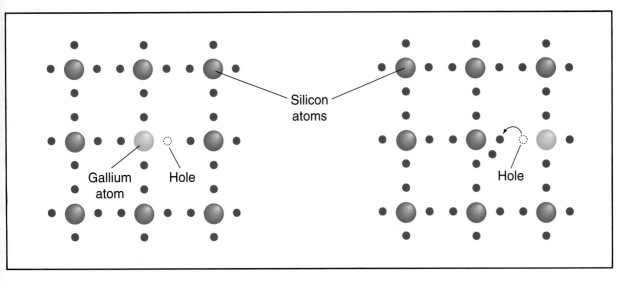

Silicon
atoms

Gallium
atom

Hole

Hole

Figure 22–4 *When an atom of gallium is added to a silicon crystal, a hole is created because gallium does not have another electron to fill it. An electron from a silicon atom can jump into the hole, only to leave another hole behind it.*

Figure 22–5 *Devices that used vacuum tubes were large, heavy, and cumbersome. They also gave off a considerable amount of heat. Devices that use semiconductors can be made extremely small. In addition, they are more dependable, last longer, use less energy and give off less heat.*

Now suppose a small amount of an impurity with three outer electrons, such as gallium, is added to the semiconductor. In this case, there is a "hole" in the crystal structure next to a gallium atom as shown in Figure 24–4. Electrons from nearby silicon atoms can jump into this hole and fill it. But when the electron jumps, it leaves a "hole" where it had been. Another electron can jump into that hole and the process continues. Silicon atoms require four electrons to be neutral. Thus the hole, which is a lack of a negative charge, can be thought of as a positive charge. This type of semiconductor is called a p-type because it is the positive holes that allow for the movement of electrons, or current.

Both n-type semiconductors and p-type semiconductors are electrically neutral. However, when an n-type semiconductor is joined to a p-type semiconductor (a p-n junction diode), a few electrons move across the junction where the two are joined. The electrons move from n-type into the p-type, where they fill in a few of the holes. The n-type, which loses negative electrons, becomes positively charged and the p-type, which gains negative electrons, becomes negatively charged. The result is a potential difference between the two semiconductors. If a battery is connected to the diode in one way, current can flow. But if the battery is connected in reverse, no current will flow. Because a p-n junction allows current to flow in one direction, it can serve as a **rectifier,** or device that changes alternating current into direct current.

Transistors

When one type of semiconductor is sandwiched between two of the opposite type semiconductors, a **transistor** is formed. What are the two arrangements of transistors? You are correct if you said pnp and npn as shown in Figure 22–6. The center semiconductor of a transistor is called the base. One of the end semiconductors is called the collector and the other is called the emitter.

The arrangement of the impurities in the semiconductors enables a transistor to act as an amplifier. A weak signal, corresponding to a weak current, enters the transistor and is amplified so that a strong signal is produced.

Transistors are commonly used in radios, televisions, stereos, computers, and calculators. The properties of small size, light weight, and durability have also enabled transistors to play an important role in the development of instruments essential to modern wireless communication.

Integrated Circuits

Although individual transistors are tiny compared to vacuum tubes, they are huge compared to **integrated circuits,** or **chips.** An integrated circuit combines many diodes, transistors, and other devices on a thin slice of silicon crystal.

When you studied electric circuits in Chapter 19, you learned that a circuit can consist of many parts connected by wires. Complicated circuits organized in this fashion, however, become very large. In response, scientists found a way to place an entire circuit on a tiny board.

To form an integrated circuit, tiny amounts of impurities can be placed at particular locations within a single silicon crystal. These can be arranged to form diodes, transistors, and resistors. (Resistors are simply undoped semiconductors.) Other electronic devices can be formed as well. A chip only 1cm on a side can contain thousands of circuit elements in a variety of complex combinations.

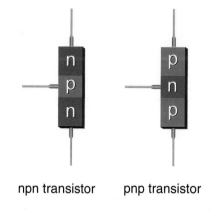

npn transistor   pnp transistor

Figure 22–6 *Different types of transistors can be formed depending upon the arrangement of semiconductors (top). Once formed, transistors come in a variety of shapes and sizes. What does a transistor do?*

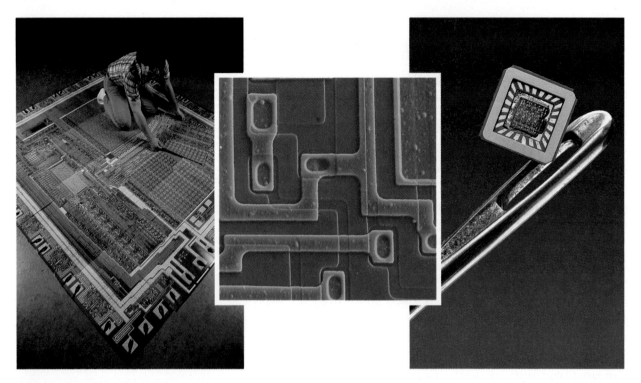

Figure 22–7 *An integrated circuit, or chip, contains thousands of diodes and transistors on a thin slice of silicon crystal (right). A computer scientist designs a new computer chip by first drawing a large version and then having the design miniaturized (left). Magnified 175 times by a scanning electron microscope, the integrated circuit paths can be seen (center). A human hair is wider than 150 of these paths!*

Integrated circuits are used as amplifiers and switches in a wide variety of devices. Computers and microcomputers, calculators, radios, watches, washing machines, refrigerators, and even robots use integrated circuits.

22–1 Section Review

1. What is electronics? How is it different from the study of electricity?
2. How are electrons used in a vacuum tube? How is a vacuum tube used as a rectifier? As an amplifier?
3. What is a semiconductor?
4. How are semiconductors used to make integrated circuits? What are some advantages of the use of integrated circuits?

Connection—*Language Arts*
5. The words rectify and amplify are not limited to scientific use. Explain what these words mean and give examples of their use in everyday language. Then explain why they are appropriate for the electronic devices they name.

22–2 Transmitting Sound

Since the first telegraph line was connected and the first telegraph message was sent in 1844, people have become accustomed to instant communication. Each improvement in the speed, clarity, and reliability of a communication device has been based on a discovery in the field of electronics.

One particular discovery that is the basis for many devices used to transmit information is an interesting relationship between electricity and magnetism. The discoveries made by Oersted, Faraday, and others that you have read about in Chapter 21 clearly illustrate that electricity and magnetism are related. Another scientist, James Clerk Maxwell, used the discoveries of his predecessors to open a new world of scientific technology.

Maxwell showed that all electric and magnetic phenomena could be described by using only four equations involving electric and magnetic fields. Thus he unified in one theory all phenomena of electricity and magnetism. These four equations are as important to electromagnetism as Newton's three laws are to motion.

Perhaps the most important outcome of Maxwell's work is the understanding that not only does a changing magnetic field give rise to an electric field, but a changing electric field produces a magnetic field. In other words, if a magnetic field in space is changing, like the up and down movements of a wave, a changing electric field will form. But a changing electric field will also produce a changing magnetic field. The two will keep producing each other over and over. The result will be a wave consisting of an electric field and a magnetic field. Such a wave is called an **electromagnetic wave.** Electromagnetic waves are like waves on a rope except that they do not consist of matter. They consist of fields.

You are already more familiar with electromagnetic waves than you may realize. The most familiar electromagnetic wave is light. All the light that you see is composed of electromagnetic waves. The microwaves that heat food in a microwave oven are also electromagnetic waves. The X-rays that a doctor takes are electromagnetic waves. And as you will

Guide for Reading

Focus on this question as you read.

▶ *How do sound-transmitting devices work?*

ACTIVITY

WRITING

Telephone and Radio History

The invention of the telephone and the invention of the radio were two important advances in electronic technology. Using books and other reference materials in the library, find out about the invention of each. Be sure to include answers to the following questions.

1. Who invented the device?

2. When was it invented?

3. Were there any interesting or unusual circumstances surrounding the invention?

4. How was the invention modified through the years?

Present the results of your research in a written or oral report. Accompany your report with illustrations.

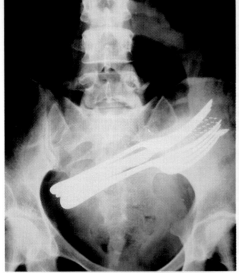

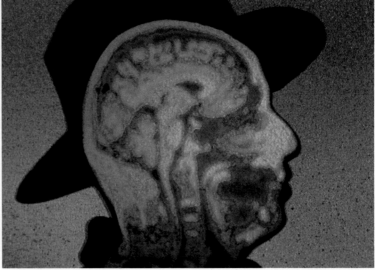

Figure 22-8 *Electromagnetic waves in the form of X-rays enable you to see the forks, pen, and toothbrush in this person's intestine! Another type of EM wave allows scientists to study the composition of the brain and other parts of the body. Believe it or not, this photograph of a river was taken in total darkness using infrared waves. What type of electromagnetic wave can be seen in the bottom photograph?*

soon learn, the prediction and verification of electromagnetic waves opened up a whole new world of communication—from the first wireless telegraph to radio and television to artificial space satellites.

Radio Communication

Would you be surprised to learn that radio broadcasting once played the same role that television plays today? People would gather around a radio to listen to a variety of programs: musical performances, comedy shows, mystery hours, and news broadcasts. Today, radio broadcasting is still a great source of entertainment and information. But its role has been greatly expanded.

Radios work by changing sound vibrations into electromagnetic waves called radio waves. The radio waves, which travel through the air at the speed of light, are converted back into sound vibrations when they reach a radio receiver.

A radio program usually begins at a radio station. Here, a microphone picks up the sounds that are being broadcast. An electric current running through the microphone is disturbed by the sound vibrations in such a way that it creates its own vibrations that match the sound.

The electric signals that represent the sounds of a broadcast are now sent to a transmitter. The transmitter amplifies the signals and combines them with a radio wave that will be used to carry the information. How the wave carries the information determines if the information will be broadcast as AM or FM radio. The final wave carrying the signal is then sent to a transmitting antenna. The antenna sends

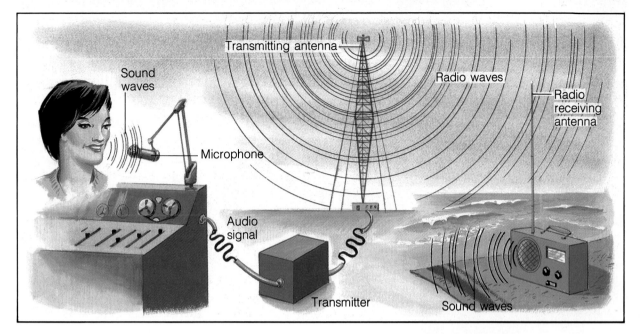

Sound waves

Transmitting antenna

Radio waves

Microphone

Radio receiving antenna

Audio signal

Transmitter

Sound waves

the radio waves out into the air. Why do you think many radio stations locate their antennas at high elevations, in open areas, or on top of towers?

Radio waves are converted back into sound waves by means of a radio receiver. A radio receiver picks up and amplifies the radio waves originally sent out from a radio station. When a radio receiver picks up sounds corresponding to a specific frequency, it is described as being tuned in.

Have you ever wondered how a telephone call can be made from a moving vehicle such as a car or an airplane? Cellular telephones (movable telephones) use signals that are sent out by an antenna as radio waves. Other antennas pick up the radio waves and convert them back into sound. To understand more about cellular telephones, you must first learn how a telephone operates.

Figure 22–9 *Radios work by converting sound vibrations into electromagnetic waves. The waves are amplified and sent out into the air. Picked up by a receiving antenna, the radio waves are converted back into sound waves. What else does the receiver do with the radio waves?*

Telephone Communication

Have you ever stopped to think about the amazing technology that enables you to talk to someone else, almost anywhere in the world, in seconds? The device that makes this communication possible is the telephone. The first telephone was invented in 1876 by Alexander Graham Bell. Although modern telephones hardly resemble Bell's, the principle on which all telephones work is the same. A telephone sends and receives sound by means of electric signals. In addition to a base, a telephone has two main parts.

TRANSMITTER The transmitter is located behind the mouthpiece of a telephone. Sound waves produced when a person speaks into a telephone cause a thin metal disk located in the transmitter to vibrate. These vibrations vary according to the particular sounds. The vibrations, in turn, are converted to an electric current. The pattern of vibrations regulates the amount of electric current produced and sent out over telephone wires. You can think of the electric current as "copying" the pattern of the sound waves. The electric current travels over wires to a receiver.

RECEIVER The receiver, located in the earpiece, converts the changes in the amount of electric current sent out by a transmitter back into sound. The receiver uses an electromagnet to produce this conversion.

When the electric current transmitted by another telephone goes through the coil of the electromagnet, the electromagnet becomes magnetized. It pulls on another thin metal disk, causing it to vibrate. The vibrations produce sound waves that the listener hears.

Early telephones used carbon grains in the transmitter to convert sound to electricity. Today's telephones use a small semiconductor crystal. Transistors then amplify the electric signal. In modern telephone earpieces, semiconductor devices have replaced electromagnets. And fiber-optic systems, in which the vibrations travel as a pattern of changes in a beam of laser light, are replacing copper cables used for ordinary transmission.

Figure 22–10 *The first telephone was invented in 1876 by Alexander Graham Bell. Today, you push buttons or dial to make calls. But up until the early 1900s, telephone calls were placed by switchboard operators, whose familiar phrase was "Number, please."*

Figure 22–11 *A telephone, consisting of a transmitter and a receiver, sends and receives sounds by means of electric signals. Where are transistors used? For what purpose?*

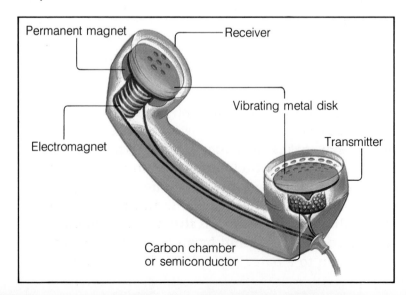

Permanent magnet
Receiver
Electromagnet
Vibrating metal disk
Transmitter
Carbon chamber or semiconductor

22-2 Section Review

1. Describe the relationship between sound and electric current in devices that transmit sound.
2. Describe the two main parts of a telephone.
3. Describe the broadcast of a radio program.
4. How do you think solid-state devices have affected telephones and radios?

Connection—*You and Your World*
5. How do you think radio communication has affected the development of business and industry?

22-3 Transmitting Pictures

Guide for Reading

Focus on this question as you read.

▶ How does a cathode-ray tube operate?

You would probably agree that a video game would be far less exciting if the images were unclear and did not move very quickly. The same is true of your favorite television show. The images on a video screen and a television screen are produced by a special type of vacuum tube.

Cathode-ray Tubes

Television images are produced on the surface of a type of vacuum tube called a **cathode-ray tube,** or CRT. Cathode-ray tubes are also responsible for images produced by video games, computer displays, and radar devices.

A cathode-ray tube is an electronic device that uses electrons to produce images on a screen. This special type of vacuum tube gets its name from the fact that inside the glass tube, a beam of electrons (cathode rays) is directed to a screen to produce a picture. The electrons, moving as a beam, sweep across the screen and cause it to glow. The screen glows because it is coated with fluorescent material. Fluorescent material glows briefly when struck by electrons.

The electrons in a CRT come from the negatively charged filament within the sealed glass vacuum tube. An electric current heats the metal filament

Figure 22-12 *When you play a video game, you are taking advantage of a cathode-ray tube.*

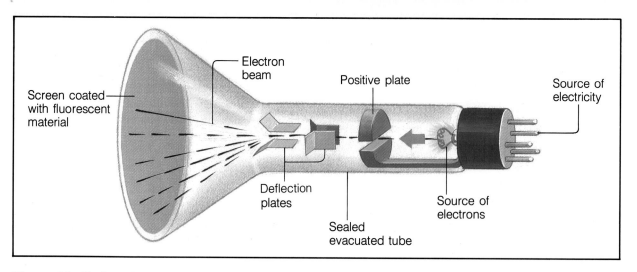

Figure 22–13 *A cathode-ray tube is a sealed evacuated tube in which a beam of electrons is focused on a screen coated with fluorescent material. As electrons strike the fluorescent material, visible light is given off and an image is formed.*

and causes electrons to "boil" off it. The electrons are accelerated toward the screen and focused into a narrow beam. Because the electrons move so quickly in a concentrated beam, the source is sometimes referred to as an electron gun. The moving electrons produce a magnetic field that can be used to control the direction of the beam. Electromagnets placed outside the CRT cause the beam to change its direction, making it move rapidly up and down and back and forth across the screen.

At each point where the beam of electrons strikes the fluorescent material of the CRT screen, visible light is given off. The brightness of the light is determined by the number of electrons that strike the screen. The more electrons, the brighter the light. The continuous, rapid movement of the beam horizontally and vertically across the screen many times per second produces a pattern of light, or a picture on the screen. In the United States, the electron beam in a CRT traces 525 lines as it zigzags up and down, creating a whole picture 30 times each second. In some other countries the beam moves twice as fast, creating an even clearer image.

Television Transmission

A cathode-ray tube in a color television set differs from a simple cathode-ray tube in two important ways. First, the screen of a color television set is coated with three different materials placed close together in clusters of dots or in thin stripes at each point on the screen. Each material glows with a different color of light—red, blue, or green—when struck by a beam of electrons. Various colors are

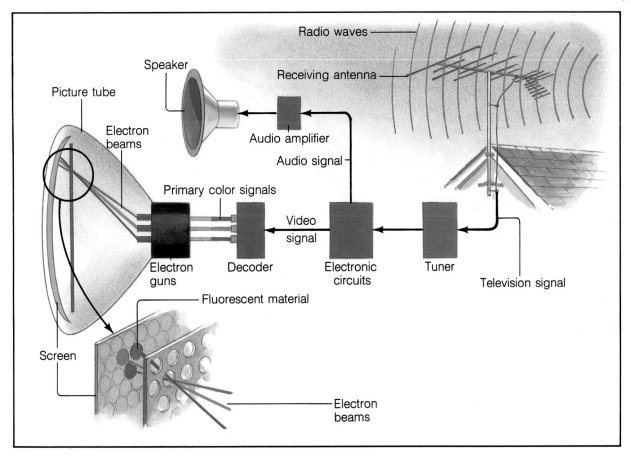

Radio waves

Receiving antenna

Speaker

Picture tube

Electron beams

Audio amplifier

Audio signal

Primary color signals

Video signal

Electron guns

Decoder

Electronic circuits

Tuner

Television signal

Fluorescent material

Screen

Electron beams

produced by adjusting the strengths of the electron beams. For example, red is produced when electrons strike only the red material. Purple is produced when electrons strike both red and blue material. When do you think white is produced?

Second, a color television CRT contains three electron guns—one for each color (red, green, and blue). The information for controlling and directing the beams from the three electron guns is coded within the color picture signal that is transmitted from a TV station.

Figure 22–14 *The CRT in a color television contains three electron guns—one each for red, blue, and green signals. The screen of the CRT is coated with three different fluorescent materials, each of which glows with a different primary color of light when struck by a beam of electrons.*

22–3 Section Review

1. What is a cathode-ray tube? Describe how it works.
2. How does a color television CRT differ from a simple CRT?

Critical Thinking—*Making Inferences*
3. Photographs of a TV picture taken with an ordinary camera often show only part of the screen filled. Explain why.

22–4 Computers

Computers have quickly become a common sight over the past few decades. You see computers in stores, doctors' and dentists' offices, schools, and businesses. Perhaps you even have one in your home. **A computer is an electronic device that performs calculations and processes and stores information.** A modern electronic computer can do thousands of calculations per second. At equally incredible speed, it can file away billions of bits of information in its memory. Then it can rapidly search through all that information to pick out particular items. It can change numbers to letters to pictures to sounds—and back to numbers again.

Using these abilities, modern computers are guiding spaceships, navigating boats, diagnosing diseases and prescribing treatment, forecasting weather, and searching for ore. Computers make robots move, talk, and obey commands. Computers can play games and make music. They can even design new computers. The pages of this textbook were composed and printed with the help of a computer (although people still do the writing)!

Computer Development

The starting point of modern computer development is thought to be 1890. In preparation for the United States census that year, Herman Hollerith

Figure 22–15 *Early computers, which used large vacuum tubes were neither fast nor reliable. And like the ENIAC, they certainly were enormous in size! A modern computer that fits on a desk top once required an entire room.*

devised an electromagnetic machine that could handle information punched into cards. The holes allowed small electric currents to pass through and activate counters. Using this system, Hollerith completed the 1890 census in one fourth the time it had taken to do the 1880 census! Hollerith's punch card became the symbol of the computer age.

The first American-built computer was developed in 1946 by the United States Army. The Electronic Numerical Integrator and Calculator, or ENIAC, consisted of thousands of vacuum tubes and occupied a warehouse. It cost millions of dollars to build and maintain. It was constantly breaking down and had to be rebuilt each time a new type of calculation was done. ENIAC required great amounts of energy, generated huge amounts of heat, and was very expensive. By today's standards, ENIAC was slow. It could do only 6,000 calculations per second.

The first general-purpose computer was introduced in 1951. It was called the Universal Automatic Computer, or UNIVAC. UNIVAC was certainly an improvement over ENIAC, but it was still large, expensive, and slow.

Increased demand for computers encouraged more advanced computer technology. Technical breakthroughs such as transistors and integrated

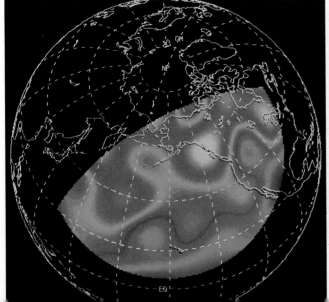

Figure 22–16 *The uses of computers are wide and varied. Computer applications include the identification of worldwide ozone concentrations (bottom left), the analysis of the body mechanics of a runner (top), and the study of fractal geometry in mathematics (bottom right).*

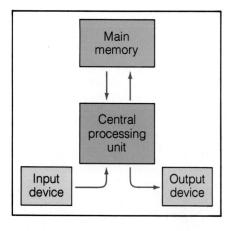

circuits reduced the size and cost of computers. They also increased the efficiency, speed, and uses of computers. And equally important, they brought the computer within everyone's reach.

The future of computers lies in both the very small and the very large. Integrated circuits called microprocessors can hold an entire processing capability on one small chip. At the other extreme, groups of computers are being linked together to form supercomputers.

Computer Hardware

Computer **hardware** refers to the physical parts of a computer. **Computer hardware includes a central processing unit, main storage, input devices, and output devices.**

The "brain" of a computer is known as the **central processing unit,** or CPU. A CPU controls the operation of all the components of a computer. It executes the arithmetic and logic instructions that it receives in the form of a computer program. A computer program is a series of instructions that tells the computer how to perform a certain task. A computer program can be written in one of several different computer languages.

The main storage of a computer is often referred to as the **main memory.** The main memory contains data and operating instructions that are processed by the CPU. In the earliest computers, the main memory consisted of thousands of vacuum tubes. Modern computer memory is contained on chips. The most advanced memory chip can store as much information as 1 million vacuum tubes can.

Data are fed to the central processing unit by an **input device.** One common input device is a keyboard. A keyboard looks very much like a typewriter. Using a keyboard, a person can communicate data and instructions to a computer. Other input devices include magnetic tape, optical scanners, and disk drives.

Figure 22–17 *Computer hardware includes a central processing unit, main memory, an input device, and an output device. What is the function of each?*

574

A **disk drive** reads information off a disk and enters it into the computer's memory or into the CPU. Information from a disk drive can be placed into a computer very quickly.

Information produced by a computer can be removed and stored on a disk. So a disk drive is also an **output device.** An output device receives data from the central processing unit. Output devices include printers, cathode-ray tubes, magnetic tape drives, and voice synthesizers. Even robots are output devices.

CONNECTIONS

The Human Computer

The organization of the human body is pretty amazing, isn't it? Think of all the various organs constantly working independently as well as interacting with one another to keep you alive, healthy, and functioning normally. What's even more amazing is that the body does all its work without your having to think about it! You don't even have to worry about nourishing your body because it reminds you to do so by making you feel hungry. Now that's pretty awesome! What is even more incredible, perhaps, is that you have the ability to think, reason, reach conclusions, and use your imagination. What a wonderful device the human body is!

The organ of your body that controls the various body systems and is also the seat of intelligence is the *brain.* Different parts of the brain have different functions. One part enables you to coordinate your movements quickly and gracefully. Another part controls body processes, such as heartbeat, breathing, and blood pressure—not to mention swallowing, sneezing, coughing, and blinking. And still another part is responsible for your ability to think.

Many attempts have been made to simulate the activities of the brain. There is, in fact, a field of computer research that aims to create artificial intelligence—that is, computers capable of thinking and reasoning like humans. Currently, however, such attempts to unravel the interconnections of the human brain have proved largely unsuccessful. For now, at least, the human brain still holds its many secrets.

Like a disk drive, a **modem** is an input and output device. A modem changes electronic signals from a computer into signals that can be carried over telephone lines. It also changes the sounds back into computer signals. A modem allows a computer to communicate with other computers, often thousands of kilometers away. As computers link in this way, they form a network in which information can be shared. A modem allows use of this network by accessing (getting) information from a central data bank. A data bank is a vast collection of information stored in a large computer.

The Binary System

Computer hardware would be useless if computer **software** did not exist. **Software is the program or set of programs the computer follows.** Software must be precise because in most cases a computer cannot think on its own. A computer can only follow instructions. For example, to add two numbers, a program must tell a computer to get one number from memory, hold it, get the other number from memory, combine the two numbers, and print the answer. After completing the instruction, the computer must be told what to do next.

A computer can execute instructions by counting with just two numbers at a time. The numbers are 0 and 1. The system that uses just these two numbers is called the **binary system.**

Computer circuits are composed of diodes. As you learned in the previous sections, diodes are gates that are either open or closed to electric current. If the gate is open, current is off. If the gate is closed, current is on. To a computer, 0 is current off and 1 is current on. Each digit, then, acts as a tiny electronic switch, flipping on and off at unbelievable speed.

Each single electronic switch is called a **bit.** A string of bits—usually 8—is called a **byte.** Numbers, letters, and other symbols can be represented as a byte. For example, the letter A is 01000001. The letter K is 01001011. The number 9 is 00111001.

You do not need to be reminded of the importance of computers. You have only to look around you. The uses of computers are many, and their presence is almost universal. Any list of computer

Activity Bank

Computer Talk, p. 767

ACTIVITY

THINKING

Helpful Prefixes

Several terms related to electronic devices may be easier for you to understand if you know the meaning of their prefixes. Find out the meaning of each prefix that is underlined in the words below. Then write a sentence explaining how the prefix will help you to learn the definition of the word.

binary system
diode
integrated circuit
microprocessor
semiconductor
triode
transistor

PROBLEM Solving

Go With the Flow

A computer follows a series of activities that take place in a definite order, or process. If you think about it, so do you. You get dressed one step at a time. When you follow a recipe, you add each ingredient in order.

It is useful to have a method to describe such processes, especially when writing computer programs. A flowchart is one method of describing a process. In a flowchart the activities are written within blocks whose shapes indicate what is involved in that step.

Designing a Flowchart It is a good thing you know how to write a flowchart because you are hosting the class luncheon today. But the chef that you have hired can cook only from a flowchart. Write a flowchart showing the chef how to prepare today's menu.

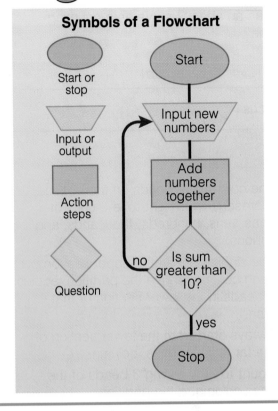

Symbols of a Flowchart

Start or stop

Input or output

Action steps

Question

Start → Input new numbers → Add numbers together → Is sum greater than 10? → no (loop back to Input new numbers) / yes → Stop

applications cannot really be completed today. For by the time today is over, another application will have been devised. The future of computers is exciting, indeed!

22–4 Section Review

1. What is a computer? How are its hardware and software involved in its operation?
2. What is a modem? How is it related to a data bank?
3. How is the binary system used by a computer?

Critical Thinking—*Making Calculations*
4. Show how the following numbers would be represented by a byte: 175, 139, 3, 45, 17.

ACTIVITY READING

Artificial Intelligence

It is difficult to imagine using wires and crystals to construct a device that can think as you can. Read David Gerrold's *When H.A.R.L.I.E. Was One* and discover what such a device would be like.

Laboratory Investigation

The First Calculator: The Abacus

Problem

How can an abacus serve as a counting machine?

Materials   *(per group)*

abacus

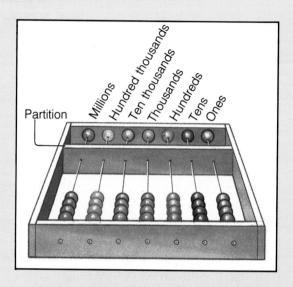

Procedure

1. The columns of beads on the abacus represent, from right to left, units of ones, tens, hundreds, thousands, and millions.

2. The single bead in the upper section of each column, above the partition, equals 5 beads in the lower section of that column.

3. Always start from the lower section of the far right, or ones, column.

4. Count to 3 by sliding 3 beads of the ones column to the partition.

5. Continue counting to 8. Slide the fourth bead up to the partition. You should be out of beads in this section. Slide all 4 beads back down and slide the single bead from the upper section of this column down to the partition. Remember that the top bead equals 5 lower beads. Continue counting from 6 to 8 by sliding the beads in the lower section of the ones column up to the partition. Before doing any further counting, check with your teacher to see that you are using the abacus correctly.

6. Continue counting to 12. Slide the last bead in the ones column up to the partition. You should now have a total of 9. And you should be out of beads in the ones column. Slide all these beads back

to their original zero position. Slide 1 bead in the lower section of the tens column up to the partition. This represents 10. Continue counting in the ones column until you reach 12.

Observations

1. Count to each of these numbers on the abacus: 16, 287, 5016, 1,816,215.

2. How would you find 8 + 7 on the abacus? Start by counting to 8 on the abacus. Then continue adding 7 more beads Find the following sums: 7 + 8, 3 + 4, 125 + 58.

Analysis and Conclusions

1. On what number system is the operation of the abacus based?

2. How does this compare with the operation of a computer?

3. **On Your Own**   Try designing a number system that uses more than 2 numerals but fewer than 10. Count to 20 in your system.

Study Guide

Summarizing Key Concepts

22–1 Electronic Devices

▲ Electronics is the study of the release, behavior, and control of electrons as it relates to use in practical devices.

▲ In a tube in which most of the gases have been removed—a vacuum tube—electrons flow in one direction.

▲ A rectifier is an electronic device that converts alternating current to direct current.

▲ An amplifier is an electronic device that increases the strength of an electric signal.

▲ Semiconductors are materials that are able to conduct electric currents better than insulators do but not as well as true conductors do.

▲ Adding impurities to semiconductors is called doping.

▲ An integrated circuit combines diodes and transistors on a thin slice of silicon crystal.

22–2 Transmitting Sound

▲ Radios work by changing sound vibrations into electromagnetic waves, or radio waves.

▲ A telephone sends and receives sound by means of electric signals. A telephone has two main parts: a transmitter and a receiver.

22–3 Transmitting Pictures

▲ A cathode-ray tube, or CRT, is an electronic device that uses electrons to produce images on a screen.

▲ A cathode-ray tube in a color television set contains three electron guns—one each for red, blue, and green signals.

22–4 Computers

▲ Integrated circuits called microprocessors can hold the entire processing capability on one small chip.

▲ Computer hardware consists of a central processing unit, main storage, input devices, and output devices.

▲ A computer program is a series of instructions that tell the computer how to perform a certain task.

Reviewing Key Terms

Define each term in a complete sentence.

22–1 Electronic Devices
electronics
vacuum tube
diode
triode
amplifier
solid-state device
semiconductor
doping
rectifier
transistor
integrated circuit
chip

22–2 Transmitting Sound
electromagnetic wave

22–3 Transmitting Pictures
cathode-ray tube

22–4 Computers
hardware
central processing unit
main memory
input device
disk drive
output device
modem
software
binary system
bit
byte

Chapter Review

Content Review

Multiple Choice

Choose the letter of the answer that best completes each statement.

1. Diode vacuum tubes are used as
   - a. transistors.
   - b. rectifiers.
   - c. amplifiers.
   - d. triodes.
2. Which electronic device was particularly important to the rapid growth of the radio and television industry?
   - a. triode
   - b. diode
   - c. punch card
   - d. disk drive
3. Which of the following is a semiconductor material?
   - a. copper
   - b. plastic
   - c. silicon
   - d. oxygen
4. A sandwich of three semiconductor materials used to amplify an electric signal is a(an)
   - a. diode.
   - b. transistor.
   - c. integrated circuit.
   - d. modem.
5. Radios work by changing sound vibrations into
   - a. cathode rays.
   - b. gamma rays.
   - c. electric signals.
   - d. bytes.
6. Which is not an advantage of solid-state devices in telephones and radios?
   - a. smaller size
   - b. increased cost
   - c. better amplification
   - d. greater energy efficiency
7. The physical parts of a computer are collectively referred to as computer
   - a. software.
   - b. peripherals.
   - c. programs.
   - d. hardware.
8. Which is computer software?
   - a. printer
   - b. disk drive
   - c. program
   - d. memory

True or False

If the statement is true, write "true." If it is false, change the underlined word or words to make the statement true.

1. A device that converts alternating current to direct current is a <u>rectifier</u>.
2. A telephone sends and receives sound by means of <u>electric</u> current.
3. The beam of electrons in a <u>cathode-ray tube</u> produces a picture.
4. A color television CRT has <u>two</u> electron guns.
5. The first American-built computer was <u>UNIVAC</u>.
6. <u>Microprocessors</u> are integrated circuits that can hold the entire processing capability of a computer on one chip.
7. <u>Output</u> devices feed data to a computer.
8. A <u>data bank</u> is a vast collection of information stored in a large computer.
9. A string of bits, usually eight in number, is called a <u>byte</u>.

Concept Mapping

Complete the following concept map for Section 22–1. Then construct a concept map for the entire chapter.

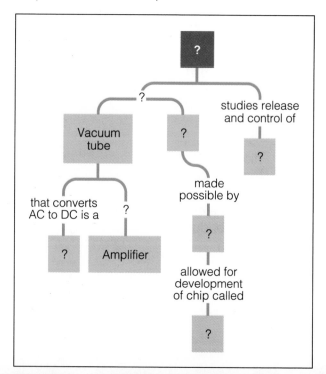

Concept Mastery

Discuss each of the following in a brief paragraph.

1. Why are electrons important to electronic devices? Give some examples.
2. Compare the functions of rectifiers and amplifiers. What type of vacuum tube is used for each?
3. Describe a semiconductor. Why are semiconductors doped?
4. What connection between electricity and magnetism is used in radio communication systems?
5. How does a telephone work?
6. How is a radio show broadcast?
7. In what ways are semiconductor diodes better than their vacuum tube ancestors?
8. Describe how a cathode-ray tube creates a picture.
9. What is a computer? What are some uses of computers?
10. What system is used in computers and calculators? Explain how it works.

Critical Thinking and Problem Solving

Use the skills you have developed in this chapter to answer each of the following.

1. **Making diagrams** Draw a diagram that shows how the four main hardware components of a computer are related.
2. **Sequencing events** The sentences below describe some of the energy conversions required for a local telephone call. Arrange them in proper order.
   a. Sound vibrates a metal plate.
   b. An electromagnet is energized.
   c. A vibrating magnet produces sound.
   d. Vibrating vocal cords produce sound.
   e. Mechanical energy is converted into an electric signal.
3. **Classifying computer devices** Many methods for putting data into a computer are similar to methods for getting data out of a computer. Identify each of the following as an input device, an output device, or both: typewriter keyboard, CRT, printer, optical scanner, magnetic tape, disk drive, punched cards, voice synthesizer.
4. **Applying concepts** A program is a list of instructions that tells a computer how to perform a task. Write a program that describes the steps involved in your task of waking up and arriving at school for your first class.
5. **Making calculations** The pictures on a television screen last for one thirtieth of a second. How many pictures are flashed on a screen during 30 minutes?
6. **Using the writing process** The electronics industry and the development of computers have evolved quite rapidly. You yourself are even witnessing obvious changes in the size and capabilities of electronic devices such as calculators, video games, computers, VCRs, compact disc players, and videodiscs. Write a story or play about how you think electronic devices will affect your life thirty or forty years from now.

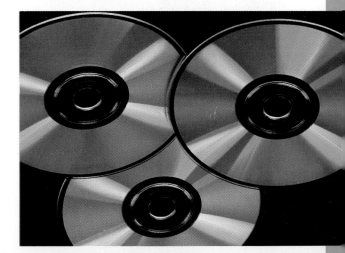

GAZETTE

THE SEARCH FOR
SUPERCONDUCTORS

Imagine trains that fly above their tracks at airplane speeds and powerful computers that fit in the palm of your hand. Picture unlocking the secrets of the atom, or skiing on slopes made of air. Purely imagination? Not really. All of these things—and more—have been brought closer to reality by the work of Dr. Karl Alex Mueller and Dr. Johannes Georg Bednorz. These two dedicated scientists have changed fantasy to fact through their work with superconductors.

SEARCHING FOR A BETTER CONDUCTOR

Much of our electricity runs through copper wire. Copper is an example of a conductor, or a material that carries electricity well. However, copper is not a perfect con-

ductor because it offers resistance to the flow of electricity. As a result of resistance, about 15 percent of the electric power passing through a copper wire is wasted as heat.

A superconductor has no resistance. Therefore, it can conduct electricity without any loss of power. With superconductors, power plants could produce more usable electricity at lower costs and with no waste. Electric motors could be made smaller and more powerful. Superconducting wires connecting computer chips could produce smaller, faster computers.

Scientists have known about superconductors for more than 75 years. But although the principle of superconductivity was understood, the method of creating one remained a secret...a secret that seemed to be "locked in a deep freeze." For until the time of Mueller and Bednorz's discovery, materials would not become superconductors unless they were chilled to at least –250°C!

Superconductivity pioneers Karl Mueller (left) and Johannes Bednorz.

To cool materials to such extremely low temperatures, scientists had to use liquid helium, which is very costly. The supercold superconductors were just too expensive to be of general use.

If a substance could become superconducting at −196°C or higher, then it could be cooled with liquid nitrogen. Liquid nitrogen costs as little as a nickel a liter—less expensive than milk or soda. But what substances might become superconductors at these relatively high temperatures? That was the problem Dr. Mueller and Dr. Bednorz had to solve.

LOOKING IN A NEW DIRECTION

Many experts thought that superconductors simply did not exist at temperatures higher than −250°C. But Dr. Mueller, a highly respected physicist at IBM's research laboratory in Zurich, Switzerland, remained fascinated by high-temperature superconductors. In fact, he had already devised a new approach to finding one!

To some, his idea seemed impossible. But Dr. Mueller and his partner Dr. Bednorz were willing to follow their unusual approach under the guidance of what Dr. Mueller describes as "my intuition."

For almost three years, the two scientists mixed powders, baked them in ovens to form new compounds, and then chilled them to see if they would lose their resistance to electricity. And for three years, the two scientists kept their work a secret. "We were sure anybody would say, 'These guys are crazy,'" Dr. Bednorz later said. But despite endless hours of hard work and dedication, none of the new compounds was the superconductor Mueller and Bednorz sought.

Then in December 1985, Dr. Bednorz read about a new copper oxide. He and Dr. Mueller thought the oxide looked promising. They decided to test it for superconductivity. On January 27, 1986, Dr. Mueller and Dr. Bednorz broke the temperature barrier to superconductivity—and broke it by a

▲ This magnetic disk may seem to be defying gravity. Actually, it is floating above a disk made of a superconductive material. The superconductive disk repels magnetic fields and causes the magnet to float in midair.

large amount. They achieved superconductivity at −243°C. By April, Mueller and Bednorz had raised the temperature of superconductivity to a new record, −238°C. Around the world, scientists began to duplicate the experiments and make even greater advances in high-temperature superconductors.

In February 1987, a team of researchers at the University of Houston led by Dr. C.W. Chu created a new oxide that shows superconductivity at −175°C. This is the first superconductor that can be cooled with liquid nitrogen—the first superconductor that might be used for everyday purposes.

Dr. Mueller and Dr. Bednorz received the 1987 Nobel Prize for Physics for their pioneering work on superconductors. Their work, however, does not end here. They look forward to the development of a room-temperature superconductor!

UNIT SIX
Sound and Light

The description of amber waves of grain in the familiar song "America the Beautiful" produces a stunning image of golden fields of wheat rhythmically blowing in the breeze. Simply from the use of the word wave, you form a complete picture of the motion of the wheat. It blows back and forth in a smooth, repeating pattern—perhaps not unlike the motion of a flag flying on a windy day. In fact, the expression "Long may it wave" is applied to the flag. You probably use the word wave to describe a variety of motions. You wave hello, wave good-bye, wave a banner, make waves in water.

◀ Beautiful flags of different countries blow rhythmically in the wind.

▼ A variety of appealing sounds is produced as the band marches proudly down the street.

CHAPTERS

But do you say you hear waves of sound or see waves of light? Probably not. Yet wave motion is necessary to describe both sound and light. Waves are also necessary to describe forms of energy that surround you every day, as well as many technologies that affect your life and your future. In this Unit you will learn about the actual nature of wave motion. You will discover that each type of wave has certain characteristics that make it different from other types of waves, along with characteristics that account for the qualities that make a wave in a wheat field different from a wave of light. And you will become familiar with the wave energy that flies a flag, disturbs a pool of water, warms you and your food, carries sound and light, and transmits information. As you read this Unit, the word wave will become an even more important part of your vocabulary.

Majestic waves rock the ocean waters over and over again without ever stopping.

Discovery Activity

Making Waves

1. Fill a pan or tub with water.

2. Float a narrow instrument such as a pencil on the water.

3. Push the pencil up and down and observe the waves that are made in the water. Draw a wave on a piece of paper.

   ■ What characteristics do you notice about the wave?

   ■ What happens to the waves when they hit the sides of the container?

   ■ What happens if you push the pencil at different speeds?

Characteristics of *Waves*

Guide for Reading

After you read the following sections, you will be able to

23–1 Nature of Waves
- Explain how waves are related to energy.

23–2 Characteristics of Waves
- Describe the basic characteristics of waves.

23–3 Types of Waves
- Classify waves as transverse, longitudinal, or both.

23–4 Speed of Waves
- Relate wave speed to frequency and wavelength.

23–5 Interactions of Waves
- Identify basic wave interactions.

Way out in the ocean, far from the eyes of eager surfers, the wind stirs a small ripple into the water's calm surface. As the wind continues to blow, gaining speed and strength, the ripple grows into a full, surging wave. By the time it travels thousands of kilometers to the Hawaiian shore, the wave rises several meters above the surface—forming the famous Hawaiian Pipeline.

Uninterested in its origin and development, the surfers see the wave as the challenge of the day. They run into the water, surfboards in hand. A few quick strokes and they catch the monstrous wave. Most cannot keep ahead of the crushing weight of water for long and are soon pulled under. But one surfer holds on. She steers back and forth as the wave towers over her. The water thunders around her, but success is hers. With a sense of accomplishment and an appreciation of nature's power, she rides the wave all the way to shore.

What is a wave? What do ocean waves have to do with wind? How can a wave travel several thousand kilometers? As you read this chapter, you will find the answers.

Journal *Activity*

You and Your World If you have ever been under an ocean wave as it broke, you know how powerful waves can be. In your journal, describe an experience you have had with any type of water waves—ocean waves, waves in a lake, waves that you made in a pan of water or bathtub. Explain what you were doing and how the waves affected you. Then describe three scenes that illustrate different aspects of ocean waves. Center each description around one of the following words: beauty, destruction, fun.

◄ *Although the powerful wave can't last forever, its awesome energy has given this surfer a wonderful ride.*

Figure 23–1 *A pebble tossed into a still pond creates a disturbance that moves outward along the surface of the water as a wave. The continuous blowing of the wind causes wheat to move in a wavelike pattern.*

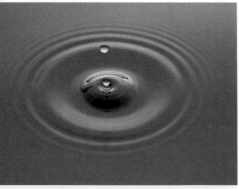

23–1 Nature of Waves

Have you ever dropped a pebble into a still pond and observed the circular waves moving outward? Maybe you have watched the waves moving across a field of wheat on a windy day. Or perhaps you have observed huge waves in the ocean during a storm. All these examples illustrate waves. You might be surprised to learn that even light and sound are examples of waves.

Waves and Energy

Think again about ocean waves. Ocean waves continuously roll into the shore, one after the other, night and day. Have you ever wondered how ocean waves can do this without flooding the beaches? The reason is that ocean waves do not actually carry water. As a wave rushes to the shore, the ocean water is moved up and down—but not forward. So even though it looks as if the water itself is moving toward shore, it is actually not. Only the wave moves forward.

To help you understand this, consider another example of waves. What happens to a nearby canoe or pile of leaves in a lake when a motorboat speeds by? The motorboat creates waves that move past the object, causing the object to bob up and down. The waves continue to move forward, but the object remains in approximately the same place. Why? The motorboat disturbs the flat surface of the lake. The disturbance moves outward along the surface of the water as a series of **waves.**

The meaning of the word disturbance should not be new to you. Suppose that you are taking a nap one day in a comfortable hammock when a friend comes along and tilts you out. Your friend has moved you from your resting position. Among other things, you might say that your friend has disturbed you from your rest, or that your friend is a disturbance! After your friend leaves, you return to your nap. In much the same way, particles of water are disturbed from their resting positions by water waves. Once the disturbance has passed, the water particles return to their resting positions. They are not carried by the wave.

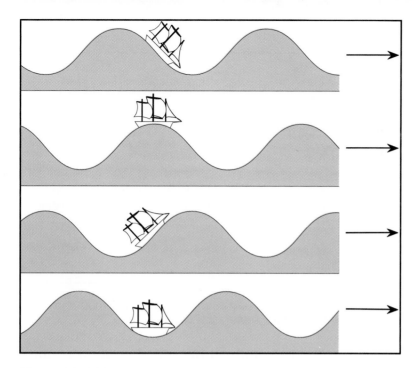

Figure 23–2 *The boat in the water simply bobs up and down as waves roll by. What is a wave?*

What, then, makes up the disturbance? You already learned that it is not matter. The fact that water waves do not carry matter—such as water, canoes, or piles of leaves—is true of any wave. So what is carried by a wave? Waves carry energy. Recall from Chapter 16 that energy is the ability to do work or cause change. **A wave is a traveling disturbance that carries energy from one place to another.**

Where Do Waves Get Energy?

To understand how waves are made, try making a wave on your own. Tie a rope to a fixed object such as a doorknob or post. See Figure 23–4 on page 590. Jerk the free end of the rope and observe the "bump," or wave motion, that travels to the other end. Now try moving your hand up and down or back and forth over and over again. You have just created a series of waves. How did you do this?

You made the wave motion on the rope by moving your hand up and down or back and forth. Any movement that follows the same path repeatedly is called a **vibration.** You created a vibration. Vibrations are probably quite familiar to you already. The top of a drum vibrates after it is struck by a drumstick. It moves up and down several times, creating

Figure 23–3 *Just the slightest touch, carried like a signal, knocks over a long row of dominoes. Like a falling row of dominoes, a wave can move over a long distance. The substance through which it moves, however, has limited movement.*

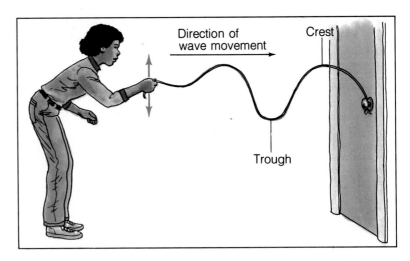

Figure 23–4 *A rope attached at one end to a doorknob and pulled up and down will generate a wave.*

Seeing Sound, p. 769

Activity Bank

its characteristic sound. In fact, the vibration of your eardrum in response to sound enables you to hear. A stretched rubber band that is plucked also vibrates for a few seconds. So does a guitar string. Even the Earth can vibrate during a powerful earthquake.

An object that is vibrating is moving. And an object that is moving has energy. A vibrating object gives off some of its energy to nearby particles, causing them to vibrate as well. These particles, in turn, give off energy to the particles next to them, and so on. This movement of energy from a vibrating source outward is a wave. Waves—whether they be ocean waves, waves on a rope, sound waves, or microwaves—have a vibration as their source. The motorboat you just read about gave energy to the water particles in the lake. You gave some of your energy to the rope by moving your hand. Wind blowing back and forth over the ocean creates ocean waves. Electric charges (like the ones you see and feel when you receive a shock) can vibrate to create light and microwaves. Energy is given to the air by the vibration of a guitar string to create a sound wave.

Waves Through Matter and Space

In most of the previous examples, energy from a vibration traveled through a substance. The matter, or substance, through which a wave is transmitted is called a **medium**. Water is a medium for ocean

Figure 23–5 *When a piano key is struck, a string is hit and set into vibration. Notice the vibrating string in the center of the photo. Energy is given to the string by the player's finger. What gives energy to the sound wave?*

waves. Air is a medium for sound waves. All phases of matter (solid, liquid, and gas) can act as a medium. Waves that require a medium are called **mechanical waves**.

For certain waves, a medium is not required. These waves can be transmitted through a vacuum (space free of particles). Instead of matter, these waves disturb electric and magnetic fields. For this reason, they are called **electromagnetic waves**. Because they do not depend on particles of matter, electromagnetic waves can exist with or without a medium. Light is an electromagnetic wave. Light from the sun can travel to the Earth through the vacuum of space. Light can also travel through air across your room. Microwaves in an oven are electromagnetic waves, as are X-rays used in medicine.

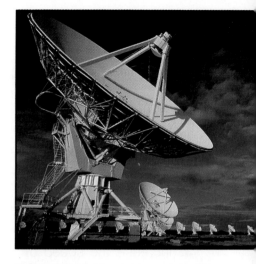

Figure 23–6 *The telescopes of the Very Large Array in New Mexico collect invisible waves that travel with or without a medium. What are these types of waves called?*

23–1 Section Review

1. How are waves and energy related?
2. Where do waves get their energy?
3. What is a medium? A mechanical wave?
4. Describe an electromagnetic wave. How does it differ from a mechanical wave?

Connection—*You and Your World*
5. The programs you watch on television are made up of all sorts of sounds and colors. How do waves make television possible?

23–2 Characteristics of Waves

You just learned that there are many different kinds of waves. Sound waves, light waves, X-rays, microwaves, and ocean waves are but a few examples. All waves, however, share certain basic characteristics. **All waves have amplitude, wavelength, and frequency.**

In order to understand these characteristics of waves, it may help you to represent a wave as a drawing on a graph. The X-axis (the horizontal line)

ACTIVITY

Figure 23–7 *The basic characteristics of a wave are shown here. What is the high point of a wave called? The low point? What does wave amplitude measure?*

represents the normal, or resting, position of the medium, or field, before it is disturbed by a wave. For example, the X-axis might represent a calm sea or a tight rope. The vibrational movements of the wave are shown on the Y-axis (the vertical line). See Figure 23–7. The highest points on the graph are called peaks or **crests.** The lowest points are called **troughs** (TRAWFS).

Amplitude

If the wave disturbs a medium, the particles of the medium are moved from their normal (resting) positions. The distance the particles are moved from their resting positions is shown by the up and down pattern of the graph. Similarly, if the wave disturbs electric or magnetic fields, the graph shows the rise and fall of the fields. In any wave, the amount of movement from rest is shown by the distance above or below the X-axis. The maximum (or greatest) movement from rest is called the **amplitude** (AM-pluh-tood) of the wave. The amplitude can be found by measuring the distance from rest to a crest or from rest to a trough.

The amplitude of a wave indicates the amount of energy carried by the wave. As energy increases, particles of the medium are moved a greater distance from rest. Thus the amplitude of the wave also increases. The amplitude decreases as the wave loses energy. What happens to the crests and troughs of a wave as amplitude increases? As it decreases?

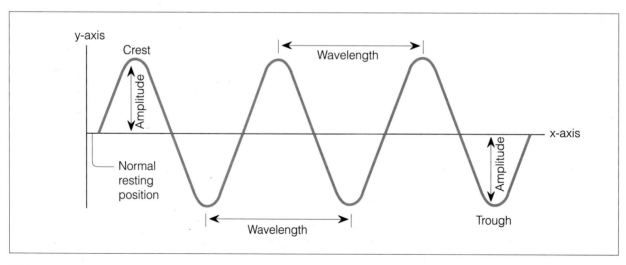

Wavelength

The distance between two consecutive (one after another) crests or troughs of a wave is called the **wavelength**. Actually, the wavelength can be measured from any point on a wave as long as it is measured to the same point on the next wave. Wavelength is usually measured in meters or centimeters. The symbol for wavelength is the Greek letter lambda (λ).

Frequency

The number of complete waves, or complete cycles, per unit of time is called the **frequency** (FREE-kwuhn-see). Because every complete wave has one crest and one trough, you can think of the frequency as the number of crests or troughs produced per unit time. The unit used to measure wave frequency is called the hertz (Hz). This unit is named after Heinrich Hertz, who was one of the first scientists to study certain types of waves. A frequency of one hertz is equal to one wave, or cycle, per second: 1 Hz = 1 wave/sec.

The frequency of a wave depends on the frequency at which its source is vibrating. Think about

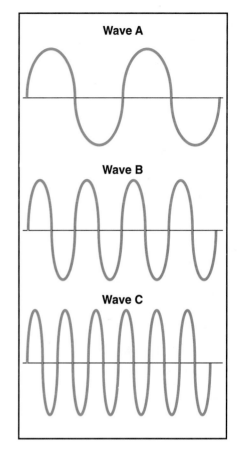

Figure 23–8 *Frequency is the number of complete waves per unit time. What is the frequency of Wave A? Wave B? Wave C?*

Figure 23–9 *Electromagnetic waves of different frequencies produce rainbows. In fact, the same kinds of waves at lower frequencies are used to heat food in microwave ovens. A curious pooch can detect sounds of higher frequencies than you can.*

the rope again. If you move your hand slowly, the rope vibrates slowly. Perhaps you will create one new wave every two or three seconds. If you move your hand rapidly, the rope vibrates rapidly. This way, you may create several waves each second. Try it and see!

Frequency, which is often used to describe waves, is an important characteristic. Frequency is used to distinguish one color of light from another, as well as one sound from another. For example, red light is different from blue light because red light has a lower frequency. A dog can hear a whistle that you cannot hear because dogs can hear sounds at higher frequencies than humans can.

23–2 Section Review

1. Define three basic characteristics of a wave.
2. What is the unit of wave frequency? How is it defined?
3. If the horizontal distance from a crest to a trough is 1.0 m, what is the wavelength?

Critical Thinking—*Making Calculations*
4. Suppose you notice that 20 waves pass a point in 5 sec. What is the frequency? How many waves would pass a point in 1 sec if the wave frequency were two times greater?

Guide for Reading

Focus on this question as you read.

▶ *What is the difference between a transverse wave and a longitudinal wave?*

23–3 Types of Waves

You learned that mechanical waves require a medium through which to travel. Although they share this characteristic, all mechanical waves are not the same. Ocean waves are a different type of wave from sound waves. Why? Although they both transfer energy through a medium, the movement of the disturbance, or wave, through the medium is quite different. Depending on the motion of the medium as compared to the movement of the wave, waves are classified as either transverse or longitudinal.

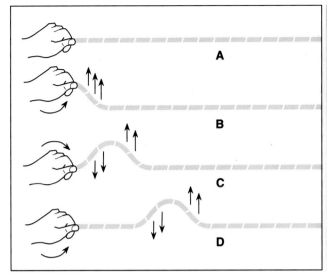

Figure 23–10 *A wave on a rope is the same type of wave as a wave that carries sunlight to your eyes. What type of wave is it?*

Transverse Waves

When one end of a rope is jerked, energy is given to the nearby particles of rope. These particles start to move up and down (vertically) as a result of the energy. As they move, they transfer energy to neighboring particles, which in turn move up and down. As each neighboring rope particle begins to move up and down, energy is transferred from one place to another (horizontally). Each particle moves up and down, but the wave moves horizontally along the rope. Thus the movement of the particles is vertical while the movement of the wave is horizontal. The two movements are at right angles to each other. **A wave in which the motion of the medium is at right angles to the direction of the wave is called a transverse wave.** A wave on a rope is a **transverse wave**. Light and other electromagnetic waves are transverse waves.

Longitudinal Waves

Clap your hands together near your face. Do you hear a clap? Do you also feel air striking your face? When you clap your hands, you move the particles of air away from their resting positions and crowd them together. A space in the medium in which the particles are crowded together is called a compression (kuhm-PREHSH-uhn). Because you give the particles energy, they begin to vibrate back and forth.

ACTIVITY
READING

Mysteries of the Sea

The wonders of the sea have been the topic of many beautiful works of art and literature throughout time. Obtain and read "Sea Songs" by Myra Cohn Livingston. This is a wonderful poem about the magic and mysteries of nature.

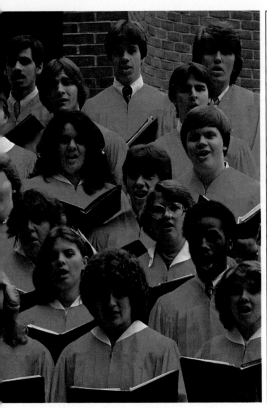

Figure 23–11 at top showing direction of wave movement with compressions and rarefactions labeled.

Figure 23–11 *The vibration of a drum head produces compressions and rarefactions in the air. So do the melodious voices of singers in a choir. What type of a wave is a sound wave?*

Figure 23–12 *Longitudinal waves can be represented on a graph. The crests of a longitudinal wave represent the compressions. The troughs represent the rarefactions.*

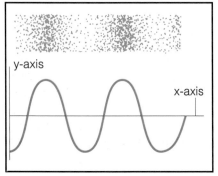

See Figure 23–11. As the particles of air move to the right, they pass their resting positions and collide with the particles of air next to them. These particles also become compressed. Then the first set of air particles moves to the left while the second set of particles begins to vibrate and moves to the right. This leaves a space that contains many fewer particles. A space in the medium in which there are fewer particles is called a rarefaction (rair-uh-FAK-shuhn).

Each layer of particles pushes the next layer as the compressions move forward through the medium. Each compression is followed by a rarefaction. So rarefactions also move forward. As the layers of particles move back and forth through a medium, compressions and rarefactions develop and move in a regular, repeating way. Energy is transmitted as a wave. A wave that consists of a series of compressions and rarefactions is a **longitudinal** (lahn-juh-TOOD-uhn-uhl) **wave.**

As you can see, longitudinal waves are quite different from transverse waves. **In a longitudinal wave, the motion of the medium is parallel to the direction of the wave.** In other words, the particles of the medium move in the same direction in which the wave moves. Sound waves are longitudinal waves.

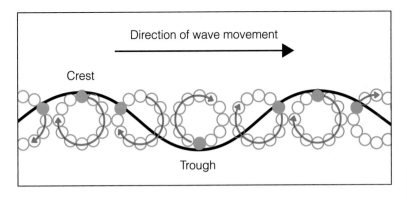

Crest

Direction of wave movement

Trough

Figure 23–13 *The particles affected by a surface wave move in circular patterns. The energy of the wave is transmitted without the movement of the medium as a whole.*

Longitudinal waves can be represented on a graph in the same way transverse waves can. The crests represent the crowded areas, or compressions. The troughs represent the least crowded areas, or rarefactions. The wavelength of a longitudinal wave is the distance between compressions or rarefactions. Frequency is the number of compressions or rarefactions that pass a point per second.

Combinations of Waves

Some waves cannot be described as only transverse or longitudinal. That is because these waves are a combination of the two types of waves. An example of such a wave is a **surface wave**. Surface waves (as their name implies) occur at the surface between two different mediums. Water waves on the surface of the ocean are an example of surface waves. They travel between water and air. The motion of each particle is neither up and down nor back and forth. It is a combination of both movements. The combination produces a wave in which each particle moves in a circle.

23–3 Section Review

1. What is the difference between a transverse wave and a longitudinal wave?
2. What is a compression? A rarefaction?
3. What is an example of a transverse wave? Longitudinal wave?
4. Describe a surface wave.

Critical Thinking—*Making Connections*

5. Describe an example of a transverse wave that gives rise to a longitudinal wave.

CAREERS

Geophysicist

Scientists who study and map out the Earth's layers and discover its treasures are called **geophysicists**. A common technique used by geophysicists is to send sound waves downward through rock. The sound waves are reflected from the rock layers back to the surface. By recording the time it takes for the waves to travel through the various regions, geophysicists can determine the components of the rock layers.

A college degree in geology is required to become a geophysicist. For more information, contact the American Geophysical Union, Meetings and Members Program, 2000 Florida Avenue, NW, Washington, DC 20009.

23–4 Speed of Waves

Have you ever noticed that you hear thunder several seconds after you see lightning? Even though thunder and lightning are produced at the same time, you see the lightning first because light travels at a much faster speed than sound. Different waves travel at different speeds.

The speed of a wave is determined by the number of waves passing a point in a certain amount of time (frequency) and the length of the wave (wavelength). The speed of a wave is equal to the frequency times the wavelength.

Speed = Frequency × Wavelength

When the frequency of a wave is measured in hertz and the wavelength is measured in meters, the speed of the wave is measured in meters per second.

A wave with a frequency of 4 hertz (Hz) and a wavelength of 2 meters has a speed of 8 meters per second (4 Hz × 2 m = 8 m/sec). If the frequency of the wave were increased to 8 hertz, the wavelength would decrease to 1 meter in the same medium. Why? **In a given medium, the speed of a wave is constant.** Thus the speed must still be 8 meters per second. If the frequency is now 8 hertz, the wavelength must be 1 meter (8 Hz × 1 m = 8 m/sec). An increase in frequency requires a corresponding decrease in wavelength. What would happen to the frequency if the wavelength were increased?

The speed of a wave does not depend on the source or the speed of the source. For example, the speed of sound does not depend on whether it is produced by an airplane or by the snap of your fingers. Nor does the speed of sound depend on the

Figure 23–14 *You see lightning, even at a great distance, before you hear thunder because light travels at a greater speed than sound. Nothing is known to travel faster than the speed of light.*

speed of the airplane that caused it. **The speed of a wave depends upon the medium through which it is traveling.**

One property of a medium that affects the speed of mechanical waves is the density. The density of a medium is a measurement of the medium's mass divided by its volume. A substance that is very dense has more particles or more massive particles than a less dense substance. It may help you to consider some examples: Molasses is more dense than water; water is more dense than air.

If you stir molasses, you will discover that your spoon moves more slowly than it does when you stir water because molasses is more dense than water. The movement of the spoon is slower in the denser medium. The same is true of waves. A wave moves more slowly in a denser medium. The more dense the medium, the slower the speed of a wave in that medium. Why? A denser medium has more inertia to overcome. It is harder to get all of the particles of a denser medium to respond to the energy of the wave and start moving.

Another property of a medium that affects the speed of waves is elasticity. Elasticity refers to the ability of a medium to return quickly to its original shape after being disturbed. A wave moves faster in a more elastic medium. This is because the particles return to their rest positions more quickly.

ACTIVITY
DOING

Waves of Straw

1. Stretch out 2m of masking tape, sticky side up. At right angles to the tape, place a soda straw every 6 cm. When all the straws are in place, place another piece of tape over the straws on top on the first piece of tape.

2. Attach one end of the tape to a stationary object. a doorknob or ring stand will do.

3. Rotate the free end by turning your wrist. Observe the motion of the straws.

What is the role of the straws and tape?

4. Now move the first straw up and down. With a stopwatch, measure the time it takes for the wave to travel to the end of the tape. (Speed = Distance/Time)

5. Attach paper clips to the ends of the straws. Repeat step 4.

How does the speed of this wave differ from the speed of the wave in step 4. Why?

23–4 Section Review

1. What is the relationship between wave speed, frequency, and wavelength?
2. If the frequency and wavelength of a wave are changed, what happens to the speed? Why?
3. A wave has a frequency of 10 Hz and a wavelength of 30 m. What is its speed?
4. If the frequency of the wave in question 3 were 20 Hz, what would be the wavelength?

Critical Thinking—*Applying Concepts*

5. At 25°C, the speed of sound in air is 346 m/sec. At 0°C, the speed of sound in air is 331 m/sec. Explain why the speed decreases as the temperature decreases.

23–5 Interactions of Waves

You learned that waves traveling in the same medium move at a constant speed and in a constant direction. What would happen, however, if the waves encountered a different medium, reached an obstacle, or met another wave? Depending on the conditions, the waves would interact in a certain way. **The four basic wave interactions are reflection, refraction, diffraction, and interference.**

Reflection

Have you ever seen water waves strike a rock or the side of a swimming pool? What happens? You are correct if you have observed that the waves bounce back. When a wave strikes a barrier or comes to the end of the medium it is traveling in, at least part of the wave bounces back. Figure 23–15 shows waves striking a barrier and bouncing back. This interaction is called **reflection** (rih-FLEHK-shuhn). Reflection is the bouncing back of a wave after it strikes a boundary that does not absorb all the wave's energy.

In order to better describe and illustrate reflection (as well as other wave interactions), certain diagrams are used. A line drawn in the direction of motion of a wave is called a ray. Rays are used to show wave activity. The incoming wave is called

Figure 23–15 *According to the law of reflection, the angle of incidence equals the angle of reflection. The green laser beam dramatically illustrates this point as it bounces off three mirrors before it enters the jar.*

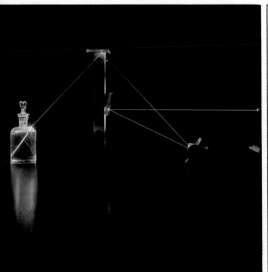

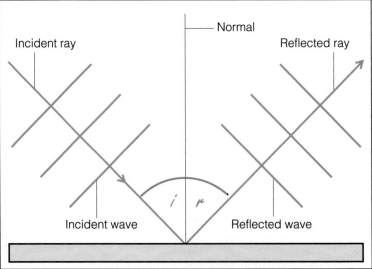

Figure 23–16 *Thanks to the reflection of sunlight from the surface of the moon, you can enjoy a moonlit night.*

an incident wave. The wave that is bounced back is called a reflected wave. The angle formed by the incident ray and an imaginary line drawn perpendicular to the barrier is called the angle of incidence (i). The angle formed by the same perpendicular line and the reflected ray is called the angle of reflection (r). The line drawn perpendicular to the barrier is called the normal. **The law of reflection states that the angle of incidence (i) is equal to the angle of reflection (r).** This means that the angle the incident wave makes with a surface is equal to the angle the reflected wave makes with the same surface.

You are probably already familiar with reflection in your everyday life. For example, when you look in the mirror, you are taking advantage of the reflection of light to see yourself. Concert halls and theaters are designed to use reflection to make the sound more powerful. An echo is another example of reflection.

Refraction

Waves do not bend as they travel through a medium unless an obstacle gets in the way. Waves travel in straight lines. The light from your flashlight, for example, travels straight across the room. However, when waves pass at an angle from one medium to another—air to water or glass to air, for example—they bend. The waves bend because the speed of the waves changes as the waves travel from one medium to another. Remember, wave speed is constant only for a particular medium. As a wave enters a different medium, its speed changes.

The bending of waves due to a change in speed is called **refraction** (rih-FRAK-shuhn). Refraction occurs because waves move at different speeds in different mediums. As waves pass at an angle from one medium to another, they may speed up or slow down.

You can easily see for yourself the results of the refraction of light by trying the following activity. Place a pencil diagonally in a glass of water. What do

Activity Bank

Sound Around, p. 770

ACTIVITY

DISCOVERING

Handball Physics

1. Choose a spot on a wall. Roll a rubber ball directly to that spot so that the direction of movement of the ball is perpendicular to the wall. How is the ball reflected?

2. Change your position and again roll the ball to the spot, but this time at an angle to the wall.

3. Change your position again and roll the ball to the wall from a different angle.

■ Do your observations confirm the law of reflection?

■ How can you improve your handball or racquetball game?

601

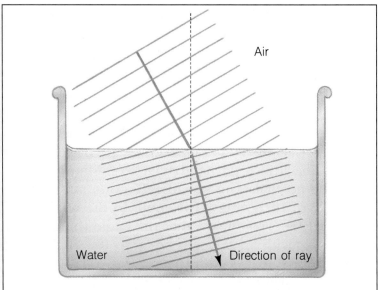

Figure 23–17 *Waves bend as they pass from air into water. Notice how the light beam in the photograph demonstrates refraction.*

Figure 23–18 *The refraction of light as it passes from one medium to another makes this flower stem look as if it were broken. Why does refraction occur?*

you see? The pencil appears to be split into two pieces. The light waves traveling through air are slowed down and bent when they travel through water. Here's another way to observe refraction. Place a coin in the bottom of an empty cup. Move the cup so that the coin is out of your line of sight. Then fill the cup with water. Does the coin become visible? Explain what has happened.

Diffraction

If you duck around a corner to escape an oncoming snowball, you avoid getting hit. The snowball will continue past you. But if you try the same tactic to avoid someone who is yelling at you, you can still hear the shouting. Why? Sound travels as a wave, whereas the snowball does not. And although waves travel in straight lines through a medium, if an obstacle is encountered, waves bend around it somewhat and pass into the region behind it.

The bending of waves around the edge of an obstacle is called **diffraction** (dih-FRAK-shuhn). Diffraction is a result of a new series of waves being formed when the original waves strike an obstacle. The amount of diffraction depends on the wavelength and the size of the obstacle.

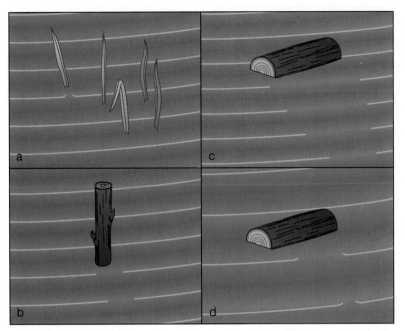

Figure 23–19 *The larger the wavelength of the waves compared with the size of the object, the more the waves will bend around the object, or diffract. In frames a, b, and c the wavelength of the waves is the same, but less bending occurs as the size of the object increases. Frames c and d show the same object, but because the wavelength is greater in frame d, more bending is observed.*

Activity Bank

Presto Chango, It's Gone, p. 771

ACTIVITY

DISCOVERING

Rough Riding

Assemble the following materials: 2 rubber or wooden wheels, firmly attached to an axle, and a large piece of velvet cloth or course sandpaper.

1. Roll the wheels and axle across a smooth tabletop. Describe the direction of motion.

2. Place the velvet cloth or course sandpaper on the tabletop.

3. Roll the wheels again but in such a way that only one wheel moves across the rough surface. Describe the motion.

4. What effect does this motion have on the direction of the wheels? What causes this to happen?

■ What does this activity illustrate about wave interactions?

Interference

Suppose that you and a friend are holding the ends of a piece of rope. You both snap the ends at the same time. Two waves are sent toward each other. What will happen when the waves meet at the middle of the rope?

When two or more waves arrive at the same place at the same time, they interact in a process called **interference.** The waves combine to produce a single wave. To see how two waves combine, the displacement, or distance from rest, of one wave is added to the displacement of the other wave at every point along the wave. If the displacement of one wave is below the resting position (the X-axis), it is subtracted from the displacement of the other wave. Waves can combine in two different ways.

CONSTRUCTIVE INTERFERENCE If waves combine in such a way that the disturbance that results is greater than either wave alone, constructive interference occurs. For example, if the crests of one wave meet the crests of the other wave, constructive interference occurs. The crests of the two waves add together to form a single wave. The amplitude of the single wave is equal to the sum of the amplitudes of the two original waves.

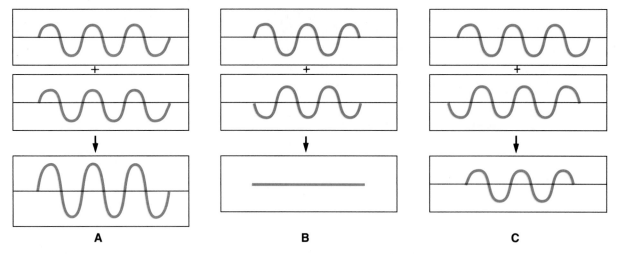

A	B	C

Figure 23–20 *When two waves arrive at the same place at the same time, they interfere with each other. If the same points on each wave combine, they add together (A). If opposite points combine, they cancel out (B). And if the waves meet at different points, some parts add and some parts subtract, causing the wave to vary (C).*

DESTRUCTIVE INTERFERENCE If waves combine in such a way that the disturbance that results is less than either wave alone, destructive interference occurs. For example, if the crests of one wave meet the troughs of the other wave, destructive interference occurs. The crests and troughs combine by subtracting from each other to form a single wave. The amplitude of this wave is the difference between the amplitudes of the original waves.

If the crest of one wave occurs at the trough of the other wave and both waves have the same amplitude, the waves will cancel each other out. The combination of the waves will result in no wave at all.

Standing Waves

If you continuously shake the end of a rope up and down, the waves you create will travel to the opposite end of the rope and be reflected back. After a few vibrations, there will be quite a jumble of waves. But if you vibrate the rope at just the right frequency (move your hand up and down a certain number of times each second), something interesting happens. A wave that does not appear to be moving results. This type of wave is called a **standing wave**.

The points on a standing wave where destructive interference results in no energy displacement are called nodes (NOHDZ). Nodes are located on the X (resting) axis. The points at which constructive interference causes maximum energy displacement are called antinodes. Any crest or trough may be called an antinode.

Standing waves can occur at more than one frequency for waves on a rope. The lowest frequency that produces a standing wave causes the first pattern shown in Figure 23–21. Twice that frequency will cause two loops. Three times that frequency will cause three loops, and so on for any multiple of the frequency.

The frequency at which a standing wave occurs is called the natural frequency, or **resonant frequency**, of the object. When an object is vibrating at its natural frequency, little effort is required to achieve a large amplitude. Perhaps you have pushed a friend or a child on a swing. At first it may be difficult to push the swing. But once the swing reaches its natural frequency of moving back and forth, you need only push lightly to keep the swing moving.

An object that is vibrating at its natural frequency can cause a nearby object to start vibrating if that object has the same natural frequency. The ability of an object to vibrate by absorbing energy of its own natural frequency is called resonance (REZ-uh-nuhns). A singer can shatter glass by singing a clear, strong high-pitched note. If the natural frequency of the glass is the same as the natural frequency of the note sung by the singer, the glass will vibrate due to resonance. Glass is not very flexible. So if it absorbs enough energy, it will shatter.

You are already familiar with other examples of resonance—although you may not realize it! You are applying the principle of resonance every time you tune in your radio or turn the station on your television. Each station broadcasts at a specific frequency.

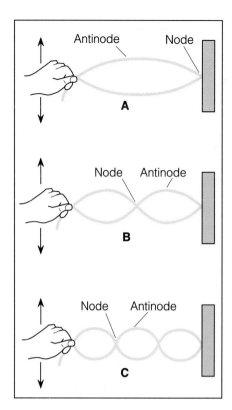

Figure 23–21 *Standing waves occur when an object vibrates at its resonant frequency and multiples of that frequency. How many nodes are there in the standing wave that occurs at four times the resonant frequency of this rope?*

Figure 23–22 *Raindrops on a lake show what happens when waves interfere. At the regions where the circular waves overlap, the waves exhibit greater amplitudes than in the center of each circle.*

Figure 23–23 *When the tuning fork on the left is set in motion, it begins to vibrate at its natural frequency. These vibrations travel through the air and the wooden resonance box, which strengthens them. The tuning fork on the right will begin to vibrate "in sympathy" because it absorbs energy at its own natural frequency. Resonance caused the collapse of the Tacoma Narrows Bridge in November 1940.*

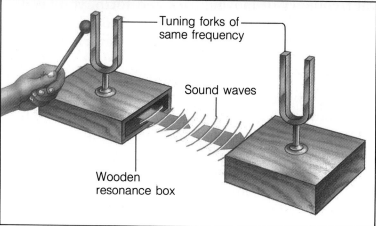

Tuning forks of same frequency

Sound waves

Wooden resonance box

When you tune into a station, you are matching the frequency of your radio or television with the frequency of the broadcasting station.

23–5 Section Review

1. Name the four wave interactions.
2. What is reflection? What is the law of reflection?
3. What is refraction? Diffraction?
4. Compare constructive and destructive interference.
5. What is a standing wave?

Critical Thinking—*Applying Concepts*

6. If you drop a perfectly transparent piece of glass into perfectly clear water, you can still see the glass. Why?

CONNECTIONS

Shake, Rattle, and Roll

About one million times a year, some part of the Earth's surface shakes and trembles in a violent release of energy. Such an event is called an *earthquake*. An earthquake occurs when energy stored in the Earth's crust builds up to the extent that it causes different sections of rock to move. From the point at which the earthquake originates, waves ripple out in all directions. Earthquake waves are known as seismic waves.

There are three different types of *seismic waves*. Those that travel the fastest are called primary waves, or P waves, because they are recorded first. P waves are longitudinal waves. They move through solids, liquids, and gases. The next type of seismic wave is a secondary wave, or S wave. S waves are recorded after P waves. S waves are transverse waves that move through solids but not through liquids and gases. The last type of seismic wave is a surface wave, or L wave. When P waves and S waves reach the surface, they are converted into L waves. L waves travel along the Earth's surface, causing the ground to move up and down. L waves cause the most damage because they are responsible for bending and twisting the Earth's surface.

Scientists have learned a great deal about earthquakes by studying seismic waves. By using an instrument called a seismograph, which records seismic waves, scientists can determine the presence and strength of an earthquake. The greater the amplitude of the seismic waves, the greater the amount of energy they carry—and thus the more powerful the earthquake.

Studying earthquake wave activity has enabled scientists to gain insight into predicting and describing earthquakes and also to think about preventing them someday.

Notice the destruction caused by seismic waves that traveled across the surface of the Earth during the 1989 California earthquake.

Laboratory Investigation

Observing Wave Properties of a Slinky®

Problem

What are the characteristics of a wave?

Materials *(per group)*

Slinky® or other coiled spring

Procedure

1. On a smooth floor, stretch the spring to about 3 m. Have one person hold the spring at each end. **CAUTION:** *Do not overstretch the spring.*
2. Make a loop at one end of the spring, as shown in the accompanying figure.

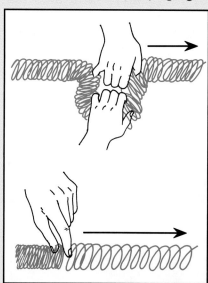

3. Release the loop and observe the motion of the wave. Observe the reflected wave.
4. Move one end of the spring back and forth on the floor. Draw a diagram of the wave you observe.
5. Repeat step 4, increasing the rate at which you move the spring back and forth.

6. Now squeeze together the first 20 cm of the spring, as shown in the accompanying figure.
7. Release the compressed section of the spring and observe the wave as it moves down the spring.

Observations

1. In step 3, is the reflected wave on the same or the opposite side as the original wave?
2. What happens to the frequency when you increase the rate at which the spring is moved back and forth?
3. What happens to the wavelength when you increase the rate at which the spring is moved back and forth?

Analysis and Conclusions

1. Are the waves generated in steps 1 through 5 transverse or longitudinal? Explain your answer.
2. Are the waves generated in steps 6 and 7 transverse or longitudinal? Explain your answer.
3. What is the relationship between the rate at which the spring is moved back and forth and the frequency? And the wavelength?
4. What are three characteristics of a wave?
5. **On Your Own**   How are the properties of ocean waves related to the wind that causes them? Design an investigation to test your answer.

Study Guide

Summarizing Key Concepts

23-1 Nature of Waves

▲ A wave is a disturbance that carries energy from one place to another.

▲ Mechanical waves require a medium. Electromagnetic waves can travel through a vacuum or through a medium.

23-2 Characteristics of Waves

▲ When a wave is graphed, the highest points are called crests and the lowest points are called troughs.

▲ The maximum displacement of a wave is its amplitude.

▲ The distance between two consecutive similar points on a wave is its wavelength.

▲ The frequency of a wave is the number of waves that pass a point per unit time.

23-3 Types of Waves

▲ In a transverse wave, the motion of the medium is at right angles to the direction of the motion of the wave.

▲ The motion of the medium is parallel to the direction of a longitudinal wave.

23-4 Speed of Waves

▲ Wave speed equals frequency times wavelength.

▲ The density and elasticity of a medium affect the speed of a wave.

23-5 Interactions of Waves

▲ Reflection occurs when a wave strikes a barrier and bounces back.

▲ The law of reflection states that the angle of incidence equals the angle of reflection.

▲ Refraction is the bending of waves due to a change in speed.

▲ The bending of waves around the edge of a barrier is called diffraction.

▲ Waves traveling through the same space at the same time interfere with each other.

▲ A wave produced at the resonant frequency of a material is a standing wave.

Reviewing Key Terms

Define each term in a complete sentence.

23-1 Nature of Waves
wave
vibration
medium
mechanical wave
electromagnetic wave

23-2 Characteristics of Waves
crest
trough
amplitude
wavelength
frequency

23-3 Types of Waves
transverse wave
longitudinal wave
surface wave

23-5 Interactions of Waves
reflection
refraction
diffraction
interference
standing wave
resonant frequency

Chapter Review

Content Review

Multiple Choice

Choose the letter of the answer that best completes each statement.

1. A wave transports
   a. energy.
   b. matter.
   c. water.
   d. air.
2. An example of an electromagnetic wave is a
   a. water wave.
   b. light wave.
   c. wave on a rope.
   d. sound wave.
3. The maximum displacement of a wave is measured by its
   a. wavelength.
   b. frequency.
   c. amplitude.
   d. speed.
4. The distance between two consecutive troughs is the
   a. frequency.
   b. amplitude.
   c. medium.
   d. wavelength.
5. Light travels as a
   a. transverse wave.
   b. mechanical wave.
   c. longitudinal wave.
   d. wave in a medium.
6. In a given medium, if the frequency increases,
   a. wavelength increases.
   b. speed increases.
   c. speed stays the same.
   d. speed decreases.
7. The bending of waves due to a change in speed is called
   a. diffraction.
   b. refraction.
   c. reflection.
   d. interference.
8. The bending of waves around the edge of an obstacle is called
   a. diffraction.
   b. reflection.
   c. refraction.
   d. interference.
9. The interaction of waves that meet at the same point is called
   a. reflection.
   b. diffraction.
   c. interference.
   d. refraction.

True or False

If the statement is true, write "true." If it is false, change the underlined word or words to make the statement true.

1. Waves transfer <u>matter</u>.
2. A <u>vibration</u> gives rise to a wave.
3. The energy carried by a wave is indicated by its <u>wavelength</u>.
4. In a transverse wave, the particles of the medium move <u>parallel</u> to the direction of the wave.
5. Frequency is measured in <u>hertz</u>.
6. When a wave strikes an obstacle, part of the wave is <u>reflected</u>.
7. The incoming wave is the <u>incident</u> wave.
8. When two waves combine to subtract from each other, <u>constructive</u> interference occurs.

Concept Mapping

Complete the following concept map for Section 23–1. Then construct a concept map for the entire chapter.

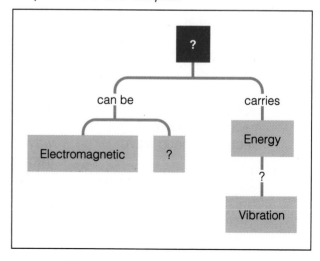

Concept Mastery

Discuss each of the following in a brief paragraph.

1. Explain how waves are related to energy and vibrations.
2. Why can microwaves travel both through empty space and through air and food?
3. A pendulum makes 32 vibrations in 20 sec. What is its frequency?
4. Suppose a red spot is painted at one point on a spring. Describe what happens to the red spot as a transverse wave passes by. Describe what happens as a longitudinal wave passes by.
5. Must a wave be transverse or longitudinal? Explain.
6. How does the density and the elasticity of a medium affect the speed of a wave?
7. Describe what happens to an incident wave after it hits an obstacle at an angle.
8. Explain the wave activity that enables you to hear a marching band before it rounds the corner.
9. Two waves occur in the same place at the same time, yet no wave can be detected there. Explain how this can be true.

Critical Thinking and Problem Solving

Use the skills you have developed in this chapter to answer each of the following.

1. **Applying concepts** Explain how a long line of people at a concert can be a medium for a longitudinal wave.
2. **Making inferences** Satellites above the Earth that are used to relay communications such as radio and television must rely on electromagnetic waves. Why?
3. **Identifying relationships** Red light has a longer wavelength than blue light. Why must it have a lower frequency?
4. **Identifying relationships** Energy is neither created nor destroyed. How does this law require that waves be reflected when their medium ends abruptly?
5. **Making calculations** Complete the following table.

Speed (m/sec)	Frequency (Hz)	Wavelength (m)
150	2.0	
	250	1.5
200		0.5
	200	1.0

6. **Applying concepts** Short races in a track meet are run over straight courses. Timers at the finish line start their watches when they see smoke from the starting gun, not when they hear the shot. Why? (The speed of sound in air is 340 m/sec.)
7. **Applying concepts** If you watch people trying to carry a large pan full of water, you will see that some are quite successful at it while for others, who are equally as careful, the water sloshes around badly. What makes the difference?
8. **Using the writing process** You are a sportswriter with a background in science. While covering an exciting game one Sunday, you cannot help but notice the enthusiasm of the crowd. Quite often throughout the game, entire sections of people stand up and sit down again in groups, from left to right, in an activity called "The Wave." Write a short newspaper article on the crowd's participation.

611

Sound and Its Uses

24

It is another hot, dry day on the African plain. All is quiet. Among the many animals that make their home in this region is a large herd of elephants. Silently the elephants walk along single file—all, that is, except the young ones who run alongside to keep up with their mothers. The herd's destination is uncertain—perhaps it is a watering hole or an area with a fresh supply of food. Their motion is slow but constant. Then suddenly, for no obvious reason, all the elephants freeze in place. Some stop with their trunks up in the air. Others halt in midstep. But just as quickly and unexpectedly as they stopped, they resume motion. Only this time, they make a sharp turn to head in a different direction.

You may be wondering why you are reading about elephants in a chapter on sound. After all, what did their behavior have to do with sound? It was done in silence. Or was it? Actually, elephants can communicate over several kilometers using sounds that cannot be heard by humans. As you read this chapter you will learn about sound—what it is, how it is made, and why you cannot hear the language of the elephants.

Journal *Activity*

You and Your World Go to a quiet place. Close your eyes for a minute and just listen. You will probably find out that it is not as quiet as you think. You may hear a light fixture humming above your head, a truck passing in the distance, or a clock ticking on the wall. You are almost always surrounded by sounds. In your journal, describe the sounds you hear.

◀ *African elephants, of assorted sizes, out for an afternoon stroll*

24-1 What Is Sound?

Have you ever noticed that if you lean on a piano while it is being played, you can feel the beat of the music? Or if you place your hand over a loudspeaker, you can actually feel a sensation in the air directly in front of it? And did you also know that if you could take your radio to the moon, you would not be able to hear it (or any noise, for that matter)? In order to understand these facts, you must learn about the nature of sound.

How Sounds Are Made

A bell shaking rapidly, a drum moving up and down, and a harp string bouncing back and forth are all examples of objects that make sounds. What do these examples have in common? They each vibrate when they are making sounds. As an object vibrates, it gives energy to the particles of matter around it. The energy causes the particles of matter to vibrate as well—and in such a way that a series of compressions (crowded areas) and rarefactions (less-crowded areas) moves outward from the source. Recall from Chapter 23 that a moving series of compressions and rarefactions is called a longitudinal wave. **Sound, which is produced when matter vibrates, travels as a longitudinal wave.**

Anything that vibrates produces sound. Your vocal cords, for example, vibrate to produce sound. When you speak, air from your lungs rushes past

Figure 24-1 *Although a tuning fork does not appear to vibrate, you can clearly see that it does from the splashes it makes when placed in water. If there are no particles of a medium to vibrate, there will be no sound. Why can't the astronaut riding along in a lunar vehicle hear the engine?*

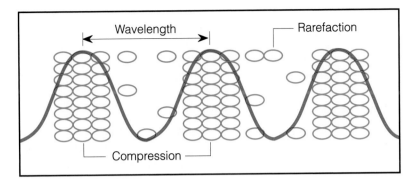

your vocal cords (two folds of tissue located in your throat), causing them to vibrate. As your vocal cords move inward, the air between them is pushed together, forming a compression. As your vocal cords move outward, an area with fewer particles of air is left, creating a rarefaction. A series of compressions and rarefactions travels outward from your vocal cords, making up the sound of your voice. When you speak, therefore, it is not the air you breathe that travels to the receiver; it is the sound waves that travel. The particles of air simply move back and forth.

Think about your radio again. The mechanism in the speaker of your radio actually moves the air in front of it by causing the particles to vibrate. If there were no air (medium) in front of the speaker, there could be no sound. Without a medium to transmit vibrations, there can be no sound. On the surface of the moon, where there is no atmosphere, there is no medium to transmit sound. Thus there can be no sound on the moon or in any vacuum.

Perhaps you are familiar with the age-old question, "If a tree falls in the forest and no one is present to hear it, is there a sound?" Although some people might answer no, you would probably say yes now that you know about sound. A falling tree sends a disturbance through the air and the ground. This disturbance travels as a longitudinal wave—a sound wave. Thus a sound is produced.

Speed of Sound

You learned in Chapter 23 that the speed of a wave depends on the properties of the medium and not on the source of the wave. For example, if a flute and a trumpet are both played in the same orchestra, both sounds will travel through the same

Activity Bank

Bells A' Ringing, p. 772

ACTIVITY
DOING

Viewing Vibrations

Sounds are caused by vibrations. You can observe this by experimenting with a tuning fork.

1. Strike the prongs of a tuning fork with a pencil and then hold the fork close to your ear. What happens? What happens when you touch the prongs of the fork?

2. Again strike the prongs of a tuning fork and place the ends of the prongs in a glass of water. What happens?

3. Tie a small piece of cork to a string and hold the string in one hand so the cork can swing freely. Strike the prongs of a tuning fork and hold one prong against the cork. Observe what happens.

Figure 24–3 *The pioneering flight of Chuck Yeager made possible the now-commonplace flights of airplanes at more than three times the speed of sound.*

Figure 24–4 *Vibrations of the vocal cords cause air particles to vibrate and thus produce sound. This is how the sounds you make when you speak, sing, or yell are produced. It is also the way the operatic artist Jessye Norman produces the beautiful notes of the aria. Norman is an accomplished singer with the New York Metropolitan Opera.*

air and arrive at your ear at the same time. Both sounds will travel at the same speed. **The speed of sound is determined by the temperature, elasticity, and density of the medium through which the sound travels.**

TEMPERATURE   One important characteristic of the medium that determines the speed of sound is temperature. Lowering the temperature of a substance makes the motion of the particles more sluggish. The particles are more difficult to move and slow to return to their original positions. Thus sound travels slower at lower temperatures and faster at higher temperatures.

In 1947, Captain Chuck Yeager took advantage of the relationship between the speed of sound and temperature to set a historic record. Captain Yeager was the first person to fly faster than the speed of sound. When he "broke the sound barrier," he was flying at a speed of 293 meters per second. But if the speed of sound in air averages about 340 m/sec (faster than he was traveling), how could Yeager have broken the sound barrier? Yeager was flying at an altitude of 12,000 meters. At this altitude, the temperature is so low that the speed of sound is only 290 m/sec, which is 3 m/sec less than the speed achieved by Yeager. A vehicle on the ground would have to travel about 50 m/sec faster to beat the speed of sound.

ELASTICITY AND DENSITY   Although most sounds reach you by traveling through air, sound waves can travel through any medium. To return to the example of the piano, sound waves cause the particles in the wood of the piano to vibrate. That is what you feel when you lean on the piano. Years ago, Native Americans put their ears to the ground in order to find out if herds of buffalo or other animals were nearby. By listening for sounds in the ground, they could hear the herds much sooner than if they listened for sounds in the air. The speed of sound in the ground at 20°C is 1490 m/sec—more than four times as fast as in air. Can you think of an example where you listen through some material other than air?

Perhaps from these examples you have realized that sound travels at its greatest speed in solids and at its slowest speed in gases. What is it about the phase of the medium (solid, liquid, or gas) that determines the speed of sound? For one thing, the speed depends on the elastic properties of the medium. This means that if the particles of the substance are disturbed, they must be able to return to their original positions easily.

To understand this, consider the following: You decide to run 1 kilometer down a paved road. You are able to run quickly and steadily because your feet spring off the solid blacktop. By the time you get to the end, you are hardly tired. This is similar to sound traveling through materials in which the particles are rigidly bound together and return to place quickly. Sound travels fastest in elastic materials such as these. But suppose you run the same distance on a wet beach where each time you step, the sand sinks under your feet. This time you have to put more energy into each step. When you finish this jog, you will be more tired. This is what happens to sound waves in less-elastic mediums. The sound waves travel more slowly and lose energy more quickly.

Solids are generally more elastic than either liquids or gases. The particles in a solid do not move very far and bounce back and forth very quickly as the compressions and rarefactions of a sound wave go by. Thus sound travels more easily through solids than it does through liquids and gases. Most liquids are not too elastic. Sound is not transmitted as well in liquids as it is in solids. Gases are even more inelastic than liquids. So gases are the poorest transmitters of sound.

In materials in the same phase of matter, the speed of sound is slower in the denser material.

SPEED OF SOUND	
Substance	**Speed (m/sec)**
Rubber	60
Air at 0°C	331
Air at 25°C	346
Cork	500
Lead	1210
Water at 25°C	1498
Sea water at 25°C	1531
Silver	2680
Copper	3560
Brick	3650
Wood (Oak)	3850
Glass	4540
Nickel	4900
Aluminum	5000
Iron	5103
Steel	5200
Stone	5971

Figure 24–5 *The speed of sound varies in different mediums. In what medium does sound travel the fastest? The slowest?*

Just Hanging Around, p. 774

Figure 24–6 *A piano can be made to send melodious tunes through the air to your ear. But the sound waves also travel through the wood of the piano and can be felt as vibrations. Does sound travel! faster through wood or through air? Why?*

Because the denser medium has greater mass in a given volume, it has more inertia. Its particles do not move as quickly as those of the less-dense material. The speed of sound in dense metals such as lead and gold is much less than the speed of sound in steel or aluminum. Lead and gold are also less elastic—another reason why the speed of sound is slower in these metals.

24–1 Section Review

1. What is sound? What kind of wave carries sound?
2. What characteristics of the medium affect the speed of sound?
3. Compare the transmission of sound in solids, liquids, and gases.

Connection—*Earth Science*

4. Light travels faster than sound. Thunder and lightning occur at the same time. However, thunder is heard after a flash of lightning is seen. How can the time in between the two be used to calculate how far away a storm is?

Guide for Reading

Focus on this question as you read.

▶ *How are the characteristics of sound related to the physical characteristics of the wave?*

24–2 Properties of Sound

Now you know that all sounds originate in the same basic way. They are produced by vibrations and transmitted as longitudinal waves. Yet there are millions of different sounds in everyday life—each having certain characteristics that make it unique. Think about the many sounds you hear every day. How you hear and describe a sound depends on the physical characteristics of the sound wave. As you have read in Chapter 23, the physical characteristics of a wave are amplitude, frequency, and wavelength. These are the factors that determine the sounds you hear.

Frequency and Pitch

Certain sounds are described as high, such as those produced by a piccolo, or low, such as those produced by a bass drum. A description of a sound

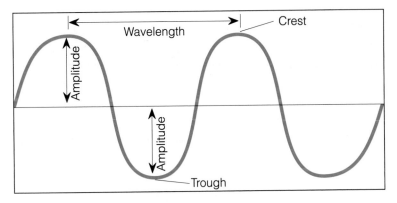

Figure 24–7 *Some of the basic characteristics of sound can be seen in this wave diagram. What three characteristics can you identify?*

as high or low is known as the **pitch** of the sound. The pitch of a sound depends on how fast the particles of a medium vibrate. Each complete vibration— one compression and one rarefaction—makes up a wave. So the pitch of a sound depends on the number of waves produced in a given time. This is a definition of frequency. **Thus the pitch of a sound depends on the frequency of waves.**

Sound waves that have a high frequency are heard as sounds of high pitch. A violin produces high-pitched sounds. Sound waves that have a low frequency are heard as sounds of low pitch. A tuba produces low-pitched sounds. A high note sung by a soprano may have a frequency of 1000 hertz. You will recall that a frequency of 1 hertz is equal to one wave, or cycle, per second. Thunder has a low pitch—its frequency is less than 50 hertz.

Frequency is an especially important characteristic of sound because the ear can respond to only certain frequencies. The normal human ear is capable of detecting from about 20 to 20,000 vibrations per second, or hertz. Sounds with frequencies higher than 20,000 hertz are called **ultrasonic** (uhl-truh-SAHN-ihk) because they are above the range of human hearing. Some animals hear quite well at this level. If you have ever used a dog whistle, you know that when you blow on it, your dog comes running even though you do not hear any sound. Dogs can hear sounds with frequencies up to 35,000 hertz. Or perhaps you have seen a cat appear startled although you have heard nothing. Cats can hear sounds with frequencies up to 65,000 hertz. So the cat probably did hear a noise! Porpoises can hear sounds with frequencies up to 150,000 hertz. And bats actually produce ultrasonic sounds and then use the echoes

Figure 24–8 *The pitch of a sound depends on the frequency of the waves. How would you describe the frequency of the high-pitched sound of a flute? Of the low-pitched sound of a sousaphone?*

Figure 24–9 *Your pet may be aware of activities you do not notice because it can hear sounds that you cannot. Similarly, dolphins can hear and communicate with one another by using sounds with frequencies more than seven times those heard by humans.*

Figure 24–10 *Certain natural phenomena such as volcanoes and earthquakes emit sounds with frequencies lower than humans can hear. Many animals become aware of the danger of such Earth movements before humans do because the animals hear the infrasonic warnings.*

to locate prey or to avoid bumping into objects. In this way, bats can fly about safely in the dark.

Sound waves with frequencies below 20 hertz are referred to as **infrasonic** (ihn-fruh-SAHN-ihk) because they are below the range of human hearing. You might have wondered earlier why, if sound is produced by all vibrations, you do not hear a sound from vibrations such as your arm swinging back and forth. The truth is, you actually do produce a sound, but the frequency is much too low for your ear to hear it. Think back to the elephants you read about in the beginning of this chapter. Elephants communicate by infrasonic sounds. Earthquakes and volcanoes emit infrasonic sound waves. Even certain kinds of machinery vibrate at frequencies in the infrasonic region. This can be dangerous to workers exposed to these vibrations for long periods of time, because although the sound is not heard, the energy carried by the waves can alter body processes over time.

Doppler Effect

There is another common occurrence that depends on the frequency of sound waves. You experience it quite often without even realizing it. Have you ever stood on the side of the road as a police car sped by with its siren on? If so, then you

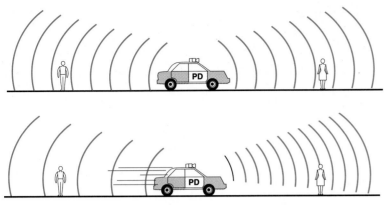

Figure 24–11 *When there is no movement between the source of a sound and its receiver, the sound waves are sent out equally in all directions. When there is motion, however, the sound waves either pile up or spread out, depending on the motion. This changes the frequency of the sound. How does this affect the pitch of the sound?*

should have noticed that the pitch of the siren was higher as it approached you and then lower as it moved away from you. Or perhaps you have been in a moving car that passed a fire station as the alarm was sounding. You may recall a similar change in the pitch of the alarm as you drove toward and then away from the station. This change in pitch is referred to as the **Doppler effect**. The Doppler effect occurs whenever there is motion between the source of a sound and its receiver. Either the source of a sound or the receiver must move relative to the other.

Consider again the police car moving toward you. Each time the siren sends out a new wave, the car moves ahead in the same direction as the wave. This causes the waves to be pushed together. Because they are pushed together, the waves have shorter wavelengths and higher frequencies as they reach you, the receiver. Higher frequency results in higher pitch. As the car passes you, it is traveling in the opposite direction of the sound waves that reach you. Thus the waves are more spread out, causing lower frequency and a lower pitch to the sound. Can you think of some other examples in which you experience the Doppler effect?

Intensity and Loudness

What is the difference between the sound of thunder and the sound of a handclap? You might say that one sound is louder than the other. Do you know what makes one sound louder than another?

Figure 24–12 *Decibel levels of some familiar sounds are shown in this chart. Which sounds would be considered painful?*

INTENSITY OF SOUND

Sound	Decibels	Sound	Decibels
Threshold of human hearing	0	Heavy street traffic	70–80
Rustling leaves	10	Vacuum cleaner	75–85
Whisper	10–20	Loud music	90–100
Very soft music	30	Rock concert	115–120
Classroom	35	Threshold of pain	120
Average home	40–50	Jet engine	140
Conversation	60–70	Rocket engine	200

Perhaps this example will help. If you pound your fist lightly on a table top, you hear a sound. But if you strike the table top much harder, you hear a louder sound. By striking the table top harder, you put more energy into the sound. Loudness is related to the amount of energy carried by a wave.

The amount of energy carried by a wave in a certain amount of time is called the **intensity** of the wave. As you may recall from Chapter 23, the energy of a wave is indicated by the amplitude. The larger the amplitude, the greater the intensity. For sound waves, this means that the compressions are more crowded and the rarefactions are less crowded. **Intensity determines the loudness of a sound.** The greater the intensity of a sound, the louder the sound is to the ear. Thunder sounds louder than a handclap because the intensity of thunder is much greater than the intensity of a handclap.

A scale has been developed to measure the relative intensity of sounds. The scale is based on a unit called the decibel (dB). A sound with an intensity level of 0 decibels is so soft that it can barely be heard. Thunder, on the other hand, has an intensity level of 120 decibels. Thunder is a tremendously loud sound. Sounds with intensities greater than 120 decibels can actually cause pain in humans.

A jet engine has an intensity level of about 140 decibels. The sound is really painful to human ears. So ground crews exposed to this sound must wear special ear protection to avoid injuring their ears.

Figure 24–13 *Elevated trains and subways produce sounds with high intensity levels. What are some other high-intensity sounds that you encounter every day?*

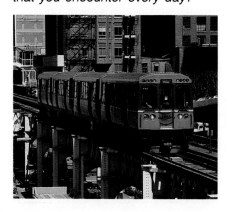

Music with an intensity above 85 decibels also can cause ear damage. Many rock stars wear ear plugs at their own concerts to prevent hearing loss.

24–2 Section Review

1. What characteristic of sound is determined by frequency? By amplitude?
2. Compare ultrasonic and infrasonic waves.
3. Describe the Doppler effect.

Critical Thinking—*Applying Concepts*
4. How might the Doppler effect be used to measure velocity?

24–3 Interactions of Sound Waves

Have you ever found yourself tapping your foot to the beat of a good tune? Perhaps you have even said that you liked one song better than another because it had a faster or a slower beat. Beats result from interactions between waves. As you learned in Chapter 23, waves that occur at the same place at the same time combine, or interfere. Because sound is a wave, sound experiences interference.

Combining Sounds

Interference of sound waves, like the interference of any other waves, can be constructive or destructive. **When sound waves combine in such a way that the resulting disturbance is greater than either wave alone, constructive interference occurs.** As a result of constructive interference, the intensity of a sound is increased. The sound is louder. Outdoor amphitheaters use band shells to amplify (increase the loudness of) the music through constructive interference. The sound waves produced by the orchestra or the singers bounce off the ceiling and walls so that they join together.

Guide for Reading

Focus on this question as you read.

▶ *What happens when sound waves combine?*

Figure 24–14 *Sound waves from these loudspeakers interfere constructively at point A but destructively at point B. Why is this important when setting up a radio or stereo system?*

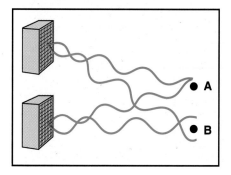

If an amphitheater is not designed properly, the resulting sound waves heard by parts of the audience will have smaller amplitudes than in a properly designed amphitheater. **When sound waves combine in such a way that the resulting disturbance is less than either wave alone, destructive interference occurs.** As a result of destructive interference, the intensity of a sound is decreased. The sound is softer.

Destructive interference can produce spots in which sounds cannot be heard at all. These areas are referred to as dead spots. Dead spots are especially troublesome in large halls that have hard surfaces which reflect (bounce back) sounds into the room. The reflected sounds interfere destructively and cancel each other. Engineers who work in **acoustics,** or the science of sound, try to design concert halls and auditoriums with no dead spots. Acoustical engineers must carefully design the shape, position, and materials of an auditorium to eliminate interference problems and prevent the sound waves from being absorbed.

You may still be wondering where beats come from. If two sources of sound are close in frequency but not exactly the same, the sound waves they produce combine in such a way that the amplitude and loudness of the resulting wave changes at regular intervals. At some points the interference is constructive and at others it is destructive. It gets louder and softer at intervals that depend upon the difference in frequencies. The repeated changes in loudness are called beats.

In addition to giving music its characteristic tune, beats have useful applications as well. For example, a

Figure 24–15 *Beats occur when two waves of slightly different frequencies add together. What happens at the beat?*

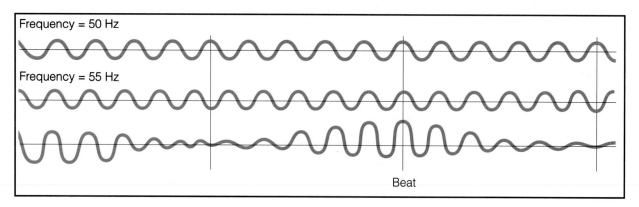

Frequency = 50 Hz

Frequency = 55 Hz

Beat

Figure 24–16 *Even the early Greeks knew about the importance of acoustics when they designed this theater in Italy. Although material and construction have improved, as illustrated by the Sydney Opera House in Australia, architects and acoustical engineers must still design theaters to take advantage of the action of sound waves.*

piano tuner strikes a tuning fork and the matching string on a piano at the same time. If beats exist between the two sound waves, the piano tuner knows that the string is vibrating at a different frequency from the tuning fork. When the string is adjusted so that the beats disappear, the string is tuned to the same frequency as the tuning fork.

24–3 Section Review

1. What happens when two sound waves combine if the crest of one wave meets the crest of the other? If the trough of one wave meets the crest of the other?
2. What is the difference between constructive and destructive interference in terms of sound intensity?
3. What are beats? How are they produced?

Connection—*You and Your World*

4. Why does putting a carpet and furniture in a room decrease the amount of sound in the room?

A jackhammer vibrates to produce sound, yet you would probably not call it music. Most likely, you would call it noise! You might call the squeak of chalk across a chalkboard noise too (and it probably is not one of your favorite sounds). A talented musician, however, makes an instrument produce melodious, pleasing music. What is the difference between music and noise? The difference is in the quality of the sound.

Sound Quality

Every different sound has its own quality. You would not mistake a flute for a trumpet even when they are both playing the same note. This is because the instruments have a different **sound quality**. Sound quality is also called **timbre** (TAM-ber).

Sounds are produced by a source vibrating at a certain frequency. In reality, however, most objects that produce sounds vibrate at several different frequencies at the same time. Each frequency produces a sound with a different pitch. The blending of pitches gives the sound its timbre.

In Chapter 23 you learned that every object has a natural, or resonant, frequency. When the object vibrates at that frequency, or multiples of that frequency, it produces a standing wave. The lowest frequency at which this occurs is the fundamental. The note that is produced is called the **fundamental tone**. The fundamental tone has the lowest frequency and pitch possible for that object. While the whole object (a string, for example) is vibrating at its resonant frequency, sections of the string are vibrating faster than the fundamental tone and producing sounds with higher frequency and pitch. The sounds of higher frequencies are called **overtones**. Sounds normally have a fundamental tone and one or more overtones. **The blending of the fundamental tone and the overtones produces the characteristic quality, or timbre, of a particular sound.**

Without overtones, a trumpet and a flute would sound exactly the same. In fact, a violin, a clarinet, and your friend's voice would all have the same

Figure 24–17 *A fundamental tone is produced when the whole string vibrates. When sections of the string vibrate faster than the fundamental tone, notes called overtones are produced. How does the pitch of the overtones compare with that of the fundamental tone?*

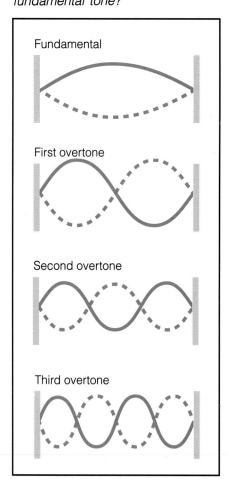

Fundamental

First overtone

Second overtone

Third overtone

sound quality if it were not for overtones. Sound quality is so unique for each person's voice that voiceprints have been used to identify a person.

Music

Now that you know about sound quality, you can understand the difference between music and noise. If the relationship between the fundamental tone and the overtones results in a sound with a pleasing quality and a clear pitch, the sound is considered music. **A sound is music if it has a pleasing quality, a definite identifiable pitch, and a repeated timing called rhythm.**

The design of a musical instrument is responsible for establishing the relationship between the fundamental and the overtones. In musical instruments, as in any source of sound, a vibration must exist. The material that vibrates can vary. Percussion instruments (drums, bells, and cymbals) are made to vibrate by being struck. Stringed instruments (guitars and violins) are either plucked or rubbed to produce regular vibrations. In woodwind and brass instruments (flutes, trombones, pipe organs), columns of air are made to vibrate.

Consider a stringed instrument such as a guitar. When a string is plucked, it begins to vibrate. The vibration produced has a certain frequency and thus a certain pitch. But by changing the length, tightness, or thickness of the string, the string can be made to produce different pitches.

A shorter string vibrates at a higher frequency and produces a sound of higher pitch. The short strings of a ukulele (yoo-kuh-LAY-lee) produce higher pitched notes than the longer strings of a cello. The vibrating length of a string can be changed by the proper positioning of the fingers along the string. Musicians do this to produce the pitches they desire.

The tighter the string, the higher the frequency of vibration and the higher the pitch. A stringed instrument is tuned either by tightening or loosening each string on the instrument. If a string is tightened, it produces a higher pitched sound. If it is loosened, it produces a lower pitched sound.

Strings of different masses also have different sounds. Because the speed of a wave on a heavy

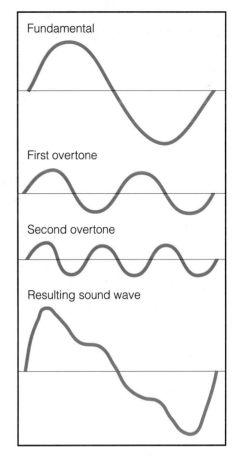

Figure 24–18 *At any point, the amplitude of the fundamental wave is added to those of the overtones. The result is the actual sound wave.*

ACTIVITY
DOING

Making Music

1. Fill six empty bottles, each with a different amount of water.

2. Blow across the top of each bottle and observe the sound that is produced. Compare the pitches.

How could you change the pitch of the bottles without changing the amount of water in the bottles?

Figure 24-19 *Musical instruments are made in a variety of ways. A pipe organ and unusual horns native to Peru are made to produce music when a column of air vibrates. The Korean instrument known as a kayakum makes music by the plucking of strings. And when the Guatemalan musician strikes his marimba made of gourds, unique sounds are produced.*

Figure 24-20 *This construction worker is producing sound, but it certainly is not music. It is noise. How is noise different from music?*

string is less than on a lighter string, a sound on a thicker string will have a lower frequency for the same wavelength. So thicker strings produce lower pitched sounds. The strings on a bass guitar are thicker than the strings on a lead guitar. The strings on a piano or a harp are of different lengths and masses. What kinds of sounds do thinner strings produce?

In woodwind and brass instruments, columns of air vibrate. Like waves on a string, the waves in air produce a sound with a pleasing quality. The characteristics of the sound are determined by the medium—the length of the air column and its temperature. Have you ever blown air across the top of a bottle to make a noise? When you do this, you set up waves in the air inside the bottle, thereby creating a sound.

Noise

So why is the squeak of chalk on a chalkboard so unpleasant? The answer is quite simple: It is noise.

Noise has no pleasing quality, no identifiable pitch, and no definite relationship between the fundamental tone and the overtones. A sound such as that made by a jackhammer or a piece of chalk on a chalkboard does not have a clear pitch or a repeating pattern. It does have a certain quality, but it is not a pleasing one. Rather than a small collection of frequencies, all of which are multiples of the fundamental, noise has a mixture of frequencies that have no relation to one another.

When noise reaches a level that causes pain or stress, it becomes noise pollution. Noise pollution has become a major concern of society because noise can have a serious effect on people's health. The stress of listening to loud noises can eventually cause high blood pressure and ulcers, as well as damage hearing.

What can be done about noise pollution? In many countries, laws have been passed to prohibit noise pollution. People are not allowed to bring loud radios into public places. Of course, you don't have to wait for a law to follow this example. You can look for sources of noise pollution in your home. Then you can determine which sources are within your control. You may not want to stop using a loud appliance in your kitchen. But by placing a rubber pad under the appliance, you can lessen its noise level. In what other ways can you help prevent noise pollution?

ACTIVITY

DISCOVERING

Changing Pitch

1. Obtain a stringed instrument such as a guitar or a violin. Notice the relative thickness of each string.

2. Pluck each string. Which string has the lowest pitch?

3. Pluck one of the strings again and quickly place your finger on the string at the halfway position. What happens to the pitch when you shorten the string like this?

4. Pluck another string and loosen the tension of the string with the tuning peg. What happens to the pitch when the tension is decreased?

■ The pitch of a male voice becomes lower during a period of development known as puberty. What must happen to the vocal cords at this time?

24–4 Section Review

1. Describe sound quality.
2. Explain how music is produced by a stringed instrument. By a woodwind instrument. By a percussion instrument.
3. What is the difference between music and noise?

Critical Thinking—*Classifying Information*
4. Sounds with dB levels between 60 and 100 can be annoying. Sounds above 100 dB can cause damage to hearing. Classify the following sounds as either annoying or damaging: snowmobile, food blender, power mower, jet plane, loud rock band, subway train, police siren.

24–5 Applications of Sound

When you think about the importance of sound in your life, different thoughts probably come to mind. The voices that are part of your daily interactions with people, the hustle and bustle of a busy city, the birds chirping in a country meadow, and the songs you enjoy listening to or singing are just a few examples. But in addition to making life more colorful and enjoyable, sound also has some important applications.

Sonar

Perhaps you think of bats only as scary creatures of the night. But bats display an important use of sound. Bats live and are most active in total darkness, yet they can reach a desired target with pinpoint accuracy. (And they never bump into the walls of the cave!) How do they manage this? Bats send out high-frequency sound (ultrasonic) waves as they fly. The waves bounce off objects such as walls or insects or mice and reflect back to the bat. Such reflected sound is called an echo. Bats use echoes to determine the location of dinner and to navigate around the black interior of their cave.

In this way bats are similar to many ships and submarines. Ships also use sound waves to navigate and to locate objects in the dark depths of the ocean. Suppose, for example, that the cargo of a

Figure 24–21 *You may find them a little unnerving, but bats are actually interesting creatures. They use sound waves to "see." If their eyes are covered, their travel is not impaired at all. But if their ears are covered, they are helpless. What is the use of sound for navigation called?*

ship sinks in the middle of the ocean. The water is far too deep to send divers down in search of the lost merchandise. How then can the cargo be located so that it can be retrieved? **High-frequency ultrasonic waves are used in a system called *Sound Navigation And Ranging*, or sonar.**

A research ship on the ocean surface sends a sound wave into the water. The sound wave travels in a straight line until it reaches a barrier, such as the ocean floor or the sunken cargo. When it hits the barrier, it is reflected back to the ship as an echo. The time it takes for the wave to travel down to the bottom and back up is carefully measured. Using this time and the speed of sound in ocean water, researchers are able to calculate the distance the wave traveled (Distance = Speed × Time). By dividing the total distance by two (half going down and half going up), the depth of the barrier can be determined. If the calculated distance is less than the distance shown on a map of the ocean floor, researchers know that the cargo is located in that spot. (The cargo reflected the sound wave, not the ocean floor.)

Sonar devices are often used in commercial fishing to locate large schools of fish. Sonar is also used to find oil and minerals within the interior of the Earth.

Have you ever seen or used a camera that adjusts the focus automatically? Such a camera may use sonar. Some cameras send ultrasonic waves toward the subject being photographed. After the echo

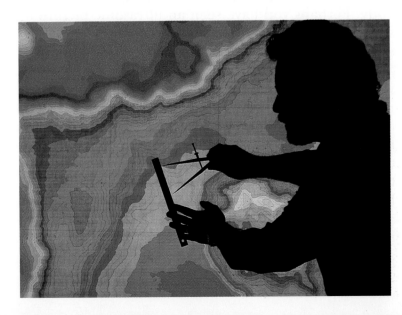

Figure 24–22 *More than a colorful diagram, this map of the ocean made by sonar shows elevation, obstacles, and temperature. Why is a map of the ocean floor useful?*

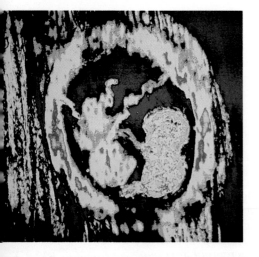

Figure 24–23 *These twins don't know it, but they have had their first picture taken—even before they are born. Ultrasonic waves enable doctors to observe the development of unborn babies, as well as the condition of other structures within the body.*

returns to the camera, the camera calculates the distance to the subject and sets the proper focus.

A type of sonar is presently being tested in cars. A system in which sonar is used to calculate the distance from a car to nearby objects such as curbs and other vehicles could be used to prevent accidents and to enable cars to park more easily and safely.

Ultrasonic Cleaning

Some objects are too delicate to clean with rough sponges or harsh detergents. Are you surprised to learn that you can clean these objects with sound? Ultrasonic waves are used to clean jewelry, electronic components, and delicate machine parts. To do this, the object is placed in a mild liquid. Sound waves are then sent through the liquid, causing it to vibrate with great intensity. The vibration knocks the dirt off the object without harming it.

Sound and Medicine

A technique much like sonar is used in medicine to diagnose medical problems. An ultrasonic wave is directed into the body. Its reflection from barriers within the body—such as organs and bones—is then detected. The technique is referred to as ultrasound. Using this technique, abnormal growths or pockets of fluid can be discovered.

Images much like X-rays are produced during an ultrasound procedure. But unlike X-rays, which are taken at one instant, ultrasonic waves can be used continuously to show motion occurring within the body. Perhaps you have seen an ultrasonic picture of a developing fetus (unborn baby). Doctors actually watch the movement of the fetus for several minutes at a time on a screen similar to the screen of a television set. Ultrasound has the added advantage that normal ultrasonic waves do not alter body cells.

In addition to allowing doctors to "see" inside the body, ultrasonic waves can be used to treat certain medical conditions. Sometimes unwanted tissue must be destroyed. By focusing ultrasonic waves of high intensity on the unwanted material, larger than normal amounts of energy are transferred to the material, causing it to be destroyed. Ultrasound is also used in physical therapy to provide local heating of injured muscles.

24–5 Section Review

1. What is sonar? What does sonar stand for? How does sonar work?
2. How are ultrasonic waves used in medicine?
3. What are some advantages of ultrasound over X-rays?
4. The speed of sound in ocean water is 1530 m/sec. If it takes 3 seconds for a sound wave to make a round trip from a sonar device, what is the distance to the reflecting object?

Connection—*Earth Science*
5. What are some of the advantages of using sonar to locate oil and mineral deposits in the Earth?

24–6 How You Hear

Guide for Reading

Focus on this question as you read.

▶ *How does the body detect sounds?*

Do you remember the famous question posed at the beginning of this chapter about a tree falling in the forest? You learned that even if no one is around to hear the tree fall, a sound is still produced. Sound is a form of energy that causes particles of a medium to vibrate back and forth.

If the question had been whether a sound is heard, the answer would have been no. In order for a sound to be heard, three things are needed. One, there must be a source that produces the sound. Two, there must be a medium to transmit the sound. And three, there must be an organ of the body that detects the sound. **In humans, the organ of the body that detects sound is the ear.**

How do you hear a series of compressions and rarefactions? Look at Figure 24–24 on page 634. Hearing begins when sound waves enter the **outer ear**. The outer ear acts as a funnel for the waves. The waves move through the ear canal and strike a lightly stretched membrane called the **eardrum**. The vibrating air particles cause the eardrum to vibrate much like a musical drum.

Vibrations from the eardrum enter the **middle ear**. The middle ear contains the three smallest bones in the body. The first bone, the hammer, picks up the vibrations from the eardrum. The hammer

Figure 24–24 *The illustration shows the structure of the human ear. What are the three main parts of the ear?*

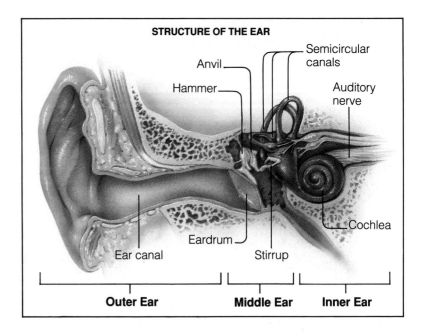

STRUCTURE OF THE EAR

Anvil

Hammer

Semicircular canals

Auditory nerve

Cochlea

Ear canal

Eardrum

Stirrup

Outer Ear | **Middle Ear** | **Inner Ear**

passes the vibrations to the second bone, the anvil. The anvil transmits the vibrations to the third bone, the stirrup. The stirrup then sets another membrane vibrating. This membrane transmits the vibrations to a liquid-filled **inner ear**.

The vibrations in the inner ear are channeled into the **cochlea**. The cochlea, which is shaped like a snail shell, contains a liquid and hundreds of cells attached to nerve fibers. The nerve fibers join together to form one nerve that goes to the brain. The cells detect movements in the liquid of the cochlea and convert them to electrical impulses. The nerve fibers transmit the electrical impulses to the brain, where they are interpreted as sound.

24–6 Section Review

1. Where does hearing begin in humans?
2. What are the three main parts of the ear?
3. What is the function of the eardrum?
4. Where are the nerve impulses interpreted as sound?

Connection—*Life Science*
5. Sometimes an extremely loud sound actually tears the eardrum. Explain what characteristic of the sound wave causes the injury and how the injury affects hearing.

CONNECTIONS

Seeing Sound

"Ooooouuut" yells the umpire as he throws his right hand wildly up over his shoulder, his thumb stretched outward. A little dramatic, you might think as you dust yourself off. But hand signals in baseball have some important origins.

At the turn of the twentieth century, a deaf professional baseball player played outfield. Because he was deaf, he could not hear the umpires' calls. To help him, several hand signals, or signs, were developed. These signals enabled him to "see" the calls and follow the game. A great variety of signs are still used in baseball today.

Silent signals are certainly not limited to baseball. In fact, complex languages of manual symbols and gestures are used for communication in many cultures—in particular, among the deaf community. These languages are known as *sign languages*. Sign language combines signs, gestures, facial expressions, and body movements to communicate ideas. For example, by cradling your right arm in your left arm to rock an imaginary infant, you make the sign for baby. By positioning your hand as though tipping the brim of a baseball cap, you create the sign for boy. And by moving your closed hand, thumb extended, along your jaw line as if tying an imaginary bonnet string, you make the sign for girl. For many proper nouns, names, addresses, and words that have no sign, a system called finger spelling is used. Finger spelling involves using hand positions to represent the letters of the alphabet.

Just as one culture may communicate by speaking English, Spanish, French, or any other language, the deaf community communicates by using sign language. One language of signs, the American Sign Language, is used by so many people that it is the fourth most common language in the United States. But signing is even more than a means of communication. It is actually a beautiful form of expression.

Laboratory Investigation

Investigating Properties of Sound Waves

Problem

What are sympathetic vibration, resonance, interference, beats, and the Doppler effect?

Materials *(per group)*

2 tuning forks, 320 Hz
rubber band
resonance box
400-mL beaker filled with water

Procedure ⚗

1. *Vibration in a medium:* Strike a tuning fork against the heel of your shoe and then insert the prongs into a beaker of water. Observe what happens.

2. *Sympathetic vibration:* Strike a tuning fork against the heel of your shoe and bring it within a few centimeters of a second tuning fork with the same frequency. Place the second tuning fork a few centimeters from your ear. Observe what happens.

3. *Resonance:* Strike a tuning fork against the heel of your shoe and note the loudness of the sound. Strike the tuning fork once again and then touch the base of its stem to the top of the resonance box. Note the loudness of the sound.

4. *Interference:* Strike a tuning fork against the heel of your shoe and bring one of the prongs 2 or 3 centimeters from your ear. Slowly rotate the tuning fork completely. Carefully note any change in the loudness of the sound.

5. *Beats:* Fasten a rubber band securely on the middle of one prong of a tuning fork. Obtain a second tuning fork of the same frequency. Strike both forks against the heel of your shoe and place the bases of the stems of the forks on the resonance box. If the sound is constant, reposition the rubber band and try again. Carefully note the sound emitted by the forks.

6. *Doppler effect:* Strike a tuning fork against the heel of your shoe with an extra force. Rapidly move the tuning fork in a wide arc round your head. The effect can best be heard by a second observer several meters away. Note what you hear.

Observations

1. In which steps of the procedure did the loudness of the sound change?

2. In which steps of the procedure did the pitch of the sound change?

Analysis and Conclusions

1. What does sound do to its medium?

2. What is sympathetic vibration? How does it happen?

3. Why does sound increase with the use of a resonance box?

4. Is sound louder during constructive or destructive interference?

5. How are beats produced?

6. When the tuning fork was moving in a circle, the pitch alternately increased and decreased. Did it increase when the fork moved toward you or away from you?

Study Guide

Summarizing Key Concepts

24-1 What Is Sound?

▲ Sound is a form of energy that causes particles of a medium to vibrate back and forth.

▲ Sound is a longitudinal wave.

▲ The speed of sound depends on the properties of the medium. Sound travels faster at higher temperatures, in more elastic mediums, and in less dense mediums.

24-2 Properties of Sound

▲ The frequency of a sound wave determines the pitch of the sound.

▲ The Doppler effect is a change in the frequency and pitch of a sound due to the relative motion of the source or the observer.

▲ The amplitude of a sound wave determines its intensity. The loudness of a sound depends on the intensity of the wave.

24-3 Interactions of Sound Waves

▲ Sound waves can interfere constructively, making the sound louder, or destructively, making the sound softer.

▲ Two sources of sound that have slightly different frequencies produce beats.

24-4 Quality and Sound

▲ A sound has quality, or timbre. The blending of the fundamental tone and overtones produces quality.

▲ Music has a clear relationship among the fundamental tone and the overtones. Noise does not.

24-5 Applications of Sound

▲ Sound navigation and ranging, or sonar, is used to measure distances in the ocean, in the Earth, and in the body.

24-6 How You Hear

▲ The ear is the human organ that detects sound.

▲ The outer ear collects sound waves and sends them into the ear canal. The waves cause the eardrum to vibrate.

▲ The vibrations of the eardrum are transmitted to three small bones in the middle ear and then into the fluid in the cochlea.

▲ Special cells in the cochlea change the vibrations into electric nerve impulses that are sent to the brain by nerve fibers.

Reviewing Key Terms

Define each term in a complete sentence.

24-2 Properties of Sound

pitch
ultrasonic
infrasonic
Doppler effect
intensity

24-3 Interactions of Sound Waves

acoustics

24-4 Quality and Sound

sound quality
timbre
fundamental tone
overtone

24-5 Applications of Sound

sonar

24-6 How You Hear

outer ear
eardrum
middle ear
inner ear
cochlea

Chapter Review

Content Review

Multiple Choice

Choose the letter of the answer that best completes each statement.

1. Sound travels as a(an)
   a. transverse wave.
   b. electromagnetic wave.
   c. light wave.
   d. longitudinal wave.
2. The speed of sound is fastest in a
   a. vacuum.   c. liquid.
   b. gas.   d. solid.
3. An increase in the speed of sound may be due to an increase in
   a. temperature.   c. amplitude.
   b. density.   d. pitch.
4. Pitch is related to
   a. frequency.   c. speed.
   b. interference.   d. amplitude.
5. The loudness of a sound depends on its
   a. frequency.   c. Doppler effect.
   b. amplitude.   d. pitch.

6. The quality of sound depends on its
   a. amplitude.   c. speed.
   b. loudness.   d. overtones.
7. The lowest frequency at which an object can vibrate is called its
   a. timbre.   c. fundamental
   b. resonance.   tone.
                       d. overtone.
8. Using sound to measure distance is called
   a. sonar.   c. cochlea.
   b. resonance.   d. acoustics.
9. Vibrations from the eardrum enter the
   a. outer ear.   c. inner ear.
   b. middle ear.   d. brain.
10. The hammer, anvil, and stirrup are in the
    a. outer ear.   c. cochlea.
    b. inner ear.   d. middle ear.

True or False

If the statement is true, write "true." If it is false, change the underlined word or words to make the statement true.

1. The source of a sound is a <u>vibrating</u> object.
2. The speed of sound in hydrogen gas is <u>faster</u> than in oil.
3. An increase in elasticity <u>decreases</u> the speed of sound.
4. As the energy of a sound wave increases, the <u>frequency</u> of the wave also increases.
5. The loudness of a sound depends on the <u>intensity</u> of the sound wave.
6. <u>Constructive</u> interference of sound waves may result in dead spots.
7. <u>Noise</u> has a definite repeating pattern.

Concept Mapping

Complete the following concept map for Section 24–1. Then construct a concept map for the entire chapter.

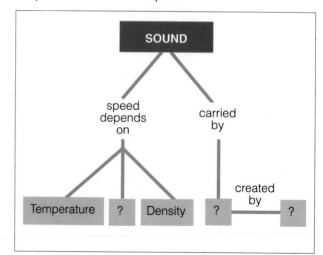

Concept Mastery

Discuss each of the following in a brief paragraph.

1. Describe why a bell ringing inside a vacuum chamber cannot be heard.
2. If you sit in the last row of an auditorium during a concert, why might you see the drummer hit the drum before you actually hear it?
3. Explain why your voice and the voices of your friends do not sound alike.
4. Trace the path of the sound of a hand-clap from the moment the clap is made to the moment you interpret the sound.
5. How come you do not hear a sound when you bat your eyelashes?
6. Suppose that a few pipes of a pipe organ are next to a heating unit. How would this affect the performance of the organ?
7. Describe the sound of a car whose horn is stuck as it approaches you and then passes you.
8. Describe the factors that affect the sound of a guitar string.

Critical Thinking and Problem Solving

Use the skills you have developed in this chapter to answer each of the following.

1. **Making comparisons** List the following materials from best to worst as transmitters of sound: (a) iron, (b) oxygen gas, (c) soup. Explain the reasoning behind your list.
2. **Making graphs** Using the following data, plot a graph showing how the speed of sound in air varies with temperature:

Temperature (in °C)	Speed (in m/sec)
−10	325
0	331
10	337
20	343

3. **Interpreting graphs** From your graph in question 2, determine the speed of sound in air at 18°C and at 25°C. By how much does the speed of sound change if the temperature changes 1°C?
4. **Identifying relationships** Draw a wave diagram to illustrate each of the following sounds: (a) high pitched and loud, (b) low pitched and soft, (c) low pitched and loud.
5. **Relating concepts** Sometimes a whistling sound is heard in a room when a window is slightly open on a windy day. How is this observation related to the principle of a wind instrument?
6. **Designing an experiment** How could two observers on opposite banks of a river use sound to measure the river's width?
7. **Applying definitions** Overtones that sound good together are said to be in harmony. In order for sounds to be harmonic, their overtones must have frequencies that are whole-number multiples of the fundamental. Which of the following frequency combinations will produce harmonic sounds? What will the other combinations produce? (a) 256, 512, 768, 1024 Hz; (b) 128, 256, 1024 Hz; (c) 288, 520, 2048 Hz; (d) 128, 288, 480 Hz; (e) 512, 1024, 4096 Hz
8. **Using the writing process** Use what you have learned about sound and your imagination to write a short story entitled "The Day There Was No Sound."

Light and the Electromagnetic Spectrum

Guide for Reading

After you read the following sections, you will be able to

25–1 Electromagnetic Waves
- Describe the properties of electromagnetic waves.
- Explain how electromagnetic waves are produced.

25–2 The Electromagnetic Spectrum
- Identify the regions of the electromagnetic spectrum.
- Describe the uses of electromagnetic waves of different frequencies.

25–3 Visible Light
- Explain three ways by which luminous objects produce light.

25–4 Wave or Particle?
- Describe the particle nature of electromagnetic waves.

Bzzzz. Bzzzz. A determined honeybee descends on a delicate white flower for a delicious meal of nectar. No big deal, you might think. But in the world of plants, this is an extremely important event.

When a honeybee lands on a flower to drink nectar, pollen sticks to the bee. When the honeybee flies to another flower to feast again, some of the pollen falls on that flower. Thus the honeybee pollinates the plant without even realizing it.

The trick is to get the honeybee to fly to a flower. Nature has devised some clever methods for attracting honeybees to flowers. Brightly colored flower petals are one such method. Why, then, in a field of fabulously colored flowers, does the honeybee choose a white one? The answer is that some flowers have markings on them that are invisible to humans—like a secret code for bees only! These markings are seen only in ultraviolet light. Ultraviolet markings direct the honeybee to the center of the flower—the source of nectar.

What is ultraviolet light, and how is it produced? What other types of rays exist around you? You will find the answers to these and other questions in this chapter.

Journal *Activity*

You and Your World Different types of lights are an important part of your everyday life that you may perhaps take for granted. Imagine what it must have been like to live before electric lights were invented. In your journal, describe how your life might have been different.

A hungry honeybee gathers nectar and pollen from a tiger lily flower.

25–1 Electromagnetic Waves

What does sunlight have in common with the X-rays used in a doctor's office? Are you surprised to learn that they are both waves? They're not matter waves that you can feel or hear. They are electromagnetic waves. You may remember reading about electromagnetic waves in Chapter 23. Although you might not realize it, you are constantly surrounded by thousands of electromagnetic waves every day. Sunlight (visible light) and X-rays are only two types of electromagnetic waves. Other types are radio waves, infrared rays, ultraviolet rays, and gamma rays.

Nature of an Electromagnetic Wave

An electromagnetic wave, as its name suggests, is both electric and magnetic in nature. An electromagnetic wave consists of an electric field and a magnetic field. These fields are not made up of matter like that in a football field or a soccer field. Electric and magnetic fields are the regions through which the push or pull of charged particles and magnets is exerted. (Charged particles and magnets can push or pull certain other objects without even touching them.) **An electromagnetic wave consists of an electric field and a magnetic field positioned at right angles to each other and to the direction of motion of the wave.** See Figure 25–2. Because the electric and magnetic fields are at right angles to the direction of motion of the wave, electromagnetic waves are transverse waves.

Like other waves, such as water waves and waves on a rope, electromagnetic waves carry energy from one place to another. But unlike other waves, electromagnetic waves do not carry energy by causing matter to vibrate. It is the electric and magnetic fields that vibrate. This explains why electromagnetic waves can travel in a vacuum (where there is no matter). But it does not mean that electromagnetic waves cannot travel through a medium. They certainly can. Light, for example, can be transmitted with a medium—as through the atmosphere—or without a medium—as through space.

Figure 25–1 *The colors of light produced by fireworks are one familiar form of electromagnetic waves. What type of wave is light?*

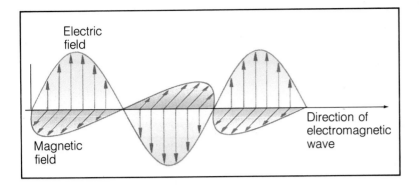

Electric field

Magnetic field

Direction of electromagnetic wave

Figure 25–2 *In a transverse wave, the direction of the wave energy is at right angles to both the electric and the magnetic fields.*

Production and Transmission of Electromagnetic Waves

When you first started studying waves, you learned that the source of any wave is a vibration. For example, a vibrating bell causes air particles to move back and forth, producing a sound wave. This same idea about a vibrating source is true for electromagnetic waves as well. However, rather than a source setting up vibrations in a medium, the source of an electromagnetic wave sets up vibrating electric and magnetic fields.

To understand how electromagnetic waves are produced, you need to recall the structure of the atom. Atoms are the building blocks of matter. An atom consists of a central core, or nucleus, surrounded by tiny particles called electrons. Electrons do not have set positions. Instead, they constantly move about the nucleus.

Electrons are charged particles that can produce electric and magnetic fields. But in order to create the vibrating electric and magnetic fields that are characteristics of an electromagnetic wave, electrons must move. A charged particle, such as an electron, moving back and forth creates electric and magnetic fields that move back and forth, or vibrate. **The source of all electromagnetic waves is charge that is changing speed or direction.** Visible light, for example, is produced by electrons jumping between different positions in an atom. According to modern theories used to describe atoms, electrons move at different distances from the nucleus according to the amount of energy they have. But an electron can absorb more energy and thereby move to another

ACTIVITY

THINKING

Electromagnetic Waves in Your Life

1. Look around your home at the devices and appliances you use every day. Name four objects in your home that produce electromagnetic waves.

2. Describe the type of electromagnetic wave that each object produces.

What type of electromagnetic wave is most common on your list?

Do electromagnetic waves play an important role in your life?

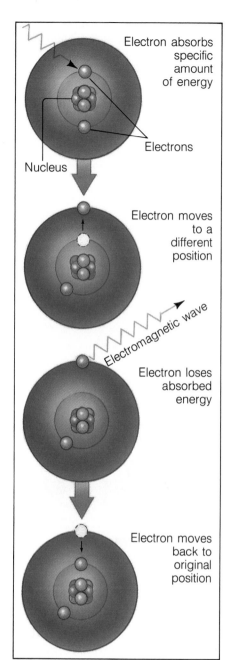

Electron absorbs specific amount of energy

Electrons

Nucleus

Electron moves to a different position

Electromagnetic wave

Electron loses absorbed energy

Electron moves back to original position

Figure 25–3 *All forms of electromagnetic waves have their source in the atom. In particular, visible light is produced when an excited electron returns to its normal position, releasing energy in the form of an electromagnetic wave.*

position. This move, however, is not a stable one. That is, the electron will not remain in its new position for long. Eventually, it will lose the extra energy and fall back to its original position. As it falls back, it creates vibrating electric and magnetic fields. These fields form the electromagnetic waves that carry the released energy.

Other types of electromagnetic waves are also created in atoms. For example, electrons moving back and forth in an antenna create radio waves. X-rays are produced when electrons slow down abruptly as they collide with a target in an X-ray tube. Gamma rays are produced when the nucleus of an atom gives up extra energy.

The speed of all electromagnetic waves is the same—300 million meters per second in a vacuum. This speed is usually referred to as the speed of light. The speed is slightly slower in air, glass, and any other material. To appreciate just how great this speed is, consider the following: Light from the sun travels 150 million kilometers to Earth in about 8 minutes! Nothing known in the universe travels faster than the speed of light.

Figure 25–4 *Electromagnetic waves carry light from distant stars. If light required a medium for transmission, it would not be able to travel through space to Earth.*

25–1 Section Review

1. What is an electromagnetic wave?
2. What are the physical characteristics of an electromagnetic wave?
3. What is an electric or magnetic field?
4. How is visible light produced?

Critical Thinking—*Relating Concepts*
5. How are sound and light alike? How are they different?

PROBLEM Solving

Reaching for the Stars

Suppose you have been given the following assignment: Determine the composition of three distant stars. How can you possibly do it? After all, you cannot travel billions of kilometers to get a sample of each. And, what's more, all you have been given is a few strips of paper with what seem like some silly lines on them. Whatever will you do?

Luckily for you, those strips of paper are all you need. All elements produce a characteristic set of lines when they are heated, and the light given off is passed through a device known as a spectroscope. The lines are called spectral lines. Every element has its own set of spectral lines—much like a fingerprint.

Examine the spectral lines of the following elements. Compare them with the spectral lines labeled A, B, and C. Determine which elements are in the stars that produced A, B, and C.

Hydrogen

Helium

Sodium

Calcium

A

B

C

Guide for Reading

Focus on these questions as you read.

▶ *How is the electromagnetic spectrum organized?*

▶ *What types of waves make up the electromagnetic spectrum?*

25–2 The Electromagnetic Spectrum

Now that you know what electromagnetic waves are, you might be wondering how sunlight is different from X-rays if both are electromagnetic waves that travel at the same speed. Electromagnetic waves, like all types of waves, are described by their physical wave features: amplitude, wavelength, and frequency. And it is these characteristics that can vary and thereby produce many different kinds of electromagnetic waves.

Electromagnetic waves are often arranged in order of wavelength and frequency in what is known as the electromagnetic spectrum. Because all electromagnetic waves travel at the same speed, if the frequency

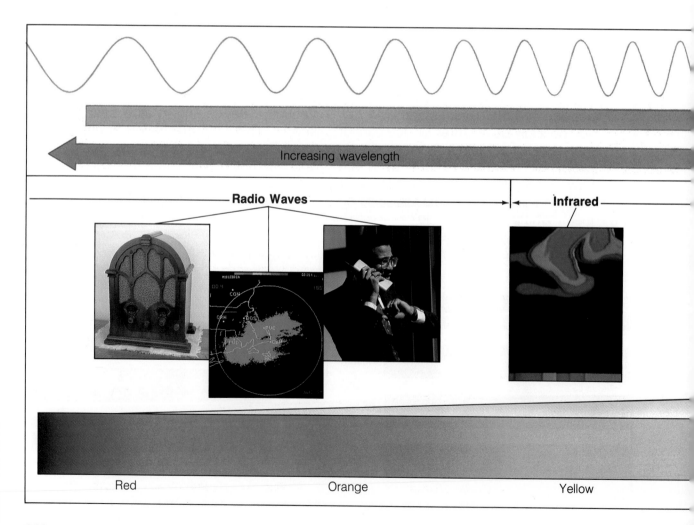

Increasing wavelength

◄——————— Radio Waves ———————► ◄—— Infrared ——

Red   Orange   Yellow

of a wave changes, then the wavelength must change as well. (Remember: Speed = Wavelength × Frequency.) Waves with the longest wavelengths have the lowest frequencies. Waves with the shortest wavelengths have the highest frequencies. Look again at the formula for wave speed. Do you see why these statements must be true? The **electromagnetic spectrum** ranges from very long-wavelength, low-frequency radio waves to very short-wavelength, high-frequency gamma rays. The amount of energy carried by an electromagnetic wave increases with frequency. Figure 25–5 gives you a good idea of the nature of the electromagnetic spectrum. Notice that only one small region is visible. The rest of the spectrum is invisible!

The electromagnetic spectrum covers a tremendous range of frequencies and wavelengths. Comparing the frequencies of radio waves to those of visible

Figure 25–5 *Electromagnetic waves are arranged according to their increasing frequency and decreasing wavelength in the electromagnetic spectrum. Although the many applications of electromagnetic waves are very different, they all depend on the same basic type of waves.*

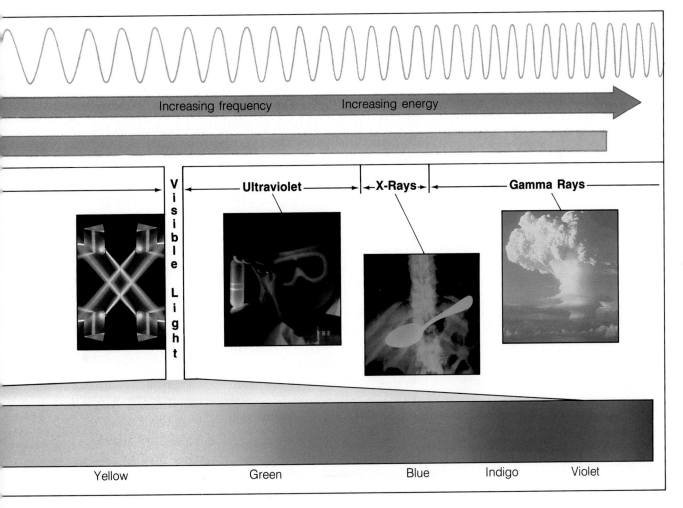

Increasing frequency   Increasing energy

Visible Light

Ultraviolet — —X-Rays→— Gamma Rays

Yellow   Green   Blue   Indigo   Violet

light is like comparing the thickness of this page to the Earth's distance from the sun! Because the differences are so great, the various regions of the spectrum are given different names.

Radio Waves

The waves in the electromagnetic spectrum that have the lowest frequencies and longest wavelengths are called **radio waves**. Radio waves are produced when charged particles move back and forth in instruments such as antennas. When you think of radio waves, do not confuse them with the waves you hear coming out of your radio. Those waves are sound waves. Radio waves are the waves used to transmit information from the antenna of a broadcasting station to the antenna on your radio or television.

Perhaps you are wondering how your favorite song or television show can be carried by a wave. The answer is rather interesting. When radio waves are transmitted, one of two characteristics of the wave can be varied—either the amplitude of the wave or the frequency of the wave. The variation in either amplitude or frequency of a wave is called **modulation** (mahj-uh-LAY-shuhn). The setting on your radio indicates the type of modulation used to carry the information to your radio: AM means amplitude modulation, and FM means frequency modulation. At the broadcasting station, information (music or words or pictures) is converted from its original form to an electronic signal and then to a pattern of changes in either the amplitude or frequency of a radio wave. When the radio wave is received by an antenna of a radio or television, the pattern is converted back to its original form. The sound portions of most television broadcasts are carried as AM waves while the picture portions are carried as FM waves.

When radio waves are sent out from a broadcasting station, they spread out through the air. Any antenna tuned in to the frequency of the waves receives the waves. Usually radio waves are used when a message is being sent to many antennas—as in a television or radio broadcast. However, radio waves can be disturbed by obstacles or weather

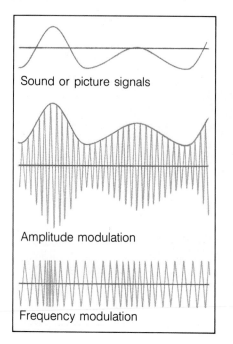

Figure 25–6 *Sounds at a broadcasting station are converted into electric sound signals. The sound signal is then used either to adjust the frequency (FM) or amplitude (AM) of a radio wave. Notice how the crest of the sound signal affects each of the radio waves.*

Sound or picture signals

Amplitude modulation

Frequency modulation

conditions. Suppose, for example, a small town is located deep in a valley. Many of the radio waves will be unable to pass through or around the surrounding mountains and the town will be unable to receive the signals. In situations such as this, it is important to protect the radio waves from being disturbed. One way that this can be accomplished is to send the radio waves through a cable wire that travels directly to the destination of the signal. This is basically how cable television works. Perhaps you have heard that cable television is often used in areas where television reception is poor. Cable television is, as its name suggests, television signals carried by radio waves through cables that protect the signal.

Radio waves are also used in medicine. Radio waves and strong magnetic fields are used to cause different atoms in the body to vibrate. By analyzing the response of different sections of the body to different frequencies, doctors can create pictures of parts of the human body, including the brain, without harming the cells. This procedure is known as magnetic resonance imaging.

In astronomy, radio waves have a different application. Observations of space are often blocked by conditions in Earth's atmosphere. Radio waves pass through the atmosphere unaffected, however. For this reason, astronomers have constructed telescopes that study radio waves from space. The main part of a radio telescope is shaped like a huge dish. The curved dish collects radio waves emitted from space

Figure 25–7 *Satellite dishes are used to record electromagnetic waves from space and form images of distant objects, such as this remnant of an exploding star, or supernova. Radio waves are also used to form images of structures within the human body. This image shows the hips and pelvic region.*

and focuses the waves toward an antenna. The radio waves are then fed to a computer, which processes the information and converts it into an image. Only in the past few decades have scientists learned that electromagnetic waves are radiated from space across the entire electromagnetic spectrum—not just the visible portion. So in addition to radio telescopes, devices for collecting information in every region of the spectrum have been developed.

MICROWAVES One particular group of radio waves is that of **microwaves.** Microwaves are the highest frequency radio waves. The wavelengths of microwaves are only a few centimeters long.

The application of microwaves that is probably most familiar to you is a microwave oven. One of the advantages of a microwave oven is that food can be heated in a short amount of time without heating the dish that the food is in. How can this happen? The answer is that microwaves pass right through some substances but are absorbed by others. Water and other molecules in the food absorb energy from the microwaves, causing the food to heat up. Glass and plastic containers do not absorb microwaves and therefore do not become hot in a microwave oven. Metals, however, absorb microwaves. In fact, metals can absorb enough electromagnetic energy from microwaves to create a current of electricity. That is why metal containers should never be used in a microwave oven.

An application of microwaves with which you may be less familiar is communication. Yet actually, transmitting information is the most common use of microwaves. For example, microwaves are used for communication in cellular, or portable, telephones. Microwaves transmit information efficiently because they are not easily blocked by structures such as mountains, trees, and buildings.

Microwaves are also used in weather forecasting. Microwaves can penetrate clouds of smoke, but they are spread out by water droplets. By observing what happens to microwaves sent out into the atmosphere, weather forecasters can locate storms.

RADAR Short-wavelength microwaves are used in **radar.** Radar, which stands for *r*adio *d*etecting *a*nd *r*anging, is used to locate objects and monitor speed.

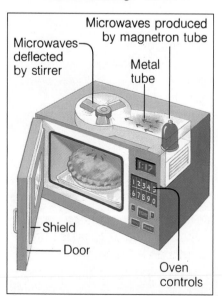

Figure 25–8 *Because microwaves are absorbed by most foods, they are used in cooking. Microwaves cause the molecules of the food to vibrate, which increases the temperature of the food. How does the speed of microwave cooking compare with conventional cooking methods?*

Microwaves produced by magnetron tube

Microwaves deflected by stirrer

Metal tube

Shield

Door

Oven controls

The procedure is the same as sonar for sound waves. A radar device operates by sending out short pulses of radio waves. Any object within a certain distance will reflect these waves. A receiver picks up the reflected waves, records the length of time it takes for the waves to return, and then calculates the distance to the object. Radar is used to monitor the positions of airplanes taking off and landing at airports and to locate ships at sea—especially in heavy fog. Radar is used to keep track of satellites that are orbiting the Earth. In addition, weather forecasters use radar to locate and track storms.

In Chapter 24, you learned about the Doppler effect, which is caused when either the source of a sound or the receiver is moving. The sound waves bunch up or spread out, changing the frequency (and thus the pitch) of the sound. The Doppler effect also exists for electromagnetic waves. It is what enables a police officer on the side of the road to determine the speed of a moving car. If a police officer sends microwaves to a moving car, the waves will be reflected. But because the car is moving, the rays coming back will have a different frequency from the rays sent out. The radar device uses the change in frequency to calculate the speed of the car.

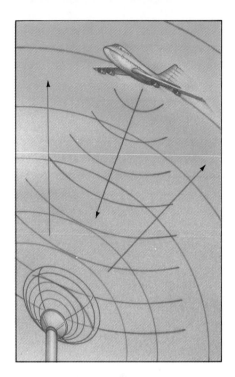

Figure 25–9 *In a radar device, a radio transmitter sends out high-frequency waves that bounce off objects and return as echoes picked up by a receiver. Can you think of other important uses for radar?*

Infrared Rays

Electromagnetic waves with frequencies slightly lower than visible light are called **infrared rays**. Although infrared rays cannot be seen, they can be felt as heat. You can feel infrared rays as heat from a light bulb, a stove, or the sun. Nearly 50 percent of the rays emitted by the sun are in the infrared region.

All objects give off infrared rays. The amount of infrared given off by an object depends on the temperature of the object. Warmer objects give off more infrared rays than colder objects do. Cool objects can absorb the energy from infrared waves and become hotter. For this reason, infrared lamps are used to keep food hot, relieve sore muscles, and dry paint and hair.

Infrared cameras are devices that take pictures using heat instead of light. Such cameras allow

ACTIVITY DOING

Heat and Light

1. Place a thermometer on a dinner plate.

2. Position an incandescent light bulb 10 cm above the thermometer.

3. Turn on the bulb. After about 5 minutes, record the temperature.

4. Repeat the procedure, but this time use a fluorescent bulb.

Which light source operates at a higher temperature? Is this an advantage?

Figure 25-10 *Infrared light cannot be seen, but it can be detected as heat and used to produce a thermogram. Hotter areas appear white, and cooler areas appear black or blue. Note the dog's cold nose!*

pictures to be taken at night. This ability has special applications for researchers who wish to observe the habits of animals during the night, for security systems, and for military operations.

Certain types of photographs that are taken using heat are called thermograms. Thermograms can identify the warm and cold areas of an object or person. Thermograms can be used to detect heat loss in a building. They are also used in medicine. Sometimes, unhealthy tissue will become hotter than surrounding healthy tissue. Thermograms can be used to identify such tissue.

People studying pieces of art—either to learn from them or to determine their authenticity—make use of infrared rays. To the unaided eye, a painting on a canvas is all that appears on the surface. But sometimes there is more than meets the eye. During certain periods in history (and for various reasons), artists painted on used canvas—one painting right on top of another. A painting thought to be lost or missing may have been painted over. In other

Figure 25-11 *You probably think these photographs were taken on beautifully bright days. Quite the contrary. The photographs were taken in the darkness of night using an infrared camera.*

instances, it is discovered that an artist changed his or her style as the painting progressed. And in some cases, the original signature on a painting may be painted over with a more well-known one so that the owner can sell the painting for more money. How do art experts find out the truth? One technique involves shining infrared rays onto a painting. Infrared rays are able to penetrate the thin upper layers of an oil painting and reveal the layers beneath the surface. Other forms of electromagnetic energy—X-rays and ultraviolet rays—are also used for the same purpose.

The Visible Spectrum

The electromagnetic waves that you can see are called **visible light**. Notice that visible light—red, orange, yellow, green, blue, indigo, and violet—is only an extremely small portion of the spectrum. The rest of the electromagnetic spectrum is invisible to the unaided eye. This explains why you can be surrounded by electromagnetic waves every day but never see them!

Despite its small range, the visible spectrum is of great importance. Life on Earth could not exist without visible light. Nearly half the energy given off by the sun is in the form of visible light. Over billions of years, plants and animals have evolved in such ways as to be sensitive to the energy of the sun. Without such adaptations, life would be impossible. Visible light is essential for photosynthesis, the process by which green plants make food. Other forms of life eat either green plants or animals that have eaten green plants. Forms of energy taken from the sun by plants and microorganisms millions of years ago are locked up in the coal and oil used as energy resources today. You will learn more about visible light in the next section and in Chapter 26.

Ultraviolet Rays

Electromagnetic waves with frequencies just higher than visible light are called **ultraviolet rays**. The energy of ultraviolet rays is great enough to kill living cells. So ultraviolet lamps are often used to kill germs in hospitals and to destroy bacteria and preserve food in processing plants.

ACTIVITY READING

By Land or by Sea

Light has played an important role in history. One use of light has been as a signal in situations where sound could not be used. Read *Midnight Alarm: The Story of Paul Revere's Ride* by Mary K. Phelan and enjoy a story about the use of light in the American Revolution.

Figure 25–12 *Some scientific research combines more than one area of science. For example, Dr. Shirley Ann Jackson is a talented physicist who works in the field of optoelectronics. Her research involves designing electronic devices that produce, regulate, transmit, and detect electromagnetic radiation. Some of the applications of her research are improving the nature of communication throughout the world.*

Figure 25–13 *The sunflowers you are accustomed to seeing resemble the cheerful yellow flower shown on the right. A honeybee, however, sees something quite different. The photo on the left shows the sunflower seen in ultraviolet light.*

Figure 25–14 *When rocks containing fluorescent minerals are exposed to invisible ultraviolet light, they glow. Why might this property be important to geologists?*

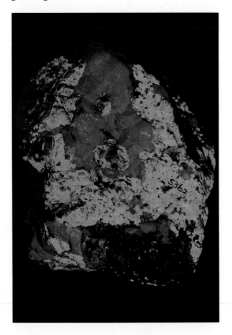

Although ultraviolet light is invisible to humans and many other animals, it can be seen by many insects. Flowers that appear to be the same color in visible light are much different under the ultraviolet rays seen by insects. Do you remember the honeybee you read about at the beginning of this chapter? The honeybee took advantage of its ability to see into the ultraviolet region of the electromagnetic spectrum.

As you may already know, ultraviolet rays are present in sunlight. Although the eyes cannot see them, their effects can be felt as sunburn. When your body absorbs sunlight, ultraviolet rays cause your skin cells to produce vitamin D. Vitamin D is needed to make healthy bones and teeth. Despite this benefit, ultraviolet rays are harmful to body cells. (All electromagnetic waves beyond the visible region—ultraviolet, X-rays, and gamma rays—are harmful to living cells.) Tanning is the body's way of protecting itself against these harmful rays. But overexposure to ultraviolet rays can cause serious damage to the skin, eyes, and immune system.

Fortunately, a layer of ozone in the atmosphere absorbs most of the sun's damaging ultraviolet rays before they reach the Earth. Without this protective ozone layer, life on Earth would be impossible. Many scientists believe that this protective ozone layer is now being destroyed by chemicals released into the atmosphere by aerosol propellants, air-conditioning coolants, and various other sources.

X-Rays

Electromagnetic waves with frequencies just above ultraviolet rays are called **X-rays**. The energy of X-rays is great enough to pass easily through many materials, including your skin. Denser materials, however, absorb X-rays. Bone absorbs X-rays. When an X-ray picture of a part of your body is taken, the bones absorb the rays but the soft tissues do not. The picture that results shows the bones as white areas and the soft tissues as black areas.

Strong sources of X-rays have been detected deep in space. The sources are believed to be certain star formations. In addition to these star formations, exploding stars are known to give off most of their energy at the time of explosion in the form of X-rays.

Despite their usefulness in medical diagnosis, X-rays are a potential health hazard. Exposure of body cells and tissues to large amounts of X-rays over a lifetime can cause defects in cells. Lead absorbs almost all the X-rays that strike it. Can you think of an important use of lead, based on this property?

Gamma Rays

The electromagnetic waves with the highest frequencies and shortest wavelengths are called **gamma rays**. Gamma rays have the highest energy of the electromagnetic spectrum. Certain radioactive materials and nuclear reactions emit gamma rays.

Gamma rays have tremendous penetrating ability—even greater than that of X-rays. The energy of gamma rays is so great that they can penetrate up to 3 meters of concrete! Excessive exposure to gamma rays can cause severe illness.

Gamma rays have positive applications in medicine. A patient under observation can be injected with a fluid that emits gamma rays. A camera that

Figure 25–15 *Doctors can observe the result of a skier's unfortunate accident—a broken leg—by taking an X-ray. Similarly, doctors can use images formed by a gamma camera to study the skeleton of a healthy person.*

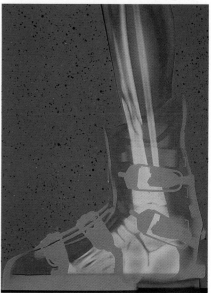

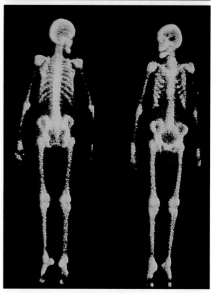

X-Ray Vision

Wilhelm Roentgen discovered X-rays in 1896. Within a few months, X-rays were being used in hospitals. Using books and other reference materials in the library, find out about Roentgen and his work with X-rays. Write a report on your findings. Include information on the benefits and dangers of X-rays.

Activity Bank

A Sunsational Experiment, p.775

detects gamma rays—a gamma camera—can then be moved around the patient to form an image of the inside of the body according to how the rays are given off.

25–2 Section Review

1. What is the electromagnetic spectrum? List the kinds of waves that make it up.
2. Moving along the spectrum from radio waves to gamma rays, what happens to frequency? Wavelength? Energy?
3. What is the difference between AM radio waves and FM radio waves?
4. Describe a use of each of the following: infrared rays, ultraviolet rays, X-rays, and gamma rays.

Connection—*Life Science*
5. Why is the destruction of the ozone layer dangerous? Design a poster to express the importance of protecting the ozone layer.

Guide for Reading

Focus on this question as you read.

▶ *How do luminous objects produce light?*

25–3 Visible Light

You are not capable of giving off light. But a firefly is. Have you ever seen a firefly light up? Certain organisms and objects give off their own light. Anything that can give off its own light is called a **luminous object**. The sun and other stars, light bulbs, candles, campfires, and fireflies are luminous objects.

Other objects are lit up, but not by their own light. When you stand in a spotlight, you are lit up by a luminous object (the spotlight). You can be seen because the light given off by a luminous object bounces off you. An object that can be seen because it is lit up is called an **illuminated object**. You see the moon because sunlight is reflected off its surface. The moon does not give off its own light. How would you describe the pages of this textbook? The lamp in your room?

Production of Light

There are several ways in which a luminous object can be made to give off energy in the form of light. Three of the ways in which objects produce light are described here. **A luminous object can produce incandescent light, fluorescent light, or neon light.**

INCANDESCENT LIGHT   Have you ever seen the coils of a toaster oven heat up until they were red hot? Or the coals of a barbecue turn bright orange? Certain objects can be heated until they glow, or give off light. Light that is produced from heat is called **incandescent light**. An object that gives off incandescent light is said to be incandescent.

Have you ever touched a light bulb after it has been lit for a while? It is quite hot to the touch. Ordinary light bulbs in your home are incandescent. They produce light when electricity is applied to them. Inside the glass bulb of a light bulb is a thin wire filament made of the metal tungsten. Tungsten can be heated to over 2000°C without melting. When the light is switched on, electrons flow through the tungsten wire. Because the filament is thin, there is resistance to the electron flow. Electric resistance produces heat. Enough heat will cause the tungsten to glow, creating visible light.

FLUORESCENT LIGHT   You have probably seen long and narrow or circular white lights in your school, an office, or a department store. These lights are called **fluorescent lights**. Fluorescent light is cooler and uses much less electricity than incandescent light. Instead of being used to build up heat, electrons in fluorescent lights are used to bombard molecules of gas kept at low pressure in a tube.

Normally, you cannot see ultraviolet light. The inside of a fluorescent light, however, is coated with special substances called phosphors. Phosphors absorb ultraviolet energy and begin to glow, producing visible light. The color that a fluorescent bulb produces depends on the phosphors used.

Phosphors are sometimes added to laundry detergents to make white clothes appear whiter. Ultraviolet light in sunlight will cause the phosphors to glow, making the color appear brighter. Have you ever seen your clothes glow in the haunted house or fun

Figure 25–16 *A firefly is a luminous source of light. Although Jupiter and its moons shine brightly, they are not luminous objects. What type of objects are they? Why can we see them?*

Figure 25–17 *Light bulbs and hot coals are examples of objects that produce light as they are heated. What are these types of luminous objects called?*

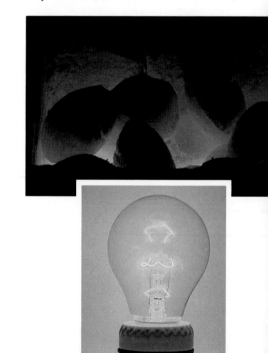

Figure 25–18 *Fluorescent lights have a number of industrial applications, such as illuminating eggs for inspection. Neon lights are usually more brightly colored and used for decoration or advertisement.*

Activity Bank

Mystery Message, p.776

Guide for Reading

Focus on this question as you read.

▶ *Is light a particle, a wave, or both?*

house at an amusement park? What kind of light do you think is used to make this happen?

NEON LIGHT   Perhaps you have seen thin glass tubes of brightly colored lights in an advertisement or sign. These lights were probably **neon lights**. Neon light is similar to fluorescent light in that it is cool light. When electrons pass through glass tubes filled with certain gases, light is produced. The most common type of gas used is neon gas. The light produced from neon gas is bright red. If other gases are added, however, different colors are produced.

Mercury vapor produces greenish-blue light that does not create much glare. So mercury vapor lamps are used to light streets and highways. Sodium vapor lamps, which give off a bright yellow-orange light, use less electricity than mercury vapor lamps. In many locations, sodium vapor lamps are replacing mercury vapor lamps.

25–3 Section Review

1. What is a luminous object? An illuminated object?
2. How does an incandescent bulb produce light?
3. How does a fluorescent source produce light?
4. How is fluorescent light similar to neon light?

Critical Thinking—*Drawing Conclusions*
5. Why are fluorescent lights helpful in preserving Earth's natural resources?

25–4 Wave or Particle?

Throughout this chapter you have read about light as a wave and about the properties of electromagnetic waves. The wave model of light, which has been the prevailing theory since the early 1800s, successfully explains most of the properties and behavior of light. In the early 1900s, however, scientists discovered something unusual about light— something that made them modify the wave theory.

Scientists shone violet light onto the surface of certain metals. The energy carried by the light was absorbed by electrons in the atoms of the metal

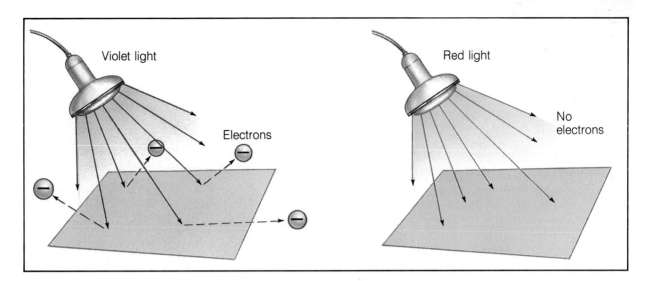

Violet light

Electrons

Red light

No electrons

plate. This energy knocked electrons out of some of the atoms in the metal plate. In fact, enough electrons were knocked off the metal plate to cause an electric current to flow.

The scientists then repeated the experiment with red light. To their surprise, nothing happened! No matter how long the red light was shone or how bright it was, no electrons were ever knocked out of the metal's atoms. The dimmest violet light produced a current, but the strongest red light did not!

As you can imagine, this caused confusion. According to the wave theory, if red light strikes a metal as a continuous wave, eventually the electrons should "soak up" enough energy to escape from their atoms. But that does not happen.

Suppose, though, that light acts more like a stream of particles than like a wave. Each individual particle would be a tiny bundle of energy related to the amount of energy absorbed by an electron. Each individual bundle, or **photon,** of red light acting on its own could never knock an electron from its atom. Each photon must have a different amount of energy for each color of light. However, no single red light photon contains enough energy to do the job, no matter how long the light is on or how bright it is. On the other hand, violet light photons carry more energy than red light photons. So a single violet light photon can impart enough energy to an electron to knock it right out of its atom.

Further experimenting showed that photon energy increases as frequency increases and wavelength decreases. Thus, photon energy increases across the electromagnetic spectrum from radio

Figure 25–19 *The energy of individual photons of violet light can produce an electric current. The energy of individual photons of red light cannot. What theory of light explains this effect?*

Figure 25–20 *Solar cells, such as these on a satellite in orbit around the Earth, use the energy of sunlight to produce a useful electric current. Why are solar cells becoming increasingly important to energy conservation and ecology?*

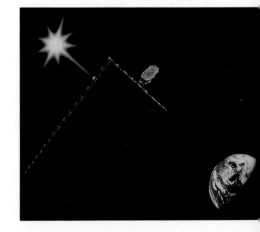

Figure 25–21 *When two beams of light from two slide projectors intersect, they pass through each other without colliding. The images produced on the screen are clear. What theory of light explains this behavior?*

ACTIVITY

DISCOVERING

Light: Particle or Wave?

1. CAUTION: *Do this step outdoors.* Turn on two water hoses. Aim the stream of water from one hose across the path of the stream of water from the other hose. Observe what happens to the stream of water from the second hose.

2. Darken a room and project a slide from a slide projector on the wall. Shine a flashlight beam across the projector beam in the same way you did the stream of water in step 1. Observe any effect it has on the projected picture.

Do the two streams of water particles act in the same way that the two beams of light do? Explain your answer.

■ Does this activity support a wave theory or a particle theory of light? Explain your answer.

waves to gamma rays. Because the experiments involved both electrons and photons, the result came to be known as the **photoelectric effect**.

The photoelectric effect can only be explained by a particle theory of light. But many other properties of light can only be explained by a wave theory of light. Confused? Don't be. **Scientists today describe light and other electromagnetic waves as both particlelike and wavelike.** Although it may be difficult for you to picture both a particle and a wave at the same time, both models are necessary to explain all the properties of light. And this problem provides a good opportunity for you to remember that science is a way of explaining observations; it is not absolute knowledge.

25–4 Section Review

1. Why is light said to have two natures—wave and particle?
2. What convinced scientists of the particle nature of light?
3. Which carry more energy, ultraviolet photons or photons in gamma rays? Explain.

Connection—*You and Your World*
4. Many security systems are composed of a beam of light shining on a metal plate. As the electrons are knocked out of the plate, they create a current of electricity. If something crosses the beam of light, the flow of electricity stops and an alarm sounds. Why is the photoelectric effect necessary to explain this type of alarm?

CONNECTIONS

The World at Your Fingertips

Click. The television goes on. Click again and the volume goes up. Click once more and the channel changes. Remote control, or controlling a device from a distance, has become a standard feature of many household products, ranging from television sets to garage-door openers. Beyond the household, remote control is used to control faraway devices such as satellites and guided missiles. Remote control makes many devices easier to operate—with just the push of a button. It also helps to perform tasks that would otherwise be difficult, dangerous, or even impossible.

There are different kinds of remote-control mechanisms. Consider the television again. When you push a button on the remote control, you set a tiny device into vibration. The vibration produces an infrared beam carrying a signal that is sent to the television. The signal depends on the button you push. A detector on the television receives the infrared beam signal and converts it to an electronic signal. The electronic signal controls several switches—on/off, channel selector, and volume. The switch that is activated by the electronic signal depends on which button you pressed. Infrared waves are also used to carry signals to VCRs and cable television boxes.

Other remote controls use radio waves. For example, radio waves are used to drive toy cars, fly model airplanes, and open garage doors. A remote-control device sends radio waves carrying signals to the object. A receiver decodes the signal and passes on the message to tiny motors controlling the object's movements. Some radio-control systems work with the aid of computers. Controllers on the ground use the combination of radio signals and computers to position antennas and operate other equipment on artificial satellites in orbit.

The next time you effortlessly push a remote-control button, think about the electromagnetic energy involved. From toy cars to guided missiles, electromagnetic waves really do put the world at your fingertips!

Laboratory Investigation

In the Heat of the Light

Problem

How do the effects of the various regions of the electromagnetic spectrum differ?

Materials *(per group)*

scissors
light bulb
convex lens
cardboard shoe box
prism
black paint
sensitive thermometer

Procedure 🜀 ▭ ᛝ

1. Place the convex lens in front of the light bulb so that the light focuses through a small hole cut in the side of the shoe box. See the accompanying diagram.

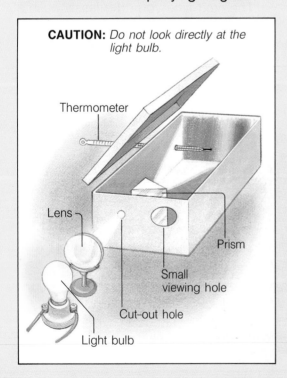

CAUTION: *Do not look directly at the light bulb.*

Thermometer

Lens

Small viewing hole

Prism

Cut-out hole

Light bulb

2. Position the prism in front of the hole in the box. A prism separates light into various wavelengths.

3. Use the black paint to paint the thermometer bulb so that it will absorb all the light energy that strikes it.

4. Place the thermometer bulb in the corner of the box. Allow a few minutes for the thermometer to register the temperature. Record the temperature.

5. Repeat Step 4 at several points, moving the thermometer bulb over slightly each time. Be sure to place the thermometer at points beyond the visible spectrum.

Observations

1. Record the temperatures in a data table.

2. Starting at the red end of the spectrum and moving toward the violet end, explain what happens to the temperature.

Analysis and Conclusions

1. Where is the warmest part of the spectrum?

2. Did you detect infrared or ultraviolet waves? How do you know?

3. How is the change in temperature related to the amount of energy carried by each wave?

4. If your temperatures did not vary in a regular pattern, what reasons can you give for the observation?

5. **On Your Own** Repeat the experiment with a bottle of water (or other fluid) outside the box and in front of the hole. How does this change your results?

Study Guide

Summarizing Key Concepts

25–1 Electromagnetic Waves

▲ An electromagnetic wave consists of an electric field and a magnetic field at right angles to each other and to the direction of motion of the wave.

▲ Electromagnetic waves can travel through a vacuum because they do not require matter to exist.

▲ Electromagnetic waves are produced by charge that is changing direction or speed.

▲ All electromagnetic waves travel at the same speed in a vacuum—300 million m/sec.

25–2 The Electromagnetic Spectrum

▲ The electromagnetic spectrum is an arrangement of electromagnetic waves according to wavelength and frequency.

▲ The electromagnetic spectrum includes radio waves, infrared rays, visible light, ultraviolet rays, X-rays, and gamma rays.

25–3 Visible Light

▲ Luminous objects give off light. Illuminated objects are lit up because light bounces off them.

▲ Incandescent light is produced from heat.

▲ Fluorescent light is produced when electrons are used to bombard gas molecules contained at low pressure.

▲ Light that is produced when electrons pass through glass tubes filled with gas is called neon light.

25–4 Wave or Particle?

▲ Visible light and other electromagnetic waves have a particlelike nature as well as a wave nature.

▲ The fact that light rays can knock electrons out of their atoms is referred to as the photoelectric effect.

Reviewing Key Terms

Define each term in a complete sentence.

25–2 The Electromagnetic Spectrum
electromagnetic spectrum
radio wave
modulation
microwave
radar
infrared ray
visible light

ultraviolet ray
X-ray
gamma ray

25–3 Visible Light
luminous object
illuminated object
incandescent light
fluorescent light
neon light

25–4 Wave or Particle?
photon
photoelectric effect

Chapter Review

Content Review

Multiple Choice

Choose the letter of the answer that best completes each statement.

1. Which of the following does not belong?
   a. X-rays
   b. sound waves
   c. gamma rays
   d. radio waves
2. The source of all electromagnetic waves is the
   a. air.
   b. sun.
   c. Earth.
   d. atom.
3. The electromagnetic spectrum arranges waves in order of
   a. frequency and wavelength.
   b. the alphabet.
   c. discovery.
   d. use and applications.
4. Microwaves are a type of
   a. X-ray.
   b. gamma ray.
   c. ultraviolet light.
   d. radio wave.
5. Thermograms are produced using
   a. infrared rays.
   b. gamma rays.
   c. X-rays.
   d. visible light.
6. The waves with the highest energy in the electromagnetic spectrum are
   a. gamma rays.
   b. radio waves.
   c. ultraviolet rays.
   d. visible light.
7. Light produced from heat is called
   a. neon light.
   b. fluorescent light.
   c. incandescent light.
   d. illuminated light.
8. Substances that glow when exposed to ultraviolet light are called
   a. phosphors.
   b. photons.
   c. photoelectric.
   d. neon.

True or False

If the statement is true, write "true." If it is false, change the underlined word or words to make the statement true.

1. Electromagnetic waves are <u>longitudinal</u> waves.
2. The <u>invisible</u> spectrum contains all the colors of the rainbow.
3. <u>Ultraviolet</u> rays can be felt as heat.
4. Waves with frequencies just above the ultraviolet region are called <u>gamma</u> rays.
5. Objects that can be seen because light bounces off them are called <u>luminous</u>.
6. In fluorescent lights, phosphors glow in response to <u>infrared</u> rays.
7. A particle of <u>light</u> is called a <u>photon</u>.
8. The movement of electrons because of energy absorbed from photons of light is called the <u>Doppler</u> effect.

Concept Mapping

Complete the following concept map for Section 25–2. Then construct a concept map for the entire chapter.

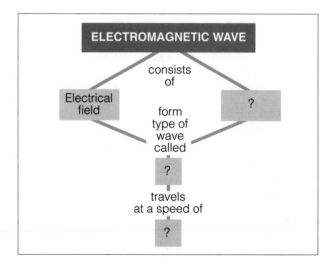

Concept Mastery

Discuss each of the following in a brief paragraph.

1. How is visible light produced?
2. How is the electromagnetic spectrum organized in terms of frequency, wavelength, and photon energy?
3. What happens to the wavelength of an electromagnetic wave if its frequency increases? Why is this true for all electromagnetic waves?
4. Are the wavelengths of radio and television signals longer or shorter than those detectable by the human eye? Describe the type of waves that carry these signals.
5. Explain why the wave theory of light cannot explain the photoelectric effect.

6. A person lost in the forest at night may signal for help by turning a flashlight on and off according to a code known as Morse code. This is actually a modulated electromagnetic wave. Is it AM or FM? Explain.
7. List five examples of luminous objects.
8. How is light produced in an incandescent light bulb? In a fluorescent light bulb? In a neon light?

Critical Thinking and Problem Solving

Use the skills you have developed in this chapter to answer each of the following.

1. **Applying concepts** How is it that someone in the United States listening on the radio to a music concert taking place in London, England, can hear the music before someone sitting in the audience can?
2. **Making calculations**
   a. A police radar signal has a frequency of about 11 billion Hz. What is the wavelength of this signal?
   b. What is the frequency of a microwave that has a wavelength of 1.50 cm?
3. **Drawing conclusions** What important information can be gathered from a thermogram of a house?
4. **Applying concepts** Suppose you are building an incubator and you need a source of heat. Would you use an incandescent or fluorescent light bulb? Explain your answer.

5. **Recognizing relationships** Describe the relationship between ultraviolet waves and the ozone layer.
6. **Making comparisons** Explain how a row of billiard balls rolling across a table in single file illustrates the particle nature of light.
7. **Using the writing process** Develop an advertising campaign praising the merits of fluorescent lights.

Light and Its Uses

Guide for Reading

After you read the following sections, you will be able to

26–1 Ray Model of Light
- Describe the nature of a light ray.

26–2 Reflection of Light
- Compare regular and diffuse reflections.

26–3 Refraction of Light
- Describe the process of refraction.

26–4 Color
- Account for the color of opaque and transparent objects.

26–5 How You See
- Explain how you see.

26–6 Optical Instruments
- Describe the operation and uses of several optical instruments.

26–7 Lasers
- Explain how a laser works.

Imagine a sturdy glass disc, smaller than a record album, that can hold enough information so that if it were printed and stretched out it would span over 5 kilometers! And imagine that the information on the disc could be used over and over without scratching or wearing out the disc. Well, you don't really have to imagine. This amazing disc is already in use. It is called a compact disc, or CD. You have probably even seen the pretty colors of a compact disc shimmering in the light.

Besides their small size, CDs have many advantages over vinyl record albums. CDs produce extremely clear sound with no background noise. And information on a CD is found with a push of a button. How can all this be accomplished?

The answer is through the use of light. Instead of sharp instruments such as needles, CDs depend on beams of light. A beam of light creates a code on the disc, and a beam of light reads the code when it is popped into a compact-disc player.

Sound strange? In this chapter you will learn about light—how it bounces and bends, how colors are produced, and how light is used in a great variety of instruments and devices.

Journal *Activity*

You and Your World Have you ever stopped to admire a beautiful rainbow? Describe a rainbow in your journal. Include the conditions that formed the rainbow you saw. Then write a short poem about rainbows.

Spinning compact discs are a shining example of the versatility of light.

Guide for Reading

Focus on this question as you read.

▶ *What is the ray model of light?*

Activity Bank

The Straight and Narrow, p.777

26–1 Ray Model of Light

Have you ever been frightened by your own shadow? Or made shadow figures on a wall with your hands? Shadows occur due to the fact that light travels in straight lines. This is not difficult to understand. If you turn on a flashlight in a dark room, you see a straight beam of light. If an object gets into that beam, the object blocks some of the light and a shadow is created. The light does not bend around the object.

Shadows are quite common. Even the Earth and the moon create shadows with the sun's light. An eclipse occurs when either the Earth or the moon passes through the other's shadow.

Notice that neither the wave nature nor the particle nature of light is necessary to discuss shadows—only the assumption that light travels in straight lines. This assumption has led to the ray model of

Figure 26–1 *According to the ray model of light, a luminous object emits light rays in all directions. The existence of shadows supports the ray model of light. Why do shadows form?*

light. **The ray model of light assumes that light travels in straight-line paths called light rays.** Recall from Chapter 23 that straight arrows called rays were used to discuss such wave activities as reflection and refraction. Light rays are the same type of rays.

The ray model of light assumes that a luminous object sends out light rays that spread out in all directions in straight lines. An image is formed when the light rays leaving the object from the same point meet.

As you learn about light and its uses you will discover that different aspects and applications of light depend on either its particle nature or its wave nature. The ray model does not contradict the wavelike or particlelike characteristics of light. Instead, it puts aside the actual nature of light and concentrates on its behavior. In this way the ray model makes it easier for you to understand and describe activities of light such as reflection, refraction, and the formation of images.

ACTIVITY

DISCOVERING

Shadows

A shadow is an area of darkness that is formed when an object blocks light from striking a surface. Often a shadow has two parts. When the light is completely blocked, the very dark umbra forms. The area outside the umbra receives some light and appears gray. This area is the penumbra.

With the sun or another light source behind you, observe your shadow or that of another object. Identify the umbra and penumbra.

■ Does the shadow change with the type of light source?

26–1 Section Review

1. Describe the ray model of light.
2. What is a light ray?
3. When is an image formed?

Connection—*Mathematics*
4. What must happen to at least one of the light rays if two light rays that leave a point in different directions eventually meet?

26–2 Reflection of Light

When you bounce a ball on the pavement, it bounces back to you. If you bounce it at an angle, it bounces off the pavement at the same angle it bounced on the pavement. But what happens if you try to bounce the ball on a bumpy field or a rocky playground? The ball bounces off in a wild direction. You have no way of predicting where it will go.

Guide for Reading

Focus on these questions as you read.

▶ *What is the relationship between kinds of reflection and reflecting surfaces?*

▶ *How are mirrors classified according to shape?*

Light behaves in much the same way as the ball. When light strikes a surface, some of the light bounces back. (The rest is either absorbed by the material or is transmitted through it.) **The bouncing back of light is called reflection.** Recall what you learned about reflection in Chapter 23. Like the ball, light will be reflected off a surface at the same angle as it strikes the surface. Does this sound familiar to you? It should! This is the law of reflection. Like all waves, light obeys the law of reflection. This means that when light is reflected from a surface, the angle formed by the incoming, or incident, ray and the normal equals the angle formed by the outgoing, or reflected, ray and the normal. The normal is an imaginary line perpendicular to the surface.

Kinds of Reflection

Why can you see your reflection in a piece of glass but not in a wall? In both cases light is reflected off a surface. The answer lies in how the light is reflected. **The type of surface the light strikes determines the kind of reflection formed.**

A piece of glass has a smooth surface. All the rays reaching the glass hit it at the same angle. Thus, they are reflected at the same angle. This type of reflection is called **regular reflection.** It is similar to the ball bouncing off the pavement.

The surface of a wall is not really smooth. This may surprise you because you probably think that most walls have a smooth surface. If you were to magnify the surface of a wall, however, you would see that it is rough and uneven. If the surface of a wall were smooth, you would be able to see yourself in it! Sometimes surfaces are made to shine by coating them with materials that fill in the uneven spots. Many waxes and polishes make surfaces shinier by doing that.

Because the surface of a wall is not smooth, each light ray hits the surface at a different angle from the other light rays. Each ray still obeys the law

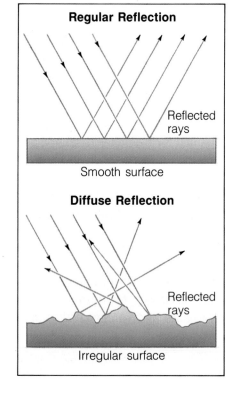

Regular Reflection

Reflected rays

Smooth surface

Diffuse Reflection

Reflected rays

Irregular surface

Figure 26–2 *Reflection from a smooth surface, or regular reflection, does not produce much scattering of light rays. Reflection from an irregular surface, or diffuse reflection, produces considerable scattering of light rays.*

Figure 26–3 *At first glance, it appears that there are two birds standing toe to toe. But actually there is only one bird. Reflection off the smooth surface of the water creates a clear image of the bird. What kind of reflection occurs when sunlight hits this grumpy-looking gorilla?*

of reflection, so each is reflected at a different angle from the others. Thus the reflected rays are scattered in all directions. Reflected light that is scattered in many different directions due to an irregular surface is called **diffuse reflection.** It is similar to the ball bouncing off the uneven field.

Although diffuse reflections are not desirable for seeing your image, they are important. If the sun's rays were not scattered by reflecting off uneven surfaces and dust particles in the air, you would see only those objects that are in direct sunlight. Anything in the shade of trees and buildings would be in darkness. In addition, the glare of the sunlight would be so strong that you would have difficulty seeing.

Reflection and Mirrors

The most common surface from which light is reflected is a mirror. Most mirrors are pieces of glass with a silver coating applied to one side. Glass provides an extremely smooth surface through which light can pass easily. Silver, which is not usually smooth, reflects almost all the light that hits it. Applying silver to the smooth surface of glass makes a very smooth reflecting surface.

ACTIVITY DOING

Mirror, Mirror on the Wall

1. Stand 1 or 2 meters away from a full-length mirror. Have a friend or classmate place pieces of masking tape at the points on the mirror where you see the top of your head and your feet.

2. Compare the distance between the pieces of tape with your height.

3. Without changing the position of the mirror, move so that you are a distance of 4 or more meters from it. What happens to your image?

Derive a relationship between your height and distance from the mirror and the size and location of your image.

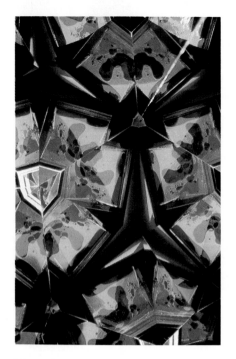

Figure 26–4 *Have you ever looked into a kaleidoscope? The magic of a kaleidoscope is created by a particular arrangement of mirrors.*

Figure 26–5 *This diagram shows how an image is formed by a plane mirror. Notice that the reflected rays do not actually meet. The brain, however, perceives them as having come from the point at which they would have met had they been straight.*

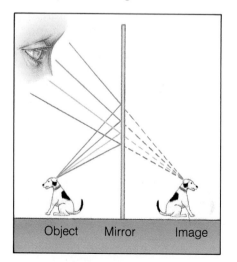

Any smooth surface that reflects light and forms images can be used as a mirror. The surface of a mirror can be perfectly flat or it can be curved. **Based on the shape of its surface, a mirror is classified as plane, concave, or convex.**

PLANE MIRRORS A mirror with a perfectly flat surface is a **plane mirror.** An ordinary wall or pocket mirror is a plane mirror. Think about the image you see when you look into a mirror. Figure 26–5 shows how an image is formed. As you look at the figure, you should notice two things about the image. It is right side up, and the same size as the original object. And, as you know from experience, left and right are reversed. If you raise your left hand, the right hand of your image appears to be raised.

Where is the image when you look into a plane mirror? The image appears to be on the other side of the mirror—where you could almost reach forward and touch it. But you know this is not really so. Your brain is playing a trick on you. The human brain always assumes that light rays reach the eyes in a straight line. So even if the rays are reflected or bent, the eye records them as though they had traveled in a straight line. To better understand this, consider the bouncing ball again. If you did not know that the ball had bounced, it would seem as if the ball had come straight up through the pavement. This is what happens in a mirror. The brain traces light rays back to where they would have come from if they had been straight. They appear to have come straight through the mirror.

The light rays from an object reflected in a plane mirror do not actually meet. But the brain interprets an image at the point at which the light rays would have met had they been straight. This type of image is called a virtual image. As used here, the word virtual means not real. A virtual image only seems to be where it is. In other words, it can be seen only in the mirror.

CONCAVE MIRRORS A mirror can be curved instead of flat. If the surface of a mirror curves inward, the mirror is called a **concave mirror.** You can experiment with a concave mirror by looking at the inner surface of a shiny metal spoon. Move the spoon back and forth and observe what happens to your image.

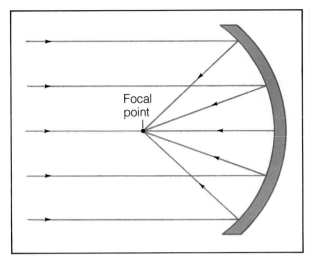
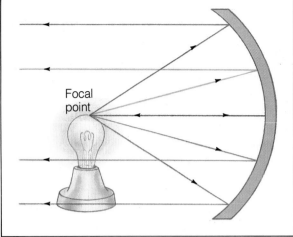

Figure 26–6 *Parallel light rays reaching a concave mirror are all reflected to the same point, the focal point. Light rays coming from the focal point, on the other hand, are reflected parallel to one another.*

Light rays coming parallel into a concave mirror are all reflected through the same point in front of the mirror. For this reason, concave mirrors are used in reflecting telescopes to gather light from space. The point in front of the mirror where the reflected rays meet is called the **focal point.** Figure 26–6 shows the focal point of a concave mirror. The distance between the center of the mirror and the focal point is called the focal length. Images formed by concave mirrors depend on the location of the object with respect to the focal point.

Notice the paths of the light rays in Figure 26–6. Light rays follow the same paths in the opposite direction if they are coming from the focal point rather than from space. All the light rays are reflected back parallel to one another in a concentrated beam of light. If you open a flashlight, you will find a concave mirror behind the bulb. The bulb is placed at the focal point of the mirror so that the reflected light forms a powerful beam. Concave mirrors are placed behind car headlights to focus the light beam. Concave mirrors are also used in searchlights and in spotlights.

CONVEX MIRRORS If you turn a shiny spoon over, you will notice that the surface curves outward. This is a **convex mirror.** The surface of a convex mirror curves outward like the surface of a ball. Reflected rays spread out from the surface of a convex mirror, as you can see from Figure 26–8 on page 674. The

Figure 26–7 *The image produced by a concave mirror depends on the position of the object in relation to the focal point. Where must the object be placed to produce a virtual image?*

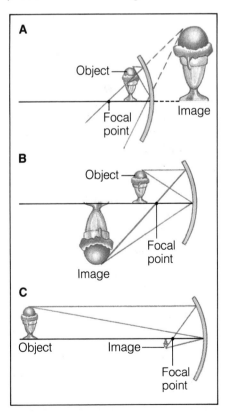

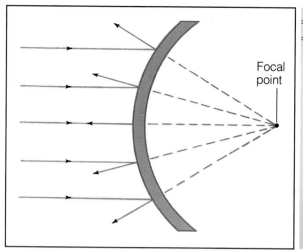

Figure 26–8 *Because a convex mirror spreads out reflected light rays from its very large area of reflection, it is often used to increase traffic visibility. What type of image does a convex mirror form?*

image formed by a convex mirror is always right side up and smaller than the object. Like the image formed by a plane mirror, the image appears behind the mirror. It is a virtual image.

Convex mirrors provide large areas of reflection. For this reason, they are used in automobile side-view and rear-view mirrors to obtain a wider view. They are also used in stores to provide security guards with a wide view of the shopping area. Convex mirrors, however, give a distorted indication of distance. Objects appear farther away than they actually are. Why is this an important concern when using a car mirror?

26–2 Section Review

1. How are regular and diffuse reflections related to the characteristics of the reflecting surface?
2. Describe the surface of and the images formed by a plane mirror. A concave mirror. A convex mirror.
3. What are some uses of each type of mirror?
4. A slide projector projects the image of a slide on a screen. Is this image real or virtual?

Connection—*Social Studies*

5. Archimedes is said to have burned the entire Roman fleet in the harbor by focusing the rays of the sun with a huge curved mirror. Explain if this is possible and what type of mirror it would have been.

26–3 Refraction of Light

You can win the stuffed animal at the carnival if you can throw a penny into the cup at the bottom of a fish bowl. Sounds easy, doesn't it? Actually, it is rather difficult—unless you know that the bending of light makes the cup appear to be where it is not!

You have just learned that light travels in straight lines. This means that it travels at a constant speed in a straight path through a medium. But light travels at different speeds in different mediums. So what happens when light passes from one medium to another? When light passes at an angle from one medium to another, it bends. (Do you remember learning in Chapter 23 that waves bend when they enter a new medium because part of the wave changes speed before the rest of the wave does?) **The bending of light due to a change in its speed is called refraction.**

When light passes from a less dense medium to a more dense medium, it slows down. This is the case when light passes from air to water. When light passes from a more dense medium to a less dense medium, it speeds up. This is the case when light passes from glass to air. To find out which way light bends, draw the normal to the boundary. If the wave speeds up, it bends away from the normal. If it slows down, it bends toward the normal. See Figure 26–9.

Because of refraction, a stick may look bent or broken when placed in a glass of water. If you are standing on the bank of a lake and you see a fish, it may appear closer to the surface than it actually is. Remember, the eyes see and the brain interprets light rays as if they were straight. The brain does not know that the rays were bent along the way.

Every medium has a specific **index of refraction,** which is a measure of the amount by which a material refracts light. **The index of refraction is the comparison of the speed of light in air with the speed of light in a certain material.** Because the

Guide for Reading

Focus on these questions as you read.

▶ *What is refraction?*

▶ *How do concave and convex lenses form images?*

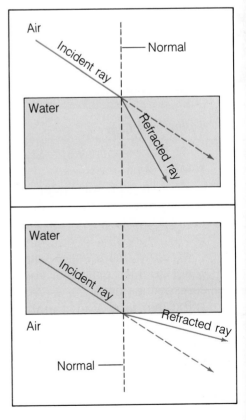

Figure 26–9 *As light passes from a less dense medium to a more dense medium, its speed decreases and it is refracted toward the normal (top). As light passes from a more dense medium to a less dense medium, its speed increases and it is refracted away from the normal (bottom).*

Figure 26–10 *The normal to this block of glass is horizontal across its length. When the light enters the glass, it bends up, toward the normal. When it leaves the glass on the other side, it bends down away from the normal. Notice how the light breaks up as some of it is reflected.*

ACTIVITY

DOING

Penny in a Cup

1. Place a penny in a Styrofoam cup.

2. Fill a glass with water.

3. Position yourself so that the cup blocks the view of the penny.

4. Slowly fill the cup with water from the glass until you can see the penny.

Explain why you cannot see the penny without the water but you can see it with the water.

speed of light in air is always greater than in any other material, the index of refraction in any other material is always greater than one. The larger the index of refraction, the more light is bent.

Mirages

Perhaps you have had this experience: You were traveling in a car on a dry day when up ahead you saw a puddle of water shimmering on the roadway. But when you reached the spot where the puddle should have been, it was not there. And what's more, you saw another imaginary puddle farther ahead. The disappearing puddle is a type of mirage—not unlike the famous desert mirages sometimes seen in the movies.

A mirage is an example of refraction of light by the Earth's atmosphere. The index of refraction of air depends on the temperature of the air. When light passes from air at one temperature to air at another temperature, it bends. The greater the change in temperature, the greater the bending.

The puddle mirage exists because under certain conditions, such as a stretch of pavement or desert heated by intense sunshine, there are large temperature changes near the ground. Light from an object bends upward as it enters the hot air near the ground. It is refracted to the observer's eyes as if it had come from the ground or even from underground. So, for example, light from the sky can be refracted to look like a body of water.

Figure 26–11 *A small island with palm trees in the middle of a desert lake, right? No, wrong! This is only a mirage.*

Bending and Separating

Have you ever seen a beautiful rainbow? Or the colors of a rainbow as sunshine passed through a window, a drinking glass, or even a diamond? If so, have you wondered where rainbows come from?

You have learned that white light is made up of all the visible colors. Each color corresponds to a particular wavelength. If white light passes at an angle from air into another medium, its speed changes and it is refracted. Each wavelength is refracted by a different amount. Although the variation is small, it is enough to separate the different wavelengths in a beam of white light.

The longer the wavelength, the less bending there will be. Red, with the longest wavelength, is refracted the least. Violet, with the shortest wavelength, is refracted the most. The result is the separation of white light into the colors of the visible spectrum, which always appear in the same order— red, orange, yellow, green, blue, indigo, and violet. This process is called dispersion. If combined again, the various colors of the spectrum would form a beam of white light.

The piece of glass that forms the spectrum is called a prism. Notice that light bends as it enters the prism and as it leaves. The bending occurs as the light leaves the prism because the speed of light changes again as the light passes from glass back to air. Real rainbows are produced when tiny water droplets in the air act as prisms.

Figure 26–12 *The colorful rainbow seen above an irrigation device is produced by the dispersion of light. Because each wavelength of light is refracted a different amount in the droplets of water, sunlight is spread into an array of colors.*

Figure 26–13 *Passing white light through a prism separates the light into the various colors of the rainbow.*

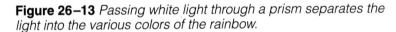

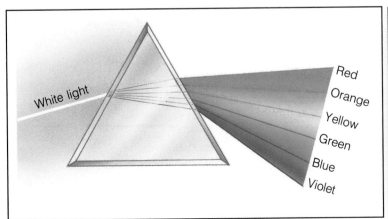

White light

Red
Orange
Yellow
Green
Blue
Violet

ACTIVITY READING

Refraction and Lenses

Have you ever used a magnifying glass, a camera, or a microscope? If so, you were using a **lens** to form an image. **A lens is any transparent material that refracts light.** The light is said to be focused through the lens. Most lenses are made of glass or plastic and have either one or two curved surfaces. As parallel rays of light pass through the lens, the rays of light are refracted so that they either come together or spread out. A lens that converges, or brings together, light rays is a **convex lens;** a lens that diverges, or spreads out, light rays is a **concave lens.**

CONVEX LENSES A lens that is thicker in the center than at the edges is called a convex lens. As parallel rays of light pass through a convex lens, they are bent toward the center of the lens. The light rays converge. The point at which the light rays converge is the focal point.

Light is refracted as it enters a lens and again as it leaves the lens. The amount of refraction depends on the degree to which the lens is curved. A very curved lens will refract light more than a lens whose surface is only slightly curved.

Figure 26–14 *A convex lens converges light rays toward the center. The degree to which the lens is curved determines the amount of refraction. How does the focal length of a very curved lens compare with that of a slightly curved lens?*

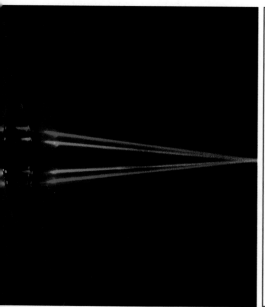

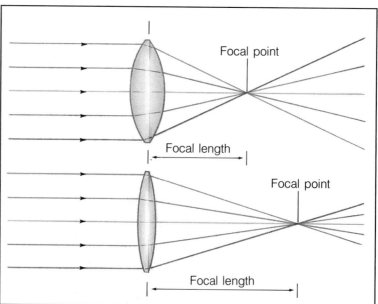

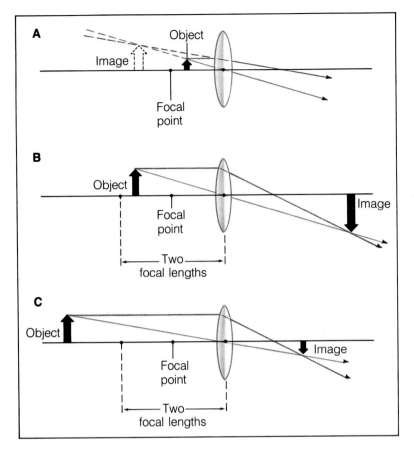

Figure 26–15 *The type of image formed by a convex lens depends on where the object is placed relative to the focal length of the lens. What type of image is formed in A? In B? In C?*

ACTIVITY

DOING

Firewater!

1. Place a candle 15 cm in front of a piece of clear glass or plastic.

2. Place a glass filled with water 15 cm behind the glass or plastic.

3. Put on safety goggles and then carefully light the candle. **CAUTION:** *Exercise care when working with matches and a lighted candle.*

4. Stand in front of the candle and hold a book or piece of cardboard between you and the candle so that your view of the candle is obscured. Look at the drinking glass. What do you see? Explain why you see what you do.

CONCAVE LENSES A lens that is thicker at the ends and thinner in the center is called a concave lens. As parallel rays of light pass through a concave lens, they are bent outward toward the ends of the lens. The light rays diverge.

Figure 26–16 *A concave lens diverges light rays toward the edges. The brain perceives the rays as if they were straight. How does the image compare with the object?*

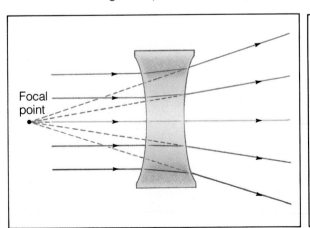

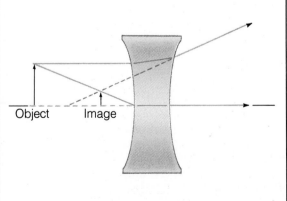

26-3 Section Review

1. Describe the process of refraction.
2. What is the index of refraction?
3. How can you determine which way a light ray will bend when it enters a new medium?
4. Which color of light is refracted the most? The least?

Critical Thinking—*Applying Concepts*

5. A magnifying glass is a simple lens. Explain which type of lens can be used as a magnifying glass and draw a diagram showing how light rays would be bent.

Guide for Reading

Focus on this question as you read.

▶ *How is color related to the reflection, transmission, and absorption of light?*

26-4 Color

You have just read that white light is broken into its individual colors by prisms. Yet you do not need a prism to see color. If all the colors of the rainbow are locked up within white light, how do objects have particular colors?

When Light Strikes

In order to understand why objects have color, you must know what happens when light strikes the surface of an object. **When light strikes any form of matter, the light can be transmitted, absorbed, or reflected.**

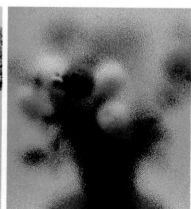

Figure 26–17 *A transparent material transmits light readily, so objects seen through it are clear (left). A translucent material does not transmit light readily, so objects seen through it are unclear and lack detail (right).*

When light is transmitted, it passes through the substance it strikes. If the light is transmitted readily, the substance is said to be **transparent.** Objects seen through transparent substances are very clear. Glass, water, and air are transparent.

If light is transmitted through a substance that scatters the light, the image is unclear and lacks detail. A substance that transmits light but no detail is said to be **translucent.** Waxed paper and frosted glass are translucent substances. A translucent substance produces a fuzzy image when you look through it.

A substance that does not transmit light is said to be **opaque.** A block of wood, a sheet of metal, and a piece of black cloth are opaque substances.

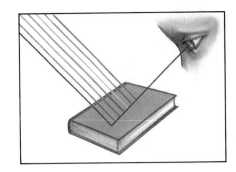

Figure 26-18 *The color of an object is the color of light reflected from the object to your eye.*

The Color of Objects

Why is grass green, an apple red, and a daffodil yellow? The answer to this question depends on the nature of the object and the colors of the light striking the object.

If an object does not allow any light to pass through it (the object is opaque), the light falling on the object is either reflected or absorbed. If the light is absorbed, can it reach your eyes? Obviously not. Only the light that is reflected reaches you. So the color of an opaque object is the color it reflects.

Think for a moment of a red apple. A red apple reflects red and absorbs all the other colors. You see the red apple only by the light it reflects. What color do the green leaves and the stem of the apple reflect?

Now think about an object that is white. White is the presence of all the colors of the visible spectrum. So what is being reflected from a white object? You are right if you said all the colors are reflected. No color is absorbed. If, on the other hand, all the colors are absorbed, then no color is reflected back to you. The object appears black. Black is the absence of color. Have you ever noticed that many items of clothing, such as tennis clothes, that are worn in warm weather or in sunlight are made of white material? This is because white reflects the sunlight and thus the heat, keeping you cooler. Why are many cold-weather clothes made of dark-colored materials?

Figure 26-19 *In white light, the apple appears red because it reflects red light. If only green light shines on it, the apple appears black. Why?*

ACTIVITY WRITING

Color Photography

Color film is sensitive to the various frequencies of light. It can record the colors of an object.

Using books and other reference materials in your library, find out how color film works. Write a report that describes how the various colors are recorded on the film.

Activity Bank

Spinning Wheel, p.778

Figure 26–20 *This plus sign looks quite colorful, but on a television screen it is actually white. The colors of images on a television screen are produced by combinations of tiny dots of the primary colors of light. The primary colors of light combine to form white light.*

If an object allows light to pass through it, the color that is transmitted is the color that reaches your eyes. The other colors are absorbed. So the color of a transparent object is the color of the light it transmits. Red glass absorbs all colors but red, which it transmits. Green glass transmits only green light. Ordinary window glass transmits all colors and is said to be colorless.

Adding Primary Colors of Light

Three colors can be mixed to produce light of any other color. These colors are called the primary colors. The primary colors of light are red, blue, and green.

Adding the proper amounts of these three colors produces any color, including white. For example, red and green light add together to produce yellow light. Blue and red add together to make magenta.

The color picture on a television screen or a computer screen is produced by adding the primary colors together. A screen contains groups of red, blue, and green dots. The correct mixture of these dots makes the pictures that you see.

Subtracting Colors of Pigments

You have just learned that all the colors of light combine to form white. But have you ever mixed all the colors in a paint set? Was the mixture white? Definitely not.

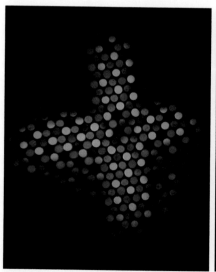

Paints are not sources of light. Paints are pigments. And the blending of pigments is different from the way your eyes blend the various colors of light. The primary pigments are yellow, cyan, and magenta. When the three primary pigments are mixed in equal amounts, all colors are absorbed and the result is black. Each different-colored pigment absorbs at least one color out of the visible spectrum of light that hits it. By mixing more and more pigments together, more of the visible spectrum is absorbed, or subtracted, from what you see. A movie film is made in this way.

Pigments have a certain color because they can absorb only certain wavelengths of the visible spectrum. All the rest are reflected. Does this sound similar to the explanation of why an apple is red? There is a good reason for the similarity. All objects contain pigments. The color of an object is a result of the pigments it contains.

Figure 26–21 *The primary pigments can be combined to form all the other colors. The pure colors can be lightened by adding white. Mixing together the three primary pigments produces black.*

Polarized Light and Filters

You can probably recall several instances in which you found yourself squinting because of the glare of the sun. But have you ever put on a pair of polarizing sunglasses to make the problem disappear? Sunglasses that reduce glare use polarizing filters.

You have learned that the waves of light from a normal light source vibrate in different directions at the same time. A polarizing filter is made up of a large number of parallel slits. When light passes through a polarizing filter, only those waves vibrating in the same direction as the slits can pass through. The light that passes through the filter is

Activity Bank

Color Crazy, p.780

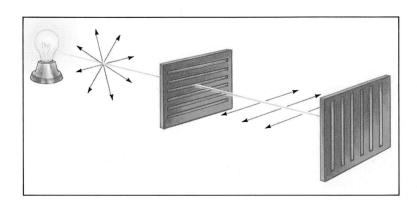

Figure 26–22 *Light waves that vibrate in all directions can be passed through a special filter to produce light waves that vibrate along a single plane. This light is called polarized light. What is a common use of polarizing filters?*

Figure 26–23 *Because of glare, all you can see are reflections on the surface of the water. When viewed through a polarizing filter, however, you can see the more detailed structure of the branch below the water.*

said to be **polarized light.** The rest of the light is either reflected or absorbed.

The glare of sunlight that makes you squint is mostly horizontal. Polarized sunglasses are vertically polarized. So the glare is reduced without affecting the rest of the light that enters your eyes.

Different types of filters are used to block certain colors of light. A color filter is a material that will absorb some wavelengths of light while allowing others to pass through. A common use of color filters is in slides. A color slide contains three filters. When white light from the projector is sent through the slide, each filter absorbs some colors and allows the other wavelengths to pass through. The combination of filters allows each image to appear in its natural color.

Activity

DISCOVERING

Colors and Filters

1. Obtain six color filters: red, green, blue, cyan, yellow, and magenta.

2. Look at a source of white light through each filter. Notice the colors you see.

3. Put the green filter behind the red filter. Look at the light through both filters.

4. Repeat step 3 for all combinations of filters.

■ How do the filters and combinations of filters affect the colors you see? Explain how color filters can be used to make slides.

■ How do you think tinted or colored eyeglasses or sunglasses affect what you see?

26–4 Section Review

1. Compare transparent, translucent, and opaque substances.
2. What are the primary colors of light? Of pigments?
3. What happens when the primary colors of light are mixed in equal amounts? When the primary pigments are mixed in equal amounts?
4. What is polarized light?

Critical Thinking—*Applying Concepts*

5. Why would a purple-people eater appear black under yellow light?

PROBLEM Solving

Round and Round It Goes

You have been given a very strange-looking but intriguing device and only one instruction: Place it in sunlight. At first glance it appears to be useless. Upon closer inspection, you notice that it consists of four squares, and each square is silver on one side and black on the other. You're still not impressed, however.

So you place the contraption in front of a window. Suddenly it starts spinning wildly. The brighter the sunlight, the faster the device spins.

Making Inferences

1. Explain why the act of placing this device in sunlight makes it move.

2. What practical application might this device have?

26–5 How You See

You have learned what light is, how it is produced, how it reflects and refracts, and how colors appear. But how do you see light? **You see light through a series of steps that involve the various parts of the eye and the brain.**

Light enters the eye through an opening called the **pupil.** The pupil is the black circle in the center of your eye. It is black because no light is reflected from it. (Remember, black is the absence of color.) The colored area surrounding the pupil, called the **iris,** controls the amount of light that enters the pupil. When the light is dim, the pupil is opened wide. When light is bright, the pupil is partially closed, or small.

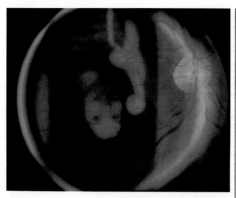

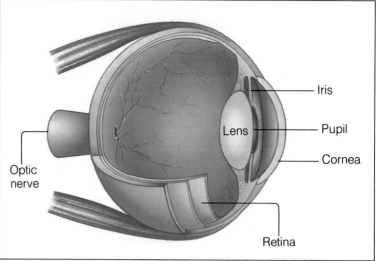

Figure 26–24 *The eye is the organ of sight. This photograph is an image as it is formed on the retina. What is true about the position of the image on the retina?*

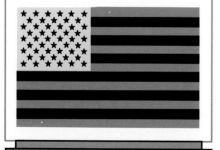
The light that enters the eye is refracted and focused on the curved rear surface of the eye, called the **retina.** The image that falls on the retina is upside down and smaller than the object. Most of the refraction is done by the protective outer covering of the eye, called the **cornea.** The lens of the eye makes adjustments for focusing on objects at different distances. Muscles attached to the lens control its shape. To see distant objects, the muscles relax, leaving the lens thin. To see nearby objects, the muscles contract, producing a thick lens.

The image that falls on the retina is then transferred to and interpreted by the nervous system. The retina is made of light-sensitive nerves that transfer the image to the brain. Some of the nerve cells in the retina are called **rods.** Rods are sensitive to light and dark. Other nerve cells called **cones** are responsible for seeing colors. Each cone is sensitive to a particular color.

Lenses and Vision

The lens of your eye is a convex lens. It is not a hard, rigid lens but rather a soft, flexible one. So it can easily change shape to allow you to see clear images of objects both near and distant.

NEARSIGHTEDNESS Ideally, the image formed by the lens should fall directly onto the retina. If the eyeball is too long, the image forms in front of the retina. This condition is called **nearsightedness.** A

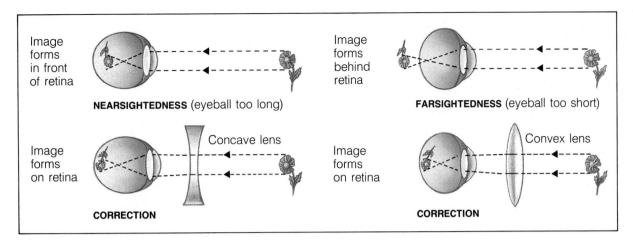

NEARSIGHTEDNESS (eyeball too long)

Image forms in front of retina

Image forms on retina

Concave lens

CORRECTION

FARSIGHTEDNESS (eyeball too short)

Image forms behind retina

Image forms on retina

Convex lens

CORRECTION

Figure 26–25 *Nearsightedness is corrected by using a concave lens. Why? Farsightedness is corrected by using a convex lens. Why?*

nearsighted person has difficulty seeing objects at a distance but has no trouble seeing nearby objects.

The lens of a nearsighted person is too convex. The rays of light converge at a point in front of the retina. A correcting lens would have to make the light rays diverge before they enter the eye. So a concave lens is used to correct nearsightedness.

FARSIGHTEDNESS If the eyeball is too short, the image is focused behind the retina. This condition is called **farsightedness.** A farsighted person can see distant objects clearly but has difficulty seeing nearby objects. These objects appear blurred.

The lens of a farsighted person is not convex enough. The rays of light converge at a point behind the retina. A correcting lens would have to make the rays converge before they enter the eye. So a convex lens is used to correct farsightedness.

26–5 Section Review

1. Describe the parts of the eye and their role in vision.
2. Where in the eye is the image formed?
3. What is nearsightedness, and how is it corrected? What is farsightedness, and how is it corrected?

Critical Thinking—*Making Inferences*
4. What causes colorblindness?

CONNECTIONS

It's All an Illusion

Look at the two figures of circles. The center circle in the figure on the right is larger than the center circle on the left. Right? Wrong! Both circles are the same size. Sometimes your eyes play tricks on you. The way that you perceive an image to be is different from its true measurement, color, depth, or movement. This is called an *optical illusion.*

In the case of the circles, your brain compares the size of the center circle with those around it. Because the outer circles in the figure on the right are smaller, the center circle appears larger. A similar optical illusion occurs when you look at the moon or the sun. If it is close to the horizon, your brain compares it with houses and trees. It then appears much larger.

Now look at the spiral. Ooops, caught you again. The figure actually shows a series of circles. The background causes your eyes to perceive the circles as spiraling into the center.

Some optical illusions are so convincing, you cannot believe it until you actually measure the objects or separate the colors. Look at the various figures shown below. Can you determine what is real and what is illusion?

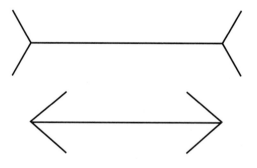

26–6 Optical Instruments

Reflection and refraction of light can be useful. Certain devices, known as optical instruments, produce images through reflection and refraction of light. Optical instruments use arrangements of mirrors and lenses to produce images.

Cameras

Like the eye, a camera works by allowing light to enter through a lens or a series of lenses. The major difference is that a camera permanently records an image on film. The film contains chemicals that are sensitive to light and that undergo change when light strikes them. Where does the image produced by the eye fall?

A camera contains a convex lens. When the shutter is opened, light from objects that are being photographed is focused by the lens as an image on the film. The image formed by a camera is real and upside down. It is also smaller than the actual object. The size of the image depends on the focal length of the lens.

It is important that not too much or too little light reaches the film. The opening in the camera through which light enters is called the aperture. The size of the aperture controls the amount of light that passes through the lens and reaches the film. What part of the eye plays the role of the aperture?

Guide for Reading

Focus on this question as you read.

▶ *What is the role of mirrors and lenses in cameras, telescopes, and microscopes?*

Figure 26–26 *These three photographs were taken with lenses of different focal lengths. The size of the image depends on the focal length of the lens. Which photograph was taken with a camera lens of short focal length? Of long focal length?*

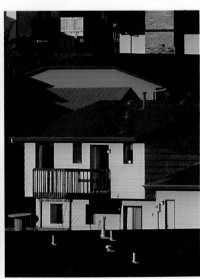

ACTIVITY

Telescopes

Telescopes are used to view objects that are very far away. Astronomers use telescopes to collect light from space. Because the light from many events that occur in space spreads out so much by the time it reaches Earth, the events are impossible to see with the unaided eye. The amount of light that can be gathered by the eye is limited by the eye's small size. By using large lenses and mirrors, telescopes can gather a great deal of light and capture images that otherwise could not be seen.

One type of telescope is called a refracting telescope. A refracting telescope consists of two convex lenses at opposite ends of a long tube. The lens located at the end of the telescope closest to the object is called the objective. This lens gathers light and focuses it to form an image. The other lens magnifies the image so that it can be observed by the eye. Sometimes the second lens is replaced with a camera so that the image can be recorded on film.

The larger the lens used in a refracting telescope, the greater the light-gathering power. But the construction of very large lenses is difficult. For this

Figure 26–27 *A refracting telescope uses a series of lenses to form an image of a distant object. The telescope at Yerkes Observatory in Wisconsin is the world's largest refracting telescope.*

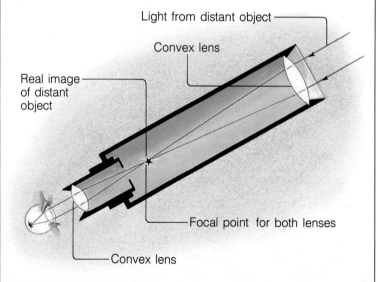

Light from distant object

Convex lens

Real image of distant object

Focal point for both lenses

Convex lens

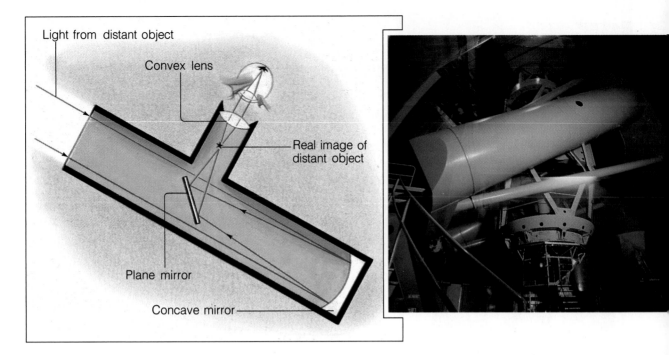

Light from distant object

Convex lens

Real image of distant object

Plane mirror

Concave mirror

Figure 26–28 *Light rays from a distant object are reflected from one mirror to another to produce an image in a reflecting telescope. The Hale Telescope at Mount Palomar Observatory in California is one of the world's largest reflecting telescopes.*

reason, telescopes were developed that use a large mirror instead of an objective lens. Large mirrors are easier to construct and support. A telescope that uses mirrors to gather light is called a reflecting telescope. The 200-inch Hale telescope at Mount Palomar in California is one of the world's largest reflecting telescopes.

Microscopes

When you want to get a better look at the detail of a nearby object, you bring it closer to your eye. But a person with normal eyesight cannot see an object clearly if it is closer than 15 centimeters from the eye. In addition, sometimes the object is just too small to see with the unaided eye. A microscope is used to aid the eye in magnifying nearby objects.

A microscope is similar to a refracting telescope, except that its goals are different. A microscope uses two convex lenses to magnify extremely small objects. One lens of the microscope, the objective, is placed at the end of the body tube close to the

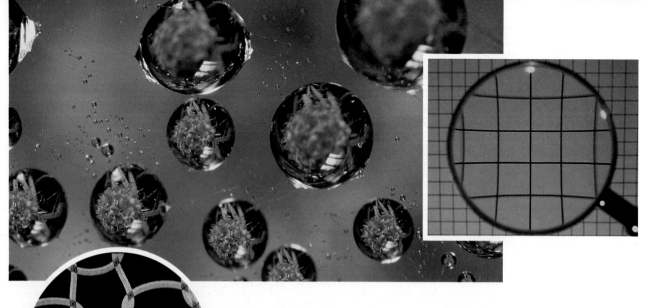

Figure 26–29 *These water droplets, captured by the web of a spider, show a clear image of a nearby flower. Droplets of water can act as convex lenses. A convex lens can also be used as a magnifying glass by placing the object within the focal length of the lens. A microscope uses two convex lenses to magnify images. This microscopic image shows the actual structure of a nylon stocking.*

object under inspection. The other lens, the eyepiece, is used to magnify the image formed by the objective. The total magnification produced by the microscope is the product of the magnification of the two lenses.

26–6 Section Review

1. Name three optical instruments. Explain what each does.
2. How are the parts of a camera similar to the parts of the eye?
3. Compare a refracting and a reflecting telescope.
4. How is a microscope similar to a refracting telescope? How is it different?

Critical Thinking—*Drawing Conclusions*
5. In some microscopes, oil rather than air is placed in the space between the two lenses. What effect might the oil have?

Guide for Reading

Focus on these questions as you read.

▶ What are the characteristics of laser light?

▶ How is laser light used in technology?

26–7 Lasers

A **laser** is a device that produces an intense beam of light of one color. The light given off by a laser is different from the light given off by an ordinary luminous object, such as the sun or a flashlight. Look at the light given off by the flashlight in Figure 26–30.

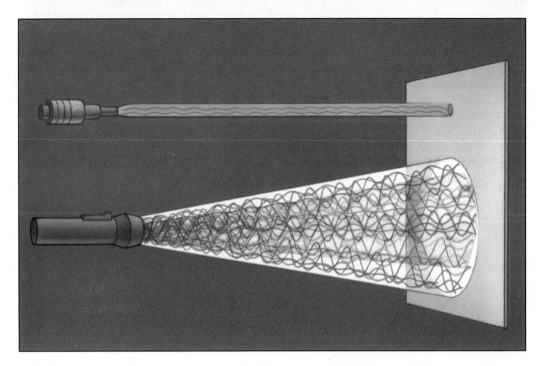

The light is a mixture of all the wavelengths of the visible spectrum. The light from the laser, however, is of only one wavelength. In the light given off by the flashlight, there is a mix of crests and troughs. The waves interfere, sometimes adding together and sometimes cancelling out. Eventually the light spreads out, decreasing its power. At a good distance from the flashlight, no light will be seen by an observer. In the laser, however, all the waves travel in step. The crests all travel next to one another and the troughs all travel next to one another. Light of the same wavelength that travels in step is said to be coherent light. **A laser is a device that produces coherent light.**

How Are Lasers Made?

In Chapter 25 you learned that electromagnetic waves are produced by moving charge. In the case of visible light, an electron in an atom absorbs a photon of energy and moves to a new position. The atom is said to be excited. When the electron releases the photon, it returns to its original position. But what happens if a photon hits an atom that is already in an excited state? The photon will not be absorbed by the excited atom. Instead, the photon will cause the excited atom to lose the energy it has already absorbed. The energy will be released in the form of a photon. Thus two identical photons that

Figure 26–30 *White light consists of a combination of wavelengths all traveling randomly. Laser light, however, consists of light of only one wavelength. All the crests and troughs of laser light travel together.*

Light Up Your Life

Your life would not be the same without the effects of light and its uses. Look around you and take note of the importance of light in your daily life. In addition to lighting up everything for you to see, consider the colors you notice and the instruments you use—including eyeglasses, telescopes, binoculars, and so on. Organize a list of at least ten examples. Explain how each example is made possible by light.

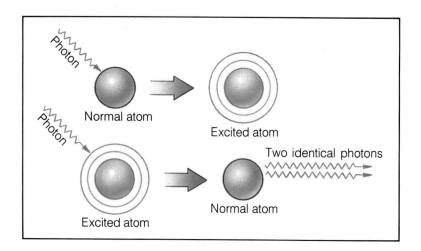

Figure 26–31 *When a photon hits a normal atom, its energy is absorbed and the atom becomes excited. When another identical photon hits the excited atom, the atom does not absorb the additional photon. Instead, it emits its extra energy so that two identical photons leave the atom, traveling in step with each other. What happens to the atom then?*

Photon

Normal atom

Excited atom

Photon

Excited atom

Normal atom

Two identical photons

Figure 26–32 *Earlier scientists were often unable to test their scientific theories because the necessary technology did not exist. But today, researchers such as Dr. Raymond Chiao of the University of California at Berkeley have a wide variety of sophisticated devices at their disposal. This gives them the exciting ability to test and witness the predictions of their predecessors. Dr. Chiao has used lasers to experiment with light and to confirm theories proposed by Albert Einstein.*

are traveling in step with each other will leave the atom. If these two photons hit two more excited atoms, the process will be repeated, ending with four photons. Then four photons will hit four more excited atoms, and so on. This process is called stimulated emission. The word laser comes from *l*ight *a*mplification by *s*timulated *e*mission of *r*adiation.

A laser uses this process to produce a huge number of identical photons. A laser consists of a tube containing gases, liquids, or solids. The element used is chosen by the properties of the laser light it produces. Different elements produce different wavelengths of light. A mirror is placed at each end of the tube. The mirrors will cause any photons traveling down the tube to bounce back and forth between the ends. As they move back and forth, the photons will strike more and more atoms and keep producing millions of identical photons. One of the mirrors is a partial mirror. Instead of reflecting all the light that strikes it, it lets a tiny bit go through. As the beam becomes strong enough, a small percentage of the coherent light escapes through this mirror. This light becomes the laser beam.

Although there are many kinds of lasers, they all have certain features in common. They all consist of a narrow rod with mirrored ends containing a material that can produce identical photons. One of the earliest types of lasers was the solid ruby laser. A ruby laser consists of a solid rod made of ruby crystals. The most common type of laser is the helium-neon laser.

A laser also needs a source of energy that can put as many atoms as possible in an excited state. If the atoms are not excited, they will absorb the photons that hit them rather than emit more photons. Many lasers use electricity, but others use intense flashes of light or chemical reactions.

Uses of Lasers

Lasers have uses in medicine, manufacturing, communication, surveying, entertainment, and even measuring the distance to the moon. Lasers are used in audio and videodiscs, computers, and printers. In the future, lasers may be used to produce an almost limitless supply of energy for nuclear fusion.

MEASUREMENTS Laser beams can be made so strong and can be focused so well that they can be bounced off the moon. By carefully timing how long it takes for a laser beam sent from the Earth to reflect off a mirror on the moon's surface (put there by Apollo missions) and return back to Earth, the distance to the moon has been calculated within a few centimeters.

Because laser light travels in such a straight line, a focused laser beam makes an exceptionally accurate ruler. Lasers were used to lay out the tunnels of the Bay Area Rapid Transit (BART) system in California.

MEDICINE Sometimes the retina of the eye becomes detached from the inner surface of the eye and produces a blind spot. To treat this condition, surgeons use laser beams to focus light at the tip of the detached retina and thereby weld it back without cutting into the eye.

Surgeons also use lasers as knives to cut through human skin and tissue. Lasers are replacing scalpels in certain kinds of surgery. Lasers have the special advantage of heating while they cut. The heat closes the blood vessels, thus reducing bleeding.

INDUSTRY Do you remember the compact discs you read about at the beginning of this chapter? Compact discs are produced and interpreted by laser beams. When a CD is made, sound is converted to electrical signals. The electrical signals are fed to the laser, which emits light as flashes that cause a pattern of flat areas and pits on the disk. The disk is then coated for protection.

When the CD is played, another laser beam shines on the disc as it spins. A small device records the reflection of the beam. However, the reflection

Figure 26–33 *You may have seen lasers used to produce entertaining light shows or to read bar codes at the local grocery store. But laser light is also commonly used in surgery. This argon laser beam is passing into the bone of the ear.*

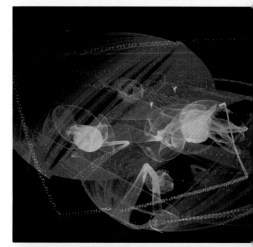

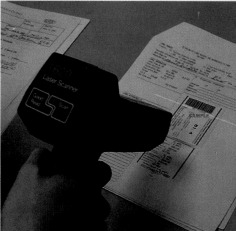

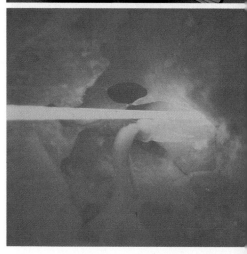

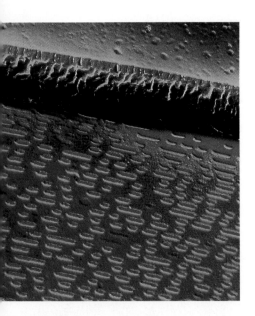

Figure 26–34 *The highly magnified surface of a compact disc shows the series of flats and pits that code the information it contains. The white portion at the top is its outer covering.*

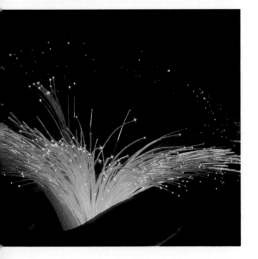

Figure 26–35 *Fiber optic cables carry laser light for use in communication, medicine, and industry.*

is not constant, due to the flats and pits. The device reads the changes as a code that is converted to electrical signals. This time, the electrical signals are sent to speakers, which reproduce the original sound waves. Video discs carrying both sound and pictures are now being produced in a similar manner.

Most products you buy in the supermarket contain UPC codes (Universal Product Codes). These codes are read when a laser beam bounces off them. The information is fed into a computer, which automatically puts the price into the cash register. This process minimizes mistakes and helps keep track of inventory.

Fiber Optics

Imagine strands of glass, some of them ten times finer than a human hair, replacing copper wire in cables used to transmit telephone and television signals. The strands of glass are so pure that you can see clearly through a block of them 20 kilometers thick. The glass cables can carry more information at higher speeds than copper cable can—and they occupy only one tenth the space.

Pure imagination? Absolutely not! These strands of glass are called **optical fibers.** Optical fibers transmit signals as flashes of light. You learned in Chapter 25 that information is often carried on radio waves. But the amount of information that can be carried on an electromagnetic wave increases as the frequency increases. Since light has higher frequencies than radio waves, much more information can be carried on a light beam than on a radio wave. The study and use of optical fibers is called fiber optics.

TOTAL INTERNAL REFLECTION The principle that allows glass fibers to carry light involves both reflection and refraction. You know that when light crosses into a new medium in which its speed changes, it bends, or refracts. The greater the angle at which it enters the new medium (the angle of incidence), the more it is bent. If the angle of incidence is great enough, the light is bent so much that it is reflected rather than transmitted through the new medium. This type of reflection is known as **total internal reflection.** Very little light is lost when it is totally reflected.

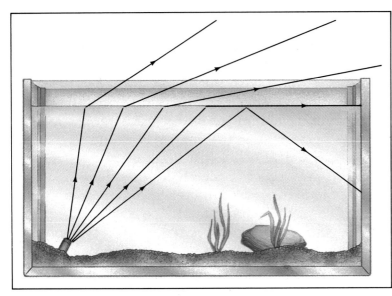

Figure 26-36 *Perhaps you have seen a light in the bottom of a fishtank or swimming pool. The angle at which the light is placed determines whether or not the light can leave through the top of the water. At any position greater than a certain angle, all light will be reflected back into the water. What is this principle called?*

Did you ever see a diamond sparkle brilliantly in the light? Diamonds would not sparkle if it were not for total internal reflection. In fact, raw diamonds are quite rough and dull. The angles cut into a diamond are precisely calculated so that all the light entering the diamond is reflected internally and emerges at the top. Diamond has a high index of refraction. This means that with proper cutting, all the light entering it can be reflected and directed to one point—the top. A poorly cut diamond will not sparkle. A diamond's brilliance is also caused by dispersion. The light that enters a diamond is broken up into the colors of the spectrum, making its reflections multicolored. In this case, what other object does a diamond act like?

You may be wondering what total internal reflection has to do with transmitting information through glass fibers. Well, it has everything to do with it! An optical fiber is like a "light pipe." If a beam of light is directed into one end of an optical fiber at the proper angle, it will always strike the walls at angles great enough to cause total internal reflection. Thus a ray of light is reflected so that it zigzags its way through the length of the fiber. Light entering one end of a fiber is internally reflected many times—as many as 15,000 times per meter—without being lost through the walls of the fiber. So signals do not fade away as easily as they do in copper wire.

When you talk on the telephone, your voice is converted into an electrical signal that goes to a tiny laser, no larger than a grain of salt. The laser transmits your voice as a series of flashes of light that

697

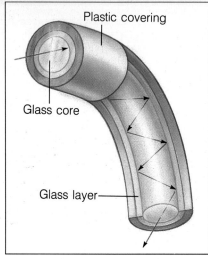

Figure 26–37 *By a continuous series of total internal reflections, laser light can be transported through an optical fiber. A tiny laser at the end of a fiber can shine light through a fiber, around a spool, and all the way to the end of the fiber.*

Plastic covering

Glass core

Glass layer

travel through the glass fiber. When you speak, you leave spaces between words and syllables. In the fiber, these spaces are filled with someone else's conversation. In this way, an optical fiber can carry a tremendous amount of information at one time. Optical fibers now in use can carry about 20,000 telephone calls at once! Just think of that the next time you are using the telephone. In addition, sound, pictures, and computer information can all be carried in the same cable.

The applications of fiber optics are not limited to communication. Advances in the field have made it possible for doctors to see inside a patient's body without having to perform surgery. Surgeons can snake a thin optical fiber through a portion of the body to a specific region such as the heart or the intestines. In this way, particular organs can be studied without the risks of surgery.

Holography

When you take a photograph of an object or scene, does the photograph turn out to be quite the same as you remember the scene to be? Probably not. The major difference between what you see and what a photograph records is dimension. You see objects in three dimensions. The reason for this is that light waves are reflected from every point on the object. At certain points, the reflected light waves overlap and interfere with one another. The interference pattern of the reflected waves gives the object its depth. A camera cannot capture that information. So photographs are only two dimensional.

There is a technology, however, that uses laser beams to form three-dimensional images. The technology is called **holography,** and the three-dimensional image is called a hologram. The word hologram comes from the Greek words *holos* and *gramma,* meaning whole message. Because holography captures all the information coming from an object, it provides depth as well.

Instead of recording an image, holography uses a laser beam to record the entire interference pattern created by the light reflected from an object—just as your eyes do. A laser beam is split into two parts. One part is sent directly to the film, and the other is sent to the object. The object then reflects this part of the beam to the film. At the film, the two halves of the beam interfere with each other, producing the same interference pattern that is recorded by your eyes.

A hologram is a record of the interference pattern. When you look at the piece of film that makes up a hologram, you do not see the image. In fact, a hologram looks more like a transparent piece of plastic with smudges on it. But when you shine the same type of laser beam that made the hologram through it, you see the object in three dimensions. What you are doing when you shine a laser beam through a hologram is making a set of light waves exactly like those originally reflected from the object. Just as with a real object, the image changes when you look at it from different angles.

Holography is currently being used in many interesting ways. Holograms are used on credit cards and clothing labels as security devices because the pictures are almost impossible to forge. Holograms are also used to test products for structural flaws. For example, technicians make holograms of new tires before and after subjecting them to stress. Putting one image on top of the other shows the flaws. Inside the human body, holograms can be used to give three-dimensional views of organs. And because holograms can store a tremendous amount of data in a limited space, they may someday be used to store books and other reference materials. Eventually, holography may even bring three-dimensional television pictures and artwork into your home.

Figure 26–38 *Holograms capture three-dimensional images on film. Notice the depth of the fruit hologram. By recording the interference pattern of light reflected off an object, such as a statue, a hologram can be made.*

26–7 Section Review

1. What is a laser? How is laser light made? How are lasers used?
2. Distinguish between white light and laser light.
3. What is total internal reflection? How is it related to fiber optics?
4. What are some applications of fiber optics?
5. What is a hologram? What are some uses for holography?

Critical Thinking—*Applying Concepts*
6. Why is it dangerous to look into a laser beam?

Laboratory Investigation

Convex Lenses

Problem

What kinds of images are formed by convex lenses?

Materials (per group)

convex lens
lens holder
light bulb and socket
blank sheet of paper
meterstick

Procedure 🧪 ▯▮

1. Place the convex lens in the lens holder and position them at least 2 meters in front of the lighted bulb.

2. Position the paper behind the lens so a clear image of the bulb can be seen on the paper. The sheet of paper must be positioned vertically. Record the position and relative size of the image.

3. Measure the distance from the lens to the paper. This is the focal length of the lens. Record the distance in centimeters.

4. Turn off the light bulb.

5. Move the bulb to a position that is greater than twice the focal length of the lens. Turn on the light bulb. Record the position and relative size of the image.

6. **CAUTION:** *Turn off the light bulb each time you move it.* Move the bulb to a position that is exactly twice the focal length. Record the position and relative size of the image.

7. Move the bulb to a position equal to the focal length. Record the position and relative size of the image.

8. Move the bulb to a position between the lens and the paper. This position is less than one focal length. Record the position and relative size of the image.

Observations

Describe the image formed in each step of the procedure for which you have made observations.

Analysis and Conclusions

1. Is the image formed by a convex lens always right side up? If not, under what conditions is the image upside down?

2. What happens to the size of the image as the bulb moves closer to the focal length? To the position of the image?

3. What happens to the size of the image as the bulb moves to less than the focal length? To the position of the image?

4. **On Your Own** Design and complete an experiment to study the images formed by concave lenses.

Study Guide

Summarizing Key Concepts

26-1 Ray Model of Light

▲ According to the ray model, light travels in straight-line paths called rays.

26-2 Reflection of Light

▲ The bouncing back of light when it hits a surface is called reflection.

▲ A plane mirror has a flat surface. A concave mirror curves inward. A convex mirror curves outward.

26-3 Refraction of Light

▲ The bending of light due to a change in speed is called refraction.

▲ A convex lens converges light rays. A concave lens diverges light rays.

26-4 Color

▲ The color of an opaque object is the color of light it reflects.

▲ The color of a transparent object is the color of light it transmits.

26-5 How You See

▲ Light enters the eye through the pupil. The amount of light that enters is controlled by the iris. The cornea and the lens refract light to focus it on the retina. The brain interprets the image.

26-6 Optical Instruments

▲ The image formed by a camera is real, upside down, and smaller than the object.

▲ A refracting telescope uses lenses to focus and magnify light. A reflecting telescope uses mirrors to gather light.

▲ A microscope uses lenses to magnify extremely small objects.

26-7 Lasers

▲ Light from a laser has one wavelength and forms an intense, concentrated beam.

▲ Optical fibers are long, thin, flexible fibers of glass or plastic that transmit light.

▲ A hologram is a three-dimensional picture made from laser light.

Reviewing Key Terms

Define each term in a complete sentence.

26-2 Reflection of Light
regular reflection
diffuse reflection
plane mirror
concave mirror
focal point
convex mirror

26-3 Refraction of Light
index of refraction
lens
convex lens
concave lens

26-4 Color
transparent
translucent
opaque
polarized light

26-5 How You See
pupil
iris
retina
cornea
rod
cone

nearsightedness
farsightedness

26-7 Lasers
laser
optical fiber
total internal reflection
holography

Chapter Review

Content Review

Multiple Choice

Choose the letter of the answer that best completes each statement.

1. Shadows can be explained by the fact that light travels as
   a. waves.   c. photons.
   b. curves.   d. rays.
2. The scattering of light off an irregular surface is called
   a. diffuse reflection.
   b. refraction.
   c. regular reflection.
   d. total internal reflection.
3. The point in front of a mirror where reflected rays meet is the
   a. aperture.
   b. focal length.
   c. focal point.
   d. index of refraction.
4. Crests and troughs of each wave are lined up with crests and troughs of all the other waves in
   a. incandescent light.   c. neon light.
   b. fluorescent light.   d. laser light.

5. A substance that does not transmit light is
   a. translucent.   c. transparent.
   b. opaque.   d. polarized.
6. The colored part of the eye is the
   a. iris.   c. retina.
   b. pupil.   d. cornea.
7. A nerve cell that responds to light and dark is a(an)
   a. cone.   c. rod.
   b. iris.   d. pupil.
8. Farsightedness is corrected by a
   a. convex mirror.
   b. convex lens.
   c. concave mirror.
   d. concave lens.
9. The process by which white light is separated into colors is
   a. reflection.   c. transmission.
   b. absorption.   d. dispersion.

True or False

If the statement is true, write "true." If it is false, change the underlined word or words to make the statement true.

1. An image that only seems to be where it is seen is a <u>real</u> image.
2. <u>Convex</u> mirrors are placed behind car headlights to focus the beam of light.
3. A mirage is an example of the <u>reflection</u> of light by the Earth's atmosphere.
4. A lens that is thicker at the ends than in the middle is a <u>concave</u> lens.
5. Frosted glass is an example of a <u>transparent</u> substance.
6. A telescope that uses mirrors to gather light is a <u>reflecting</u> telescope.
7. A <u>laser</u> is a device that produces coherent light.

Concept Mapping

Complete the following concept map for Section 26–2. Then construct a concept map for the entire chapter.

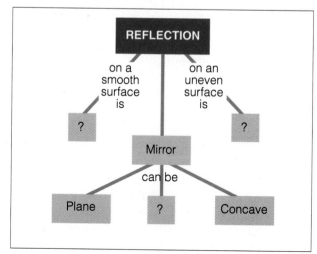

702

Concept Mastery

Discuss each of the following in a brief paragraph.

1. What is the ray model of light?
2. Compare a regular and a diffuse reflection.
3. Compare a real image and a virtual image. When you go to the movies, do you see a real or a virtual image on the screen?
4. When light passes from air into glass, which characteristic does not change: wavelength, frequency, or speed?
5. Explain why mirages form.
6. Explain why a spoon looks bent when you place it in a glass of water.
7. Describe the role of each part of the eye in sight.
8. How do polarized sunglasses help you to see in sunlight without squinting?
9. Why do you see a rose as red?
10. Describe two vision problems. How is each corrected?
11. What are two advantages of using large reflecting mirrors in astronomical telescopes?
12. What is the purpose of mirrors in a laser? Why is one less than 100 percent reflecting?
13. Explain how an optical fiber transmits light.
14. What is a hologram? How is it formed?

Critical Thinking and Problem Solving

Use the skills you have developed in this chapter to answer each of the following.

1. **Applying concepts** Why must the moon have a rough surface rather than a smooth, mirrorlike surface?

2. **Making calculations** The speed of light in a glass block is 150,000,000 m/sec. What is the index of refraction of the material?
3. **Applying concepts** A prism separates white light into the colors of the spectrum. What would happen if a second prism were placed in the path of the separated colors? Use a diagram in your answer.
4. **Making diagrams** Explain why you still see the sun setting just after it has truly set. Use a diagram in your answer.
5. **Identifying relationships** Why are roadways usually made of materials that are dark in color?
6. **Making inferences** Cones stop working in dim light. Explain why color seems to disappear at night.
7. **Making comparisons** Compare the structure and operation of a camera to that of the eye.
8. **Applying definitions** The lens at the end of a microscope tube has a magnification of $10\times$. The eyepiece lens has a magnification of $6\times$. What is the total magnification achieved by the microscope?
9. **Using the writing process** The technology is available to place a series of mirrors in orbit. These mirrors would reflect light back to Earth to illuminate major urban areas at night. Write a letter expressing your opinions about such a project. What do you think are some of the problems that would result from such a project? What are some of the benefits?

GAZETTE

ALLAN HOUSER:

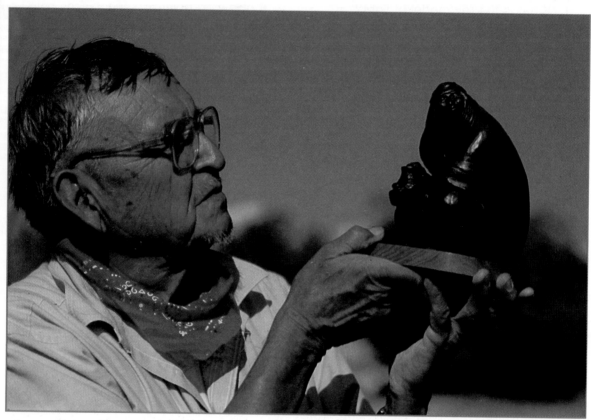

AN ARTIST'S ADVENTURE

Are you surprised to find a story about an artist in Adventures in Science? Perhaps you do not realize that a painter must be something of a scientist in order to use colors and light creatively. Sculptors also need to know scientific principles of force and balance to create a statue. One artist who has been both a painter and a sculptor is the Native American artist Allan Houser.

Allan Houser was born in Oklahoma to Apache Indian parents with the surname Haozous. His Apache background is evident in his appearance: keen glance, wide cheek-

bones, and sharply angled brows. His family was descended from a line of chiefs and leaders. In fact, his father, Sam Haozous, was one of Geronimo's warriors. Houser is what is known as a first-generation transitional Indian. This means that he has successfully built his life within the majority culture while still preserving a distinct sense of his Native American heritage.

Houser's parents lived and worked on a government-grant farm. For American Indians to survive as farmers was a continual challenge, and life was difficult. Although Allan began high school at Chilocco Indian School in northern Oklahoma, he had to drop out after the first year in order to work on the family farm. He never did return to high school. But after five years of working on the farm, he was able to begin art studies at the Painting Studio of Santa Fe Indian School.

Houser's career as a painter developed rapidly. After just two years of art school, he gained international recognition by having his paintings on display at the 1936 New York World's Fair. Three years later, he was commissioned to paint murals in the Department of the Interior building in Washington, DC. That same year, his paintings were displayed at the National Gallery of Art in Washington and at the Art Institute of Chicago.

Houser began sculpting in 1941. By this time, however, he was faced with financial problems. In order to support his family, he took a job as a construction worker and pipe-fitter's assistant. He continued painting and sculpting at night. After long years of struggle, in 1949 he received a Guggenheim Fellowship. With the fellowship, he once again had the freedom to devote himself to his work as an artist.

Houser draws much of the inspiration for his work from nature and the land. Granite cliffs, crumbling sandstone walls, rolling foothills, and valleys scooped by wind and rain all find their way into his painting and sculpture.

His love of nature keeps Houser in New Mexico. He often speaks of "doing research" there in much the same way that a scientist does. And, indeed, he is something of a scientist as he studies interesting rocks, fossils, and bones—especially skulls. Houser explains, "There are many very sculptural pieces in a skull. You can pull them apart and find unusual things, like the jaw bone [which is] a very strong form."

Since the beginning of his career, Houser's work has been drawn entirely from Native American themes. Yet, like all great art, his work transcends race and language. Houser's work is a link between modern life and the spirit of primitive culture. As a result, he has been able to do a great deal to advance the status of work by Indian artists.

Today, Houser is considered by many to be the greatest Native American artist. He has received many honors, but none that means more to him than the installation of one of his bronze sculptures in the United States Mission at the United Nations. Entitled *Offering of the Sacred Pipe*, the statue depicts a slender figure clothed in a feathered headdress and a cloak of animal skin. The figure holds aloft a sacred pipe as an offering to the Great Spirit. The strong upward lines of the figure symbolize humanity's search for lofty ideals, hope, and expanded potential. Former United Nations Ambassador Jeane Kirkpatrick described the statue as "A prayer for peace...a symbol of this country's identity and roots."

When he is not working as an artist, Houser enjoys playing music. So, as you can see, every aspect of Allan Houser embodies a wondrous spirit filled with vigor and life. His work and his life are composed of a beautiful union of color, light, sound, and nature.

▼ **Standing proudly outside the United Nations building, this bronze statue is a tribute to the strong spirit of Allan Houser and all that he believes in.**

For Further Reading

> If you have been intrigued by the concepts examined in this textbook, you may also be interested in the ways fellow thinkers—novelists, poets, essayists, as well as scientists—have imaginatively explored the same ideas.

Chapter 1: Exploring Physical Science

Freeman, Ira, and Mae Freeman. *Your Wonderful World of Science.* New York: Random House.

Kohn, Bernice. *The Scientific Method.* Englewood Cliffs, NJ: Prentice Hall.

Chapter 2: General Properties of Matter

Lipsyte, Robert. *One Fat Summer.* New York: Bantam.

Verne, Jules. *Twenty Thousand Leagues Under the Sea.* New York: Pendulum Press.

Chapter 3: Physical and Chemical Changes

Hawthorne, Nathaniel. "The Birthmark," in *Tales and Sketches.* New York: Viking Press.

McKillip, Patricia. *The Changeling Sea.* New York: Ballantine.

Chapter 4: Mixtures, Elements, and Compounds

Mahy, Margaret. *The Catalogue of the Universe.* New York: Macmillan.

Plotz, Helen. *Imagination's Other Place: Poems of Science and Math.* New York: Crowell.

Chapter 5: Atoms: Building Blocks of Matter

Asimov, Isaac. *How Did We Find Out About Atoms?* New York: Walker & Co.

Keller, Mollie. *Marie Curie.* New York: Watts.

Chapter 6: Classification of Elements: The Periodic Table

Konigsburg, E. L. *Father's Arcane Daughter.* New York: Atheneum.

Lowell, Amy. "Patterns," in *Selected Poems of Amy Lowell.* Cambridge, MA: Riverside Press.

Chapter 7: Atoms and Bonding

Bond, Nancy. *The Voyage Begun.* New York: Macmillan.

Botting, Douglas. *The Giant Airships.* New York: Time-Life Books.

Chapter 8: Chemical Reactions

Fox, Mary V. *Women Astronauts: Aboard the Space Shuttle.* Englewood Cliffs, NJ: Messner.

Krementz, Jill. *The Fun of Cooking.* New York: Knopf.

Chapter 9: Families of Chemical Compounds

Dolan, Edward F., Jr. *Great Mysteries of the Ice and Snow.* New York: Putnam.

Hendershot, Judith. *In Coal Country.* New York: Knopf.

Chapter 10: Petrochemical Technology

Merrill, Jean. *The Pushcart War.* New York: Addison-Wesley.

Whyman, Kathryn. *Plastics.* New York: Watts.

Chapter 11: Radioactive Elements

Dank, Milton. *Albert Einstein.* New York: Watts.

Nardo, Don. *Chernobyl.* San Diego, CA: Lucent.

Chapter 12: What Is Motion?

Cormier, Robert. *I Am the Cheese.* New York: Pantheon.

Sillitoe, Alan. *The Loneliness of the Long-Distance Runner.* New York: Knopf.

Chapter 13: The Nature of Forces

Store, Josephine. *Green Is for Galaxy.* New York: Argo Books.

Wells, H. G. *The Invisible Man*. New York: Watermill Press.

Chapter 14: Forces in Fluids

Ferber, Edna. *Giant*. Garden City, NY: Doubleday.
Gallico, Paul. *The Poseidon Adventure*. New York: Coward.

Chapter 15: Work, Power, and Simple Machines

Foster, Genevieve. *The Year of the Flying Machine: 1903*. New York: Scribner.
Gardner, Robert. *This Is the Way It Works: A Collection of Machines*. New York: Doubleday.

Chapter 16: Energy: Forms and Changes

Bograd, Larry. *Los Alamos Light*. New York: Farrar.
Bond, Nancy. *The Voyage Begun*. New York: Argo Books.

Chapter 17: What Is Heat?

Adler, Irving. *Hot and Cold: The Story of Temperature From Absolute Zero to the Heat of the Sun*. New York: John Day.
Doolittle, Hilda. *Collected Poems*. New York: AMS Press.

Chapter 18: Uses of Heat

Bradbury, Ray. *Fahrenheit 451*. New York: Ballantine.
Schneider, Stephen. *Global Warming*. New York: Random House.

Chapter 19: Electric Charges and Currents

Cosner, Sharon. *The Light Bulb: Inventions that Changed Our Lives*. New York: Walker.
Franklin, Benjamin. *Autobiography of Benjamin Franklin*. New York: Airmont.

Chapter 20: Magnetism

Averons, Pierre. *The Atom*. New York: Barron.
Vogt, Gregory. *Electricity and Magnetism*. New York: Watts.

Chapter 21: Electromagnetism

Farr, Naunerle C. *Thomas Edison—Alexander Graham Bell*. West Haven, CT: Pendulum Press.
Snow, Dorothea J. *Samuel Morse: Inquisitive Boy*. New York: Macmillan.

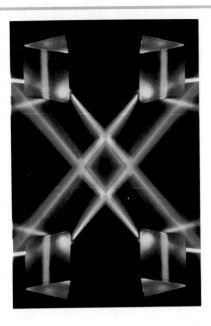

Chapter 22: Electronics and Computers

Chetwin, Grace. *Out of the Dark World*. New York: Lothrop, Lee & Shepard Books.
Clarke, Arthur C. *2001: A Space Odyssey*. New York: New American Library.

Chapter 23: Characteristics of Waves

Christopher, Matt. *Earthquake*. Boston: Little, Brown.
Olney, Ross. *A Young Sportsman's Guide to Surfing*. Nashville, TN: Thomas Nelson.

Chapter 24: Sound and Its Uses

Goffney, Timothy R. *Chuck Yeager: First Man to Fly Faster Than Sound*. Chicago: Children's Press.
Neimark, Anne E. *A Deaf Child Listened: Thomas Gallaudet, Pioneer in American Education*. New York: William Morrow.

Chapter 25: Light and the Electromagnetic Spectrum

Benchley, Nathaniel. *The Electromagnetic Spectrum: Key to the Universe*. New York: Harper & Row Junior Books.
Faraday, Michael. *Faraday's Chemical History of a Candle*. Chicago: Chicago Review.

Chapter 26: Light and Its Uses

Butler, Beverly. *Light a Single Candle*. New York: Pocket Books.
O'Neill, Mary. *Hailstones and Halibut Bones*. New York: Doubleday.

Activity Bank

Welcome to the Activity Bank! This is an exciting and enjoyable part of your science textbook. By using the Activity Bank you will have the chance to make a variety of interesting and different observations about science. The best thing about the Activity Bank is that you and your classmates will become the detectives, and as with any investigation you will have to sort through information to find the truth. There will be many twists and turns along the way, some surprises and disappointments too. So always remember to keep an open mind, ask lots of questions, and have fun learning about science.

CALCULATING DENSITY

Calculating the density of a regular solid such as a cube is easy. Measure the sides of the object with a metric ruler and calculate the volume. Place the object on a balance to determine its mass. Then use the formula D = M/V to calculate the object's density. But can you determine the density of an object that has an irregular shape and is not easy to measure? A rock, for example. It's easy when you know how. Follow along and you can become the density calculator for your class.

Materials

graduated cylinder
rock
small piece of metal pipe
large nut or bolt
triple-beam balance
metric ruler
string

Procedure and Observations

1. Select one of the objects whose density you wish to calculate. Place the object on a balance and determine its mass. Enter the mass in a data table similar to the one shown on page 713.

2. Place some water in the graduated cylinder. Look at the water in the cylinder from the side. The water's surface will be shaped like a saucer. Notice that the water level dips slightly in the center. Add water carefully until the lowest part of the water's surface (the bottom of the dip) is at one of the main division lines on the side of the graduated cylinder. Enter the water-level reading in your data table.

3. You are going to determine the volume of your irregularly shaped object by water displacement. To do this, first tie a piece of string around the object you are going to use. Make sure the string is well tied.

4. Hold the end of the string and carefully lower the object into the water in the graduated cylinder. Read the new water level. Enter this reading in your data table. Subtract the first water-level reading from the second to determine the volume of the object. Enter this volume in your data table.

5. Repeat this procedure for each remaining object.

6. Use the formula D = M/V to calculate the density of each object you selected.

DATA TABLE

Object	Mass	First Water Level	Second Water Level	Water Displaced (mL)

Analysis and Conclusions

1. What is the volume of an object whose dimensions are 1.0 cm × 6.0 cm × 2.0 cm? Remember to include the proper units.
2. If the mass of this object is 60 g, what is its density?
3. What are the densities of the objects you measured?
4. Which object is made of the densest material?

Think About This

1. If an object with a density of 10 g/cm^3 is cut into two equal pieces, what is the density of each piece? Why?
2. Could the water displacement method be used to determine the volume of a rectangular object as well as an irregularly shaped object?
3. Why is the density of a substance important?

WHAT "EGGS-ACTLY" IS GOING ON HERE?

This simple investigation can help you observe and better understand the concept of density and the effects of different densities. You might like to share the results of this investigation with your family and friends. It may amaze and astound them.

You Will Need

hard-boiled egg   teaspoon
saucer   box of table salt
large clear plastic
   container

spoon to remove the egg from the water. Place the egg in a small saucer and let it cool. As an alternative, you can also place the pan in the sink and let cold water run into the pan. The egg will cool more quickly this way.

2. Carefully place the egg at the bottom of your plastic container. Add enough water so that the container is three-quarters full. The egg should be covered by at least 10 cm of water.

3. Describe what you see and make a drawing of your setup.

4. Gradually add salt to the water in your container. Add the salt 1 teaspoon at a time. Stir the water carefully. Do not break the egg. If you are careful you can make egg salad at the end of this investigation! Describe what happens after you add each teaspoon of salt.

Now You Can Begin

1. You might be able to buy a hard-boiled egg from a delicatessen or your school's cafeteria. If you cannot, it won't take long to cook a hard-boiled egg yourself. *Ask a parent or other adult to help you with this procedure.* Place the egg in a small pan filled with cool water. Put the pan on a heat source. When the water starts to boil, begin to count off 10 minutes. At the end of this time, the egg is properly cooked. *Again ask an adult to help you now.* Use a large

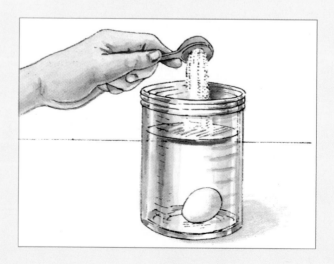

Seeing and Explaining

1. The position of the egg changed at some point. Describe any changes that occurred after adding salt.

2. Why do you think the changes occurred?

A Different View

Your family is undecided about where to spend summer vacation. Traditionally the family takes a vote, with each member casting one vote. The choice is between a cabin at a mountain lake or a trip to the seashore. Your younger brother likes to swim, although he does not swim very well. He will, however, cast the deciding vote. Be a "good egg" and apply what you have learned in this investigation to help your brother make a wise choice. Outline your thinking here.

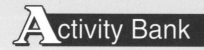
CRYSTAL GARDENING

Diamonds, sugar, and table salt have something in common. They all form crystals. In fact, many substances form crystals, but usually only under certain conditions. In this investigation you will be able to "grow" some salt or sugar crystals in the laboratory. You probably would also like to grow diamonds, but unfortunately the conditions needed to produce diamond crystals cannot be duplicated in the laboratory! You can work with a partner in this investigation.

Materials Needed

table sugar
table salt
2 small metal washers or nuts
2 wooden tongue depressors or sticks
    from an ice cream bar
2 heat-proof plastic jars
sauce pan
source of heat
teaspoon
string

What to Do

1. Pour a cup of water into a sauce pan and place the pan on a source of heat. **CAUTION:** *You will need an adult's permission and help during this part of the investigation.*

2. Add 1 teaspoon of salt to the water as it heats. Do not let the water boil. Keep stirring the solution. Keep adding salt, 1 teaspoon at a time. Observe the water as you add the salt. At some point, after you have added a quantity of salt, any additional salt will appear to take a long time to dissolve. At this point, add 1 more teaspoon of salt. Remove the pan from the heat.

3. Put the pan on a heat-resistant surface. Prepare the rest of your apparatus as the water cools. Tie one end of a piece of string to the washer or nut. Wind the other end of the string around the piece of wood as shown in the diagram. Adjust the length of the string so that when the piece of wood is placed across the top of the jar, the washer at the other end of the string does not touch the bottom of the jar.

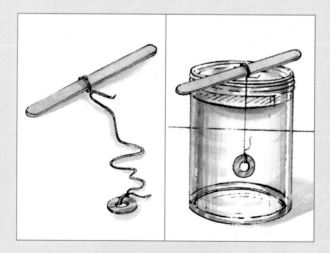

4. When the pan has cooled, carefully pour the saltwater solution into the jar. Place the jar in a spot where it can remain undisturbed for several days.

5. Repeat the above procedure using table sugar instead of table salt.

Observations

1. After several days examine the two jars. Describe what you see. Accompany your description with a drawing.

2. What was the solvent and the solute in each of the solutions from which you grew your crystal gardens?

Something to Think About

On June 25, 1992, NASA launched space shuttle Columbia on its longest mission yet. One of the experiments that was conducted on this mission was to grow crystals of zeolite, a compound formed from aluminum and silica. Scientists wanted to see if larger and more perfect crystals of this compound could be produced in space. What variable do you think scientists were testing in this experiment? Explain your answer.

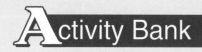

Activity Bank

HOW TO WATCH THE FOODS YOU EAT

Today almost everyone is watching their weight and is showing concern about the foods they eat. To be a wise consumer you should know what nutrients are contained in the foods you eat. This investigation will show you ways in which you can test the foods you eat to see if they contain fats and starches.

Materials

small samples of cooking oil, butter, bread, cut piece of potato, carrot, cooked bacon, potato or corn chip, other food samples
iodine solution
2 medicine droppers
large brown paper bag
scissors

Before You Start 📛

You will use two simple tests to find out if your food samples contain fats and starches. You can use the results of the first two tests you perform as comparisons for your other samples.

1. Use a medicine dropper to place a drop of the iodine solution on the cut side of a piece of potato. **CAUTION:** *Be careful not to spill the iodine solution on your clothing. It will stain.* A potato con-

tains starch. The reaction you observe when iodine is placed on a potato is considered a positive test for starch. Record your observations in a data table.

2. Test other food samples with the iodine solution. Compare these results with the potato-iodine test you performed in step 1. Record these results in your data table.

3. Use your scissors to cut the brown paper bag along the sides. Open up the bag to form a single sheet of paper. Use a clean medicine dropper to place a drop of cooking oil on an area of the paper bag. Hold the paper up to a source of light and observe the spot. Record your observations in your data table. The spot you observe is considered to be a positive test for the presence of fats.

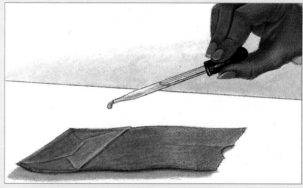

4. Test other food samples by rubbing a small amount of each sample on brown paper if it is a solid or by placing a drop of the sample on the brown paper if it is a liquid. Compare the results to the result you obtained with the cooking oil. Record your observations in your data table.

Observations

1. What is a test for starch?
2. What foods contain starch?
3. What is a test for fats?
4. What foods contain fats?

Using What You Learned

1. Did the results of any of these tests surprise you? Why?
2. These two tests are qualitative tests; that is, they show whether a food contains fats or starches. However, they do not show how much fat or starch a food contains. Why would it be important to know how much fat or starch is in a particular food?

On Your Own

Prepared foods list the amounts of nutrients they contain on their label. Collect some food labels and analyze them. Prepare a report for your classmates about your findings.

ACID RAIN TAKES TOLL ON ART

You may have read headlines similar to the one above and wondered how a gentle rain, pitter-pattering on your window panes, could be strong enough to wear away stone. Imagine that a city government has hired you to investigate how acid rain and other forms of acid precipitation are affecting its buildings and outdoor statues. How would you go about this task? What problems would you encounter? What solutions would you propose? Building a model in your laboratory might help you to study the problem of acid rain.

You Will Need

piece of soft chalk
nail
clear vinegar
medicine dropper
shallow pan
petri dish
plastic wrap

Now to Work 👁

1. Place the shallow pan in front of you on your desk or table. Working over the shallow pan will make cleanup easier when you are finished. Use the nail to carve a figure from the piece of chalk. (Chalk is calcium carbonate, the compound that makes up limestone and marble.) Include some surface details in your carving—eyes and hair are

good. Remember, you will not be graded on your artistic abilities!

2. Place your carving in the middle of the pan. Fill a medicine dropper with vinegar. Let several drops of the vinegar drip onto your "work of art." Vinegar contains acetic acid diluted in water.

3. Repeat the vinegar treatment five more times. Observe the effects each time.

4. Place a petri dish in the pan and set your carving on its side in the dish. Pour enough vinegar into the petri dish to just cover your carving.

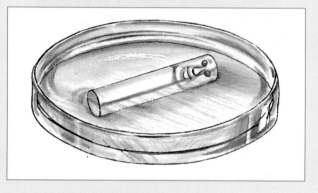

5. Cover the petri dish with plastic wrap and store it overnight in a place where it will not be disturbed.

6. Observe your carving after the overnight treatment.

Observing and Thinking

1. What happened to your carving when vinegar was dropped on it?

2. How did the length of time your carving was exposed to vinegar affect the details on your carving? How do your findings relate to city buildings and sculptures?

3. Studies have shown that the rate at which acid rain dissolves limestone and

marble is much slower than the rate at which vinegar dissolves chalk. How would this fact affect your study?

4. What steps could be taken to prevent further damage to city buildings and sculptures from acid rain? Be innovative in your suggestions.

5. What long-term action should be taken to eliminate the problem of acid rain?

Cooperating With Others

Library research: Find out the causes of acid rain and other forms of acid precipitation. Make a report on your findings. Offer suggestions to deal with this problem.

Field work: With a teacher's or parent's permission, make a survey of the effects of acid precipitation on the buildings or statues in your city or town. If you are fortunate enough to live in an area where acid rain is not a problem, you might like to make a survey of the effects of other environmental conditions on buildings and statues. You might like to make drawings or take photographs to illustrate your findings.

Several friends or classmates can work with you on this project. Their skills, ideas, and abilities can improve the quality of a project.

HUNTING FOR TREASURE IN TRASH

This is a long-term research project you can do with several of your classmates. What you discover should be shared with your class—maybe even with other classes in your school.

Some Help Before You Begin

All substances—the foods you eat, the clothes you wear, the bus that takes you to school, and the spaceship that may some-day take you to the moon—are made of matter. You already know that all matter is made of elements—elements alone or ele-ments combined with other elements to form compounds.

Planet Earth, in fact, can be thought of as a giant "element bank or storehouse" in which elements are withdrawn, used, and eventually discarded or recycled. The ways in which we live our lives determine whether these materials are used wisely.

Located below are several ideas that offer some direction for your research pro-ject. Your project should begin in your li-brary and is limited in scope only by your desires. A good book for you to borrow from your local library is: *How to Do Suc-cessful Science Projects* by Norman F.

Smith (Revised Edition), published by Julian Messner in 1990.

1. Find out which elements used by mod-ern society to make different substances are reusable. Find out if your community is recycling materials. You might like to develop, with your classmates, a program to recycle mate-rials in your school. Check your plan with your teacher.

2. Nature also recycles materials. When an animal or a plant dies, the substances that make it up are used again as part of the continuous cycle of life on Planet Earth. You might like to investigate the rate at which different kinds of materials break down in the environment. A series of experiments can be set up to determine the rate of breakdown, or even if materials will break down. After you develop a plan of study, check with your teacher for his or her ideas about the soundness of your proposed project.

Eventually you might like to make a pre-sentation to your school board or even to the mayor of your town about your findings and suggestions.

Activity Bank

WHAT IS THE EFFECT OF PHOSPHATES ON PLANT GROWTH?

One warm, sunny day, Frank and Marie decide to go for a hike in the country. After walking for some time, they see a lake in the distance. It looks beautiful, and from afar seems like an ideal place to stop and rest. As they approach the water, however, they notice an awful smell. It smells as if something is rotting. When they reach the shore, Frank and Marie notice that the lake is covered with a green mat of water plants. They notice dead fish floating. What could have caused this disaster?

Sometimes seemingly harmless chemicals have effects that are not easily predictable. For example detergents are often used to clean clothes and dishes. Phosphates, a group of chemicals found in some detergents, have been banned by some communities. In this investigation you will measure the effects of phosphates on plant growth. Then, maybe, you will have a clue to explain the observations of the two unhappy hikers.

Materials

2 large test tubes with corks or stoppers to fit
test-tube holder, or large plastic jar or beaker
2 sprigs of *Elodea*
detergent that contains phosphates
medicine dropper
sunlight or a lamp
small scissors

Before You Begin

Make sure that the detergent you use contains phosphates. Many do not. *Elodea*

is a common water plant used in home aquariums. A local pet store is a good source of supply.

Procedure

1. Take two sprigs of *Elodea*. Use your scissors to cut the sprigs to the same length. Measure the length of the sprigs and record the length in a data table similar to the table below. Place a sprig of *Elodea* into each test tube.

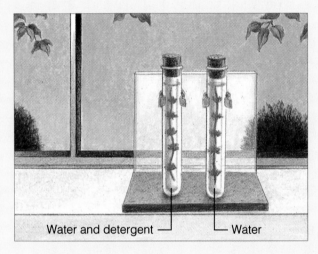
Water and detergent — — Water

2. Add enough water to each test tube to fill it nearly to the top. Be sure to cover the *Elodea* sprig with water.

3. Place a small pinch of detergent into one test tube. Gently swirl the test tube to mix the water and detergent. Leave plain water in the other test tube.

4. Stopper each test tube.

5. Place the test tubes in a test-tube rack or jar. Place the rack or jar in a sunny window or under another source of light.

(continued)

6. Every three days for a month, carefully remove and measure each *Elodea* sprig. Record your measurements in your data table. Place the sprigs back into the test tubes from which they were removed. **Note:** *Do not mix up the sprigs.*

DATA TABLE

	Day	3	6	9	12	15	18	21	24	27	30
Water											
Water + Detergent											

Observations

1. What was the control in this experiment? Why?

2. Describe the *Elodea* that was placed in plain water.

3. Describe the *Elodea* that was placed in water that contained the detergent drops.

4. Why was it important to return each sprig to the correct test tube?

Analysis and Conclusions

1. Did the detergent affect the *Elodea's* growth?

2. How do you explain the result of this investigation?

Going Further

Most of the communities that ban the use of detergents that contain phosphates are concerned about the quality of their water supply. How might the effect of phosphates on water plants affect a community's water supply?

HOT STUFF

If you look around, you will find that many of the objects and structures you depend on every day are made of metal. Metals have quite interesting and useful characteristics. One of the most important of these is the fact that metals are excellent conductors of both heat and electricity. In this activity you will find out just how well metals conduct heat.

For this activity, you will need several utensils (spoons or forks) made of different materials, such as silver, stainless steel, plastic, wood, and so forth. You will also need a beaker (or drinking glass), hot water, a pat of frozen butter, and several small objects (beads, frozen peas, popcorn kernels, or raisins).

Press a small glob of butter onto the top of each utensil. Make sure that when the utensils are stood on end, the butter is placed at the same height on each. Be careful not to melt the butter as you work with it. Press a bead, or whatever small object you choose, into the butter. Stand the utensils up in the beaker (leaning on the edge) so that they do not touch each other. Pour hot water into the beaker until it is about 6 cm below the globs of butter.

Watch the utensils for the next several minutes. What do you see happening?

Make a chart listing the material each utensil is made of, and the order in which the bead fell into the water.

Which do you expect to fall first? Which actually does?

Combine your results with those of your classmates. Make a class chart showing all of the materials used and the order in which the beads fell.

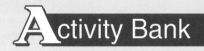
Have you ever squeezed a drop of dishwashing detergent into a pot full of greasy water to watch the grease spread apart? The reason this happens has to do with the molecular structure of both the grease and the detergent. Rather than bonding together, these molecules (or at least parts of them) repel each other and move away. In this activity, you will experiment with a similar example of substances that rearrange themselves when mixed together.

What You Will Need

baking sheet or roasting pan
milk (enough to cover the bottom of the sheet or pan)
food coloring of several different colors
dishwashing detergent

What You Will Do

1. Pour the milk into the baking sheet or pan until the bottom is completely covered.

2. Sprinkle several drops of each different food coloring on the milk. Scatter the drops so that you have drops of different colors all over the milk.

3. Add a few drops of detergent to the middle of the largest blobs of color. What do you see happening?

■ Can you propose a hypothesis to explain your observations?

Can you picture a meadow filled with wild flowers ranging through all the colors of the rainbow? The beautiful colors of flowers depend on combinations of chemicals carefully selected by Nature. But just as they are formed, they can also be destroyed. In this activity you will create a chemical reaction that affects flower colors.

You will need several flowers of different kinds and colors, a large jar or bottle with a lid (a clean mayonnaise jar or juice bottle will do and a plastic lid is preferable), a rubber band, scissors, and household ammonia (about 50 mL).

Procedure

1. Gather the flowers so that all of the stems are in a bunch. Use the rubber band to hold the stems together. You may have to twist it around the stems more than once.

2. Cut a large hole in the jar lid with the scissors. The gathered stems of the flowers must be able to fit snugly through the hole. **CAUTION:** *Be careful when using sharp instruments.*

3. Push the stems through the hole so that when the lid is placed on the jar, the flowers will be suspended inside the jar.

4. Pour a little ammonia into the jar—enough to cover the bottom. **CAUTION:** *Do not breathe in the ammonia vapors.*

5. Carefully place the lid with the flowers on the jar. Look at the flowers after 20 to 30 minutes. Do you observe any changes in them? If so, what do you see happening?

6. Compare your results with those of your classmates who may have used different flowers. Record the overall results.

Thinking It Through

■ The pigments that give flowers their beautiful colors are present along with chlorophyll, which is green. Chlorophyll is the substance that makes photosynthesis (the food-making process in plants) possible. What do you think happened during this activity to explain your observations?

■ In tree leaves, colorful pigments are also present along with chlorophyll, but in this case the green chlorophyll hides the colorful pigments. What must happen to give leaves their stunning autumn colors?

POPCORN HOP

What do you see when you pour soda or other carbonated drinks into a glass? From experience, you probably know that you see bubbles continually rising to the top—thanks to the carbonation. In this activity you will create a chemical reaction similar to the one occurring in soda and you will use it to make popcorn kernels hop!

Materials

large, clear drinking glass, beaker, or jar
15 mL (1 Tbsp) baking soda
food coloring (a few drops)
45 mL (3 Tbsp) vinegar
popcorn kernels or raisins or mothballs (handful)
stirrer (or long cooking utensil)

Procedure

1. Fill the glass container with water.

2. Add about 15 mL of baking soda, a few drops of food coloring, and stir well.

3. Drop in the popcorn kernels (or raisins/mothballs) and stir in 45 mL of vinegar. Watch the kernels for the next several minutes. What do you observe happening? (If the action slows down, add more baking soda.) Explain what you see in terms of chemical reactions.

■ In an effort to preserve the natural environment, people are beginning to use Earth-friendly cleaning products. For example, rather than dumping poisonous chemicals into a sink, a mixture of hot water, vinegar, and baking soda can be used to clean drains. Why do you think this works?

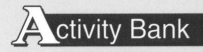
TOASTING TO GOOD HEALTH

Have you ever been given toast when you weren't feeling well? For some reason, toasted bread seems easier on your digestive system than untoasted bread does. In actuality, the reason is no mystery. It has to do with a chemical reaction involving the heat from your toaster. In this activity you will discover the difference between plain bread and toasted bread.

Materials

slice of white bread
slice of white toasted bread
household iodine (5 mL or 1 tsp)
drinking glass or 250-mL beaker
baking dish (or bowl with a flat bottom)
spoon (measuring spoon would be helpful)

Procedure

1. Fill the drinking glass or beaker half-full with water.

2. Mix 5 mL (about 1 tsp) of iodine into the water. Carefully pour the water-iodine solution into the baking dish.

3. Tear off a strip (about 2 cm wide) from the plain slice of bread. Dip the strip in the solution.

   ■ Do you observe any changes in the bread?

4. Tear off a strip of the same size from the toasted bread. Dip this strip in the solution.

■ Do you observe any changes in the toast?

■ When starch and iodine are combined, they react to form starch iodide, which is a bluish-purple. For this reason, iodine is used to test for starch. Knowing this, what can you learn from your observations?

■ What type of chemical reaction is involved in toasting—endothermic or exothermic?

■ The process of food digestion begins in your mouth. Part of this process involves breaking starches down into simpler substances. As a result of doing this activity, can you now explain why toast is sometimes recommended when you are not feeling well?

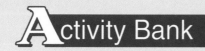

IN A JAM

You have probably seen or used litmus paper to determine whether a substance is an acid or a base. But did you know that litmus paper is not the only material that can be used as an acid-base indicator? It may surprise you to learn that many foods can also do the job in a pinch! In this activity you will experiment with just such an indicator.

Materials

blackberry jam (a spoonful is enough)
warm water
small drinking glass
household ammonia (several drops)
lemon juice or vinegar (several drops)
spoon
medicine dropper

Procedure

1. Fill the drinking glass half-full with warm tap water.

2. Put a spoonful of jam into the water and gently stir it with the spoon until it is dissolved. The water-jam solution should turn a reddish color.

3. Use the medicine dropper to put a few drops of ammonia into the solution. Stir the solution once or twice. What happens to the color of the solution?

4. Clean the medicine dropper. Use the clean dropper to add several drops of lemon juice or vinegar to the solution. Clean the spoon and again stir the solution. What happens to the color of the solution this time?

5. Compare your observations with those of your classmates who added the substance that you did not—lemon juice or vinegar. What happened to their solutions?

■ The jam solution is red when an acid is added to it and greenish-purple when a base is added. From your experiment, determine whether ammonia, vinegar, and lemon juice are acids or bases.

The Next Step

Repeat the experiment several more times, each time using a different test substance. You may choose such substances as milk, juice, soda, or fruit. Be sure to clean the spoon between each stirring. Make a chart showing which substances are acids and which are bases. Combine your observations with those of your classmates.

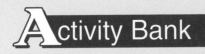

Activity Bank

OIL SPILL

You have probably seen television news reports or read newspaper articles about the devastation caused by an oil spill from a supertanker or other holding vessel. But initial reports often underestimate the full spectrum of the damage. In this activity you will simulate interactions with oil so that you can more clearly understand the dangerous consequences of an oil spill.

Materials

medicine dropper
small graduated cylinder
motor oil, used
fan
tongs
3 hard-boiled eggs, not peeled
paper towels
shallow baking pan, about 40 cm × 20 cm
white paper, 1 sheet
graph paper, 1-cm grid
beaker or jar (must be able to hold 3 eggs)

Procedure

1. Partially fill a shallow baking pan two-thirds full with water.

2. Pour the motor oil into the graduated cylinder.

3. Use the medicine dropper to remove 1 mL of oil from the graduated cylinder. Gently squeeze the oil out of the dropper into the center of the pan of water. Describe the interaction between the water and oil.

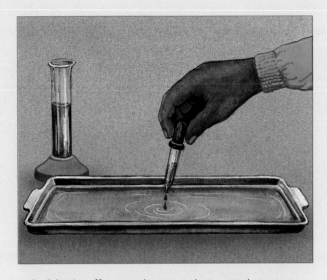

4. Mark off a region on the graph paper that is the same size as the baking pan. After several minutes, sketch the arrangement of oil in the pan of water. When you are finished drawing, count up the number of squares on the graph paper covered by oil. Remember, the area now covered was produced by only 1 mL of oil! Assuming that oil always spreads proportionately, make a chart showing the area that would be covered by 2 mL, 10 mL, 100 mL, and 1 L.

5. Place a fan beside the pan of water and oil. Turn it on and determine if the flow of air affects the spread of oil. What do you discover?

6. Now try shaking the pan slightly. Be careful not to spill the contents. Does this reaction affect the oil at all?

(continued)

7. Gently place the three hard boiled eggs in the jar or beaker. Pour oil into the container until it is full. Place the container under a strong light.

8. After 5 minutes use the tongs to carefully remove one egg. Remove the excess oil with a paper towel. Peel the egg. What do you observe?

9. Remove the second egg after 15 minutes. Peel this egg and record what you observe. Remove the third egg after 30 minutes. Again peel the egg and record your observations.

The Big Picture

1. Supertankers carry millions of liters of oil. In light of your calculations, what can you say about the implications of a large oil spill?

2. What did you learn by blowing air on the oil and by shaking the water? What conditions did these procedures represent? How do these conditions affect the severity of oil spills?

3. What effect could oil have on the eggs of birds nesting near ocean water that becomes contaminated with oil?

THE DOMINO EFFECT

Have you ever played with dominoes? If so, you know that dominoes can be arranged into all sorts of complicated patterns that enable you to knock them all down from a gentle tap on just one domino. Beyond playing, the falling action of dominoes can be used to represent a very complex phenomenon—a nuclear chain reaction. In this activity, you will need 15 dominoes and a stopwatch to learn more about nuclear chemistry.

Procedure

1. Place the dominoes in a row so that each one is standing on its narrow end. Each domino should be about 1–1.5 cm from the next one.

2. Gently tip the first domino in the line over so that it falls on the one behind it. You have just initiated a chain reaction.

   ■ What keeps the reaction going?

   ■ How can the row of dominoes be likened to a nuclear chain reaction?

3. Now arrange the dominoes as shown in the accompanying figure.

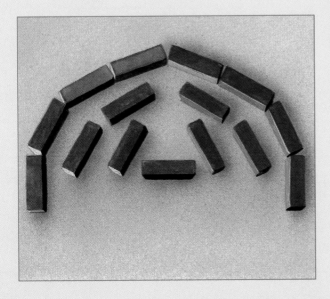

4. Gently tip over the center domino. How does this arrangement differ from the first one?

   ■ If the dominoes again represent atomic nuclei, how is this chain reaction different from the first one?

5. Which arrangement of dominoes do you think falls faster? Find out. Arrange the dominoes back into a single row. Use the stopwatch to measure the length of time from when you tip the first domino until the last domino falls. Record the measurement. Return the dominoes to the second pattern. Again record the time from the tip of the first domino to the fall of the last one. Which arrangement falls faster?

6. Now set up the dominoes as shown in the accompanying figure.

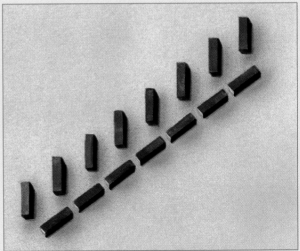

7. Tip the leftmost domino. Record the amount of time it takes for the dominoes to fall.

   ■ How does the length of time it takes for the dominoes to fall in this pattern compare with the times for the other two patterns?

(continued)

■ How can you explain this arrangement in terms of a nuclear chain reaction?

8. Design your own arrangement for the dominoes. Determine how long it takes for all the dominoes to fall from this arrangement. Compare this time with those of the other arrangements and with those of your classmates. Make a chart or a poster showing the different arrangements and the length of time recorded for each one.

What This All Means

■ Why might it be important to slow down a reaction?

■ After completing this activity, can you think of how nuclear chain reactions can be controlled in nuclear power plants?

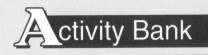

Activity Bank

Did you get into trouble the last time you launched a paper airplane across a room? Under the right circumstances (such as during a classroom activity), however, paper airplanes can be used to learn a lesson or two about motion. In this activity you will build and fly paper airplanes so that you can practice calculating speed and distance as well as learn a bit about designing an airplane.

What You Need

sheets of paper of various weights and sizes

stopwatch with a second hand

meterstick

string

adhesive tape

paper clips

stapler with staples

What You Do

1. As a group, construct a paper airplane using the materials provided. Design it any way that you would like.

2. Once all of the groups in your class have finished building their airplanes, get together to set up a flight-test area for the airplanes. This is the location in which you will hold an airplane-flying contest. It should be a large open space with few obstacles. You should also devise a set of rules by which the flights will be judged. For example, all flights should begin from the same spot. You may wish to place a piece of tape on the floor to mark the starting point for the flights. You should also decide when the time measurement begins (such as at the release of the airplane), and to where distance is measured (some airplanes will slide after they reach the floor). **CAUTION:** *The test area should be carefully controlled so that no one walks into the flight pattern. A pointed airplane nose can be quite dangerous.*

3. Now assign each group member one of the following roles: Thrower, Timer, Distance measurer, Recorder. Throw several test flights with your airplane. Each time measure the duration of the flight and the distance the airplane flew. Record this information in a data table similar to the one shown. Then use the information to calculate the airplane's speed. Take turns assuming the role of the thrower so that each group member gets a chance.

(continued)

4. Now you are going to have a friendly competition with your classmates. When everyone is ready, take turns throwing your airplanes. Have independent recorders take the measurements and record them in another data table.

What You Saw

DATA TABLE

	Time (sec)	Distance (m)	Speed (m/sec)
Trial 1			
Trial 2			
Trial 3			

What You Learned

1. How did you calculate speed? What was the slowest speed for your group's airplane? The fastest? What about in the entire class?

2. How would you want your data to change if you are trying to decrease speed? (*Hint:* How would you change distance and time?)

3. Were the speeds you calculated actual or average speeds?

4. Did you notice anything about the slowest airplanes and the shape of their flight paths? You may need to see them flown again.

5. Compare the designs of the fastest airplanes with those of the slowest. How are they alike? Different? How would you redesign your airplane to make it move more quickly? More slowly?

The Next Step

Redesign your airplane to make it move faster. Repeat the activity, but this time see if the change in design achieves a faster speed.

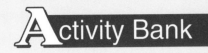
SMOOTH SAILING

If you have ever watched a rocket being launched, you know what a spectacular sight it can be. But what you may not have realized is that a rocket's blastoff can be described by Newton's third law of motion. Newton explained that for every action there is an equal and opposite reaction. In the case of a rocket, the burning fuel pushes out in one direction, forcing the rocket to move in the other direction. In this activity you will experiment with Newton's third law of motion by designing a "rocket-powered" boat.

Materials

1.89 L (half-gallon) milk or juice carton
scissors
balloon (hot-dog shaped)
bathtub or sink filled with water

Procedure

1. Wash the carton thoroughly. Using scissors, carefully cut one long side from the carton. You may find it helpful to begin your cut by poking a small hole in the carton with the sharp end of the scissors.

2. Again using the scissors, carefully cut a small hole near the center of the bottom of the carton. Do not make the hole too big.

3. Place the hot-dog shaped balloon in the carton and run its neck through the hole in the bottom of the carton.

4. Blow up the balloon but do not tie it. Instead, use your fingers to keep the neck of the balloon closed and the air in the balloon.

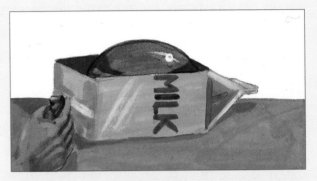

5. Place your balloon boat in a bathtub or sink filled with water. Let go of the balloon's neck and observe what happens.

Analysis and Conclusions

1. What happened when you released the balloon?

2. What did the boat use as fuel?

3. What would happen if you blew less air into the balloon? More air? Try it.

4. How is the balloon boat an example of Newton's third law of motion?

The Next Step

Predict what will happen to the boat's speed if you place some cargo in the boat. To find out, use small masses such as marbles, stones, or coins. Repeat the boat run several times, each time gradually increasing the mass of the cargo. Make sure that you blow the same amount of air into the balloon each time.

- What happens to the boat's speed and the distance it travels as you continue to add cargo to it?

- Which of Newton's laws of motion explains these observations?

737

AT THE CENTER OF THE GRAVITY MATTER

Have you ever balanced a ruler on your finger? If so, you know that it balances only when its center is placed on your finger. Placing any part of the ruler other than its center on your finger will not provide the desired result. This is because the center of the ruler is where the ruler's center of gravity is located. All objects have a center of gravity. The center of gravity of an object is the point on which gravity seems to pull. In reality, gravity pulls downward on every point on an object. Yet when the forces on all of the points are added together, it is as if the total force of gravity pulls on only one point—the center of gravity.

Not all objects are quite as predictable as a ruler. In fact, the center of gravity for some objects is not even on the object! Do you know where your center of gravity is? Find out by gathering a bandana or handkerchief and a wooden block or chalkboard eraser and performing the following steps.

What to Do

1. Stand with the entire left side of your body against a wall. Make sure your left foot is up against the wall. Now try to lift your right foot. What happens?

2. Now stand with your back against a wall. Be sure your heels are touching the wall. Drop a bandana or handkerchief just in front of your toes. Try to pick it up without bending your knees or moving your feet. Describe what happens.

3. Place a mat or blanket on the floor. Get down on your elbows and knees on top of the mat or blanket. Place your elbows on the floor right in front of your knees. At the tip of your middle fingers, place a wooden block or blackboard eraser on its edge. With your hands

behind your back, lean forward and try to knock the block over with your nose. Can you do it?

What to Think About

Make a chart showing the results for your class—who was able to hit the eraser and who wasn't. Overall, are girls or boys more successful? Why do you think this is so?

Try Again

Repeat step 3 but this time place weights in your back pockets or on your ankles. If weights are not available, have a friend hold your ankles down. Does this change your results?

What to Understand and Apply

1. Why do you think it is important for the center of gravity of a car or truck to be located in a proper position? What can happen if it is too high?

2. Why do you think tightrope walkers use long poles to help balance themselves?

LIGHT ROCK

In the Activity Bank activity on page 738, you learned about the center of gravity—what it is and how it affects you in many different ways. You can alter the center of gravity of an object only by altering the object. In this activity you will investigate the rather interesting results of altering an object's center of gravity.

Materials You Will Need

standard cork from a bottle (2.5 cm to 3 cm in diameter)
sewing needle
knitting needle or bamboo skewer
2 candles about 8 cm long and 1.5 cm in diameter
2 drinking glasses of equal height
several sheets of newspaper
box of matches

Procedure 🔥

1. Push the sewing needle sideways through the cork. **Note:** *Be careful not to break the needle and do not place your hand in such a way that the needle can poke you as it goes through the cork.*

2. Carefully slide the bottom of one candle onto one end of the sewing needle so that the needle extends to the center of the candle and the candle extends out

from the cork. See the accompanying diagram. Repeat this procedure for the other candle.

3. Push the knitting needle lengthwise (bottom to top) through the cork. Be careful not to hit the sewing needle. (You may need to direct the knitting needle slightly above or beneath the sewing needle.) Place the setup over two drinking glasses that have been turned upside down. Make sure the glasses are placed on top of several sheets of newspaper.

4. Light both candles. **CAUTION:** *Be careful when using matches.* Observe the setup for several minutes.

Observations and Conclusions

1. What happens when the candles are lighted? Why?

2. How could you alter the center of gravity of other objects, such as cars?

PUTTING GRAVITY TO WORK

If someone asked you what gravity does, you might say that it is responsible for pulling you to the ground when you stumble over a stone or fall off your bicycle. While these answers are painfully correct, it is important to realize that gravity is more often an extremely helpful force. In addition to keeping you from flying off the Earth's surface, gravity has important applications in the operation of many modern devices. In this activity you will find out how gravity can be used to test the strengths of various materials.

Materials

ring stand and ring

masking tape

plastic or paper cup

strips of several different kinds of paper
(14 cm x 3 cm); examples include
paper towels, tissue paper, toilet paper,
wrapping paper, writing paper, and
typing paper

250-mL beaker

sand, 250 mL

balance

several sheets of newspaper

Procedure

1. Tape one end of the first paper strip to the ring. Tape the other end to the rim

of the plastic or paper cup. Spread some newspapers below the cup.

2. Fill the beaker with sand. Slowly pour the sand from the beaker into the cup. Stop pouring when the paper begins to tear. Be careful not to let the cup fall because the sand will spill out of it.

3. Remove the cup with the sand in it and discard the paper strip. Use the balance to measure the mass of the cup with the sand in it. On a separate sheet of paper, make a data table similar to the one shown on the next page. Make sure your data table includes all of the different types of paper you have. Record the mass in the appropriate column in your data table and return the sand to its container.

4. Repeat steps 1, 2, and 3 using each of the different strips of paper. Make sure the cup is clean each time.

5. Calculate the weight held by each paper strip by multiplying the mass you recorded by 9.80 N/kg. (**Note:** *Make sure you convert the masses from grams to kilograms first by dividing them by 1000.*)

Observations and Calculations

DATA TABLE

Sample	Mass (g)	Weight (N)
A		
B		
C		
D		

Analysis

1. Which type of paper supports the greatest weight? The least?
2. How did the investigation differentiate the types of paper by their strengths?
3. Why is gravity a good choice of force to use to measure the strength of the different materials?

The Next Step

Repeat the experiment but this time cut the papers at a 90° angle to the direction in which you cut them the first time. For example, if you cut a letter size sheet of paper lengthwise, cut it widthwise this time. How does this affect your results? Can you propose a hypothesis as to why?

WATERING YOUR GARDEN GREEN

Have you ever grown a plant or kept a garden? Whether you have or have not, the first item you probably think is required for such an endeavor is soil. After all, how can you grow a plant without soil? But you can! In this activity you will grow a small garden without soil—thanks to the principles of fluid pressure.

Materials

large plastic container	small plastic container with a lid
nail	hammer
nylon stocking	twist tie
white glue	Perlite or sand
water	houseplant fertilizer
spoon	seedlings
plastic aquarium tubing (60 cm)	

Procedure

1. Using the hammer and nail, punch a hole in one side of each container near the bottom. The hole must be large enough to accommodate the plastic tubing. Take care, however, not to crack the containers. If you find it easier, you may want to use clean milk or juice cartons instead of plastic containers. Make another hole in the center of the lid of the smaller container.

2. Place a piece of nylon stocking over one end of the aquarium tubing. Secure it there with the twist tie. Push this end into the hole in the large container. Push the other end of the aquarium tubing into the bottom hole in the small container.

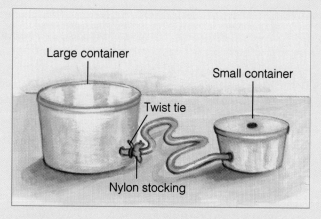

3. Surround the holes with glue so that they become watertight. Let the glue dry thoroughly.

4. Fill the large container with wet Perlite and the small container with water. Add a pinch of fertilizer to the water in the small container, stir, and put on the lid. Place the seedlings in the large container. You have completed the construction of your garden.

5. To make your garden grow, put it on a sunny windowsill. Feed it once a day by lifting the water container higher than the plant container. When the water container empties, place it lower than the plant container and it will fill up again. There, you have fed your garden for the day.

6. Once a month add fresh water to the water container and stir in a pinch of fertilizer. Enjoy the results of your "green thumb"!

Analysis

1. Why does lifting the small container affect the plants in the large container?

2. Why do you need to put fertilizer in the water?

3. What would happen if a small leak or hole developed in the tubing?

4. What is the purpose of using the nylon stocking?

5. Can you think of a common device that operates in a manner that is somewhat similar to this water garden?

DENSITY DAZZLERS

One scorching summer afternoon, while out in a row boat with your friend Alex and your dog Sam, you learn a quick lesson about density. It all begins when Sam jumps up to bark at a duck, then Alex stands up to grab Sam, and before you know it, you are all in the water. After putting on your life vests, you begin to look around for the rest of your belongings. The boat is floating nearby—upside down, unfortunately. The soccer ball you brought is floating beside the plastic utensils that were with your lunch. But where is your lunch? And where is your radio? Why did they sink if everything, and everyone, else is floating?

The answer to why some objects float and others do not has to do with density. An object can float only if it is less dense than the substance it is in. In this activity you will complete your own investigations into density. But don't worry—you won't get wet!

Materials

2 250-mL beakers
cooking oil (about 125 mL)
ice cube
salt
spoon or small sheet of tissue paper
   (optional)
hard-boiled egg or raw potato
medicine dropper
dishwashing liquid
food coloring

Procedure

1. Fill a beaker half-full with cooking oil. Very gently place an ice cube on the surface of the oil. What happens to the ice cube? Watch the ice cube for the next 15 to 20 minutes. What happens as the ice cube melts?

2. Use the dishwashing liquid to thoroughly clean the beaker. Fill the beaker half-full with water. Make sure you know the volume of water you put in.

3. Dissolve plenty of salt in the water. The amount of salt will vary depending on exactly how much water you use. Stop adding salt when the water becomes cloudy.

4. Add the same amount of water you used in step 2 to another beaker. Do not add salt this time. Slowly pour the water into the beaker containing the salt water in such a way that it does not mix with the salt water. You may need to pour it over a spoon or sheet of tissue paper so that it hits the salt water more gently.

5. Gently place an egg or small potato in the beaker. Describe and draw what you see.

6. Clean out the two beakers. Add a small amount of hot tap water, about 10 mL, to one of the beakers. Add food coloring to the hot water. You can choose any color that you wish, but make sure you add enough food coloring to the water so that you can see the color well.

7. Fill the other beaker with cold tap water.

8. Use a medicine dropper to pick up a few drops of the hot colored water.

9. Place the tip of the medicine dropper in the middle of the cold water. Now slowly squeeze a drop of the hot colored water into the cold water. Describe and draw a picture of what you see.

Analysis and Conclusions

1. Explain the observations you made when watching the ice cube you placed in the oil in step 1.

2. Explain your observations regarding the egg in the beaker of water.

3. What does your experiment tell you about the density of hot water as compared to that of cold water?

4. Predict what will happen if you repeat steps 6 to 9 but this time add cold colored water to hot water. Try it. Are you correct?

BAFFLING WITH BERNOULLI

Have you ever tried to perform a magic trick for your friends or family? What makes a magic trick work is knowing the secret. Well, now you can use Bernoulli's principle to amaze and baffle others who don't know about forces and fluids, as you do!

What You Will Need

2 drinking straws	Ping-Pong ball
drinking glass	thumbtack
2 balloons	halved index card
fine thread	wooden spool (the
tape	kind used for
small funnel	cotton thread)

What You Will Do

Part A

1. For the first "trick," hold a drinking straw upright in a glass of water so that the bottom of the straw is slightly above the bottom of the glass.

2. Use a second straw to blow a stream of air across the top of the first straw. (If you have only one straw, you can cut it in half to make two straws.) Vary the force with which you blow the stream of air.

- What happens when you blow into the second straw?

- What happens when you blow harder?

- Can you explain why this "trick" is possible?

Part B

If your audience was impressed with what happened with the straws, they'll really be excited by this next "trick."

1. Blow up two balloons. Tie about 60 cm of thread to each one. Use tape to hang them from the top of a door frame, light fixture, or low ceiling, about 5 cm apart.

2. Have your audience predict what will happen to the balloons if you blow a stream of air between them. Go ahead and do it. (You may find it easier to blow through a straw that you hold between the balloons.)

- What happens? Was your audience correct in their prediction?

Part C

In this next display, you will set out to defy gravity. Do you think it can be done?

1. Hold the small funnel upright and place a Ping-Pong ball in it. Blow through the narrow end of the funnel.

- Can you blow the ball out? Why or why not?

2. Now turn the funnel downward and hold the Ping-Pong ball inside it with your hand. Blow on the funnel again and let go of the ball. What do you think will happen when you let go?

- What does happen? Why?

Part D

This last "trick" will surprise everyone— maybe even you!

1. Push a thumbtack through the middle of a halved index card.

2. Hold the index card and tack under the wooden spool so that the pin projects into the hole of the spool. Blow hard down through the other hole in the spool and let go of the card. What do you expect will happen?

- What happens to the index card?

The Next Step

Design a poster that relates each of these "tricks" to Bernoulli's principle. Together with your classmates, come up with additional examples of Bernoulli's "trickery" and add them to your poster.

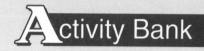

Activity Bank

CRAZY EIGHTS

Have you ever watched the pendulum swinging in a grandfather clock? There is something about it that truly captures one's attention. The pendulum always swings as far to the right as it does to the left in a regular repeating pattern. But what do you think would happen if a pendulum was made to swing on another pendulum? In this activity you will find out.

Materials

plastic funnel
heavy wire (about 120 cm long)
sheet of paper
several sheets of newspaper or wrapping paper
sand (or salt or sugar)
3 lengths of string, about 1 m each
scissors
metric ruler
compass
adhesive tape

Procedure

1. Use the scissors to poke three small holes in the funnel near the edge of the larger end. The holes should be evenly spaced around the opening.

2. Tie an end of one string to one of the holes. Repeat this for the remaining two strings and two holes.

3. Wrap the heavy wire around the rim of the funnel to make it heavy. You may wish to have a partner hold the strings out of the way so that they do not become tangled in the wire.

4. Use the compass to draw a circle on the sheet of paper. The radius of the circle (the distance from the center to

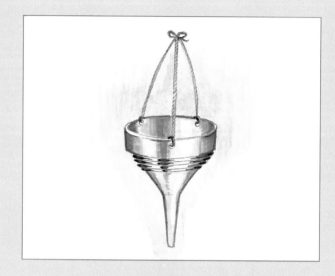

the edge) should be slightly less than the height of your funnel. Cut out the circle. Then make one straight cut from the edge to the center.

5. Fold the circular piece of paper into a cone that will fit into your funnel. When you have found the right size, tape it so that it holds it shape. Then cut a small hole in it at the point and place the cone in the funnel.

6. Arrange two chairs or desks about 60 cm apart with several sheets of newspaper or wrapping paper spread on the floor between them. Tie one string to the back of each chair or desk. With your fingers, pull these two strings together about 30 cm above the funnel. Pull the remaining string up to this point. Secure the three strings together at this point with a narrow piece of adhesive tape. (If the adhesive tape is not strong enough, you may want to use a small piece of wire or twist tie. Do not tie the strings together because you will need to adjust this length later on.)

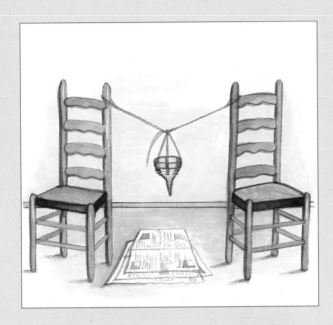

7. Cover the narrow funnel opening with your finger. Pour fine sand (or salt or sugar) into the funnel. Pull the funnel to the side and let go, removing your finger as you do so.

■ What do you see happening to the sand or salt?

■ What would happen if the funnel was supported by only two strings?

8. Make a chart listing the distance between the funnel and the gather where you placed the adhesive tape. Next to that information, draw the pattern created by the sand (or salt or sugar). Leave room on your chart for several more trials.

9. Carefully pick up the edges of the newspaper or wrapping paper so that the sand moves to the center. Then pour it back into its container. Repeat the activity several times, each time changing the length of the string below the gather where you placed the adhesive tape by moving the tape up or down. Add the data and the drawings to your chart.

■ When you are finished, share your observations with those of your classmates. How are your observations similar to theirs? How are they different? Did anyone find any surprising or unusual observations?

■ Do you think your results would change if you pulled the funnel back further to start the motion? What about if you pulled it less? Why? Try it and see.

MAY THE FORCE (OF FRICTION) BE WITH YOU

When you rub your hands together, they feel warmer. What causes your hands to warm up? The answer is friction. Friction is a common force that resists motion. Friction is caused by one surface rubbing against another surface. In this activity you will measure and compare the force of friction on two different surfaces, one smooth and one rough. Where do you think the force of friction will be greater—on the smooth surface or the rough surface?

Materials

spring scale
small weight
sandpaper
tape

Procedure

1. Attach a small weight to a spring scale. A spring scale measures weight in units called newtons. What is the weight of the object in newtons?

2. Place the weight on a smooth, flat surface, such as a table top. Use the spring scale to pull the weight across the surface of the table. How much force is shown on the spring scale? Subtract the weight of the object from

the amount of force shown on the spring scale. The result is the force of friction for the table top. What is this force in newtons?

3. Tape a piece of sandpaper to the table top. Repeat step 2, but this time use the spring scale to pull the weight across the sandpaper. What is the force of friction for the sandpaper? Is the force of friction greater for a smooth surface or for a rough surface? Was your prediction correct?

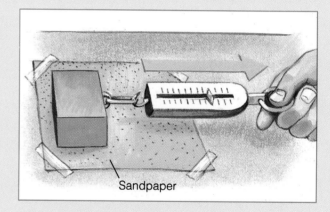
Sandpaper

Do It Yourself

Have you ever used sandpaper to smooth the rough edges of a piece of wood? What happens to the wood when you rub it with the sandpaper? Try it and find out.

Think for Yourself

You may have seen beautifully polished samples of rocks and minerals as part of a display in a museum of natural history. During the grinding and polishing process, water is sprayed onto the rock surface. Based on what you know about friction, why do you think this is done?

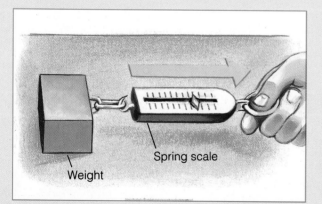
Spring scale
Weight

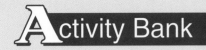

ONE HUNDRED DEGREES OF SEPARATION

Temperature is measured with a thermometer. All thermometers have a scale, or a set of numbers, that allows you to read the temperature. On a Celsius thermometer, the scale runs from 0°C (the freezing point of water) to 100°C (the boiling point of water). In this activity you will calibrate, or mark the scale on, an unmarked thermometer.

Materials

unmarked thermometer
2 beakers
ring stand and ring
Bunsen burner
ice
glass-marking pencil
metric ruler

Procedure

1. Place the unmarked thermometer in a beaker of water. Heat the water over a Bunsen burner until the water begins to boil. **CAUTION:** *Be careful when using a Bunsen burner.*

2. When the column of liquid in the thermometer stops rising, remove the thermometer from the beaker.

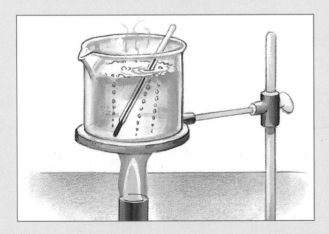

CAUTION: *The thermometer will be hot.* Mark the point at which the liquid stopped rising. What is the temperature at which the liquid rose as high as it would go in the thermometer? Write this temperature next to the mark you made on the thermometer.

3. Allow the thermometer to cool a bit. Then place the thermometer into a beaker of ice water. When the liquid stops falling, remove the thermometer from the beaker. Mark the point at which the liquid stopped falling. What is the temperature at which the liquid fell as low as it would go? Write this temperature next to the mark you just made on the thermometer.

4. Using a metric ruler, divide the space between the high point and the low point into 10 equal parts. Mark these divisions. How many degrees does each mark represent?

Think for Yourself

Suppose you wanted to calibrate your thermometer using the Kelvin scale instead of the Celsius scale. What number would you write next to the highest mark? The lowest mark?

THESE "FUELISH" THINGS

Just as rocket fuel provides the energy needed to launch the Space Shuttle, so the food you eat contains fuel that provides your body with the energy you need every day. This fuel is in the form of stored energy called potential energy. You cannot measure the amount of potential energy in food directly. Instead, you can measure the heat energy, in calories, gained by water when a sample of food is burned. The heat energy gained is equal to the heat energy lost by the burning food.

Food sample

Paper clip

Pie plate

Materials

triple-beam balance
assorted food
   samples
   (peanuts, bread,
   and so forth)
flask
matches

ring stand and
   clamp
paper clip
aluminum pie plate
Celsius thermometer
clock or watch

Procedure 🧪 🔥 👉

1. Find the mass of the empty flask in grams.

2. Half fill the flask with water and find the mass of the flask and the water. Then subtract to find the mass of the water alone. Record this mass in a data table similar to the one shown.

3. Clamp the flask onto the ring stand. Measure and record the temperature of the water (T_i).

4. Carefully straighten the paper clip and stick it through the food sample.

5. Position the paper clip so that the ends rest on the edges of the pie plate.

6. Use a match to ignite the food sample. **CAUTION:** *Be careful when using matches.* Once the food begins to burn, blow out the match and dispose of it safely.

7. Place the pie plate directly below the flask. Let the food burn for 3 minutes and then blow out the flame. Record the temperature of the water as T_f in your data table.

Observations

DATA TABLE

Food Sample	Mass of Water (g)	Temperature (°C)	
		T_i	T_f

Analysis and Conclusions

1. Use the following equation to calculate the heat energy gained by the water in the flask as the food burned:

Heat gained = Mass x Change in temperature x Specific heat

= Mass x (T_f - T_i) x 1 cal/g•°C

2. How much heat energy was lost by the burning food sample? (Remember, heat gained = heat lost.)

3. Share your results with the rest of the class. Make a class data table showing the results for the different food samples tested. Which food sample released the most heat energy? The least?

4. Most of the heat energy lost by the burning food was absorbed by the water in the flask. What might have happened to any heat energy that was not absorbed by the water?

LET THE SUN SHINE IN

How does a passive solar-heating system work? In this activity you will build a simple model to find out. You will need two shoe boxes, plastic wrap, tape, scissors, and two Celsius thermometers.

1. Cut a square "window" at one end of each shoe box.

2. Tape a piece of clear plastic wrap over each window.

3. Place a thermometer inside each box. Be sure that the temperature inside the boxes is the same (near normal room temperature, about 20°C). Then place the lid on each box.

4. Place both shoe boxes in direct sunlight. Position one box so that its window faces the sun. Position the other box so that its window faces away from the sun. Which box do you predict will get warmer? Why?

5. After about 30 minutes, open the boxes and read the temperature on each thermometer. Which shoe box got warmer? Was your prediction correct? Based on your results, how do you think the windows of a house should be oriented to get the most benefit from a passive solar-heating system?

On Your Own

As a class project, you might want to design and build a more elaborate model of a passive solar home. What conditions should you consider when designing your model?

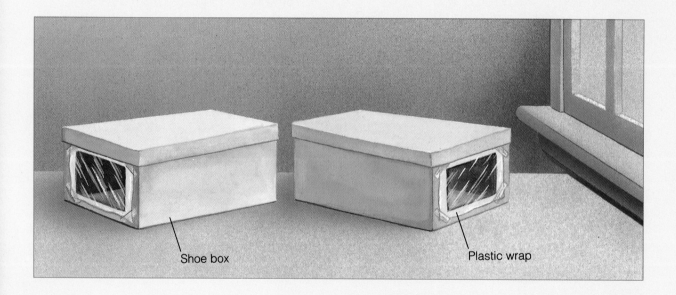

Shoe box

Plastic wrap

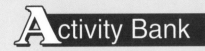

TURN DOWN THE HEAT

Most of the energy we use every day comes from fossil fuels—coal, oil, and natural gas. Unfortunately, supplies of fossil fuels on Earth are limited. How can we make supplies of fossil fuels last longer? Most environmentalists recommend using fuel-efficient engines as one way to conserve energy. Another solution is the use of proper insulation for homes and other buildings. The better insulated a building is, the less fuel it will need for heating and cooling. There are many kinds of insulating materials. Which one is the best insulator? Let's find out.

Materials

assorted insulating materials
2 bowls
2 baby food jars
graduated cylinder
2 Celsius thermometers
clock or watch

Procedure

1. Choose a material that you think would be a good insulator. Place a layer of the material in the bottom of a small bowl.

2. Place an empty baby food jar on top of the insulation. Then pack more of the insulation around the sides of the jar.

3. Place a second jar directly into another small bowl. Do not put any insulation around this jar.

4. Carefully fill each jar with the same amount of hot water. **CAUTION:** *Do not use boiling water.*

5. Place a thermometer in each jar and record the temperature of the water as T_i in a data table similar to the one shown.

6. After 15 minutes, record the temperature of the water in each jar as T_f in your data table. To find the change in temperature, subtract T_f from T_i. Record the change in temperature in your data table.

7. Repeat this procedure using different insulating materials.

(continued)

Observations

DATA TABLE

Insulating Material	Temperature (°C)		Temperature Change
	T_i	T_f	

Analysis and Conclusions

1. Which of the insulating materials you tested was most effective in preventing heat loss? How do you know? Is this material currently being used for insulation? If so, where?

2. Do you think any of the insulating materials you tested could be used to insulate buildings? Why or why not?

Going Further

Share your results with the class. Prepare a class data table listing all the different types of insulating materials tested. Which material was the best insulator?

Think for Yourself

1. Suppose you had discovered a new, more efficient insulating material. How would you convince a builder to use this insulation even though it is more expensive than other insulating materials?

2. Do you think the government should encourage private citizens to make better use of insulation in their homes? Why or why not?

GIVE IT A SPIN

An object can acquire charge in a number of ways. One way is by friction, a process in which two objects are rubbed together. Another way is by conduction. In this case, two objects that are in contact with each other transfer charge between them. Still another way is by induction, in which a charged object brought near but not in contact with another object causes charges to rearrange themselves. In this activity you will make a normal drinking straw spin about by experimenting with two of these methods of charging.

What Materials to Gather

2 soda straws
jar (medium to large in size)
fine thread, 20 cm long
rubber comb
cloth made out of wool
scissors

What Procedure to Do

1. Tie the thread around the middle of one of the drinking straws. Lay this drinking straw across the mouth of the jar so that the thread hangs at least a few centimeters above the bottom of the jar. If the thread is too long, trim it with the scissors until it is the correct length.

2. Cut the other drinking straw in half. If you have a narrow jar, you may need to cut it shorter. The straw must be able to fit horizontally in the jar.

3. Tie this piece of drinking straw to the end of the thread attached to the first straw.

4. Lay the full straw back across the mouth of the jar so that the thread with the smaller straw hangs inside.

5. In a room where humidity is low, rub the comb briskly with the wool cloth. Hold the comb up to the outside of the jar. Observe what happens.

6. Rub the comb again and touch it to the jar in a different location. Observe what happens.

7. Repeat the process several more times, but each time place the comb on the jar in a different spot—even drag it around the jar. Observe what happens.

8. Try this activity in a humid environment. You can choose a steamy bathroom or a sink filled with hot water. Observe what happens in this environment.

What Ideas to Think About

1. What observations did you make in step 5?

2. What happens to the small straw in step 6?

3. Describe your observations in step 7.

4. What forms of electrical charging occurred in this activity?

5. Can you explain your observations?

6. What did you observe in step 8?

7. Why won't this activity work in high humidity?

757

SNAKE CHARMING

Do you think static electricity and snakes have anything to do with each other? They may if the snake is made out of tissue paper. In this activity, you will take advantage of static electricity to charm a snake.

Materials You Need

large sheet of tissue paper
silk handkerchief or scarf
plastic pen
metal plate or tray
scissors
compass
metric ruler

What You Do

1. Use the compass to gently draw a circle on the tissue paper. Be very careful not to tear the paper. The diameter of the circle should be about 20 cm. Then use the scissors to cut the circle out of the tissue paper.

2. Place the pen at the center of the circle and draw a spiral that extends out to the edge of the circle. Again, draw very delicately so as not to tear the paper.

3. Slowly cut along the spiral line you drew on the paper. Cut only along the line so that when you are finished you are left with a continuous length of tissue paper.

4. Lay the tissue paper spiral on the metal plate or tray.

5. Rub the pen vigorously with the silk handkerchief or scarf.

6. Place the end of the pen slightly above the center of the spiral and slowly lift the pen.

What You Saw and Why

1. What happens to the spiral as you lift the pen?

2. What was the purpose of rubbing the pen with silk?

3. How would you describe static electricity?

4. What eventually happens to the tissue-paper snake?

COVER UP

Have you ever heard an object described as having been electroplated? Electroplating is the process in which one metal is gradually deposited on another metal by means of electricity. Modern pennies, in fact, are made primarily of zinc and then electroplated, or covered, with copper. Sometimes jewelry is made of less expensive metals and then electroplated with gold to give it the appearance of gold. In this activity you will investigate a simple example of electroplating.

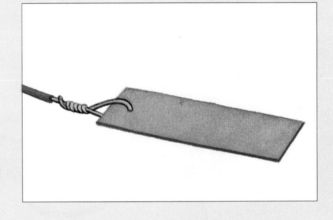

Materials

milk or juice carton, 95 mL (1 qt)

copper strip (about 2.5 cm x 7.5 cm)

several tablespoons of salt

100 mL of vinegar

2 lengths of wire, 30 cm each

key or other metal object that you have permission to use

fresh battery

scissors

tablespoon

Procedure ◀▌▊

1. Use the scissors to carefully cut around the carton about 5 to 6 cm from the bottom. Discard the top of the carton and make sure that the bottom is thoroughly cleaned.

2. Poke a small hole in the end of the copper strip about 1 cm from the end.

3. Remove the insulation from the ends of the wire. Thread the end of one length of wire through the hole in the copper strip and twist it tightly back onto itself as shown in the accompanying diagram.

4. Bend the end of the copper strip with the wire attached so that it can hang on the edge of the carton. Carefully hang it on the edge so that the wire is on the outside of the carton.

5. Pour vinegar into the container until most of the copper strip is submerged.

6. Add a tablespoon of salt to the vinegar and stir. If all the salt dissolves, keep adding salt and stirring until no more salt can be dissolved. You will know this point because the salt will begin settling to the bottom. This means that you have made a saturated solution.

7. Attach the free end of the wire to the anode on the top of the battery.

8. Connect one end of the other piece of wire to the cathode and the other end to the key (or other metal object) by looping the wire through the keyhole and twisting it. *Remember, you must obtain permission to electroplate the object.* Electroplating will not affect the use of the object. Make sure the object is clean and dry.

(continued)

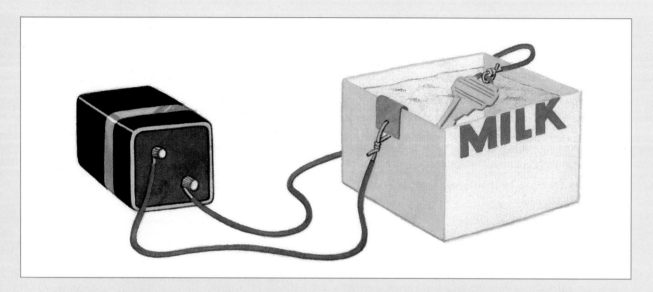

9. Immerse the key in the vinegar-salt solution except for the very top where it is connected to the wire. Make sure that the two pieces of metal, the copper strip and the key, do not touch each other.

Observations and Conclusions

■ Do you see anything happening to the solution?

■ What do you see on the key?

■ What happens to the metal object after a while? Can you explain why? [**Note:** If the process you are observing seems to be slowing down, you may need to remove the key, wipe off the bubbles, and then return it to the solution.]

■ Can you suggest reasons why electroplating is useful?

A SHOCKING COMBINATION

You probably learned long ago that electricity and water are an extremely dangerous combination. This is because water (other than pure water) is an excellent conductor of electricity. But what about ice? Does water conduct electricity even when it is frozen? Michael Faraday asked this same question, and in this activity you will discover the answer just as he did.

Materials Needed

3 lengths of insulated wire, 30 cm each

2 strips of copper, 2.5 cm x 7.5 cm

milk or juice carton, 95 mL (1 qt)

6-volt battery
galvanometer
scissors
ice pick
wire cutter
salt

Procedure

1. Use the ice pick to punch a small hole in one end of each of the copper strips about 1 cm from the end. **CAUTION:** *Be careful when using sharp instruments.*

2. Remove the insulation from the ends of the connecting wires. Thread the end of one length of wire through the hole in one of the copper strips and twist it tightly back onto itself as shown in the accompanying diagram. Do the same with another length of wire and the remaining copper strip.

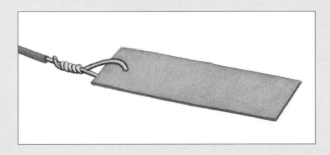

3. Use the scissors to carefully cut around the milk or juice carton about 7 cm from the bottom. Discard the top of the carton and make sure the bottom is clean.

4. Bend the copper strips so that they can hang on the sides of the carton. The bend should be closer to the end with the wire attached. With the wire on the outside of the container, hang the copper strips on opposite sides of the carton.

5. Angle the part of the strips inside the carton inward so that the two ends come within about 2.5 cm of each other.

6. Connect the wire hanging from one of the copper strips to the galvanometer. Then attach the wire from the other copper strip to one of the battery terminals. Use the remaining piece of wire to connect the galvanometer to the other battery terminal.

(continued)

761

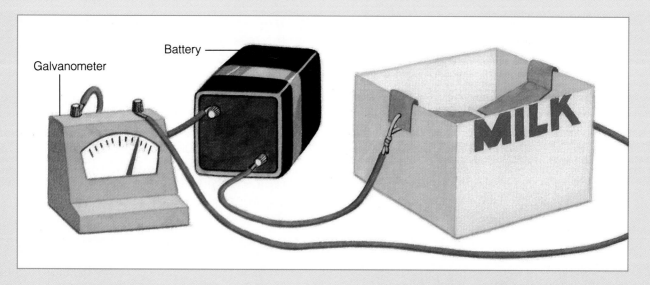

Galvanometer

Battery

MILK

7. Now all you need is something to complete the circuit—to bridge the gap between the copper strips. Fill the carton to about 2.5 cm from the top with ordinary tap water. Make sure the sections of the copper strips inside the carton are submerged in water.

At the same time, have a partner keep an eye on the galvanometer. You may or may not get a response depending on what part of the country you live in. If the water in your area is hard (has a high mineral content), it will conduct current. But if the water is soft, it may not be able to conduct enough current to deflect the galvanometer. **CAUTION:** *Don't be misled by this, however. Soft water can still conduct dangerous quantities of electricity in other circumstances.*

8. If the galvanometer needle did move, your local water conducts electricity and you can move on to the next step. If your galvanometer needle did not move, add salt to the water until it does.

9. Now detach the connections between the copper strips and the battery and galvanometer by untwisting the wires. Do not cut them because you will need them again. Place the carton, with the copper strips attached, in the freezer.

10. When the water in the carton is frozen solid, reconstruct the original circuit. Do you get a reading on the galvanometer with the frozen water? Keep an eye on the galvanometer as the ice melts. What do you observe?

■ What can you conclude from this experiment?

■ Compare your results with those of your classmates. Are your results the same? If not, can you suggest reasons why? Perhaps mistakes were made in the procedure. Can you hypothesize as to what mistakes may occur during this activity?

■ Why do you think you should never do such things as use your hair dryer near water or swim during a lightning storm?

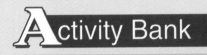

JUST DUCKY

A traditional compass is not the only device that can determine the direction of the Earth's magnetic field. A pair of cute little ducks can do the job too. That is if you design the ducks, of course. In this activity you will discover for yourself what happens when two magnets are placed together, and also how the magnets behave in reaction to the magnetic field of the Earth.

Materials Needed

2 steel pins
strong magnet
sheets of colored
  paper
2 cork disks, about
  4 cm in diameter

baking dish
scissors
glue
magnetic compass
  (optional)

Steps to Follow

1. Fold a sheet of paper in half widthwise. Draw the outline of a duck. (You can draw anything you like, but for these instructions, it will be called a duck.)

2. Use the scissors to carefully cut the duck out of the paper. Make sure you cut through both pieces of paper so that you have two identical shapes when you are finished.

3. Rub a strong magnet over the two steel pins repeatedly so that the pins become magnetized.

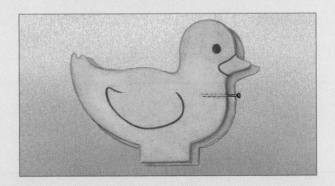

4. Place one pin between the duck cutouts. Glue the two pieces of paper together with the pin between them.

5. Repeat steps 1 and 2 to cut another two duck shapes. Glue the remaining magnetized pin between these duck cutouts, but this time place the magnetized pin facing in the opposite direction. For example, if you put the first pin's head near the duck's beak, put the second pin's head near the duck's tail.

6. Glue each figure upright on its own cork disk. (If you have trouble making it stand up, you may have to make a small base for it out of the remaining paper.) When the glue is dry, place the figures upright in a dish of water. Shake the dish slightly so that the figures move.

Observations and Conclusions

1. What happened to the ducks after a few minutes?

2. Can you explain why they moved as they did?

3. If you have a compass, compare the direction in which the ducks face with the direction of north on the compass.

4. Compare your results with those of your classmates. Are they the same as yours? If not, what may have gone wrong? Did anyone make unusual figures?

MAGNETIC PERSONALITY

It is sometimes difficult to imagine a phenomenon that exists but cannot easily be seen or felt—for example, the Earth's magnetic field. But the Earth's magnetic field is real and you are in it all the time! In this activity, you will experiment with the Earth's magnetic field.

Materials

crowbar
magnetic compass
hammer
sheet of paper
several paper clips

Procedure

1. Use the compass to determine the directions of north and south. Mark the directions on a sheet of paper.

2. Place the crowbar over the marks so that its ends point north and south. The north end should point slightly downward so you will need to place a book under the south end.

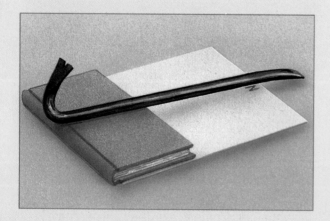

3. Place several paper clips on top of the crowbar. Observe what happens to them.

4. Now hit the crowbar solidly several times with the hammer. **CAUTION**: *Be careful when using the hammer. Do not swing it high and make sure that no one's hands or fingers are near where you hit it.* Wait a few minutes and then place the paper clips on the crowbar again. Observe what happens this time. If you do not observe any changes, hit the crowbar again.

Observations and Conclusions

1. What happened when you first placed the paper clips on the crowbar?

2. What happened to the paper clips after you hit the crowbar with the hammer?

3. How can you explain your observations?

4. Why do you think the crowbar had to be positioned with its north end pointing downward?

The Next Step

Take a second crowbar, or the same one after it is no longer magnetized, and again place it in a north-south position. Do not hit it this time. Simply let it remain in that position for several days to a week to find out if it becomes magnetized. If it does, what was the purpose of hitting the crowbar in the original activity?

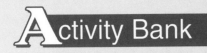

SLUGGING IT OUT

Have you ever wondered how a vending machine differentiates between a real coin and a fake one, or a slug? As you may know, a vending machine accepts only real coins—not just any coin-sized piece of metal. In this activity you will construct a device that distinguishes between real coins and impostors.

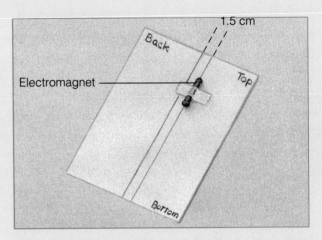

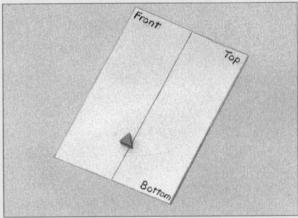

Materials

thin, stiff cardboard, about 25 cm x 30 cm

various coins

coin-sized iron washers

6-volt battery

electromagnet (If you cannot get one, you can build one by following the directions on page 537.)

small triangular piece of wood, with an altitude of about 2 cm and a base of about 2 cm

2 insulated wires, about 40 cm each

tape

glue

metric ruler

Procedure

1. Mark the cardboard to show front, back, top, and bottom. Draw a line down the center of both the front and back from top to bottom.

2. Turn the cardboard so that the back is facing you. Draw a line parallel to the center line but about 1.5 cm to the right of it. Tape the electromagnet on this line about one-third of the way down from the top.

3. Turn the cardboard so its front is facing you. Glue the triangular piece of wood onto the front of the cardboard. The bottom of the triangle should be about 8 cm from the bottom of the cardboard. The top of the triangle should be about 0.5 cm to the left of the center line.

4. Use alligator clips to connect the end of one of the wires to one terminal of the battery and the other end to the electromagnet.

5. Connect the second wire to the other end of the electromagnet.

6. Prop the cardboard against something sturdy at a 45° angle. To complete the circuit, attach the loose wire to the remaining terminal of the battery. **Note**: *Only do this momentarily each time you test a coin.* The electromagnet will drain a lot of energy from the battery.

7. From the top of the center line, let a coin slide down the cardboard. Observe what happens.

(continued)

765

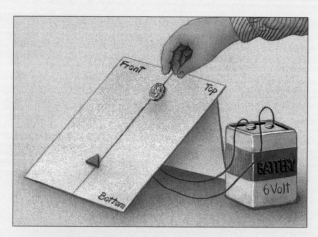

8. Slide a slug down the center line. Observe what happens.

9. Continue to slide several more slugs and coins down the center line. Look for a pattern in your observations.

Observations and Conclusions

1. Describe your observations in steps 7, 8, and 9.

2. How can you explain your observations?

Where It All Started

In the 1880s, it was believed that iron ore, the source of useful iron, was scarce. But Thomas Edison knew that this was not the case. The reason was because the valuable iron ore was mixed with worthless sand. Edison designed a processing plant that separated the iron ore from the sand in a device much like your slug rejector. Explain how such a device could have been used to achieve Edison's goal.

At first glance, the binary system of numbers seems quite confusing. However, someone who knew only the binary system would find the number system with which you are familiar equally as confusing. Believe it or not, the number systems operate on the same basic principles. The only difference is how many different numerals there are, or the base of the number system. You are familar with a base 10 number system in which there are ten different numerals. The binary system is to the base 2. It contains only two numerals. In this activity you will become accustomed to recognizing and using the binary system.

Materials

several sheets of white construction paper
several sheets of black construction paper
scissors

Procedure

1. Form a group with three other classmates. Draw light bulbs (about 10 cm tall) on the sheets of construction paper. Draw as many as you can fit on the paper you have.

2. Use the scissors to carefully cut out each bulb.

3. The binary system has only two numerals, 0 and 1. In an electronic device, such as a calculator, a circuit or light is shut off to show a 0. In this activity, the black bulbs represent lights that are off, or 0s. A circuit or light is turned on to show a 1. The white bulbs represent lights that are on, or 1s.

4. Form numbers by standing next to each other and holding up the construction-paper bulbs. Practice counting to 8 until you get the hang of it. Make sure you each know how to read binary numbers by using the information in the number guide that follows.

Number Guide

In any number system, each place holds a power of the base of the system. For example, the first place is always the base of the system to the zero power. Any number to the zero power is equal to 1. So the numeral one (white bulb) in the first place represents the number 1. A zero (black bulb) represents a zero.

The second place is the base, in this case 2, to the first power, so 2 ($2^1=2$). The numeral one in the second place thus represents the number 2. Notice how each time you move one place to the left, the power increases by one. The number 3 is represented by showing a 1 and a 2 at the same time—a numeral one (1 in the first place) and a 2 (1 in the second place). All other numbers are formed by making combinations of 1s and 0s in that manner.

2^5	2^4	2^3	2^2	2^1	2^0
32	16	8	4	2	1

(continued)

5. Now it's time for some friendly competition. Join together with another group. Take turns holding up numbers and testing each other.

6. Once your two groups are satisfied with your mastery of the binary system, join together as one large group. You need more than four people to count to 16 and higher. Organize a game with the rest of your classmates in which teams (sizes will vary depending on the size of your class) will figure out binary numbers held up by other teams. You should set up rules that determine how points are scored, how long each contestant has to figure the number out, and how the contestants from each team should buzz in to answer.

Analysis

1. Rewrite the chart shown and extend it five more places.

2. How high can you count with one place? Two places? Five places? Seven places? Do you see a pattern?

3. A certain number of people (digits) are required to make each number. How can you determine how many people you need? How many people are needed to show the number 33?

4. Design a chart like the one shown for the base 10 number system. Do you see how they are similar?

SEEING SOUND

A wave originates when a vibrating source gives it energy causing it to vibrate as well. This may be easy to remember, but it can be difficult to understand. After all, it is often hard to picture something that you cannot see. In this activity, however, you will have an opportunity to create and indirectly observe the vibrations of sound waves.

What You Need

cardboard cylinder, such as from a container of oatmeal
balloon
rubber band
sugar or salt
wooden spoon
metal baking tray
scissors
graph paper

What You Do

1. Remove both ends from the cardboard cylinder.

2. Cut the balloon and stretch it tightly over one end of the cylinder. Secure it by stretching the rubber band around the balloon and the cylinder. It is important that the balloon be stretched tightly for this to work. You have made a simple drum.

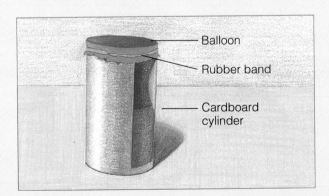

Balloon

Rubber band

Cardboard cylinder

3. Sprinkle sugar (or salt) on the drum head (stretched balloon). Tap the edge of the drum head several times with the wooden spoon. What happens to the sugar? Hit it harder and observe any further changes.

4. Spread the sugar out on the drum head again. Have a classmate hold the drum head level while you shout into the open end. What happens to the sugar this time? Use graph paper to draw your observations. Repeat this step, but this time have your classmate shout and you observe what happens. Again draw your observations.

5. Spread the sugar out over the drum head once more. At a distance of about 20 cm above the drum head, tap a metal baking tray with the wooden spoon. What happens to the sugar?

Observations and Conclusions

1. What do you observe when you tap on the drum head in step 3?

2. How can you explain what happens to the sugar or salt?

3. What gave energy to the drum head?

4. What happens when you shout into the cylinder in step 4? Is energy involved this time?

5. Compare the graph you made when you shouted into the cylinder with those of your classmates. Are they alike? Do they show any differences?

6. What do you observe when the baking tray is hit with the wooden spoon in step 5?

7. Explain how the metal tray being hit can affect the drum without even touching it.

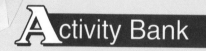
SOUND AROUND

You know that a ball will bounce off a sidewalk and that light will reflect off a mirror. But will sound bounce off a hard surface as well? Because sound is a wave and waves are reflected, it should. But by doing this activity you can prove it for yourself!

Materials

two sturdy cardboard tubes without ends (poster or art tubes, for example)

small wind-up toy or ticking watch

large smooth piece of sturdy cardboard or plastic, about 40 cm × 40 cm

pieces of fabric and foam

Procedure

1. Have a classmate hold the cardboard or plastic upright on a large table or on the floor.

2. Place the tubes on the surface of the table or floor at an angle to the cardboard and to each other. Leave a gap of about 6 cm between the cardboard and the ends of the tubes.

3. If the tubes have caps, place a cap on the outer end of one tube. If the tubes do not have caps, ask a second classmate to cover the outer end of one tube with his/her hand or a book. Listen through the end of the uncovered tube. Cover your outer ear with your hand so that the only sounds you hear are coming through the tube. What do you hear?

4. Have your classmate uncover or take the cap off the other tube. Place the watch or toy just inside the end of the tube and put the cap back on the tube or cover it again. Listen in the other tube as you did before. What do you hear? Explain your observations.

5. Switch places with your classmate so that you cover the tube and your classmate listens. What does your classmate hear in each case?

Going Further

Repeat the activity several times, but each time cover the cardboard with a different material, such as a variety of fabrics and foam. Determine how these materials affect what you hear. Explain why.

■ Why is a carpeted room more quiet than an uncarpeted room?

■ Some automobiles are very noisy when you ride in them. How can automobile manufacturers make cars less noisy?

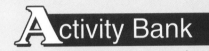

PRESTO CHANGO, IT'S GONE

Do you think that you can make an object disappear before your very eyes? You can—and in this activity you will find out how! The secret is understanding refraction—in this case the bending of light as it travels from one medium into another.

You will need an empty jar with a lid (preferably a short jar such as a peanut-butter jar), a postage stamp, and some water.

Procedure

1. Put the stamp on a tabletop.
2. Place the jar, open end up, over the stamp. Look at the stamp.
3. Fill the jar with water and put the lid on it.
4. Look at the stamp now.

What You Saw

1. What did you observe when you placed the jar over the stamp?
2. Did adding water to the jar affect how you saw the stamp?
3. Can you explain your observations?
4. How is this activity different from the one that appears at the end of the first paragraph on page 602? Draw diagrams in your explanation.

BELLS A'RINGING

Can you imagine shouting as loud as you can yet not making any sound? This is exactly what would happen if you tried to shout in outer space. And the reason is that in space there are no air molecules for sound to travel through. Although you cannot reproduce the characteristics of space, this activity will give you an idea of how dependent sound is on molecules of matter.

Materials

glass jar with a lid, about 236–250 mL (8 oz)
string, 10–12 cm long
tape
small bell
hot water

Procedure

1. Tape the string to the center of the inside of the lid.
2. Tie a small bell to the free end of the string.
3. Carefully screw the lid with the bell attached onto the jar. Make sure the bell does not touch the sides or bottom of the jar. If it does, adjust it by either cutting the string or moving the taped end of the string.
4. Gently shake the jar and listen to the bell.
5. Remove the lid with the bell attached and pour about 2 to 3 cm of hot tap water into the jar.
6. Allow the jar to stand for about 30 seconds and then replace the lid and bell. Be sure the bell does not touch the water.

7. Gently shake the jar again and listen to the bell.
8. Add more hot water and repeat steps 5, 6, and 7. Adjust the length of the string if necessary.

Observations and Conclusions

1. What did you observe in this activity?
2. How can you explain your observations?
3. What do your observations indicate about sound?
4. How does this activity relate to the lack of sound in space?

CUP-TO-CUP COMMUNICATION

When you were young, did you ever try to make a telephone out of paper cups and string? If so, your simple telephone may have been one of your first scientific endeavors! What you may not have realized, however, is that such a device utilizes the most basic principles of sound—the fact that sound is created by a vibration and travels as a disturbance that moves through materials such as air and string. In this activity you will get another chance to build a telephone, but this time you will be able to explain why it works.

Materials Needed

2 paper cups
frozen-dessert stick (or drinking straw or toothpick)
4 m cotton sewing thread (or dental floss)
sharpened pencil or scissors

Procedure

1. Use the sharpened end of a pencil or scissors to poke a small hole in the center of the bottom of each cup.
2. Pull the thread through the holes in the cups so that each cup has one end of the thread in it.
3. Break the frozen-dessert stick (or cut the straw or toothpick) in half. Tie each

end of the thread to one of the halves so the thread cannot pull out of the hole in the cup.
4. Hold one cup in your hand and give the other cup to a classmate. Move apart from each other so that the thread is pulled tight. Be sure the thread does not touch anything.
5. Put your cup to your ear and have your classmate speak into the other cup. What do you hear? Now you talk and have your classmate listen. What does your classmate hear?
6. Switch roles again and this time try touching the thread while your classmate is talking. What happens?

Analysis and Conclusions

1. What is sound and how is it transmitted?
2. Use your definition of sound to explain how the paper-cup telephone works.
3. Can you explain why your observations changed when you touched the thread while your classmate spoke into the cup?
4. Compare the telephone you made to a real telephone.

Going Further

Would your results have been different if you had used aluminum or plastic containers instead of paper cups? If you had used knitting yarn or thin wire instead of thread (or dental floss)? Find out by repeating this activity using different materials. Remember, however, that to be truly scientific in your investigation, you can have only one variable!

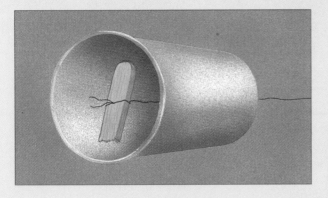

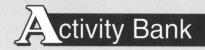
JUST HANGING AROUND

You read that sound travels better through solids than it does through gases. Want to prove this idea for yourself? Try this activity.

Procedure

1. To begin, tie two strings (each about 30 cm long) to a metal hanger as shown in the accompanying diagram. (If you do not have a hanger, you can use two spoons.)

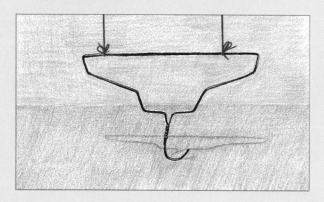

2. Hold the end of one string in one hand and the end of the other string in the other hand. Bump the hanger against a desk or other hard solid object. Listen to the sound produced.

3. Now wrap the end of each string around one of your index fingers.

4. Put your index fingers up against your ears and bump the hanger against the object again.

What I Proved

1. Describe the sound you heard the first time you bumped the hanger.

2. How does the first sound compare with the sound you heard with your fingers up against your ears?

3. What can you say about how sound travels through different mediums?

4. Can you now explain why people sometimes put drinking glasses up to doors or walls to hear through them?

Going Further

Try other solid materials in place of the hanger. How are they alike? How do they differ?

A SUNSATIONAL EXPERIMENT

Perhaps you have seen that old movie trick in which someone starts a fire using only a magnifying glass. Do you think it's a trick or can it really happen? Try the following activity to find out.

Materials

sheet of white paper
small glass bowl
magnifying glass

Procedure

1. Select a location that receives bright sunlight with no wind.
2. Crumple a sheet of paper and place it in a small glass bowl.
3. Hold a magnifying glass between the paper and the sun so a beam of light is focused on the paper.

4. Move the magnifying glass closer to and farther away from the paper. As you do so, notice how the point of light on the paper changes from a tiny bright circle to a hazy undefined shape. Adjust the distance between the paper and the magnifying glass to make the point of light very small and bright.
5. Once you have positioned the magnifying glass so that it forms a small bright circle, pull it back about 1 cm and watch the paper. **CAUTION:** *Under the right conditions, the paper may ignite.*

Observations

What did you see happening once you had positioned the magnifying glass correctly?

Conclusions

1. What do you think happened?
2. Why do you think this occurred?
3. How do your observations and conclusions compare with those of your classmates? How do you explain differences?
4. With this activity in mind, can you explain why a lawn will burn if it is watered during daytime sun?

MYSTERY MESSAGE

Have you ever imagined yourself to be an international spy using secret technology and writing messages in code—or better yet with disappearing ink? If so, you may be happy to discover that not all of your spy supplies are just in your imagination. In this activity, you will write a secret message that can be read only by someone who knows to use incandescent light to create the chemical reaction necessary to make the message visible.

Materials

toothpick
white paper, 1/2 sheet
lamp with light bulb
lemon juice (or lemon)

Procedure

1. Dip the toothpick into the lemon or lemon juice and use it as a pen to write a message on the white paper. Let the lemon juice dry. Observe the lemon juice as it dries.

2. Once the lemon juice has dried, hold the paper close to a lighted light bulb for several minutes.

Observations and Conclusions

1. What happens to the lemon juice as it dries?

2. What do you see when you hold the paper up to the light bulb?

3. A chemical reaction occurred when the paper was held up to the light. What are the two variables that could have caused the reaction?

4. The reaction you observed was an endothermic reaction. If you are not familiar with that term, look up the prefix *endo-* and the root *therm* to figure out what they mean. Now can you determine why the incandescent light bulb was used? Would a fluorescent bulb have worked as well?

5. Can you explain your observations in terms of chemical reactions?

THE STRAIGHT AND NARROW

You learned that although light travels in waves, light can be described by its straight-line paths. In this activity you will observe the straight path of a beam of light.

Materials

4 large index cards
flashlight or projector
metric ruler
scissors
8 chalkboard erasers (or small books or boxes)
thread or string (optional)

Procedure

1. Measure and mark the center of each index card. Then cut out a small circle (about 1 cm in diameter) in the center of each card.

2. In a room in which you can shut or dim the lights, space the cards about 30 cm apart. Hold each card upright so that the long side of the index card is on the floor or on a tabletop. Place chalkboard erasers on both sides of each card so that the cards stand upright without being held.

3. Make sure that the holes align. You may want to run a piece of string or thread through the holes in the cards and pull it tightly. This will help you to line up the holes.

4. Shut the lights so that the only light you see comes from the flashlight or projector. Now hold your light source so that it shines through the hole in one of the end cards. The light should not be able to shine around the first card. Have a classmate stand at the other end and observe.

5. Reverse roles with your classmate so that he or she holds the light source and you observe. What do you see?

6. Now move one of the cards about 3 cm to the side and repeat steps 4 and 5. Determine whether this changes what you observe.

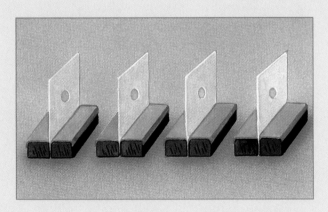

Observations and Conclusions

1. What did you and your classmate observe in steps 4 and 5? In step 6?

2. What does this activity tell you about the path of light?

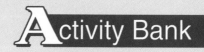
SPINNING WHEEL

As any painter knows, many of the colors you see are actually combinations of several colors. In this activity you will observe the results of combining different colors.

Materials

white posterboard
compass
metric ruler
scissors

crayons or markers
string, 1 m
India ink
several sheets of newspaper

Procedure

1. Use a compass to draw a circle with a diameter of 10 cm on white posterboard. Carefully cut out the circle using the scissors.

2. Divide the circle into three equal pie-shaped sections and color one section red, one section green, and the third section blue. Crayons or markers are the easiest coloring instruments to use.

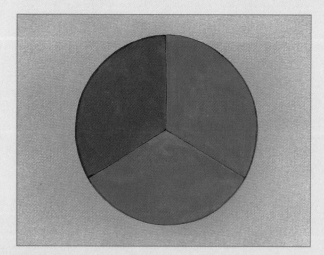

3. Use the pointed end of the compass or scissors to make two small holes on opposite sides of the center of the circle. They should be placed about 2 cm

from each other. Your circle should look like a giant button.

4. Thread a string (about 1 m long) through the holes and tie the ends of the string together so that the thread forms a loop which passes through the holes. See the accompanying diagram.

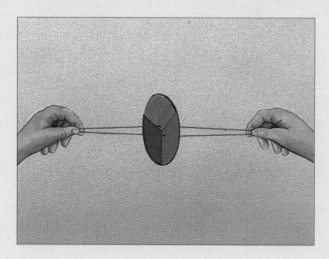

5. Center the circle on the thread, wind up the circle, and make it spin by alternately stretching and relaxing the string. It may take a little practice to keep it going. If you have trouble spinning the circle, you can try increasing its weight by doubling the thickness of the posterboard or pasting the circle onto cardboard.

The Next Step

Try the same thing with another circle with different colors and/or different numbers of sections. Predict each time what you expect to see.

6. Sometimes you see colors even when they are not there. Use the compass to draw another circle on the posterboard with a diameter of 10 cm. Cut out the circle with scissors.

7. Cover your working surface with several layers of newspaper and place your white disk on top of the paper.

8. Use India ink and a paintbrush to paint your disk with one of the patterns shown.

9. When the ink is dry, again use the pointed end of the compass or scissors to make two small holes on opposite sides of the center. Thread string through the holes as you did before. Wind up the circle and make it spin. Observe how the circle looks.

Observations and Conclusions

1. What did you see when you spun the colored circle?

2. How can you explain your observations?

3. What did the inked circle look like when it spun? Can you hypothesize as to why you see what you do?

Activity Bank

COLOR CRAZY

The color of an object is the color of light it reflects. A banana looks yellow because it reflects yellow light. However, in a beam of light that does not contain yellow, the banana looks black because there is no yellow light to reflect. In this activity you will have an opportunity to test this color theory for yourself.

Materials

shoe box
red and green cellophane (enough to cover the top of the shoe box)
scissors
flashlight
black construction paper
green object (such as a lime or green tomato)
yellow object (such as a banana or lemon)
red object (such as a red tomato or red playing card)

Procedure

1. Use the scissors to carefully cut a large rectangular hole in the lid of the shoe box. The hole should be large enough so that you can look through it and see anything placed in the shoebox.

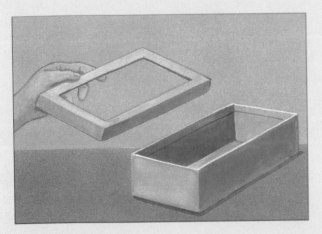

2. Cut a small hole in the center of one of the narrow ends of the shoe box.
3. Tape the green cellophane under the lid of the shoe box so that it entirely covers the hole you cut in step 1.
4. Line the inside of the shoe box with black construction paper.
5. Place the objects in the box and put the lid on.
6. In a darkened room, shine the flashlight into the shoebox through the small hole you cut out in the end. Record your observations.

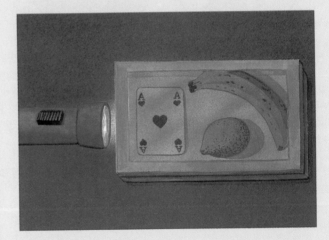

7. Replace the green cellophane with red cellophane and again shine the flashlight into the box. Again record your observations.

Observations and Conclusions

1. What did you see when the green cellophane was in place in step 6?
2. How can you explain your observations when looking through the green cellophane?
3. What did you observe when the red cellophane was in place in step 7?

4. Were your observations different through the red cellophane? If so, why?

5. What is the purpose of the black construction paper?

6. What do you think would happen if you put a white object or an object with white on it in the box? Try it to see if you are correct.

7. Describe the role played by the cellophane in this activity. Draw diagrams to show what it does.

The Next Step

Repeat the activity using different objects inside the box and additional colors of cellophane.

THE METRIC SYSTEM

The metric system of measurement is used by scientists throughout the world. It is based on units of ten. Each unit is ten times larger or ten times smaller than the next unit. The most commonly used units of the metric system are given below. After you have finished reading about the metric system, try to put it to use. How tall are you in metrics? What is your mass? What is your normal body temperature in degrees Celsius?

Commonly Used Metric Units

Length   The distance from one point to another

meter (m)   A meter is slightly longer than a yard.
               1 meter = 1000 millimeters (mm)
               1 meter = 100 centimeters (cm)
               1000 meters = 1 kilometer (km)

Volume   The amount of space an object takes up

liter (L)   A liter is slightly more than a quart.
               1 liter = 1000 milliliters (mL)

Mass   The amount of matter in an object

gram (g)   A gram has a mass equal to about
               one paper clip.

               1000 grams = 1 kilogram (kg)

Temperature   The measure of hotness or coldness

degrees   0°C = freezing point of water
Celsius (°C)   100°C = boiling point of water

Metric–English Equivalents

2.54 centimeters (cm) = 1 inch (in.)
1 meter (m) = 39.37 inches (in.)
1 kilometer (km) = 0.62 miles (mi)
1 liter (L) = 1.06 quarts (qt)
250 milliliters (mL) = 1 cup (c)
1 kilogram (kg) = 2.2 pounds (lb)
28.3 grams (g) = 1 ounce (oz)
$°C = 5/9 \times (°F - 32)$

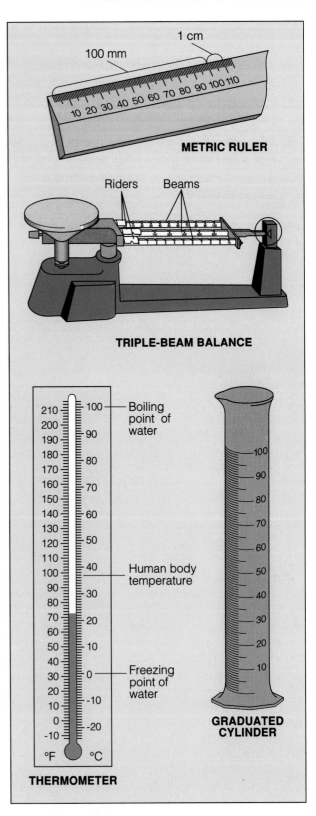

METRIC RULER

TRIPLE-BEAM BALANCE

THERMOMETER

GRADUATED CYLINDER

$\mathbb{A}$ppendix B

The laboratory balance is an important tool in scientific investigations. You can use the balance to determine the mass of materials that you study or experiment with in the laboratory.

Different kinds of balances are used in the laboratory. One kind of balance is the double-pan balance. Another kind of balance is the triple-beam balance. The balance that you may use in your science class is probably similar to one of the balances illustrated in this Appendix. To use the balance properly, you should learn the name, function, and location of each part of the balance you are using. What kind of balance do you have in your science class?

The Double-Pan Balance

The double-pan balance shown in this Appendix has two beams. Some double-pan balances have only one beam. The beams are calibrated, or marked, in grams. The upper beam is divided into ten major units of 1 gram each. Each of these units is further divided into units of 1/10 of a gram. The lower beam is divided into twenty units, and each unit is equal to 10 grams. The lower beam can be used to find the masses of objects up to 200 grams. Each beam has a rider that is moved to the right along the beam. The rider indicates the number of grams needed to balance the object in the left pan. What is the total mass the balance can measure?

Before using the balance, you should be sure that the pans are empty and both riders are pointing to zero. The balance should be on a flat, level surface. The pointer should be at the zero point. If your pointer does not read zero, slowly turn the adjustment knob so that the pointer does read zero.

The following procedure can be used to find the mass of an object with a double-pan balance:

1. Place the object whose mass is to be determined on the left pan.

2. Move the rider on the lower beam to the 10-gram notch.

3. If the pointer moves to the right of the zero point on the scale, the object has a mass less than

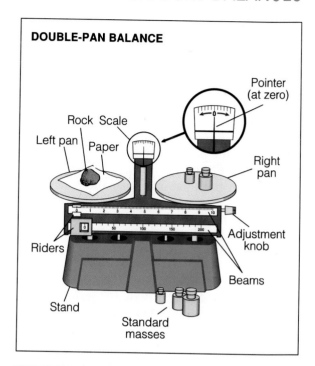

DOUBLE-PAN BALANCE

Rock Scale
Left pan Paper
Pointer (at zero)
0
Right pan
Riders
Adjustment knob
Beams
Stand
Standard masses

Parts of a Double-Pan Balance and Their Functions

Pointer Indicator used to determine when the mass being measured is balanced by the riders or masses of the balance

Scale Series of marks along which the pointer moves

Zero Point Center line of the scale to which the pointer moves when the mass being measured is balanced by the riders or masses of the balance

Adjustment Knob Knob used to set the balance at the zero point when the riders are all on zero and no masses are on either pan

Left Pan Platform on which an object whose mass is to be determined is placed

Right Pan Platform on which standard masses are placed

Beams Horizontal strips of metal on which marks, or graduations, appear that indicate grams or parts of grams

Riders Devices that are moved along the beams and used to balance the object being measured and to determine its mass

Stand Support for the balance

10 grams. Return the rider on the lower beam to zero. Slowly move the rider on the upper beam until the pointer is at zero. The reading on the beam is the mass of the object.

4. If the pointer did not move to the right of the zero, move the rider on the lower beam notch by notch until the pointer does move to the right. Move the rider back one notch. Then move the rider on the upper beam until the pointer is at zero. The sum of the readings on both beams is the mass of the object.

5. If the two riders are moved completely to the right side of the beams and the pointer remains to the left of the zero point, the object has a mass greater than the total mass that the balance can measure.

The total mass that most double-pan balances can measure is 210 grams. If an object has a mass greater than 210 grams, return the riders to the zero point.

The following procedure can be used to find the mass of an object greater than 210 grams:

1. Place the standard masses on the right pan one at a time, starting with the largest, until the pointer remains to the right of the zero point.

2. Remove one of the large standard masses and replace it with a smaller one. Continue replacing the standard masses with smaller ones until the pointer remains to the left of the zero point. When the pointer remains to the left of the zero point, the mass of the object on the left pan is greater than the total mass of the standard masses on the right pan.

3. Move the rider on the lower beam and then the rider on the upper beam until the pointer stops at the zero point on the scale. The mass of the object is equal to the sum of the readings on the beams plus the mass of the standard masses.

The Triple-Beam Balance

The triple-beam balance is a single-pan balance with three beams calibrated in grams. The back, or 100-gram, beam is divided into ten units of 10 grams each. The middle, or 500-gram, beam is divided into five units of 100 grams each. The front, or 10-gram, beam is divided into ten major units of 1 gram each. Each of these units is further divided into units of 1/10 of a gram. What is the largest mass you could find with a triple-beam balance?

The following procedure can be used to find the mass of an object with a triple-beam balance:

1. Place the object on the pan.

2. Move the rider on the middle beam notch by notch until the horizontal pointer drops below zero. Move the rider back one notch.

3. Move the rider on the back beam notch by notch until the pointer again drops below zero. Move the rider back one notch.

4. Slowly slide the rider along the front beam until the pointer stops at the zero point.

5. The mass of the object is equal to the sum of the readings on the three beams.

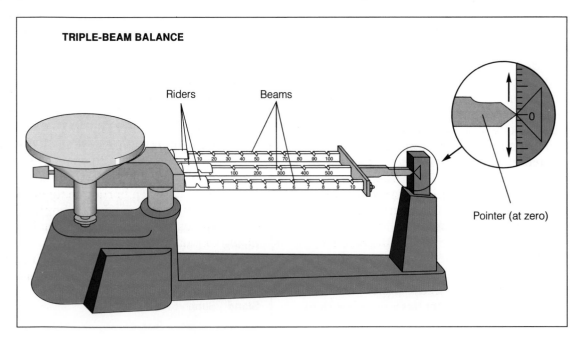

TRIPLE-BEAM BALANCE

Riders   Beams

Pointer (at zero)

Appendix C

One of the first things a scientist learns is that working in the laboratory can be an exciting experience. But the laboratory can also be quite dangerous if proper safety rules are not followed at all times. To prepare yourself for a safe year in the laboratory, read over the following safety rules. Then read them a second time. Make sure you understand each rule. If you do not, ask your teacher to explain any rules you are unsure of.

Dress Code

1. Many materials in the laboratory can cause eye injury. To protect yourself from possible injury, wear safety goggles whenever you are working with chemicals, burners, or any substance that might get into your eyes. Never wear contact lenses in the laboratory.

2. Wear a laboratory apron or coat whenever you are working with chemicals or heated substances.

3. Tie back long hair to keep it away from any chemicals, burners and candles, or other laboratory equipment.

4. Remove or tie back any article of clothing or jewelry that can hang down and touch chemicals and flames.

General Safety Rules

5. Read all directions for an experiment several times. Follow the directions exactly as they are written. If you are in doubt about any part of the experiment, ask your teacher for assistance.

6. Never perform activities that are not authorized by your teacher. Obtain permission before "experimenting" on your own.

7. Never handle any equipment unless you have specific permission.

8. Take extreme care not to spill any material in the laboratory. If a spill occurs, immediately ask your teacher about the proper cleanup procedure. Never simply pour chemicals or other substances into the sink or trash container.

9. Never eat in the laboratory.

10. Wash your hands before and after each experiment.

First Aid

11. Immediately report all accidents, no matter how minor, to your teacher.

12. Learn what to do in case of specific accidents, such as getting acid in your eyes or on your skin. (Rinse acids from your body with lots of water.)

13. Become aware of the location of the first-aid kit. But your teacher should administer any required first aid due to injury. Or your teacher may send you to the school nurse or call a physician.

14. Know where and how to report an accident or fire. Find out the location of the fire extinguisher, phone, and fire alarm. Keep a list of important phone numbers—such as the fire department and the school nurse—near the phone. Immediately report any fires to your teacher.

Heating and Fire Safety

15. Again, never use a heat source, such as a candle or burner, without wearing safety goggles.

16. Never heat a chemical you are not instructed to heat. A chemical that is harmless when cool may be dangerous when heated.

17. Maintain a clean work area and keep all materials away from flames.

18. Never reach across a flame.

19. Make sure you know how to light a Bunsen burner. (Your teacher will demonstrate the proper procedure for lighting a burner.) If the flame leaps out of a burner toward you, immediately turn off the gas. Do not touch the burner. It may be hot. And never leave a lighted burner unattended!

20. When heating a test tube or bottle, always point it away from you and others. Chemicals can splash or boil out of a heated test tube.

21. Never heat a liquid in a closed container. The expanding gases produced may blow the container apart, injuring you or others.

22. Before picking up a container that has been heated, first hold the back of your hand near it. If you can feel the heat on the back of your hand, the container may be too hot to handle. Use a clamp or tongs when handling hot containers.

Using Chemicals Safely

23. Never mix chemicals for the "fun of it." You might produce a dangerous, possibly explosive substance.

24. Never touch, taste, or smell a chemical unless you are instructed by your teacher to do so. Many chemicals are poisonous. If you are instructed to note the fumes in an experiment, gently wave your hand over the opening of a container and direct the fumes toward your nose. Do not inhale the fumes directly from the container.

25. Use only those chemicals needed in the activity. Keep all lids closed when a chemical is not being used. Notify your teacher whenever chemicals are spilled.

26. Dispose of all chemicals as instructed by your teacher. To avoid contamination, never return chemicals to their original containers.

27. Be extra careful when working with acids or bases. Pour such chemicals over the sink, not over your workbench.

28. When diluting an acid, pour the acid into water. Never pour water into an acid.

29. Immediately rinse with water any acids that get on your skin or clothing. Then notify your teacher of any acid spill.

Using Glassware Safely

30. Never force glass tubing into a rubber stopper. A turning motion and lubricant will be helpful when inserting glass tubing into rubber stoppers or rubber tubing. Your teacher will demonstrate the proper way to insert glass tubing.

31. Never heat glassware that is not thoroughly dry. Use a wire screen to protect glassware from any flame.

32. Keep in mind that hot glassware will not appear hot. Never pick up glassware without first checking to see if it is hot. See #22.

33. If you are instructed to cut glass tubing, fire-polish the ends immediately to remove sharp edges.

34. Never use broken or chipped glassware. If glassware breaks, notify your teacher and dispose of the glassware in the proper trash container.

35. Never eat or drink from laboratory glassware. Thoroughly clean glassware before putting it away.

Using Sharp Instruments

36. Handle scalpels or razor blades with extreme care. Never cut material toward you; cut away from you.

37. Immediately notify your teacher if you cut your skin when working in the laboratory.

Animal Safety

38. No experiments that will cause pain, discomfort, or harm to mammals, birds, reptiles, fishes, and amphibians should be done in the classroom or at home.

39. Animals should be handled only if necessary. If an animal is excited or frightened, pregnant, feeding, or with its young, special handling is required.

40. Your teacher will instruct you as to how to handle each animal species that may be brought into the classroom.

41. Clean your hands thoroughly after handling animals or the cage containing animals.

End-of-Experiment Rules

42. After an experiment has been completed, clean up your work area and return all equipment to its proper place.

43. Wash your hands after every experiment.

44. Turn off all burners before leaving the laboratory. Check that the gas line leading to the burner is off as well.

Appendix D

This mathematics refresher is designed to review those topics that may trouble you when you study physical science. You may wish to study this material before working on problems presented in the text. The material in this Appendix, although not presented in great detail, is sufficient to enable you to solve the chapter problems.

Working with Fractions

1. Addition and Subtraction: Same Denominators
To add or subtract fractions that have the same denominator, add or subtract the numerators, then write the sum or difference over the denominator. Express the answer in lowest terms. (See Examples 2 and 3.)

Examples

1. $\dfrac{1}{5} + \dfrac{2}{5} = \dfrac{1+2}{5} = \dfrac{3}{5}$

2. $\dfrac{5}{14} + \dfrac{1}{14} + \dfrac{1}{14} = \dfrac{5+1+1}{14} = \dfrac{7}{14} = \dfrac{1}{2}$

3. $\dfrac{11}{12} - \dfrac{5}{12} = \dfrac{11-5}{12} = \dfrac{6}{12} = \dfrac{1}{2}$

4. $\dfrac{4}{7} - \dfrac{2}{7} - \dfrac{1}{7} = \dfrac{4-2-1}{7} = \dfrac{1}{7}$

2. Addition and Subtraction: Different Denominators
To add or subtract fractions that do not have the same denominator, find the least common denominator. Express the fractions as equivalent fractions using the least common denominator. Then add or subtract the numerators. Write the sum or difference over the denominator. Express the answer in lowest terms. (See Example 2.)

Examples

1. $\dfrac{1}{2} + \dfrac{1}{3} = \dfrac{3}{6} + \dfrac{2}{6} = \dfrac{3+2}{6} = \dfrac{5}{6}$

2. $\dfrac{2}{5} + \dfrac{1}{10} = \dfrac{4}{10} + \dfrac{1}{10} = \dfrac{4+1}{10} = \dfrac{5}{10} = \dfrac{1}{2}$

3. $\dfrac{7}{8} - \dfrac{1}{4} = \dfrac{7}{8} - \dfrac{2}{8} = \dfrac{7-2}{8} = \dfrac{5}{8}$

4. $\dfrac{7}{8} - \dfrac{1}{3} = \dfrac{21}{24} - \dfrac{8}{24} = \dfrac{21-8}{24} = \dfrac{13}{24}$

3. Multiplication
To multiply two or more fractions, multiply the numerators to obtain the numerator of the product. Multiply the denominators to obtain the denominator of the product. Because it is easier to work with smaller numbers, whenever possible divide any numerator and denominator by their greatest common factor before multiplying. (See Examples 3 and 4.) Express the answer in lowest terms. (See Example 2.)

Examples

1. $\dfrac{7}{8} \times \dfrac{3}{5} = \dfrac{7 \times 3}{8 \times 5} = \dfrac{21}{40}$

2. $\dfrac{1}{2} \times \dfrac{1}{3} \times \dfrac{2}{5} = \dfrac{1 \times 1 \times 2}{2 \times 3 \times 5} = \dfrac{2}{30} = \dfrac{1}{15}$

3. $\dfrac{\cancel{4}^{1}}{\cancel{5}} \times \dfrac{\cancel{15}^{3}}{\cancel{16}_{4}} = \dfrac{1 \times 3}{1 \times 4} = \dfrac{3}{4}$

4. $\dfrac{1}{\cancel{2}} \times \dfrac{\cancel{8}^{4}}{\cancel{15}_{3}} \times \dfrac{\cancel{5}^{1}}{7} = \dfrac{1 \times 4 \times 1}{1 \times 3 \times 7} = \dfrac{4}{21}$

4. Division
To divide one fraction by another, invert the divisor and then multiply the two fractions. Express the answer in lowest terms.

Examples

1. $\dfrac{1}{2} \div \dfrac{1}{3} = \dfrac{1}{2} \times \dfrac{3}{1} = \dfrac{1 \times 3}{2 \times 1} = \dfrac{3}{2} = 1\dfrac{1}{2}$

2. $\dfrac{2}{5} \div \dfrac{8}{15} = \dfrac{2}{\cancel{5}} \times \dfrac{\cancel{15}^{3}}{\cancel{8}_{4}} = \dfrac{1 \times 3}{1 \times 4} = \dfrac{3}{4}$

3. $\dfrac{2}{3} \div \dfrac{4}{5} = \dfrac{\cancel{2}^{1}}{3} \times \dfrac{5}{\cancel{4}_{2}} = \dfrac{1 \times 5}{3 \times 2} = \dfrac{5}{6}$

4. $\dfrac{9}{16} \div \dfrac{3}{4} = \dfrac{\cancel{9}^{3}}{\cancel{16}_{4}} \times \dfrac{\cancel{4}^{1}}{\cancel{8}_{1}} = \dfrac{3 \times 1}{4 \times 1} = \dfrac{3}{4}$

Converting a Fraction to a Decimal

To convert a fraction to a decimal, divide the numerator by the denominator, carrying the answer to the required number of decimal places.

Examples

1. Convert $\frac{2}{5}$ to a decimal.

$$
\begin{array}{r}
.4 \\
5\,\overline{\big)2.0} \\
2\,0 \\
\end{array}
\quad = \quad .4
$$

2. Convert $\frac{2}{7}$ to a two-place decimal.

$$
\begin{array}{r}
.285 \\
7\,\overline{\big)2.000} \\
1\,4 \\
\hline
6\,0 \\
5\,6 \\
\hline
4\,0 \\
3\,5 \\
\hline
5 \\
\end{array}
\quad = \quad .29
$$

3. Convert $\frac{45}{85}$ to a three-place decimal.

$$
\begin{array}{r}
.529 \\
85\,\overline{\big)45.000} \\
425 \\
\hline
250 \\
170 \\
\hline
800 \\
765 \\
\hline
35 \\
\end{array}
\quad = \quad .529
$$

Converting a Fraction to a Percent

To convert a fraction to a percent, divide the numerator by the denominator and multiply the result by 100 percent.

Examples

1. Convert $\frac{18}{25}$ to a percent.

$$
\begin{array}{r}
.72 \\
25\,\overline{\big)18.00} \\
17\,5 \\
\hline
50 \\
50 \\
\end{array}
\quad .72 \times 100\% = 72\%
$$

2. Convert $\frac{7}{50}$ to a percent.

$$
\begin{array}{r}
.14 \\
50\,\overline{\big)7.00} \\
5\,0 \\
\hline
2\,00 \\
2\,00 \\
\end{array}
\quad .14 \times 100\% = 14\%
$$

3. Convert $\frac{7}{4}$ to a percent.

$$
\begin{array}{r}
1.75 \\
4\,\overline{\big)7.00} \\
4 \\
\hline
3\,0 \\
2\,8 \\
\hline
20 \\
20 \\
\end{array}
\quad 1.75 \times 100\% = 175\%
$$

Converting a Percent to a Decimal

To convert a percent to a decimal, write the number without the percent sign and move the decimal point two places to the left.

Examples

1. Convert 84% to a decimal.
84% = .84

2. Convert 0.6% to a decimal.
0.6% = .006

3. Convert 160% to a decimal.
160% = 1.60, or 1.6

4. Convert 27.5% to a decimal.
27.5% = .275

Working with Ratios and Proportions

A ratio compares two numbers. A ratio is often written as a fraction in which the number being compared is the numerator and the number to which it is compared is the denominator. The fraction is then expressed in lowest terms. A ratio also may be written with a colon.

Examples

1. Express the ratio of 12 to 4.

$$12 \text{ to } 4 = \frac{12}{4} = \frac{3}{1}, \text{ or } 3 : 1$$

2. Express the ratio of 4 to 12.

$$4 \text{ to } 12 = \frac{4}{12} = \frac{1}{3}, \text{ or } 1 : 3$$

3. Express the ratio 25 cm to 75 cm.

$$\frac{25 \text{ cm to } 75 \text{ cm}}{} = \frac{25}{75} = \frac{1}{3}, \text{ or } 1:3$$

Proportions

A proportion is a mathematical sentence that states that two ratios are equivalent. To write a proportion, place an equal sign between the two equivalent ratios. In this case, the equal sign stands for "is the same as." You can use a colon instead of a fraction.

Examples

1. Write as a proportion: 6 compared to 9 is the same as 8 compared to 12.

$$\frac{6}{9} = \frac{8}{12}, \text{ or } 6:9 = 8:12$$

2. Write as a proportion: 56 is to 14 as 76 is to 19.

$$\frac{56}{14} = \frac{76}{19}, \text{ or } 56:14 = 76:19$$

To write a proportion in which the value of one number is unknown, use X to represent the unknown number.

Examples

1. Some number compares to 45 as 8 compares to 10.

$$\frac{X}{45} = \frac{8}{10}, \text{ or } X:45 = 8:10$$

2. Some number compares to 30 as 9 compares to 54.

$$\frac{X}{30} = \frac{9}{54}, \text{ or } X:30 = 9:54$$

To find the value of the unknown number in a proportion, cross multiply, then divide both sides of the equal sign by the number that precedes X. Check your answer by substituting the value you found for X in the original proportion.

Examples

1. $\dfrac{X}{45} \diagdown \dfrac{8}{10}$

$10 \times X = 8 \times 45$
$10X = 360$
$\dfrac{10X}{10} = \dfrac{360}{10}$
$X = 36$

2. $\dfrac{X}{30} \diagdown \dfrac{9}{54}$

$54 \times X = 9 \times 30$
$54X = 270$
$\dfrac{54X}{54} = \dfrac{270}{54}$
$X = 5$

Working with Equations

An equation is a mathematical sentence that contains a variable and an equal sign. An equation expresses a relationship between two or more quantities. A formula is a special kind of equation. A formula shows relationships between quantities that are always true. A formula is a mathematical rule. In physical science, you will be dealing with formulas. In Appendix E, you will find a list of the formulas used in this textbook.

To solve a formula, follow these three steps:
Step 1 Write the formula.
Step 2 Substitute given numbers and units.
Step 3 Solve for the unknown variable.

Examples

1. Using the formula for the area of a circle, $A = \pi r^2$, calculate the area of a circle whose radius is 2 cm:

Step 1 Write the formula. $A = \pi r^2$
Step 2 Substitute given numbers and units.
$A = \dfrac{22}{7} \times (2 \text{ cm})^2$
Step 3 Solve for the unknown variable.
$A = \dfrac{22}{7} \times 4 \text{ cm}^2 = \dfrac{88 \text{ cm}^2}{7} = 12.5 \text{ cm}^2$

2. Using the formula for density, $D = \dfrac{m}{v}$, find the mass of a sample of aluminum whose volume is 5 cm^3 and whose density is 2.7 g/cm^3:

Step 1 Write the formula. $D = \dfrac{m}{v}$

Step 2 Substitute given numbers and units.
$$2.7 \text{ g/cm}^3 = \frac{m}{5 \text{ cm}^3}$$

Step 3 Solve for the unknown variable.
$m = 2.7 \text{ g/cm}^3 \times 5 \text{ cm}^3$
$m = 13.5 \text{ g}$

1. Density (Chapter 1)

$$\text{Density} = \frac{\text{Mass}}{\text{Volume}} \qquad D = \frac{m}{v}$$

2. Volume of a Regular Solid (Chapter 1)

Volume = Height × Length × Width

$$V = h \times l \times w$$

3. Speed (Chapter 12)

$$\text{Speed} = \frac{\text{Distance}}{\text{Time}}$$

4. Acceleration (Chapter 12)

$$\text{Acceleration} = \frac{\text{Final Velocity} - \text{Original Velocity}}{\text{Time}}$$

5. Momentum (Chapter 12)

Momentum = Mass × Velocity

6. Force (Chapter 13)

Force = Mass × Acceleration

7. Weight (Chapter 13)

Weight = Mass × Acceleration due to gravity

$$w = m \times g$$

8. Pressure (Chapter 14)

$$\text{Pressure} = \frac{\text{Force}}{\text{Area}}$$

9. Work (Chapter 15)

Work = Force × Distance

$$W = F \times d$$

10. Power (Chapter 15)

$$\text{Power} = \frac{\text{Work}}{\text{Time}}$$

$$P = \frac{W}{t} \ \text{or} \ P = \frac{F \times d}{t}$$

11. Kinetic Energy (Chapter 16)

$$\text{Kinetic energy} = \frac{\text{Mass} \times \text{Velocity}^2}{2}$$

$$\text{K.E.} = \frac{m \times v^2}{2}$$

12. Gravitational Potential Energy (Chapter 16)

G.P.E. = Weight × Height

13. Heat Gained or Lost (Chapter 17)

$$\begin{array}{c}\text{Heat gained} \\ \text{or lost}\end{array} = \text{Mass} \times \begin{array}{c}\text{Change in} \\ \text{temperature}\end{array} \times \begin{array}{c}\text{Specific} \\ \text{heat}\end{array}$$

Heat gained or lost = m × ΔT × s.h.

14. Ohm's Law (Chapter 19)

$$\text{Current} = \frac{\text{Voltage}}{\text{Resistance}}$$

$$I = \frac{V}{R}$$

$$\text{Amperes} = \frac{\text{Volts}}{\text{Ohms}}$$

15. Electric Power (Chapter 19)

Electric power = Voltage × Current

$$P = V \times I$$

Watts = Volts × Amperes

16. Electric Energy (Chapter 19)

Electric energy = Power × Time

$$E = P \times t$$

17. Wave Speed (Chapter 23)

Speed = Frequency × Wavelength

18. Law of Reflection (Chapter 23)

Angle of incidence = Angle of reflection

Appendix F

THE CHEMICAL ELEMENTS

NAME	SYMBOL	ATOMIC NUMBER	ATOMIC MASS†		NAME	SYMBOL	ATOMIC NUMBER	ATOMIC MASS†
Actinium	Ac	89	(227)		Neodymium	Nd	60	144.2
Aluminum	Al	13	27.0		Neon	Ne	10	20.2
Americium	Am	95	(243)		Neptunium	Np	93	(237)
Antimony	Sb	51	121.8		Nickel	Ni	28	58.7
Argon	Ar	18	39.9		Niobium	Nb	41	92.9
Arsenic	As	33	74.9		Nitrogen	N	7	14.01
Astatine	At	85	(210)		Nobelium	No	102	(255)
Barium	Ba	56	137.3		Osmium	Os	76	190.2
Berkelium	Bk	97	(247)		Oxygen	O	8	16.00
Beryllium	Be	4	9.01		Palladium	Pd	46	106.4
Bismuth	Bi	83	209.0		Phosphorus	P	15	31.0
Boron	B	5	10.8		Platinum	Pt	78	195.1
Bromine	Br	35	79.9		Plutonium	Pu	94	(244)
Cadmium	Cd	48	112.4		Polonium	Po	84	(210)
Calcium	Ca	20	40.1		Potassium	K	19	39.1
Californium	Cf	98	(251)		Praseodymium	Pr	59	140.9
Carbon	C	6	12.01		Promethium	Pm	61	(145)
Cerium	Ce	58	140.1		Protactinium	Pa	91	(231)
Cesium	Cs	55	132.9		Radium	Ra	88	(226)
Chlorine	Cl	17	35.5		Radon	Rn	86	(222)
Chromium	Cr	24	52.0		Rhenium	Re	75	186.2
Cobalt	Co	27	58.9		Rhodium	Rh	45	102.9
Copper	Cu	29	63.5		Rubidium	Rb	37	85.5
Curium	Cm	96	(247)		Ruthenium	Ru	44	101.1
Dysprosium	Dy	66	162.5		Samarium	Sm	62	150.4
Einsteinium	Es	99	(254)		Scandium	Sc	21	45.0
Erbium	Er	68	167.3		Seaborgium	Sg	106	(263)
Europium	Eu	63	152.0		Selenium	Se	34	79.0
Fermium	Fm	100	(257)		Silicon	Si	14	28.1
Fluorine	F	9	19.0		Silver	Ag	47	107.9
Francium	Fr	87	(223)		Sodium	Na	11	23.0
Gadolinium	Gd	64	157.2		Strontium	Sr	38	87.6
Gallium	Ga	31	69.7		Sulfur	S	16	32.1
Germanium	Ge	32	72.6		Tantalum	Ta	73	180.9
Gold	Au	79	197.0		Technetium	Tc	43	(97)
Hafnium	Hf	72	178.5		Tellurium	Te	52	127.6
Helium	He	2	4.00		Terbium	Tb	65	158.9
Holmium	Ho	67	164.9		Thallium	Tl	81	204.4
Hydrogen	H	1	1.008		Thorium	Th	90	232.0
Indium	In	49	114.8		Thulium	Tm	69	168.9
Iodine	I	53	126.9		Tin	Sn	50	118.7
Iridium	Ir	77	192.2		Titanium	Ti	22	47.9
Iron	Fe	26	55.8		Tungsten	W	74	183.9
Krypton	Kr	36	83.8		Unnilennium	Une	109	(266?)
Lanthanum	La	57	138.9		Unniloctium	Uno	108	(265)
Lawrencium	Lr	103	(256)		Unnilpentium	Unp	105	(262)
Lead	Pb	82	207.2		Unnilquadium	Unq	104	(261)
Lithium	Li	3	6.94		Unnilseptium	Uns	107	(262)
Lutetium	Lu	71	175.0		Uranium	U	92	238.0
Magnesium	Mg	12	24.3		Vanadium	V	23	50.9
Manganese	Mn	25	54.9		Xenon	Xe	54	131.3
Mendelevium	Md	101	(258)		Ytterbium	Yb	70	173.0
Mercury	Hg	80	200.6		Yttrium	Y	39	88.9
Molybdenum	Mo	42	95.9		Zinc	Zn	30	65.4
					Zirconium	Zr	40	91.2

†Numbers in parentheses give the mass number of the most stable isotope.

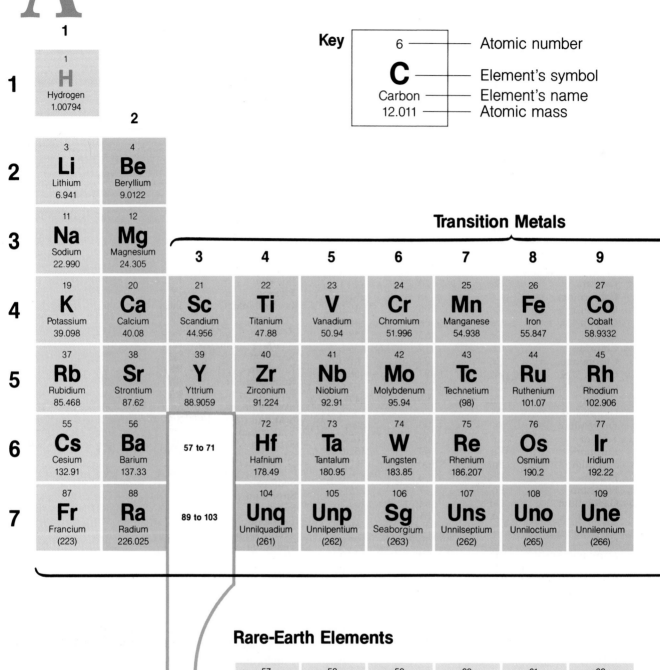

Key

6	Atomic number
C	Element's symbol
Carbon	Element's name
12.011	Atomic mass

1

1
H
Hydrogen
1.00794

2

2
3
Li
Lithium
6.941

4
Be
Beryllium
9.0122

3
11
Na
Sodium
22.990

12
Mg
Magnesium
24.305

Transition Metals

3	4	5	6	7	8	9

4
19 **K** Potassium 39.098 | 20 **Ca** Calcium 40.08 | 21 **Sc** Scandium 44.956 | 22 **Ti** Titanium 47.88 | 23 **V** Vanadium 50.94 | 24 **Cr** Chromium 51.996 | 25 **Mn** Manganese 54.938 | 26 **Fe** Iron 55.847 | 27 **Co** Cobalt 58.9332

5
37 **Rb** Rubidium 85.468 | 38 **Sr** Strontium 87.62 | 39 **Y** Yttrium 88.9059 | 40 **Zr** Zirconium 91.224 | 41 **Nb** Niobium 92.91 | 42 **Mo** Molybdenum 95.94 | 43 **Tc** Technetium (98) | 44 **Ru** Ruthenium 101.07 | 45 **Rh** Rhodium 102.906

6
55 **Cs** Cesium 132.91 | 56 **Ba** Barium 137.33 | 57 to 71 | 72 **Hf** Hafnium 178.49 | 73 **Ta** Tantalum 180.95 | 74 **W** Tungsten 183.85 | 75 **Re** Rhenium 186.207 | 76 **Os** Osmium 190.2 | 77 **Ir** Iridium 192.22

7
87 **Fr** Francium (223) | 88 **Ra** Radium 226.025 | 89 to 103 | 104 **Unq** Unnilquadium (261) | 105 **Unp** Unnilpentium (262) | 106 **Sg** Seaborgium (263) | 107 **Uns** Unnilseptium (262) | 108 **Uno** Unniloctium (265) | 109 **Une** Unnilennium (266)

Rare-Earth Elements

Lanthanoid Series
57 **La** Lanthanum 138.906 | 58 **Ce** Cerium 140.12 | 59 **Pr** Praseodymium 140.908 | 60 **Nd** Neodymium 144.24 | 61 **Pm** Promethium (145) | 62 **Sm** Samarium 150.36

Actinoid Series
89 **Ac** Actinium 227.028 | 90 **Th** Thorium 232.038 | 91 **Pa** Protactinium 231.036 | 92 **U** Uranium 238.029 | 93 **Np** Neptunium 237.048 | 94 **Pu** Plutonium (244)

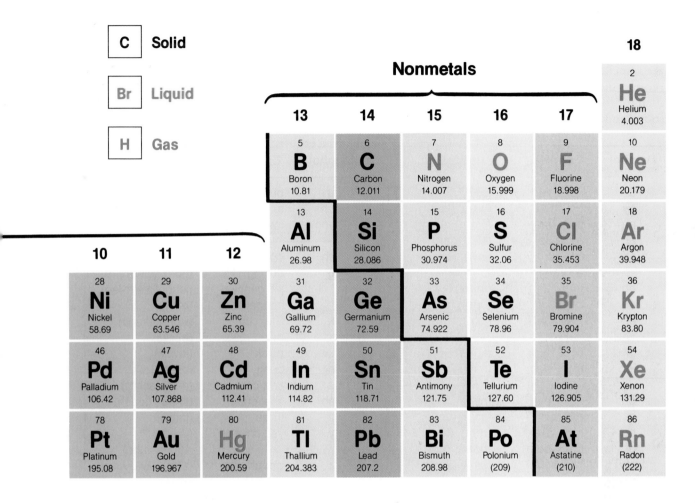

C	Solid
Br	Liquid
H	Gas

Nonmetals

	13	14	15	16	17	18
						2 **He** Helium 4.003
	5 **B** Boron 10.81	6 **C** Carbon 12.011	7 **N** Nitrogen 14.007	8 **O** Oxygen 15.999	9 **F** Fluorine 18.998	10 **Ne** Neon 20.179

10	11	12	13 **Al** Aluminum 26.98	14 **Si** Silicon 28.086	15 **P** Phosphorus 30.974	16 **S** Sulfur 32.06	17 **Cl** Chlorine 35.453	18 **Ar** Argon 39.948
28 **Ni** Nickel 58.69	29 **Cu** Copper 63.546	30 **Zn** Zinc 65.39	31 **Ga** Gallium 69.72	32 **Ge** Germanium 72.59	33 **As** Arsenic 74.922	34 **Se** Selenium 78.96	35 **Br** Bromine 79.904	36 **Kr** Krypton 83.80
46 **Pd** Palladium 106.42	47 **Ag** Silver 107.868	48 **Cd** Cadmium 112.41	49 **In** Indium 114.82	50 **Sn** Tin 118.71	51 **Sb** Antimony 121.75	52 **Te** Tellurium 127.60	53 **I** Iodine 126.905	54 **Xe** Xenon 131.29
78 **Pt** Platinum 195.08	79 **Au** Gold 196.967	80 **Hg** Mercury 200.59	81 **Tl** Thallium 204.383	82 **Pb** Lead 207.2	83 **Bi** Bismuth 208.98	84 **Po** Polonium (209)	85 **At** Astatine (210)	86 **Rn** Radon (222)

The symbols shown here for elements 104-105 and 107-109 are being used temporarily until names for these elements can be agreed upon.

Metals

Mass numbers in parentheses are those of the most stable or common isotope.

63 **Eu** Europium 151.96	64 **Gd** Gadolinium 157.25	65 **Tb** Terbium 158.925	66 **Dy** Dysprosium 162.50	67 **Ho** Holmium 164.93	68 **Er** Erbium 167.26	69 **Tm** Thulium 168.934	70 **Yb** Ytterbium 173.04	71 **Lu** Lutetium 174.967
95 **Am** Americium (243)	96 **Cm** Curium (247)	97 **Bk** Berkelium (247)	98 **Cf** Californium (251)	99 **Es** Einsteinium (254)	100 **Fm** Fermium (257)	101 **Md** Mendelevium (258)	102 **No** Nobelium (259)	103 **Lr** Lawrencium (260)

Glossary

Pronunciation Key

When difficult names or terms first appear in the text, they are respelled to aid pronunciation. A syllable in SMALL CAPITAL LETTERS receives the most stress. The key below lists the letters used for respelling. It includes examples of words using each sound and shows how the words would be respelled.

Symbol	Example	Respelling
a	hat	(hat)
ay	pay, late	(pay), (layt)
ah	star, hot	(stahr), (haht)
ai	air, dare	(air), (dair)
aw	law, all	(law), (awl)
eh	met	(meht)
ee	bee, eat	(bee), (eet)
er	learn, sir, fur	(lern), (ser), (fer)
ih	fit	(fiht)
igh	mile, sigh	(mighl), (sigh)
oh	no	(noh)
oi	soil, boy	(soil), (boi)
oo	root, rule	(root), (rool)
or	born, door	(born), (dor)
ow	plow, out	(plow), (owt)

Symbol	Example	Respelling
u	put, book	(put), (buk)
uh	fun	(fuhn)
yoo	few, use	(fyoo), (yooz)
ch	chill, reach	(chihl), (reech)
g	go, dig	(goh), (dihg)
j	jet, gently, bridge	(jeht), (JEHNT-lee), (brihj)
k	kite, cup	(kight), (kuhp)
ks	mix	(mihks)
kw	quick	(kwihk)
ng	bring	(brihng)
s	say, cent	(say), (sehnt)
sh	she, crash	(shee), (krash)
th	three	(three)
y	yet, onion	(yeht), (UHN-yuhn)
z	zip, always	(zihp), (AWL-wayz)
zh	treasure	(TREH-zher)

absolute zero: temperature at which all molecular motion ceases; lowest possible temperature (0 K, −273°C)

acceleration: rate of change in velocity

acid: compound with a pH below 7 that tastes sour, turns blue litmus paper red, reacts with metals to produce hydrogen gas, and ionizes in water to produce hydrogen ions; proton donor

acoustics: science of sound and its interactions

actinoid series: second row of rare-earth elements in the periodic table; radioactive; all but four are synthetic

activation energy: energy required for a chemical reaction to occur

active solar-heating system: heating system that uses a solar collector to store heat from the sun and an arrangement of a hot-water heater and pipes to circulate heat throughout a building

alkali metal: member of element Family 1 that has 1 valence electron

alkaline earth metal: member of element Family 2 that has 2 valence electrons

alkane: straight-chain or branched-chain saturated hydrocarbon

alkene: unsaturated hydrocarbon in which at least one pair of carbon atoms is joined by a double covalent bond

alkyne: unsaturated hydrocarbon in which at least one pair of carbon atoms is joined by a triple covalent bond

alloy: a solution of two metals or a metal and a nonmetal that has the properties of a metal

alpha (AL-fuh) **particle:** weakest type of nuclear radiation; consists of a helium nucleus released during alpha decay

alternating current: current in which the electrons reverse their direction regularly

amplifier: device that increases the strength of an electric signal

amplitude (AM-pluh-tood): greatest distance from crest of a wave

Archimedes' principle: explanation that says that the buoyant force on an object is equal to the weight of the fluid displaced by the object

artificial transmutation: changing of one element into another by unnatural means; involves bombarding a nucleus with high-energy particles to cause change

atom: smallest part of an element that has all the properties of an element

atomic mass: average of the masses of the existing isotopes of an element

atomic mass unit (amu): unit used to measure the masses of subatomic particles; a proton has a mass of 1 amu

atomic number: number of protons in the nucleus of an atom

aurora: glowing region of air caused by solar particles that break through the Earth's magnetic field

base: compound with pH above 7 that tastes bitter, is slippery to the touch, turns red litmus paper blue, and ionizes in water to produce hydroxide ions; proton acceptor

battery: device that produces electricity by converting chemical energy into electrical energy; made up of electrochemical cells

Bernoulli's principle: explanation that the pressure in a moving stream of fluid is less than the pressure in the surrounding fluid

beta (BAYT-uh) **particle:** electron, created in the nucleus of an atom, released during beta decay

bimetallic strip: strip consisting of two different metals that expand at different rates and cause the strip to bend; switch in a thermostat

binary system: number system consisting of two numbers, 0 and 1, that is used by computers

binding energy: energy required to break up a nucleus into its component protons and neutrons

bit: single electronic switch, or piece of information

boiling: process in which particles inside a liquid as well as those on the surface of a liquid change to a gas

boiling point: temperature at which a substance changes from the liquid phase to the gas phase

boron family: Family 13 of the periodic table; elements have 3 valence electrons

bubble chamber: device that uses a super-heated liquid to create bubbles when radioactive particles pass through it

buoyant (BOI-uhnt) **force:** upward force in a fluid that exists because the pressure of a fluid varies with depth

byte: string of bits; usually 8 bits make up a byte

calorie: unit used to measure heat

calorimeter (kah-luh-RIHM-uht-er): instrument used to measure the heat given off in chemical reactions

carbon family: Family 14 of the periodic table; elements have 4 valence electrons

catalyst: substance that increases the rate of a chemical reaction without being changed by the reaction

cathode-ray tube: type of vacuum tube that uses electrons to produce an image on a screen

Celsius scale: metric temperature scale on which water freezes at 0° and boils at 100°

centimeter: one hundredth of a meter

central heating system: system that generates heat for an entire building or group of buildings from a central location

central processing unit: part of a computer that controls the operation of all the other components of the computer

charge: physical property of matter that can give rise to an electric force of attraction or repulsion

chemical bonding: combining of atoms of elements to form new substances

chemical change: process by which a substance becomes a new and different substance

chemical energy: energy that bonds atoms or ions together

chemical equation: expression in which symbols, formulas, and numbers are used to represent a chemical reaction

chemical formula: combination of chemical symbols usually used to represent a compound

chemical property: property that describes how a substance changes into a new substance

chemical reaction: process in which substances undergo physical and chemical changes that result in the formation of new substances with different properties

chemical symbol: shorthand way of representing an element

chip: thin piece of silicon containing an integrated circuit

circuit: complete path through which electricity can flow

circuit breaker: reusable device that protects a circuit from becoming overloaded

cloud chamber: device to study radioactivity, which uses a cooled gas that will condense around radioactive particles

cochlea: part of the ear that contains hundreds of nerve cells attached to nerve fibers

coefficient (koh-uh-FIHSH-uhnt): number that is placed in front of a symbol or a formula in a chemical equation that indicates how many atoms or molecules of this substance are involved in the reaction

collision theory: theory that relates collisions among particles to reaction rate; reaction rate depends on such factors as concentration, surface area, temperature, and catalysts

colloid (KAHL-oid): homogeneous mixture in which the particles are mixed together but not dissolved

combustion: process in which fuels are combined with oxygen at a high temperature; the burning of fuel

compound: substance made up of molecules that contain more than one kind of atom; two or more elements chemically combined

concave lens: lens that is thicker at the ends than in the middle

concave mirror: mirror with a surface that curves inward

condensation (kahn-duhn-SAY-shuhn): change of a gas to a liquid

conduction (kuhn-DUHK-shuhn): heat transfer through a substance or from one substance to another by direct contact of molecules; method of charging an object by allowing electrons to flow through one object to another object

conductor: material which permits electrons to

flow freely or transfers heat more easily than other substances

cone: nerve cell in the eye that sees color

control: an experiment run without a variable in order to show that any data from the experimental setup was due only to the variable that was being tested

convection (kuhn-VEHK-shuhn): heat transfer in liquids and gases by means of convection currents

conversion factor: fraction that always equals one, which is used for dimensional analysis

convex lens: lens that is thicker in the middle than at the edges

convex mirror: mirror with a surface that curves outward

cooling system: system that removes heat from a building, room, or other enclosed space by evaporation

cornea: protective outer covering of the eye that refracts light

corrosion: gradual wearing away of a metal due to a chemical reaction in which the metal element is changed into a metallic compound

covalent bonding: bonding that involves the sharing of electrons

crest: high point of a wave

crystal: solid in which the particles are arranged in a regular repeating pattern

crystal lattice: regular, repeating arrangement of atoms

cubic centimeter: metric unit used to measure the volume of solids; equal to a milliliter

current: flow of charge

data: recorded observations and measurements

decay series: sequence of steps by which a radioactive nucleus decays into a nonradioactive nucleus

decomposition reaction: chemical reaction in which a complex substance breaks down into two or more simpler substances

density: measurement of how much mass is contained in a given volume of an object; mass per unit volume

diatomic element: element whose atoms can form covalent bonds with another atom of the same element

diffraction (dih-FRAK-shuhn): bending of waves around the edge of an obstacle

diffuse reflection: bouncing back of light from an uneven surface

dimensional analysis: method of converting one unit to another

diode: vacuum tube or semiconductor that acts as a rectifier

direct current: current consisting of electrons that flow constantly in one direction

disk drive: part of a computer that can act as an input device by reading information off a disk and entering it into the computer or as an output device removing information from a computer and storing it on a disk

doping: process of adding impurities to semi-conducting materials

Doppler effect: change in sound or light that occurs whenever there is motion between the source and its observer

double-replacement reaction: chemical reaction in which different atoms in two different compounds replace each other

ductile: able to be drawn into a thin wire

eardrum: stretched membrane in the ear that vibrates at the same frequency as the sound waves that enter the ear

efficiency: comparison of work input to work output

electric discharge: loss of static electricity as electric charges move off an object

electric field: region of space around a charged particle in which a force is exerted on other charged particles

electric motor: device that uses an electromagnet to convert electrical energy to mechanical energy that is used to do work

electrolyte (ee-LEHK-troh-light): substance whose water solution conducts an electric current

electromagnet: solenoid with a magnetic material such as iron inside its coils

electromagnetic energy: energy associated with moving charges

electromagnetic force: force of attraction or repulsion between particles in an atom

electromagnetic induction: process by which a current is produced by a changing magnetic field

electromagnetic spectrum: arrangement of electromagnetic waves in order of wavelength and frequency

electromagnetic wave: wave that consists of electric and magnetic fields and does not require a medium to exist

electromagnetism: relationship between electricity and magnetism

electron: negatively charged subatomic particle found in an area outside the nucleus of an atom

electron affinity: tendency of an atom to attract electrons

electron cloud: space in which electrons are likely to be found

electron-dot diagram: diagram that uses the chemical symbol for an element surrounded by a series of dots to represent the electron sharing that takes place in a covalent bond

electronics: study of the release, behavior, and control of electrons as related to use in practical devices

electroscope: device consisting of a metal rod with two thin metal leaves at one end that can be used to detect radioactivity or charge

element: simplest type of pure substance

endothermic reaction: chemical reaction in which energy is absorbed

energy: ability to do work

energy conversion: change of energy from one form to another

energy level: most likely location in an electron cloud in which an electron can be found

evaporation (ee-vap-uh-RAY-shuhn): vaporization that takes place at the surface of a liquid

exothermic (ek-soh-THER-mihk) **reaction:** chemical reaction in which energy is released

external-combustion engine: engine in which fuel is burned outside the engine; a steam engine

family: column of elements in the periodic table; group

farsightedness: condition in which the eyeball is too short, causing images to form behind the retina; corrected with a convex lens

fiberglass: common insulating material consisting of long, thin strands of glass packed together

flammability (flam-uh-BIHL-uh-tee): ability to burn

fluorescent light: light produced by bombarding molecules of gas in a tube

focal point: location at which light rays reflected from a mirror meet

force: push or pull that gives energy to an object, sometimes causing a change in the motion of the object

fraction: petroleum part with its own boiling point

freezing: change of a liquid into a solid

freezing point: temperature at which a substance changes from the liquid phase to the solid phase

frequency (FREE-kwuhn-see): number of waves that pass a certain point in a given amount of time

friction: force that acts in the opposite direction of motion; will cause an object to slow down and finally stop

fulcrum: fixed pivot point of a lever

fundamental tone: note produced at the lowest frequency at which a standing wave occurs

fuse: thin strip of metal used for safety because when the current flowing through it becomes too high, it melts and breaks the flow of electricity

galvanometer: device that uses an electromagnet to detect small amounts of current

gamma (GAM-uh) **ray:** high-frequency electromagnetic wave released during gamma decay; strongest type of nuclear radiation

gas: phase in which matter has no definite shape or volume

Geiger counter: device that can be used to detect radioactivity because it produces an electric current in the presence of a radioactive substance

generator: device that uses electromagnets to convert mechanical energy to electrical energy

gram: one thousandth of a kilogram

gravitational potential energy: potential energy that is dependent on height above the Earth's surface

gravity: force of attraction that depends on the mass of two objects and the distance between them; responsible for accelerating an object toward the Earth

group: column of elements in the periodic table; family

half-life: amount of time it takes for half the atoms in a given sample of an element to decay

halogen family: Family 17 of the periodic table; elements have atoms that contain 7 valence electrons

hardware: physical parts of a computer

heat: form of energy caused by the internal motion of molecules of matter

heat energy: energy involved in the internal motion of particles of matter

heat engine: machine that changes heat energy into mechanical energy in order to do work

heat of evaporation: amount of heat needed to change a substance from the liquid phase to the gas phase

heat of fusion: amount of heat needed to change a substance from the solid phase to the liquid phase

heat-pump system: heating system that takes heat from the outside air and brings it inside

heat transfer: movement of heat from a warmer object to a cooler one

heterogeneous (heht-er-oh-JEE-nee-uhs) **mixture:** substance that does not appear to be the same throughout

holography: technology that uses lasers to produce three-dimensional photographs

homogeneous (hoh-moh-JEE-nee-uhs) **mixture:** mixture that appears the same throughout

hot-water system: heating system in which hot water is pumped through pipes to a convector that heats a room by means of convection currents

hydraulic device: machine that takes advantage of the fact that pressure is transmitted equally in all directions in a liquid; obtains a large force on a large piston by applying a small force with a small piston

hydrocarbon: organic compound that contains only hydrogen and carbon

hypothesis (high-PAHTH-uh-sihs): proposed solution to a scientific problem

illuminated object: object that can be seen because it is lit up

incandescent light: light produced from heat

inclined plane: flat slanted surface that multiplies force

index of refraction: comparison of speed of light in air with speed of light in a certain material

induced current: current produced in a wire exposed to a changing magnetic field

induction: method of charging an object by rearranging its electric charges into groups of positive charge and negative charge

inertia (ihn-ER-shuh): tendency of objects to remain in motion or to stay at rest unless acted upon by an outside force

infrared ray: electromagnetic wave in the frequency range just below visible light; felt as heat

infrasonic (ihn-fruh-SAHN-ihk): sound below the range of human hearing (20 Hz)

inner ear: liquid-filled portion of the ear; receives vibrations from the middle ear

input device: device through which data are fed into a computer

insoluble: unable to be dissolved in another material, such as water

insulation: prevention of heat loss by reducing the transfer of heat by conduction and convection

insulator: material made up of atoms with tightly bound electrons that are unable to flow freely; substance that does not conduct heat easily

integrated circuit: circuit consisting of many diodes and transistors that are all placed on a thin piece of silicon, known as a chip

intensity: amount of energy carried by a wave; indicated by the amplitude of a wave

interference: interaction of waves that occur at the same place at the same time

internal-combustion engine: engine in which the burning of fuel takes place inside the engine; a gasoline engine

ion: an atom that has become charged due to the loss or gain of electrons

ionization: process of removing electrons and forming ions

iris: colored area surrounding the pupil that controls the amount of light entering the eye

isomer: one of a number of compounds that have the same molecular formula but different structures

isotope (IGH-suh-tohp): atom that has the same number of protons (atomic number) as another atom but a different number of neutrons

joule: unit of work and energy; 1 newton-meter

Kelvin scale: metric temperature scale on which 0 K represents absolute zero, the freezing point of water is 273 K, and the boiling point of water is 373 K

kilogram: basic unit of mass in the metric system

kilometer: one thousand meters

kinetic (kih-NEHT-ihk) **energy:** energy that a moving object has due to its motion; energy of motion

kinetics: study of the rates of chemical reactions

lanthanoid series: first row of rare-earth elements in the periodic table; soft, malleable metals that have a high luster and conductivity

laser: *l*ight *a*mplification by *s*timulated *e*mission of *r*adiation; device that produces coherent light

law: summarizing statement of observed experimental facts that has been tested many times and is generally accepted as true

Law of Conservation of Energy: law that states that energy can neither be created nor destroyed by ordinary means.

lens: transparent material that refracts light

lever: rigid bar free to move about a single point; may be first-class, second-class, or third-class depending on the positions of the effort force, resistance force, and fulcrum

light ray: straight-line path of light

liquid: matter with no definite shape but with a definite volume

liter: basic unit of volume in the metric system

longitudinal (lahn-juh-TOOD-uhn-uhl) **wave:** wave in which the motion of the medium is parallel to the direction of the wave

luminous object: object that is capable of giving off its own light

luster: shininess

machine: device that makes work easier by changing force and distance or by changing the direction of a force

magnetic domain: region of a material in which the magnetic fields of individual atoms are aligned

magnetic field: area over which the magnetic force is exerted

magnetism: force of attraction or repulsion of a magnetic material due to the arrangement of its atoms

magnetosphere: region in which the magnetic field of the Earth is found

main memory: part of a computer that contains data and operating instructions that are processed by the central processing unit

malleable: able to be hammered out into a thin sheet

mass: amount of matter in an object

mass number: sum of the protons and neutrons in the nucleus of an atom

matter: anything that has mass and volume

mechanical advantage: number of times a machine multiplies the effort force

mechanical energy: energy associated with motion

mechanical wave: wave that disturbs a medium

medium: material through which a mechanical wave travels

melting: change of a solid to a liquid

melting point: temperature at which a substance changes from the solid phase to the liquid phase

meniscus (mih-NIHS-kuhs): point at the bottom of the curve of a liquid in a graduated cylinder

metal: element that is a good conductor of heat and electricity, is shiny, has a high melting point, is ductile and malleable, and tends to lose electrons

metallic bond: bond formed by atoms of metals, in which the outer electrons of the atoms form a common electron cloud

metalloid (MEHT-uh-loid): element that has properties of both metals and nonmetals

meter: basic unit of length in the metric system

metric system: standard system of measurement used by all scientists

microwave: high-frequency radio wave used primarily for communication

middle ear: part of the ear that receives vibrations from the eardrum and contains the hammer, anvil, and stirrup

milligram: one thousandth of a gram

milliliter: one thousandth of a liter

millimeter: one thousandth of a meter

mixture: matter that consists of two or more substances mixed but not chemically combined

modem: device that changes electronic signals from a computer into messages that can be carried over telephone lines

modulation (mahj-uh-LAY-shuhn): variation; in particular, in the amplitude or frequency of an electromagnetic wave

molecule (MAHL-ih-kyool): combination of atoms formed by a covalent bond

momentum: mass of an object times its velocity; determines how difficult it is to stop the object's motion

monomer: smaller molecule that joins with the other smaller molecules to form a chain molecule called a polymer

motion: change in position in a certain amount of time

natural polymer: polymer molecule found in nature; for example, cotton, silk, and wool

nearsightedness: condition in which the eyeball is too long, causing images to form before the retina; corrected with a concave lens

neon light: cool light produced when electrons flow through a glass tube filled with gas

network solid: covalent substance whose molecules are very large because the atoms involved continue to bond to one another; have rather high melting points

neutralization (noo-truhl-ih-ZAY-shuhn): reaction in which an acid combines with a base to form a salt and water

neutron: subatomic particle with no charge located in the nucleus of an atom

newton: unit of force; 1 kg × 1 m/sec/sec

nitrogen family: Family 15 of the periodic table; elements with 5 valence electrons

noble gas: member of Family 18 of the periodic table; elements have atoms with 8 valence electrons and are extremely unreactive

nonmetal: element that is a poor conductor of heat and electricity, has a dull surface, low melting point, is brittle, breaks easily, and tends to gain electrons

nuclear chain reaction: series of fission reactions that occur because the products released during one fission reaction cause fission reactions in other atoms

nuclear fission (FIHSH-uhn): splitting of an atomic nucleus into two smaller nuclei of approximately equal mass

nuclear fusion: joining of two atomic nuclei of smaller mass to form a single nucleus of larger mass

nuclear radiation: particles and energy released from a radioactive nucleus

nuclear strong force: force that overcomes the electric force of repulsion among protons in an atomic nuclei and binds the nucleus together

nucleus (NOO-klee-uhs): small, dense positively charged center of an atom

Ohm's law: electrical law that states that the current in a wire (I) is equal to the voltage

(V) divided by the resistance (R); also can be stated as $V = I \times R$

opaque: material that does not transmit light

optical fiber: thin tubes of glass used to transmit information as flashes of light

organic compound: a carbon-containing compound with a few inorganic exceptions, such as calcium carbonate, carbon dioxide, and carbon monoxide

outer ear: part of the human ear that funnels sound waves into the ear

output device: part of a computer through which information is removed

overtone: tone produced at frequencies higher than the fundamental at which a standing wave occurs

oxidation number: number of electrons an atom gains, loses, or shares when it forms chemical bonds

oxygen family: Family 16 of the periodic table; elements have atoms with 6 valence electrons

parallel circuit: circuit in which different parts are on separate branches; if one part does not operate properly, current can still flow through the others

passive solar-heating system: heating system in which a building is heated directly by the rays of the sun

period: horizontal row of elements in the periodic table

periodic law: law that states that the physical and chemical properties of the elements are periodic functions of their atomic numbers

petrochemical product: product made either directly or indirectly from petroleum

petroleum: substance believed to have been formed hundreds of millions of years ago when dead plants and animals were buried beneath sediments such as mud, sand, silt, or clay at the bottom of the oceans; crude oil

pH: measure of the hydronium ion concentration of a solution; measured on a scale from 0 to 14

phase: state in which matter can exist: solid, liquid, gas, or plasma

phase change: change of matter from one phase (solid, liquid, or gas) to another

photocell: device that uses electrons emitted from a metal during the photoelectric effect to produce current

photoelectric effect: process by which light can be used to knock electrons out of a metal; can only be explained using the particle nature of light

photon: tiny bundle of light energy

physical property: characteristic that distinguishes one type of matter from another and can be observed without changing the identity of the substance

pitch: property of sound that depends on frequency

plane mirror: mirror with a perfectly flat surface

plasma: phase in which matter is extremely high in energy and cannot be contained by ordinary matter; very rare on Earth

polarized light: light in which all the waves are vibrating in the same direction

pole: regions of a magnet where the magnetic effects are the strongest

polyatomic ion: group of covalently bonded atoms that acts like a single atom when combining with other atoms

polymer: large molecule in the form of a chain whose links are smaller molecules called monomers

polymerization (poh-lihm-er-uh-ZAY-shuhn): process of chemically bonding monomers to form polymers

potential (poh-TEHN-shuhl) **difference:** difference in charge as created by opposite posts of a battery

potential energy: energy of shape or position; stored energy

power: rate at which work is done or energy is used

pressure: force that particles of a fluid exert over a certain area due to their weight and motion

product: substance produced by a chemical reaction

property: characteristic of a substance

proton: positively charged subatomic particle located in the nucleus of an atom

pulley: rope, belt, or chain wrapped around a wheel; can change either the amount of force or the direction of the force

pupil: opening in the center of the eye through which light enters

pure substance: substance made of one kind of material having definite properties

quark (kwork): particle that makes up all other known particles in the nucleus of an atom

radar: use of short-wavelength microwaves to locate objects and monitor speed

radiant electric system: heating system in which electricity is passed through wires or cables that resist the flow of electricity, thus producing heat

radiant hot-water system: heating system in which hot water runs through a continuous coil of pipe in the floor of a room and heats the room through radiation

radiation (ray-dee-AY-shuhn): heat transfer through space

radioactive: description for a nucleus that gives off nuclear radiation in the form of mass and energy in order to become stable

radioactive decay: process in which a nucleus spontaneously emits particles or rays to become lighter and more stable

radioactivity: release of energy and matter that results from changes in the nucleus of an atom

radioisotope: radioactive isotope often used in medicine or industry

radio wave: electromagnetic waves with the longest wavelengths and lowest frequencies in the electromagnetic spectrum

rare-earth element: general term for any element in the lanthanoid and actinoid series

reactant (ree-AK-tuhnt): substance that enters into a chemical reaction

reaction rate: measure of how quickly reactants change into products

rectifier: device that converts alternating current to direct current; accomplished by a diode

refining: process of separating petroleum into its fractions

reflecting telescope: telescope that uses a large mirror at its objective end

reflection (rih-FLEHK-shuhn): bouncing back of waves upon reaching another surface

refracting telescope: telescope consisting of two convex lenses at opposite ends of a long tube

refraction (rih-FRAK-shuhn): bending of waves due to a change in speed

regular reflection: bouncing back of light from a smooth, even surface

resistance: opposition to the flow of electric charge

resonant frequency: frequency at which a standing wave occurs

retina: light-sensitive region that lines the eye and on which images are formed

rod: nerve cell in the eye that is sensitive to light and dark

salt: compound formed from the positive ion of a base and the negative ion of an acid

saturated hydrocarbon: hydrocarbon in which all the bonds between carbon atoms are single covalent bonds

scientific method: systematic approach to problem solving

screw: inclined plane wrapped around a central bar to form a spiral

semiconductor: material that is able to conduct electric currents better than insulators but not as well as true conductors

series circuit: circuit in which all parts are connected one after another; if one part fails to operate properly, the current cannot flow

single-replacement reaction: chemical reaction in which an uncombined element replaces an element that is part of a compound

software: set of instructions, or program, a computer follows

solar-heating system: heating system that uses the energy of the sun to produce heat

solenoid: long coil of wire that acts like a magnet when current flows through it

solid: phase in which matter has a definite shape and volume

solid-state device: device made of semiconductors through which electrical signals flow

solubility (sahl-yoo-BIHL-uh-tee): measure of how much of a solute can be dissolved in a given amount of solvent under certain conditions

soluble (SAHL-yoo-buhl): can be dissolved in another material, such as water

solute (SAHL-yoot): substance that is dissolved in a solution

solution (suh-LOO-shuhn): homogeneous mixture of two or more substances in a single physical state

solvent (SAHL-vuhnt): substance that does the dissolving in a solution

sonar: *so*und *na*vigation *r*anging, a technique of using sound waves to measure distance

sound quality: blending of pitches to produce sound; timbre

specific heat: ability of a substance to absorb heat energy

speed: rate at which an object moves

standing wave: wave that does not appear to be moving; occurs at the natural frequency of the material

static electricity: movement of charges from one object to another without further movement

steam-heating system: heating system in which steam is forced through pipes from a boiler to a convector that heats a room by means of convection currents

strong force: force that binds protons and neutrons in the nucleus

structural formula: description of a molecule that shows the kind, number, and arrangement of atoms in a molecule

subatomic particle: proton, neutron, or electron

sublimation (suhb-luh-MAY-shuhn): change from the solid phase directly into the gas phase

subscript: number placed to the lower right of a chemical symbol to indicate the number of atoms of the element in the compound

substituted hydrocarbon: hydrocarbon formed when one or more hydrogen atoms in a hydrocarbon ring or chain are replaced by a different atom or group of atoms

superconductor: material in which resistance is essentially zero at certain low temperatures

surface wave: wave that consists of a combination of transverse and longitudinal waves and occurs at the surface between two different mediums

synthesis (SIHN-thuh-sihs) **reaction:** chemical reaction in which two or more simple substances combine to form a new, more complex substance

synthetic polymer: polymer that does not occur naturally, but is formed artificially from petrochemicals

temperature: measure of the motion of molecules

theory: a logical, time-tested explanation for events that occur in the natural world

thermal expansion: expansion of a substance due to heat

thermal pollution: damage to the environment due to waste heat that causes an unnatural rise in temperature

thermocouple: device that produces electrical energy from heat energy

thermometer: instrument used to measure temperature

thermostat (THER-muh-stat): device that helps control the temperature in an indoor area or in an appliance

timbre (TAM-ber): blending of pitches to produce sound; sound quality

total internal reflection: reflection that occurs if the angle of incidence for light is too great to be transmitted and is instead reflected back into its original medium

tracer: radioactive element whose pathway can be followed through the steps of a chemical reaction or industrial process

transformer: device that increases or decreases the voltage of alternating current

transistor: device consisting of three layers of semiconductors used to amplify an electric signal

transition metal: element that has properties similar to other transition metals and to other metals but whose properties do not fit in with those of any other family

translucent: material that transmits light but no detail

transmutation: process in which one element is changed into another as a result of changes in the nucleus

transparent: material through which light is transmitted easily

transuranium element: element formed synthetically; has more than 92 protons in its nucleus

transverse wave: wave in which the motion of the medium is at right angles to the direction of the wave

triode: type of vacuum tube used for amplification that consists of a wire grid as well as its electrodes

trough (trawf): low point of a wave

ultrasonic (uhl-truh-SAHN-ihk): sound above the range of human hearing (20,000 Hz)

ultraviolet ray: electromagnetic wave in the frequency region just above visible light

unsaturated hydrocarbon: hydrocarbon in which one or more of the bonds between carbon atoms are a double covalent or triple covalent bond

vacuum tube: glass tube, in which almost all gases are removed, which contains electrodes that produce a one-way flow of electrons

valence electron: electron in the outermost energy level of an atom

vaporization (vay-per-ih-ZAY-shuhn): change of a liquid to a gas

variable: the factor being tested in an experimental setup

velocity: description of speed in a given direction

vibration: movement that follows the same path over and over again

visible light: wavelengths of the electronmagnetic spectrum that can be seen with the unaided eye

voltage: potential difference; energy carried by charges that make up a current

volume: amount of space an object takes up

warm-air system: heating system in which heated air is forced through ducts to vents and moves throughout a room by convection currents

watt: unit of power; 1 joule per second

wave: traveling disturbance that carries energy from one place to another

wavelength: distance between two consecutive similar points on a wave

wave speed: frequency of a wave times its wavelength

weak force: force that is the key to the power of the sun; responsible for a process known as radioactive decay

wedge: inclined plane that moves

weight: measure of the force of attraction between objects due to gravity

wheel and axle: machine made up of two circular objects of different sizes; a force that is applied to the wheel and transferred to the axle

work: force acting over a distance to move an object

work input: work that goes into a machine; effort force exerted over a distance

work output: work that comes out of a machine; output force exerted over a distance

X-ray: electromagnetic wave in the frequency range just above ultraviolet rays

Index

Tesla, Nikola, 546
Tevatron, 276, 277
Thallium (Tl), 154
Theory, scientific, 8–9
Thermal expansion, 443–447
Thermal pollution, 470
Thermocouples, 494
Thermogram, 420, 462, 652
Thermograph, 462
Thermometer, 432–433, 494
    Celsius, 29
Thermonuclear reaction, 282
Thermostat, 446–447
Thompson, Benjamin (Count
    Rumford), 424–425, 431, 466
Thomson, J.J., 115–116, 120
Thorium, 273
Thunder, 490
Timbre, 626–627
Titanic, sinking of, 52
Tone, fundamental, 626, 627, 629
Tools of measurement, 26–31
Total internal reflection, 696–698
Tracer, 287
Transformers, 548–550
Transistors, 563
Transition metals, 135, 142,
    152–153
Translucent substances, 681
Transmitter, telephone, 568
Transmutation, 273
    artificial, 276–278
Transparent substances, 681
Transuranium elements, 277
Transverse waves, 595, 642, 643. *See
    also* Electromagnetic waves
Triode, 560–561
Triple-beam balance, 27–28
Tritium, 123
Troughs, 592, 593, 597, 604
Tungsten, 657
Turbines, 467, 546–547

Ultrasonic cleaning, 632
Ultrasonic sounds, 619–620
Ultrasonic waves, 630–632
Ultrasound technique, 632
Ultraviolet light, 641, 657
Ultraviolet radiation, 465
Ultraviolet rays, 647, 653–655
Unbalanced force, 325, 330
Unequal pressure, principle of,
    352–353
Universal Automatic Computer
    (UNIVAC), 557, 573
Universal gravitation, law of,
    339–340
Unsaturated hydrocarbons, 237,
    239–240
UPC codes (Universal Product
    Codes), 696
Uranium, 115–116, 158, 175, 267

Uranium-238, 272–273
    decay series for, 276
Urea, 233

Vaccuum tubes, 559–561. *See also*
    Computers
    cathode-ray tube (CRT),
    569–571
Valence (bonding power),
    137–138
Valence electrons, 147, 148, 150,
    175, 202. *See also* Chemical
    bonding; Chemical families
Valence numbers, 160
Valenzuela, Frank, 631
Van Allen, James, 527
Van Allen radiation belts, 527
Van de Graaff generator, 486
Van Leeuwenhoek, Anton, 551
Vaporization, 72
    heat of, 441, 443
Variable, 13
Velocity
    changes in, 309–313
    combining velocities, 307–308
    defined, 307
    kinetic energy and, 400–401
    momentum and, 313–314
    motion and, 307–308
    terminal, 338–339
Verdigris, 78
Verne, Jules, 47
Vibration, 589–590, 593–594, 643.
    See also Electromagnetic
    waves; Sound; Wave(s)
Videotape, induced currents in,
    547–548
Virtual image, 672, 674
Viscosity, 64
Visible light, 643, 644, 647, 653,
    656–658
Vision, 685–687
    lenses and, 686–687
Vitamin D, 654
Vocal cords, sound produced by,
    614–615
Voltage, 496–497
    electric power and, 506
    Ohm's Law and, 499–500
    transformers to adjust, 548–550
Volts (V), 496
Volume, 48–49
    defined, 49
    mass and, 22–23
    measuring, 28–29
    in metric system, 20, 21
    pressure and, 66–67, 68
    temperature and, 67–68

Warm-air heating system, 457
Waste disposal, problem of, 79

Water
    formula for, 104
    high specific heat of, 436
    molecule, 101
    phases of, 62
    pollution of, 162–163, 470
    salt vs. fresh, freezing
        temperature of, 12, 13–17
    as universal solvent, 93
Watt (W), 374–375, 506
Wave(s), 584–585, 587–611. *See
    also* Electromagnetic waves;
    Sound
    characteristics of, 591–594
    combinations of, 597
    crests of, 592, 593, 597, 603, 604
    defined, 589
    in Earth's surface, 607
    energy and, 588–590
    interactions of, 600–606
    through matter and space,
        590–591
    mechanical, 591, 594, 599
    nature of, 588–591
    radio, 566, 646, 648–651, 661
    sound, 309, 596, 623–625
    speed of, 598–599, 601–602
    troughs of, 592, 593, 597, 604
    types of, 594–597
Wavelength, 593
    electromagnetic spectrum
        arranged by, 646–648
    refraction and, 677
    speed of waves and, 598
Wave model of atom, 117–118
Wave model of light, 658–659
Wax (petroleum product), 254
Weak force, 128
Weather, power of, 376
Weatherstripping, 462
Wedge, 381–382
Wegener, Alfred, 529
Weight, 45–48, 341–342
    changeability of, 45–46
    defined, 45, 341
    formula for, 342
    gravitational potential energy
        and, 403
    gravity and, 46–48, 341–342
    mass and, 341–342
Wheel and axle, 388–389
White color, 681
White light, dispersion of, 677
Wind, solar, 526–527
Wöhler, Friedrich, 233
Woodwind instruments, 627, 628
Work, 372–374. *See also* Energy,
    conservation of, 378, 379
    defined, 372
    energy and, 410
    formula for, 373
    kinetic energy and, 431–432
    machines and, 377–389